To Paul ~omson

Charles Knighton

BRISTOL RECORD SOCIETY'S
PUBLICATIONS

General Editors: MADGE DRESSER
ROGER LEECH
JONATHAN BARRY

VOL. 65

CLIFTON COLLEGE:

FOUNDATION TO EVACUATION

pledge ourselves always to remember that
the chief aim of a Public School is to train
up faithful men to serve their Queen and
Country in church and state, at home and
abroad, in peace and in war.

Address to Queen Victoria on her Diamond Jubilee, 1897; with watercolour by
H. Whatley (Art master). The text is printed as Document 378.

CLIFTON COLLEGE: FOUNDATION TO EVACUATION

EDITED

BY

C.S. KNIGHTON

Published by
BRISTOL RECORD SOCIETY
in association with
CLIFTON COLLEGE
2012

ISBN 978 0 901538 34 5

BRISTOL RECORD SOCIETY

The Society exists to encourage the preservation, study and publication of documents relating to the history of Bristol, and since its foundation in 1929 has published sixty-four major volumes of historic documents concerning the city. All the volumes are edited and introduced by scholars who are experts in their fields.

Recent volumes have included: *The Topography of Medieval and Early Modern Bristol* (Vols 48 and 52); *William Worcestre: The Topography of Medieval Bristol* (Vol. 51); *The Diary of Sarah Fox* (Vol. 55); *The Pre-Reformation Records of All Saints' Church, Bristol* (Vols 46, 53 and 56); *Bristol Probate Inventories* (Vols 54, 57 and 60); *Robert Sturmy's Commercial Expedition to the Mediterranean 1457–8* (Vol. 58); *Records of Bristol Cathedral* (Vol. 59); *Bristol's Trade with Ireland and the Continent, 1503–1601* (Vol. 61); *Westbury-on-Trym: Monastery, Minster and College* (Vol. 62); *The Ledger of Thomas Speed, 1681–1690* (Vol. 63); and *The Diary of William Dyer: Bristol in 1762* (Vol. 64).

The subscription for private members is £10 per annum, for UK institutions £12.50, and for overseas membership £20. In return, members of the Society receive the volumes as they are published.

The Society acknowledges with thanks the continued support of the University of Bristol and of the Bristol Record Office.

Correspondence to the Secretary, Hardings Cottage, Swan Lane, Winterbourne, S. Glos. BS36 1RJ. Subscriptions to the Treasurer, 20 The Willows, Yate, S. Glos. BS37 5XL.

Orders for past volumes to the Bristol Record Office, 'B' Bond Warehouse, Smeaton Road, Bristol BS1 6XN. Website: http://www.bris.ac.uk/Depts/History/bristolrecordsociety

Produced for the Society by
4word Ltd
Unit 15 Bakers Park
Cater Road
Bristol BS13 7TT

CONTENTS

LIST OF ILLUSTRATIONS AND MAPS

Frontispiece   Address to Queen Victoria on her Diamond Jubilee 1897

Plates (between pp. 200 and 201)

All from Clifton College Archives; nos 1, 6 and 16 from a set of engravings by Edward J. Burrow published in 1898

Maps (on pp. 410–12)

ACKNOWLEDGEMENTS

I am most grateful to the President and Council of Clifton College for permission to print the documents from the College Archives on which this volume is principally based; to the Head Master Mr M.J. Moore, the Bursar Mrs L.K.J. Hanson, and the Secretary of the Old Cliftonian Society Mr S.J.M. Reece for their endorsement and encouragement; to the Warden and Fellows of Keble College, Oxford for permission to include items from their collection of Dr D.G.A. Fox's papers, and to the College Archivist Mr R. Petre for making these available; to Dr R. Darwall-Smith, Archivist of Magdalen College, Oxford, and to the College Library staff; to Miss T. Wilkinson, Assistant Archivist of King's College, Cambridge; to Mrs Hatfield, Archivist of Eton College; to Mr J. Wisdom, Librarian of St Paul's Cathedral; to Messrs Harrison and Harrison, organ builders of Durham, for extracts from their archive, and to the Administrator Mrs Radford for much assistance; to Mr J.R. Drinkwater for help in obtaining this material at the company's premises and at Durham County Record Office; to the Hon. Laura Ponsonby and the Hon. Mrs Russell for permission to include extracts from the diary and correspondence of their great-grandfather Sir Hubert Parry at Shulbrede Priory; to Mrs A.P. Mason, Archivist of King's College, Taunton; to Miss A. Metcalfe of the National Library of Scotland for help in obtaining a copy of an item from the Haig MSS; to Mr R.H. Martin for allowing the use of his vivid letters describing the Bristol Blitz; to Mr R.K.G. MacEwen for sharing his memoirs of the day school which stayed at Clifton during the war; and to both of them for help in editing their writings; to Mr M.J. Polack for permission to use extracts from the journal of his great-aunt Sophie; to Mr A.W. Hasthorpe for his advice in selecting and describing the scientific material; to Mr M.J. Butterfield, Mr G.V. Hardyman, and Miss H. Williams for taking much trouble to look over the proof pages; to them also, and to Mr T.C.W. Gover, Mr D.O. Winterbottom, and Mr B. Worthington for guidance in local custom; to Professor R. Coates of the University of the West of England for sharing his knowledge of local place-names; to Dr M.J. Whitfield for much advice on medical matters, and for giving me an advance copy of his study of those of his profession who lived in Victoria Square; to the staffs of the Bodleian Library, Oxford, Cambridge University Library, Bristol University Library, Bristol Record Office and the Bristol Central Library for all manner of assistance in the research; and finally to Dr M. Dresser and Dr J. Harlow of the Bristol Record Society for their kindness and expertise in speeding the path of this volume, enabling it to appear before its time by way of celebrating Clifton's 150th anniversary.

C.S.K.

The Bristol Record Society is indebted to Clifton College for a generous grant towards the cost of publication.

BIBLIOGRAPHICAL AND GENERAL ABBREVIATIONS

All works listed here and cited in the text are published in London unless otherwise stated.

AA	Anti-Aircraft
A.F.S.	Auxiliary Fire Service
A.R.P.	Air Raid Precaution(s)
BAC	Bristol Aeroplane Company *later* (1959) British Aircraft Corporation
Bamford, *Public Schools*	T.W. Bamford, *Rise of the Public Schools: A Study of Boys' Public Boarding Schools in England and Wales from 1837 to the Present Day* (1967)
Best, 'Militarism'	G.F.A. Best, 'Militarism and the Victorian Public School', in Simon and Bradley, *Victorian Public School*, pp. 129–46
Birdwood, *Khaki and Gown*	Lord Birdwood (W.R.), *Khaki and Gown: An Autobiography* (1941)
Birley, 'Organs'	J. I. Birley, 'The organs in Clifton College', *The Organ*, no. 137 (July 1955), pp. 34–40
Bond and Cave, *Haig*	B. Bond and N. Cave (eds), *Haig: A Re-Appraisal 80 Years On* (1999)
Bradley, *Marlborough*	A.G. Bradley, A.C. Champneys, and J.W. Baines, *A History of Marlborough College*, rev. J.R. Taylor, H.C. Brentnall, and G.C. Turner (3rd edn, 1927).
BRO	Bristol Record Office
Bromwich, *Taunton*	D. Bromwich, *King's College Taunton: The First Hundred Years, 1880–1980* (Taunton, 1980)
Brown, *Letters*	S.T. Irwin (ed.), *Letters of Thomas Edward Brown* (4th edn, Liverpool, 1952)
Brown, *Newly Discovered Letters*	A.G. Dakyns and B. Robinson (eds), *Newly Discovered Letters of T.E. Brown* (Douglas, 2004)
BRS	Bristol Record Society
BSL /B.S.L.	Big Side Levée
Casey and Hale, *College, Club & Country*	P.J. Casey and R.I. Hale, *For College, Club and Country: A History of Clifton Rugby Football Club* (2009)
CC	Clifton College
Centenary Essays	N.G.L. Hammond (ed.), *Centenary Essays on Clifton College* (Bristol, 1962)

Chandos, *Boys Together*   J. Chandos, *Boys Together: English Public Schools 1800–1864* (Oxford, 1984)

Charteris, *Haig*   J. Charteris, *Field-Marshal Earl Haig* (1929)

Chitty, *Newbolt*   S. Chitty, *Playing the Game: A Biography of Sir Henry Newbolt* (1997)

Christie, *History*   O.F. Christie, *A History of Clifton College 1860–1934* (Bristol, 1935)

Cottle and Sherborne, *University*   B. Cottle and J.W. Sherborne, *The Life of a University* (2nd edn, Bristol, 1959)

De Groot, *Haig*   G.J. De Groot, *Douglas Haig 1861–1928* (1988)

Crockford   *Crockford's Clerical Directory* [with date of issue]

Directory   *Matthews' Annual Directory for the City and County of Bristol* continued as *J. Wright & Co.'s Bristol & Clifton Directory* then *Kelly's Directory of Bristol and Suburbs* [with date of issue]

Dunning, 'Origins of football'   E.G. Dunning, 'The origins of modern football and the Public School ethos', in Simon and Bradley, *Victorian Public School*, pp. 168–76

Foster, *Al. Oxon.*   J. Foster, *Alumni Oxonienses. The Members of the University of Oxford, 1715–1886* (Oxford, 1887–8)

Fox, *Douglas Fox*   W. Fox, *Douglas Fox (D.G.A.F): A Chronicle* (privately printed, 1976)

Gardner, *Public Schools*   B. Gardner, *The Public Schools: An Historical Survey* (1973)

Freeman, *Worthies* (1909)   A.B. Freeman, *Bristol Worthies* (Bristol, 1909) [second set]

Haig, *Private Papers*   R.N.W. Blake (ed.), *The Private Papers of Douglas Haig, 1914–1919* (1952)

Hill, *History of BGS*   C.P. Hill, *The History of Bristol Grammar School* (1951)

HMC   Headmasters' Conference

Hope Simpson, *Rugby since Arnold*   J.B. Hope Simpson, *Rugby since Arnold: A History of Rugby School from 1842* (1967)

Hyam, *Imperial Century*   R. Hyam, *Britain's Imperial Century: A Study of Empire and Expansion* (3rd edn, 2002)

Jones, *Clifton*   D. Jones, *A History of Clifton* (Chichester, 1992)

Le Neve, *Fasti*   J. Le Neve, *Fasti Ecclesiae Anglicanae, 1541–1857*, ed. J.M. Horn *et al.* (1969–)

McGrath, *Merch. Venturers*   P. McGrath, *The Merchant Venturers of Bristol: A History of the Society of Merchant Venturers of Bristol from its Origins to the Present Day* (Bristol, 1975)

Matthews, *God's Grace*   B. Matthews, *By God's Grace ... : A History of Uppingham School* (Maidstone, 1964)

Meadows and Brock, 'Science'   A.J. Meadows and W.H. Brock, 'Topics fit for gentlemen: the problem of Science in the Public School curriculum', in Simon and Bradley, *Victorian Public School*, pp. 95–114

Milford, *Two Brothers*   T.R. Milford, *Two Brothers: A Milford Memoir, 1895–1935* (priv. pr. 1986)

Morgan, *Cheltenham*	M.C. Morgan, *Cheltenham College: The First Hundred Years* (Chalfont St Giles, 1968)
Mozley, *Memories*	J.R. Mozley, *Clifton Memories* (Bristol, 1927)
Newbolt, *Later Life*	Lady Newbolt (ed.), *The Life and Letters of Sir Henry Newbolt* (1942)
Newbolt, *My World*	Sir H.J. Newbolt, *My World as in my Time: Memoirs of Sir Henry Newbolt* (1932)
Newsome, *Wellington*	D. Newsome, *A History of Wellington College 1859–1959* (1959)
OC / O.C.	Old Cliftonian
OCS	Old Cliftonian Society
ODNB	H.C.G. Matthew and B. Harrison (eds), *The Oxford Dictionary of National Biography* (Oxford, 2004)
OTC / O.T.C.	Officers' Training Corps
Parker, *Old Lie*	P. Parker, *The Old Lie: The Great War and the Public-School Ethos* (1987)
Parkin, *Thring*	G.R. Parkin, *Edward Thring, Headmaster of Uppingham: Life, Diary and Letters* (1898)
Percival, *Superior Men*	A.C. Percival, *Very Superior Men: Some early Public School Headmasters and their Achievements* (1973)
Potter, *Headmaster*	R. J. Potter, *Headmaster: The Life of John Percival, Radical Autocrat* (1998)
RCM	Royal College of Music
Register (1925)	F. Borwick (ed.) *Clifton College Annals and Register 1862–1925* (Bristol, 1925) [Subsequent editions of the *Register* (1947, 1962, 1978, 1994) omit the introductory *Annals*]
Reg. Univ.	*University of Bristol. Register of Graduates with Lists of Former and Present Officers and Professors of the University 1909–1959* (Bristol, 1909)
Shrosbee, *Clarendon Commission*	C. Shrosbee, *Public Schools and Private Education: The Clarendon Commission, 1861–4, and the Public School Acts* (Manchester, 1988)
Simon and Bradley, *Victorian Public School*	B. Simon and I. Bradley (eds), *The Victorian Public School: Studies in the Development of an Educational Institution* (Dublin, 1975)
Smith, *History of BRI*	G. Munro Smith, *A History of the Bristol Royal Infirmary* (Bristol, 1917)
Spender, *Dunn*	J.A. Spender *et al.* (eds), *Thomas William Dunn: Fellow and Dean of Peterhouse, Assistant Master at Clifton College, Founder and Head Master of Bath College* (priv. pr. 1934)
Temple, *Percival*	W. Temple, *Life of Bishop Percival* (1921)
Terraine, *Haig*	J. Terraine, *Douglas Haig: The Educated Soldier* (1963)
Thorn, *Road to Winchester*	J.L. Thorn, *The Road to Winchester* (1989)
Transactions	*Transactions of the Clifton College Scientific Society*
Venn, *Al. Cant.*	J.A. Venn (comp.), *Alumni Cantabrigienses. A Biographical Register of all known Students,*

	Graduates and Holders of Office at the University of Cambridge from the earliest Times to 1900, II, *From 1752 to 1900* (Cambridge, 1940–54)
Whitfield, *Victorian Doctors*	M.J. Whitfield, *The Victorian Doctors of Victoria Square: The Medical Occupants of a Square in Clifton, Bristol, from 1837–1901* (Bristol, 2012)
Wilson, *Autobiography*	A.T. and J.S. Wilson (eds), *James M. Wilson: An Autobiography 1836–1931* (1932)
Winterbottom, *Brown*	D.O. Winterbotton, *T.E. Brown: His Life and Legacy* (Douglas, 1997)
Winterbottom, *Dynasty*	D.O. Winterbottom, *Dynasty: The Polack Family and the Jewish House at Clifton* (Bristol, 2008)
Winterbottom, *Clifton after Percival*	D.O. Winterbottom, *Clifton after Percival: A Public School in the Twentieth Century* (Bristol, 1990)
Winterbottom, *Hallward*	D.O. Winterbottom, *Bertrand Hallward: First Vice-Chancellor of the University of Nottingham 1948–1965. A Biography* (Nottingham, 1995)
Winterbottom, *Newbolt*	D.O. Winterbottom, *Henry Newbolt and the Spirit of Clifton* (Bristol, 1986)
Winterbottom, *Rossall*	D.O. Winterbottom, *The Tide flows On: A History of Rossall School School* (Rossall, 2006)

LOCAL ABBREVIATIONS

Houses and Towns

Originally the boarding houses were known by the names of their incumbent masters. In 1922 permanent names were adopted, and in the Register *these are applied retrospectively. Likewise 'Pre' is used for the original Preparatory and Junior Schools as well as the modern Preparatory School into which they merged in 1933. These practices are followed here.*

BH	Brown's House
DH	Dakyns' House
HHP	Hartnell's House (Pre)
MHP	Matthews' House (Pre)
NT	North Town
OH	Oakeley's House
PH	Polack's House
PHP	Poole's House (Pre)
SH	School House
ST	The South Town
Town	The Town [*before division in 1875 into North/South; the latter won retention of the definite article*]
UH	United House [*grouping of 'small' or 'waiting' Houses*]
WaH	Watson's House
WiH	Wiseman's House

Hartnell's and Matthews' were formerly HH and MH but these abbreviations have now been taken by new Upper School Houses (out of range of this volume).

Forms

For most of this period the forms of the Classical Side below the Sixth were denoted by Roman numerals and subdivided (or 'streamed') α β γ; the Modern Side had an equivalent sequence of Arabic numbers subdivided *a b c*, and the Military and Engineering Side had Arabic numbers subdivided *x y z*. This precision was not always observed, but the usage of the original documents is here followed.

Head Masters

A.A.D.	Albert Augustus David [*HM4*]
B.L.H.	Bertrand Leslie Hallward [*HM7*]
J.E.K.	John Edward King [*HM5*]
J.M.W.	James Maurice Wilson [*HM2*]
J.P.	John Percival [*HM1*]
M.G.G.	Michael George Glazebrook [*HM3*]
N.W.	Norman Whatley [*HM6*]

EDITORIAL CONVENTIONS

Documents are numbered and cross-referenced in bold figures within square brackets thus **[1]**. All are printed verbatim except for some formal sections of the Clifton College Company's Articles **[7]**, and those parts of the Charter **[36]** which are copied from the Articles. The spelling of the originals is retained even where defective or variant. Consistent orthography has not been one of Clifton's strong points: in his letter of resignation John Percival described his office as both 'Head Master' and 'Headmaster' **[24]** These forms were used indifferently and have been retained as they appear. Abbreviations and contractions have been silently expanded, though retained in dating forms and proper names. Capitalisation has in general been reduced to a level more in keeping with modern practice. It is accepted that something of the flavour of the originals is lost, and in particular the hectoring emphasis of rules and regulations. But with material drawn from so many sources over a prolonged period, the fluctuations in usage would have been perplexing. Dating forms have been preserved as written. Punctuation, which in many of the originals is seriously obstructive, has been adjusted; missing apostrophes have been silently added. Insertions in the original texts are set within angled brackets <thus>. Marginal summaries in the longer formal documents have been omitted. Letter headings have been broadly standardised, and the addressees' details are omitted (save where part of a larger text). In printed letter-heads telephone numbers and telegraphic addresses have been omitted, as have other such details in commercial stationery.

All editorial insertions within the documents are contained within square brackets: words in italic are supplied to assist sense; words in Roman type supply what is clearly lost where the original has been cropped or torn; deletions and corrections are specifically explained.

Within the documents open italic is used to represent underlining for emphasis in MS and typescript, and for headings and sub-headings which have some distinctive character in the originals.

Editorial comment between documents is in italic and prefaced by □.

Entries in the printed *Clifton College Register* are flagged throughout the text, footnotes and index as explained below. This saves the duplication of much biographical detail already published, and which is in process of being made available online. Further details are added only where these have some particular relevance to the context.

The index uses the (arabic) entry numbers of the documents, not pages.

Clifton College Register citations

Since the 1947 edition pupils have been numbered in a single numeric sequence retrospectively assigned from 1862. Within each term of entry (and its sub-sections for the Junior and Preparatory Schools) the names are listed alphabetically. These numbers are used throughout this volume, either within the text thus [*12345*] or in the footnotes, where they are followed by the House abbreviations and years of attendance. There are separate sequences preceded by *HM* (Head Masters) and *M* (masters), with years of service. The numbers are normally given only at the first occurrence of each individual in the text or notes; they are also used in the index.

The successive volumes of the printed *Register* (last published 1994) will be found in the Bristol Central Library and the Bristol Record Office, and in major reference libraries elsewhere. While stocks last, copies may be bought from Clifton College Office, 32 College Road, Bristol BS8 3JH. A new and composite edition is being prepared for online publication, notice of which will be made by via http://www.cliftoncollegeuk.com/.

† here indicates years of attendance or service closed by death

PRINCIPAL PERSONS OF THE COLLEGE
during the period of this volume

Presidents of the College

1860	Henry John Reynolds-Moreton, 3rd Earl of Ducie *died 1921*
1921	Douglas Haig, 1st Earl Haig [*1981*] *died 1928*
1928	The Rt Hon. John Henry Whitley [*2252*] *died 1935*
1935	William Riddell Birdwood, 1st Baron Birdwood [*2054*] *died 1951*

Chairmen of the Council

1860	Canon John Guthrie *died 1865*
1865	Canon Henry Moseley *resigned 1868*
1868	James Heyworth *died 1880*
1880	Francis Nonus Budd *resigned 1894*
1895	John Percival, Bishop of Hereford [*HM1*] *resigned 1917*
1917	Sir (Thomas) Herbert Warren [*607*] *died 1930*

1930 Sir Rowland Edward Whitehead, Bt [*2127*] *resigned 1934*
1934 Sir Robert Clermont Witt [*3198*] *resigned 1946*

Head Masters

1861 [*HM0*] Charles Evans *resigned 1862*
1862 [*HM1*] John Percival *resigned 1879*
1879 [*HM2*] James Maurice Wilson *resigned 1890*
1891 [*HM3*] Michael George Glazebrook *resigned 1905*
1905 [*HM4*] Albert Augustus David *resigned 1909*
1910 [*HM5*] John Edward King [*943*] *resigned 1923*
1923 [*HM6*] Norman Whatley *resigned 1939*
1939 [*HM7*] Bertrand Leslie Hallward *resigned 1948*

Secretaries to the Council and (from 1930) Bursars

1860 Edward James *Hon. Secretary of Provisional Committee*
1860 John Page
1862 E.C. Boville
1864 John Bacon Medley
1864 William Douglas Lawson Macpherson
1912 W.J. Lewis
1930 Nicholas Robin Udal
1936 Gerald Eliot Badcock
1939 Alan Durant Imlay [*5233/M194*] *to 1945*

CLIFTON GLOSSARY

Beggar's Bush — Playing fields at Abbots Leigh, on the Somerset side of the Avon Gorge.

Big School — Great open schoolroom and general auditorium (now storeyed).

Big Side — Originally, all boys not fags; in continuing usage for (a) first divisions in cricket and football; (b) area of the Close where such divisions play.

Big Side Levée — Boys' council regulating games and general customs (originally comprising all except fags; from 1870 limited to certain seniors, with House and Form representatives).

Call-over — Evening roll-call in the Houses; applied to the order of the names as listed for this purpose.

Close — The enclosed playing field south of the main buildings.

Cock House — Winner of inter-House contest (sports and other activities).

Commem — Commemoration (formally 'the Guthrie Commemoration'), originally held to mark the completion of the Chapel; annual celebration combining prize-giving, entertainments, exhibitions &c.; at this period in late June but now normally at the end of May, before the division of the Summer term.

Council — The executive governing body.

Governors — Body of distinguished OCs and others, to whom the Council is formally answerable.

Grubber	Tuck and stationery shop.
Holder of Big-Side Bags	Head of the Upper Pack (*q.v.*); i.e. Captain of Running.
House Tutor	Assistant House Master.
Junior School	Subsidiary department of the College (from 1863 to 1930), for boys from 11 to 13.
Long Pen/the Long	The Long Penpole run.
Marshal	Official in charge of attendance and general discipline (not a master; normally a retired NCO or equivalent).
New Field/~Close	Detached playing field west of the Close.
Penpole/Pen	Cross country run (Long~, Short~), originally routed via Penpole Point (by Avonmouth)
Praepostor	Prefect.
Pre	Preparatory School: (a) 1874–1930, subsidiary department of the College for boys from 7 to 11; (b) from 1930, combined with Junior School, for boys from 7 to 13, and institutionally distinct from the Upper School.
President	Constitutional head of the College.
Short Pen/the Short	The Short Penpole run.
Sixth Power	Sixth Form boy as House Prefect.
Superannuation	Automatic expulsion for failing to advance through the forms.
Upper Pack	Top group in cross-country runs.
Upper School	The whole main School or 'the College', as distinct from the Preparatory and Junior Schools; hence 'Upper' boys.
XXII	Those playing the top cricket game who were not in the XI (so in effect the 2nd XI, but not originally a representative team as such).

INTRODUCTION

Much has already been published about Clifton's history, the institutions of the School and its personalities.[1] What follows is therefore principally a guide to the documents printed below. These have been grouped thematically, and within each section the entries are chronological. The foundation and evacuation which form the terminal points of the volume make natural brackets for the rest. The first part of this introduction links together documents from all parts of the volume which illustrate the constitutional history of the College up to the start of the Second World War. Other main topics are then discussed by casting Cliftonians in a variety of roles.

Selection of documents has been among the most difficult editorial decisions. Some formal items were obligatory and these tended to be the longest. One principle was to avoid what was already in print, and only in a few cases have exceptions been made. There already exists the great reservoir of *The Cliftonian*, on which it would have been all too easy to draw. It is in any case intended that this and the other official magazines should be made available online. The choice has also been conditioned by the present state of the College Archives. For some years these were stored in a commercial warehouse, and they only returned to the College in 2009 at the urging of the Governors.[2] Much still remains to be sorted and catalogued, doubtless including many papers which, had they been to hand, would have claimed a place here. There has been a measure of personal preference as well. It is hoped that a fair range of interests has been served, though some topics are poorly represented or wholly absent.

---

[1] Principally: O.C. Christie, *A History of Clifton College, 1860–1934* (Bristol, 1935), still a valuable respository of fact and lore; N.G.L. Hammond (ed.), *Centenary Essays on Clifton College* (Bristol, 1962); D.O. Winterbottom, *Clifton after Percival* (1990); C. Trafford (ed.), *'The Best School of All': 150 Years of Clifton College* (2009), the title alluding to the School song. Jeremy Potter's *Headmaster: The Life of John Percival, Radical Autocrat* (1998) adds much to the early story. *The Cliftonian*, first issued in 1867, is in itself the history of the School (and for its own early history see Christie, pp. 337–50). Over the years its format and frequency have much varied; since 2007 it has been combined with the Old Cliftonian Society's *Annual Report* (latterly *The Old Cliftonian*) as *The Clifton Magazine*. The *Clifton College Register* provides biographical detail on masters and pupils. Volumes have been issued periodically since 1880; that of 1947 was the last to include all individuals. Editions of 1962, 1978 and 1994 contained only new entrants and updated information for earlier ones, with cumulative indexes. A new edition combining data from all its predecessors will be issued online. The older printed volumes (to 1925) remain useful for details of parentage not given thereafter; they also contain introductory historical essays, lists and maps known collectively as the *Annals* (also issued separately).

[2] Particular mention should be made of the efforts of Mr S.M. Andrews [*HM11*].

I: CLIFTON COLLEGE 1860 TO 1940

Back to the start

If any individual may be called Clifton's founder it is Henry Sidney Wasbrough, partner in the firm of solicitors which still looks after the College's interests. On Maundy Thursday 1860 he hosted a meeting at his house in Gloucester Row to discuss the setting up of a new school for the neighbourhood. Though the record of that meeting [1] is brief, it pinpoints fundamental elements of the school which duly appeared. In the first place it was to be a 'proprietary College'; this was a relatively new expression, well understood to mean a commercial venture disguised as a medieval foundation. It was to be a school for boys, and to attain the 'highest branches of learning', which signalled the primacy of the Classics while allowing for modern studies. The projectors were clearly looking to the template created by Thomas Arnold at Rugby, from which replicas were being generated across the country.[3] This was reinforced by ensuring that the principal was to be a graduate of Oxford or Cambridge.

The unstated premiss was that none of the existing schools in Bristol was or could be converted into a 'first class' establishment on the Rugby model. There were already a good many private schools in Clifton itself, but these were small and ephemeral, wholly dependent on the circumstances of the individuals who owned and ran them.[4] Of the City's long established schools only one might have evolved into the kind Clifton's founders had in mind. In the first half of the nineteenth century Bristol Grammar School had been in such decay that only total reorganisation seemed likely to revive it. For two decades the school had been clinically dead, with no pupils at all. Although recovery then followed, its existing site in Unity Street offered little opportunity for expansion. A scheme was nevertheless devised to turn it into a boarding school, only to be quashed by a ruling from Master Romilly in 1860. Its place, he maintained, was as a day school for 'the necessary instruction of the lower classes of the community'; boarding was only appropriate for the higher classes.[5] So the Grammar School stayed as it was, and for the time being where it was.

The momentum for the new foundation came in any case from the villas and terraces of Clifton. Bristol was represented by the Mayor, John Bates, who took the chair at early meetings and summoned the public forum [2–3]. Also present and elected to the provisional Committee was Odiarne Lane, who was to become the next Mayor and later Master of the Society of Merchant Venturers. But both these City magnates were residents of Clifton. Wasbrough and his friends had no doubt talked up the proposal before the first formal meeting. The eighteen then present included

---

[3] It has been said with only slight exaggeration that during the 1860s and 1870s 'new public schools were founded almost every month': B. Gardner, *The Public Schools: An Historical Survey* (1973), p. 181; including some foundations only later accepted as public schools, there were four in 1860, four in 1862 (including Clifton and Haileybury), four in 1863–4 and three in 1865 (including Malvern): *ibid.*, pp. 181–90.

[4] D. Jones, *A History of Clifton* (Chichester, 1992), pp. 137–8, noting 20 'genteel private academies' in 1845; one of them educated the future Empress of the French. Among several Catholic schools was the foundation of Bishop Clifford (1860) which might have become the alternative Clifton College had it not moved to Prior Park, Bath, in 1867: J.A. Harding *The Diocese of Clifton 1850–2000* (Bristol, 1999), pp. 42–3.

[5] C.P. Hill, *The History of Bristol Grammar School* (1951), pp. 75–6, 84.

the cream of Clifton's professional classes; there were five medical men (among them Bristol's leading physician William Budd), five lawyers and three bankers (including the Mayor), and just one merchant. The only hint of commerce was the presence of the journalist Joseph Leech, who may have been asked for the sake of publicity. A full report of the proceedings was duly carried in the next edition of his *Bristol Times*.[6] Yet Leech too was a Clifton man.

Via media

The stipulation that the principal of the College was to be an Oxbridge graduate may also have been meant to ensure that he was an Anglican. In fact religious tests had been abolished by statutes of 1854 and 1856,[7] but the laymen at the first meeting may have been unaware of this or its imminent relevance.[8] As soon as clergy were involved, the Anglican character of the proposed foundation was made explicit. The religious pitch was crucial because two previous attempts to set up a superior school in Bristol had failed on that count. Bristol College in Park Row, which opened 1831, antagonised the Anglican establishment by admitting nonconformists. As an antidote the Bishop of Gloucester and Bristol set up Bishop's College, which succeeded in driving the competitor out of business without finding wide enough backing for itself. It struggled on until 1861, by which time the leading members of the Cathedral Chapter had already switched their support to the Clifton project.

It was one of the Canons, Henry Moseley, who formally proposed that the School be committed to the teaching of the Church of England. Later in the year the Dean of Bristol (Gilbert Elliot) and one of his Chapter colleagues were named as Vice-Presidents, while Canon John Guthrie became first Chairman of the Council. On Guthrie's death in 1865 Moseley succeeded him in the chair. However, the Dean soon left the picture. In 1863 he married a woman much younger than himself, a writer of travel books, and for the next few years the Dean travelled much in her company. It was only after the collapse of the marriage that Elliot became again a significant presence in Bristol.[9]

Bishop William Thomson (1861–3) also lent support in the early days, not least in helping to secure the Head Mastership for his former charge John Percival.[10] Shortly before the College opened it was announced that the Bishop was to be its Visitor [25]. That may have been mere courtesy, but collegiate visitors sometimes have substantive powers. The exact status is not explained here.[11] Within a few months Thomson was translated to York, and no more is heard of any organic connexion

---

[6] 19 May. The paper came out on Saturdays only.

[7] 17 & 18 Vict. *c*. 81 (Oxford), sect. 43; 19 & 20 Vict. *c*. 88 (Cambridge), sect. 45.

[8] The first man appointed Head Master would have sworn to the 39 Articles on matriculation; Percival, arriving at Oxford in 1855, was in the first generation freed from that requirement.

[9] J. Bettey, 'Contrasting clerics in nineteenth-century Bristol: Dean Elliot and Canon John Pilkington Norris', *Historic Churches and Church Life in Bristol: Essays in Memory of Elizabeth Ralph 1911–2000*, ed. Bettey (Bristol, 2001), pp. 196–201, summarised in the same editor's *Records of Bristol Cathedral* (BRS, LIX, 2007), p. 198. Later Elliot had a major part in establishing University College, serving as its first President until his death in 1891: B. Cottle and J.W. Sherborne, *The Life of a University* (2nd edn, Bristol, 1959), p. 5.

[10] He had been Provost of The Queen's College, Oxford in Percival's time.

[11] Thomson became first Visitor of Cheltenham College at the same period: M.C. Morgan, *Cheltenham College: The First Hundred Years* (Chalfont St Giles, 1968), pp. 38, 39.

between Clifton College and the See of Bristol. The only residual trace of that is in the College's Arms.[12] The disappearance of both Bishop and Dean in the year after the foundation may have been to Clifton's advantage; for without compromising its Anglican credentials, the College was not too closely bound to the local hierarchy.

Sure foundations

Clifton succeeded where other schemes had failed because the impetus came not from above but from within a community elite able to underwrite its aspirations. The mechanism by which this could be achieved came from the world in which those men were already familiar. The ancient schools had evolved gradually or been created by the large generosity of individual or corporate founders. The Victorians had no time for the former, and although some schools were still founded from endowments, the usual option was to set up a limited company. Recent commercial legislation provided the blueprint for these 'proprietary' schools, and enabled capital to be raised very quickly. Shareholders had privileges in nominating pupils as well as the usual right of calling the directors to account at company meetings. The directors constituted the governing body, styled 'President and Council' to suggest affinity with ancient collegiate bodies like the Provost and Fellows of Eton and the Dean and Chapter of Westminster.[13]

This was the pattern for Clifton. The two flagships in the proprietary fleet lay close at hand. Marlborough (1843) had some peculiarities because of its principal concern to educate the sons of the clergy. Nevertheless it was tremendously successful, being aided, as Rugby had been, by proximity to a hub of the railway system. The joint-stock school in its purest form is represented by Cheltenham (1841), and the circumstances of its foundation are matched exactly by what took place in Clifton twenty years later.[14] Although no evidence for this has yet appeared, Wasbrough and his friends must have looked closely at the Cheltenham model, and in all probability had contacts there.

Once the founders' proposals had been endorsed by the public meeting of Clifton residents, there were four major objectives, all secured with astonishing speed. The first was to raise the capital, the second to find and secure a site, the third to build on it, and the fourth to appoint a Head Master of sufficient distinction to justify the whole effort. By the beginning of July three sites had been short-listed; none was quite as large, flat, or unencumbered as it might have been, but there was little doubt as to the best **[4]**. The idea had been to rent the land, but the owner then realised that if the School failed he would be left with a great pile useless for any other purpose. Fortunately funds were already available to buy the property outright **[5]**. Altogether about thirteen acres were acquired. A competition was then announced for design of the buildings, for which detailed guidelines were provided. These included the stipulation that the structure must be Gothic or Elizabethan in style **[82]**. This was

---

[12] D. Riddle, 'Heraldry of public schools', *The Escutcheon*, 11, no. 1 (Michaelmas 2005); C.S. Knighton, 'Harking to the heralds', *Clifton Magazine* (2011), pp. 26–7.

[13] T.W. Bamford, *Rise of the Public Schools* (1967), pp. 23–34.

[14] A.G. Bradley *et al.*, rev. J.R. Taylor *et al.*, *A History of Marlborough College* (3rd edn, 1927), pp. 78–86; Morgan, *Cheltenham*, pp. 3–15.

not merely aesthetics, but made further pretension to the status of Eton, Winchester and Westminster. The adjudicator Benjamin Ferrey [9] chose the design of Charles Francis Hansom, who had worked extensively in the West Country. Just one detail of Hansom's work is featured here [84]. Some elements of the plan (including the Chapel) were to be deferred until more funds were available. The construction of the rest was completed on schedule within two years of purchasing the land [13].[15]

Of the eighteen founding fathers, only half became members of the original Council; a further five became shareholders.[16] By September 1860, when the Company was formed, a distinctly different group of names appears [6, 7]. At the head as President was a young nobleman, the 3rd Earl of Ducie; in support were twelve Vice-Presidents, mostly local gentry and MPs. William Gale Coles, who promoted the business aspect of the foundation, was named Treasurer, and there were twelve ordinary councillors. There is evidence that the promoters had hunted around for influential figures, and several of those named here had no large or lasting involvement.[17] However significant figures do arrive at this point: Canon Guthrie, who was to be the first Chairman of Council, James Heyworth, later to hold that post, and the physician John Addington Symonds of Clifton Hill House. The Company's Articles of Association [7] are primarily concerned with the shareholders and the Council, and are in large part the common form for a joint-stock company as then regulated by statute. Some of the provisions are therefore merely summarised here. The sections dealing with the school itself (67–87) are more significant, and many of them passed *verbatim* into the Royal Charter of 1877 [36].

In 1860 the Mayor had given notice that Clifton's new school was to be for the sons of gentlemen [2], and this was repeated in the Articles and early prospectuses [6, 10]. However the status was never defined, unlike at Cheltenham where social distinction was categorically stated in relation to the shareholders.[18] Bristol is however not Cheltenham, and no evidence has been found of anyone being turned away on the grounds of inadequate gentility. An extract from the first register of shareholders [8] tells us exactly who was putting money into the project. Professional men predominate, with a few from the forces; but there are merchants there as well, and public officials significantly further down the social scale. The most noteworthy name is that of the banker and constitutional theorist Walter Bagehot, himself a product of the short-lived Bristol College and a protégé of Dr Symonds.[19] The Clifton College Company could not have had a better endorsement than the money of the future editor of *The Economist*.

---

[15] Sir John Betjeman conducted an elegant survey of the Clifton buildings in *Centenary Essays*, pp. 21–7. A volume could be filled in documentary support; in the present collection this is limited to a few features which can be treated in some detail: the Holman Hunt mosaic [86–92], the Glazebrook memorial pulpit [107–16], the Science School [147–51], the Memorial Arch [428–36] and the Haig Memorial [445–52].

[16] Original Councillors: Bates, Black, F.N. Budd, Coles, Colthurst, Cooke, Cox, Saunders, and Wasbrough; Savile became a Councillor later. Shareholders: Burroughs, Daniel, Lane, Leech, McArthur. See notes to [1] for identification.

[17] The Company's first petty cash book, from which extracts are given as [9] and [16], also includes payment for a list of members of the House of Commons.

[18] It was resolved that 'no person should be considered eligible who should not be moving in the circle of gentlemen. No retail trader being under any circumstances to be considered': Morgan, *Cheltenham*, p. 3.

[19] Lord St John of Fawsley (N.A.F. St John-Stevas), *Walter Bagehot* (1963), pp. 5–8.

Head men

While the business and building operations were proceeding the Council was arranging the direction of the School itself. Soon after the Company had been set up Wasbrough went to see Edward Thring, the Headmaster who was transforming Uppingham into a major school. Thring was glad to hear that 'the Bristol people' were adopting his system 'as the best of all the public schools', and invited Wasbrough to send him fuller details. He was duly impressed by the 'zeal and liberality' with which Clifton's founders were creating 'an immense engine of power for reforming education.'[20] Thring had himself introduced facilities such as a gymnasium and a swimming bath, which Clifton would acquire at an early stage; but he also gave boys more privacy and met their failings with more tolerance than Clifton's early rulers would allow. It was in any case to another school in the Midlands that the Council looked for the all-important figure of the first Head Master. Frederick Temple of Rugby obliged by releasing from his staff, Charles Evans, who was manifestly qualified by his scholarly record and twelve years of teaching in the country's most prestigious school. Evans was duly appointed in January 1861, and began recruiting staff and pupils [11]. Premises were hired for a 'preliminary school' in Arlington Villas. This was run by one of Thring's former housemasters T.H. Stokoe, who had been chosen by Evans in August [9, 11].[21]

Less than a month before the College was due to open the Council heard with dismay that Evans had applied for the Headmastership of his own old school, King Edward's, Birmingham. [12] He was not of course prepared to surrender one appointment before securing the other, so the Councillors could do no more at their next meeting than to look round the completed buildings [13]. Guthrie had meanwhile consulted Temple again, and held a reserve candidate *in pectore*. This was John Percival, much younger than Evans and not so natural a teacher, but even more academically distinguished and formidably self-confident. Evans was duly appointed at Birmingham; telegrams were exchanged to co-ordinate this news with that of Percival's appointment to Clifton [16].[22] Evans rather fatuously offered his future services should the College have need of them. It did not, and the first Head Master was as nearly as possible wiped from the Clifton memory [14]. On 30 September 1862 Clifton College formally opened for business, the first part of which was to hear Percival tell his new charges to be truthful and manly,[23] to avoid idleness and impurity, and above all to pray [15].

The pulpit remained the central instrument of Percival's government, as indeed it was for other public school headmasters of the heroic age. On a more mundane level his directives usually came by printed notice; incidentally an early letter shows his concern to keep down printing costs [17]. A few miscellaneous examples indicate the style of these communications. Circulars announce the almost simultaneous

---

[20] G.R. Parkin, *Edward Thring, Headmaster of Uppingham: Life, Diary and Letters* (1898), i, pp. 103–5; B. Matthews, *By God's Grace ... : A History of Uppingham School* (Maidstone, 1964); Potter, *Headmaster*, pp. 145–6 first noticed the reference to Clifton in Thring's diary.

[21] CC Company Minute Book 1, p. 99; Parkin, *Thring*, i, pp. 96–7; Matthews, *God's Grace*, p. 85; Percival, *Superior Men*, pp. 235–8.

[22] These negotiations are documented in W. Temple, *Life of Bishop Percival* (1921), pp. 11–14.

[23] This 'cardinal Victorian virtue' is discussed by D. Newsome, *Godliness and Good Learning* (1961), pp. 195–259, and N. Vance, 'The idea of manliness', in Simon and Bradley, *Victorian Public School*, pp. 115–28.

provision of a Chapel **[85]** and of a Laboratory **[139]**.[24] Parents are informed of each new facility, and of how much extra it will cost them **[207, 277, 279]**. They were, however, instructed not to give their sons too much pocket money; for this the weekly limit was set at one shilling **[73]**.[25] On the other hand an apparent ban on food hampers had to be explained as mere discouragement **[75]**. School uniforms were introduced around the time Clifton was founded, and the flouting of the dress rules became as much a tradition as the making of them. The opening of the Junior School is announced in 1863, and the benefits of what is now called a 'tied cottage' are politely explained. Boys from elsewhere, it suggests, were likely to be 'imperfectly prepared or badly grounded' **[72]**. Rules made in 1872 include precise instructions on the writing of lines **[77]**. A compendium of 'Bye-Laws and Regulations' was drawn up by Percival's successor in 1882 **[79]**. This was reissued periodically for many decades, with little alteration save for the rise in fees and charges.

So successful was the School that it was soon full to capacity, and in 1872 Percival had to warn prospective parents that boarding-house places should be booked well in advance **[78]**. By that time there were already around 450 boys in the Upper and Junior Schools, and when the Preparatory School for younger boys was added in 1875, the combined roll was 576. This peaked at 680 four years later, and was then pegged back to avoid overcrowding.[26] For the boarding house masters (who until 1921 included the Head Master in School House), keeping up numbers was essential, since the houses were run as private businesses. Some alleviation came from fees extracted from parents who had not given the required notice of removal **[80]**.

Town boys

A distinctive feature of Clifton is the town house system. Many other schools had a mixture of boarding and day boys, but the latter were generally an inferior species, imperfectly integrated into the collegiate body.[27] At Clifton the town boys were progressively accepted as full members of the School; they were eligible for the same scholarships **[127]** and were admitted to the Sanatorium **[207]**. In the all-important deliberations of Big Side Levée the Head of the Town was from the start ranked with the Heads of Houses **[278]**. In 1868 a day boy became the fourth Head of the School,[28] and seven more attained that place over the next twenty years. In 1875 the Town was split not quite equally into North Town and the South Town (retention of the article being won by the latter). Another advance came in 1888 when North Town was Cock House at cricket; within two years the town boys had matched the boarders in athletics and football as well.[29] The downside was that out of hours town boys were still subject to regulation by the School. They were considered as 'home

---

[24] The coincidence noted as 'a piece of symbolism that would not have impressed Arnold': Gardner, *Public Schools*, p. 185.

[25] The editor distinctly recalls this sum as being his own weekly allowance about a hundred years later.

[26] *Register* (1925), p. cxxix (figures include day boys and boarders). Numbers fluctuated around 600 until after the First World War, then rose considerably (792 in 1924), falling back again in the economically depressed 1930s: Winterbottom, *Clifton after Percival*, pp. 111–12.

[27] One of Percival's enduring achievements as Headmaster of Rugby was to give Town House parity with boarders such as he had created at Clifton: Hope Simpson, *Rugby since Arnold*, pp. 124–5.

[28] E.N.P. Moor: below **[55]**.

[29] This position was retained in the following year, when the South Town became Cock House in athletics; then in 1890 North Town was jointly Cock House at football with School House: *Register* (1925), p. cii.

boarders', with their parents as their unpaid masters and tutors, and they had to keep the same bounds as those who boarded within the School [79(14,19)]. Their homes were in effect detached areas of Clifton sovereign territory. The parents accepted this because it saved them a good deal of money. The School was likewise relieved of the expense and trouble of erecting boarding houses for everyone. Percival himself saw the arrangement as a positive virtue, his humble origins having persuaded him that 'the best education in English life was not to be had in a boarding school but by the boy who ... attended a good school near his home'.[30]

Percival was not, however, the only begetter of the Clifton towns. At the public meeting in May 1860, one speaker had stressed the advantages of locating a public school within a residential community. The minutes record only that Dr Symonds, having described the lack of a first-class public school as a 'serious detriment to Clifton', moved that one such be forthwith established [3]. From the press report we know that he wanted this new school to 'come under home influences, in conjunction with the intellectual culture and training of the college'.[31] Though he rather overdid it by invoking 'the blessed, purifying, sanctifying influence of home, and the society of mothers and sisters', this was the manifesto for the 'home boarder' system.

Its origins may be traced to events at Harrow, where Symonds' son, John Addington junior, had recently been a boarder. There he learned that the Headmaster, C.J. Vaughan, was conducting an *amour* with another boy. Though Symonds junior was himself consumed by homophile passion, this relationship between master and pupil appalled him and he told his father what he knew. Symonds senior proceeded to blackmail Vaughan into resignation and the declining of all high preferment in the church. It seems very likely that these events encouraged the high-minded doctor to promote the sanctity of home boarding.[32]

It might be supposed that Clifton's substantial provision for day boys was all to the benefit of established local residents. In fact many public schools drew clients into their neighbourhood; most of the incomers were well-heeled widows, but sometimes complete families uprooted themselves. At Rugby such folk were so thick on the ground from the 1820s that they acquired a name, 'sojourners'.[33] How many of Clifton's day-boy parents were of this migratory kind cannot yet be assessed. In one extreme instance of a boarder threatened with expulsion, it was suggested that he might stay as a day boy if his mother set up house in Clifton to keep him straight [265]. Sojourning of a more regular sort is evident in a very prominent case. When Henry and Francis Newbolt joined the School in September 1876, their mother moved from Staffordshire to take up residence in Worcester Crescent.[34] The boys were therefore placed in the South Town, since at first there was a fixed horizontal division between north and south on the latitude of the old Pavilion. This simplistic arrangement failed to reflect demographic reality, and to achieve a better numerical balance a new boundary was drawn in 1877. North Town extended its catchment area

---

[30] Temple, *Percival*, p. 37; admittedly this remark was made at the prize-giving of a day school.

[31] *Bristol Times*, 19 May 1860; longer extract in Winterbottom, *Clifton after Percival*, pp. 12–13, though mis-ascribed to 'Bristol *Daily Post*'.

[32] P. Grosskurth, *John Addington Symonds: A Biography* (1964), pp. 33–41; *idem* (ed.), *The Memoirs of John Addington Symonds* (1984), pp. 25, 97–8, 112–16. The scandal was recast in fiction by Frances Vernon as *The Fall of Doctor Onslow* (1994); its relevance to Clifton was suggested in Potter, *Headmaster*, pp. 103–4.

[33] T.W. Bamford, 'Public School Town in the nineteenth century', *British Journal of Educational Studies*, VI, 1 (Nov. 1957), pp. 25–36, summarised in his *Public Schools*, pp. 21–2.

[34] D.O. Winterbottom, *Henry Newbolt and the Spirit of Clifton* (Bristol, 1986), p. 17.

down to Oakfield Road, and this brought in Worcester Crescent. **[404]**. The Newbolt brothers did not have the two-years' qualification which would have kept them *in situ*, so they were re-allocated to North Town.

Despite all the efforts at integration there was some lingering resentment of the town boys. When debating the unlikely prospect of the School re-locating across the Gorge, one boarder saw advantage in eliminating what he called the 'nuisance' of town boys **[295]**. By the 1920s perspectives had changed, and Norman Whatley advocated a discreet policy of refusing as day boys those whose parents could afford to send them as boarders **[68(5)]**.

Reforming Commissions

Before the end of the nineteenth century Clifton would acquire much of its present appearance; the buildings were yoked together by the central tower of 1890, funded by and named after the second Head Master, J.M. Wilson **[83]**. The rise in numbers already noted was checked as the site became surrounded by new streets. The College itself attracted these developments, so in a sense it was to be the prisoner of its own success. Its academic reputation was very soon acknowledged by external examiners who commended its blend of traditional Classical and modern erudition **[121–2]**. It was unfortunate that no sooner had the founders' intentions of creating a 'great public school' **[3, 10]** begun to materialise, than this status was exclusively defined by the Clarendon Commission of 1861–4.[35] Although the nine ancient schools investigated by that body resented the meddling in their domestic concerns, they were thereby set apart for ever from the rest.[36] They were not, as one of their headmasters had feared, engulfed by 'the tide of Joint stock education'[37] but surfed above it. No matter how the relative status of schools is calibrated, there can be no retrospective promotion to Lord Clarendon's premier league.[38] At best an affinity with the 'great public schools' could be claimed by operating the same rules **[235]**. Although outside the Commission's chosen terms of reference, the leading proprietaries Cheltenham and Marlborough were commended for their promotion of science and modern studies.[39] Clifton was soon to excel in these areas, but was still too young to be taken by Clarendon as a model.

Another and much more sweeping reform could have restructured the infant Clifton far more radically than had been done for the senior nine. As soon as Clarendon's work was completed, a new Commission headed by Lord Taunton began to review the whole area of secondary education. Its particular concern was to channel

---

[35] The best account is C. Shrosbee, *Public Schools and Private Education: The Clarendon Commission 1861–4 and the Public School Acts* (Manchester, 1988), though allowance should be made for the author's distaste for his subject.

[36] Eton, Winchester, Westminster, Charterhouse, Merchant Taylors', St Paul's, Harrow, Rugby and Shrewsbury; the key to the elite is found in the borderline case of Shrewsbury: *ibid.*, pp. 88–90.

[37] B.H. Kennedy of Shrewsbury, in his evidence to the Commission, quoted in A.C. Percival, *Very Superior Men: Some early Public School Headmasters and their Achievements* (1973), p. 145.

[38] A useful criterion is inter-action through sporting fixtures and other competitions; on this basis Clifton is by 1902 in a top group of 22 including (besides the Clarendon nine) its two closest rivals Cheltenham and Marlborough: J.R. Honey, 'Tom Brown's universe: the nature and limits of the Victorian Public School community, in B. Simon and I. Bradley (eds), *The Victorian Public School: Studies in the Development of an Educational Institution* (1975), pp. 27–8.

[39] Shrosbee, *Clarendon Commission*, pp. 52, 91.

under-used endowments into more efficient areas.[40] These efforts were accelerated when the Liberals won the General Election of 1868 and Gladstone formed his first ministry. The Endowed Schools Act of 1869 empowered local Commissioners to redistribute existing endowment funds (including those of general charities), and to devise schemes for this purpose. Existing fee-paying schools would be invited to participate by taking extra pupils, supported by the revenues taken from less efficient bodies. This was an echo of the dissolution of the monasteries and chantries in the sixteenth century, when the Crown re-deployed seized assets towards new educational foundations (such such as Bristol Cathedral School). More closely it prefigured the direct grant system of the mid-twentieth century, in which the Cathedral School again featured.

In Bristol the Commissioners had only limited success in trying to help the still enfeebled Grammar School. They met fierce opposition to the enforced transfer of non-educational endowments, and to the creation of a single governing body for all City's non-Anglican endowed schools. A renewed proposal to introduce boarders was rejected as a misguided attempt to compete with the College on the hill. In the event a modified scheme was adopted, improving the revenue without compromising independence.[41]

At Clifton the Commissioners' approach was awaited with apprehension, except by the Head Master, for whom it represented a wonderful opportunity for the social engineering to which he was committed. He knew what was in the wind and even before the Council set up a Committee to consider the issue [27], he had informal meetings with the local Commissioner, Joshua Fitch. What the Commissioners really wanted was a single 'first-grade' school for Bristol, which would merge the College with the Grammar School [28]. While Percival was not prepared to go that far, he and Fitch devised a scarcely less radical scheme which was presented to the Council on 18 June 1870 [29]. This would have amounted to a hostile take-over, with the Commissioners using the sequestered Bristol endowments to buy out the shareholders. They would then cap fees at £25 year, and dispense with the social and religious requirements on which the founders had insisted. Cliftonians would no longer have to be the sons of gentlemen, and their religious instruction would not be bound by the Articles of the Church of England. If the Council did not agree to all this, the Commissioners were minded to set up the Grammar School as a rival and cheaper establishment on a new site 'somewhere in Clifton', such as Tyndalls Park.[42]

Clifton's founders and shareholders had not invested their money and their efforts to provide for the poor of Bristol, however deserving, but for the upbringing of their own kind. They had no wish to see the princely character of the College diluted by a rabble of uncouth paupers, even if their fees were paid from public funds. It fell to Canon Moseley to articulate these views at some length [30]. He raised as many technical objections to the scheme as he could muster, but the essence of his argument was that 'it was distinctly not as a Citizen School that Clifton College was established'. He called the Commissioners' bluff about re-siting the Grammar School, predicting that this would absorb so much of its new income that it could never prosper. Somewhat illogically he nevertheless expected the College to thrive on the competition.

---

[40] Bamford, *Public Schools*, pp. 168–91 and *passim*.
[41] Hill, *History of BGS*, pp. 96–103.
[42] To which the reinvigorated Grammar School did move in 1879, though without imperilling the College.

These meetings must have been more heated that the minutes reveal; Moseley had merely called the Percival-Fitch scheme 'most undesirable', to which Percival responded by finding it 'exceedingly inadvisable' not to negotiate with the Commissioners. In fact detailed discussions did follow, but came to nothing. The Commission was wound up after the Conservatives returned to government in 1874, its powers being transferred to the Charity Commissioners, and then in 1899 to the newly established Board of Education. Under these auspices a good many schemes were implemented, and some schools rose to prominence as a result.[43] The Clifton projects retain much interest for what they tell us of the School as it then was, and for the vision of what it might have become [31–5].

The fuss over the Endowed Schools Act had one immediate and significant side-effect. Thring of Uppingham was so fearful of State control that he invited the Headmasters of other threatened schools to close ranks by meeting together. Only fourteen Headmasters turned up to the first conference at Uppingham in December 1869. The Clarendon schools, being exempt from the Act, were not on the list, and Thring derided the suggestion that the Head Master of Eton had a natural right to preside. Percival, to whom the Act was welcome, did not attend; but he was at the second conference at Sherborne, so geography may explain his earlier absence. Marlborough and Cheltenham, the market leaders among the proprietaries, were also unrepresented at the first meeting. Harper of Sherborne had been the only West Country Headmaster there, most of the others being from the south-east. One of the two northern delegates was Stokoe of Richmond, the former master of the preliminary School at Clifton [11].[44] At Christmas 1875, towards the end of his time at Clifton, Percival would bring the Conference to Bristol.[45]

Instrument of government

By this time, and influenced by these events, large questions had arisen about the governance of the College. The proprietary system had worked admirably in bringing Clifton into being, but the feeling grew that this was an undignified and possibly unstable basis for a great academic institution. If a high-minded Government agency could threaten a buy-out, was there not even more reason to fear unscrupulous speculators? Proprietary schools did fail, though generally because of inherent weakness rather than external pressure.[46] The solution was hinted at in the

---

[43] B=amford, *Public Schools*, pp. 136–7.
[44] G. Baron, 'The origins and early history of the Headmasters' Conference', *Educational Review*, VII (1955), pp. 223–4; Bamford, *Public Schools*, pp. 183–4; Matthews, *God's Grace*, pp. 99–100; Potter, *Headmaster*, p. 146. Those attending the first HMC are listed in Percival, *Superior Men*, p. 242.
[45] Potter, *Headmaster*, p. 146; *cf.* S.T. Irwin (ed.), *Letters of Thomas Edward Brown* (4th edn, Liverpool, 1952), p. 51.
[46] Taunton College, founded as a proprietary in 1865, suffered a series of misfortunes, including the loss of its patron Lord Taunton, two epidemics of scarlet fever, and the undercutting of local food products by cheap American imports; like Bristol College it also alienated Anglicans by admitting nonconformists. It closed in 1879, but was then revived by Canon Nathaniel Woodward: D. Bromwich, *King's College, Taunton: The First Hundred Years, 1880–1980* (Taunton, 1980), pp. 6–9. Bath Proprietary College as founded in 1853 did not survive beyond 1878. It was revived under the former Clifton master T.W. Dunn and enjoyed a high reputation for Classics; but this specialisation was also a weakness, as was the Governors' refusal to admit the sons of tradesman, and the College finally closed in 1909: J.A. Spender *et al.* (eds), *Thomas William Dunn* (priv. pr, 1934), pp. 11–30, 33–4, 37.

recommendation that Clifton should have 'a constitution similar to Marlborough' **[31]**. This meant incorporation by Royal Charter (letters patent under the Great Seal), creating a perpetual collegiate body which could not be bought and sold. Marlborough had achieved this status in 1845, just two years after the school had opened.[47] Incorporation was not available on demand, and Cheltenham was refused a Charter in 1869. Another attempt in 1890 was frustrated by difficulties over the traffic in nominations. Cheltenham eventually found a quicker route to incorporation through a Local Act of Parliament in 1894.[48] Malvern, founded three years after Clifton, was encouraged by its example to open negotiations for a Charter in 1879, but it would be fifty years before this could be secured. Here also the problem of buying out the existing interests became all the more difficult with the passage of time.[49]

For Clifton the process was relatively swift. There is a colourful tradition that Percival struck a deal with the Jewish MP Lionel Cohen, whom he had met while taking the waters of Hotwells. If Cohen would use his influence to obtain a Charter, Clifton would set up a boarding house for Jewish boys.[50] The tale eventually acquired dialogue, with Percival saying 'We do not have a charter as yet, and I would welcome your assistance in piloting one for us through the House.'[51] The Jewish House was indeed started at this time **[18]**; a Charter is not, however, an Act of Parliament or any business of the Legislature, but an instrument of the Crown's prerogative. As such it is a matter for the Privy Council, and since Clifton's President was himself a member of that body there is no reason to suppose that the College's suit needed any other promoter.[52] So in February 1876 the College resolved to petition the Crown for a Charter, at the same time 'throwing the College open to all classes'.[53] In October the Chairman described the successful outcome of a delegation to London:

Mr Heyworth reported that acting on Mr Cave's[54] advice he had requested to have an interview with Mr Peel the Secretary to the Duke of Richmond[55] and that he had applied to Mr Peel for an interview. That Mr Peel had made an appointment and that he the Chairman, Dr Percival, and Mr Cox[56] had attended at the Privy Council Office and had an interview with Mr Peel (with Mr Self the Chief Clerk) and fully informed him of the position of the College in every respect and the want of some new incorporation and the course which had been taken, and he stated that he had since received a letter from Mr Peel stating that he had <as> arranged communicated with the Duke of Richmond, the Lord President of the Council, and was informed that if an application

---

[47] Bradley, *Marlborough*, p. 111.
[48] Morgan, *Cheltenham*, pp. 63–6. Local Act 57 & 58 Vict. *c.* ciii.
[49] R. Blumenau, *A History of Malvern College 1865–1965* (1965), pp. 97–9.
[50] D.O. Winterbottom, *Dynasty: The Polack Family and the Jewish House at Clifton 1878–2005* (Bristol, 2008).
[51] J. Samuel, *The Jews of Bristol* (Bristol, 1997), pp. 152–6 (where the exchange is rightly called 'romantic').
[52] Lord Ducie became a Privy Counsellor on joining Palmerston's government as Captain of the Yeomen of the Guard in 1859; he retained that post until the fall of Russell's ministry in 1866.
[53] CC Company Minute Book 4, p. 9.
[54] The banker Charles Daniel Cave, later Baronet, who had been involved in setting up the College, though not appointed to the Council: see below **[3]**.
[55] Charles Lennox Peel, later Clerk of the Council and knighted; a nephew of Sir Robert Peel, and first cousin of the 6th Duke of Richmond (Lord President 1874–8).
[56] Alfred Cox, an original member of the College Council: below **[1]**.

was made for a Royal Charter for Clifton College the circumstances were so exceptional that it would be favourably entertained.[57]

Back in Bristol the draft Charter was approved, and the shareholders were persuaded to accept appointment as Governors with continuing rights to nominate pupils. On 28 November the Council made their formal petition with the comfortable assurance that it would be granted.[58] At a special meeting on 18 December the Clifton College Company dissolved itself [27].

The Charter issued on 16 March 1877 [36] notionally created a new Clifton College, although it made not the smallest difference to the School's daily life. The granting of a Charter to an existing institution is sometimes taken to be a new foundation and sometimes not. The Mayoralty of Bristol does not date from Charles II's Charter of 1684, although this purports to create it.[59] On the other hand Westminster School chooses to date itself from Elizabeth's I Charter of 1560 establishing Westminster Abbey as a collegiate church, even though the School had existed for many centuries. Clifton, with its shorter history, has not chosen to write off its first fifteen years. It was not in any case the direct creation of Queen Victoria. Even medieval founders were not always personally involved in the process in the manner of William of Wykeham and Henry VI. The only Victorian school conceived in this way was Wellington.[60] Even so Clifton's Charter has much of the character of its medieval forebears, outlining the purposes of the foundation, nominating its first governing body, and regulating its internal life. What is missing is the accompanying grant of endowment by which the medieval founder gave his creation the means to survive.[61] The royal connexion brought no substantive privileges, save the right to address the Sovereign on solemn occasions. The Queen was therefore sent an elegantly crafted address on her Golden Jubilee in 1887 [375], and a more ponderous one ten years later [378]. When Edward VII came to Avonmouth in 1908 there was an opportunity to present such an address directly, and for the King to reply [381].

Most of the Charter is concerned with the higher governance of the College and with the conduct of Council meetings. The former shareholders are reborn as Original Governors, with rights to nominate pupils, transferable one time only; those who subsequently give £50 become Life Governors with non-transferable rights of nomination; Donors, paying £20, have rights of nomination but not of voting. By the 1930s the Original Governors had all but disappeared. Although it was still possible for anyone with £50 to buy a Life Governorship, the Council tried to mould the Governing Body into an extended family by inviting Old Cliftonians to subscribe [53]. In special cases the subscription was made nominal, so that a Governorship could be bestowed somewhat like an Honorary Fellowship [54].

The Charter's relatively few regulations for the management of the School (sections 66–77) are closely modelled on and sometimes exactly follow the Company's Articles of Association [7]. The Head Master's comprehensive jursidiction is thereby sustained, and indeed invested with royal authority. Only in one instance is

---

[57] CC Company Minute Book 4, p. 69.

[58] CC Company Minute Book 4, p. 81.

[59] R.C. Latham (ed.), *Bristol Charters 1509–1899* (BRS, XII, 1947), pp. 178–9 / 182–3.

[60] Here the Charter was granted five years before the first Master was appointed; the distinctive features of this foundation are explained in D. Newsome, *A History of Wellington College 1859–1959* (1959), pp. 33–83.

[61] See E.F. Jacob, 'Founders and foundations in the later Middle Ages', in his *Essays in later Medieval History* (Manchester, 1968), pp. 154–74.

this qualified: where the Articles (sect. 71) gave him absolute authority to dismiss assistant masters, the Charter (sect. 69) allowed for reinstatement on appeal to the Council. In reality no Head Master could survive such a humiliation; this is one area in which even the most liberal of the species must assert his autocracy.[62]

Top brass

At the head of the foundation was still the President. Under the Company management the President had not actually been a member of the Council; his inclusion in their number was specifically requested by Council in petitioning for the Charter.[63] The President's sole statutory function was to preside at general meetings [sect. 25]; it is implied that he would sit in the Council as an ordinary member, and a later President-designate sought to do just that [44]. The President was to be appointed by vote of the Governors in general meeting [sect. 33]; nothing is said of his qualifications or the term he should serve. This was of no immediate concern because everyone was content for Lord Ducie to remain in office, which he did until he died at the age of 94 in 1921. Earl Haig was the obvious choice for his successor and sustained the role with great distinction. When he died seven years later there was no clear idea of the procedure for replacing him. The Chairman of the Council thought the nominee ought to be a Governor, but being a practical man he was confident that 'could be got over'. He would meanwhile look up a list of OCs in the House of Lords [41]. One name suggested was that of Clifton's other Field Marshal, Sir William Birdwood; but the first choice was to be Earl Buxton, a former Governor-General of South Africa. When he turned down the post it was accepted by the Speaker of the House of Commons, J.H. Whitley [42–6]. Following Whitley's death in 1935, the Chairman wanted to strengthen links with the City by choosing Lord Dulverton, head of the Wills family [52]. This did not persuade the Governors, and Birdwood was elected instead.

At Clifton the President is by Bagehot's celebrated distinction the *dignified* part of the constitution. The *efficient* part is represented by the Council and its Chairman. Lord Ducie's retention of the Presidency into extreme old age gave the subordinate position rather more prominence. The first Chairman, Canon Guthrie, is remembered chiefly for bequeathing funds which paid for the Chapel. This was duly named after him [85], as was the Commemoration festival which became the high point of the Clifton year [405]. Canon Moseley, Chairman from 1865 to 1868, had secured Clifton's original dedication to Anglican teaching. As a Fellow of the Royal Society and holder of the chair of Natural Philosophy and Astronomy at King's College, London, he was also manifestly committed to the advancement of science. He had resigned the Chairmanship before the controversy over the Endowed Schools Act, and his intervention in the debate was therefore that of an ordinary member of the Council. The new Chairman was James Heyworth, also in orders and another of the founding fathers. He presided over the transition from the Company to the Corporation, and he was to be found a scholarship [127].

---

[62] A former Clifton master, when Headmaster of Repton, even succeeded in facing down that school's formidable President, Archbishop Lord Fisher, over the dismissal of a master: J.L. Thorn, *The Road to Winchester* (1989), p. 82.
[63] CC Company Minute Book 4, p. 81.

Dropping the pilot

The most difficult period of Heyworth's chairmanship came when, after fifteen years rich in achievement, John Percival resigned the Head Mastership. Despite his devotion to Clifton he had twice tried to escape from it by applying for the Headmastership of Rugby, and was twice spurned by the electors there.[64] Clifton rejoiced to retain him, though by the end it gave him nightmares, and with some relief he accepted the Presidency of Trinity College, Oxford in 1879. This proved an unhappy choice, and in 1887 he returned to his last when the electors of Rugby finally called for him. A regime of great severity rescued that school from recent traumas, though Percival was ridiculed for ordering footballers to cover their knees as a deterrent to lust.[65] In 1895 he was elevated to the Bishopric of Hereford, where his radical opinions caused much disquiet, as they were meant to do. Disappointed of the Primacy of England, he occupied his see until the year before his death in 1918. He then came home to lie in Clifton Chapel, as he had long intended, and despite advice that his doing so would be illegal **[94–106]**.

Yet he had never really been away. Shortly after he had moved to Oxford he was elected to the Council, and in 1895 he became Chairman. As such he remained closely involved in all aspects of the School's life, from the expulsion of wicked boys **[271, 273]** to the design of a departing master's present **[371, 373]**. Most especially he was concerned in the appointment of successive Head Masters. In 1879 he had been invited to name his own heir, and had no hesitation in recommending James Maurice Wilson, a former colleague at Rugby. Wilson was an eminent mathematician, though a little rusty in the Classics, and the Council duly appointed him. Then followed what Wilson recalled drily as 'a very curious incident'. One of the senior Clifton masters appended to his congratulations a regret that the post had not been advertised, as he felt sure that the Master of Marlborough would then have been chosen. Others in the Common Room, it was suggested, felt the same way. Wilson at once withdrew and the Council, much to its displeasure, had to go through the motions of a fair contest.[66] Only with great reluctance did Wilson agree to stand **[20]**. He had good reason to be wary because of Rugby's recent experience of a Headmaster in whom the staff had no confidence.[67] When he did apply he acknowledged his shortcomings as a Classicist, but at the same time unequivocally stated his terms **[21]**. Even then he did his best to promote the cause of a rival **[23]**. Among these was one of Percival's protégés, whose backers included Bell of Marlborough (never in fact a candidate himself) **[22]**. To nobody's surprise the Council chose Wilson again, and Percival was able to inform parents of the passing of the torch **[24]**.

---

[64] Temple, *Percival*, pp. 43–52; Potter, *Headmaster*, pp. 77–83.
[65] It has been noted that his edict is all too often quoted 'as if it were a freakish aberration': J. Chandos, *Boys Together: English Public Schools 1800–1864* (Oxford, 1984), p. 338; here, and frequently, it is ascribed to Percival's Clifton days. For an attempt to absolve Percival of silliness in the matter see A.C. Percival, 'Some Victorian Headmasters', in B. Simon and I. Bradley, *The Victorian Public School* (1975), pp. 77–8.
[66] A.T. and J.S. Wilson (eds), *James M. Wilson: An Autobiography 1836–1931* (1932), pp. 87–9.
[67] In 1870 the Rugby Trustees, having rejected Percival and other highly qualified applicants, chose the undistinguished Henry Hayman as Headmaster. This provoked a public outcry and a savage remonstrance from the Rugby staff impugning Hayman's credentials and character. In this Wilson had taken a leading part. The masters could not prevent Hayman from being foisted upon them, but after four years of conflict they engineered his dismissal: Wilson *Autobiography*, pp. 69–82; Hope Simpson, *Rugby since Arnold*, pp. 66–100.

Apostolic succession

Wilson had not taken orders until his appointment to Clifton, but he had always been intent on an ecclesiastical career, and to this he departed in 1890. Percival had no doubt that the man to succeed him should be his own most distinguished pupil and a former Head of the School, T.H. Warren [55]. Warren had gone on to collect a host of Oxford's most glittering prizes [26], and since 1885 he had been President of Magdalen. From this eminence not even Percival could persuade him to descend to the Head Mastership of Clifton.[68] Warren did however join with Percival and Wilson in proposing the name of H.A. James, the recently appointed Principal of Cheltenham. James accepted, only to withdraw after a fortnight because Cheltenham had begged him to stay. At the third attempt the Council secured the services of M.G. Glazebrook, High Master of Manchester Grammar School [56–7]. Glazebrook was competent but unappealing, and it was not only the collectors of pin-ups who engaged his disapproval [81]. Clifton's livelier side nevertheless owes much to him, for he allowed drama to begin [358], and he institutionalised the teaching of music. His actual memorial is the Chapel pulpit [107–16].

There were no difficulties in replacing Glazebrook when he moved to an Ely canonry in 1905. Percival, who had by then been running the Council for a decade, wanted A.A. David, a former Rugby master, and the Council appointed him. The main interest is in the financial arrangements which were made for him. The Head Master's salary was exactly matched by the rent he had to pay for School House, which until 1922 was attached to his office. His actual income came from a capitation fee for each boy in the College and its two junior departments, so that the Head Master's livelihood was directly pegged to the numbers in the School [61]. David was popular and progressive; he introduced Swedish drill and the study of current affairs [381]. He did not stay for long enough to make any greater mark, for Rugby poached him back in 1910. Then, after declining many bishoprics including that of Bristol, he accepted St Edmundsbury and Ipswich, and was later translated to Liverpool.[69]

To the vacated Head Mastership Percival was most anxious to promote his godson and former Rugby pupil William Temple, destined to follow his father Frederick to Canterbury. In this however he failed, being outvoted in the Council, as the minutes most unusually reveal [62]. Temple was already widely known as a radical, like his father; indeed that was part of his appeal in Percival's eyes. The majority of the Council took another view, and Temple's name was removed from the shortlist. Perhaps some who were sympathetic to Temple suspected that, like David, he would not stay for long.[70] Temple's service to Clifton was to write Percival's biography, in which he made no reference to this incident. Once Temple was discounted, four candidates remained, all of whom were laymen and eminent Classicists, and three of them Old Cliftonians. The choice fell on J.E. King, Headmaster of Bedford Grammar

---

[68] Winterbottom, *Clifton after Percival*, p. 38. Percival, it was noted, had just made such a move; but this was and remains the only instance of an Oxbridge Head of House moving to a headmastership.

[69] His career resembled Percival's also in that towards the end of his headmastership he went slightly mad; in his case by sending delinquents to a homespun psychoanalyst in whom he had great faith: Hope Simpson, *Rugby since Arnold*, pp. 159, 183–5.

[70] As suggested in Winterbottom, *Clifton after Percival*, p. 44.

School, who thus became Clifton's first lay Head Master, and as yet the only one to have been an O.C.[71]

Another remarkable aspect of this election was that Temple's candidacy was common knowledge among the smallest boys, and caused apprehension:

> When Albert David left there was speculation about who would succeed him, and word went round that it might be one William Temple. But he was said to be a socialist, and wouldn't that be frightful, said the fags in School House. Apparently the Governors [*sic*] were of the same opinion, for they appointed J.E. King, who wore wing collars and side-whiskers and looked exactly like Beach, the Blandings butler ... the dullest teacher of Classics imaginable.[72]

King's forbidding manner may have been adopted to compensate for lack of clerical *gravitas*. Yet many remembered him with affection **[71]**, and there was a whimsical side to his erudition.[73]

The Great War

King's headmastership was momentous. It saw the extension of the Chapel to its present form **[93]**, and the acquisition of the additional playing fields at Beggar's Bush over the Bridge. In 1912 the College celebrated its Golden Jubilee, and received a visit from the King and Queen **[382–4]**.

The war cast all else into shadow, and its impact was immediate. Six masters at once enlisted, including two who never had the chance to take up their appointment **[422]**. Among those who did not return was the House Master and Corps Commander Harry Clissold, whose name features prominently in these documents **[329, 425]**. Of the 3,100 Old Cliftonians who fought, 578 were lost.[74] This was equivalent to the entire population of the School, a grim statistic shared with many others.[75] It is argued that the public schools were the agents of their own calamity, having moulded a military caste whose zeal for war outran its technical ability to command. However this may be quantified, the special vulnerability of junior officers added significantly to the public school casualties.[76] There is no doubt too that the chivalric code induced a casual disregard for danger which cost many lives. Clifton in particular had been

---

[71] The first lay headmasters of 'leading public schools' are reckoned to be: Frank Fletcher, appointed Master of Marlborough in 1903; W.W. Vaughan [*M138*], appointed Master of Wellington in 1910, on the strength of a reputation for 'modern views' established when Head of Clifton's Modern Side; and Cyril Norwood, who moved from the headmastership of Bristol Grammar School to become Master of Marlborough in 1917, and thereafter went to Harrow: Newsome, *Wellington*, pp. 275–6, followed by Hope Simpson, *Rugby since Arnold*, pp. 189–90. There were, however, lay headmasters before the seventeenth century (notably William Camden at Westminster).

[72] T.R. Milford [*7027*: SH 1909–14], *Two Brothers: A Milford Memoir, 1895–1935* (priv pr. 1986), p. 35.

[73] He made an English verse translation of *Carmina Blagdonensis*, a fanciful Latin epic celebrating the fishing on Blagdon Lake, written by H.S. Hall [*235/M59*]. King's version was to have been put in this volume, but had to make way for heavier matter; it will now be printed in the *Clifton Magazine*.

[74] Christie, *History*, pp. 182–91, gives an account of the losses, and of the honours.

[75] Christie, *History*, p. 204 n. 9; R. Hyam, *Britain's Imperial Century: A Study of Empire and Expansion* (3rd edn, 2002), pp. 335–6; P. Parker, *The Old Lie: The Great War and the Public-School Ethos* (1987), pp. 16–17, 279 & n. 1.

[76] Parker, *op.cit.*, deals comprehensively with these issues. See also G.F.A. Best, 'Militarism and the Victorian School', in Simon and Bradley, *The Victorian Public School*, pp. 129–46.

encouraged by the verse of Sir Henry Newbolt to see warfare as an extended cricket match. One of the earliest casualties was A.E.J. Collins, who as a boy in the Junior School had made cricket's highest individual innings score [285]. In the last days of battle another of Clifton's most cherished players was killed. G.W.E. Whitehead had made the highest individual score for the School, and he had captained the XI of 1914; six of that team died, and four were wounded. From a compilation of Whitehead's letters two in particular recall Clifton with special affection and poignancy [423–4]. It was scarcely surprising that the memory had already turned to gold, and that from the perspective of the Western Front the architecture of Clifton seemed like heaven on earth.

The horror of the mounting casualty lists was tempered by pride in the achievements of Clifton's fighting sons and the recognition they received. In 1915 Sir Douglas Haig *alumnus praeeminens* assumed command of the greatest army the nation had ever put in the field. When he received his baton two years later the School was prompt in its salute [443]. Haig had already showed his appreciation of efforts made by the Old Cliftonian Society to assist sons of war victims [442]. As victory approached the OCS paid tribute to Haig's great part in achieving it, though the Society's own sacrifice was not yet complete [427].

Remembering them

Even before an end was in sight the planning of a war memorial had begun. This was commonplace, as was the feeling that some of the money raised should be spent in support of education, and in other practical ways.[77] Since the South African War memorial already occupied the prime site, and in purely artistic terms could scarcely be bettered, the new monument had to be some distance away and in a different form. The simple extent of the names posed a problem, and there was thought of setting them up separately. These issues were sensibly delegated to the acknowledged expert in the field, Major Charles Holden. He proposed an archway within which the names would be carved, creating a feature both solemn and functional [428]. This was accepted in principle; the actual design was then opened to competition, and Holden's own entry was chosen [429–30]. Care was taken to find stone matching that of the existing buildings [432], though the College baulked at the cost of erecting a full-size model [433]. Much thought was given to the protocol for the dedication, including the hospitality which followed [435–9]. The Memorial Arch has been greatly admired, even when Clifton's main prospect has been found unremarkable.[78] It was soon obliged to carry another great burden of names.

End of the first age

John Percival died three weeks after the end of the First World War. For Clifton the year 1918 is thereby all the more emphatic a watershed. Percival had retired from Hereford in the summer of the previous year, when at the age of 82 his physical powers began at last to fail him. In the following November the Council received

---

[77] *Register* (1925), pp. cxxiii–cxxv; other school memorials are surveyed in Parker, *Old Lie*, pp. 275–8.
[78] M. Jenner, *Bristol's Best 100 Buildings* (Bristol, 2010), p. 126 (where only the Chapel and the Arch earn Clifton its place).

'with sincere sympathy and regret' the news that he was also laying down his Chairmanship [**37**]. It has always been supposed that Percival resigned solely for reasons of infirmity and old age. That was understood when the Old Cliftonian Society sent their own sympathetic tribute [**426**]. It can now be revealed that his resignation was hastened if not caused by the departure from Clifton of his grandson Jack. The evidence comes in two letters to the Head Master from the boy's father, Percival's fourth and only surviving son Lancelot [**254–5**]. The details are still obscure, and are muddled with some bizarre fuss over a pilfered sausage. The serious business was a theft of money, in which Jack was seemingly an accessory. Quite probably the boy had been goaded into an act of bravado. He had been victimized as Head Master's kin; not unusual in itself, but striking testimony to the aura of a Head Master who had left 38 years before. Although Lancelot Percival accepted his son's assertion of innocence, he did not invoke the law to prove it.[79] He simply asked to be allowed to give the news to his father, certain that this would mean his immediate resignation from the Chairmanship, and would prevent him from attending another meeting of the Council. So it was, and a deep sadness must have clouded the great man's final months.

Between the wars

While he yet lived Percival's place at the head of the Council was taken by the man whom he had hoped to see as Head Master, Sir Herbert Warren [**38**]. The twelve years of his chairmanship were generally prosperous, and much credit for this is owed to Warren's unrelenting efforts. He is a presence still in the archives, which contain a formidable quantity of his letters and memoranda. In 1922 King retired as Head Master, and Warren superintended the search for his successor [**64**]. The four short-listed candidates included an O.C. and former master M.R. Ridley, who among other distinctions inspired the physical appearance of Lord Peter Wimsey.[80] The chosen man, however, was Norman Whatley, Fellow of Hertford College, Oxford, the first of four successive dons enticed to Clifton [**65**]. Of these Whatley was perhaps the most committed to school-mastering; at any rate the other three returned to university posts.[81] It was nevertheless a venturesome appointment, for which Warren was largely responsible.[82] Whatley set high standards of scholarship, and his termly reports to the Council, though business-like, had touches of donnish whimsy. He also made a careful record of his decisions [**152**]. After two years he submitted a comprehensive survey of his inheritance and his vision for the future [**68**]. Apart from the recurring fantasy of buying the Zoo, most of his main aspirations were achieved, though not all in his time.

In his first decade Whatley pushed through two major and inter-related projects. From the outset he had advocated merging the Junior and Preparatory Schools, and

---

[79] There are echoes of the *cause célèbre* of 1908 concerning an Osborne cadet and a stolen postal order, the story on which Terence Rattigan based his play *The Winslow Boy* (1946).

[80] It may be noted that as well as providing Dorothy L. Sayers with her great sleuth, the Clifton Common Room also gave Agatha Christie the model for one of her master-villains: below [**361**].

[81] B.L. Hallward left in 1948 to become first Vice-Chancellor of Nottingham University; Sir Desmond Lee, after serving as Headmaster of Winchester from 1954 to 1968, ended his career as President of Hughes Hall, Cambridge; N.G.L. Hammond left in 1962 to become Professor of Greek at Bristol. Even Whatley retired to the orbit of Academe, becoming Mayor of Oxford.

[82] Winterbottom, *Clifton after Percival*, p. 57.

making the combined department much less dependent on the Upper School. What was thereafter to be called the Preparatory School was housed in a new building on Guthrie Road, the site for which was acquired cheaply because of the slump. On the site formerly occupied by the Junior School, east of the Chapel, there arose the Science School, its gleaming modernities gracefully hidden behind an Elizabethan facade [147].

Surprisingly the Head of Science, Dr E.J. Holmyard, had not wanted this new building at all. Clifton science was already in awe of its own traditions, and Holmyard was reluctant to abandon the laboratories where Sir William Tilden and W.A. Shenstone had taught [148]. Eventually a satisfactory design was agreed, and the various rooms were embellished to commemorate their donors [149–51]. Holmyard warmed to the scheme, not least because he was able to set his own stamp upon it. He was a man of letters as well as of science (indeed his doctorate was in the former), and he collected a great treasure of early scientific books and manuscripts [185]. He therefore ensured that the laboratories were complemented by a substantial library. The new building was opened in 1927 by the Prince of Wales [391–402].

After ten years Whatley's regime began to falter. This was partly because of external economics, though there were also domestic problems. Whatley lost his patron and supporter Warren, who died in 1930 after 47 years on the Council [47–51]. Whatley himself was in failing health, and was out of action a whole term in 1933 [70]. One of the assistant masters had been a prolonged nuisance, and there was also trouble below stairs. The College's early success had been helped by the continuous service of its senior administrators. At the head of the office was and is Secretary to the Council. This position was taken up in 1864 by A.D.L. Macpherson, who retained it until the year of the College's golden jubilee. His successor W.J. Lewis had been chief clerk since 1882, and he carried on himself until 1930. So between them these two men ran Clifton's administration for sixty-eight years. They worked well with successive Head Masters, and assisted the transition from one reign to the next. The orderliness of the system is still evident in the great series of ledger books bound in crimson leather which range along the shelves of the Archive Room. In Lewis's place, and with the additional title of Bursar, Whatley appointed N.R. Udal, who had administered the Sudan with evident competence. Clifton however proved to be beyond him, as it was for his successor G.E. Badcock. This was disruptive in itself, and exacerbated conflict between Whatley and the new Chairman of Council, Sir Robert Witt.[83] The upshot was that Whatley was bullied into retiring, though he chivalrously agreed to serve another term. Announcing this to the Governors while Whatley was still *in situ*, the Chairman referred only, and with great warmth, to the Head Master's many achievements [66]. He did not feel it necessary to repeat himself at the AGM after Whatley had left [71].

Whatley was not an inspiring figure. He looked more like a businessman than an academic, and even when in gown and hood the camera always seemed to catch him with these garments in disarray. His successor was by contrast a man of imposing physical presence and immaculate bearing. Bertrand Hallward was a Classics Fellow of Peterhouse, where Birdwood, to general astonishment and his own, had become Master.[84] Though Hallward was starting to publish, his interests were more

---

[83] Winterbottom, *Clifton after Percival*, pp. 112–16.
[84] D.O. Winterbottom, *Bertrand Hallward, First Vice-Chancellor of the University of Nottingham: A Biography* (Nottingham, 1995), p. 68; Lord Birdwood (W.R.), *Khaki and Gown: An Autobiography* (1941), pp. 409–11.

in administration, and he had already tried for the Headmastership of Felsted.[85] Not even Birdwood's recommendation could help him to that, but it secured Clifton for him. It was an inspired act of patronage, for Hallward was destined to guide the School securely through its darkest days.

Under attack

Clifton prepared to face the Second World War in full expectation of being in the front line [**453–7**]. This did not happen immediately, because until the fall of France the West Country lay beyond the range of German bombers. Thereafter Bristol did become a prime target, and from September to December 1940 the City was repeatedly attacked. There are many graphic accounts of that time, to which the despatches of Richard Martin can now be added [**457–60, 463**]. His letters to his mother, written as bombs were falling round about him, present a characteristically Cliftonian blend of informed reportage and *sang froid*. Spitfires appear from nowhere, dive straight down on the bombers and push them back to the Channel. Some of the younger boys are understandably 'rather frightened' but only for a moment. School life carries on as best it can in and out of the shelters. Eventually, however, the bombs came too close. Incendiaries fell all over the premises, and disaster was only averted by the efforts of the School's own fire brigade. Then on 2 December 1940 explosives landed on the New Field, and the two adjacent boarding houses (Polack's and Wiseman's) became uninhabitable. As a result the Head Master sent all the boarders home the following day [**461**]. Four days later the Council decided to evacuate the whole School before the next term [**462**]. No destination had yet been fixed, though various possibilities had been considered. This now became a matter of urgency, and after some high-powered lobbying the War Office allocated a group of hotels in Bude on the north Cornish coast. These had been requisitioned for military use; in return the College premises were handed over to the War Office for the duration. In due course Clifton became a base for American troops: initially V Corps and then General Bradley's First Army. Much of the planning for D-Day was done at Clifton. That however is another story, beyond the terminal point of this volume. Or not quite: because Clifton did not go away entirely. The Preparatory School took up residence at Butcombe Court fifteen miles to the south – relatively safe in the country though still in the Luftwaffe's flight-path. A small group of Pre day boys nevertheless stayed in Bristol and were taught in Matthews' House. Their story has never been fully told before; but happily one of their number, Robert MacEwen, has committed his memories to paper. These are printed with his permission as the tailpiece to this volume [**464**].

II: CLIFTONIANS

Inmates

Domestic life is best documented from the volumes compiled in the Houses, variously styled annals, journals or simply 'the House Books' [**403–21**]. The House

---

[85] The competition was exceptionally strong, including 32 incumbent headmasters: M. Craze, *A History of Felsted School 1564–1947* (Ipswich, 1955), p. 291.

commands its inmates' primary loyalties, and that is reflected in these volumes. Each House had its own style. Some kept bare records of sporting fixtures, scholarships, and other formalities. Elsewhere discursive journals were compiled. In many cases photographs, programmes and suchlike are inserted. Some books were kept by the boys themselves, others by the House Masters. For Polack's there is the personal journal kept by the wife of the first House Master of that name [19, 405–7, 410–11]. Survival is sporadic; School House in this period is represented only by a photograph album, for most of the House archive disappeared during the American occupation of 1942–3. Not all formats are suitable for presentation here, and the examples chosen are of the more literary kind.

Scholars

The central function of the School is among the most difficult to illustrate from the archives. That large part of the the educational process conducted *viva voce* is by definition unrepresented there. Little survives of written classwork, and what there is would not have been especially illuminating. The Classics curriculum is outlined in a notice of 1873 [128], and the enduring value of Classics as training for public life is endorsed by the Head Master in 1929 [132]. Scholarships and prizes were progressively founded, some by way of memorial, others linking College and City [67, 71, 125–7, 130–1]. The first external assessment dates from 1864, and while making allowance for Clifton's immaturity, the examiners found it 'abundantly evident that a thorough system of public school education has been established' [121]. The report at the end of the first decade was equally enthusiastic, though it must be noted that the author was a former Clifton master [122]. In 1880 Jowett of Balliol was able to congratulate the School on what he believed to be the unprecedented achievement of three simultaneous entrance awards [129]. By later standards this would have been unremarkable. Indeed in 1925 Whatley told the Council that winning ten Oxbridge awards in the previous term was 'not very good', merely what was expected [67]. Three years later the external examiners (admittedly a massively learned team) were even more sparing with their praise. The scientists received the best report; in the Classics and Modern Languages a few boys excelled, but many weaknesses were exposed; the historians and the divines were inclined to ramble aimlessly [123].

The examiners' reports single out the achievements of some pupils; individual reports in this period are rather meagre. Haig's celebrity has ensured the survival of one examination report in which he distinguished himself [440]. By far the best documented Clifton schoolboy of this period is T. Tunstall-Behrens.[86] The large volume containing his letters to and from home includes facsimiles of his reports from 1893–5, along with examination papers and other material.[87] Another format of report survives from 1879 to 1919. The 'Record Sheets' contain very brief comments on each term's performance, epitomising entire school careers in a few lines. These reports were not sent to parents, which is why they remain in the College Archives. Haig left the term before the extant series begins. The report on Birdwood, the other

---

[86] Tankred Tunstall-Behrens [*4605*: BH 1892–5].

[87] D.L. Crane (ed.), with J. Crane and R.L. Bland, *Letters between a Victorian Schoolboy and his Family, 1892–1895* (priv. pr. 1999), Documentary appendix, pp. I–XV (reports), XVI–XVIII (curriculum), XX (timetable), XXI–II (mathematics papers). Without having been so planned, the documents selected for the present volume range either side of Tunstall-Behrens' schooldays.

Field Marshal whom Clifton educated, gives little hint of future greatness **[133]**. It seemed appropriate to add the report on C.W.E. Bean **[134]**, who chronicled Birdwood's command of ANZAC.[88] Bean, son of one of the original pupils of 1862, later founded the Australian War Memorial; father and son were among several early Cliftonians influential in Australia.[89] The report on J.M. Wilson's son Arnold is notable for the improvements it charts, from 'careless and conceited' to 'shows public spirit' **[135]**. This group is completed with reports for three inter-connected Cliftonians of a very different stamp, Bloomsbury groupies Roger Fry and Thoby Stephen, and Fry's schoolfriend the philosopher J.E. McTaggart **[136–8]**.

Scientists[90]

One of the great criticisms levelled against the old public schools was that they taught no science, and were slow to introduce it even when prevailed upon to do so.[91] Clifton on the other hand, provided science teaching from its early days, and this rapidly developed into a major department. Percival laid the foundations by including a botanist, F.A. Leipner, among his original staff as teacher of German and Natural Philosophy.[92] In 1867 the first laboratory was opened **[139]**, and Percival brought in Colonel E.C. Plant to teach Mechanical and Engineering Drawing, and W.T. Rowden to teach Physics, both men trained at the Bristol Trade and Mining School.[93] The original Physics course was charted with precision **[124]**. The following year Dr H. Debus joined the team, also engaged to teach 'Physical Science' but in fact a chemist, the pupil and successor of Bunsen at Marburg, and already an FRS.[94] It is significant than none of these first four science staff members came from Oxford or Cambridge, which had themselves barely begun to manufacture scientists in any quantity.[95] As already noted the Chairman of the Council from 1865–8, Henry Moseley, was an FRS with a science chair at King's College, London.

---

[88] During the Gallipoli campaign, Bean wrote in his diary: 'It is the quietest day we have had ... with only an occasional sniping shot, exactly like the crack of a cricket ball ... I could scarcely believe that this crack, crack, crack, was not the nets at Clifton College': K. Fewster (ed.) *Bean's Gallipoli: The Diaries of Australia's War Correspondent* (3rd edn, 2007), p. 105.

[89] In 1891 one of Sydney's leading schools defined its object as to become 'the Clifton of Australia': G. Sherington, *Shore: A History of Sydney Church of England Grammar School* (Sydney, 1983), p. 38.

[90] See particularly T.I. Williams, 'Clifton and Science', in *Centenary Essays*, pp. 195–212; S.M. Andrews, 'A century of science teaching', in *Science at Clifton* (priv. pr. 1977), pp. 3–6.

[91] A.J. Meadows and W.H. Brock, 'Topics fit for gentlemen: the problem of science in the Public School Curriculum', in Simon and Bradley, *Victorian Public School*, pp. 95–114; Shrosbee, *Clarendon Commission*, pp. 50–3 and *passim*.

[92] Frederick Adolph Leipner [*M7*: 1862–9]; after leaving Clifton became Lecturer in Botany, Zoology and German at University College, Bristol, then first Professor of Botany from 1886 to his death in 1894; also established the University's first Botanic Garden at Woodland Road: *Reg. Univ.*, p. 234.

[93] For Plant see below **[194]**; William Thomas Rowden [*M35*: 1867–8] also studied at the Royal School of Mines and the Royal College of Chemistry, collecting a London BSc and numerous medals; later Professor of Applied Mechanics at Anderson's College, Glasgow.

[94] Heinrich Debus [*M37*: 1868–70]; later Professor of Chemistry at the Royal Naval College, Greenwich.

[95] Cf. Shrosbee, *Clarendon Commission*, p. 51, noting many of institutions from which the public schools might have drawn science teachers had they been so minded. The first Clifton science master to come from Oxbridge was Arnold William Reinold [*M41*: 1869], who had been a Fellow of Merton; later FRS and Professor of Physics at Greenwich.

Percival appointed two more scientists of distinction. The mathematician Dr J. Perry, like several of these other figures, moved on swiftly.[96] But the chemist W.A. (later Sir William) Tilden stayed for eight years, being elected to the Royal Society in his last term.[97] This was indeed a brief time, before Oxford and Cambridge science asserted itself, when many an FRS was engaged in school teaching.[98] Clifton science received a new champion when Wilson succeeded as Head Master in 1877. Mathematics was his main subject, but he had taught some general science at Rugby, and had a particular interest in Astronomy. Although he had not been able to achieve much, it had made him an acknowledged expert on science teaching in public schools.[99] In 1880 Wilson appointed W.A. Shenstone, whose pioneering research into the working of silica was relayed to pupils as it developed [165]. He was elected to the Royal Society in 1898, and Clifton managed to retain him until his death ten years later. Yet for all this fine teaching, before the start of the twentieth century the number of Cliftonians taking up careers in science was insignificant.[100]

Alongside the formal instruction was the Scientific Society, founded in 1869, from whose minutes a large and varied section is here offered [153–86]. So rich is this material that selection was again a problem. One consideration was not to duplicate reports already published in the Society's *Transactions*; another was to achieve a balance in the branches of science. Naturally the great names from the science staff are featured. Tilden takes a leading part in one discussion [155], and another time cuts short a speaker waffling after a failed experiment [156]. Shenstone demonstrates the properties of Phosphorus and the preparation of Oxygen, as well as his own recently developed technique for the working of silica [156, 160, 165]. Some eminent outsiders appear by proxy. The veteran geologist Adam Sedgwick sends his greetings, and recalls his own study of the Gorge [154]. Reference is made to a demonstration of wireless telegraphy in Big School by Marconi himself [173].

J.M. Wilson became the Society's President and encouraged its members to look to the stars [158, 166]. The Society's Secretaries included the future Nobel Chemistry Prize-winner Sir John Kendrew [183, 185], though the only report of his work is not encouraging [187].[101] Of particular note is a lecture which clearly inspired another Secretary to embark on a successful career in the oil industry [179]. Conversely there is interest in the scientific enthusiasms of those who were to achieve distinction in other fields. It is surprising to know that Roger Fry was an authority on moss [162], and that Sir David Piper was expert in optics [187]; perhaps less so to find a future bishop with an enthusiasm for railways [163]. Members learned about the science of sport [176] and war [177]; they were instructed in the making of soap [181], dynamite

[96] John Perry [*M50*: 1871–3], later FRS and Professor of Mathematics and Mechanics at the Royal College of Science.

[97] For Tilden see below [155–6].

[98] The phenomenon was identified by Sir Brian Pippard, FRS [*10478*] in 'Schoolmaster-Fellows and the campaign for science education', *Notes and Records of the Royal Society* 56 (2002), pp. 63–81.

[99] Hope Simpson, *Rugby after Arnold*, p. 92; Shrosbee, *Clarendon Commission*, p. 62; Meadows and Brock, 'Science', pp. 104–6.

[100] Bamford, *Public Schools*, pp. 219–21, analysing Cheltenham and Clifton leavers up to 1905, finds no evidence for increase in science careers, and concludes that though the forces (by far the largest occupation in both cases) gained a higher level of technical skill, there was no general benefit to the nation and its industry. It must be noted that the statistical base for this (the printed Registers) is very imperfect.

[101] The reader will however look in vain beyond this point for the names of two other Nobel laureates: Sir John Richard Hicks [*8183*: WiH 1917–22], who shared the Economic Sciences Prize for 1972, and Sir Nevill Francis Mott [*8430*: PHP, SH 1918–23], who shared the Physics Prize for 1977.

[157], and talking pictures [182]. In 1909 members were shown the flickering light of a 'kathode ray' [175]; twenty-five years later two boys built a television [187]. There were also outings to local industries and businesses to see how science made the modern world work [178, 183]. For the Archaeological Section there were chances to explore Bristol's abundant heritage [184].

The Science School of 1927 is documented with details of its planning [147–51] and with papers concerning its opening by the Prince of Wales [391–402]. The new building became the venue for an annual *Conversazione* when the members of the Scientific Society demonstrated their skills. This is illustrated by the programme for the 1934 event, from a copy which the Society's President has annotated [187].

Keepers

Another but rather less successful scientific venture was the Museum. It was set up, with great enthusiasm in the early days, as was a related Botanic Garden, and abundant donations were received for both [140–2]. The sensible guidelines made at the outset were not observed, and the Museum was swamped with a disorderly jumble of miscellaneous objects, soon to be a laughing stock. In 1925 Whatley had hope of reviving it, but crisply analysed the problem of maintaining such a collection [68].

Flyers

Bristol's prominence in aero-engineering is properly represented. Sir Roy Fedden, BAC's chief engine designer, was the Old Cliftonian most eminent in this field. He showed enthusiastic members of the Scientific Society round the Filton works [178] and later offered encouraging prospects of careers in the industry [180]. During the First World War the fledgling Air Ministry provided an engine for teaching purposes [181]. This was lodged somewhat incongruously under the Chapel, which might have been a safer place for the monoplane given to his old School by the daredevil aviator Douglas Gilmour. After a spell hanging in the Gym, Gilmour's 'Bat' was given to the City Museum, where it perished as a result of a less welcome development in aviation [191–2]. It should also be recorded that Clifton educated the pioneering British dirigible pilot Ernest Willows.[102]

Talkers

The minutes of the School and House debating societies for this period are rather disappointing. Early reports give nothing but the names of the speakers and the outcome of the vote. It is interesting to learn that Henry Newbolt spoke against the second Afghan War, but it would be more so to know what he said [291]. When the minutes do become more expansive, it is primarily because the Secretaries enjoy writing them up in a facetiously condescending manner [292–4, 296]. Only

---

[102] Ernest Thompson Willows [*5207*: ST 1897–1901]; killed in a ballooning accident 1926: see A. McKinty, *The Father of British Airships: A Biography of E.T. Willows* (1972).

the Polack's House debates have more substance; indeed any larger selection from them would have unfairly balanced this section. The debate about moving Clifton to Somerset raises some realistic issues, even though the motion itself was illusory [295]. In October 1933 Polack's staged its own version of the 'King and Country' debate held at the Oxford Union earlier in the year. Some of the observations were a little off the point, such as the warning from a future Lord Mayor of London that a German invasion would put up income tax. Nor can the speech by Corps Commander and Great War veteran C.H.R. Gee have been quite as belligerent as is represented. The substance of serious argument is none the less presented. In the end the noes had it, and Polack's stood prepared to fight for Country, though not specifically for King.[103]

Patients

Health care was not promoted as a selling point when the College was established. A Sanatorium was opened in 1865,[104] and five years later its facilities were opened to day boys [207]. It remained, however, only for those whose parents had already subscribed for the term; other invalids who turned up at the door were presumably sent away. Moreover since the subscription did not cover medical attendance, food, or washing, it was probably easier to catch an infection there than to recover from one [207]. Diseases of one sort or another regularly disrupted the life of the School throughout this period, and not infrequently terms began or ended prematurely by way of precaution [208, 214]. Fortunately the College was well placed to employ medical advisers of high quality, having many of Bristol's leading physicians as neighbours,[105] and not a few of them already involved as Governors and parents. It is therefore astonishing that J.M. Wilson's sensible proposal to appoint a Medical Officer was twice rejected by the Council before being implemented. Even after a boy in Brown's had died from typhoid, the Council felt that the Head Master and House Masters between them were adequate authorities on sanitation [209–10]. But then T.E. Brown himself, the most compassionate of pastors, seems to have regarded the whole affair as a nuisance.[106]

When the sense of Wilson's argument was at last acknowledged, Dr William Fyffe was charged with overseeing the prevention as well as the cure of disease. The thoroughness of his sanitary reports is matched by that of the Head Master's responses to them. It was a matter of some satisfaction that the Russian 'flu epidemic of 1890 resulted in only one death [211–12]. A further outbreak of typhoid on 1897 was successfully controlled, and the only contention was over a mother's complaint about access to her son [217].

Less serious but still debilitating illnesses feature prominently in the journal of Sophie Polack [406–7, 410]. It cannot be supposed that her charges were especially frail, so it must be concluded that she had not yet cooled to the public school ethos. This is better evident in the School House boy who, having suffered a scalding and a

---

[103] *Cf.* Whatley's patronising compliment that the Jewish House was 'wonderfully patriotic' [68].

[104] *Register* (1925), p. lxv.

[105] One part of Clifton notably well populated with medical expertise is surveyed in M.J. Whitfield, *The Victorian Doctors of Victoria Square* (Bristol, 2012).

[106] See Brown, *Newly Discovered Letters*, p. 101: 'All drains to be turned up, "whole sanitary system to be reconstructed" in all the houses. Fancy! in three weeks!'

fractured wrist, and had undergone a throat operation, collapsed in a faint. The doctor diagnosed indigestion and gave him a tonic; after half an hour's rest this 'plucky boy' was asking to be allowed back into School so as not to miss any more work [242]. Progressively more comprehensive health care was provided. Dr Fyffe gave his attention to the ethics of dental anaesthesia [215]. Vaccination against diphtheria was introduced following an expensive outbreak in Brown's [230–1]. Even when boarding fees had come to include use of the Sanatorium and general medical attendance, vaccination and anaesthetics were still distinctly noted as extras.[107] In 1910 one of the Medical Officers was particularly keen to have the boys weighed and measured, according to the system used at Oxford [218]. In a School which sent so many of its sons into the army this had significance beyond medical statistics. During the Boer War there was alarm about the inadequate height and weight of military recruits, and concern to maintain the physical prowess of the 'Imperial Race'.[108]

The Pollard case of 1914–15 shows how a potentially damaging suit for medical negligence was diplomatically resolved; in passing it offers striking insights into contemporary perspectives on health treatment. The formal record of the Council minutes tells us merely that Dr Reginald Pollard, himself an O.C., threatened to sue the College following the death of his son shortly after leaving school [219]. The sum claimed was considerable (£750) and the College thought it best to obtain the opinion of a prominent K.C. [220–1]. After some ritual exchanges the solicitors settled out of court for about half the sum claimed, which was admitted as the plaintiff's real expense [223–4]. There was no suggestion that Pollard held the College accountable for his son's death, only for certain treatment. The key to this is provided by the Headmaster of a Cheshire school, A.G. Grenfell (another O.C.), to whom King had written for advice [222]. There was apprehension that the mother of one of Grenfell's pupils, having heard of the Pollard boy's death, no longer wanted her own son to proceed to Clifton. Grenfell reassured King on that point, and dismissed the plausibility of any action for negligence. By analogy of another case, it appears that the School's Medical Officer A.W. Prichard, unaware that the Pollard boy had terminal cancer, induced complications by treating him in the ordinary way for a minor injury. Grenfell's assertion that 'boys at Public Schools are supposed to be *normally* healthy' has special resonance within the context of the war. It was almost saying that those who died before reaching military age were deserters. The unhesitating defence of the doctor is also very much of its time, though as soon as legal action had been threatened, Prichard had resigned on the grounds of failing eyesight.

Amidst all the other tragedies of the war, Clifton was affected by a serious outbreak of meningitis, from which two boys died [225–9]. A detailed report provided by a specialist from the University demonstrates how the infection spread through the School [228]. Despite the deaths of two of his pupils King felt able to report in February 1916 that the health of the School was very much better. He was pleased that the precautionary spraying of throats had much reduced coughing in Chapel [227]. Later the Sixth wanted to make coughing (or rather the non-reporting of a cough) a punishable offence [288].

---

[107] *Bye-Laws* (1937), p. 7.
[108] Hyam, *Imperial Century*, pp. 274–5.

Leavers

Those who departed under clouds have usually remained hidden by them. It is now fashionable to boast, after a decent interval, of being sacked from a famous school, but this special form of inverted snobbery took a while to evolve. Publicity was bad for all concerned, and historians have consequently been frustrated. 'An expulsion register or two' wrote T.R. Bamford in 1967, 'would be a gold-mine of information.'[109] The Clifton Archives may not be quite that, but they offer prospectors some reward. In this matter the Head Master had absolute discretion by virtue of section 70 of the Charter **[36]**. He was obliged to report his actions immediately to the Council, and the minutes record his doing so. Sometimes the offences are specified, but they are more often glossed over as 'gross misbehaviour' **[70]**. The most puzzling case is that of a Greek boy Constantine Voltos, who entered Clissold's House in January 1914; or rather he ran away from it on his first day, was recaptured and then expelled on his second.[110] Attempted escape could not in itself have justified expulsion, and it is hard to imagine how adequate mischief could have been wrought in so short a stay. Much more significant is a recently-discovered file of documents about forced departures from the 1880s and the end of the First War. The contents proved to be, quite literally, explosive.

The selection begins with exchanges between Glazebrook and the father of a boy being expelled for mere incompetence **[232–6]**. The boy had not passed up from the Junior School by the appointed age, and so was required to leave by the rule of superannuation **[79(7)]**. Faced with the father's annoyance, the Head Master replied that his son was 'quite extraordinarily stupid'. He was later more open, offering his views on the Cliftonians of 1891 – 'below the average of the Public Schools in ability' but with exceptional freedom to 'follow their particular bent'. He also accepted that the food in School House had been awful, but stressed that he had improved it **[234]**. When the father persisted, Glazebrook told him bluntly and quite correctly that he was wasting his time, as the Finance Committee's decision was to prove **[235–6]**.

A sadder story is told of a boy withdrawn because his father considered he was being unreasonably punished for academic weakness **[237–53]**. The papers form a printed submission to the Council in a subsidiary argument over liability for fees. There are two letters from the boy himself, brave in adversity, and cheerfully describing an outing to mark the relief of Mafeking **[243–4]**. The father comes to Clifton but Glazebrook, busy with Commem guests, cannot meet him. The exchange of letters becomes sharper, and the boy is duly taken home **[245–51]**. At least the Finance Committee agrees to waive the outstanding fees **[252–3]**.

The matter of superannuation was straightforward because it was manifestly the School's right to make its own rules and enforce them. Moral policing was altogether more complex, and sexual disorder accounts for the largest body of papers in this file. There is an immensely long printed correspondence between J.M. Wilson and the father of a boy who had allegedly contrived an act of indecency in the Zoo.[111]

---

[109] *Rise of the Public Schools*, p. 71.
[110] WiH House Master's Book 1913–33, p. 52; his brief Clifton career is known only from this entry, for his name was not put in the *Register*.
[111] Though Wilson was even by the standards of his day reticent in speaking of sex, he wrote about it a great deal. His presidential address to the Education Society (1881), printed in that Society's *Journal*, was reprinted as *Morality in Public Schools and Relation to Religion: A Fragment Journal of Education* and distributed to the Clifton staff; *cf.* Chandos, *Boys Together*, pp. 287–9; Brown, *Newly Discovered Letters*, p. 105 n. 2.

For reasons of space rather than delicacy this is left unexplored. The subject is represented by a dilemma faced by J.E. King during 1915–16 **[256–73]**. As so often the major issue only emerged through the investigation of a minor one. A master casually spying into a School House study saw what he persuaded himself was 'something indecent'. This may have been no more than routine bullying, but in any case the victim got his own back by saying that one of his molesters had been in bed with another boy on the last morning of Christmas term. There were further hints of 'filthy talk and ... misconduct' in the House, but none of this reached the Head (and House) Master until March. He then examined all concerned, only to find a morass of further accusations and shifting evidence. The Sixth Power (dormitory prefect) changed his story, and another boy became so confused in trying to remember all his activities that he dissolved into tears.

After King had sent home the ringleaders, he was confronted by the pained disbelief of the fathers, who knew one another and co-ordinated their response. King's diary of the whole affair is presented, along with the correspondence in one case, where the father had demanded actual evidence of sexual congress. King explained that the mere fact of boys being together in bed was proof enough, but nevertheless agreed to forego the shaming formality of expulsion. The House closed ranks, petitioning for a lesser punishment, and some thought was given to letting the minor culprits remain as day boys. That was rejected after discussion with the College lawyers **[265–70, 272]**. Percival, as Chairman of the Council, made his own contribution to the debate. He advised King to stand firm, despite weaknesses in the evidence. He thought only a madman would take legal action, but should that happen it might even benefit the School by advertising its high moral tone **[271, 273]**. The letters relating to the removal of Percival's grandson (p. xxxv above) are also in this file **[254–5]**.

A boy who breaks into the Armoury, goes round the School touting a revolver, and smashes up scientific equipment, can expect no mercy. So it was with Clifford Philpott in 1918. He did not shoot anybody, because this was *When* not *If* ... , and his weapon was not in fact loaded. He was, however, carrying a live .22 round, which emerged when King made him turn out his pockets. The Corps Commander identified it as Armoury issue, and the bullet was put with the papers on the case. There it remains, though after discovery in 2011 it was de-activated by the present Commanding Officer. Philpott's father accepted his son's dismissal philosophically, though still convinced of his essential goodness, and that the jemmy found under his bedroom floorboards was for lifting carpet tacks **[274–6]**.

Musicians[112]

The early prospectuses make no mention of music, for despite its long tradition as an academic discipline, it had as yet no place in the public school curriculum. This was because music offered very little prospect of respectable employment. Such music as flourished did so informally, and its development was only mildly encouraged by the mid-century reformers.[113] This changed quite quickly. Harrow led the way by

---

[112] See principally D.G.A. Fox and Y.P. Lidell, 'Music at Clifton', in *Centenary Essays*, pp. 95–127, and W. Fox, *Douglas Fox (D.G.A.F.): A Chronicle* (priv. pr. 1976), which reprinted (pp. 58–65) Lidell's section on Fox from *Essays*; for individual recollections see Milford, *Two Brothers*, pp. 39–40, and W. Owen, *My Life in Music: Conversations with Sir David Willcocks and Friends* (2008), pp. 45–7.

[113] Shrosbee, *Clarendon Commission*, pp. 139, 148–9.

appointing a Director of Music in the year that Clifton opened its doors, and three years later Uppingham followed suit. Also in 1865 Rugby appointed a professor from the Royal College of Music to be its Adviser and Examiner in Music. He was husband of the celebrated singer Jenny Lind, whose voice was heard in Rugby Chapel while Percival still taught there.[114] What Percival thought of the 'Swedish nightingale' is not on record. Music as recreation was not among his enthusiasms but he recognised its importance in corporate worship. When he gave his inaugural sermon **[15]** the music had been led by the Cathedral choir. Two years later the Cathedral's Deputy Organist W.F. Trimnell became Clifton's first designated Organist and Choirmaster **[298]**. When services were still being held in Big School an organ was borrowed from the parish church, Percival personally paying half the fee **[299]**.

That arrangement came to an end when the Chapel opened in 1867, with an organ of its own provided wholly by the Head Master's generosity. This instrument was relocated when the Chapel was first extended in the 1880s, and was not deemed complete until 1890 **[302]**. Only at that point is it identified as the work of the celebrated craftsman Henry ('Father') Willis. Meanwhile another and much better remembered Willis had been bought for Big School by the Concert Society, which needed support for the large-scale works it regularly performed **[301]**. Clifton music was given a solid base in 1896–7 with the appointment of A.H. Peppin as first Director and the building of the Music School in Guthrie Road.

For the further extension of the Chapel which began in 1909 a new organ was installed by Harrison and Harrison of Durham. The whole cost was met by H.H. Wills, also one of the principal benefactors of the University. The relevant papers printed here **[303–14]**, though only a small selection from our own archives and those of Messrs Harrison and Harrison, illustrate the complex negotiations between the donor, the Director of Music, and the organ builders. Wills, an amateur organist himself, suggests a few changes to the specification which he confidently expects builders to accept **[307]**; Peppin argues passionately for certain stops, disguising his directives in an appeal to compromise **[308]**. After two years' planning the instrument is installed, and passes the inspection which the donor has required **[309–11]**. Since then, as the Head Master predicted, it has proved valuable and permanent, although there were some awkward problems in the early days **[312–14]**.

School songs are an artistic sub-species contemporary with Clifton, rarely of much literary or musical merit. Clifton has at least the distinction of a song with an impeccable pedigree. The words of 'The Best School of All' are by Newbolt – though they have been judged 'not really up to his own standards';[115] the richly sonorous tune is unmistakably Parry. The composer was persuaded to the task by his O.C. son-in-law Harry Plunket Greene, and by Peppin, who had worked for Parry's predecessor as Director of the RCM, Sir George Grove. For Parry it was a very minor piece of work,[116] despatched in a couple of morning sessions before going to the office **[315]**. He could not attend the first performance **[316]**, and seemingly never consulted with Newbolt, even when there were matters to be settled about the publishing of the score **[317]**.

---

[114] Hope Simpson, *Rugby since Arnold*, pp. 50–1. Jenny Lind (Mrs Otto Goldschmidt) stayed in Clifton as the guest of Dr J.A. Symonds: A. Burnside, *A Palladian Villa in Bristol: Clifton Hill House and the People who lived there* (Bristol, 2009), p. 29. The first Director of Music at Rugby (1886) was Basil Johnson, who had had an influence on Clifton music **[303]**.

[115] G. Ewart (comp.), *Forty Years On: An Anthology of School Songs* (1969), introduction (unpag.).

[116] J. Dibble, *C. Hubert H. Parry; His Life and Music* (1988), p. 426; see also C.S. Knighton and M.J. Butterfield, 'The best song of all?', *Clifton Magazine* (2009), pp. 20–1.

Although Peppin established Clifton's musical reputation, it was his pupil and eventual successor Douglas Fox whose teaching and performances are most prominent in Clifton's memory. This is partly because of the discipline and expertise by which he sustained his musical life after losing an arm in the Great War. Fox was also assiduous in documenting his own achievements, and we have in the College Archives more material from him than from any other individual. While this volume was in preparation another large group of his papers was discovered at Keble College, Oxford. This collection had been sorted by Fox's sister Winifred in preparing her memoir (1976); several items from it are printed below, alongside material from our own files **[318–33, 341–57]**.

Fox's keyboard talent had been immediately spotted by Peppin, who arranged for the boy to be heard by Sir Walter Parratt, the Organist at Windsor and Master of the King's Musick **[318–19]**. Parratt advised extra tuition at the expense of regular schoolwork, and to this the Head Master agreed. In fact the boy was bright enough to shine in Classics as well. He also had a chance to perform before another master of music, Sir Charles Stanford **[321–3]**. Parratt had recommended that Fox should work towards an Oxbridge organ scholarship, and plotted a path which would take him first to the Royal College of Music and then to Keble **[324]**.

Fox was still at Oxford when the war broke out, but he was determined to join the army as soon as he could be released from his studies. Peppin tried without success to persuade him that this was neither necessary nor a good use for his talent **[325]**. The injury which resulted in the amputation of his right arm appeared to vindicate that argument. The great career which had been predicted for him as an organist was no longer in prospect. Parry, whose star pupil Fox had been at the Royal College,[117] felt this to be 'one of the most cruel things that has happened in the war'; all he could do was to write a strongly word testimonial in soliciting generous compensation **[326, 331]**. Others who sent messages of sympathy were two former Head Masters, and the sister of a House Master who had himself been killed **[328–30]**. The letter from Stanford stands out with its breezy tone and its frivolous references to Nelson and Wagner **[327]**.

But Stanford was right; Fox did adapt with astonishing speed, and taught himself to play the organ again with his three remaining limbs. Within a year he was capable of giving public recitals, and although his repertoire was necessarily limited he became renowned as a versatile performer. Though the higher reaches of the profession were closed to him, he was able to channel his skill into teaching. At first that took him to Bradfield, and so for a time out of Clifton's story.

He might have returned as Director in 1926 but chose not to apply, once again declining Peppin's advice **[332–3]**. Instead the post went to a bright young man from Melbourne, William McKie, who was strongly recommended by the Precentor of Eton and a former Head Master, Glazebrook **[334–5]**. The latter's opinion carried weight because, though not himself a musician, he had been responsible for building the Music School and hiring Peppin as the first Director.[118] So McKie was chosen, and entered upon his task with uncharacteristic diffidence **[336–8]**. Indeed it is hard to recognise here the man who would later have a reputation for toughness as Organist and Master of the Choristers of Westminster Abbey. Four years of Clifton were all

---

[117] The College Archives has a sequence of letters from Parry to Fox between 1913 and 1915, inviting his opinion on organ pieces he was composing: M302 file.

[118] His concern for music appears to have been prompted by his wife, who was an accomplished pianist.

he could stand. He then asked the Head Master for six months' leave of absence to return home in the hope of securing another post [339]. Whatley's response is not preserved and does not need to be, since no employer would have been so indulgent. Six months later McKie writes again, clearly on the verge of breakdown; and the next paper in the file is the advertisement for his job [340–1]. This time Fox did apply; and from the unlikely venue of a five-star hotel in Switzerland he accepted the call back to Clifton [342–3].

Although Fox now felt ready for this larger responsibility, the four-manual Harrison in Clifton Chapel still presented a challenge. With his one hand he could play two manuals simultaneously, and he put more work on the pedals.[119] But he did need some extra gadgets, and asked for two to be installed. When he saw Harrisons' estimate Fox restricted his request to a sub-octave coupler on the Swell, offering to pay half its cost himself. Rather ungraciously the Council accepted this, and Fox's first month's salary disappeared before he had left Bradfield [344–8]. Another sequence of letters shows Fox negotiating a tidy deal for tuning the two Clifton organs [349–53].

It would have been possible to fill an entire volume with tributes to Fox's musicianship and teaching. That would in any case move beyond the timescale of this book, since Fox remained Director until 1957, soon afterwards becoming parish organist of Great St Mary's in Cambridge. Across the road in King's College, Fox's most distinguished pupil had just been appointed Director of Music; this was David Willcocks, who had taken over from another Old Cliftonian and Fox's own contemporary, Boris Ord.[120] Willcocks had secured the King's organ scholarship in 1938 with the help of a glowing but not unqualified testimonial from Fox [354]. Fox was congratulated by his predecessor on his pupil's success [355]. The selection from Fox's papers concludes with two kindly letters from the retired Whatley, one of them with more congratulations on a successful pupil, Fox's eventual successor Evan Prentice [356–7].

Players and rulers

Sport is not to be contained within the bounds of a single documentary section.[121] Balls are liable to come flying over any wall [280]. Sport permeates the various House books [403–21], it infiltrates the minutes of the Scientific Society [161, 176], and is only halted by the arrival of a Royal visitor [389]. The first and only functional consideration in finding a site for the College in the first place had been that there

---

[119] It is alleged that *in extremis* he would play a note with his nose: Thorn, *Road to Winchester*, p. 55.

[120] Bernhard ('Boris') Ord [*6750*: ST 1908–14]; Organist of King's 1929–58. Willcocks was appointed in 1957 with the title of Director of Music so as not to displace Ord.

[121] Since the documentary section makes no mention of Clifton's most illustrious athlete, he will be given his place here. John Frederick ('Jerry') Cornes [*9273*: SH 1923–8], won Silver in the 1500 metres at the Los Angeles Olympics of 1932, and competed in the same event at Berlin in 1936. His classmate R.H. Oakeley [*9128*: WiH 1922–7], in a memoir deposited in the Archives in his 102nd year, dictated this 'epic story' of Jerry Cornes: 'He was told in the morning when he got up that there was going to be skating in the Zoo, and when he got to class he held up his hand and said could he pleased be excused and the master said 'yes, off you go' so he went off and 'borrowed' a bicycle in inverted commas from one of the town boys and bicycled down to Clifton and bought himself a pair of skates and bicycled back to Clifton and damaged the bicycle on the way, and got back to his class and the master took no notice.': P9128 file; with thanks to the Dr H.F. Oakeley [*13611*: OH 1954–60] for editing his father's recollections and transmitting them.

should be a generous playing area **[4]**. The Close defines Clifton, so that it seems to be a playing field surrounded by a School. And the Close has, through the relentlessly quoted opening and closing lines of Newbolt's *Vitaï Lampada*, become the τόπος of muscular Anglicanism.

Percival had not been among the most zealous adherents of that doctrine, which was in any case barely rooted in the public schools when he arrived at Clifton. Compulsory organised games were first introduced at Marlborough, during the Mastership of G.E.L. Cotton (1852–8).[122] Cotton had been one of Arnold's assistants, but in this respect went much further than his mentor. Percival, though he had not served Arnold directly, was closer to him. He encouraged a variety of sports **[277, 279]** but for their own sake rather than as an element of faith. Whereas for many later headmasters the chief function of organised games was to exhaust boys beyond the possibilities of mischief, Percival warned that games 'engross a great deal too much of the average boy's energy at school'.[123] Quite how much of that there could be is suggested by the first entry in the Brown's House Annals **[403]**, where the sole item recorded for the term was a rugger match occupying 40 boys over four days, during which no tries were scored **[403]**.[124]

The sport culture at Clifton was driven not from above but from within, and was so closely bound up with the Arnoldian version of pupil power that even the Head Master had little say in it. A key element of the system which Percival brought with him from Rugby was the Levée, the quaintly named boys' council.[125] From the start Big Side Levée regulated almost everything to do with the conduct of organised games, including hours of play and rules of engagement. The only decision left to the Head Master was the fitness of the weather conditions **[278–9, 281–2]**. BSL originally comprised the whole Upper School except fags. In 1870 it was restricted to Praepostors (prefects), Heads of Houses,[126] captains of major sports, and a few other dignitaries. Over all presided the Head of the School, whose office had first been held by a great-nephew of Wellington.[127] BSL ceased to function during the First World War, to be revived by the Acting Head Master in 1933, a year not otherwise fortunate for democracy **[70]**.

The Sixth Form Levée (usually just 'the Sixth') was superior to BSL in that there were no representatives of the lower forms. In practice the two bodies overlapped and since their minutes were kept in the same books, it is sometimes difficult to distinguish between them. The Sixth held itself to be the repository of all custom, exercising a large measure of self-regulation. Newly-appointed Head Masters had to be instructed in these matters, lest they tried (as they always do) to change things. It was also no doubt possible to con a new head man into confirming as immemorial tradition some rule which the Sixth had just invented. There is a suspicion of this

---

[122] J.A. Mangan, 'Athleticism: a case study in the evolution of an educational ideology', in Simon and Bradley, *Victorian Public School*, pp. 147–67; *cf.* E.G. Dunning, 'The origins of modern football and the Public School Ethos', *ibid.*, pp. 171–2; Parker, *Old Lie*, pp. 77–84.

[123] Address to the HMC 1873, quoted Potter, *Headmaster*, p. 76.

[124] The entertainment came perhaps from the 'good deal of hacking', a Clifton proclivity which caused the first foreign match in 1864 to end in chaos: Bradley, *Marlborough*, p. 276.

[125] Christie, *History*, pp. 71–2; *cf.* Dunning, 'Origins of football', pp. 172–3. 'Big Side' meant in the first instance the members of the Upper School, and by extension the area of the Close on which the top division played, and then those divisions themselves. 'Levée' means an assembly or court. All this came from Rugby.

[126] These were deemed to include the Head of the (as yet undivided) Town.

[127] Henry William Wellesley [69: SH 1862–3]; he entered the Indian Civil Service.

in the condescension with which they told Glazebrook that beating was the proper punishment for cutting a School game. Contempt for those 'authorities' who had deemed this as 'unconstitutional' is barely concealed. Glazebrook agreed to the resolution, asking only for firm evidence of intent, and that young boys might be spared the 'extreme penalty' on the first offence [283].

In 1899 the Sixth drew up a compendium of current regulations; the first concern is fagging, and the second (surprisingly) the Library; after cricket and football in the sporting hierarchy comes running, which was the main and compulsory sport of the Lent term. This was another import from Rugby, with Penpole replacing Crick as the terminal point. It was valued in itself, but also essential in allowing the Close to recover from football to be ready again for the summer game [285]. Just a month after those regulations were compiled the most celebrated match in Clifton's history was played on the Lower Close. The 628 (or thereabouts) not out achieved by A.E.J. Collins has held its place in the record books. Here for the first time the full match scorecard is printed [285].

Not everything that the Sixth proposed was rubber-stamped by the Head Master. King's counter-minutes dealt briskly with schemes he judged impractical or unnecessary [286, 288]. Hallward stifled attempts by BSL to offer its views on non-sporting matters such as Sunday opening for the 'Grubber' (tuck shop) and the recreational use of bicycles [290]. Meanwhile Hallward's own *modus operandi* was being carefully monitored from the opposing camp. It was customary for the Head of the School to sum up his experiences in a notebook which was then passed, with expressions of encouragement, to his successor. The example chosen to illustrate this *genre* is from 1940 when R.M. Jenkins was preparing to hand over to R.J. Potter. Jenkins explains how to cope with Hallward, feeding him regularly with information and giving only the pretence of attention to his bright ideas. In dealing with the other masters, the advice was to let them feel that they were superior [289].

Masters

The assistant masters appear throughout the book, and have been allocated only a brief documentary section to themselves. This presents three different forms of farewell. When Edward Miller died playing golf on the Downs in 1889 the letters of condolence sent to his family were collected into a small volume. Two examples are given here, one from Percival, and the other, much more expressive, from the prolific letter-writer T.E. Brown [369–70]. The retirement of C.W.A. Tait in 1904 produced some correspondence about the most suitable gift [371–3]. When A.H. Peppin left in the middle of the First World War he felt it would be inappropriate to accept anything costly; so instead his pupils and admirers gave him a handsomely illuminated address [374].

Appointment procedure is illustrated in some detail in the section on Directors of Music [332–48]. A Head Master must constantly monitor the deployment of his staff, and Whatley's interview book shows one instance of how this was done [152]. The masters' general terms of employment are laid down in the Charter [36(66–9)], which clearly sets them under the direction of the Head Master. There was however a right of appeal to the Council against the Head Master's sentence of dismissal. Only one discordant note is heard. In the 1930s considerable controversy was generated by the attempts of a master to win a seat on the City Council, a position which would necessarily have impinged on his School duties. This would have infringed the bye-laws, which obliged the masters to refrain from any other work 'remunerated or otherwise' during term [**79**(23)]. The Council and the Acting Head Master were more concerned by the spectacle of a Clifton master canvassing for Labour votes on the streets of Bristol. But since they could not openly admit to that, they issued a blanket prohibition on political activity by the staff. Masters were nevertheless encouraged to undertake work in the community of a non-contentious kind [**70**].

Citizens

The most direct way in which masters and boys could show that they belonged to Bristol was through the College Mission.[128] Clifton's efforts in this direction predated by a decade the Eton Mission in Hackney, which began in 1880 and encouraged many imitators.[129] These operations were thought to benefit the givers as much as the receivers. For Henry Newbolt, mixing with working class boys in Notting Hill 'enlarged [his] sense of patriotism', which was already extensive.[130] Percival, determined that his School should not stand aloof from the social problems of the City below, would walk over the Downs just to 'hear Bristol'. In a practical way he began by dedicating all the Chapel offertories to the local poor. The College briefly ran a 'Ragged School' in Sidney Street; then in 1875 a longer link was forged with the parish of St Barnabas, Ashley Road. Percival's enthusiasm was shared and sustained by his successor Wilson. The district developed into a separate parish, served by the new church of St Agnes consecrated in 1886. A handsomely appointed church hall was built, complemented by boys' and girls' club rooms and a gymnasium. There were cricket matches and bunfights at the College, and outings to the countryside. As noted below, Clifton's dramatic tradition has its origins in entertainments to raise money for the Mission and its clubs [**358–61**]. A few extracts from the minutes show how masters, boys and Old Cliftonians combined in running the scheme [**117–20**]. They also reveal that, with the College's own buildings still under construction, there was some criticism of this diversion of funds. Once the new parish was set on its feet the College's involvement became less formal. By the 1920s it had become minimal, and Whatley saw no useful purpose in reviving it [**68**]. Eventually public welfare and social change undermined ventures of this kind and the attitudes which underlay them.

Actors

By contrast with the profuse documentation of Clifton's music, its drama is poorly represented in the archives except at the very start. The story of the Clifton stage is more readily followed in the pages of *The Cliftonian*. The few items collected here illustrate the way in which the drama tradition began. Percival had regarded acting

---

[128] *The History of Saint Agnes Parish compiled by members of Clifton College* (Bristol, 1890); *Register* (1925), pp. cx–cxvi; Christie, *History*, pp. 122–8. The significance of the Clifton Mission within its local and social context is discussed in H.E. Miller, *Leisure in the Changing City, 1870–1914* (1976), pp. 149–60, 174–5.

[129] Parker, *Old Lie*, pp. 141–6.

[130] Newbolt, *My World*, p. 154.

as frivolous if not positively depraved, and Wilson had been no more minded to encourage the boys to act. It was only under the generally glum gaze of Glazebrook that *tableaux vivants* were presented in Big School, to raise money for the College Mission **[358]**. Soon afterwards scenes from classic plays were introduced at Commemoration, though only as semi-staged interludes between the speeches.

The first real plays seen at Clifton had the same charitable intentions as the *tableaux*, though they involved only masters, O.C.s and friendly neighbours. At the start of King's regime these shows were stopped because of fear that admitting a paying audience would imperil the College's own charitable status **[359–62]**.[131] Only after the First World War (and after Percival had been consigned to his vault) was the College Amateur Dramatic Society founded. Now for the first time the boys took to the stage, and it was not long before a star appeared. Michael Redgrave shone not only as an actor, but as a pianist as well, winning the Kadoorie Cup **[415]**. His early performances were all in women's roles (if Lady Macbeth can be so included); he finally made a triumphant transfer to trousers (or rather breeches) as Captain Absolute in *The Rivals* **[363]**. Redgrave's contemporary Trevor Howard never shared the same stage; here he features as a sportsman **[416]**.

Some further dramatic interludes are provided by the Polack's House Reading Society, which once a term varied its programme by going to watch a fully staged play **[364–8]**. One would wish the minutes less frivolous and rather more informative. Even so we learn that the Polack's drama students were incompletely amused by the talent of Noël Coward, and found larger hilarity in the lyrics of Kaufman and Ryskind **[366–7]**. That Ibsen should have been found too severe as an antidote is less surprising **[368]**.

Fighters

Military training in schools began in the year that Clifton was conceived, with Rossall in the vanguard.[132] In retrospect it seems natural development, indeed integral to the manufacture of gentlemen. In fact it was grafted on to the public school system when Napoleon III was regarded as a threat (despite having a Clifton-educated Empress). That particular menace had passed by the time the College was authorised to establish a Rifle Corps in 1875 **[193]**. Its development was to a pattern shared with many other schools. Although attached to the local Volunteer Corps, it was little more than a shooting club, and was regulated with other sporting activities **[194]**. In its early days it was resented as an encroachment upon the serious business of cricket and football. This began to change after 1875 when a 'Military and Engineering Side' was set up, albeit a rather poor alternative to the Classical Side or even the Modern. Clifton nevertheless grew in repute as an army school, and for intending soldiers at least the Corps became integral to the curriculum.[133] Most Cliftonians who joined the army went not to Sandhurst but to Woolwich, the training school for the Engineers

---

[131] On the other hand Gloucestershire CCC adopted the Close as its ground in 1871 precisely because admission could be charged there, which had not been possible when playing on Durdham Down. First class cricket continued at Clifton until 1932: CC Company Minute Book 3, p. 11 and *passim*; D. Green, *The History of the Gloucestershire County Cricket Club* (1990), pp. 23–4, 231.

[132] D.O.Winterbottom, *The Tide Flows On: A History of Rossall School* (Rossall, 2006), pp. 21–2; Parker, *Old Lie*, p. 63.

[133] Christie, *History*, pp. 39–40; Best, 'Militarism', pp. 132–3.

and Artillery.[134] This was a reflection of Clifton's predominantly middle-class intake, and also dictated the predominant concern of the Corps, which was building bridges **[200–1]**.

A sombre landmark was reached in 1885 when for the first time an Old Cliftonian died fighting for Queen and Country.[135] By 1886 the Rifle Corps had become the 150-strong Engineer Corps, and the Head Master backed the CO's claim for additional funding. Even so, his having to explain to the Council that the Corps was 'an important element in the life of the School' rather suggests that it was still on the periphery **[195–6]**. The South African War changed that. The celebrations of Mafeking and Pretoria **[243]** had been premature, and it took two more gruelling years to interest the Boers in the possibilities of defeat. Forty-four Old Cliftonians were killed, far more than in any previous campaign. The great sense of loss is reflected in the prominence given to the memorial unveiled with much ceremony in 1904 **[197–8]**. A noble figure of St George stands on a pedestal on which are carved the names, and an inscription composed by Sir Henry Newbolt:

> Clifton, remember these thy sons who fell
> Fighting far over sea
> For they in a dark hour remembered well
> Their warfare learned of thee.

Two years after Lord Methuen had unveiled the Memorial, an even more illustrious commander came to review the troops. Lord Roberts made it his particular mission to encourage military training in the public schools,[136] but he had a special reason for coming to Clifton, having spent part of his childhood in Royal York Crescent **[199]**.

As a result of this war and in preparation for the next, there was a major extension and reshaping of the army reserve. One aspect of which was that in 1908 school OTCs came under the direct control of the War Office and training was standardised. When war was declared in 1914 the Clifton Corps had just arrived for its annual camp at Mytchett in Surrey. A lively account of this time is given in a letter from one of the Cadets, later to become Chairman of the Council and President of the College **[202]**. At the start of the war the CO still had to work hard to secure classrooms for his men, and for permission for newly-raised troops to train in the Close **[203–4]**. Thereafter soldiering became so popular that, a month before Haig launched the real army into the mud of Passchendaele, the Corps subscription could be reduced by six shillings **[205]**.

Commander

In the vast literature on Haig relatively little attention has been paid to his schooldays, yet even here there has been argument, and what has been said is not always on

---

[134] *Ibid.*, p. 133.
[135] Joseph W.W. Darley [*822*: SH 1870–2], Capt, 4th Bn Royal Irish Dragoon Guards, killed at the battle of Abu Klea in the Sudan (17 Jan. 1885); this is the action alluded to in the second verse of *Vitaï Lampada* (beginning 'The sand of the desert is sodden red'). The printed *Register* identified Darley as the first Cliftonian killed on the field of battle. However that distinction belongs to John Stuart Forbes [*256*: BH 1864], 7th Regt US Cavalry, who stood and died with Custer at Little Bighorn in June 1876.
[136] Best, 'Militarism', p. 137.

target. In his classic study John Terraine has only one sentence about Clifton, and it is mistaken. Haig is said to have proposed the motion 'The Army has done the country more service than the Navy' at the School Debating Society.[137] There is no such debate in the Society's minutes of the relevant period. The story comes from Lady Haig's memoir, in one of several unattributed recollections from contemporaries, where it is clearly said to be the *School House* Debating Society,[138] and of this no records survive. More recently it has been noted that Haig's school was one specially driven by Christian principles as interpreted by Dr Arnold, but the detail is awry.[139] Lady Haig admitted to knowing little of her husband's schooling, but she noted with pride that, despite his struggles with Latin, in his final year he was top of the form.[140] This report is reproduced here [**440**].

Brigadier John Charteris, who had been Haig's Intelligence Officer and really did know him, detected Clifton's firmest imprint in his frequent use of the phrase 'it is the spirit that quickeneth';[141] that is the Christian version of *Spiritus intus alit*, though this did not become Clifton's motto until after Haig's time.[142] A later writer has asserted that Clifton implanted in him 'all the qualities which Public Schools then tried to inculcate', and also saw Percival's influence as the 'key to Haig's adult character and much of his subsequent attitude to life.'[143] Against this a biographer in general unsympathetic to his subject felt it 'safe to conclude that the values the public schools encouraged ... were only partially absorbed by him'.[144]

Whatever effect Clifton had on his career, and although he did not choose it for his own son's education, Haig recalled his schooldays with obvious affection [**449**].[145] Writing to his mother in his last year at School, he appreciated the efforts made to prepare him for Oxford [**441**]. The debt he acknowledged to one of his Clifton masters is expressed with characteristic charm [**440n**], and it pleased him that the School should display his armorial bearings [**444**]. Above all he re-engaged in Clifton by accepting the post of President, which for him was no sinecure. He took an active part in the appointment of a new Head Master in 1922.[146] It was particularly appropriate that he presided at the dedication of the War Memorial in the same year [**435–7**]. Although he could not be present when the Prince of Wales made his first

---

[137] J. Terraine, *Douglas Haig: The Educated Soldier* (1969), p. 4.

[138] Dorothy, Countess Haig, *The Man I Knew* (1935), p. 15.

[139] N. Cave, 'Haig and religion', in *Haig: A Re-Appraisal 80 Years On*, ed. B. Bond and Cave (1999), p. 242, where it is said that Clifton was founded by 'one of Arnold's housemasters'. Percival was not Clifton's founder, he had not been a housemaster at Rugby, and he joined the staff there 20 years after Arnold's departure.

[140] Lady Haig, *loc. cit.*

[141] J. Charteris, *Field-Marshal Earl Haig* (1929), p. 5. The point is picked up in J. Hussey, 'Portrait of a Commander-in-Chief', in Bond and Cave, *Haig*, p. 15, though without reference to Clifton.

[142] The English phrase is John 6:63, the Latin from *Aeneid*, vi.726. When the College was granted arms in 1895, this motto proposed by S.T. Irwin was chosen by the masters: C.S. Knighton, 'Harking to the heralds', *Clifton Magazine* (2011), p. 27.

[143] P. Warner, *Field Marshal Haig* (1991), pp. 14, 16.

[144] G.J. De Groot, *Douglas Haig, 1861–1928* (1988), p. 17; *cf.* W. Reid, *Architect of Victory: Douglas Haig* (2006), p. 31 ('minimal impact at Clifton').

[145] Haig arrived at Clifton soon after the Military and Engineering Side was established; had he joined it, he would have gone to Woolwich rather than Oxford and Sandhurst, and so into the Engineers rather than the 17th Lancers.

[146] Winterbottom, *Clifton after Percival*, p. 57; *cf.* Potter, *Headmaster*, pp. 127–31, describing the exchanges when four of Clifton's great men – Haig, Speaker Whitley, Sir Henry Newbolt and Sir Francis Younghusband – travelled down by train together to attend the key meeting of the Council.

visit **[386]**, he was host when His Royal Highness returned to open the Science School in 1927 **[401]**.

In return Clifton has acknowledged Haig as her greatest son. In terms of mere public celebrity there is no serious competition, and the unrelenting argument about Haig's claim to greatness has in itself elevated his profile as an historical figure. At Clifton he is truly an enduring presence, more visible even than Percival, albeit some modern Cliftonians think he is Kitchener. The fine statue by William MacMillan casts Clifton in bronze as resonantly as *Vitaï Lampada* does in verse. Haig looks intently towards the Close, as if thinking it might be just the place for a bit of a show. It is therefore surprising to learn that neither the Sixth nor the masters wanted the statute at all **[445]**, and that Lady Haig thought the sculptor had altogether failed to capture the chin she knew **[449]**.

SECTION I: FOUNDATION

[1]   5 April 1860. First meeting to discuss the foundation of a College
[*CC Company Minute Book 1, pp. 1–3. MS*]
Minutes of the proceedings of the promoters of a Proprietary College at Clifton
7 Gloucester Row, Clifton.
At a meeting held the 5th April 1860 <at the residence of Mr Wasbrough, 7 Gloucester
[*Row*], Clifton> the following gentlemen <being present>:
The Mayor of Bristol <John Bates Esq.>[1] in the chair

Mr J.B. Burroughs[2]	Mr H.B. Ford[3]
Mr W. Gale Coles[4]	Major Savile[5]
Mr <Edward> Daniel[6]	Mr Alfred Cox[7]
Mr J. McArthur[8]	Dr Budd[9]
Mr Joshua Saunders[10]	Mr F.N. Budd[11]
Mr <Joseph> Leech[12]	Mr John Colthurst[13]

---

[1] Mayor 1859–60, General Manager of the West of England and South Wales Bank, and resident in Royal York Crescent; member of Clifton College Council until 1867: *Directory* (1860), p. 82.

[2] John Beames Burroughs, surgeon, resident in West Mall: *Directory* (1860), p. 96, and **[8]** below.

[3] Henry Bell Ford, of Vyvyan Terrace, Clifton: *Directory* (1861), p. 128.

[4] William Gale Coles, of the Somersetshire Bank, resident in Victoria Square; Sheriff of Bristol 1867–8; member of Council until his death in 1890: *Directory* (1860), p. 105.

[5] Henry Bouchier Osborne Savile, Chairman of the Bristol and South Wales Railway Waggon Co.; Sheriff of Bristol 1883–4; member of Council from 1871 until his death in 1917.

[6] Solicitor, resident in Worcester Terrace: *Directory* (1860), p. 113, and **[8]** below.

[7] Solicitor, resident in Shannon Court; member of Council until 1886; father of A. (presumably Alfred) [*16*: Town 1862–4], an original Cliftonian, and three others [*144, 212, 581*].

[8] John McArthur, iron merchant, of Charlotte Street, and Park House, Queen's Road: *Directory* (1860), p. 176, and **[8]** below; father of Charles [*41*: Town 1862–4], an original Cliftonian.

[9] Of Lansdown Place: see M. Dunnill, *Dr William Budd: Bristol's most famous Physician* (Bristol, 2006); Whitfield, *Victorian Doctors*, pp. 10–31.

[10] Bristol Agent for the Bank of England and Sheriff of Bristol 1860–1, resident at Thornton Villa, Richmond Hill, Clifton; member of Council until 1900: A.B. Freeman, *Bristol Worthies* (Bristol, 1909), p. 98.

[11] Francis Nonus Budd (brother of William), barrister, and member of Council until 1899 (Chairman 1880–94); also first Chairman of the Council of University College, Bristol 1876–82: Dunnill, *Budd*, p. 145.

[12] Publisher of the *Bristol Times* which he founded in 1839; author of *Brief Romances from Bristol History* (1884) and (as reprinted) *Rural Rides of the Bristol Churchgoer*, ed. A. Sutton (Gloucester, 1982); resident at Albert Villas, Lower Harley Place: Matthews (1860), p. 170.

[13] Surgeon, of The Mall, Clifton; member of Council until 1867: **[8]** below.

Dr Black[14]   Mr <William> Cross[15]
Mr George Cooke[16]   Mr H.S. Wasbrough[17]
Mr O.C. Lane[18]

The following resolutions were unanimously adopted.

That the want of a first class educational establishment for boys is much felt at Clifton. It is therefore desirable to establish a Proprietary College where an education in the highest branches of learning might be provided on moderate terms. The Principal of which institution should be a graduate of either of the Universities of Oxford or Cambridge.

That with a view to the establishment of such an institution a meeting of the residents of Clifton be convened at an early day by circular.

That Mr Budd, Mr Cox, Mr Ford and Mr Wasbrough be requested to settle a prospectus to be submitted to a second meeting of the gentlemen now present, previous to such general meeting.

That in the mean time inquiry be made for premises which might be rented temporarily, until a permanent building can be provided. And to report thereon to the meeting.

☐ *A second meeting on 27 April approved the texts of the prospectus and the circular.*

[2]   27 April 1860. The Mayor's invitation to a general meeting
[*CC Company Minute Book 1, p. 5. MS*]

Clifton,
May 7th 1860.

Dear Sir,

Several influential residents of Clifton having represented to me that the want of a first class school for the sons of gentlemen in Clifton is much felt, and requested that I would convene a meeting with a view to the establishment of a college similar to those at Cheltenham, Marlborough and other places, I have much pleasure in acceding to their request, and would beg the favour of your attending a meeting on the subject on Wednesday the 16th day of May inst. at 4 o'clock in the afternoon at the Clifton Subscription Rooms, Mall, which have been kindly granted by the committee for that purpose.

I remain, dear Sir, faithfully yours,
John Bates, Mayor.

---

[14] Physician, of Lansdown Place; member of Council to his death in 1883, and donor of lectern to the Chapel; father of Francis [*7:* Town 1862–3], an original Cliftonian, and Alfred [*248*]; author of *Treatise of the Principles and Practice of Homoeopathy* (1842), and pioneer of this branch of medicine in Bristol:Whitfield, *Victorian Doctors*, pp. 12–18.

[15] Surgeon, of Caledonia Place, Clifton: *Directory* (1860), p. 112.

[16] Solicitor, of The Paragon, Clifton; member of Council to his death in 1894; father of Edward Annesley [*15:* Town 1862–5], an original Cliftonian.

[17] Henry Sidney Wasbrough, solicitor; member of Council to his death in 1892; father of Charles Whitchurch [*120:* Town 1862–3], who came in the second term.

[18] Odiarne Coates Lane, bookseller, stationer and binder, of Somerset House, Somerset Place, Clifton; Mayor of Bristol 1860–1; Member of the Society of Merchant Venturers 1860 (Warden 1863, Master 1864): *National Commercial Directory ... Gloucestershire* (Pigot & Co., 1830); *Directory* (1860), p. 107; McGrath, *Merch. Venturers*, p. 554.

[3]   16 May 1860. Residents' meeting.
[*CC Company Minute Book 1, pp. 6–10. MS*]

At a meeting held at the Clifton Subscription Rooms, the 16th of [April *corrected to*] May 1860.
    Present: John Bates, Esq., Mayor of Bristol, in the chair.
    The Revd Canon Moseley.[19] The Revd James Heyworth.[20] The Revd Edward Young.[21]
    [*two half pages blank*]
The following resolutions were unanimously adopted:
    Moved by Dr Symonds,[22] seconded by Joseph Cookson, Esq.:[23]
    That the want of a first class establishment in the nature of a public school for the education of the sons of gentlemen has long been felt to be a serious detriment to Clifton, and it is desirable that such a school should be forthwith established.
    Moved by Wm. Gale Coles, Esq., seconded by J.B. Burroughs, Esq.:
    That a Company be formed under the Limited Liability Act[24] for the purpose of raising the necessary capital to accomplish this object.
    Moved by the Revd Canon Moseley, seconded by T. Sawer, Esq.:[25]
    That the religious teaching be in accordance with that of the Church of England and the constitution as nearly as possible that of the great public schools.
    Moved by the Chairman:
    That the following gentlemen to act as a provisional committee with power to add to their number, for the purpose of taking the necessary steps for the establishment of the institution: the Mayor of Bristol, the Very Revd the Dean of Bristol,[26] the Revd Canon Moseley, [the Revd Canon Hensman *deleted*],[27] the Revd J. Heyworth, [the Revd W.W. Gibbon[28] *deleted*], Jos. Cookson, Esq.re, Dr Symonds, Wm. Gale Coles,

---

[19] Henry Moseley, FRS, Canon of Bristol 1852–72: Le Neve, *Fasti*, viii, p. 30; also Chaplain-in-Ordinary to the Queen, Professor of Natural Philosophy and Astronomy at King's College, London and an Inspector of Schools; Member of the Clifton College Council from 1865 to his death in 1872 (Chairman 1865–8); a prominent educationalist and founder of a scientific dynasty (his son Henry Nottidge Moseley, FRS, gave his name to a penguin, *Eudyptes c. moseleyi*).
[20] Resident at Henbury Hill 1847–79 (unbeneficed); Chairman of the College Council from 1868; President and Treasurer of Bristol General Infirmary from 1869, and also involved in setting up the Fine Arts Academy; died at Cannes Dec. 1879: Venn, *Al. Cant.* iii, p. 355; Smith, *History of BRI*, pp. 362–3.
[21] Resident in Clifton Park since 1849 (unbeneficed); author of *Pre-Raffaellitism* (1857) and other works attacking Ruskin; died 1890: Venn, *Al. Cant.* vi, p. 621; *Directory* (1860), p. 258.
[22] John Addington Symonds snr; first physician at Bristol General Hospital, with practice in Berkeley Square; resident at Clifton Hill House; member of Council until his death in 1871: C.B. Perry, *The Bristol Medical School* (Bristol Branch of the Historical Association pamphlet 58, 1984), p. 13.
[23] Resident in Royal York Crescent: *Directory* (1860), p. 108.
[24] Of 1855: 18 & 19 Vict. *c*. 133.
[25] Had attended the second meeting (27 April); father of John Ryde [*58*: Town 1862–5], an original Cliftonian.
[26] Gilbert Elliot, Dean from 1850 till his death in 1891, and first President of University College, Bristol from 1876: Le Neve, *Fasti*, viii, pp. 18–19; *Univ. Reg.*, p. 231.
[27] John Hensman, an Evangelical leader; Curate of Wraxall 1803–9, of Clifton (St Andrew) 1809–22, of the Dowry Chapel, Hotwells 1822–30; Perpetual Curate of Holy Trinity, Hotwells 1830–44, of Christ Church, Clifton 1844–7, and of St Andrew, Clifton 1847–64; Canon of Bristol from 1858 until his death in 1864; a Chapel of Ease was consecrated in his memory: Venn, *Al. Cant.* iii, p. 334; *ODNB*.
[28] William Wynter Gibbon, Curate of St Mary Magdalene, Bridgnorth 1846–8, and of Clifton 1848–62; Minor Canon of Bristol Cathedral 1852–62; Vicar of Wapley (Glos.), 1862–70; later Canon of Ripon: Venn, *Al. Cant.* iv, p. 37.

Esq.re, H.H. Harford, Esq.re,[29] Chas. D. Cave, Esq.re,[30] Joshua Saunders, Esq.re, Wm. Cross, Esq.re, Dr Budd., Dr Black, Major Savile, John Colthurst, Esq.re, J.B. Burroughs, Esq.re, O.C. Lane, Esq.re, Edward Daniel, Esq.re, Thos. Sawer, Esq. re, H.B. Ford, Esq.re, F.N. Budd, Esq.re, James Hassell,[31] Esq.re, John McArthur, Esq.re, George Cooke, Esq.re, Edward James, Esqre,[32] R.J. Ramsden, Esq.re,[33] the Revd Edward Young, Joseph Leech, Esq.re, Ralph Bernard, Esq.re,[34] Isaac A. Cooke, Esq.re.[35]

Moved by Joshua Saunders, Esq., seconded by W. Gale Coles, Esq.:

That Messrs Henry Sidney Wasbrough and Alfred Cox be appointed Solicitors to the undertaking.

Moved by the Chairman:

That the thanks of the meeting be given to the committee of the Clifton Subscription Rooms Association for the use of their room.

The Mayor having quitted the chair, the same was taken by Joseph Cookson, Esq., when it was proposed by J.B. Burroughs, Esq., and carried by acclamation:

That the thanks of the meeting be given to the Mayor for his able conduct in the chair.

[4] 9 July 1860. The search for a site
[*CC Company Minute Book 1, pp. 28–31. MS*]

At a meeting of the Sub Committee held 9 July 1860.

Present: W. Gale Coles Esqre., Messrs A. Cox, G. Cooke, Dr Budd, F.N. Budd, Joshua Saunders, H.B. Ford, H. Wasbrough, Dr Black.

The following report with reference to the sites inspected by the Sub Committee was settled.

Proposed College at Clifton.

Report of the Sub Committee appointed at a meeting of the Provisional Committee, held 18 day of June last for the purpose of considering a site for the College and to report thereon.

Before proceeding to describe the sites viewed by the Sub Committee, they would state that having given their best consideration to the requirements of the proposed College, based on information derived from Cheltenham and other places, they are of opinion that one and a most important element of success in an institution of the kind is the provision of a good and open play ground for the boys,[36] for although the advantages that the Clifton Downs afford cannot well be over estimated, yet these never can take the place of a home ground, kept distinct for the boys themselves

---

[29] William Henry Harford, jnr, banker; member of Council from 1860 until his death in 1865.

[30] Sir Charles Daniel Cave, banker, created Baronet 1896; Sheriff of Bristol 1862–3; President and Treasurer of Royal Infirmary (succeeding Heyworth) 1880 to 1904: Smith, *History of BRI*, pp. 363, 407; son-in-law of Dr J.A. Symonds, and father of Daniel Charles Addington, member of the Council from 1901 to his death *vitae patris* 1901.

[31] Leather factor of Hill Side, Cotham; at the second meeting: *Directory* (1860), p. 146, and **[8]** below.

[32] Also at the second meeting; first Hon. Secretary of the Provisional Committee.

[33] Father of Edward Plumptre [*53*: Town 1862–4], Charles Arthur [*54*: Town 1862–4], Algernon Fielden [*55*: Town, DH 1862–5], original Cliftonians, and John Pemberton [*106*: Town, DH 1863–5], who joined his brothers in the second term.

[34] Ralph Montague Bernard, of Victoria Square, Clifton: Whitfield, *Victorian Doctors*, pp. 95–9.

[35] Isaac Allen Cooke, solicitor, of Windsor Terrace, Clifton; **[8]** below.

[36] *Cf.* M.C. Morgan, *Cheltenham College: The First Hundred Years* (Chalfont St Giles, 1968), p. 18.

which they will naturally take a pride in, and in which most of their sports will be enjoyed.

The Sub Committee are therefore unanimously of opinion that the site should contain an area of not less than twelve acres;[37] and they particularly draw the attention of the Committee to this point as it must be considered in connection with the sites which they will now mention.

There are only three sites in Clifton which appear to the Committee to meet the requirements of the College.

1. A large field immediately beyond Buckingham Villas and opposite Oakfield House, with a field adjoining, both belonging to the Society of Merchants but at present in lease to Mr Samuel Worrall.[38] The two fields together contain a little more than ten acres.

2. A large field lying on the north side in Pembroke Road beyond Pembroke House containing six and a half acres belonging also to the Society of Merchants, with a field adjoining it on its north side the property of Mr Haynes containing about five acres.

And 3rd. A field lying on the south side of the Zoological Gardens and on the right hand side of the pathway leading from Worcester Terrace to the Downs, the property of Mr Adams[39] and containing nearly nine acres.

With respect to the first mentioned site, it lies remarkably well for a public building, but there is a serious objection to it in consequence of the ground falling away towards the north, and it is so uneven as to prevent its conversion into a play ground except at very considerable expense. The best site too for the building is intersected by a footpath which there would probably be much difficulty in diverting so as to render it available for building.

With regard to the second site, it also lies well for building and does not present the same difficulties for the formation of a play ground as the other, but it has been objected to by several residents in Clifton who take an interest in the establishment of the College (and the Sub Committee are inclined to share in this objection) that the site is too distant for boys residing in the more frequented parts of Clifton as the Upper and Lower Crescent, The Paragon, Windsor Terrace &c.

The third field is certainly free from this objection for whilst it lies within an easy distance of all parts of Clifton, it is also conveniently placed as regards Redland and West Clifton, particularly as it will be approached by a roadway to be constructed from Pembroke Road. It will also be fronted by a road on the west and is altogether admirably adapted <both> for the purposes of building and a play ground.

Adjoining this field are lands belonging to Mr Haynes and Farnell's Trustees,[40] both of whom have been communicated with and are prepared to treat with the Company so that no difficulty lies in the way of obtaining an area of the extent suggested by the Sub Committee. A pathway crosses Mr Adams' field, but having regard to the new roads about to be carried out, there is very little doubt that it may be diverted so as not in any way to interfere either with the building or play ground.

---

[37] Malvern began with fourteen: R. Blumenau, *A History of Malvern College 1865–1965* (1965), pp. 4–5.
[38] Lawyer and Town Clerk of Bristol; another major local landowner: Jones, *Clifton*, pp. 116, 135.
[39] Francis Adams, of Cotswold Grange, Cheltenham, who in 1844 owned 80 acres in Clifton, and who was in the process of selling a large part of his estate, assisted by a private act of 1832 (15 & 16 Vict. *c. 8*): D. Jones, *A. History of Clifton* (Chichester, 1992), pp. 100, 125, 134; see also map, p. 121, from *Register* (1925), p. xviii.
[40] George Rooke Farnall had owned 117 acres in Clifton in 1844: Jones, *Clifton*, p. 100.

The several properties above enumerated may be procured on ground rents which will avoid the expenditure of any part of the capital for the purchase of land.

Taking into consideration the requirements of the institution, both as regards position and the convenience of the inhabitants of the surrounding neighbourhood, the Sub Committee would recommend that Mr Adams' land with a sufficient quantity of Mr Haynes' <land> or that of Farnell's Trustees to make up the twelve acres should be procured for the purposes of the College.

The Sub Committee would also recommend that although it would be desirable to procure plans for an establishment suitable for not less than five hundred boys, yet that at first a part only of the plan sufficient for two hundred or two hundred and fifty should be carried out, which from enquiries they have made may it is considered be completed for about four thousand pounds.

The next point for consideration is the appointment of an architect, and the Sub Committee recommends that the Bristol architects should be invited to send designs for the necessary buildings upon instructions to be drawn up for that purpose.

[5]   29 August 1860. Site to be purchased rather than rented
[*CC Company Minute Book 1, pp. 38–40. MS*]

Clifton College
Report of Sub-Committee to Provisional Committee

The Sub-Committee have been engaged since the last report in conjunction with the Solicitors in endeavouring to carry into effect the resolutions adopted by the Committee and have had prepared the Memorandum of Association and the Articles connected therewith, which are now before you for your consideration and approval **[6, 7]**. The Articles are of the highest importance and have been carefully written, and when approved, your Sub-Committee recommends that they be engrossed and the Company duly formed.

In addition to the consideration of its details, it will be necessary at this meeting to nominate the gentlemen to form the Council and the Treasurer.

The Sub-Committee has also proceeded to arrange a contract for the purchase of the land of Mr Adams. In the course of the treaty great if not insuperable difficulties presented themselves in arranging the purchase in consideration of an annual rent. The first of these was the difficulty of securing the payment in consequence of the buildings required for the College being so little suitable for other purposes. This difficulty might probably be overcome if the whole of the pile of buildings which will be necessary should the College be prosperous were at once completed, but your Committee cannot think it prudent to make a further outlay in building at the onset than would be required for a moderate number of boys, taking care in their arrangements that additions may be made in due harmony with the buildings as occasion shall require. Under these circumstances they have deemed it prudent to arrange for the absolute purchase of the land of Mr Adams at the rate mentioned at the last meeting. The terms of the contract have been considered and there exists no obstacle to the same being completed by the Council when constituted.

The purchase money will be about £10,000 and your Committee have arranged for the immediate payment of £1000 only and the residue at the end of a year, by which time much progress will be made with the College buildings and the value of the land will be, it is anticipated, much enhanced, so that it is considered that there will be little difficulty in obtaining the residue of the purchase money by mortgage or on debentures of the Company.

Your Committee have thought it undesirable to treat for a further purchase of land either of Mr Haynes or Mr Farnell until the contract with Mr Adams is signed, but when that is completed your Committee think it desirable to pursue their negotiations so as to secure for the College the 12 acres already deemed by the Committee requisite.[41]

Your Committee have reconsidered the question of the limit of the issue of shares, and finding that there are applications above the number of 250 they think that 50 further shares of Class A might be issued, limiting the present total issue to 300.

Your Committee think it extremely desirable immediately on the signing of the contract with Mr Adams that steps be taken to divert the footpath across the land proposed to be purchased.

Your Committee have prepared instructions to be issued to architects for the College buildings which are now before you for your consideration and approval [82], but they do not consider that they can be issued until there is a probability of concluding whether the footpath can be diverted or not.

Committee Room, 29 August 1860.

[6]   5 September 1860. Memorandum of Association
[*Printed*][42]

Memorandum of Association
of the
'Clifton College Company, Limited'.

1st. – The name of the Company is 'The Clifton College Company, Limited'.

2nd. – The Registered Office of the Company is to be established in England.

3rd. – The object for which the Company is formed is the establishment and conduct of a College, for the education of the sons of gentlemen, to be situate at Clifton, in the City of Bristol, and to provide, on moderate terms, a classical, mathematical, and general education of the highest class; the religious teaching of the College to be in accordance with that of the Church of England.

4th. – The liability of the shareholders is 'limited'.

5th. – The nominal capital of the Company is £10,000, divided into 400 shares of £25 each.

We, the several persons whose names and addresses are subscribed, are desirous of being formed into a Company in pursuance of this Memorandum of Association, and we respectively agree to take the number of shares in the capital of the Company set opposite our respective names.

---

[41] The original purchase of 9 acres of Adams' land between Worcester Terrace and the Zoo was made in October 1860; a further three acres to the north and east of this of was bought from Haynes in March 1861, and 2¾ acres to the south, also once belonging to Haynes, was bought from Dr Black in June 1862: *Register* (1925), p. xxi; Jones, *Clifton*, pp. 120, 134.

[42] Printed as booklet by Joseph Leech at the *Bristol Times and Journal* Office, Small Street, Bristol.

Names and addresses of subscribers	Number of shares taken by each subscriber
John Guthrie,[43] Dorset House, Clifton, Bristol	Two shares.
Joshua Saunders, Thornton Villa, Clifton, Bristol	Two shares.
Francis Nonus Budd, 6, Harley Place, Clifton, Bristol	Two shares.
George Cooke, The Paragon, Clifton, Bristol	Four shares.
Francis Black, 12, Lansdown Place, Clifton, Bristol	Eight shares.
William Gale Coles, 11, Victoria Square, Clifton, Bristol	Eight shares
William Henry Harford, Junr., Lawrence Weston, Gloucestershire	Four shares.
Alfred Cox, Shannon Court, Bristol	Four shares.
Henry Sidney Wasbrough, 7, Gloucester Row, Clifton, Bristol	Four shares.

Dated the fifth day of September, 1860.
Witness to the above signatures,
Henry J. Gorton, Clerk to Messrs Stanley & Wasbrough, Solicitors, Bristol.
Registered with Articles of Association.
Certificate of incorporation dated the 13th day of September, 1860.

[7]   5 September 1860. The Company's Articles of Association
[*Printed*]

ARTICLES OF ASSOCIATION
OF THE
𝕮𝖑𝖎𝖋𝖙𝖔𝖓 𝕮𝖔𝖑𝖑𝖊𝖌𝖊 𝕮𝖔𝖒𝖕𝖆𝖓𝖚, 𝕷𝖎𝖒𝖎𝖙𝖊𝖉.

It is agreed as followed:

1. The regulations in the table marked B. in the schedule to the 'Joint Stock Company's [*sic, ter*] Act, 1856',[44] shall not apply.

2. The College shall be established and governed and the affairs of the Company conducted by a Council constituted as hereinafter mentioned.

SHARES.

3. The original shares by which the capital of £10,000 shall be raised shall be divided into two classes – class **A** and class **B** – and shall confer upon the holders thereof respectively the respecive rights and privileges hereinafter mentioned, and the number of original shares which shall be issued in each class shall be in the discretion of the Council. No person shall be admitted a shareholder unless approved of by the Council, nor be deemed to have accepted any share unless he has testified his acceptance thereof by writing under his hand, in such form as the Company may from time to time direct.

4, 5. [*The Company may upon due notice make calls upon shareholders in respect of moneys unpaid, and may charge interest for calls unpaid.*]

6. [*The Company may pay interest on additional moneys advanced by shareholders.*]

7. [*Any one of joint shareholders may give receipts.*]

8. [*Share certificates will be issued for 2/6d.*]

---

[43] Vicar of Calne (Wilts) 1835–65; Canon of Salisbury and Prebendary of Bedminster and Redclyffe in Salisbury Cathedral 1852–8; Canon of Bristol from 1858; Chairman of the Council to his death in 1865: Freeman, *Worthies* (1909), pp. 38–9; Le Neve, *Fasti*, vi, p. 24. The College Chapel was erected in his memory at the expense of his widow Caroline. She laid the first stone in December 1865 but died herself the following year, before the building was completed.

[44] 19 & 20 Vict. *c*. 47.

TRANSMISSION OF SHARES.

9. The executors and administrators of a deceased shareholder shall be the only persons recognized by the Company as having any title to the share of such shareholder.

10. [*No transfer allowed unless approved by the Council.*]

11. [*Any person entitled to a share by transmission but not approved by the Council may transfer his share.*]

12, 13. [*Registration of transfers.*]

FORFEITURE OF SHARES.

14, 15. [*Forfeiture of shares on which calls are not paid.*]

RIGHTS OF SHAREHOLDERS IN CLASS A.

16. The registered holder for the time being of any share in class **A** shall have the privilege of nominating to the College one pupil in respect of each such share; and as often as a vacancy shall occur by the departure or removal or death of any pupil so nominated, then of nominating another to supply his place, and so on as often as occasion shall require; but no pupil shall be admitted to the College without the express sanction of the Council previously obtained.

17. If it appear to the Council at the commencement of any half-year or term that in respect of any share in class **A**, no pupil shall have been nominated or be attending the College, the Council shall have the power (with a special view of keeping up the number of pupils) of nominating and sending to the College a pupil on every such share, subject to the usual tuition fees, and to such extra charges (if any) as the Council may think fit. Provided always, that if the proprietor of any such share shall at any subsequent period wish to nominate and send to the College a pupil on such share, he shall be at liberty to do so notwithstanding the nomination previously made by the Council, but the pupil nominated by the Council shall not be affected thereby.

18. Every nomination of a pupil, except when made by the Council in pursuance of the last clause, shall be made in writing, under the hand of the nominating shareholder, and shall state the time at which it is intended that the pupil nominated shall attend the College, from which time the tuition fees for such pupil shall be payable, whether he then attend the College or not, unless in case of his non-attendance the College, in consequence of some reasonable excuse, shall waive the payment of such fees in respect of any period of time to be fixed by them. And such nomination shall be as nearly as circumstances will admit in the form marked C. in the schedule hereto, and shall be accompanied by the declaration at the foot thereof, under the hand of the nominating shareholder, and of the parent or guardian of the pupil, in the form marked D. in the said schedule, or as near thereto as circumstances will admit. And every such nomination shall be delivered to the Secretary, and a memorandum thereof shall be entered by him in the Register of Pupils.

RIGHTS OF SHAREHOLDERS IN CLASS B.

19. The registered holder of any share in class **B** shall be entitled to receive interest on the amount of capital paid up on such share at the rate of £4 per cent. per annum, from the time of the opening of the College for the reception of pupils, but shares in this class shall not confer upon the proprietors thereof any right of nominating pupils to the College.

20. [*Shareholders in class* **B** *may be transferred to class* **A**, *whereupon their right to interest will cease and they will acquire the rights of class* **A**.]

21. [*Interest for shares in class* **B** *payable annually.*]

INCREASE OF CAPITAL.

22. [*The Company may increase the capital by issuing new shares in class* A.]

GENERAL MEETINGS.

23–9. [*Regulations for the calling and quorum of meetings.*]

30. The President of the College, or (in his absence) one of the Vice-Presidents (to be chosen, if there shall be more than one, by the shareholders present) shall preside as chairman at every meeting of the Company. And if neither the President nor any of the Vice-Presidents be present at the time of holding a meeting, the shareholders present shall choose some one of their number to be chairman of such meeting. The chairman, whether a shareholder or not, shall, in case the votes at any general meeting shall be equally divided, have a casting vote, and if the chairman shall be a shareholder, such casting vote shall be in addition to the vote or votes to which he may be entitled as a shareholder.

31. [*Chairman may adjourn meetings.*]

32–3. [*Declaration by chairman that a resolution has been carried to be evidence of the fact, unless a poll be demanded by at least five shareholders; in which case the poll to be taken in the manner the chairman directs.*]

34. In addition to the powers given to general meetings by the Joint Stock Company's Acts 1856, 1857,[45] or these presents, any general meeting may, from time to time, make any new rules or regulations which they may consider proper for the government or management of the College or Company, or for the guidance or control of the Council ... Provided ... that no such new rule or regulation, and no special resolution passed in pursuance of the Joint Stock Company's Act 1856, shall repeal, alter, or affect the provision that the religious teaching of the College shall be in accordance with the Church of England.

VOTES OF SHAREHOLDERS.

35. Every shareholder shall have one vote for every share up to five, but no shareholder shall in any case have more than 5 votes, nor be entitled to vote at any meeting unless all calls due from him have been paid.

36. If any shareholder is a lunatic or idiot he may vote by his committee curator bonis, or other legal curator; and if any shareholder is a minor, he may vote by his guardian, tutor, curator, or any one of his guardians, tutors, or curators, if more than one.

37. [*Among joint shareholders only the first-named in the Register to vote.*]

38. [*Arrangements for proxies.*]

THE COUNCIL AND OFFICERS OF THE INSTITUTION – THEIR POWERS AND DUTIES.

39. The officers of the institution shall consist of a President, any number of Vice-Presidents not exceeding 12, a Council constituted as hereinafter mentioned, a Head Master, a Second Master, and such other masters as the Council shall think proper, a Treasurer (who shall, subject as regards the first Treasurer to the proviso contained in the 44th clause, be the holder in his own right of one share at least), a Secretary, Solicitor, two Auditors, and such other officers as the Council shall, from time to time, think necessary.

40. The first President, Vice-Presidents, and Treasurer shall be the following persons (that is to say):

---

[45] The second being 20 & 21 Vict. *c.* 14.

President.
The Right Honourable the Earl Ducie.[46]
Vice-Presidents:
William Jerdone Braikenridge, Esq.[47]
Joseph Cookson, Esq.
The Very Rev. Gilbert Elliot, Dean of Bristol.
Sir Arthur Hallam Elton, Bart.[48]
The Rev. Edward Girdlestone, Canon of Bristol.[49]
The Rev. James Heyworth.
Matthew Davenport Hill, Esq.[50]
Thomas Hill, Esq.[51]
William Henry Gore Langton, Esq., M.P.[52]
Philip William Skinner [*recte* Skynner] Miles, Esq.[53]
John Addington Symonds, Doctor of Medicine.
Arthur Edwin Way, Esq., M.P.[54]
Treasurer:
Wm. Gale Coles, of the City of Bristol, Banker.
All future vacancies in the offices of President, Vice-President, or Treasurer, shall be filled up by a general meeting.

41. The Council shall (except so far as the present clause is modified by the next) consist of the Treasurer for the time being (who shall be an *ex officio* member thereof) and twelve ordinary members, each of whom shall (subject as regards the first Council to the proviso contained in the 44th clause) be the registered proprietor, in his own right, of one share at least, and the first Council shall consist of the following persons:

John Bates, Esq.
Francis Black, Doctor of Medicine.
Francis Nonus Budd, Esq.
Robert Bush, Esq., a Lieut.-Colonel in the Army.[55]
John Colthurst, Esq.

[46] Henry John Reynolds-Moreton, succeeded as 3rd Earl of Ducie 1853, PC 1859, Captain of the Yeoman of the Guard 1859–66, Lord Lieutenant of Gloucestershire 1857–1911; created the fine arboretum, still largely intact, at his seat at Tortworth Court. He remained President of the College until his death in 1921.

[47] Son of the Bristol antiquary George Weare Braikenridge (d. 1856), whose great collection of topographical pictures and MSS passed to the City Museum and Art Gallery, the Central Library, and the Bristol Record Office on William's death in 1907.

[48] The 7th Baronet, of Clevedon Court (d. 1883); Liberal politician (MP for Bath 1857–9) and High Sheriff of Somerset.

[49] Canon of Bristol from 1854 until his death in 1884: Le Neve, *Fasti*, viii, p. 26; P.J. Perry, 'Edward Girdlestone 1805–84: a forgotten Evangelical', *Journal of Religious History* 9 (1977), pp. 292–301.

[50] Lawyer, penologist, author and Liberal politician; a Commissioner in Bankruptcy for Bristol District (d. 1872): see R. and F. Davenport Hill, *A Memoir of Matthew Davenport Hill, the Recorder of Birmingham* (1878).

[51] Of Sumeleigh House, Clifton Park: *Directory* (1861), p. 152.

[52] William Henry Powell Gore-Langton (d. 1873), Conservative MP for Somerset Western 1851–7 and from 1863 to his death.

[53] Of King's Weston (d. 1881); senior MP for Bristol 1837–52 (succeeded by a cousin of Gore-Langton), and member of the Society of Merchant Venturers 1864: McGrath, *Merch. Venturers*, p. 554.

[54] Conservative MP for Bath 1859–65 (in succession to Sir Arthur Elton).

[55] Of Brislington; member of Council until his death in 1877; father of Alfred George de L'Isle [*124: Town 1863–5*] and James Arthur [*125: Town 1863–8*] who came in the third term, and three others [*333, 723, 934*].

George Cooke, Esq.
The Rev. John Guthrie, Canon of Bristol.
William Henry Harford, Esq., the younger.
The Rev. James Heyworth.
Thomas Lowten Jenkins, Esq.[56]
Joshua Saunders, Esq.
John Addington Symonds, Doctor of Medicine.

42. Until the annual general meeting in the year 1863, the Solicitors of the Company shall, in addition to the other members of the Council, be *ex officio* members thereof; and the first Solicitors of the Company shall be Henry Sidney Wasbrough and Alfred Cox, both of the City of Bristol, Gentlemen.

ROTATION OF MEMBERS OF COUNCIL AND TREASURER.

43. [*At the AGM of 1863 and thereafter annually the Treasurer and four ordinary members of the Council shall retire, and shall be eligible for re-election.*]

44. [*Cycle of retirements. Treasurer and members to retire if they cease to hold shares; with proviso that the first Treasurer and members need not be shareholders until three months after the incorporation of the Company.*]

45. [*The Council may increase or reduce the number of members of Council, and may by special resolution remove the Treasurer or any ordinary member.*]

46. [*Casual vacancies may be filled up by existing members.*]

47. Every election to the office of Treasurer or member of the Council shall be made by ballot.

POWERS OF THE COUNCIL.

48. The appointment from time to time of the Head Master, Solicitors, and Secretary, and all other officers, the appointment of whom is not hereby otherwise expressly provided for, shall be vested solely in the Council. The Second and all other masters shall be from time to time appointed by the Council, associated with the Head Master, who, as regards such appointments, shall be considered to have the same rights and powers as if he were an ordinary member of the Council.

49. The Council shall have power to fix the amount of the respective salaries and remunerations of all the officers appointed by them, or by them associated with the Head Master as aforesaid, and the conditions and terms of their respective tenures of office; and also, except where it is otherwise provided by these presents, to prescribe and regulate their respective duties, and the Council shall likewise have power from time to time to remove any of such officers.

50. The Council may employ, from time to time, on behalf of the Company, at such wages and upon such terms as they may think fit, as many workmen, policemen, and servants as they may consider necessary, and may dismiss such workmen, policemen, and servants when and as they shall think proper.

51. The Council shall have power to purchase or acquire, from time to time, on behalf of the Company, all such sites and buildings as they may think necessary for the purposes of the College or Company, and particularly to purchase the whole or such part as they may think proper of a messuage known as 'The Gardener's Arms' and certain pieces of land adjoining, situate in Clifton aforesaid, and containing between nine and ten acres, the property of Francis Adams, Esq., or his trustees; and every purchase or acquisition made by the Council in pursuance of this power may

---

[56] Barrister, of Wraxall House; **[8]** below; father of Vaughan [*151*: HHP, DH 1863–9], an original pupil of the Junior School, and his younger brother [*413*].

be either in fee simple or for a term of years, and either in consideration of a yearly or fee farm or other rent, or of a sum in gross, or partly in consideration of such rent and partly in consideration of a sum gross, and subject to such stipulations and conditions in every respect as the Council shall think fit; but every such purchase, except the purchase of the said messuage and pieces of land hereinbefore particularly mentioned, shall require the ratification of a general meeting, and the Council may authorize any one or more of their number to enter into any contract on behalf of the Company for the purchase or acquisition of any such site as aforesaid; and every contract so entered into shall be binding on the Company.

52. The Council shall have power to erect, from time to time, upon any site which may be so purchased or acquired as aforesaid, all such buildings as they may think necessary for the requirements of the College, including, if they should think it advisable, a College Chapel, and houses for the residence of the Head Master and other masters, or any of them, or any other officer or servant of the Company, and from time to time to alter, enlarge, or improve such buildings as they may think proper; and also to lay out any part of such site for roads or play-grounds, and if they think proper so to do, to dedicate such roads, or any of them, to the public, and also to divert any such public roads or pathways leading across any site which may be purchased or acquired as aforesaid, or any part thereof. And generally to do all things which they may consider necessary or proper to render any such site fitted for the purposes of a College. And for the purposes aforesaid or any of them, to enter into all necessary contracts with architects and others; and the Council may, if they think fit, offer, from time to time, any premium or premiums for designs of buildings adapted to the objects of the Company.

53. The Council shall, from time to time, furnish all buildings for the time being used for the purposes of the College or Company with such fixtures, furniture, and fittings as they may think necessary, and shall keep the same buildings, fixtures, furniture, and fittings properly repaired and insured against fire, in such sum or sums as they may consider sufficient. And they shall provide all books, stationery, mathematical and other instruments, maps, and all other things necessary and proper for use in the College or to be supplied to the pupils. And if any master's house, or houses for any other officer or servant of the Company shall be built upon any such site as aforesaid, the Council may fix, from time to time, the terms upon which the masters or other officers and servants, or any of them, shall be allowed to reside therein either rent-free or otherwise.

54. The Council shall fix the time at which the College shall be opened for the reception of pupils; and if they shall consider it advisable that the business of the College shall be commenced before the necessary buildings shall have been built, they may hire any house or houses and premises in Clifton which they may consider fitted for the purposes of the College or Company, upon such terms as they may think fit, and make all necessary alterations therein, and commence the business of the College accordingly. The Council may also at any time hire any house or houses and premises which they may think necessary for additional accommodation.

55. [*The Council may with the authority of a general meeting borrow money on mortgage of all or any part of the real property, or on debentures.*]

56. [*The Council may sell or exchange any part of the real property.*]

57. [*Everything which the Council and officers are hereby authorized to do to be at the cost of the Company.*]

58. [*All receipts to be paid direct to the Treasurer, who is to keep an account with one of the Bristol banks.*]

59. The Council shall leave in the hands of the Treasurer such a balance as they shall deem sufficient to meet the current expenses of the Company, and may either permit the residue to remain in the hands of the Treasurer, or invest the same in the names of any three or more members of the Council in any of the stocks, funds, or securities of the British Government or of India, or the stock of the Bank of England or of Ireland, or upon freehold, copyhold, or leasehold securities, in England, Wales, or Ireland, or upon the mortgages or debentures of any incorporated railway or other company in Great Britain, or in the preference or guaranteed stock or shares of any such company, with power, from time to time, to vary such investments into or for others of a like nature, as the Council shall think proper. And the Council may, if and when they think fit, set apart out of the funds of the Company the sum of £1000, and invest the same in the names of any three or more of their number in any of the securities aforesaid, to be held as a guarantee fund, at the disposal of the Council, either to pay salaries or other expenses, or to meet any contingencies which may unexpectedly arise, and any deductions made, from time to time, out of such funds, shall be replaced from the first accruing receipts of the Company that may be made so available, so that a guarantee fund of £1000 in amount may at all times be kept up for the protection of the Council, and for answering the purposes aforesaid.

60. The Council may, if they shall so think fit, apply any part of the capital or income of the Company, and also any money borrowed by the Council, and any donations or bequests to the College or Company, for all or any of the following purposes, viz.: for or towards the purchase or hire of any lands or buildings, or the erection of any buildings which the Council may deem necessary; or the altering, enlarging, or improving of any buildings for the time being belonging to the Company, or the paying off or redeeming all or any of the shares in class B., or any charge or mortgage which may at any time be existing upon any property of the Company, or any debts or liabilities to which the Company may for the time being be liable, or for the founding of exhibitions, scholarships for the universities, or other prize appointments, premiums, or School scholarships for distinguished proficiency in School studies, or for general good conduct, or for the purchase of mathematical or other scientific works or instruments, or for the general formation of a Library of reference, or for such other purposes connected with the College as may be considered advisable by the Council.

61. [*The Council may also exercise such powers of the Company as are not by the Acts of Parliament or these articles declared to be exercisable by the general meeting.*]

62. The Council may, if they shall so think fit, with the sanction of two-thirds in number and value of the shareholders present at an extraordinary general meeting, declare a dividend to be paid to the shareholders in proportion to their shares, but no dividend shall be declared without the sanction of the Council.

PROCEEDINGS OF THE COUNCIL.

63. [*The Council may regulate its own meetings.*]

64. [*The members may elect a chairman for such period as they determine, and in his absence may choose one of their number to chair a meeting.*]

65. [*The Council's acts not be invalidated by the discovery of any defect in the appointment of any member.*]

66. The Council shall cause minutes to be made in books provided for the purpose: (1) of all appointments of officers made by the Council; (2) of the names of the members of the Council present at each meeting of the Council; (3) of all orders made by the Council; and (4) of all resolutions and proceedings of meetings of the Company and of the Council. And any such minute as aforesaid if signed by any person purporting to be the chairman of any meeting of the Council shall be receivable in evidence without any further proof.

MASTERS AND PUPILS.

67. The Head Master and other masters for the time being and the Council may, in the absence of any special agreement, terminate the engagement between them by either of the parties giving to the other three months' previous notice. The Council may also in the absence of such special agreement, as aforesaid, terminate their engagement with any master by giving to him three months' salary in lieu of notice.

68. The Head Master and Second Master of the College shall be members of the Church of England and graduates of Oxford, Cambridge, or Dublin University; and no master who may be in holy orders shall serve any church on week days, or undertake any professional or other office, cure, or employment requiring the devotion thereto of any part of his time, without the sanction of the Council.

69. All masters and teachers shall sign and deliver to the Secretary a written agreement to abide by and perform the regulations of the College and Company; and such agreement shall be (as nearly as circumstances will permit) in the form marked E. in the schedule hereto.

70. The internal regulation of the College shall (subject only to such rules as may from time to time be made, under the 34th clause of these presents), be under the sole management of the Head-Master, who shall regulate the duties of all the other masters, and shall carry into effect the system of education for the time being approved of by the Council. The moral government and discipline of all the pupils, whether boarders or day scholars, in and out of the School, and the making and enforcing of all regulations in reference thereto, as well as the supervision, regulation, and control of the several boarding-houses and boarding-house masters in regard to the moral discipline and government of the boys, and their regular attention to the studies and exercises required by them out of School hours, shall also, subject as aforesaid, be confided to the Head Master; who shall, whenever requested by the Council to do so, consult with them upon all matters relating to the conduct or management of the College, or of the affairs thereof.

71. The Head Master shall have power at any time, independently of the Council, (but without prejudice to the similar power hereinbefore vested in them), to dismiss any of the other masters.

72. The Council alone shall have the power of expelling pupils from the College; and such power may be exercised in any case in which the Council may in their judgment consider the expulsion of a pupil necessary or beneficial to the College in consequence of the immorality, wilful breach of discipline, or transgression of the rules of the College, or any flagrant misconduct of such pupil, in or out of School hours; and the pupil so offending may be expelled by the Council, either on the recommendation of the Head Master or without such recommendation. In any case of a pupil so offending, the Head-Master may, if he think fit so to do, immediately place such pupil under suspension until the Council shall have adjudicated on the case; and

in every case of suspension of a pupil by the Head-Master, he shall forthwith report thereon to the Council.

73. The Head-Master shall make, or cause to be made, monthly to the parent or guardian of each pupil, a report of the progress in learning and general conduct of such pupil.

74. Neither the Head-Master nor any of the other masters shall be allowed to take any private pupil, except in vacation time, without the previous sanction of the Council. It shall not be competent for any of the masters to hold any share in the Company, but they shall have the privilege of sending their own sons to the College under the same regulations as the pupils nominated and sent to the College by the shareholders in class A.

73. Every shareholder shall, for the tuition of each pupil nominated by him, pay, during the continuance of such pupil at the College, the annual sum which shall for the time being be fixed by the Council [as payable by the class to which the pupil may belong not exceeding £20, nor less than £16 *corrected in MS to*][57] not exceeding £25 per annum, and such amount shall be paid to the Treasurer in advance by half-yearly or other periodical payments, as may be directed by the Council. In case of any default in payment of such amount, or any part thereof in advance as aforesaid, the Council may (if they think fit) suspend the entrance or return to the College of any pupil on whose account such amount shall remain unpaid till the payment of the same.

74. In the event of a pupil leaving the College, previous notice of at least one quarter must be given to the Secretary, such quarter to be reckoned from the regular Quarter Day next ensuing after the delivery of such notice, in default of which the pupil will be entered at the next opening of the College as still on the College books, and a quarter's payment reckoned from such opening shall be considered as due and demanded accordingly; and if payment thereof be not made within twenty-one days after being so demanded, the shareholder by whom such pupil was nominated shall not be allowed to nominate another pupil on his or her share until such sum shall have been paid.

77. No pupil shall be eligible for admission to the College until he shall have completed his 7th year.

78. A fine of 10s. shall be imposed upon each pupil absent from the College on the day appointed for re-assembling after a vacation, and the like sum for every subsequent day until his return to the College, unless the absence of such pupil shall be with the leave of the Head-Master, or be occasioned by ill health or unavoidable accident, a certificate of which shall be, at the time of the pupil's return, submitted to and approved by the Head-Master. And every such fine shall be paid to the Treasurer by the parent or guardian of such pupil within one calendar month after the day on which the same arose.

79. An examination of the pupils as to their progress and proficiency in the various studies and subjects taught in the College shall take place not less than once a year, at such time or times as the Head-Master shall appoint; and every such examination shall be conducted on a plan to be proposed by the Head-Master and approved of by the Council; and all the expenses incidental to such examinations, and to all prizes given to the pupils, shall be paid out of the funds of the Company.

---

[57] This correction is made to the copy of the text prefaced to the register of first shareholders, and also to other printed copies of the 'Memorandum and Articles of Association'.

80. The daily business of the College shall be opened with a short selection of prayers from the liturgy of the Church of England.

BOARDING-HOUSES AND THEIR MASTERS.

81. No person shall be qualified to receive any pupil as a boarder without having previously obtained the license [*sic, bis*] of the Council for doing so, which license the Council may, from time to time, revoke. And the Council may exclude from the College any pupil who shall be found to be boarding in any house contrary to their regulations.

82. The master of every boarding-house shall be responsible to the Head-Master of the College, and also to the Council, for the due management thereof, for the proper care and domestic comfort of the boarders, for their moral government and discipline out of School hours, and for their regular attention to the studies or exercises required by them of School hours, and to their religious duties. And the master of every boarding-house shall conform to all rules and regulations of the Head-Master of the College, or of the Council.

83. The Head-Master of the College and the Council shall have the right of access to every boarding-house, and of inspecting and regulating all that concerns the health, comfort, good conduct, discipline, and proper management of the boarders. And for this purpose, the Council may depute any one or more of their members, or any other person or persons whom they may see fit, to visit, inspect, and report to the Council on any such boarding-house as aforesaid.

84. All complaints, either from the masters of boarding-houses or from their boarders, shall be made to the Head Master of the College; and the master of every boarding-house shall send to the Head-Master of the College monthly reports of the conduct of his boarders, stating any offences which may have been committed, and any punishments which may have been inflicted by any such master.

85. No master of any boarding-house shall either hold or be interested in any share in the Company, or at any time interfere, either directly or indirectly, in regard to the sale or transfer, or the negotiation for the sale or transfer of any share.

86. The terms on which boarding-house masters shall receive pupils as boarders shall be determined, from time to time, by the Council.

87. The Head-Master and other masters may, with the sanction of the Council, receive pupils as boarders, but in such case all the foregoing regulations and clauses shall, so far as the same are applicable, apply to them respectively in their character of masters of boarding- houses.

ACCOUNTS.

88. [*The Council's accounts to be kept at the Registered Office of the Company.*]

89. [*An annual statement of account to be made in general meeting.*]

90. [*Arrangement of accounts and balance sheet.*]

AUDIT.

92. The accounts of the Company shall be examined and the correctness of the balance sheet ascertained by two Auditors, to be elected by the Company in general meeting.

93. [*Auditors need not be shareholders, but may not otherwise be interested in any transaction of the Company.*]

94–7. [*Election and remuneration of Auditors.*]

98–100. [*Processes of audit.*]

NOTICES.

101–102. [*Arrangements for delivery of notices to shareholders.*]

103. [*Notices so required shall be advertised in two or more newspapers circulating where the Company's Office is situated.*]

NAMES AND ADDRESSES OF SUBSCRIBERS.

[*List and witness as for the 'Memorandum' below.*]

SCHEDULE OF FORMS.

Form C.

Form of nomination of pupils.

The Clifton College Company, Limited.

I [*blank*], of [*blank*], being the proprietor of share no. [*blank*] in class A, in the said Company, do hereby nominate as a pupil to the College:

Pupil's name [*blank*].

Born on the [*blank*] day of [*blank*].

Relationship of pupil to nominating shareholder [*blank*].

Father's name [*blank*] address [*blank*] profession [*blank*].

If no father, mother's or guardian's name [*blank*] address [*blank*].

Form D.

Declaration at foot of Form C.

I hereby declare sincerely, and to the best of my knowledge and belief, that the above-named [*blank*] was not removed from the school at which (or from the care of the tutor with whom) he was last placed, on account of any misconduct, and that he is not subject to fits, or affected with any contagious disorder; and that, in the event of his becoming, at any time, so visited, he shall be forthwith removed from the College.

Signature of shareholder [*blank*].

Signature of parent or guardian [*blank*].

And I also agree to abide by and perform the regulations of the said Company, so far as the same are applicable to parents or guardians of pupils.

Signature of parent or guardian [*blank*].

Note – If the parent or guardian be also a shareholder, this last will be unnecessary.

Form E.

[*Undertaking on being appointed a master to abide by the regulations and resolutions of the Company and Council.*]

☐ *The names of the first shareholders are inscribed in a handsome volume which begins with the printed Articles of Association. The register is printed here so far as to include all entries for 1860. Although the signatures are authentic, the entries were evidently made retrospectively. It will be noted that at the start the gentry and professional classes are listed before the tradesmen, irrespective of date.*

[8]   26 Nov 1860 x 14 March 1862. Register of earliest shareholders

[*F20. Bound volume of vellum leaves, with MS on printed forms*]

[*Column headings*] Name, in full / Signature [*here omitted*] / Number of shares subscribed for (written) [*here italic*] /Address / Occupation, rank or usual title / Date of signature / Witness [*here italic*].

John Guthrie. *Two A*. Dorset House, Clifton. Clerk in Orders.
 Nov. 30th 1860. *John Page*.[58]
Joshua Saunders. *Two A*. Thornton Villa, Clifton. Banker.
 Nov. 27th. 1860. *John Page*
Francis Nonus Budd. *Two A*. 5 Harley Place, Clifton. Barrister at Law.
 Nov. 27th, 1860. *Alfred Cox*.
George Cooke. *Four A*. The Paragon, Clifton. Solicitor.
 15 Decr. 1860. *James K. Morgan*.
Francis Black. *Four A, Four B*; 12 Lansdown Place, Clifton. M.D.
 Nov. 30 1860. *Alfred Cox*.
William Gales Coles. *Two A, Six B*. 11 Victoria Square, Clifton. Banker.
 28 Novr. 1860. *James K. Morgan*.
William Henry Harford. *Four B*. Bristol. Banker.
 30 Nov. 1860. *Alfred Cox*.
Alfred Cox. *Four A*. Shannon Court, Bristol. Solicitor.
 27 Nov. 1860. *F.N. Budd*.
Henry Sidney Wasbrough. *Four A*. 7 Gloucester Row, Clifton. Solicitor.
 28th Nov. 1860. *James K. Morgan*.
John Bates. *Two A*. 8 Royal York Crescent, Clifton. Banker.
 28th Nov. 1860. *James K. Morgan*.
John Colthurst. *Two B*. 11 The Mall, Clifton. F.R.C.S.
 Novr. 30. 1860. *Alfred Cox*.
James Heyworth. *Two A*. Westbury on Trym, nr Bristol. Clerk.
 Nov. 27th 1860. *John Page*.
Thomas Lowten Jenkins. *Two A, Two B*. Wraxall House, Wraxall. Barrister.
 Novr. 30. *Alfred Cox*.
John Addington Symonds. *One A, Two B*. Clifton Hill House, Clifton, Bristol. M.D.
 4th Decr. 1860. *James K. Morgan*.
Robert Bush. *Two Class A*. Brislington nr Bristol. Lt. Colonel 1st Gloster R[*ifle*]
 Volunteers.
 30 Novr. 1860. *Alfred Cox*.
John Bowman. *One Class A*. 16 Buckingham Villas, Clifton. M.A.
 Novr. 26th 1860. *James K. Morgan*.
Alban Thomas Jones Gwynne. *Ten shares Class B*. 1 Chandos Place, West Clifton.
 Colonel.
 Novr. 26th 1860. *James K. Morgan*.
George Ashmead. *One share Class A*. 9 Victoria Place, West Clifton. Surveyor.
 Janry 23rd 1861. *James K. Morgan*.
[Frank *corrected to*] Francis Adams [*blank*].
William Budd. *Two A*. Lansdown Place, Clifton. M.D.
 Dec. 15. 1860. *James K. Morgan*.
Lionel Oliver Bigg. *Two shares Class B*. St Stephen St, Bristol. Solicitor.
 26 Janry 1861. *James K. Morgan*.

---

[58] Secretary of the Company 1860–2.

Fulke Tovey Barnard. *One A, one B.* Huntington Villa, Clifton. Gentleman.
    Dec. 12. 1860. *John Page.*
Ralph <Montague> Bernard. *One A, one B.* Victoria Square, Clifton. Surgeon.
    Dec. 15. 1860. *John Page.*
John Blackburn. *One A.* Horton Rectory, Chippenham. Clerk M.A.
    Mar. 14/1862. *Henry White.*
John Beames Burroughs [*blank*].
Jane Black. *Four B.* 4 Richmond Terrace, Clifton. [*Occupation blank*]
    Janry 12th 1861. *James K. Morgan.*
William Jerdone Braikenridge. *Two A.* Clevedon, Somerset. Gentleman.
    Novr. 27th 1861. *John Page.*
[Isaac Allan Cooke *deleted: entered below*]
Augustus Cooper. *Two A.* Clifton. Clerk M.A.
    Nov. 30th 1860. *James K. Morgan.*
Henry Taylor Chamberlain. *One A, one B.* Elm Cottage, Redland, nr Bristol.
Merchant.
    Dec. 6. 1860. *James K. Morgan.*
William Cross. *One A, one B.* 7 Caledonia Place, Clifton. Surgeon.
    Nov. 28th 1860. *James K. Morgan.*
Edward Daniel. *Two A, two B.* 9 Worcester Terrace, Clifton. Solicitor.
    Dec. 10th. 1860. *James K. Morgan.*
George William Edwards. *Two A.* Shannon Court. Share Broker.
    Jan. 28th 1861. *James K. Morgan.*
William Henry Edwards. *Two B.* 4 Richmond Park. Merchant.
    Feb. 1, 1861. *James K. Morgan.*
Heberden Finden Emery. *One A, one B.* Banwell. Esquire.
    28 March 1861. *Henry White.*
Charles Eales. *One A.* Mall, Clifton. Gentleman.
    4th Decr. 1860. *James K. Morgan.*
James Evens. *Four A.* Stoke Bishop. W[*ine*] Merchant.
    24 Janry 1861. *James K. Morgan.*
Henry Bell Ford. *Two A.* Clifton Park. Merchant.
    15th Dec. 1860. *James K. Morgan.*
Lewis Fry.[59] *One A.* 30 Lower Crescent. Solicitor.
    15 Decr. 1850. *James K. Morgan.*
Conrad Finzel.[60] *Two A.* Clevedon. Sugar Refiner.
    Febry 5/61. *James K. Morgan.*
William Joseph Fedden. *One B.* Bank Court, Corn St, Bristol. Merchant.
    Janry 24. 1861. *James K. Morgan.*
Edward Girdlestone. *One A.* Wapley Vicarage, Chipping Sodbury. Canon of Bristol.
    March 11 1861. *John Page.*
Henry Gribble. *Two B.* Coston Villa, Clifton. Solicitor.
    22 Janry 1861. *James K. Morgan.*
Samuel Burleigh Gabriel [*blank*].

---

[59] Bristol MP (Liberal/Lib. Unionist) 1878 x 1900, PC 1901, Chairman of the Council of University College 1903–9, honorary member of the Society of Merchant Venturers 1919, along with Sir Herbert Warren; member of the College Council 1902–20: *Univ. Reg.*, p. 231; McGrath, *Merch. Venturers*, p. 560.
[60] C.W. Finzel, father of W.R. [*130*: SH 1863–6], who came in the third term.

John Henry Hirst. *Two B*. 1 Brighton Park. Architect.
Decr. 15. 1860. *James K. Morgan*.
James Hassell. *Two A, two B*. 3 Hill Side, Cotham. Leather Factor.
Janry 28. 1861. *James K. Morgan*.
George Hall [*blank*].
Richard Hitchins. *Two A*. Horfield Lodge, Horfield. Merchant.
Decr. 16. 1861 [*sic*]. *Henry White*.
Thomas Wright Rankin.[61] *One A, Two B*. Sutton House, Clifton. Gentleman.
Decr. 27/60. *John Page*.
Samuel John Sayce.[62] *One A*. West Town, nr Bristol. Stockbroker.
Novr. 27th 1860. *John Page*
Charles Hill junior.[63] *Two A*. Windsor Villa, Clifton. Merchant.
Decr. 15. 1860. *James K. Morgan*.
Richard Charles Hanson.[64] *One A, one B*. Prince Street, Bristol. Merchant.
Janry 28th 1861. *James K. Morgan*.
Sarah Frances Henley. *One B*. Leigh House, Chard. [*blank*].
October 29th 1861. *W. Gale Coles*.
George Keddell [*blank*].
Joseph Leech. *One A*. Albert Villas, Clifton. Newspaper proprietor.
Dec. 15. 1860. *James K. Morgan*.
William Poole King.[65] *Two A*. Rodney Place, Clifton. African merchant.
March 12th 1861. *Henry S. Wasbrough*.
Odiarne Coates Lane. *Three A, three B*. Somerset House, Clifton. Esquire.
Decr. 15. 1860. *James K. Morgan*.
Thomas Todd Walton. *Two B*. 14 Victoria Square, Clifton. Head Postmaster of Bristol
District (Armiger).[66]
27th Nov. 1860. *James K. Morgan*.
Walter Bagehot. *Three B*. The Arches, Clevedon. Banker.[67]
28 Nov. 1860. *James K. Morgan*.
John Stroud. *One B*. Kingshill House, Knowle, nr Bristol. Esquire.
27 Nov. 1860. *James K. Morgan*.
Christopher S. Penny.[68] *Two A*. Hazlewood House, Sneyde Park, nr Bristol. Esquire.
30 Nov. 1860. *James K. Morgan*.
George Wills.[69] *Four B*. 9 Buckingham Villas, Clifton, Bristol. Wine Merchant.
30 Nov. 1860. *James K. Morgan*.

---

[61] Father of Francis William [*56*: Town 1862–5], an original Cliftonian, and Lionel Kentish [*159*: Town 1863–72], who came in the third term.
[62] Father of Arthur Birch [*110*: Town 1863–5], who came in the second term, and Francis William [*243*: Town 1864–5].
[63] Member of the Society of Merchant Venturers 1881: McGrath, *Merch. Venturers*, p. 556.
[64] Father of Richard Bush [*26*: Town 1862–3], an original Cliftonian.
[65] William Thomas Poole King, member of the Society of Merchant Venturers 1838; father of Edmund Ambrose [*238*: Town 1864–7], and Percy Liston [*376*: Town 1865], both also members of the Society, the latter serving as Treasurer 1901–14: McGrath, *Merch. Venturers*, pp. 265–6, 551, 555, and *passim*.
[66] Used as fanciful equivalent to 'esquire'.
[67] At this time still active in Bristol banking and shipping, but already well known as an economist and political writer, and soon to achieve celebrity with *The English Constitution* (1867).
[68] Father of Francis Henry [*50*: Town 1862–7] and Edward Stubbington [*51*: Town 1862–8], original Cliftonians, and of Christopher Stewart [*615*: Town, DH 1868–71].
[69] Uncle of Howel [*386*: Town, DH 1866–73], first of several Cliftonians from this prominent family.

Robert Neale.[70] *One A, one B.* Thingley Place, Corsham, Wilts. Esquire.
    Dec. 1st 1860. *James K. Morgan.*
Simon Alexander George Young. *Two B.* 3 Chandos Place, Clifton. Retired List,
    Madras Medical Establishment.
    Decr. 1st 1860. *James K. Morgan.*
John Wetherman, Junr. *Two A.* Devon House, Kingsdown, Bristol. Porter Merchant.
    Decr. 4th 1860. *James K. Morgan.*
John Netting. *Two A.* 7 Exeter Buildings, Redland, Bristol. Merchant.
    Decr. 7th 1860. *James K. Morgan.*
William Frederick Phillips. *One A, one B.* Clifton. Merchant.
    Decr. 7th 1860. *John Page.*
Mark Davis Protheroe.[71] *Two A, two B.* Cobourgh [*Coburg*] Villa, Clifton. Gentleman.
    Decr. 8th 1860. *James K. Morgan.*
George Rocke Woodward. *Two A, two B.* Cornwallis Grove, Clifton. Merchant.
    Decr. 10th 1860. *James K. Morgan.*
Thomas Sawer. *Two A, two B.* 45 Crescent, Clifton. Surgeon.
    Decr. 10th 1860. James K. Morgan.
John Johnson Brown. *One A.* Elmdale House, Clifton. Gentleman.
    Decr. 12th 1860. *James K. Morgan.*
Isaac Allan Cooke. *Two B.* Windsor Terrace, Clifton. Solicitor.
    Janry 21. 1861. *James K. Morgan.*
William Metcalfe [*blank*].
John McArthur. *Two A, two B.* Park House, Queen's Road, Bristol. Iron Merchant.
    Decr. 13th 1860. *James K. Morgan.*
Frederica Mulville [*deleted*]
Joseph Haynes Nash. *Four A.* Clifton Hill. Iron Merchant.
    Decr. 18. 1860. *James K. Morgan.*
George William Nalden. *Two A, two B.* Long Ashton. Solicitor.
    Janry 26. 1861. *James K. Morgan.*
Edwin Naish. *One B.* 8 Savile [*recte* Saville] Place. Clifton. [*Occupation blank*]
    Decr. 5th 1861 [*sic*]. *Henry White.*
Henry Newport. *Two A.* Exeter. Clergyman.
    March 12 1861. *John Page.*
Charles <Henry> [Pritchard *corrected to*] Prichard. *One A.* Brislington. Merchant.
    Feb. 4th 1861. *James K. Morgan.*
<John> Selwyn Payne. *One A.* Clifton. Major.
    Jan. 28th 1861. *James K. Morgan.*
Thomas Shackleton Pope. *One A.* Clifton. Architect.
    Janry 28th 1861. *James K. Morgan.*
William Bishop Peck. *One B.* 4 Park Place, Clifton. Wine Merchant.
    Decr. 31 1860. *James K. Morgan.*
Robert John Ramsden. *Four A.* 4 Victoria Square, Clifton. Gentleman.
    March 9. 1861. *John Page.*
William Rogers. *One A, one B.* 4 Chandos Place, Clifton. Carriage Builder.
    Decr. 15th 1860. *James K. Morgan.*

---

[70] Father of Robert Rufus [*46:* SH 1862–3], an original Cliftonian, and John Alexander [*99:* SH 1863–8],
who came in the second term.
[71] Member of the Society of Merchant Venturers since 1840: McGrath, *Merch. Venturers*, p. 551. Father
of Frank [*105:* Town 1863], who came in the second term and left after the next.

[9]   November 1860–July 1861. First extant Petty Cash expenses
[*D4. Petty Cash Book 1860–3. MS*]

1860

		[£]	[s]	[d]
Nov.	By nailbrush & soap		2	6
	By chimnies [*sic*] for gas lights		7	6
	By taper stand			6
	By postage stamps	1	10	0
Decr.	By telegrams B. Ferry Esqr.[72]		8	0

1861

		[£]	[s]	[d]
Feby	By postages	2	4	4
	By fly with plans to office		1	0
	By porter at Fine Arts Academy[73]		1	0
	By stationery		2	0
	By Xmas box to postman		1	0
	By men carrying iron safe		2	0
	By porterage			6
March 15	By Hallett[74] – gas filter &c.	1	14	6
20	By Baber,[75]attendance at Fine Arts Academy	1	15	0
”	By gratuity to porter do. [*ditto*]		5	0
”	By sundries			9
22	By office penknife		1	0
25	By porter at F.A. Academy at public meeting of Company		5	0
27	By carriage of Register			9
30	By do.			9
30	By postage & registration of Annual Return		1	4
Apl.	By ink 1/1½, soap 4d, gum 1/–		2	5½
12	By carriage of Annual Return book			11
24	By ” Prospectuses			9
26	By envelopes & letter clips			5
May	By soap			6
	By Board of Health rate for office in Albion Chambers		16	8
	By postages	1	17	0
June 1	By washing towels		1	3
14	By postages		7	0
July 12	By carriages of parcel		1	1
13	Guildhall porter		2	6
”	By postages		12	3
26	By [postages *corrected to*] stamping 500 letters of call	2	0	0

---

[72] Benjamin Ferrey (d. 1880), Diocesan Architect for Bath and Wells, who was adjudicator of the competition for the College buildings; in 1861 he published a memoir of A.W.N. Pugin and his father, with and under whom respectively he had studied. He was himself 'a strong Gothic man': John Betjeman in *Centenary Essays*, p. 24.
[73] Became the Royal West of England Academy in 1915.
[74] James Hallett, plumber and gasfitter of College Street: *Directory* (1860), p. 141.
[75] Harry Baber, auctioneer and City Sheriff's officer: *Directory* (1860), p. 78.

29   By Board of Health rate 11 Arlington Villas[76]   1   2   6

☐ *There were various versions of the preliminary prospectus, issued under the name of the first appointed Head Master*

[10]   1861. Prospectus
[*Guard Book 1860–77. Printed*]

Clifton College Company, Limited.
President: The Right Honourable the Earl Ducie.
Vice-Presidents:

William Jerdone Braikenridge, Esq.	Matthew Davenport Hill, Esq.
Joseph Cookson, Esq.	Thomas Hill, Esq.
The Very Rev. Gilbert Elliot, Dean of Bristol	William Henry Gore Langton Esq., M.P.
Sir Arthur Hallam Elton, Bart.	Philip William Skinner Miles, Esq.
The Rev. Edward Girdlestone, Canon of Bristol	John Addington Symonds, Esq., M.D.
The Rev. James Heyworth	Arthur Edwin Way, Esq., M.P.

Council
The Rev. John Guthrie, Canon of Bristol, Chairman
William Henry Harford, Esq., Jun., Vice-Chairman

John Bates, Esq.	Thomas Lowten Jenkins, Esq.
Francis Black, Esq., M.D.	Joshua Saunders, Esq.
Francis Nonus Budd, Esq.	John Addington Symonds, Esq., M.D.
Lieut.-Colonel Bush	William Gale Coles Esq., Treasurer
George Cooke, Esq.	Henry Sidney Wasbrough, Esq. } Solicitors
The Rev. James Heyworth	Alfred Cox, Esq.

Head Master: The Reverend Charles Evans, M.A.,
Late Fellow of Trinity College, Cambridge, Craven University Scholar, Senior
Classic, Senior Chancellor's Medallist, and for the last twelve years Assistant
Master in Rugby School

It is proposed to establish at CLIFTON a PROPRIETARY COLLEGE, on a large scale, for the purpose of providing for the Sons of Gentlemen, at a moderate cost, a thoroughly good and liberal education.

The College will consist of two departments, under the immediate superintendence of the Head Master. In the one department, the course of instruction will have special reference to the universities, and will comprise all the subjects usually taught at a public school; in the other department the study of the Classics will not be discontinued, but greater prominence will be given to Mathematics, Modern Languages, English Literature, History and Composition, so as to prepare boys directly for all military and Civil Service examinations without the intervention of a private tutor.

Drawing and, if necessary, one experimental Science, will form part of the regular work.

------

[76] Where the Preliminary School was sited.

The religious teaching will be in accordance with the doctrines of the Church of England.

The general constitution and discipline of the College will be based, as nearly as possible, upon the model of the great public schools, in the full expectation of being able to combine the manly freedom and independent spirit of such institutions with the advantages of a wide and practical system of education.

About thirteen acres of ground on the outskirts of Clifton, and in the immediate neighbourhood of Durdham Down, have been secured as a site for the College and for play-ground; the buildings are already in progress.

The College will be opened during the summer of 1862, when the Head Master will be prepared to receive boarders into his house, which will be constructed on the most approved plan; with private studies, and every requisite for the health and comfort of pupils.

Terms:

Tuition and school fees – £20 per annum.

Boarders, including tuition and school fees – £85 per annum.

There will be no extras, except for books, stationery, and instruments.

No boy will be admitted except on the nomination of a shareholder.

The shares are £25 each, and confer the perpetual right of nomination.

Information in London can be obtained on reference to T.H. Dakyns, Esq., Treasury Office, Middle Temple.[77]

Applications for boarders to be made to the Reverend Charles Evans, Rugby. All other communications and applications for shares, to be addressed to the Secretary, John Page, Esq., The Guildhall, Broad Street, Bristol.

[11] 3 May 1861. Notice to shareholders about a Preliminary School
[*Guard Book 1860–1877. Printed*]

Clifton College Company, Limited
PRELMINARY SCHOOL
Master: The Reverend T.H. Stokoe, M.A.,
Lincoln College, Oxford, First Classman in Classics 1855; Denver Theological Essay Prizeman 1859; Late Assistant Master in Uppingham School[78]

Sir,

The Council of the Clifton College, in order to meet the convenience of several shareholders, have arranged to open a PRELIMINARY SCHOOL, after the Midsummer holidays of 1861, under the direction of the Reverend T.H. Stokoe, M.A., one of the assistant masters.

As this is a temporary arrangement, the terms will be twenty pounds for tuition and School fees, and two pounds each for French and German, per annum.

The Reverend T.H. Stokoe will be prepared to receive a small number of boarders at eighty-five pounds per annum, including tuition and school fees.

As the number of pupils will be limited, an early application should be made.

---

[77] Thomas Henry Dakyns, MD, father of Henry Graham [*M3*].
[78] Thomas Henry Stokoe [*M1*: 1862–3]. The Preliminary School opened at 11 Arlington Villas on 15 August: Christie, *History*, p. 24–5, 30 n. 8 (printing an extended version of this notice appearing in the *Bristol Times* of 13 July). Stokoe had in fact been sacked from Uppingham: Matthews, *By God's Grace*, p. 100.

I have the honour to be, Sir, your obedient servant,
John Page,
Secretary.
Guildhall, Bristol, May 3rd, 1861.

☐ *Shortly before the day arranged for opening the College the Head Master announced that he was applying for the headmastership of King Edward's School, Birmingham (his own alma mater).*

[12]   20 August 1862. Council Minutes
[*CC Company Book 1, pp. 180–1. MS*]

At a meeting of the Council held at the Company offices on Wednesday the 20th of August, 1862, at half past 12 p.m.

Present: Revd Canon Guthrie in the Chair; Dr Black, Mr Cox, Mr Coles, Mr Cooke, Lieut Col Bush, Mr Saunders, Mr Wasbrough, the Secretary.

[*After other business*]
Resolution regarding the Revd C. Evans having allowed himself to be put in nomination for Birmingham School.

I. That the Revd Charles Evans having been for some months past engaged to the College as Head Master, and the School having been advertised both by him and the Council to be opened on the 9th of September next under his superintendance [*sic*], the Council have heard with the utmost surprise a few days since that Mr Evans has <now> become a candidate for the vacant Head Mastership of Birmingham School.

II. That as it is essential that a Head Master should be secured for the College to perform if possible the pledge given to the public, and as it is also due to the friends of the nominated pupils and to the public forthwith to acquaint them should a change of Head Master be made, the Chairman be requested to write to Mr Evans to inform him that the Council cannot remain in doubt as to their position with him, and request his immediate decision whether he be ready to carry out unconditionally his engagement with the Council.

[13]   22 August 1862. Council Minutes
[*CC Company Minute Book 1, pp. 181. MS*]

A Council meeting was held at the College on Friday, the 22nd of August 1862, when the buildings were inspected, and a letter from the Revd Charles Evans to the Chairman was read by the latter.

☐ *Consideration of Evans' letter of 21 August was deferred at further meetings on 27th and 29th; meanwhile arrangements for the opening went ahead. Behind the scenes, approaches were again made to Temple of Rugby. He recommended one of his younger but most gifted masters, John Percival, who undertook to accept Clifton if Evans should be chosen by the electors at Birmingham.*

[14]   4 September 1862. Council Minutes.
[*CC Company Minute Book 1, pp. 184–6. MS*]

At a meeting of the Council held at the Company's offices, Thursday, September 4th, 1862, at 12 o'clock at noon.
Present [*as for 20 August except Bush*].

Head Mastership resigned by Mr Evans.
A letter was read from the Revd C. Evans resigning the Head Mastership of the Clifton College in consequence of his appointment to that of King Edward's School at Birmingham.

[*The text of the letter is actually entered at the end of the day's other business*]
Rugby,
September 3. 1862.
Gentlemen,
In consequence of my appointment to the Head Mastership of Birmingham School I am compelled to resign into your hands the Head Mastership of Clifton College. In the prosperity however of your new institution I shall not cease to take a warm interest, and shall at all times be glad to render to it any assistance in my power. I feel sure that any loss the College may sustain by my unexpected departure will be slight and transient, and that in the high reputation and ability of my successor you have a certain opportunity of expressing my thanks for the cordial welcome and great kindness which I received at your hands when as a stranger I first came among you, and I deeply regret than an acquaintance commenced so pleasantly has been so suddenly terminated.
I remain, Gentlemen, your faithful servant,
C. Evans.

H.M. vacant.
The Head Mastership of Clifton College is hereby declared vacant.

Mr Percival appointed to the Head Mastership of Clifton College.
It was moved by the Chairman, and seconded by the Treasurer, Mr Coles, that the Revd John Percival, M.A., Fellow of Queen's College, Oxford be elected Head Master of the Clifton College in the place of the Revd Charles Evans. It was stated that Mr Percival obtained a double first class at both examinations at Oxford,[79] and also the University Mathematical scholarship, and satisfactory testimonials in his favour from the Lord Bishop of Gloucester and Bristol, late Provost of Queen's College,[80] as well as from Revd Dr Temple, Head Master of Rugby School[81] (at which Mr Percival has been an Assistant Master) having been read, it was unanimously resolved that the Revd John Percival be and is hereby elected Head Master of Clifton College.
It was resolved that the Chairman be requested to acknowledge Mr Evans' letter announcing his appointment to the Mastership of King Edward's School at Birmingham.

---

[79] That is to say he was placed first class in the Honour School of Mathematics as well as that of *Literae Humaniores* (the achievement unofficially called the Oxford double first).
[80] William Thomson, Bishop of Gloucester and Bristol 1861–3, Archbishop of York 1863–90. (The dioceses of Bristol had been merged with Gloucester by Act of Parliament in 1836.)
[81] At Rugby 1858–69, then Bishop of Exeter; translated to London 1885 and to Canterbury 1896 (d. 1902).

□ *Clifton found no occasion to ask Evans for further assistance; indeed his memory was literally obliterated. His purported arms were hacked down from the front of School House and replaced by those of Percival; his name was omitted from the printed Register, where Percival is numbered 'HM1'.*

The College was formally opened with a service at 11 o'clock on Tuesday 30 September. This took place in Big School, for no Chapel yet existed. Benches were borrowed from the Victoria Rooms and the choir came up from the Cathedral. The Head Master preached, and by the Council's order his sermon was printed and sent to all shareholders and parents.

[15]   30 September 1862. The inaugural sermon
[*A Sermon preached at the opening of Clifton College on Tuesday, September 30, 1862, by the Rev. John Percival, M.A., Fellow of Queen's College, Oxford, Head Master* (London, Bristol and Rugby, 1862)]

1 Cor. iii. 7.
Neither is he that planteth anything, nor he that watereth but God that giveth the increase.

We meet here today to begin a new life. We have been gathered from various quarters, knowing little of each other, except that we have come to live and labour in one place and with one aim.

We come together with much in each of us that might seem likely to keep us asunder in heart and mind. We have been nursed under various influences, circumstances have combined to form our characters in different moulds, the associations that crowd around our memory are not the same in any two of us, each one comes from a life which the other knows not of, where habits for evil or for good have been contracted; and thus we come, many and various, looking at each other with enquiring eyes, to be welded into one body, to be called by one name, to be united in one work. This day is the beginning of a union, the effects of which will last through all our future life.

And in spite of our many differences in character, in feeling, in association – in spite of all that might seem to make our union difficult, I address you in the full confidence that we shall live and labour together as brethren should, and be united to each other as one family under one Head – Jesus Christ.

Let us not forget that underneath all the apparent differences which previous life may have raised between us, there is a human cord that binds us, man and boy, each to each; let us not be unmindful of that feeling of our common humanity which should bind us always to each other as by the strongest bond of sympathy; and above all let us remember that there is one God watching over us, and working within us; so that as our hope of salvation is one, and our Lord and Saviour one, so also our mind should be one.

I trust, therefore, that there is no one whose life is beginning to-day in this place, but feels himself from this moment to be one with those who are round about him. We met as strangers but we are strangers no longer.

We are standing now at a starting point in life, and for the future we must walk hand in hand.

While we are standing still, looking back and looking forward, uncertain of the ground we tread upon, let us unite in raising our thoughts to the throne of Grace, as is befitting at such a season;[82] our prayers have, I trust, ascended together to our Father in heaven, and now let us unite also in registering our resolves that we will each in his appointed place do our duty as members of this College, and as faithful followers of Christ our Redeemer.

There are doubtless many trials and many troubles which our commencement of a new life here will bring upon us, but there is one circumstance connected with it which claims our gratitude: we have this day granted unto us what many pray for in vain – a *fresh start* in life.

There are few men either old or young who would not be glad to shake themselves loose from some, at least, of the influences which have gathered round them, and begin their life again, unshackled by what has gone before.

But it is not often that this is granted; such opportunities are rare events, and they form crises in the lives of those to whom they come, which few men value as they ought.

Our opportunities for the most part come silently and unobserved. How often are we entirely unconscious of them till we view them in the retrospect! We see them when they have passed away, we recognise them in some trifling event which flitted across our life unnoticed – in some insignificant act, which never assumed its due importance till we viewed it at the head of a long train of consequences which had been determined by it; and how frequently, when looking back on the little things which have gradually robbed us of our freedom of action, while we chafe under the sin from which we have not strength to flee, how frequently do we cry – 'Oh! that I could begin my life afresh!'

Men are continually endeavouring to lay the blame of their failure in duty not on themselves, but on their surroundings.

It is still as it was at first – 'The serpent beguiled me, and I did eat'.[83] On every side the cry is heard – 'If I could only shake off the evil influences that have gathered round me; if I could only escape from evil companions, and begin afresh, free and with a *fair start*, all would be well.'

And it cannot be denied that to have such a start is an inestimable blessing; at any rate, it takes away all excuse. To be able to profit by our previous experiences, to begin our life afresh, knowing something of our own weaknesses, and the sins that most easily beset us, and to have the opportunity of choosing our course, and beginning the race again unclogged and unburdened of our former weight of embarrassing circumstances; this is a cause of deepest gratitude.

And we stand to-day exactly in such a case. Whatever difficulties or obstacles may arise in our path here, we shall have to remember with gratitude that no evil influences enchained us when our life here began. If, hereafter, any of you become the slaves of sin, the chains which bind you will have been forged by your own free act; and, knowing this beforehand, feeling that your life here opens with opportunities for good, which claim your gratitude as positive blessings, you are bound to register in the secret depths of your hearts good and firm resolutions for your future guidance and support.

Beginning, as we do, with every motive, human and divine, to inspire us to a worthy life, if we fail we shall be without excuse.

---

[82] Michaelmas (the feast of St Michael and All Angels), when the church commemorates those superior beings who engage in perpetual worship.

[83] Genesis, iii.13 (Eve's feeble attempt to shift blame on to a talking reptile).

There is a heavy responsibility laid on every one, whether master or pupil, who enters a place like this, which has no tradition, no history, to guide us.

Whatever the future of this College may be, that future will be modified for good or evil, nay, in a great measure, it will be determined and acquire its character by the conduct of those who are at this moment beginning their life in it.

If you desire to belong to a place of which you may be justly proud; if you wish to hear this College spoken of as one that bears a high name; as a place where truth, and uprightness, and purity, and all Christian virtues are held in honour; as a place where all that is base or unworthy is hated and despised, then remember that it rests with you to give it that name.

There is not a single boy who now hears me, down to the very youngest,[84] but may do something to win a worthy, noble, Christian character for this place of education, if he will only do his best.

And remember all of you that, if any one among you do evil, that evil will not only defile his own heart, but will leave its stain on this unstained spot; and forget not that it is a different thing to be the first pupils of a school which has its name to make and its character to win; it is a very different thing from being members of an old establishment, where all this has been done for you. In this place you will be set on a hill, and every act that you do will have a double significance.

It is a noble privilege to be so placed; but every privilege implies self denial and circumspection; if we stand in a conspicuous place, we must take double heed lest we fall.

Now, I wish to impress most deeply on you this day that, as members of this young society, you are placed in a most responsible position. I feel this so deeply, and it is of such unspeakable importance, that you also should feel it, that I wish to impress it on all in such a way that you may remember it on your knees night by night when your day's work is done. I wish to impress it, so that the remembrance may go with you daily in your relations with each other, and may serve as a strong motive to a worthy life. It is not given to every one to be clever. The great majority among us will never be able to attain to any intellectual distinctions, let them labour as they may. Some of you probably feel this, and are discouraged by it; but remember that there is a nobler gift than any superiority of intellect, which is denied to none who seek it.

Men admire learning, and ability, and talent, and it is right that they should, for these are worthy of all admiration; but the only really great thing upon earth, the only thing by which God will judge us, is *goodness*, and this, thank God, is within the reach of all.

Your memory may be weak, and your intellect dull, and you may feel that you cannot keep pace with others round about you, but there is this one thing which none need yield to his neighbour. All cannot become distinguished for scholarship or other acquirements, but all may be truthful and upright; all can be patient and forgiving; all can be industrious and obedient; and these are the highest gifts which can be found in master or boys. Of these things I call upon you to reflect this day; and now is the time to make the resolutions that are to guide your after life. We, your teachers, have to resolve to dedicate ourselves earnestly and heartily to the work of educating you for your calling in life.

---

[84] This seems to have been Alfred George Harrison [*30*: Town 1862–3], aged 9 years 3 months 2 days; but we do not have the birth dates of 10 of the 75 admitted in that first term, of whom about 60 attended the opening: *Register* (1925), p. xx. (The number, though taken from this source, rose to 70 in Christie, *History*, p. 26.)

And we make that resolution knowing something of what it involves; we shall have to do many things which you may dislike, and which may be painful to us, but we shall do them because we are bound to do our duty, and that I trust both men and boys will do while united here.

But while we on our side have to make our resolutions, and to pray for grace to carry them out, you also have your part to perform in this act of self-dedication.

You have to resolve, first of all, to be *truthful*. Without this, there is no possibility of our doing good to each other; if once deceit enters into your relations with us, if you shut us out of your hearts by drawing a veil of untruth round them, all our labour will be in vain. We cannot hope to do you good unless you will meet us halfway. The temptations to untruth are doubtless very strong, and you will often have to struggle against them; but when you are tempted remember that untruth is a cowardly and contemptible sin, and by God's help you will cast it out.

Do not yield to the momentary weakness which makes you shrink from speaking the plain truth, even though by speaking you should condemn yourselves. Let this be your first resolve.

And, next, beware of *idleness*: this is one of the most insidious of *sins*. I call it a sin, because I desire you always to remember that it is one. Boys are apt to think little of it; they are not ashamed of it; some are even proud of it, yet there are few more determined or more dangerous. Beware of it on all grounds. If you indulge in it, you will be led you know not whither; and in any case you will find it the most unsatisfactory of all indulgences; it gives little enjoyment, and breeds nothing but discontent; whatever you do, do your work.

There is one other resolution, which must be placed side by side with these. You have resolved to be truthful, and to be industrious; resolve also to banish from among you all impurity. If it appear among you in word or deed, cast it out and fling it from you with contempt; with contempt, I say, and stamp it with the mark of infamy; beware of its touch, for it is poison, and will defile your life; and let no impure or unseemly word ever taint the air of this place.

To these resolutions you should add others. Resolve to keep watch over your tempers, and to do all things to live in harmony with each other; be patient, be forgiving, and let malice or cruelty have no place among you.

And, once more, aim at *manliness*, respect yourselves, and avoid all that is unworthy, and others will respect you; and you will soon find that the upright way of life, seemingly hard and grievous, is, in reality, easy and pleasant.

And, lastly, remember not to be ashamed of *prayer* – never shrink from this most sacred duty. This and this alone will keep you strong in the midst of temptation and trial; if you feel weak pray for strength; if you waver pray for firmness; if you are sorrowful pray for comfort, and your Father, which is in heaven, will not fail to help you.

These are plain words, but all who are in earnest feel that words cannot be too plain when we speak of our deepest interests.

I have still to remind you more directly what is the chief aim of our work here; we shall labour day by day and week by week at secular work, the chief end of which is to make you successful in the struggle of life, and we shall always urge you to strive for earthly distinction; but we may succeed in all this, as others have succeeded, and yet fail to do what ought to be, what we desire to be the real work of this place. Our aim in life is so to pass through things temporal that we lose not finally things eternal;[85] and the aim and endeavour and earnest desire of your teachers here will be to make you feel that you are being trained not only to be industrious, active, successful men, but to be soldiers of Christ, and faithful followers of Him who died for you. If you will only believe that this is our aim; if you will stand by the resolutions which I have begged you to make; if you will trust us and cling to us not as masters, but as friends, then I have no fear lest our work should fail; but when you go forth into the world to do your work, you will look back with thankfulness on this day, the beginning of your life here.

There are many around me interested deeply in this place – as parents, as friends. I feel that many yearning prayers and earnest desires will ascend to the Throne of Grace on our behalf; and in the consciousness of this we shall rise daily stronger to our work, and we trust that those prayers will never fail us. We shall doubtless stumble, and fall, and make mistakes, in spite of all that we may do to aim at perfection; and for all this I have to beg your indulgence. Judge us not too harshly if we fail to reach our high ideal. Judge us not too severely if we seem unprepared to begin this great work; we have done what we could, and the only thing which we have to require of you is that charity in judgment which, as men and as Christians, you are prepared to give.

We begin our work in no spirit of self-confidence, but trusting for support on that foundation which is laid for us, our Saviour Jesus Christ. We shall work earnestly, but we shall work humbly, remembering that we are labourers in God's vineyard; that those committed to us are God's husbandry; and we shall not labour the less heartily because we feel that 'Neither he that planteth anything, not he that watereth, but God that giveth the increase.'

[16]   July–October 1862. Petty cash expenses
[*D4 Petty Cash book 1860–3. MS*]

1862

			[£]	[s]	[d]
May	12	By Poor Rate, 11 Arlington Villas	3	15	0
	17	By John Page, telegrams		6	0
June	4	By Bingham,[86] stationery		6	9
	20	By steel pens & holders			8
	23	By 1000 envelopes		7	0
	30	By advertisement, *Manchester Guardian*	2	16	3
		By do., *Midland C[ounties] Herald*	1	10	0
		By do., P.O.O. [*Post Office Order*] for the above			9
July	7	Hire of gas metre [*sic*] as per bill		3	0
	14	5 quires of paper		2	0
August	9	By Lavars,[87] printing	2	8	6
Septr.	1	Ream of blue note paper		4	6
		Washing of towels		1	4
	3	Telegram to Birmingham[88]		2	0
	13	Bownemain to workmen		1	0
		Paid to Mr Wasbrough for telegraphing to Mr			

[85] Adapting the Collect for the 4th Sunday after Trinity.
[86] M. Bingham, who had a newspaper and periodical office in Broad Street: *Directory* (1860), p. 86.
[87] John Lavars, lithographer, of Broad Street: *Directory* (1860), p. 169.
[88] In connexion with Evans's election to the Headmastership there.

		Dakyns relative to Mr Percival's appointment as Head Master		2	0
	25	500 envelopes (opening of School)		4	0
Octr.		Advertisements. *Star of Gwent*,	1	1	0
		Salisbury & Winchester Journal		11	0
		P.O. Orders			6
		P.C. Bradley, for attending at College on opening of same 3 days		5	0
	7th	Stamps		4	0
	13th	Stamps		10	0

[17]   6 October 1863. Percival to an unidentified stationer
[*Editor's collection. Holograph*]

Clifton College.
Oct. 6. 1863

Dear Sir,
I enclose stamps for your small account.
Will you kindly send me 24 copies of Arnold's *Confirmation Questions*?
I shall also feel obliged if you will tell me your charges for printing account papers. I think that our printer here is rather high.
Yours very truly,
J. Percival.

The Jewish House

☐ *Clifton was distinctive in having a boarding house for Jewish boys, which opened in the summer of 1878.*[89] *It is difficult to accept the story that Percival's friendship with Lionel Cohen secured the Charter in return for setting up the House.*[90] *But it unquestionably established connnexions with the higher reaches of British Jewry, and once Percival had appointed Bernard Heymann*[91] *as the first House Master, the following laboured but encouraging overture was received.*

[18]   27 December 1877. Alfred H. Beddington[92] **to Bernard Heymann**
[*Polack Centre, PH Archive, no. 1. Holograph*]

8, Cornwall Terrace,
Regent's Park N.W.
27th December 1877.

Sir,
Upon having arranged to open a House at Clifton so soon as you have seven boys as boarders, and having only as yet arrangements made with you for two boys, five boys are yet deficient to make up the number of seven.

---

[89] D.O. Winterbottom, *Dynasty: The Polack Family and the Jewish House at Clifton 1878–2005* (Clifton, 2008). Cheltenham's equivalent (Corinth House) did not open until 1892: Morgan, *Cheltenham*, p. 106.
[90] See Introduction, p. xxviii.
[91] *M91*: 1878–90.
[92] Father of Gerald Ernest [*2325*: PH 1878–84] and Claude [*2349*: PH 1878–85].

In the event of your opening a House at Clifton for Jewish boys to attend Clifton School next Easter and in case you should be deficient of any one of such five boys from Easter 1878 to Easter 1880, the following gentlemen have agreed to make up to you such deficiency at the rate of £26-13-4 per term (there being three terms only in one year) for each one of such five boys that you do not obtain as boarder that is wanting to make up the number of boarders to seven during the period of two years from Easter 1878 to Easter 1880 and they will be responsible for the sums respectively attached to their names as follows:

	From Easter 1878 to Easter 1879	*From Easter 1879 to Easter 1880*
Sir Nathaniel de Rothschild[93]	One hundred pounds	One hundred pounds
Alfred H. Beddington	One hundred pounds	One hundred pounds
Baron de Stern[94]	Fifty pounds	Fifty pounds
F.D. Mocatta Esq.[95]	Fifty pounds	Fifty pounds
Louis Nathan Esq.	Fifty pounds	Fifty pounds
John H. Beddington Esq.	Fifty pounds	Fifty pounds

In any case this responsibility shall not extend to the payment for more than five boys during the said period of two years, and the payment for which each of the said gentlemen shall be responsible shall not exceed the sums herein stated attached to their names, nor shall the total amount of their responsibility for either of the two years exceed four hundred pounds per annum.[96]

Yours truly,

Alfred H. Beddington.

☐ *At first it was Hamburg House, so named by Heymann after his native city. The enduring name came from Heymann's successor Joseph Polack,[97] and the three members of his family who ran the House in succession until its closure in 2005.*

[19]   September 1890. The opening of Sophie Polack's Journal
[*Annals of Hamburg House, vol. 1, pp. 1–2. MS in possession of Polack family*] [98]

Annals of Hamburg House
Third term 1890.

We entered Hamburg House early in September 1890. My husband and James (his brother) with the help of Matron had the house fairly in order before my arrival on the 8th of the month. I came, accompanied by Martha (nurse)[99] and my infant boy (Bennie) then seven weeks old.[100] I had previously visited Hamburg House and

---

[93] Nathaniel Mayer de Rothschild, created Baron Rothschild 1885, banker and philanthropist. None of his immediate family came to Clifton.

[94] Hermann, Baron de Stern, financier (d. 1887).

[95] Frederick David Mocatta, communal worker and philanthropist; Horace Mocatta [*2526:* PH 1879–84] was the first of many of the family to arrive, but was not F.D.'s son.

[96] Only the writer himself became a parent.

[97] *M139:* 1890–1923, and House Master throughout.

[98] Longer extract printed, as corrected, in Winterbottom, *Dynasty*, pp. 41–2.

[99] Identified as Martha Griffiths on p. 4 of the journal.

[100] Benjamin James Polack [*5838:* PH 1901–9]; killed in action 1916.

had been initiated in many details concerning management through the kindness of Mrs. Heymann, the wife of our predecessor. At first many difficulties presented themselves owing to limited accommodation, our predecessors not having been obliged to provide nurseries or [a room *corrected to*] rooms for a matron. One of the chief difficulties was the impossibility of devoting a room for a study for my husband's use and he [ha(*d*) *corrected to*] was obliged to content himself with a corner of the dining-room, a most unsatisfactory arrangement. One room only was available as a nursery and had to be used both as sleeping and day-room. It had been therefore decided to build a wing to the house and on this account Mr Polack decided to purchase the property, an achievement he was able to accomplish by the help of several parents of boys, the list of whose names is as follows:

Benjamin Cohen, Nathaniel Cohen, Samuel Montagu, D.C. Stiebel, M.H. Moses, E. Lucas, C. Davis, E. Enoch, [*blank*] Montague. [101]

Percival's resignation and the appointment of his successor

☐ *When Percival told the Council of his intention to resign to become President of Trinity College, Oxford, he was invited to recommend his successor. He duly named James Maurice Wilson, his former colleague at Rugby. Wilson accepted, but after hearing that some senior masters were unhappy with his appointment, he withdrew his acceptance. The post was then advertised and Wilson cautiously put his name forward again.*

[20]   19 November 1878. J.M. Wilson to James Heyworth, Chairman of the Council
[*HM2 file. Holograph*]

Rugby
19 Nov. 78

Dear Sir,
    May I venture to lay before you and the Council a remark on the mode of election of a Headmaster which I understand has been contemplated, so far as it affects the position of the Headmaster himself.
    If a man is chosen without its being known for certain what other men were willing to accept the post it will always be said that if the competition had been open he would never have been chosen. Whether true or not the saying could not be contradicted, and it would be more than unpleasant. It would damage the Headmaster in relation to other Headmasters, to his colleagues, and to the public generally.
    My feeling on the matter may be unreasonably sensitive, but I hope no one will mistake it for anything else if I say that for myself I should not be willing to accept

---

[101] Sir B.L. Cohen, 1st Bt (1905), father of Sir Herbert Benjamin Cohen, Bt [*3770*]; N.L. Cohen father of Jacob, Sir Robert, and Charles Waley Cohen [*3846, 4264, 4573*];the 1st Baron Swaythling (1907), father of Edwin Samuel, Gerald Samuel and Lionel Montagu [*4381, 4789, 5158*]; the father of Sir Arthur, Charles and Leonard S. Stiebel [*4039, 4296, 4504*]; the fathers of E.H. Moses [*3589*], O.D. Lucas [*3607*], L.J.C. Davis [*4423*] and C.D. Enoch [*4266*]. There was no Montague in the House.

the offer of the Headmastership if made previous to ascertaining by public notice
exactly what other men are eligible.

I remain,

Yours very faithfully,

James M. Wilson.

☐ *Wilson duly submitted his formal application, though he was not afraid to state his
terms; and when he learned that he had a strong competitor, he remained equivocal.*

[21]   5 December 1878. Wilson to the Chairman
[*HM2 file. Holograph*]

Rugby

4 Dec./78.

Sir,

I beg to offer myself as a candidate for the Headmastership of Clifton College, to
be vacated at Easter by Dr Percival.

In compliance with the terms of the advertisement I have to state that I was
educated at King William's College, Isle of Man, and at Sedbergh Grammar School;
that I obtained a classical scholarship on entering St John's College, Cambridge;
and was bracketed for the second Bell's university scholarship in my second term. I
then devoted my time chiefly to mathematics, and took my degree in January 1859
as Senior Wrangler. I was prevented by a serious breakdown in health from going in
for the Classical Tripos.

I was appointed Natural Science Master at Rugby in the same year; was elected Fellow
of my College in 1860; and in 1863 became Senior Mathematical Master at Rugby.

I have had much experience in teaching mathematics at school, and some branches
of science: but I have had as [*recte* no] higher classical teaching except the occasional
taking a form for a colleague, and a little voluntary reading with boys in my own house.

References may be made to the Bishop of Exeter, to the Revd Dr Jex-Blake of
Rugby,[102] and to the Revd A.G. Butler of Oriel College, Oxford, formerly assistant
master at Rugby.[103]

I might here conclude but that I feel bound to say that, as my work of late years
has been almost exclusively mathematical, I cannot pretend to be a sufficiently good
scholar to be the chief authority in the classical teaching of the School. It may be
well therefore for me to state that if elected I should retain only the Divinity and a
subordinate part of the classical teaching of the Sixth Form in my own hands, while
I should hope to take myself some direct part in the mathematical and scientific work
of the School. I think it probable therefore that it would be necessary for me, sooner
or later, to ask the Council for a larger grant than has hitherto been given towards the
classical teaching, as I fear that it would not be possible to secure permanently such
a chief classical assistant as the College ought to have to be responsible for the work
of the Sixth Form, for less than about £600 a year. I think it right to mention this, as
it implies a probable increase of expenditure under this head if you should elect me.
I do not anticipate however that any change would be necessary at once.

---

[102] Thomas William Jex-Blake, the incumbent Headmaster of Rugby (1874–87), later Dean of Wells.
[103] Arthur Gray Butler, Fellow of Oriel since 1836; Headmaster of Haileybury 1858–68; Foster, *Al. Oxon.*
i, p. 202.

I am 42 years old, and am at present a layman; but having for some time looked forward to taking orders on retiring from Rugby, I should hope to do so, if elected, before entering on my duties as Headmaster.

I cannot refrain from adding that I should not have thought of standing for the post but for the strong wish expressed by my friends at Clifton and elsewhere that I should do so; and that I have only consented with much hesitation. It will be no easy task to follow Dr Percival. But if elected, I shall consider it a plain summons, quite unsolicited, to higher and harder work than I have hitherto had to do, and shall devote myself entirely to that work to the best of my ability. I shall endeavour to carry out loyally the wishes of the Council, and to maintain the high character and efficiency of the School, and I shall rely on the same hearty cooperation from you that Dr Percival has always received.

I remain,

Yours very faithfully,

James Maurice Wilson.

☐ *Other contenders included the Headmasters of Highgate School (Charles McDowall) and the Perse (J.B. Allen). The application of the Second Master of Dulwich College is of particular interest as he had taught at Clifton.*

[22] 7 December 1878. J.McC. Marshall[104] to the Chairman
[*HM2 file. Holograph*]

Dulwich College,

Dec. 7. 1878.

Sir,

I have the honour to offer myself as a candidate for the Head Mastership of Clifton College, and, in accordance with the desire of the Council, I beg leave to submit the following statement.

My early education was obtained at the Manchester Grammar School. In 1857 I was elected Scholar of Trinity College, Oxford, and there gained a first class in Classical Honours at Moderations in 1859, and at the Final Examination in 1861.

A year later I became a Fellow of Brasenose, and immediately undertook the principal scholarship lectures in the College, acting at the same time as Classical Lecturer at Wadham College.

After a short training in school work at Marlborough under Dr Bradley,[105] I came to Clifton, late in 1865, and served the College for more than four years as Head Master's assistant.

I must leave Dr Percival to speak of my work at this time; for myself I will only say that I was fortunate in gaining a thorough insight into the principles and practice of his most successful system. I also look back with pleasure to my association with Dr Percival in the establishment of the evening classes, which have now developed into the Bristol College.[106]

---

[104] James McCall Marshall [*M25*: 1865–9]. Though failing here, he became Headmaster of Durham School in 1884, succeeding his rival for the Clifton appointment, W.A. Fearon [**23**].

[105] George Granville Bradley, Master 1858–70, later Dean of Westminster (d. 1903).

[106] Percival, ever keen to extend the educational franchise, had founded the 'Association for the Promotion of Evening Classes' in 1869, leading to the opening of University College, Bristol, in 1879.

During my residence at Clifton I had a small Boarding House, and built the large House now occupied by Mr Oakeley.[107]

In December 1869, I was appointed Second Master of Dulwich College. The School then contained 200 boys; the present number is 570.

I have also had a seat for several years on the Council of the 'Girls Public Day School' Company,[108] and have taken an active part in the management of its affairs. The Company has already established 17 schools in different parts of the country, containing at the present time nearly 2500 pupils.

In 1874 I published an edition of Horace in the *Catena Classicorum*,[109] and I am now engaged in work for the Clarendon Press.

I should perhaps add that I am in priest's orders and am attached to no extreme party in the Church.

I have the honour to remain, Sir,

Your very obedient servant,

J.M. Marshall.

Reference may be made to:

The Rev. G.C. Bell, Master of Marlborough College, formerly Second Master of Dulwich.[110]

James Bryce, Esq., Regius Professor of Civil Law at Oxford, Governor of Dulwich College (7 Norfolk Square, W.).[111]

The Rev. William Rogers, Chairman of the Governors of Dulwich College, The Rectory, Bishopsgate, N.E.[112]

☐ *This was to no avail; but when Wilson became aware of the strength of the competition, he wrote again to the Chairman.*

[23]   12 December 1878. Wilson to the Chairman
[*HM2 file. Holograph*]

Rugby

12 Dec. 78

Dear Sir,

I hope I may be permitted to make one more communication to the Council before they proceed to the election.

I am told that Mr Fearon[113] is a candidate. I do not know him except very slightly and I would only say that if the opinion of the Council is tolerably evenly divided between us, I hope their choice will fall on Mr Fearon. He is a good many years younger than I am and could look forward to more years of efficient work at Clifton.

---

[107] Edward Murray Oakeley [*M31*: 1867–87].

[108] Founded 1872 (under the patronage of Princess Louise).

[109] *Quinti Horati Flacci Opera*, I, *The Odes, Carmen Seculare and Epodes*; he had also published, while at Clifton, *A Table of Irregular Greek Verbs: Classified according to Curtius's Greek Grammar* (1866).

[110] George Charles Bell, Master 1876–1903; see below **[121]**.

[111] Scholar, politician and diplomat, created Viscount Bryce 1914 (d. 1922).

[112] Rector of St Botolph, Bishopsgate (d. 1896).

[113] William Andrewes Fearon, an Assistant Master at Winchester. His application for the headship of Clifton (2 December) was heavily endorsed in a seven-page testimonial from his Headmaster, George Ridding (12 December). Fearon was to become Headmaster of Durham School (1882–4) before returning to Winchester as Headmaster (1884–1901).

I do not withdraw my name because I think it is my duty to take the post if the Council decide that is for the interest of the College that I should do so: but I cannot say that I much desire the appointment.

Perhaps the knowledge of this fact might turn an evenly balanced scale, and I should be sorry to withhold it.

I remain,

Very faithfully yours,

James M. Wilson.

☐ *The Council were unmoved by Wilson's doubts and rejected all other applicants. In fact the competition was a charade since the Council had no mind to rescind their first choice to satisfy the Common Room. Wilson was duly re-appointed, and Percival was able to announce the succession.*

[24]   16 December 1878. Percival to parents
[*HM2 file. Printed*]

[*Private*]   Clifton College,

Clifton, Bristol,

Dec. 16, 1878.

Dear Sir,

You have no doubt been informed, through notices in the newspapers or otherwise, of my appointment to be President of Trinity College, Oxford, which will necessitate the surrender of my Headmastership at Easter next.

Till my successor was appointed, it seemed to be premature on my part to make any communication to parents on the subject; but I now feel I ought to inform you, without delay, that the Council, on Saturday, elected Mr J.M. Wilson, of Rugby, to be the new Headmaster, and I trust it may not be thought unbecoming if I venture to add that all who are interested in the success and good name of the College are to be congratulated on the choice which the Council have made, as in Mr Wilson's hands everything that is best in our School life will be maintained and strengthened, whilst he is sure to add new elements of distinction and good tone.

He was a classical Scholar of St John's College, Cambridge, Bell University Scholar, Senior Wrangler, and Fellow of St John's College; and he has for many years been a very successful, popular, and influential master at Rugby, where he established and organized under Dr Temple the teaching of Natural Science, and took a leading part in many other important educational matters. He is also the author of various educational works, and a member of several learned societies. At the present time he is a layman, but, having intended to take orders whenever he should be called upon to leave Rugby for a more directly spiritual charge, he will be ordained before he enters on his duties here.

I cannot conclude this letter without expressing the gratitude I feel to the parents of our boys as a body, for the kindness, trust, and confidence, which they have invariably shewn towards me as Head Master. Nothing could be more encouraging to my successor than the testimony which it will be my happiness to be able to give to him on this point.

I am, dear Sir, yours sincerely,

J. Percival.

SECTION II: GOVERNANCE

The Clifton College Company

[25]   20 September 1862. Council's Report to Shareholders
[Guard Book 1860–77. Printed][114]

Clifton College Company, Limited.
Report of the Council
Presented to the shareholders at the Annual Meeting of the 20th September 1862.

The Council, in presenting their report, congratulate the shareholders that they are enabled to meet them within the walls of the College, and that the portion of the building now completed surpasses the expectations they formed when they adopted the design. The Head Master's house is also ready for occupation, and the whole of the School buildings they feel satisfied have been well constructed, and are admirably adapted to the purpose for which they were intended.

The retirement of the Rev. Charles Evans from the Head Mastership occasioned the Council more anxiety than they can adequately express. Feeling deeply that the success of the College must depend on their obtaining the assistance not only of a distinguished scholar, an able tutor and master, but also of a gentleman who would strenuously seek to develope [*sic*] a high moral and religious feeling amongst the pupils, they would have had no hesitation had it been necessary to have deferred for a time filling up the Head Mastership rather than sacrifice any essential requirement.

It was, however, found that the proposed system of education, the advantages of position, the School buildings and arrangements, were so well known and approved, that several gentlemen possessing the highest qualifications were willing to undertake the duties of Head Master, so that the Council were enabled most promptly to fill up the vacant post.

The Reverend John Percival, M.A., Fellow of Queen's College, Oxford, who has added to a career at that University of almost unsurpassed brilliancy the experience of two years' mastership at Rugby, is now the Head Master, and the Council have obtained such satisfactory testimonials to his fitness for the position, that they regard the College as eminently fortunate in securing his services.

---

[114] The first four paragraphs were reprinted in early editions of the *Register* [as (1925), p. xx].

The Rev. T.H. Stokoe, M.A., also a first class man at Oxford, whose exertions in the Preliminary School and in the present emergency entitle him to the warm thanks of the Council, will continue his valuable assistance, and Charles George Blackader, Esq., M.A., late Scholar of St John's, Cambridge, for several years assistant master at the Modern School, at Cheltenham,[115] with other gentlemen, [and *otiose*] will supply a staff for the Head Master, calculated to inspire public confidence.

The appointment of the Head Master, having been made only on the 4th instant, it was impossible for him to take possession of his House on the 9th, the day long since advertised for opening the College; but it was considered essential that the work of the School should not be on any account postponed, and arrangements have been made for receiving the pupils in the class rooms for the present, and that the Head Master should come into residence on the 30th, with his boarders, and that on that day the College should be considered as formally opened.

The Council have the gratification of announcing that the Lord Bishop of the Diocese has undertaken the office of Visitor of the College,[116] in the welfare of which he takes a deep interest.

Dr Black having become the owner of the field adjoining the College land on the south, the Council have made arrangements with him, whereby he has consented to give the College a lease of about three acres on most liberal terms, with a right of purchase within a period of 10 years.

The general balance sheet is now prepared, and will be presented to the meeting in pursuance of the Act of Parliament.[117]

This being the annual meeting the Treasurer and four members of the Council retire from office, and are eligible for re-election: the retiring members are William Gale Coles, Esq., Treasurer; Francis Black, Esq., M.D.; John Bates, Esq.; F.N. Budd, Esq.; Thomas Lowten Jenkins, Esq., who all offer themselves for re-election.

In concluding this report the Council desire to assure the shareholders that they have every confidence in the success of the College; they find that its establishment has excited a great and growing interest, not only in our own neighbourhood, but also in different parts of the kingdom, and that a confident opinion has been expressed by those eminently able to judge, that combining as we do, the advantages of such a healthy, charming, and accessible position as Clifton, and possessing admirable School buildings and ample playground; a School established on our plan, conducted by an able Master, cannot fail to obtain a very distinguished success.

[26]   30 March 1876. Council's Report to Shareholders
[Guard Book 1866–77. Printed]

Clifton College Company, Limited
Report for the Year 1875.
Presented to the shareholders and adopted at the Annual General Meeting held at the College, Clifton, on 30th March, 1876.

---

[115] *M2*: 1862–5.
[116] Generally a dignitary set distantly over a collegiate body, to whom it can turn *in extremis* for arbitration. Sometimes a Visitor has power to intervene and regulate on his own initiative, or to nominate the executive head of the society. Such powers cannot have been envisaged here. Nothing more is heard of the position, perhaps because Bishop Thomson almost immediately departed to York.
[117] 19 & 20 Vict. *c*. 47 (Joint Stock Companies Act 1856), table B sect. 70.

The Council have the pleasure to submit their report for the past year. It has always been customary in their annual statement for the Council to report upon the numerical condition of the School, and year by year they have been able to chronicle a marked increase in numbers, so that the lists showed last term the large total of 525 boys, besides 51 attending the Preparatory School. For some months past the maximum number of boarders for whom room can be found in the houses has been reached, and the College can, therefore, no longer be expected to expand in this direction. It has not, however, been thought desirable to close the doors to residents in the neighbourhood, whose sons could attend as town boys, and accordingly the increase on this head has continued as heretofore. The lists last term read as follows: Classical Side, 243; Modern Side, 139; Military and Engineering Side, 22; and Junior School, 121. The Military and Engineering Side has been expanded into a separate department, to meet more fully the requirements of boys proceeding to Woolwich,[118] the Indian Civil Engineering College, Cooper's-Hill,[119] &c., and with most satisfactory results, as shown by the places taken by those prepared in it, and proceeding direct from it to the above examinations.

Some time since the attention of the Council was drawn to the advisability of erecting a separate building for the Junior School, with a view of separating this department more thoroughly from the Upper School. As it was much desired by the Head Master, and the Council were convinced that it was decidedly for the general advantage of the College that such provision should be made, they last summer selected a site between the Chapel and the Baths, and began the erection of a building according to the plans furnished by Mr Hansom,[120] to comprise one large room in the centre, and four rooms adjoining, to give the accommodation required. The building is now roofed in, and will shortly be ready for occupation. A separate entrance will be made from the College Road, near the Workshop. The site has been so chosen as to take little or nothing from the space available for the boys' recreation, while the structure is thoroughly in character with the other buildings, pleasing in itself, and completes the handsome and substantial range which forms the southern front of the College.

But far above the mere increase in number and material, the Council would desire to call attention to certain points more likely to escape observation, but perhaps more valuable to estimating the position of the College and the work it is doing – such, for instance, as the breadth and variety of its curriculum, its capability of meeting the complex educational wants of the time, its success in doing so as evidenced by the testimony borne to the excellence and thoroughness of its teaching by examiners and others qualified to judge,[121] and to the results of its work in the positions gained by those going out from it: or to the spontaneous movements continually made from within and without to add to its usefulness by enlarging or improving its buildings, augmenting its scholarships, increasing its library, stocking its museum, beautifying its Chapel, supplying it with objects valuable for art as well as science, proving it to be not only a place of sound teaching, but a centre of high cultivation instinct with life.

The following honours, among others, have been gained by Cliftonians, old and present, during 1875: one scholarship at Exeter College, Oxford; one scholarship

---

[118] The Royal Military Academy (for Royal Artillery and Royal Engineers).
[119] The Royal Indian Engineering College; the buildings now form part of Brunel University.
[120] Charles Francis Hansom, the chosen architect.
[121] See also earlier examiners' reports below [121–2].

at Jesus College, Cambridge; two scholarships at St John's College, Cambridge; two demyships at Magdalen College, Oxford; the Synes Exhibition, at Exeter College, Oxford; one scholarship at Pembroke College, Cambridge; one scholarship, one exhibition, and two minor open exhibitions at Balliol College, Oxford; three admissions to the Indian Civil Service; three admissions into the Royal Military Academy, Woolwich; three admissions into the Indian Civil Engineering College, Cooper's Hill; a first class in the Final Classical Schools, Oxford; two first classes in Final Natural Science Schools, Oxford; and the Gaisford Greek Verse Prize,[122] at Oxford.

The following Members of Council now retire by rotation: Mr F.N. Budd, Dr Frncis Black, Mr George Cooke, and the Rev. James Heyworth. They are eligible, and the Council beg to recommend them for re-election.

[27]   6 December 1876. Notice of winding up the Company
[*Guard Book 1860–77. Printed*]

Clifton College Company, Limited.

Notice is hereby given that a special general meeting of the shareholders of the above-named Company will be held on Monday, the 18th day of December, 1876, at Clifton College, Clifton, at three o'clock in the afternoon, to consider and if approved to pass special resolutions for the following purposes, namely:

1. To resolve that the Company be dissolved and wound-up voluntarily, and to determine the time and mode and terms upon which the dissolution and winding-up shall take place, to appoint a liquidator or liquidators of the Company for the purpose of carrying out the said voluntary winding-up.

2. To pass a special resolution conferring upon the liquidator to be appointed such powers as may be considered necessary or expedient, and in particular all such powers as may be considered necessary or expedient, to transfer all the property and rights of the Company under the provisions of sec. 161 of the Companies Act, 1862,[123] or otherwise to enable the liquidator to transfer all the property and rights of the Company to a chartered Company proposed to be constituted and incorporated by Royal Charter, and intended to be entitled 'The Clifton College', a petition for which Charter has been presented to the Crown by the Right Honourable the Earl of Ducie and others, in exchange for interests in such other Company, or to enable the liquidator to transfer all the rights and property of the above-named Company, to such Company to be incorporated by Charter, upon the terms of any arrangement whereby the members of the above-named Company may, in lieu of receiving cash shares or other like interests, receive benefits from the said Chartered Company by being constituted original Governors under the said Charter, and to authorise such liquidator or liquidators to raise by mortgage, charge, debentures or otherwise, at such rate of interest, and upon such terms, and upon and over the whole or such part of the property of the Company, as to the said liquidator or liquidators shall seem advisable, the purchase money to be paid to the dissentient members (if any) under the provisions of the said 161st section.

And notice is hereby given that a special general meeting of the said Company will be held at Clifton College aforesaid, on Friday, the 5th day of January, 1877, at ten

---

[122] The future Sir Herbert Warren; below **[38]**.
[123] 25 & 26 Vict. *c*. 89.

o'clock in the forenoon, for the purpose of confirming the resolution or resolutions adopted at the special general meeting of the said Company, to be holden on the 18th day of December, 1876.

Dated at Clifton College, this 6th December 1876.

W.D. Macpherson, Secretary.[124]

Clifton and the Endowed Schools Commission

☐ *Gladstone's first administration (1868–74) laid the foundations of free State education in Britain. The principal measure was the Education Act of 1870,[125] dealing with elementary schools. Before that the Endowed Schools Act of 1869[126] sought to redistribute existing charitable endowments to better effect. A Commission was established to negotiate schemes for this purpose, which included proposals for placing deserving pupils in fee-paying schools. Like most high-minded designs of central government, it provoked fierce opposition in the localities. Many of its proposals were curtailed as a result, and some (including those for Clifton) lapsed altogether. The Commission was dissolved when the Conservatives returned to power under Disraeli in 1874. Nevertheless it laid the seeds for the Direct Grant schools created by the 1944 Education Act.[127]*

Percival was a fervent supporter of the Commission's aims, and wanted Clifton to be fully integrated into a State system. In this aspiration he was thwarted by the Council, who had no intention of diluting Clifton's elite status.[128]

[28]   3 June 1870. First notice of the Endowed Schools Commission's proposals.
[*CC Company Minute Book 2, p. 375. MS*]

Endowed Schools (Act) Commission.

The probable effect of the Endowed Schools Act upon the College was considered.

Mr Percival reported the general outline of the scheme of the Commissioners, and it was resolved: That a Sub Committee be appointed for the purpose of seeing Mr Fitch[129] and ascertaining the views of the Commissioners in regard to the establishment of a first class school for Bristol,[130] and that such Sub Committee consist of the Chairman of the Council, the Revd Canon Moseley, the Revd John Percival and Mr Wasbrough.

[*signed by the Chairman*] James Heyworth.

---

[124] William Douglas Lawson Macpherson, Secretary 1864–1912 and founder (1920) of the Macpherson Prize for sketching; father of Alexander Geldart [*4325*: NT 1891–1901], Kenneth Douglas Worsley [*4476*: NT 1891–8], and Charles Gordon [*5678*: NT 1900–5]; see obituary of the last named in *Creag Dhubh: The Annual of the Clan Macpherson Association*, no. 5 (1953), pp. 30–1.

[125] 33 & 34 Vict. *c*. 75 (the 'Forster Act').

[126] 32 & 33 Vict. *c*. 56.

[127] 7 & 8 Geo. VI. *c*. 31 (the 'Butler Act').

[128] The debate is very ably digested in Potter, *Headmaster*, pp. 84–8.

[129] Sir Joshua Girling Fitch, an Assistant Commissioner under the Act 1870–7, later a Chief Inspector of Schools; knighted 1896.

[130] Not a measure of quality, but (as in the Commission's terminology 'first grade') a school taking pupils to the most advanced level, i.e. to the age of 17 or 18.

[29]   18 June 1870. Special meeting of the Council
[*CC Company Minute Book 2, pp. 381–5. MS*]

At a special meeting of the Council held at Messrs Stanley & Wasbrough's offices, Royal Insurance Buildings, Corn Street, Bristol, on Saturday 18th June 1870.
    Present: the Rev. Jas. Heyworth (chair); the Rev. Canon Moseley, Mr Addison,[131] Dr Black, Mr Budd, Mr Cooke, Mr Cox, and Mr Saunders.
    The Head Master attended.
    [*After routine business*]
Endowed Schools Commission.
    The Sub Committee appointed to meet Mr Fitch reported as follows:
    That a meeting with Mr Fitch had taken place on June 15th (1870). Present on behalf of the College: the Rev. James Heyworth, the Rev. Canon Moseley, F.N. Budd Esq., and the Head Master.
    Mr Fitch stated that the Commissioners in their original instructions to him with reference to this district requested him to enquire about the position of Clifton College and the possibility of any union with it which would make the establishment of a first grade school for Bristol unnecessary. This to shew that the Commissioners would look upon some such union as a desirable thing if it be found feasible.
    Mr Fitch also read a letter of the Commissioners written to him after his receipt of an informal communication from the Head Master on the subject, which was made in order to elicit the views and intentions of the Commissioners.
    It may be well to explain that some months ago the Head Master mentioned informally to the Council what would probably be the general scheme of the Commissioners in regard to the Bristol endowments and its possible effect on the College, and suggested that it would be expedient in the interests of the College to open some negotiations with the Commissioners and hear their intentions before the whole matter was settled. All the members of the Council present on that occasion agreed that this was most desirable and the Head Master was accordingly requested to see Mr Fitch unofficially. Accordingly he explained to Mr Fitch the position of the College and mentioned to him his own belief that the Council would be very ready to consider any fair proposal from the Commissioners, though he carefully warned him at the same time that he had no authority whatever for saying what the opinions of the Council would be.
    In his communications with Mr Fitch he found that some change or modification of our rules would be absolutely necessary on two or three points i.e. (1) nominations, (2) scale of fees, (3) government of College, in as much as the Commissioners would not be very likely to enter into an arrangement with an institution over which they had no control at all. He accordingly expressed his own individual hope that it might be possible to make some changes on these points sufficient to authorize the Commissioners to negotiate with the College.
    The chief points raised in the letter of the Commissioners to Mr Fitch are as follows:
    (1) That union is most desirable.
    (2) The only complete union would be for the Commissioners on behalf of the Bristol Endowment Fund to take over the College by purchase from the shareholders. Would they sell? Could they if they would?

---

[131]   William Brook Addison, member of the Council from 1869 until his death in 1882.

(3) That the only alternatives would be an arrangement similar to one made at Taunton, for which see *Endowed Schools Commission Report* XII.237, or Articles of Association of Taunton College School Company.[132]

Difficulties in the way of this:

(a) Endowments could not be handed over to the College Council to administer as the first grade school here is part of a great scheme, and moreover the College system is in some points such as the Commissioners cannot approve.

(b) As to the scale of fees, local preference could scarcely be given but on the other hand £25 a year is just the maximum fee allowed by the Commissioners.

(c) How could necessary changes be made as to nominations and other points? Could a general meeting make them? Or is the Commission to propose a scheme? If so, how can the College be brought within the Act? By consent of the Governing Body or not? (see Act, sec. 14.1, sec. 8.2.)[133]

Moreover a conscience clause would be necessary. Would this be contrary to the Articles of Association (sec. 15, sec. 34)?[134] And other similar difficulties might arise.

Mr Fitch also distinctly said that unless the College makes some arrangement with the Commissioners, a rival first grade school with lower fees will be established; that the Trustees of the Grammar School are anxious for this, and that he should expect this school to be placed somewhere in Clifton, e.g. in the neighbourhood of Tyndall's Park, as the present site of the Grammar School is out of question for such a school.[135]

He further added that it is of course open to the College to represent to the Commissioners the injustice and hardship of such a course on their part, but that the Commissioners would not be likely to be influenced by such a representation. So that, as he says, it remains for the College either to stand aloof and see a new school spring up by its side, or by some arrangement to agree to provide what the Commissioners feel bound to secure.

Such an arrangement would involve at least the following changes in the constitution of the College:

(1) That the fees should not be above £25 and, as he put it, the necessity of a general revision of the scale of fees so as to make the present average the maximum.

(2) Social distinctions to be abolished.

(3) A conscience clause to be guaranteed.

Other changes affecting property might be necessary also, as it would be indispensable to secure its permanency.

---

[132] The Taunton Articles are virtually identical with Clifton's; more relevant is the Charity Commissioners' Scheme (1867) for merging the existing borough grammar school with the new College School: King's College, Taunton, Archives, Tuckwell Scrapbook 1 (containing copies of both documents), *cf*. Bromwich, *Taunton*, pp. 4–6.

[133] By section 14.1 no scheme under the Act might interfere 'with any endowment ... originally given to charitable uses ... less than fifty years before the commencement of this Act, unless the governing body of such endowment assent to the scheme'. Section 8.2 exempted from the Act any school which on 1 January 1869 was maintained 'wholly or partly out of annual voluntary subscriptions', and had no endowment except school buildings and attached grounds.

[134] See above [7] sect. 34; sect. 15 is not relevant, and the citation must be an error for 'p. 15', where sect. 34 begins in the printed Articles.

[135] The Commissioners' report on the Grammar School and their scheme for its improvement to 'first-grade' are discussed in C.P. Hill, *The History of Bristol Grammar School* (1951), pp. 86–7, 96–102, and K. Robbins, *Pride of Place: A Modern History of Bristol Grammar School* (Andover, 2010), pp. 13–14; see also F.W.E. Bowen, *Queen Elizabeth's Hospital: The City School* (Clevedon, 1971), pp. 100–2, and J.R. Avery, *'While we have time ...' 1590–1990: Queen Elizabeth's Hospital Quater Centenary* (Bristol, 1990), p. 256.

Canon Moseley's paper: Endowed Schools Commission scheme.

The Rev. Canon Moseley read a paper stating the reasons which induced him to consider that the changes necessary to be made in the College to bring it within the range of the Commissioners' scheme would be most undesirable.

☐ *Moseley's paper was read again and entered into the minutes at another special Council meeting two days later.*

[30]   20 June 1870. Canon Moseley's opposition to the Commissioners' proposals
[*CC Company Minute Book 2, pp. 386–92. MS*]

At the adjourned special meeting of the Council held at Messrs Stanley & Wasbrough's offices, Royal Insurance Buildings, Corn Street, Bristol, on Monday 20th June 1870.

Present: the Rev. Jas. Heyworth (chair); the Rev. Canon Moseley, Mr Addison, Dr Black, Major Bush, Mr Cooke, Mr Cox, Dr Goodeve,[136] and Mr Saunders.

The Head Master attended.

Endowed Schools' Commission. Canon Moseley's paper.

The minutes of the meeting of 18th were read and confirmed, and it was resolved that the paper read by the Rev. Canon Moseley at that meeting should be entered in the minutes, and the paper by request of the meeting was again read.

Memorandum of conference with Mr Fitch about Clifton College. 15th June 1870.

(1) The Endowed Schools Commissioners may purchase the interest of the shareholders in the College, becoming themselves absolutely possessed of it. It appearing doubtful whether the shareholders had the legal power to make such a sale, such power might however be obtained by Act of Parliament. Supposing the shareholders willing and able to sell, it is very doubtful whether the Commissioners would consider themselves justified in buying Clifton College with the money of the Bristol endowed schools even if otherwise they would think it expedient to do so.

(2) The College might be made a 1st grade school in the system of the Commissioners, remaining as at present the property of the shareholders. The conditions of this arrangement on the part of the Commissioners would be: (a) a reduction of the fees so that the present average fee should become the general maximum; (b) the abolition of all social restrictions; (c) the conscience clause; (d) inspection; (e) an article securing the permanent maintenance of the College.

(3) The Commissioners are open to a proposition on the part of the shareholders retaining their present independence to receive at reduced fees boys of the class of those who now attend the Bristol Grammar School, so that the College might as far as the citizens of Bristol are concerned come in the place of the 1st grade school which is proposed to be established.

(5) [*sic*] Supposing the Commissioners' 1st grade school to be established, it will still be open to exhibitioners from (that or?) the 2nd grade schools in Bristol or elsewhere to select Clifton College as the school in which by the aid of their exhibitions they receive their higher instruction.

---

[136] Henry Hurry Goodeve, member of Council from 1868 until his death in 1884; having made his fortune in India he returned to Bristol, built a great house overlooking the Gorge, and assisted many local enterprises: M.J. Whitfield, *Dr Goodeve and Cook's Folly* (Avon History & Local Archaeology Books no. 4, 2010).

With regard to the 1st plan – of buying the College if the Commission should consider it just and expedient to buy it, it will remain for the shareholders to consider whether, taking into account the reasons for which they established the College and the principles on which they established it (which principles might not be adopted by the Commission) they would be justified in giving it up, or if justified, whether there is *any* reason or a sufficient one for so giving it up.

In regard to the 2nd expedient by which the whole commercial responsibility of the undertaking would remain with the shareholders while they sacrificed a large measure of their independence, consenting to a general reduction of their fees and the removal of a social restriction on which the class and character of the boys has been supposed to depend, and in both these alterations reducing the standard (socially) of their School, it would be for the shareholders to consider what advantages were offered to them by the Commissioners to counterbalance the commercial risk they would thus run, and as the equivalent of the sacrifice they would thus make of some of the objects of the School in the class of the persons who have hitherto supported it, and whether they would be justified in doing so without consulting what are probably the views and feelings of the people of Clifton, for whose advantage the School was established. It is uncertain in what estimation socially the 1st grade schools of the Endowed Schools Commissioners will be held by the public. It is probable, however, that they will be considered a sort of Citizen School, as the Commissioners would probably wish them to be looking at sources from which their funds are derived. But it was distinctly not as a Citizen School that Clifton College was established, but rather as a school of the class of Marlborough and Cheltenham or even of Rugby (if possible) or Harrow.[137] It is for the Council to consider whether a change like this will not seriously effect [*recte* affect] the pecuniary interests of the School, all the risk of which by the 2nd scheme remains with the shareholders. On the one side is the probable gain of a certain number of town boys and [the *deleted*] on the other the probable loss of a certain number of boys by what they may consider a lowering of the tone of the School by reason of an influx of town boys, plus the certain loss upon the fees of the present boys who remain.

The 3rd scheme is open to the same objection of the alteration of the character of the School and the probable loss of as many of the present boys for that reason as would be gained of new town boys, whilst these last would not pay the same fees as the other. This plan is however recommended by its leaving the fees of the present class of boys unchanged, and its not interfering otherwise with the independence of the College in its existing arrangements.

The 4th scheme may be passed over. It scarcely affects the interest of the College at all.

The Council would probably in the present successful state of the College be disposed to pass over all these schemes (except perhaps the 1st) without further consideration were it not that if one of the 3 first be not carried out the Commissioners will probably establish a first grade school at Clifton, which will work in competition with the College although the Commissioners may not mean it to do so, and which may injuriously affect its interests. The fears of this subject are, however, probably exaggerated. The College is a great institution established at a great cost, with all the appliances of a first rate public school; it is well established in public opinion and widely known. And particularly it is valued for the gentlemanly character of the boys

---

[137] Where Moseley sent his son.

and their good treatment and the tone of the School. With these advantages and the support of public opinion in Clifton, it need not fear the competition of any school the Commissioners will be likely to establish. Endowed as it will be, such a school must necessarily be a Citizen School. No other funds in Bristol are available (justly) for its endowment than those of the Bristol Grammar School. These amount to £1200 a year. But if the Grammar School is to be moved to Clifton and a site purchased and buildings erected like those of Clifton College, the whole of this income must be sunk in interest on the capital which will have to be borrowed. The Commissioners will then have to start a *self supporting* Citizen School with fees corresponding to the character and objects of the school, and they will have to maintain it in competition with Clifton College. The experience of all such schools is unfavourable to such an experiment. It will be impossible probably under these circumstances to make it a good school. The chances of success would be too small to induce any really good head master to undertake the teaching of it as a speculation, and the under masters cannot be sufficiently paid. It will be looked upon unfavourably by everyone as an oppressive and unjust attempt to damage an institution which the people at Clifton at great cost and risk and with much pains and trouble established for themselves at a time when the State took no interest in the education of the classes for whom the School was designed.

Some few of the present day scholars of the College would probably be tempted by the lower fee of the Grammar School to go to it. They will not, however, be among the boys it would be most desirable to keep, and as they would have to accept a lower class of associates and a lower standard of public opinion of the school and probably inferior teaching, no great migration is to be feared, whilst on the other hand some good is to be reckoned upon as likely to accrue to the College from the greater zeal with which its work will be done by reason of the competition and by the way in which the advantages of its position and structure will be brought out by the rivalry of the Grammar School. It is a mistake to think that the Commissioners will galvanize the Grammar School and make of it anything very different from what it is, and a much more formidable competitor to the College, by moving it up to Clifton. Two attempts of that kind have, I believe, already been made. The Bishop's College which still existed when I came to Clifton was one – the history of those schools is not in favour of the proposed experiment of the Commissioners with the Grammar School.[138]

The Head Master stated the reasons which induced him to consider that it would be exceedingly unadvisable to refuse to negotiate with the Commissioners, and after full discussion it was resolved: That the present Committee with the addition of Messrs Budd and Cox be requested to continue to watch the proceedings of the Educational Commission in Bristol.

☐ *Percival held back his ammunition until early in the following year.*

[31]   6 January 1871. Council meeting
[*CC Company Minute Book 2, pp. 432–5. MS*]

At an adjourned meeting of the Council held at Messrs. Stanley & Wasbrough's offices, Royal Insurance Buildings, Corn Street, Bristol, on 6th January 1871,

---

[138] Bristol College (1831–41) and Bishop's College (1840–61): see Introduction, above p. xlix.

specially called to consider the Endowed Schools scheme.

Present: the Revd. Jas. Heyworth; Mr Addison, Dr Black, Mr Budd, Major Bush, Mr Coles, Mr Cooke, Mr Cox, Dr Goodeve, Mr Saunders and Mr Wasbrough.

The Head Master attended.

The minutes of the adjourned special meeting of the 3rd were read and confirmed. Endowed Schools Commission. Mr Fitch's scheme and counter proposal.

Mr Percival read the following paper.

(1) Grammar School of 300 boys near Tyndall's Park, fees 10 to 15 guineas, 1st grade. [*Endowment*]   [£]2009

(2) City School, 200 day boys, fees 6 to 8 guineas; 200 boarders, 25 to 30 guineas; present position 2nd grade.

(3) Queen's School, 200 girls, fees 10 to 15 guineas, position somewhere above new institution. } [£]5660

Total endowment   £7669

'Mr Fitch's Scheme for 1st and 2nd grade education in Bristol.

Boy scholars of 1st grade i.e. who continue education to 18 or 19 – 300.

Do, 2nd grade who continue education to 16 or 17 – 200 day boys, 200 boarders.

Girls, 1st & 2nd grade but all paying high fees – 200.

[*Percival's observations on the above and his counter-proposal*]

(1) Note deficiency in 2nd grade education, which is what a commercial community specifically wants: only 200 day boys provided for out of all Bristol.

(2) Note also absence in scheme of any girls' school corresponding to City School for boys, i.e. with fees of 6 to 8 guineas.

(3) Note also that all these educational institutions are to be in Clifton or on the very edge of it.

It is proposed that some such alternative scheme as the following should be put before the Commissioners.

(1) Grammar School to be 2nd grade i.e. educating boys who are to leave school at 16 or 17, giving special attention to Latin, English, Modern Languages, Mathematics, elements of Science &c. but not to be prohibited from teaching Greek. In other words that it should remain substantially what it now is with same fees   [£]2000

(2) City School, also 2nd grade but more scientific and day element more developed   [£]2000

(3) Queen's School. (a) 2nd grade with fees as City School; (b) 1st grade, fees as indicated in Mr Fitch's scheme   [£]2169

This arrangement would make provision:

(1) For nearly thrice as many boys of 2nd grade at the lower fee which Bristol would require.

(2) It would provide a large 2nd grade girls' school at the same lower fees.

(3) Also a sufficient 1st grade girls' school.

Also it would leave £1000 a year for 1st grade boys' education.

For this the College should provide:

(1) By getting a constitution similar to Marlborough.[139]

(2) By admitting with free nomination at a fee of 12 to 15 guineas any boys of 14 or upwards from any Bristol endowed schools nominated by the Governors of

---

[139] Incorporated by letters patent of 21 August 1845: A.G. Bradley *et al.* rev. J.R. Taylor *et al.*, *A History of Marlborough College* (3rd edn, 1927), p. 111.

those schools, as also any exhibitioners from any such school anywhere. These to be counted as foundationers.

(3) The condition being either that the College should be endowed with £1500 a year or that for every boy so nominated a fee of 10 guineas should be paid from Bristol endowments up to the number of 150, any beyond that number so nominated to be admitted at the same terms without such additional payment.

Mr Percival read a paper written by Canon Moseley proposing a joint representation from the College and Bristol Trade School[140] objecting to the Commissioners' scheme, and recommending a counter proposal agreeing in the main with the counter proposal submitted by Mr Percival.

Mr Percival reported that he had had a conversation with Dr Symonds upon the subject, who expressed an opinion that the abolishing of social distinction among the boys might have a serious effect on the College, while he did not think that the College had much to fear from the establishment of a first grade school as proposed in the Commissioners' scheme.

The Secretary reported that in reply to his letter to the Commissioners asking for an early day for the Commissioners to receive a deputation from the Council, the Commissioners had named Thursday 12th instant at 2 o'clock.

It was resolved: That the Chairman, the Rev. Canon Moseley, the Rev. J. Percival, Mr Budd, Mr Cox and Mr Wasbrough, being the Sub Committee appointed to watch the proceedings of the Commission in Bristol, be a deputation to meet the Commissioners on the basis of Mr Percival's proposal.

[32]   6 February 1871. The Secretary of the Commission[141] to the Head Master
[*CC Company Minute Book 2, pp. 448–50. MS*]

Endowed Schools Commission,
2 Victoria Street S.W.
6th Febr. 1871.

Dear Percival,

We have been thinking over the Clifton College matter and I am instructed now to ask you to submit this letter to your Council in order to see whether there is sufficient agreement between them and the Commissioners on the financial part of the question to render it *possible* for the Commissioners to accede to the Council's proposal if other difficulties are got over.

If you will turn to the Appendix of the Schools Inquiry Report[142] p. 31 you will see that the actual cost of instruction at Cheltenham College is £18 and of building

---

[140] The Bristol Trade and Mining School, which in 1885 became the Merchant Venturers' School, on being taken over by the Society (and from 1894 was called the Merchant Venturers' Technical College); later absorbed into the Engineering Department of the University: McGrath, *Merch. Venturers*, pp. 375–85; Cottle and Sherborne, *University*, pp. 33–7.

[141] Henry John Roby (d. 1915), Secretary to the Commission 1869–72, Commissioner 1872–4; previously Secretary of the Schools Inquiry Commission (1864) and author of its Report, which prompted the 1869 Act.

[142] *Report of Her Majesty's Commissioners appointed to enquire into the Revenues and Management of certain Colleges and Schools, and the Studies pursued and Instruction given therein, with an Appendix and Evidence* (HMSO, 1864): the report of the Clarendon Commission, of which the Appendix forms vol. 2.

repairs &c. a little over £4 per boy per annum. That is to say a good first grade education can be given at a cost of about £22 per boy, buildings included.

Your fee in all is £30. It may very well be that the education given by Clifton College is superior to that given in 1867 at Cheltenham College in the proportion of £30 to £22. But it would be difficult for us to say that the Bristol people ought not to be satisfied with an education at the lower cost, or that it would be wise for us to charge either the endowments or the parents with any greater expense for this purpose.

Is then Clifton College prepared to make this reduction on the average? If we are to provide for first grade education for 150 to 200 boys in all, and Clifton will accept them at an average fee not exceeding £22 instead of £30, we can weigh the educational merits of the proposed plan against that of a separate school, without feeling the danger of being tripped up by the financial argument.

The Commissioners think £22 is the outside cost at which it would be safe to put the calculation. Of course a still further reduction would make the scheme more palatable to the Bristol people, many of whom would doubtless prefer a less costly first grade education and would not be deterred by arguments showing that the education would and must be lowered in quality.

You will know best whether it is worth your while financially to receive a large number of additional boys at £8 less than your usual fee. The selection of such boys, or at least of a large portion of them, by competitive examinations would supply in some degree a noticeable compensation.

I enclose herewith a table shewing a possible scale of charges for 180 boys, based on the hypothesis of 80 being selected by competitive examination, and 40 more at a cost to their parents of not more than the maximum fee in Fitch's schedule. The remaining 60 would have to pay a fee of £25 if the endowment were not to be burdened to a greater amount than £1200 a year. Clifton would on this calculation lose £1500, which is a trifle over £8 per boy.

Of course this is only one of many possible scales of cost and help. It is framed with the notion that probably 120 boys would be as many as would be found really desirous of such an education and not able to pay a high fee. If the boys came to Clifton at between 14 and 15 years of age, 120 boys would give about 30 a year.

I shall of course be glad to give any further explanation you may require to enable you to put the matter properly before your Council and get us an answer, on receiving which the Commissioners will at once make up their minds.

Yours truly,

H.J. Roby.

Cost of educating 180 boys at Clifton College on the hypothesis that the College make a large reduction in favour of 80 boys selected by a competitive examination, and admit 100 more boys on the terms of subscribers' nominees.

The subject was discussed and adjourned to next meeting for further consideration.

Number of Boys		Cost per boy to				Aggregate cost to			
		Parent	Endow-ment	Clifton College	Total	Parent	Endow-ment	Clifton College	Total
		£	£	£	£	£	£	£	£
By Competitive Examination	{ 20	0	10	20	30	0	200	400	600
	60	10	10	10	30	600	600	600	1800
	40	15	10	5	30	600	400	200	1200
	60	25	0	5	30	1500	0	300	1800
Total 180						2700	1200	1500	5400

[33]   14 February 1871. Acceptance of an adjusted form of the Commissioners' scheme
[*CC Company Minute Book 2, pp. 451–2. MS*]

[*Attendance as for* **31**]
The minutes of meetings on 14th January and 10th February were read and confirmed. Endowed Schools Commission scheme: alternative proposal.

The consideration of the communication from the Endowed Schools Commission adjourned from last meeting was resumed and it was resolved:

That in place of the proposal made by the Commissioners in their letter of February 6th to Mr Percival as to the basis of a financial arrangement the Council agree to admit 120 boys on the clear understanding that they be selected from the bona fide pupils of some Bristol endowed school or schools, provided that the College shall receive from endowment or fees or both combined a sum of £22 on account of every boy so selected; and:

To suggest for the Commissioners' consideration some such scheme as the following:

	Boys	Endowment	Parents	Cost to Endowment	Cost to Parents	Payment to College
		£	£	£	£	£
By Competition {	5	30	0	150	0	50
	5	15		75		75
	10	10	5	100	50	150
	20	10	10	200	200	400*
	60	19	15	600	900	1500
	20	5	20	100	400	500
	120			1225		2675

(left margin: This table to be corrected)

* Corrected from 1400.

It was resolved that Mr Saunders be added to the Endowed Schools Commission Sub Committee.

[34]   7 March 1871. The Commissioners' revised proposals
[*CC Company Minute Book 3, pp. 1–9. MS*]

At a special meeting of the Council held at Messrs Stanley & Wasbrough's offices, Royal Insurance Buildings, Corn Street, Bristol, on Tuesday 7th March 1871.
   Present: the Rev. James Heyworth (chair); Mr Addison, Mr Budd, Major Bush, Mr, Coles, Mr Cox, Dr Goodeve, Mr Saunders and Mr Wasbrough.
   The Head Master attended.
   [*After reading of minutes and routine business*]
Endowed Schools Commission Scheme.
   The following letter from the Endowed Schools Commissioners was read:

Endowed Schools Commission
2 Victoria Street S.W.
1st March 1871

The Revd James Heyworth
Chairman of Council
Clifton College, nr. Bristol

Revd Sir,
   1. I have been instructed by the Endowed Schools Commissioners to acquaint you with their conclusions with reference to the proposals made to them by the Sub Committee appointed by the Council of this College. For this purpose I will first endeavour to state what the Commissioners conceive to be the present position of affairs and the proposals and wishes of the Council.
   2. The Commissioners have cast upon them the duty of so arranging the endowments of Bristol as to make them most conducive to the advancement of education. For this purpose they have to consider the present working and objects of those endowments and the demands of the locality. What they find is a Grammar School intended to give an education which may be called first grade, a somewhat loose term, but one which is sufficiently accurate in communicating for the present purpose with such a body as your Council. This School is handsomely endowed, but is unable to do more than a moderate amount of work in its proper line. They found also some richly endowed hospital schools designed for lower grades of education, the resources of which are not well husbanded. There appears to be a great lack of education for the whole middle class, and a considerable number of wealthier persons in trade who would desire a first grade school for their children. The only unendowed school of a public character supplying thoroughly good first grade education is Clifton College, and this does not supply it to the class of persons in question.
   3. Under these circumstances the Commissioners have propounded a plan of [the *deleted*] which the general features are as follows. The large revenues of the hospital schools are to be used in providing education of the lower grades, but something more than elementary, for the bulk of the poorer children who require such education, and for a substantial number of those who may find themselves able to continue their general education up to the age of 17. The Grammar School with its funds augmented

from another source [*is*] to answer the demands of the wealthier residents for a first grade school.[143]

4. Clifton College is like this Commission a body formed for the promotion of education, for although commercial in form, it never appears to have treated the institution as a means of coining money. Certainly, as far as the Commissioners can see, your Council are now addressing themselves to the problem of public education in Bristol in a very generous spirit, and with an eye to the interest of the whole community. They apprehend that if the Grammar School is constituted according to the foregoing plan it will come into direct rivalry with Clifton College, that the two institutions will not both find sufficient aliment,[144] that one will injure the other, and that there will be so much waste of power and a dead loss to the cause of education.[145]

5. The Commissioners are sensible that these objections, if well founded in fact, are substantial in their bearing, and considering from what well informed persons they proceed, the soundness of their foundation must be taken to be at least probable. Still, if the constitution of Clifton College were to remain unaltered, the Commissioners would think that to persist in the present plans was a lesser danger than to leave Bristol entirely without a school such as the more opulent residents require. The Council clearly feel on their side that Clifton College does not provide for Bristol what it may fairly ask, and they therefore propose to alter their constitution in such a way as may meet the wants of the residents.

6. The alterations proposed are to the following effect.

(a) That the qualifications of pupils shall have reference solely to their intellectual and moral and not to their social standing.

(b) That for day scholars the principle of section 15 of the Endowed Schools Act 1869 shall be accepted.[146]

(c) That the governing body established by [*the*] scheme for the principal group of the Bristol endowed schools shall have the right to nominate [say *deleted*] a certain number (say four or five members) of the Council of Clifton College.

(d) That the principle of sections 17 & 18 of the Endowed Schools Act 1869 shall be accepted, at least so far as the nominees of the Bristol governors are concerned.[147]

(e) That the College will receive at reduced cost on the nomination of the governing body of the principal group of the Bristol endowed schools, a number of boys connected with Bristol and Clifton, i.e. those who are bonâ fide residents there or who have been educated at some of the endowed schools there. On the details of this part of the proposal I will presently remark more particularly.

7. To make the arrangements of the endowed schools fit in with this altered system, the Council require:

(a) That the schemes shall not establish any school for the education of boys beyond the age of 17 or thereabouts.

---

[143] The Peloquin Gifts, founded in 1768 by Mary Ann Peloquin to assist poor householders, which had become an idle charity: Hill, *History of BGS*, p. 100

[144] Meaning sustenance; oddly prescient (*Spiritus intus alit* was not yet Clifton's motto).

[145] The Commissioners therefore recommended that the Grammar School should find a new site, which 'should not be too near Clifton College', from which it was 'essentially different'. The move to Tyndalls Park was completed in 1879: Hill, *History of BGS*, pp. 100, 103–6.

[146] This allowed parents or guardians of day pupils to withdraw their children from religious services and instruction.

[147] Providing that governors were not to be disbarred for their religious opinions or for non-attendance at services, and that masters were not required to be in or intending to take Anglican orders.

(b) That the fees to be charged at the endowed schools shall not much exceed those now charged at the Grammar School.

(c) That the schemes shall provide a competent sum (say £1400 or £1500 per annum) to be applied in promoting first grade education for Bristol and Clifton, much of will presumably, though perhaps not necessarily, be spent in defraying the tuition fees of those nominees of the governing body who would represent the class that would use the now proposed first grade school.

(d) That whatever university exhibitions are provided for the endowed schools of Bristol, shall be as open to those who have passed on to Clifton College as to those who remain at a Bristol endowed school.

8. On the best consideration they can give to the proposals, the Commissioners believe that, if made sufficiently favourable in point of finance, they offer on other grounds a fairer future to education in Bristol than the plan proposed by themselves, and they will be willing to mould the scheme already outlined by them in conformity with the new suggestions. It is however not to be disguised that the practical difficulties are somewhat formidable; owing to the circumstance that neither the Commissioners nor the Council are free contracting parties dealing with their own property, but that each body is bound by its own line of duty and subject to its own legal limitations.

9. All that is proposed for the Commissioners to do it is competent to them to embody in a scheme. But every scheme is a cumbrous and uncertain process, of which the beginning is under the control of the Commissioners but the end is not. If you will peruse the paper herewith enclosed and marked H, you will see how many tests a scheme has to pass before it is perfected. All therefore that the Commissioners can say is, that on being satisfied as to the pecuniary terms, they will promulgate a draft or provisional scheme, to the effect indicated in paragraph 7 of this letter, and will submit them to the Privy Council under two conditions. First, that they are not convinced by opposing arguments that the line taken by them is wrong; secondly, that Clifton College finds itself able to perform the intentions now entertained by the Council and indicated in paragraph 6 of this letter.

10. I turn now to the pecuniary question. It must be remembered that the thing wanted is to provide a sufficient amount of first grade education which exists in Bristol and is not met by Clifton College. And what the Commissioners aim at is to provide this advantage out of the Bristol endowments in [the most econ(*omic*) *deleted*] full measure on the most economical terms. On the best calculation they can make, they estimate that the College should be prepared to receive not less than 180 boys on the nomination of the Bristol governors,[148] that to the whole of them the nomination charge of £5 per annum should be remitted; that to a number of them other allowances should be made, according to the degree of their merit, and that in this way the College should undertake to charge itself with providing education for Bristol boys equal in value to £1200 per annum. I send you a separate paper containing a sketch of the way in which the benefits of admission to the College might be arranged. You will see that it is there contemplated that 40 boys shall be admitted by competition, receiving different degrees of emolument according to their deserts; and that the endowment should bear a charge equal to that imposed on the College. These are details which may be re-adjusted. But the totals here given must not, as the Commissioners think, be diminished if the arrangement is to stand on a sound footing.

---

[148] The existing roll (1871) including the Junior School was 422: *Register* (1925), p. cxxix.

11. How the constitution of the College shall be altered must be for the legal advisers of the Council to consider. Seeing that the object is to work in harmony with the endowed schools, the neatest plan would be to bring the institution under the operation of a scheme. The Commissioners do not know enough of the constitution and position of the College to know whether that can legally be done, but they fear it cannot. Failing this, the College must have recourse to an Act of Parliament or to the provisions of the Joint Stock Acts.[149] Either course must be subject to some uncertainty and considerable delay, and as either course would be totally independent of the fortune of the scheme, it would be necessary to provide for the revision of the constitution by the proprietary, in case the scheme failed in any of the essential points indicated in paragraph 7 of this letter.

12. The Commissioners feel very acutely the risk which they run of sacrificing the time and labour which belong to the public by making their published schemes dependent on the arrangements of a wholly independent body. But they are so impressed with the importance of the case that they are willing to run the risk in order to secure what seems to them an advantage to all parties concerned. The Council [have *deleted*] doubtless have precisely the same feeling with respect to their proprietary. All the Commissioners can ask is that the question shall be brought before the general meeting, and so far as they have power, be decided as quickly as possible.

13. The Commissioners are now anxious to publish their draft or provisional schemes as quickly as they can. If you inform me that the arrangements expressed in this letter meets [*sic*] with the sanction of the proprietary, I will forward you the first drafts as quickly as they can be got ready, for the wording will require some consideration on your part as well as in this office. On the other hand it will be desirable that you should reduce to writing the proposed alterations of the constitution of the College, whether they are to be in the shape of clauses in a scheme, or sections in an Act of Parliament, or Articles of Association; and that you should send them here for examination. But the first step is that the Commissioners should know whether the proposals are such as the proprietary will accept.

I am, Revd Sir, your obedient servant,
(signed) H.J. Roby.

It was resolved:
That the boys to be admitted in the arrangement with the Commissioners be admitted without social distinction.

It was resolved to adjourn the matter for further consideration to Tuesday 9th [*recte* 7th] March 1871.

In the meantime, the Secretary was instructed to ascertain whether the Commissioners' sub section (a) of clause 6 of this letter to apply (1) to the general public, or (2) to the Bristol public, or (3) simply to the nominees under the Commissioners' proposal.

[35]   9 March 1871. Further discussion of the Commissioners' scheme
[*CC Company Minute Book 3, pp. 10–11. MS*]

---

[149] See above [7], sect. 34.

At a meeting of the Council (adjourned from Tuesday 7th March) held at Messrs Stanley & Wasbrough's offices, Royal Insurance Buildings, Corn Street, Bristol, on Thursday 9th March 1871. Present:

The Rev. Jas. Heyworth (chair); Mr Addison, Mr Budd, Major Bush, Mr Coles, Mr Cooke, Mr Cox, Dr Goodeve, Mr Saunders and Mr Wasbrough.

The Head Master attended.

The minutes of the last meeting were read and confirmed.

Endowed Schools Commissioners' Scheme.

In reply to the inquiry ordered to be made at last meeting as to the meaning of sub section (a) of clause 6 of the Commissioners' letter, the following letter was read:

> Endowed Schools Commission
> 2 Victoria Street S.W.
> 8th March 1871

Dear Percival,

The Commissioners understood the proposal of the Council to be to alter the Articles of Association so as entirely to remove the social disqualifications.[150] This seems to them clearly the best. But they do not think it necessary that this should be done;[151] but it is quite necessary that no disqualification of this nature should exist as regards any Bristol boys – *Bristol* being liberally interpreted so as to include all the neighbourhood likely to use the School.

> Yours very truly,
> (signed) H.J. Roby.

It was resolved that the following communication be made to the Commissioners:

The Council are unanimously agreed to admit without regard to their social position such a number of boys nominated by the Endowment Trustees as may be fixed by negotiation; but a minority are opposed to removing the social restrictions to any greater extent.

The Royal Charter

☐ *Clifton soon acquired a high reputation, and established its place among the country's leading schools. This led to a feeling that it should shake off its commercial origins, a concern heightened by the controversy over the Endowed Schools Act. It was therefore decided to petition the Crown for incorporation. The Company having been wound up* **[27]**, *the Queen formally founded the College anew by the issue of letters patent.*

[36]   16 March 1877. Letters patent of foundation[152]
[Eight vellum membranes stitched at the foot, the Great Seal depending]

---

[150] Strictly the preceding Memorandum **[6]**, which refers to 'sons of gentlemen', rather than the Articles themselves **[7]**, which do not.

[151] Something (perhaps 'generally') was missed here when the letter was copied into the Minute Book.

[152] Text repeated from the Company's Articles of Association **[7]** is here abbreviated. The text of the Charter was issued as a booklet, reprinted in 1939 with a few updates inset (here given as footnotes). A few insignificant errors in the printed text are also noted below.

[*m. 1*]   VICTORIA, by the Grace of God, of the United Kingdom of Great Britain and Ireland, Queen, Defender of the Faith; to all to whom these presents shall come, greeting:

Whereas, our right trusty and right well beloved cousin Henry John, Earl of Ducie,[153] and our trusty and well beloved James Heyworth, William Henry Harford the younger, William Gale Coles, William Brook Addison, Francis Black, Francis Nonus Budd, Robert Bush, George Cooke, Alfred Cox, Henry Hurry Goodeve, Joshua Saunders, Henry Bouchier Osborne Savile, John Addington Symonds, Henry Sidney Wasbrough, presented their petition to us, setting forth that, some time since, they with divers others of our loving subjects had joined together for the purpose of establishing and founding a College for the education of the sons of gentlemen, to be situate at Clifton, in the City of Bristol, and providing on moderate terms a classical, mathematical, and general education of the highest class; the religious teaching of the College being in accordance with that of the Church of England; and had incorporated themselves under the provisions of the Joint Stock Companies Act 1856 by the name of the Clifton College Company Limited, with a nominal capital of ten thousand pounds divided into shares of twenty five pounds each; that the whole of the said shares <had been issued> and the full amount thereof paid up; and that by the capital so raised, and by money borrowed by the said Company, and by means of voluntary gifts and donations to the said Company, land had been acquired and buildings erected, comprising hall, schoolroom, chapel, dwelling houses, gymnasia, and other conveniences, and a flourishing School had been established and carried on with much success;

That the said School has been and was being carried on under the management and direction of a Council appointed according to the provisions of the Articles of Association of the said Company; and that our petitioners who comprised the said Council, and the other promoters and supporters of the School were advised and believed that the same would be more effectively carried on and prosecuted and would be permanently established if they were protected by our royal sanction by means of a Royal Charter of incorporation; that with the view of obtaining such Charter, the Company intended to pass a special resolution to wind up voluntarily and also a special resolution authorizing the liquidator of the Company to transfer its business and property to a chartered company upon such terms as in our Charter should be provided. And the said petitioners most humbly supplicated us to grant to them and the other promoters and supporters of the said School and their successors a Charter of incorporation for the purpose of constituting them a corporation for more effectually carrying on and conducting the said School, under such regulations and restrictions as to us might seem right and expedient. And whereas, since the presentation of the said petition, such special resolutions as aforesaid have been duly passed.

Now know ye, that we taking the premises into our royal consideration, of [*our*] especial grace, certain knowledge, and mere motion, have granted, constituted, and appointed, and by these our presents, for us, our heirs and successors, do grant, constitute, and appoint as follows; that is to say:

1. The persons hereinafter described shall be and they are hereby constituted a body politic and corporate by the name of The Clifton College, and by the aforesaid

---

[153]   Ducie was not actually related to the Queen. In formal letters of this kind all peers are styled 'cousin', and for each grade in the peerage there is a particular qualification of 'trusty' and 'beloved'.

name shall have a perpetual succession and have a common seal, and shall by the same name sue and be sued in any court or place of judicature within the dominions of us, our heirs, and successors.

2. And we do hereby will and ordain that by the same name they and their successors shall be able and capable in law to take, purchase, and hold to them and their successors any goods, chattels, or personal property whatsoever, and shall also be able and capable in law, notwithstanding the Statutes of Mortmain,[154] to take, purchase, and hold to them and their successors not only all such lands, buildings, hereditaments, and possessions as may be from time to time exclusively used and occupied for the immediate purposes of the corporation, but also any other lands, buildings, hereditaments, and possessions whatsoever situate within the United Kingdom of Great Britain and Ireland, not exceeding the annual value of ten thousand pounds, such annual value to be calculated and ascertained at the period of taking, purchasing, or acquiring the same.

3. The body corporate hereby constituted is hereinafter referred to as 'The College'.

4. And we hereby will and ordain that the objects for which the College is hereby constituted are to establish and conduct a College for the education of boys and young men, to be situate at Clifton, in the City of Bristol, and to provide on moderate terms a classical, mathematical, and general education of the highest class, and to do all things incidental or conducive to the attainment of the above objects.

5. It is a fundamental condition of the constitution of the College that the religious teaching of the College shall be in accordance with that of the Church of England, but so that any pupil thereat shall, at the desire of his parent or guardian expressed in such written notice as the Council of the College hereinafter referred to may prescribe, be exempted from attending any religious service or any lesson or series of lessons on any religious subject, and such pupil shall not by reason of such exemption be deprived of any advantage or enrolment to which he would be otherwise entitled.

Constitution of the College.

6. The following persons under the name of Governors shall be members of the College (the words hereinafter used in relation to them importing the masculine gender being taken to include the feminine) that is to say:

(1) Every person shall be a Governor of the College who, on the day before the date of this Charter, was registered as holder, or was entitled to be registered as holder [*m. 2*] of a share or shares in the Clifton College Company, Limited, and who did not within the provisions of section 161 of the Companies Act 1862, express his dissent from the special resolution for the transfer of the business and property of the said Company to the College.[155] Such persons who are hereinafter, for the convenience of distinction, referred to as Original Governors shall be Governors during their respective lives and shall also have the following privileges, that is to say: it shall be lawful for every Original Governor to nominate by writing under his hand some other person, subject to the approval of the Council, to replace him in his

---

[154] Enactments by Edward I in 1279 and 1290 which prohibited the alienation of real property to religious bodies. The Crown was concerned to protect feudal revenue from inheritance &c., which was lost on land transferred to the 'dead hand' of perpetual corporations. For the effect on collegiate foundations see S. Raban, *Mortmain Legislation in the English Church, 1279–1500* (Cambridge, 1982), pp. 47–8.

[155] 25 & 26 Vict. *c.* 89. Section 161, dealing with the transfer of interests from one company to another by voluntary liquidation, allowed that any member of the first company dissenting from its special resolution for the purpose might require the liquidators to purchase his interest.

lifetime or to succeed him after his death as Governor. And the person so nominated, if he claims the benefit of such nomination within twelve months after the time at which it purports to take effect, shall, unless disapproved of by the Council (such disapproval to be signified in writing within six weeks after the claim is made), become a Governor and enjoy during his life in the place, and to the exclusion of the Original Governor nominating him, all the rights, powers, and privileges of such Original Governor, but without any such power of transmitting the same as is mentioned in this clause. And in case of the death or disapproval by the Council of the person so nominated during the life of the Original Governor, such Original Governor may again exercise the aforesaid power of nomination in like manner, and so on from time to time during his life.

(2) Every person shall be a Governor of the College who shall hereafter contribute fifty pounds or upwards in one sum for the purposes of the College, and whose donation shall be accepted by the Council hereinafter mentioned. Such persons shall be Governors during their respective lives, and are hereinafter for convenience of distinction referred to as Life Governors.

7. In the event of two or more persons being or being entitled to be jointly registered as the holders of any share or shares in the Clifton College Company Limited, the person whose name stands first in the Register of Shareholders as one of the holders of such share or shares, or whose name would in the opinion of the Council of the College have stood first if the share or shares had been properly registered, shall be considered to be the holder for the purposes of the provisions herein contained.

8. All the business and property, real and personal, of the Clifton College Company Limited at the date of this Charter, shall be transferred to and vested in the College, and shall be held by the College for the general purposes of the College, subject to all charges and incumbrances thereon. And the College shall also take upon itself and pay and discharge all such debts and liabilities of the Clifton College Company Limited as at the date of this Charter shall remain due and outstanding. To the intent that, so far as we can by this Charter ordain and appoint the College may become and be the successor and representative of the Clifton College Company Limited.

9. The several persons who at the date of the resolution for winding up the Clifton College Company <Limited> held positions as Head Master, Under Master, Teacher, Solicitor, Secretary, and the officers or servants of the Clifton College Company Limited, shall have and hold positions in relation to the College on like terms and conditions as such positions were held by them respectively in relation to the Clifton College Company Limited.

Privileges of Governors and Donors.

10. Subject to such bye-laws as may from time to time be made by the College and the payment of the fees thereby fixed, every Governor shall be entitled to have always in the College one pupil nominated by him for or in respect of every qualification as Governor he may have. For the purposes of this clause every share in the Clifton College Company Limited, shall be considered as giving one qualification, and every sum of fifty pounds contributed by any Governor shall be considered as giving one qualification.

11. Subject to such bye-laws and payment of fees as aforesaid, a donation to the College of twenty pounds, paid in one sum shall entitle the giver thereof, whether a corporation, institution, society, or individual (hereinafter referred to as a Donor), to nominate one pupil to the College in respect of every such sum of twenty pounds so

given.[156] Provided always that, notwithstanding anything hereinbefore contained, the College shall have power from time to time, with the assent of the general meeting of the College (but without prejudice to rights already acquired), to alter and vary, increase or diminish the sum required by way of contribution, to entitle persons to become Life Governors of the College, or to entitle Donors to nominate pupils.[157]

12. The Council shall have power from time to time, with a special view of keeping up the number of pupils, to nominate any pupil or pupils to the College, subject to the usual tuition fees and to such extra charges, if any, as the Council shall think fit, but not so as to prejudice or delay the admission into the College of any pupil previously nominated by a Governor or Donor.

13. Neither the Original Governors nor any other Governors or members of the College shall be entitled to any share or share in the possessions, property, capital, or income of the College, or any right to participation in the receipts or profits thereof, or any proprietary or individual or transmissible estate, right, or interest whatsoever (whether actual, contingent, or otherwise) in or to such possessions, property, or capital, income, receipts, or profits, or any part thereof, but the said possessions, property, and capital income, receipts and profits shall (subject as to endowments or other property impressed with any trusts or special purposes to the due performance and observance thereof) belong wholly to the College in its corporate character, and shall be wholly appropriated to and available for the promotion of the objects for which the College is hereby incorporated.

[*m. 3*] 14. Any person claiming to be or to exercise the rights of a Governor shall from time to time give such evidence in support of his claims as the Council or the chairman of any meeting of the College may reasonably require.

General meetings.

15. The first general meeting of the College shall be held at such time as the Council may determine. Subsequent general meetings shall be held once a year, at such times as may be determined by the Council. The above-mentioned general meetings of the College shall be called ordinary general meetings; all other meetings of the College shall be called extraordinary general meetings, but at any ordinary general meeting any special business may be transacted beyond the business thereby required to be transacted thereat by due notice being given of such special business.

16. The general meetings of the College shall be held at such place as the Council shall from time to time determine on.

17. The Council may whenever they shall think fit, and they shall upon a requisition made in writing by twenty or more Governors, convene an extraordinary general meeting.

18. At an extraordinary general meeting, whether convened on a requisition or not, no business shall be transacted except that of which notice shall be given as hereinafter provided for.

19. Every requisition so made by the Governors shall express the object of the meeting proposed to be called, and shall be left, addressed to the Council, at the office of the College.

20. Upon receipt of such requisition the Council shall forthwith proceed to convene an extraordinary general meeting of the College. If they do not proceed to convene the same within twenty one days of the date of the delivery of the requisition, the

---

[156] Raised to £25 by authority of the general meeting of 27 March 1936.

[157] The AGM of March 1921 resolved that the sum required to become a Life Governor should be £5 instead of £25, and the meeting of March 1936 reduced it to a nominal £1.

requisitionists or any other equal number of Governors may themselves convene a meeting.

21. Ten days' notice at least specifying the place, the day and hour of meeting,[158] and the purpose for which any general meeting or other meeting is to be held, shall be given to the Governors by advertisement, or in such other manner (if any) as may be prescribed by the Council.

22. Any Governor may, on giving not less than seven days' previous notice, submit any resolution to any ordinary general meeting. Such notice shall be given by leaving or sending through the post in a prepaid letter a copy of the resolution, addressed to the Secretary, at the office of the College.

23. No business shall be transacted at any meetings unless a quorum of Governors are present at the commencement of such business, and such quorum shall consist of ten Governors.

24. If within thirty minutes from the time appointed for the meeting the required number of Governors are not present the meeting if convened upon the requisition of Governors shall be dissolved; in any other case it shall stand adjourned until the following working day, at the same time and place, and if at such adjourned meeting the required number of Governors is not present, those Governors who are present shall proceed to the business for which the meeting was called.

25. The President of the College shall be entitled to preside as chairman at every meeting of the College, and subject thereto the Chairman (if any) of the Council, shall preside as chairman.

26. If there shall[159] be no such President or Chairman present at any meeting at the time for holding the same, the Governors present shall choose some one of their number to be chairman of such meeting.

27. In case of an equality of votes upon any question, the chairman of the meeting shall have a casting vote, in addition to the vote he may be entitled to as a Governor.

28. The chairman of any meeting may, with the consent of the meeting, adjourn such meeting from time to time, and from place to place, but no business shall be transacted at any adjourned meeting other than the business left not commenced or unfinished at the meeting for which the adjournment took place, and the adjourned meetings shall for all intents and purposes be considered as a continuation of the original meeting.

29. At every general meeting every question shall be determined by the Governors present by a show of hands, or such other convenient way as the chairman shall think fit.

30. At any general meeting a declaration by the chairman that a resolution has been carried, and an entry signed by the chairman to that effect in the book or minutes of proceedings of the College, or of such meeting, shall be sufficient evidence of the fact without proof of the number or proportion of the votes recorded in favor [*sic*] of or against such resolution.

Votes of Governors.

31. Every Governor shall be entitled to one vote only, notwithstanding he may be a Governor under more than one qualification, and all votes must be given personally. No proxy shall be allowed.

---

[158] Misprinted 'the place, the time, the hour of meeting'.
[159] Misprinted 'should'.

Officers of the College.

32. The officers of the College shall consist of a President, a Council constituted as hereinafter mentioned, a Head Master, and such other masters as the Council shall think proper, a Treasurer, a Secretary, Solicitors, two Auditors, and such other officers as the Council shall from time to time think necessary.

33. The first President shall be the Right Honourable the Earl of Ducie, and the first Treasurer William Gale Coles, Esquire. All future vacancies in the offices of President or Treasurer shall be filled up at a general meeting; only Governors of the College shall be eligible for election.

[*m. 4*]   *The Council.*

34. The Council of the College shall consist of the President and Treasurer for the time being who shall be ex officio members thereof and thirteen ordinary members.[160] The following persons shall be the first ordinary members of the Council: the Reverend James Heyworth, Chairman, William Brook Addison, Esquire, Francis Black, Doctor of Medicine, Francis Nonus Budd, Esquire, Robert Bush, a Major in the Army, George Cooke, Esquire, Alfred Cox, Esquire, Henry Hurry Goodeve, Doctor of Medicine, William Henry Harford, Esquire, the younger, Joshua Saunders, Esquire, Henry Bouchier Osborne Savile, Esquire, John Addington Symonds, Esquire.

Rotation of the Council.

35. At the second ordinary general meeting after the date of the Charter, and thenceforth at each ordinary general meeting, the Treasurer and four ordinary members of the Council shall retire from office, and the College shall elect the like number of persons to fill the vacated offices; only Governors of the College shall be eligible for election.

36. Every retiring Treasurer and member of Council shall be eligible for reelection, and if reelected shall for the purpose of subsequent retirement be considered as if he had then for the first time come into office.

37. If at any meeting at which an election of Treasurer or ordinary members of Council ought to take place such election is not made, the meeting shall stand adjourned till the next working day at the same time and place; and if at such an adjourned meeting the election does not take place, the former Treasurer or ordinary members of Council, as the case may be, whose place shall not have been supplied, shall be considered as continuing in office until a new Treasurer or new members of Council are appointed at the next ordinary general meeting.

38. The four ordinary members of Council who shall retire shall be those who have been longest in office, and where members are on an equal footing in this respect the matter shall, unless they all agree among themselves, be determined by ballot.

39. The College may from time to time in general meeting increase or reduce the number of the members of Council, and determine in what rotation and manner such increased or reduced number is to go out of office. The College in general meeting may also, by resolution of an extraordinary meeting specially called for the purpose, remove the Treasurer or any ordinary member of the Council before the expiration of his period of office, and appoint another qualified person in the stead of the person so removed; but the person so appointed shall hold office during such time only as the person in whose place he is appointed would have held the same if he had not been removed.

---

[160] Increased to 14 at the general meeting of March 1907, to 18 in October 1930, and to 20 in 1935.

40. Any casual vacancy occurring in the office of Treasurer, or ordinary member of the Council, may be filled up by the existing members of the Council for the time being, but any person so chosen shall retain his office so long only as the vacating Treasurer or member of the Council would have retained the same if no vacancy had occurred.

41. The Treasurer or any member of the Council may retire from office by giving notice in writing to the Council of his intention so to do.

Powers of the Council.

42. The Council may exercise on behalf of the College the several powers hereinafter expressly mentioned and all other powers of the College which are not expressly declared to be exercisable by the College in general meeting, subject nevertheless to such regulations as may be from time to time prescribed by the College in general meeting; but no regulations made by the College in general meeting shall invalidate any prior act of the Council which would have been made valid if such regulation had not been made.

43. The Council shall have full power from time to time to make and also to alter or vary any bye-laws and regulations touching the government of the College, the appointment and removal, number and rank, powers and duties, stipends and emoluments of the several persons employed therein, the terms and conditions upon which pupils (whether nominated by Governors or Donors as hereinbefore provided, or not so nominated) shall be admitted, the number of such pupils, the mode and time of convening the meetings of the Governors and of the Council respectively, the mode of conducting the business to be transacted at such meetings respectively, the qualifications as regards age and other circumstances, for the nomination and admission of pupils, and all other matters relating to such nomination or admission, and in general touching all other matters whatsoever relating to the said College, so as such bye-laws and regulations be not repugnant to the laws of our realm, or to the general design and spirit of this our Charter, or to the express provision herein contained. And all such bye-laws and regulations, when reduced into writing and after the common seal of the College shall have been affixed thereto, shall be binding upon all persons properly affected thereby.

44. The appointment from time to time of the Head Master, Solicitors, and Secretary, and all other officers and servants of the College, the appointment of whom is not hereby otherwise expressly provided for, shall be vested solely in the Council.

45. The under masters shall be from time to time appointed by the Head Master, subject to a veto by the Council, and the Head Master shall have power, subject to the like veto, to appoint all subordinate teachers, officers and servants required for the educational work or for the discipline of the College.

[*m.* 5] 46. The Council shall have power to fix the amount of the respective salaries and remunerations of the Head Master, under masters, Solicitors, Secretary, and all other officers and servants of the College, and the conditions and terms of their respective tenures of office and service, and also, except where it is hereby otherwise provided, to prescribe and regulate their respective duties, and the Council shall likewise have power from time to time to remove any of such officers and servants. The Council shall have power to maintain, alter, enlarge, or improve any buildings or property for the time being belonging to the College, and to erect and provide such further buildings, appliances and conveniences for the purposes of the College, or of the students, officers, and servants thereof, as from time to time may be considered necessary or proper, and also for the purposes aforesaid or any of them to purchase or acquire any additional sites, buildings or premises. Provided always that no expenditure or liability shall be incurred in any one year by the Council under the powers of this clause beyond the capital amount of one thousand five hundred pounds or the annual liability of five hundred pounds without the ratification of a general meeting.

47. The Council may from time to time accept donations, subscriptions, and endowments in money or other form, and may apply the same, and the interest, income, and accumulations thereof for or towards the general benefit of the College, or for or towards any exhibition, scholarship, or professorship, or other special object connected with the College, according to the judgment of the Council, and the directions of the respective donors, subscribers, or founders, if any, and such donations may be accepted upon any conditions which the Council may approve of, and they shall apply the money received from the fees and payments of students in such manner for the benefit of the College as they think fit.

48. The Council may apply any part of the capital or income of the College for the purposes of the College, and in particular for the founding of exhibitions, scholarships, or other prize appointments or premiums in connection with the College for such other purposes connected with the College as may be considered advisable by the Council.

49. The Council may grant, or concur in granting, leases (with or without previous agreements) of all or any parts of the lands for the time being vested in the College, with their respective appurtenances (except the site of the principal buildings of the College and their appurtenances), for such terms, on such conditions, and at such rents, with or without fine, as the Council may think fit.

50. It shall be lawful for the Council, from time to time, to sell or exchange any part of the real, leasehold, or other personal property of the College, and to give or receive any money for equality of exchange, and to apply any monies produced by any such sale or exchange as part of the capital funds of the College. And any such sale or exchange as aforesaid may be made subject to such stipulations in such manner and for such considerations whether of a pecuniary or other nature as the Council may consider proper. Provided always that no part of the real or leasehold property of the College shall be sold or exchanged without the consent of a general meeting.

51. It shall be lawful for the Council from time to time, for the purposes of the College, to borrow any sums of money on the general credit of the College, and also with the authority of a general meeting to borrow any sums of money on mortgage of all or any parts of the then acquired or the after acquired property of the College, or on the debentures of the College. And mortgages or debentures in pursuance of this power may be made with or without the benefit of all such trusts or powers of sale and other trusts or powers for securing the principal money and interest as the Council may think fit, but for the purposes of raising money to discharge any debts, charges, incumbrances, or liabilities existing at the day of this Charter, no authority of a general meeting shall be required, and no person lending money to the College under this clause shall be bound to enquire whether such authority of a general meeting as is hereby required shall have been actually obtained.

52. Everything which the Council or other officers of the College are hereby authorized to do or cause to be done shall be done at the cost of the College, and the Council may out of the funds pay and discharge all the costs, charges and expenses of applying for and obtaining this Charter, and charges incident to the establishment

of the College. And the funds and property of the College shall at all times be liable to indemnify the members of the Council and other officers from all loss or damage arising from anything which they shall do, or cause to be done, in the exercise of any of the powers hereby conferred upon them, either individually or collectively.

53. The Council may make such regulations as they think fit for receiving, paying, issuing, investing, laying out, and disposing of all moneys, stocks, funds, and securities belonging to the College.

54. The Council shall devise and may from time to time break, alter, and renew the common seal of the College, and shall make such provision as they shall from time to time deem expedient for the safe custody and for the use of the seal.

55. The Council shall provide for the keeping of all registers, lists, books, and accounts, from time required for the purposes of the College, and in particular a Register, in which shall be entered the names, addresses, and occupations[161] of the Governors and Donors of the College, the nature and extent of their qualifications, and all such particulars of date and circimstance as shall be necessary to show their position with regard to the College.

56. If it shall happen that the number of members of the College shall at any time be reduced below twenty five, it shall be lawful for the Council from time to time to appoint any person or persons that they may think fit to be Governors of the College, and such person or persons shall thereupon be and become Governors and members of the College for their respective lives, and have and enjoy all the rights and privileges herein given to the person or persons becoming Life Governors. [*m. 6*] Provided nevertheless that no greater number of members of the College shall be created under this power than shall suffice to maintain from time to time twenty five members of the College.

Proceedings of the Council.

57. The Council may meet together for the despatch of business, adjourn or otherwise regulate their meetings as they think fit, and determine the quorum necessary for the transaction of business, so that such quorum be not less than four. Questions arising at any meeting shall be decided by a majority of votes of the members of the Council present. In case of an equity of votes, the chairman of the meeting shall have a second or casting vote.

58. Any member of the Council may at any time summon a meeting of the Council by giving not less than one day's clear notice in writing.

59. The Council may elect a chairman of their meetings and determine the period for which he is to hold office, but if there shall be no such chairman, or if at any meeting he is not present at the time appointed for holding the same, the members of the Council present shall choose some one of their number to be chairman of such meeting. The Reverend James Heyworth shall be the first Chairman of the Council, and shall hold office until the Council shall elect some one else in his stead.

60. The Council may delegate either permanently or temporarily all or any of their powers to a committee or committees consisting of such member or members of their body as they think fit. Any committee so formed shall in the exercise of the powers so delegated conform to any regulations that may be imposed on them by the Council, and from time to time report their proceedings to the Council.

61. A committee, consisting of two or more members of the Council, may elect a chairman of their meetings, but if there be no such chairman, or if at any meeting he

---

[161] Misprinted 'descriptions'.

be not present at the time appointed for holding the same, the members present shall choose one of their number to be chairman of such meeting.

62. A committee may meet and adjourn as they think proper. Questions at any meeting of a committee shall be determined by a majority of votes of the members present, and in case of an equality of votes the chairman of the meeting shall have a second or casting vote.

63. The Governors and the Council of the College respectively, and every committee of such bodies respectively, in discharging their respective duties in relation to the College, shall cause notes, minutes or copies (as the case requires) of their orders, resolutions and proceedings to be entered in books to be kept under their superintendence, and every such entry shall be signed by the chairman of the meeting at which the order, resolution, or proceeding entered was passed or taken, or by the chairman of the next subsequent meeting of the same body, and every such entry so signed shall be received as evidence in all courts and elsewhere without proof of the meeting having been duly convened or held, or of the persons making or taking any such order, resolution or proceeding, or causing the same to be entered being Governors or members of the Council, or of the committee (as the case may be), or of the signature of the person signing as chairman, or of the fact of his having been chairman, all of which matters shall be presumed until the contrary is shewn.

64. All acts done at a meeting of the Governors or of the Council, or of any committee of the Governors or Council, or by any person acting as a member of any of these bodies, shall notwithstanding it may be afterwards discovered that there was some defect in the appointment of any member of such bodies respectively, or of the person so acting, or that such member or person was disqualified, be as valid as if there had been no such defect or disqualification, and no acts of any body shall be invalidated by reason of any vacancy in such body.

65. The receipts in writing of the Treasurer of the College, or of any person or persons authorized in that behalf by the Council, for any money payable to the College for the purposes of the College, shall be sufficient discharges to the <persons> paying the same from the money therein expressed to be received, and from being bound to see to the application or being responsible for any loss or misapplication thereof.

The Masters and discipline of the College.

66. [*Masters and Council may respectively terminate engagement by three months' notice; Council may terminate engagement of masters by three months' salary in lieu of notice (as* Articles, *67), continuing*] provided always that the Council shall not be at liberty to terminate the engagement of the Head Master, except in pursuance of a resolution passed at a meeting of the Council (of which ten days' notice shall have been given) with the concurrence of members of the Council present at such meeting, representing in number at least two-thirds of the whole body of the Council.

67. The Head Master of the College shall be a member of the Church of England, and graduate of Oxford, Cambridge, or some other university of the United Kingdom; and no master who may be in holy orders shall serve any church, or undertake any professional or other office, cure, or employment requiring the devotion thereto[162] of any part of his time, without the sanction of the Council.[163]

---

[162] Word omitted in printed text.
[163] *Cf.* Articles, 68, where the Second Master was similarly bound, and which named only Oxford, Cambridge and (Trinity) Dublin; since then (in 1874) Percival had acquired an honorary doctorate from St Andrews, which conceivably prompted the recognition that there were other universities in the United Kingdom.

68. The Head Master shall alone, subject to the directions of the Council and of the College respectively, have the management and internal regulation of the College, and shall regulate the duties of all the under masters [*concluding as* Articles, 70, from 'and shall carry into effect the system of education ... the affairs thereof'].

69. [*Head Master may dismiss any under master* (*as* Articles, 71), *continuing*] but any under master so dismissed shall have the right of appeal to the Council, who may cancel the dismissal or otherwise deal with the matter in any way they may think proper.

70. The Head Master shall have the power of expelling pupils from the College, and such power may be exercised in any case in which he may consider the expulsion of a pupil necessary or beneficial to the College in consequence of immorality, wilful breach of discipline, or transgression of the rules of the College, or any flagrant misconduct of such pupil in or out of School hours. In every case of expulsion of a pupil the Head Master shall forthwith report the same to the Council.

71. [*Daily prayers* (*as* Articles, 80).]

Boarding Houses and their masters.

72. No person except as hereinafter provided shall be qualified to receive any pupil as a boarder without having previously obtained the licence[164] of the Head Master, which licence he may from time time revoke; provided that any person may, without such licence, take as boarders the children of relatives not resident in Clifton. The Head Master shall have power to exclude from the College any pupil who shall be found to be boarding with any person in contravention of the provisions of this clause.

73. [*Responsibilites of masters of boarding houses: as* Articles, 82 *omitting* 'and to their religious duties'.]

74. [*Head Master and Council to regulate boarding houses: as* Articles, 83.]

75. All complaints either from the masters of boarding houses or from their boarders, shall be made to the Head Master.

76. [*Terms for receipt of pupils: as* Articles, 86.]

77. The Head Master, and under masters if licensed by him, may receive pupils as boarders, but in such case all the foregoing regulations and clauses shall so far as the same are applicable apply to them respectively in their character of masters of boarding houses.

Accounts and reports.

78. The Council shall cause true accounts to be kept of all sums of money received and expended by the College, and the particulars of such receipt and expenditure, and of the credits and liabilities of the College, and the books of account, shall be kept at the office of the College, and (subject to any reasonable restrictions which may be imposed by the Council as to the time and manner of inspecting the same) shall be open to the inspection of any Governor. Separate accounts shall be kept of special trust funds, or funds devoted or appropriated for special purposes.

79. At the second ordinary general meetong of the College and at every subsequent ordinary general meeting the Council shall lay before the College a general report as to the College and the affairs and position thereof, as well as suggestions for its future welfare and development.

80. The said report shall also include a statement of the income and expenditure of the College since the last report, made up to a date not more than three months before

---

[164] Misprinted 'license' on each instance in this paragraph.

such meeting. The statement so made shall show, arranged under the most convenient heads, the amount of gross income, distinguishing the several sources from which it has been derived, and the amount of gross expenditure, distinguishing the expenses of the establishment, salaries, and other like matters. Every item of expenditure fairly chargeable against the year's income shall be brought into account, so that a just view may be presented to the meeting of the financial position of the College as regards the preceding year, and in cases where any item of expenditure which may in fairness be distributed over several years has been incurred in any one year, the whole amount of such item shall be stated, with the addition of the reasons why only a portion of such expenditure is charged against the income of the year.

81. A balance sheet shall also be made out and laid before the ordinary general meeting of the College at the second and every subsequent ordinary general meeting of the College, and each balance sheet shall contain a summary of the property and liabilities of the College.

Audit.

82. The accounts of the College shall be examined and the correctness of the balance sheet ascertained by two or more Auditors to be elected by the College in general meeting.

83. The Auditors need not be members of the College, but no person shall be eligible as an Auditor who is interested otherwise than as a Govenor in any transaction of the College, and no member of the Council or other officer of the College shall be eligible during his continuance in office.

84. The election of Auditors shall be made by the College at the ordinary general meeting in each year.

85. The remuneration of the Auditors shall be fixed by the College from time to time.

86. Any Auditor shall be eligible for re-election in his quitting office.

87. If no election of Auditors is made in manner aforesaid, the Council may appoint Auditors for the current year, and the Council may likewise fill up any casual vacancy in the office of Auditor, and may fix the amount of the remuneration of the Auditors appointed by them in pursuance of this article.

88. Every Auditor shall be supplied with a copy of the balance sheet, and it shall be his duty to examine the same with the accounts and vouchers relating thereto. Every auditor shall also have a list delivered to him of all books of account kept by the College, and he shall at all reasonable times have access thereto, and shall when required by the Council examine the accounts of the College, or any of them, and report thereon in writing to the Council.

89. Every Auditor may (subject to the sanction of the Council) employ, at the expense of the College, accountants or other persons to assist him in investigating such accounts, and he may in relation to such accounts examine the members of the Council, or any officer of the College.

90. The Auditors shall make a report in writing to the College upon the balance sheet and accounts and other matter of importance with the College which has come under their notice as Auditors, and in every such report they shall state when in their opinion the balance sheet is a full and fair balance sheet, containing the particulars required by these regulations, and properly drawn up so as to exhibit a true and correct view of the state of the affairs of the College, and such report shall be read, together with the report of the Council, at the ordinary general meeting.

Notices.

91. Notices or other documents required to be served upon or given to the Governors in pursuance of the regulations of the College or otherwise, may be served either personally or by sending them through the post in a prepaid letter, or leaving the same addressed to the Governors respectively at their registered place[165] of abode in the United Kingdom, and every such notice left or posted as aforesaid shall be deemed to have been duly served on the day of leaving the same, or on the day after the day on which it shall be[166] posted, although the person to[167] whom it shall have been directed be dead or never received the same, and in proving such notice it shall be sufficient to prove that the letter containing the notice was properly addressed and put into a post office.

92. As to any Governor whose registered place of abode shall not be in the United Kingdom, the office of the College shall, as regards the service of notices or other documents, be deemed his registered place of abode in the United Kingdom, but any such member may register some place in the United Kingdom at which he may desire such service to be made, and the same shall be made accordingly.

93. All notices required to be given by advertisement shall, unless otherwise directed, be advertised in two or more newspapers circulating in the district [of][168] the City of Bristol.

94. Any summons or notice requiring[169] to be served upon the College may be served by leaving the same or sending in through the post, in a prepaid letter, or leaving the same addressed to the College at their office.

Office of the College.

95. The office of the College shall be in the College buildings, Clifton, but the Council shall have power from time to time to change the situation of the office to such other place as they think fit. Provided that notice of every change in the situation of the office shall be given by advertisement once in the *London Gazette* and in four numbers of the London *Times*, or some other London newspaper, and also in four numbers of two or more newspapers circulating in the district of the City of Bristol.

96. It shall be lawful for the College, with the consent of two succcessive extraordinary general meetings of the College especially called for the purpose, to surrender this Charter and to wind up the affairs of the College, but if in winding up or dissolution of the College there shall remain after the satisfaction of all its debts and liabilities any property whatsoever, the same shall not be paid to or distributed among the members of the College or any of them, but shall be considered as held upon trust by the persons in whom the same shall be vested, and shall be given or transferred to some other institution or institutions having objects similar to the objects of the College, to be determined by the members of the College at or before the time of dissolution, or in default thereof by such Judge of our High Court of Justice as may have or acquire jurisdiction in the matter.

And, lastly, we do hereby, for us, our heirs and successors, grant and declare that these our letters patent, or the enrolment or exemplification thereof, shall be in all things valid and effectual in the law according to the true intent and meaning of the same, and shall be construed and adjudged in the most favourable and beneficial

---

[165] Printed 'places', perhaps assuming scribal error.
[166] Misprinted 'have been'.
[167] Misprinted 'on'.
[168] MS. 'in' in error, correctly replaced by 'of' in the printed text (*cf.* clause 95).
[169] Misprinted 'required'.

sense and for the best advantage of the said College, as well in all our courts as elsewhere, notwithstanding any recital, misrecital, uncertainty, or imperfection in these our letters patent.

In witness whereof, we have caused these our letters to be made patent. Witness ourself at our Palace of Westminster the sixteenth day of March in the fortieth year of our reign.

By Her Majesty's command.

Cardew.[170]

---

[170] Misprinted 'Cordew'.

SECTION III:
GOVERNING BODIES

☐ *At the head of the College is the President, elected by the whole body of Governors. Though this is largely a ceremonial office, like that of constitutional monarch or the chancellor of a university, the holder can exercise influence behind the scenes. This position was held by Earl of Ducie from 1860 until his death in 1921, acknowledging his pre-eminent social rank among the School's founding fathers. The appointment of Earl Haig in his place was equally prescriptive, and other eminent Old Cliftonians have followed him.*

The Chairman of the Council is a much more powerful figure. He may be an eminence grise unknown to most of the School community, but he is the effective head of its government. It was through his tenure of this office since 1895 that Percival had continued to shape the School's development.

Sir Herbert Warren replaces Percival as Chairman 1917

[37]   7 November 1917. Percival's resignation
[*Council minute Book 7, pp. 35–6. MS*]

Bishop Percival resigns Chairmanship.
    A letter from Bishop Percival resigning the Chairmanship of Council, but retaining his seat as member of Council, having been read, it was resolved that Council receive their Chairman's resignation with sincere sympathy and regret, and in so doing record the value and devotion of the service he has rendered to the College whilst holding office, enlarging thereby the debt of gratitude which the School will always owe to him as its Great Headmaster and under Providence the founder and architect of its good fortune and success, and Council also testify their pleasure that he still remains one of themselves and venture to hope that the benefit of his advice and experience may long be theirs.
    It was decided to hold a special meeting of Council in December to consider the question of Chairmanship.

[38]   5 December 1917. Sir Herbert Warren elected Chairman[171]
[*Council Minute Book 7, p. 46. MS*]

It was proposed by Mr Abbot[172] and seconded by Mr Bush,[173] that Sir Herbert Warren be elected Chairman of the Council, and the resolution was carried.

☐ *Complicating circumstances behind the resignation are explained below* **[254–5]**. *Percival died on 3 November 1918, and was buried, as he had long intended, in the Chapel vault* **[105–6]**. *At the next meeting of the Council a formal tribute was entered into the Minute Book.*

[39]   26 February 1919. The passing of Percival
[*Council Minute Book 7, p. 111. MS. Printed in Temple,* Percival, *p. 62*]

The Chairman proposed the following resolution which was carried unanimously:
    At the first meeting held since the death of Dr Percival the Council of Clifton College resolve, before performing any other act, to record their deep sense of the rare fortune which gave him to the College as its first Headmaster, and later enabled them to enjoy his services for so many years as a member and as Chairman of their body. Created, established and maintained in large measure by his force, his guidance and his generosity, and impressed with his genius, the School, they feel, owes him an unique debt, in gratefully acknowledging which to his relatives they desire also to add their sincere while respectful condolence with them in their personal loss through the termination of so noble and valuable a life.

J.H. Whitley replaces Haig as President 1928

☐ *Haig's death at the age of 66 on 29 January 1928 was as keenly felt. The Chairman began at once the process of choosing the next President.*

[40]   30 January 1928. The Chairman of Council to the Head Master
[*RB2/36. Holograph*]

January 30 1928

My dear Whatley,
    What a shock! Our best, our greatest man gone! I can think of nothing else. My feeling is that he died for us all, for our country and for the good of the world.
    What an example he leaves. Now it will be seen how great he was and how good, how selfless, how self-sacrificing.
                        Yours sincerely,
                        Herbert Warren.

---

[171] Sir (Thomas) Herbert Warren [*607*: Town 1868–72], Head of the School 1871–2; President of Magdalen College, Oxford from 1885, and Professor of Poetry 1911–16; President of the OCS 1900–3, and a member of the Council from 1917.
[172] Henry Napier Abbot, member of Council 1882–1920.
[173] Alfred George de L'Isle Bush [*124*: Town 1863–5], son of Robert (Council 1860–77) and himself member of Council from 1903 until his death in 1929; member of the Society of Merchant Venturers 1874: McGrath, *Merch. Venturers*, p. 556.

[41]   8 February 1928. The Chairman of Council to the College Secretary[174]
[RB2/36. Holograph]

February 8. 1928

My dear Mr Lewis,

Mr Maitland Wills,[175] writing from Switzerland, declines the offer of election to the Council, on the ground that he is so much away. He expresses himself much pleased to have been given it.

I must now write to Mr C.H. Abbot who will I expect, accept.[176]

I suppose we ought to cater[177] the election of a new President (alas!) at the Governors' meeting. We must try to get some one (1) eminent (2) attached to the School. Constitutionally, I think he must be a Governor but that no doubt could be got over.

One or two possibilities occur to me. One will doubtless occur to many.

I think I have somewhere a list of our members of the House of Lords which you gave me. But perhaps you had better let me have a new list up to date.

Yours sincerely,
Herbert Warren.

[42]   11 February [1928]. The Chairman of Council to the Secretary
[RB2/36. Holograph]

Feb. 11. 1898 [*sic*]

Dear Mr Lewis,

Many thanks for your letter. Has the name of Sir Wm. Birdwood[178] been mentioned?

I had thought of the possibility of a neighbouring magnate, tho' rather of another name than those you mention.

Yours sincerely,
Herbert Warren.

[43]   10 April 1928. The Chairman of Council to the Secretary
[RB2/36. Holograph]

April. 10 1928

My dear Mr Lewis,

Lord Buxton[179] telegraphed on Saturday to prepare me for his non acceptance. His letter has now arrived and is quite definite. He is much pleased and complimented by the proposal but does not see his way to undertake the duty. I cannot say I am

---

[174] W.J. Lewis, Secretary 1912–30.
[175] Maitland Cecil Melville Wills (d. 1966); wrote detective stories as Cecil M. Wills.
[176] Charles Hardcastle Abbot, JP duly served till 1953.
[177] Meaning to arrange (in the now obsolete transitive usage).
[178] Field Marshal William Riddell Birdwood, 1st Baron Birdwood of ANZAC and Totnes [*2054*: ST, OH 1877–82]; had commanded ANZAC and the 5th Army in the war; knighted 1917, created Baronet 1919 and Baron 1938; Master of Peterhouse 1931–8; member of the Council from 1932; passed over for the Presidency this time but elected in 1935 and served to his death in 1951.
[179] Sidney Charles Buxton, 1st Earl Buxton [*622*: BH 1868–70]; Liberal Cabinet Minister and author; Governor–General of South Africa 1914–20 (created Viscount on his appointment and Earl on retirement); died 1934. He was unquestionably the most eminent living OC, and so the first choice to succeed Haig, but in poor health.

surprised. I am glad we offered it to him first. It becomes my duty now <if I am correct> to write to the Speaker.[180] Before I do so I should like to have a copy of the resolutions of the Council dealing with the matter. Please send this.

Yours sincerely,
Herbert Warren.

[44]   17 April 1928. Mr Speaker Whitley to the Chairman of Council
[RB2/36. Holograph]

Speaker's House, S.W.1.
17 April 1928.

My dear Warren,
Clifton President
I am very glad that Buxton was asked. As for myself, Newbolt[181] and Percival[182] sounded me a while ago, and I deprecated the idea, preferring to serve just as a member of the Council. I should still prefer this, if there is anyone else who could be brought in as President. If not, I must leave myself in your hands, on the principle of fielding where you are told. Might it be a condition that I sit at the Council under you – as a Speaker can sit and vote in Committee as a private member?

Clifton has done so much for me that I cannot refuse to give to her every service within my power.

Believe me,
Yours faithfully,
J.H. Whitley.

[45]   25 April 1928. The Chairman of Council to the Secretary
[RB2/36. Holograph]

April 25 1928

My dear Mr Lewis,
Presidentship.
I am sending you herewith a letter from the Speaker [*above*]. He feels himself as you will see at our disposal. This means that we should go ahead and summon the meeting of Governors. Please consider this letter as strictly *confidential* for the Council, the Headmaster and yourself. I suppose we can follow the same order as we followed when we elected Lord Haig. Will you send me a copy of the minutes of that Governors' meeting?

Will you let me know if the H.M. has come back. If not when he is expected.

---

[180] John Henry Whitley [*2252*: WiH 1878–84]; Speaker 1919–28; member of Council since 1920; President from 1928 until his death in 1935.
[181] Sir Henry John Newbolt [*1917*: ST, NT 1876–81]; barrister, historian and poet; member of Council 1919–37. See principally *My World as in my Time: Memoirs of Sir Henry Newbolt* (1932); Lady Newbolt (ed.), *The Later Life and Letters of Sir Henry Newbolt* (1942); P. Howarth, *Play Up and Play the Game: The Heroes of Popular Fiction* (1973), pp. 1–14 ('The Nature of Newbolt Man'); D.O. Winterbottom, *Henry Newbolt and the Spirit of Clifton* (Bristol, 1986); V.F. Jackson, 'Patriotism is not enough: A Reappraisal of the Poetry of Henry Newbolt' (Ph.D. dissertation, Bowling Green State University [OH] 1990), esp. pp. 32–55; S. Chitty, *Playing the Game: A Biography of Sir Henry Newbolt* (1997).
[182] Lancelot Jefferson Percival, KCVO [*2071*: NT, SH 1877–88], only survivor of the Head Master's three OC sons; Prebendary of Brondesbury in St Paul's Cathedral, Precentor of the Chapels Royal and Sub-Almoner, and finally deputy Clerk of the Closet to George V; knighted 1936; President of the OCS 1928–9.

I hope his new house is all right.

Did I by any chance leave my copy of the College statutes in the Council Room after the last meeting? I don't think I did but should like to be assured.

> Yours sincerely,
> Herbert Warren.

[46]   2 May 1928. Notice of election
[RB2/36. Printed]

Clifton College.

An extraordinary general meeting of the Governors will be held in the Council Room at the College on Wednesday, the 16th of May 1928, at 1.30 p.m.

Agenda.

Vacancy in the office of President of the College.

Sir Herbert Warren, Chairman of the Council, will propose: 'That the Right Hon. J.H. Whitley, M.P., Speaker of the House of Commons, be and hereby is elected President of the College'.

2nd May 1928 W.J. Lewis, Secretary.

The departing of Sir Herbert Warren 1930

[47]   7 May 1930. The Chairman of Council to the Head Master
[RB2/16. Holograph]

Confidential

> 74 Woodstock Road
> Oxford
> May 7 1930

My dear Whatley,

I have just received the kind invitation of your wife and yourself to us to attend the Brown celebration on Friday May 16.[183] I am afraid we cannot accept. I have also just received the Memorial Volume.[184] Like all these things it is unequal. But I think dear old Brown on the whole comes out well, and I think it will do good to Clifton. Of course it's entirely out of proportion to say that he is in the *first rank* of English poets of the 19th century [*vertically in the margin*: i.e. with Byron and Shelley, Wordsworth, Tennyson, Browning, Mat. Arnold, Swinburne, William Morris, Hardy, Bridges].[185] Meredith is hardly that, and as a *poet* he isn't as high as Meredith?

He remains always something of an amateur. But he is I suppose the greatest of Manx poets, and has done Mona an indefeasible service. And he was a very large, generous, richly gifted soul and of a noble spirit, and Clifton must be grateful when she counts up her jewels for this large mass of precious stone <even if imperfectly cut

---

[183] Thomas Edward Brown [*M12*: 1863–92], celebrated at Clifton as founding master of the second boarding house, and by the people of Man as their national poet. The centenary of his birth was marked by a meeting in Big School on 16 May 1930: *The Cliftonian* XXXI (1929–31), p. 240.

[184] *Thomas Edward Brown: A Memorial Volume, 1830–1930*, edited by 'Q' alias Sir A. Quiller-Couch [*2666*] (Cambridge, 1930); *cf.* D.O. Winterbottom, *T.E. Brown: His Life and Legacy* (Douglas, 1997), pp. 181–3.

[185] Warren had held the Oxford chair of Poetry from 1911 to 1916.

and polished>. His House, oddly enough, certainly made a very great contribution to the vigour of the School in its earlier years.

Wilson is fairly generous.[186]

Now about the meeting on the 21st. I hope to come. My cousin Miss Thomas has asked us to stay with her <at Pitch & Pay[187]> and what we hope to do is to come down on Tuesday 20th and stay with her two nights. I hope that will be all right. But I am liable to odd temporary disturbances of my health and cannot quite count on myself. Collier[188] thinks I can venture, but will give a more decided opinion in a few days and I will write again.

Can you give me some idea of the amount and importance of the business to be expected. I had a letter from Coles[189] the other day which gave me much satisfaction, suggesting purchase of the premises near the Zoo, Durdham Hall, and I think we certainly ought to purchase *all*.

One more point. Would it be possible to hold the meeting if I ask for it not in the Council Chamber but in some room on the ground floor? Do you still use the Head Master's study in the School House? Would that be available? I find the high stairs directly after luncheon a little formidable; [and *deleted*] [*excision*] a later time I can manage them, but if I have to hurry it gives me a bad start.

I think I shall probably have to say that I think the Council should be considering a new Chairman. I might remain as an ordinary member. If I could last out till 1932 I should have been a member of Council for 50 years!

My impression is that the School is really *stronger* than it has been at any time during that period. If it [is *otiose*] does not appear so it is because the competition and the difficulties are so much greater. In Percival's time we had all the advantage of novelty, and it suited Percival's genius, as he said himself.

I hope you have all had a good holiday and came back in good spirits.

> Yours ever,
> [Herbert Warren].[190]

[48]   20 May 1930. The Chairman of Council to the Secretary
[*RB2/16. Holograph*]

> 74 Woodstock Road
> Oxford.
> May 20 1930

---

[186] J.M. Wilson wrote 'I have never known a man so lovable, so human, so truly wonderful': *Memorial Volume*, p. 79.

[187] Miss G. Thomas lived at the house called Pitch and Pay in Sneyd Park: *Directory* (1930), p. 272. One of Clifton's founders, Joseph Leech [above, **1**] popularised an implausible explanation for this place name (tossing food to plague victims in return for cash): *Brief Romances from Bristol History* (1884), pp. 89–96; its more likely derivation is from straightforward cash trading: R. Coates with J. Scherr, 'Some local names in medieval and early modern Bristol', *Transactions of the Bristol and Gloucestershire Archaeological Society* CXXIX (2011), pp. 185–6. The editor is grateful to Professor Coates for an advance copy of this article.

[188] William Collier, Consulting Physician to the Radcliffe Infirmary: G.H. Brown (comp.), *Lives of the Fellows of the Royal Physicians of London* (1955), pp. 354–5.

[189] Hugh Thomas, 4th son of William Gale Coles (Council 1860–90), himself member of Council 1890–1937; also Treasurer of the Diocesan Training College, resident in All Saints Road, Clifton: Venn, *Al. Cant.* ii, p. 93.

[190] The signature has been excised, presumably by a maladroit *autogrophile*. This accounts for the lost text on the obverse.

My dear Mr Lewis,

I am writing a letter which I will ask to have read at the Council. I have already told the Head Master that I should not be able to attend the meeting tomorrow. I told him this some few days ago. I do not know whether the President *will* be present, but in any case I think Council will be prepared to make arrangements for the chair being taken by someone in my place.

But this brings me to further considerations.

I do not want my very good, old, and kind friends of the Council, to think too seriously of my failure in health which prevents me from coming. Some ten days ago my doctor quite encouraged me to [think *corrected to*] contemplate coming and taking my place with you all as usual.

But after that I got a chill and a set back which made him doubtful, and after a day or two though I was again pretty well again he advised me that it would be unwise to make the venture with all it would involve.

What I had hoped was that I might have the pleasure of coming down and that I might see how I got through. But that it seems cannot be.

I shall then now have missed three important meetings in succession, and it is clear to me that I cannot count on attending with any regularity.

I have written therefore to the President to place my definite resignation of the position of Chairman in his hands and in those of the Council, and I write now to ask the Council to accept the same, and to relieve me of my responsibility as and when they think fit.

It may not be convenient, and they may not wish to make a permanent appointment of a successor tomorrow, and if they wish it I will continue in office at a distance for the time being. But I should definitely desire that the successor should be elected, so as to begin another School year.

If it would be for the convenience of Council to elect a new member in my place, I should wish also to resign my post on the Council at any time which would suit them, and I should like them to have this also in their minds.

As to my feelings in the matter and the regret which I feel in having to write this letter, I will not now write at length. I may do so later. I will today only say this which I trust the Council and you too will understand, that it has been my lifelong desire from boyhood to age to do honour to the College and to aid and advance its welfare, and that every hour I have spent in the business of the Council throughout the nearly 48 years during which I have been a member has been given with a sense of privilege and pleasure in the service.

I am, yours sincerely,
Herbert Warren.

I add on a separate sheet one or two notes on the business.

[49]   21 May 1930. Council minute
[*RB2/16. Typescript*]

At a meeting of the Council held on the 21st of May 1930.

A letter was read from Sir Herbert Warren [*above*] placing his resignation of the Chairmanship in the hands of the Council.

It was resolved: That the resignation of the Chairman has been received with deep regret, and that he be requested to continue for the time being as pro forma Chairman.

It was further resolved: That the Chairman of the Finance Committee be requested to act as Chairman of the Council pending further consideration of the question at the next meeting.[191]

☐ *Warren was still in office when he died on 9 June.*

[50]   September 1930. Draft Council resolution
[RB2/16. Typescript]

That <the members of> this Council desire to record their deep sense of the loss which they and the School have suffered by the death of their Chairman, Sir Thomas Herbert Warren. He had been closely connected with the School ever since he entered it in 1868, six years after its foundation. His brilliant successes as a scholar did much to win reputation for the young School, and his influential position at Oxford combined with his untiring devotion to the School enabled him to take a very leading part in organising the activities of Old Cliftonians. He was the first old Cliftonian President at Commemoration.[192]

Elected to the Council in 1882, he served on it until his death, for the last twelve years as Chairman, and during a membership lasting forty eight years he was hardly ever absent from a meeting. Throughout that period his services were untiring. He brought to its work enthusiasm and devotion, close acquaintance with the educational world, knowledge of men and movements, a remarkable memory for the past history of the School and unfailing confidence in its future.

His unceasing urbanity and consideration for others won the affection and admiration of all those who have served with him.

[Minuted] Sept. 1930. (Sent with a personal letter to Lady Warren by Mr Whitley).

[51]   27 September 1930. Lady Warren[193] to the President
[RB2/16. Holograph]

> 74 Woodstock Road
> Oxford.
> Sept. 27. 1930

My dear Mr President,

I am writing to try and express my thanks for the resolution you sent me [*above*] and for your own letter, but when I have said all I can there will still be as much unexpressed gratitude in my heart. It is a great happiness to me to receive your resolution recalling the ways in which my husband served the School from youth to old age. So much of his heart was with the School and all he did for it was a labour of love. The Council meetings were carefully noted and his plans were always made so

---

[191] Entered in slightly longer terms in Council Minute Book 8, p. 400; the Finance Committee Chairman was H.T. Coles **[47]**.

[192] In the early days a separate position from that of President of the College, though sometimes held by the same man: *Register* (1925), pp. cv–cvi,

[193] Mary Isabel, Lady Warren (d. 1940), fourth daughter of Sir Benjamin Collins Brodie, Bt, Waynflete Professor of Chemistry.

that he might be present at them. The generous words of the resolution will always be treasured by me, and that the Council have decided to institute a Sir Herbert Warren Memorial Prize that they should desire him to be remembered in perpetuity.

Believe me,

Yours very sincerely,

Mary Warren.

Sir William Birdwood replaces Whitley as President 1935

☐ *Warren's place as Chairman was taken by Sir Rowland Whitehead.*[194] *On his retirement in 1934 he was followed by Sir Robert Witt.*[195] *One of his first duties was to arrange for a President to succeed Whitley.*

[52]   11 February 1935. Circular from the Chairman of Council to Governors[196]
[*RB2/37. Typescript*]

Clifton College,

Bristol.

11th February 1935.

Dear [*blank*],

The death of our President, J.H. Whitley,[197] is a severe blow to the College. As a member of the Council since 1920 and as our President since May 1928, it is within your knowledge that he has given splendid and continuous service to the School and that some of the most important recent developments have been due to his initiative and inspiration.

A memorial service was held in the College Chapel on Thursday, the 7th February, attended by the Lord Mayor[198] and Sheriff and by several members of the Council, and, on behalf of the Council, the Vice-Chairman and I attended the memorial service held simultaneously at St Martin-in-the-Fields, London.

Under the College Charter it is provided that vacancies in the office of President shall be filled at a general meeting[199] and I have, therefore, placed the question of his successor on the agenda of the annual general meeting to be held on the 22nd March next.

I shall be much obliged if you would kindly send me any names you might feel willing to propose. The position of the President is largely an honorary one and, while there are many distinguished individuals who would fill it admirably, I should like to suggest whether this opportunity should not be taken of strengthening the connection of the School with Bristol and its local interests by offering the Presidency to some

---

[194] Sir Rowland Edward Whitehead, Bt [*2127*: SH 1877–82]; member of Council 1901–39 (Chairman 1930–4).
[195] Sir Robert Clermont Witt [*3198*: PHP, WiH 1883–90]; member of Council from 1930 until his death in 1952 (Chairman 1934–46); by profession a solicitor, he was prominent as Chairman of the National Gallery, President of the National Art Collections Fund, and much else in that field.
[196] The file copy is attached to a letter from the Secretary dated 18 February.
[197] Whitley had declined the customary offer of a Viscountcy on retiring from the Speaker's Chair in 1928.
[198] Herbert John Maggs, Lord Mayor 1934–5.
[199] Above **[36]** section 33.

distinguished Bristolian. If that view found favour, the name of Lord Dulverton[200] might well be considered in his capacity as head of the Wills family and Chairman of the Imperial Tobacco Company, as also Director of the Great Western Railway and filling other public positions. Knowing something of him personally, I think he would be a 'persona grata'; in any company, although, of course, I have no idea whether he would entertain the proposal if made.

Yours sincerely, [*blank for signature*]

□ *The Chairman's attempt to fix the election was unsuccessful, and this time the choice fell on Birdwood.*[201]

The transformation of the Governors 1936

[53]   1936. Circular letter
[*P4527 Miscellanea Box 3. Typescript*]

Clifton College,
Bristol, 8.

Dear [*blank*]

The Council of Clifton College has decided to invite a number of Old Clifonians to become Life Governors of the College. They believe that the closer association of Old Cliftonians with the Council will strengthen the School, and that many Old Cliftonians will welcome not only the privileges associated with the position but also the opportunity of thus keeping in closer touch with the School. It is hoped that it may gradually become the rule for many Old Cliftonians to become Life Governors, and thus, at the same time, provide a steady and greatly needed addition to the funds of the College. The Charter in 1877 created two classes of Governors, that is to say, Original Governors and Life Governors. Original Governors were persons who, immediately before the granting of the Charter, were shareholders in the Company, which then owned and managed the School.[202] Each Original Governor was given the right to nominate some person to succeed him as Governor, but the person so nominated has not the right to nominate a successor. In the course of time therefore, this class of Governor will cease to exist. Life Governors are persons approved by the Council who contribute £50 or upwards in one sum for the purposes of the School.

A general meeting of the Governors is held once a year to which the Council submits a general report as to the College and its affairs and position. The Governors appoint the President, Treasurer, members of Council and Auditors.

Governors have also the right of nominating pupils to the School. The Charter provides that a Governor shall be entitled to have always in the School one pupil nominated by him in respect of any qualification of Governor he may have. And by the Bye-Laws, as recently amended, a pupil nominated by a Life Governor who became qualified after 27th March, 1936, is exempted from the payment of the entrance fee, which amounts at present for boys over 13 years of age to 5 guineas,

---

[200] Gilbert Alan Hamilton Wills, formerly Liberal Unionist MP for Bristol North, created Baron Dulverton 1929.
[201] Birdwood recorded his pride in succeeding his 'old schoolfellow' Whitley: *Khaki and Gown: An Autobiography* (1941), p. 418.
[202] Above **[36]**, section 6.

for boys between 10 years and 13 years to 3 guineas and for boys under 10 years to one guinea.

We have pleasure, therefore, in inviting you to become a Life Governor of Clifton College, and would ask if, as we hope, you are able to accept this invitation, to forward your cheque to the Bursar, Clifton College, Bristol.

Yours sincerely,

[*blank for signature*] President

[*blank for signature*] Chairman of the Council.

[54]   30 November 1936. The Chairman of Council to R.F. Truscott[203]
[*P4627 Album, extra volume. Typescript*]

32, Portman Square, W.1.

30th November, 1936.

My dear Truscott,

As I think you probably know, the constitution of Clifton provides for a body of Governors who, according to the Charter, are appointed on payment of £50 or upwards in respect of their Governorships. A general meeting of the Governors is held once a year, to which the Council submits a general report as to the College and its affairs. The Governors appoint the President, Treasurer, members of Council and the Auditors, and they have the privilege of nominating a boy for entrance to the School subject to his complying with the bye-laws.

The Council also has power in special circumstances to offer Governorships in return for a nominal sum of £1 only. In the event of your being invited by the Council to accept a Governorship at the nominal figure in view of the services rendered by you to the School, particularly in respect of your long services to the Old Cliftonian Society, would you be willing to accept this, the only honour it is in the power of the Council to confer? If so, will you kindly let me know and shall have the pleasure in submitting your name to the Council.

Yours sincerely.

Robert Witt, Chairman.

☐ *Truscott promptly accepted the offer, though it was not until 12 July 1937 that the Council's invitation was formally conveyed to him; whereupon he sent off his cheque for £1.*

---

[203] Roy Francis Truscott [*4627:* PHP, BH 1892–9], Assistant Hon. Secretary of the OCS 1925–35; compiled 13 great albums and a further 8 boxes of cuttings devoted to Clifton and OCs; now in the College Archives.

SECTION IV: HEAD MASTERS

Appointment of Glazebrook 1890

[55]   30 July 1890. First moves
[*Council Minute Book 3, pp. 301–2. MS*]

At a special meeting of the Council held at the Board-room, Royal Insurance Office, Corn Street, Bristol, on Wednesday the 30th of July 1890.

Present: Mr Budd (in the chair); Mr Abbot, Mr Aiken,[204] Mr Hugh Coles, Mr George,[205] Dr Percival, Mr Saunders, Colonel Savile, Mr Warren and the Secretary.

The Head Master Mr Wilson attended.

Resignation of Head Master.

The Chairman reported that Mr Wilson had resigned the Head Mastership of the College.

Arrangements for carrying on duties.

Mr Wilson stated that the arrangements he proposed to make to carry on the Head Mastership until Christmas, that he needed rest and preparation for his new duties involving absence from the College for a considerable part of next term, but that when not at the College he would be near at hand when required. But Mr Moor[206] would take the management of the School House and Archdeacon Stead[207] would take the Divinity teaching.

Head Mastership.

Mr Wilson gave information with regard to some probable candidates for the Head Mastership and of others eligible for the post.

Dr Percival also gave information on the subject.

It was proposed by the Chairman seconded by Dr Percival and carried unanimously:

---

[204] John Chetwode Chetwood Aiken, of Stoke Bishop, banker; member of Council 1884–1903; inherited claim to Barony of Odell 1892, was rejected by the Committee of Privileges of the House of Lords.
[205] William Edwards George, member of Council 1883–1901.
[206] Edward Norman Peter Moor [*525*: Town 1867–9 (Head of the School 1868–9); *M72*: 1874–95†].
[207] Samuel Stead, Archdeacon of Bombay 1878–86, and thereafter living at Tara Lodge, Osborne Rd, Clifton: *Directory* (1890), p. 320; *Crockford* (1890); father of Charles Clement [*3340*: ST 1884–8] and Francis Bernard [*3360*: ST 1884–91; *M172*: 1901–8].

That the Head Mastership be offered to Mr Warren.
It was decided in case of need to hold another special meeting of the Council on Tuesday the 30th of September.

☐ *Warren however did not accept the nomination, and the Council had to think again. Their second choice was Herbert Armitage James, the recently appointed Principal of Cheltenham College. James accepted but almost immediately withdrew after his colleagues and pupils had begged him to stay at Cheltenham.*

[56]   30 September 1890. The second choice
[*Council Minute Book 3, p. 306. MS*]

Election of Head Master
Mr Wilson, Dr Percival and Mr Warren gave information with regard <to> gentlemen eligible for the Head-Mastership.

Appointment. Revd H.A. James
It was moved by Colonel Savile, seconded by Mr Saunders and unanimously resolved: That the appointment of the Head Mastership be offered the Revd H.A. James.[208]

Acceptance by Mr James
Dr Percival was requested to communicate the offer to Mr James by telegraph and a telegram from Mr James's [*sic*] was received accepting the post.

[57]   16 October 1890. The third man
[*Council Minute Book 3, p. 308. MS*]

Head-Mastership. Withdrawal of Mr James
Mr James's letter to the Chairman withdrawing his acceptance of the Head-Mastership on account of the pressure put upon him to remain at Cheltenham was read.[209]

Appointment. Revd M.G. Glazebrook.[210]
It was moved by Mr Wasbrough, seconded by Mr Saunders and unanimously resolved: That the Head Mastership be offered to the Revd M.G. Glazebrook.

---

[208] Herbert Armitage James, newly appointed Principal of Cheltenham, formerly Headmaster of Rossall (1875–6) and Dean of St Asaph (1886–9) He was persuaded to remain at Cheltenham despite some earlier disagreements; in 1895 he succeeded Percival at Rugby (to be followed in turn by A.A. David); he died in 1931 as President of St John's College Oxford and a Companion of Honour: Winterbottom, *Clifton after Percival*, p. 39, and his *Rossall School*, pp. 28–33; Hope Simpson, *Rugby since Arnold*, pp. 132–57.
[209] Morgan, *Cheltenham*, pp. 59–62, printing much of the speech in which James told Cheltenham that he would stay, even though 'in a good many ways the position of the Headmaster of Clifton is a better one than that of the Principal of Cheltenham.' This was not, he assured his audience, just a matter of money, but because at Clifton the Head Man was also a House Master.
[210] Michael George Glazebrook [*HM3*: 1891–1905]; High Master of Manchester Grammar School since 1889.

Appointment of David 1905

☐ *When Glazebrook resigned for health reasons the succession was relatively simple. The selection was delegated to Percival and two of his former pupils, and they chose a man whom Percival had previously appointed to the staff of Rugby.*

[58]   22 February 1905. Glazebrook's resignation received by the Council
[*Council Minute Book 5, p. 235. MS*]

The following letter from Dr Glazebrook was read:

Clifton College,
Bristol.
Feb. 11 1905.

My dear Lord Bishop,
    For the last two years my health has caused me some anxiety; and now the doctors tell me that I can only get strong again by taking a much longer rest than School arrangements allow. I therefore ask the Council to accept my resignation for next July. I cannot do so without thanking them warmly for the confidence which they have shewn me and the uniform kindness with which they have treated me.

Yours sincerely,
(signed) M.G. Glazebrook.

The Right Rev. the Chairman, Clifton College Council.
    It was resolved that the Head Master be informed that the Council had received his letter with very great regret and that it would be submitted to a special meeting to be called for the purpose on Wednesday the 8th of March.
    The Head Master attended.

☐ *The matter was deferred to a further special meeting on 23 March.*

[59]   23 March 1905. Re-structuring of Head Master's remuneration and appointment of a selection committee
[*Council Minute Book 5, pp. 250–1. MS*]

Head Mastership. Remuneration.
    The appointment of a Head Master to succeed Dr Glazebrook was considered.
    The question of the Head Master's remuneration was discussed and it was resolved to make the following alterations in the system of payments and charges:
    The rent payable to be £500 instead of £524.10[s].
    The stipend to be £500 instead of £800; and
    The capitation to be £3 per boy over the number of four hundred instead of £2.
Selection committee.
    It was resolved that the Chairman, the President of Magdalen, and Mr Cannan[211] be a Selection Committee to make enquiries with regard to those whom they might consider most suitable for the Head Mastership and to report to the Council.

---

[211] Charles Cannan [*897*: BH 1870–7], Head of the School 1876-7; member of Council from 1899 to his death in 1919.

It was resolved to hold another special meeting of the Council on Friday the 14th of April for the further consideration of the subject.

[60]   14 April 1905. Report of Selection Committee: short-list of four
[*Council Minute Book 5, p. 255. MS*]

Headmastership. Report of Selection Committe.
The question of the appointment of a Head Master was considered.
The Selection Committee reported and submitted to the Council the names of four gentlemen whom they considered specially eligible for the appointment.
It was resolved to approve the report and that the Committee be empowered to continue their labours with the view of making a final recommendation for the appointment.

[61]   31 May. Appointment of David
[*Council Minute Book 5, pp. 258–60. MS*]

Appointment of Head Master. Offer to Mr David.
The Committee appointed with regard to the selection of a Head Master reported that in accordance with the authority given to them at the last meeting they had offered the Head Mastership to the Revd A.A. David, Fellow and Dean of Queen's College, Oxford and late an assistant master of Rugby, and that it had been accepted by him.

Mr David's letter of acceptance as follows was read:

Furness Abbey Hotel,
Lancashire,
24th April 1905.
My dear Lord Bishop,
Your letter reached me in Exeter this morning just as I was starting northwards to attend a Governors' meeting at St Bees tomorrow.
May I ask your Lordship to thank the Council very heartily for the great honour they have paid me by their selection, and to say that I accept the offer you have so kindly conveyed.
I will only add that there is no position I could better desire or more eagerly strive to fill.
It is a particular pleasure to me to think that I shall be doing my utmost to maintain traditions which you created.
Believe me, my dear Lord Bishop, to be yours sincerely,
A.A. David.
P.S. I return to Oxford on Wednesday.

Appointment. Mr David.
And, it was resolved that the Revd Albert A. David be and is hereby appointed Head Master of Clifton College in succession to the Revd M.G. Glazebrook on the terms following as communicated to Mr David by the Chairman. Mr David to enter upon his duties in September next.

Remuneration of the Head Master:

1. A salary of £500 a year.

2. A capitation fee of £3 a boy on all boys over 400 in the College, Junior School and Preparatory School reckoned together.

3. Leave to take boarders in his House to the number of 68 at £72 a year.

He will be required to pay:

1. A rent of £500 a year for the School House including Stables and Kitchen Garden.

2. A sum of £5 per term on all boys in his House beyond the number of 63 for the senior masters' fund.

3. A contribution of £1 per head per annum on all boys in the House up to 63 for the scholarships' augmentation fund.

4. House Tutor and Preparation Tutors for the House estimated at £140 a year.

He also pays:

5. House exhibitions 4 at £25 – £100.[212]

There are also some prizes which the Head Master has been accustomed to give.

The above arrangements are calculated to produce a net income of about £2370 a year when the College and House are full.

Appointment of King 1909

[62]   1 December 1909. Selection process
[Council Minute Book 6, pp. 47–8. MS]

At a meeting of the Council held at the Grand Hotel, Broad Street, Bristol, on Wednesday the 1st of December 1909.

Present: the Bishop of Hereford (chair); Mr Abbot, Mr Bush, Mr Cannan, Mr Coles, Mr Cross,[213] The Right Hon.ble Lewis Fry, Mr Pope,[214] Colonel Savile, Mr Tait,[215] the President of Magdalen (Mr Warren), Mr Ward,[216] Mr Wasbrough,[217] Mr Whitehead and the Secretary.

Head Mastership. Selection Committee Report.

The Report of the Selection Committee with regard to the appointment of a Head Master was read by the President of Magdalen, stating that as the result of the information they had obtained and the enquiries they had made, they presented the names of the following five gentlemen as eligible for the appointment and gave particulars regarding them.

1. Mr R. Carter, Rector of Edinburgh Academy.[218]

---

[212] Bracketed and marked in pencil 'Subsititute'.

[213] Francis Richardson Cross, surgeon; member of Council 1900–27; see below **[164]**.

[214] George Henry Pope [*M79*: 1876.3]; member of Council 1901–21.

[215] Charles William Adam Tait [*M57*: 1873–1904]; member of Council from 1907 until his death in 1913.

[216] William Welsford Ward, member of Council from 1900 until his death in 1932.

[217] Charles Whitchurch Wasbrough [*120*: Town 1862–3]; son and successor of the original College Solicitor (H.S.) and himself member of Council from 1901 to 21.

[218] Reginald Carter [*2791*: SH 1881–6], as an undergraduate at Balliol won the Gaisford Greek Prose Prize; Fellow of Lincoln College until appointed to Edinburgh in 1902; succeeded his successful rival J.E. King at Bedford in 1910: see J. Sargeaunt, *A History of Bedford School*, ed. E. Hockliffe (1925), pp. 205–13 (on King's headmastership there), 214 and *passim* (on Carter).

2. Mr C. Cookson, Fellow and Tutor of Magdalen College, Oxford.[219]
3. Mr C.D. Fisher, Censor of Christ Church, Oxford.[220]
4. Mr J.E. King, Head Master of Bedford Grammar School.[221]
5. The Revd Wm. Temple, Fellow and Tutor of Queen's College, Oxford.[222]

It was moved by Mr Abbot and seconded by Mr Ward: That the name of Mr Temple be excluded from the consideration of the Council.

An amendment was moved by Colonel Savile and seconded by Mr Fry: That all the five names mentioned by the Selection Committee be considered by the Council.

On being put to the vote there appeared:

For the amendment, the Bishop of Hereford, Mr Cross, Mr Fry, Colonel Savile, Mr Warren and Mr Whitehead – 6.

Against: Mr Abbot, Mr Bush, Mr Cannan, Mr Coles, Mr Pope, Mr Tait, Mr Ward and Mr Wasbrough – 8.

The amendment was therefore lost.

For the resolution: Mr Abbot, Mr Bush, Mr, Cannan, Mr Coles, Mr Pope, Mr Tait, Mr Ward and Mr Wasbrough – 8

Against the resolution: the Bishop of Hereford, [Mr Cross *deleted*], Mr Fry, Colonel Savile, Mr Warren and Mr Whitehead – 5.

The resolution was therefore carried.

Head Mastership. Offer to Mr J.E. King.

It was moved by Mr Abbot, seconded by Mr Bush, and resolved to offer the Head Mastership to Mr King, and the Chairman was instructed to communicate with Mr King accordingly.

Remuneration.

It was resolved to empower the Selection Committee to increase the capitation fee of the Head Master (for boys over 400) from £3 to £4 a head if the Committee should consider it necessary to do so.

[63]   8 December 1909. Further orders about the Head Master's remuneration
[*Council Minute Book 6, pp. 50–1. MS*]

Head Mastership. Acceptance. Mr King.

A letter from Mr J.E. King to the Chairman of the Council accepting the Head Mastership of the College was read.

Details to Finance Committee.

---

[219] Christopher Cookson [*1560*: ST 1874–9]; as an undergraduate at Balliol won the Gaisford Greek Verse Prize; taught at St Paul's School 1882–94, Fellow of Magdalen 1894–1919; co-author with his successful rival J.E. King of *Principles of Sound and Inflexion in the Greek and Latin Languages* (1888) and *An Introduction to the Comparative Grammar of Greek and Latin* (Oxford, 1890).

[220] Charles Dennis Fisher (d. 1916), editor of Tacitus.

[221] John Edward King [*943*: PHP, SH, ST 1871–7; *HM5*: 1910–23]; High Master of Manchester Grammar School 1891–1903 before going to Bedford. The only OC as yet appointed Head Master of Clifton.

[222] Son of the former Archbishop of Canterbury; Headmaster of Repton 1910–14, Bishop of Manchester 1919–29, Archbishop of York 1929–42, and finally himself Archbishop of Canterbury from 1942 to his death in 1944. Percival's godson, pupil at Rugby, and future biographer.

The Selection Committee having reported as to their communications with Mr King, it was resolved that Mr King having accepted the offer of the Head Mastership made to him by the Council, the Finance Committee be authorized to settle with him the date of his entry on his duties and emoluments and other details.

The following are the main terms of remuneration, subject to any alterations which the Finance Committee may hereafter recommend.

The Finance Committee <were> further empowered to arrange for an extra week's holiday if they should <find> it desirable to do so.

Remuneration of the Head Master [*as for David in* **61** *above, save that the capitation fee is raised from £3 to £4*].

He will be required to pay [*as for David*].

He also pays:

By remission of fees of poor Scholars about £180 a year and by remission of fees another £120 for special Scholars who are received as extra boys above his maximum.

There are also some prizes which the Head Master has been accustomed to give.

Appointment of Whatley 1922

[64]   20 December 1922. Short-list of candidates and other concerns
[*Council Minute Book 7, pp. 341–3. MS with typed insertion*]

At a meeting of the Council held at the College on Wednesday the 20th of December 1922.

Present: Field Marshal Earl Haig (chair); Mr Cross, Dr McTaggart,[223] Sir Henry Newbolt, Mr Paul,[224] Mr Robinson,[225] Mr Savile,[226] Mr Tribe,[227] Sir Herbert Warren, Mr Whitehead, Mr Whitley, Sir Francis Younghusband,[228] the Headmaster and the Secretary.[229]

[*After other business*]
Headmastership.

The report of the Committee appointed to consider the question of the Headmastership was received as follows:

[*typescript*]

1. The Committee appointed by the Council have held three meetings.

A considerable number of candidates, between twenty and thirty, either made application, or were suggested by members of the Committee, or persons known to them.

The Chairman consulted the Headmasters of several of the leading schools, such as Eton, Wellington, Rugby, Charterhouse,[230] and enquiries were made by him and by Dr McTaggart in Oxford and Cambridge respectively.

---

[223] John Ellis McTaggart, FBA [*2867*: WiH 1887–5]; philosopher, Fellow of Trinity College, Cambridge; member of Council from 1913 until his death in 1925. See below **[137]**.

[224] Walter Stuckey Paul [*102*; Town 1865–6]; member of Council from 1920 until his death in 1925.

[225] Sir Foster Gotch Robinson [*4519*: NT 1892–9]; member of Council 1921–39; knighted 1958.

[226] Charles Cornelius Savile [*923*: Town 1870–1]; member of Council 1922–7.

[227] Frank Newton Tribe [*837*: Town 1870–3]; member of Council 1921–37.

[228] Sir Francis Edward Younghusband [*1849*: PHP, SH 1876–80]; member of Council 1905–37.

[229] W.J. Lewis, Bursar and Secretary to the Council 1912–30.

[230] Respectively Cyril Alington, Frederick Blagden Malim, William Wyamar Vaughan, formerly at Clifton [*M138*: 1890–1904], and Frank Fletcher.

Among the candidates thus considered were a number of Headmasters, including those of Reading, University College School, London, King William's College, Isle of Man, King Edward VI's School Southampton, Alleyne's School, Dulwich, Sedbergh School, Kingswood School, and Liverpool College.

After very careful consideration and enquiry, the Committee are of opinion that the following candidates should be considered by the Council, and recommend that they should be interviewed by the Council:

N.B. It should be noted that the names are arranged alphabetically.

(1) The Rev. R. Brook, Headmaster of Liverpool College.[231]

(2) The Rev. M. R. Ridley, Fellow, Tutor and Chaplain of Balliol College.[232]

(3) The Rev. C.F. Russell, Headmaster of King Edward VIth School, Southampton.[233]

(4) Mr Norman Whatley, Fellow and Tutor of Hertford College.

2. They think that the Council should decide the question whether it is desirable to offer the incoming Headmaster the School House; and, if so, whether it should be offered him from the date of his appointment or after the retirement of Mr Borwick, which would naturally take place not later than four years from July next.[234]

The Committee themselves were divided with regard to this question, and will take the opportunity of putting their views before the Council.

3. They think that should the Council decide to terminate Mr Borwick's tenure of the School House at the incoming of the new Headmaster, the question of some substantial pecuniary recognition of his services should be taken into consideration.

The Committee think that an arrangement should be made with an insurance office analogous to those made for the assistant masters, to provide, either a lump sum, or an annuity, for the Headmaster on his retirement, and that the Headmaster should contribute one-third, and the College two-thirds of the premium necessary to secure this.

4. The Committee think that if the Headmaster is assigned Percival House[235] his stipend should be at least £2100, together with the house, free of rates and taxes, and they would recommend the Council to consult the Finance Committee as to whether the finances of the College would admit of this being increased.

Should he occupy the School House, he should have the same stipend, and the profits of the boarding house.

[*MS resumed*]

The Committee submitted detailed information about the four candidates mentioned in their report and also about the Rev. Canon E.C. Owen, Head Master of King William's College, Isle of Man.

---

[231] Richard Brook remained at Liverpool until 1928, and thereafter advanced in the church; Bishop of St Edmundsbury and Ipswich 1940–53, as successor but one to A.A. David.

[232] Maurice Roy Ridley [*5624/6353*: NT 1900–3, 1905–9; *M230*: 1914–20]; Fellow of Balliol 1920–45 and literary scholar; allegedly the physical model for Lord Peter Wimsey (having been observed by Dorothy L. Sayers reading his winning entry for the 1913 Newdigate prize at the 1913 Encaenia).

[233] Charles Frank Russell, who was later (1929–42) Headmaster of Merchant Taylors', Crosby.

[234] The first five Head Masters were *ex officio* Masters of School House; in 1921 King had relinquished the House to Frank Borwick [*M142*: 1892–1926]. Whatley left Borwick in place, and the old arrangement has never been revived.

[235] 1 Cecil Road, built by the College as a 'small' boarding house; bought by Glazebrook and from him by Otto Siepmann [*M137*], who in 1920 sold it back to the College; it served as the Head Master's house from 1921 to 1928, when the more suitable 24 College Road was bequeathed by the widow of H.H. Wills [*1156*], who had himself funded the purchase of the Cecil Road house: RB1/30; Winterbottom, *Clifton after Percival*, pp. 58–9; for Siepmann and Wills see below [**306**] and [**424**] respectively.

It was resolved that Messrs Russell, Whatley and Owen be requested to attend a special meeting on Thursday the 11th of January for an interview.

It was resolved that the School House should revert to the new Headmaster if he desires to take it, and that he should be asked whether he would wish to accept it at once, or would prefer to defer his decision until the retirement of Mr Borwick at a date to be arranged by the Council.

[65]   11 January 1923. Election of Whatley
[Council Minute Book 7, pp. 355–6. MS]

Headmastership.

Additional information regarding the selected candidates having been submitted and considered, the following attended and were interviewed by the Council:

The Rev. Canon E.C. Owen, Headmaster of King William's College, I. of Man.[236]

The Rev. C.J. Russell, Headmaster of King Edward VI School, Southampton.

Mr Norman Whatley, Fellow and Tutor of Hertford College, Oxford.

It was proposed by Mr Ward, and seconded by Mr Coles, that Mr Norman Whatley be elected Headmaster.

Carried, *nem: con.*

The question of the emoluments of the Headmastership was considered and it was decided to adopt the recommendations of the Finance Committee on page 353 with the exception that the salary if with the boarding house should be £2200 instead of £2100 as named therein[237].

Mr Whatley was informed that he would have the option of taking the Headmastership either with or without the School House, as named in the minute of the 20 Dec. 1922 **[64]** and was asked to consider the question and communicate his decision to the Chairman.

Mr Whatley accepted the Headmastership and thanked the Council for electing him.

Appointment of Hallward 1939

☐ *After 16 years Whatley was confronted by mounting difficulties. Many of these were outside his control – notably the world economy and his declining health. The School was also poorly served by two successive Bursars. Whatley was nevertheless blamed for a decline in numbers which worsened the School's own financial plight. He had heated exchanges with the Chairman, Sir Robert Witt, and alienated another key figure on the Council.[238] Their arguments ended with Whatley's resignation on 15 November 1938, to take effect at the end of the following term.[239]*

---

[236] Edward Cunliffe Owen, Principal of King William's College 1913–30.

[237] The Committee had recommended emoluments totalling £3000 (including salary of £2100) with the boarding house, or £2600 without it; and a pension of £750/£800 based on an annual premium of about £300 (payable in full by the Head Master if taking the boarding house, two-thirds to be paid by the College if he did not).

[238] Sir Robert Waley Cohen [*4264*: PH 1890–6]; member of the Council 1931–52.

[239] See Winterbottom, *Clifton after Percival*, pp. 110–16.

[66]   28 March 1939. Extract from Council's Report for 1938; Chairman's statement to the Governors
[*Council Minute Book 13, pp. 39–41. Typescript*]

Retirement of Mr N. Whatley.
This report deals, of course, primarily with the events that took place during the year 1938. It was for this reason alone that in the report sent to you recently the announcement of the resignation of the Headmaster was merely referred to. As his resignation only takes effect at the end of the present term, that is, after April 4th, it is in next year's report that the Council will hope to place on record its appreciation of the services which he has rendered to the School during his long Headmastership of nearly 16 years, apart from Dr Percival's the longest in the history of Clifton Headmasters.

I trust, however, that you gentlemen will be glad to give me an opportunity of expressing on behalf of the Council our deep and abiding gratitude for all Mr Whatley has done for the School during this period.

He came to the School from Oxford with the reputation of a distinguished scholar and soon proved beyond question that he possessed the even more valuable attribute of being able to communicate his great intellectual gifts to those for whose education he was responsible. You have only to look at the School records over all these years to see how remarkable was the success his methods achieved in the field of scholarship and good learning. The considerable reputation of Clifton boys at Oxford and Cambridge to-day is in great measure due to the standard he set both in education and conduct.

Nor were his gifts as an administrator inferior to those as a teacher. His knowledge of business and affairs was unrivalled and outstanding. Two of the most important additions to the School, the Science Buildings and the new Preparatory School, will always be associated with his name. No aspect of the life of the School was beyond or beneath his notice. As a natural consequence the staff supported him whole-heartedly, and with a loyalty which he himself was always the first to acknowledge. By the boys he was regarded with equal respect and affection. A man of high ideals, he imposed them upon the School and maintained them with masters, boys and parents alike.

I am sure that I am voicing the wishes of all here that he may enjoy a long and happy life after his retirement.

May I move that the meeting should resolve: 'That the Governors of Clifton College desire to place on record their cordial appreciation of the great services rendered to the School by Mr N. Whatley during his long period of Headmastership'? I will ask Mr Meade-King,[240] as the representative of the staff, to second that resolution and I will now put it to the meeting.

(The passage in the Chairman's speech referring to the resignation and services of Mr Whatley has already been circulated to Governors.)

Mr B.L. Hallward appointed Headmaster.
You will doubtless have been interested to read on Wednesday last that the Council has appointed as his successor Mr B.L. Hallward, Fellow of Peterhouse,

---
[240] George Cyril Meade-King [*2451*: NT 1879–87]; member of the Council 1937–46.

Cambridge.[241] Mr Hallward is young, only 38, but his record is a brilliant one. A scholar of Haileybury and King's College, Cambridge, he took first class honours in the Classical Tripos and subsequently held the British School Studentship in Archaeology at Athens. After a short period as assistant master at Harrow he became a Fellow and Classical Lecturer at Peterhouse, and he has held a University Lectureship in Classics since 1926. He has been Deputy Public Orator at Cambridge and Senior Proctor. His publications include chapters in the *Cambridge Ancient History*;[242] he is joint editor of a forthcoming book on Homeric studies and of the *Classical Quarterly*. He has travelled in Greece, Albania and Turkey and lived in Athens and Vienna. He has distinguished himself at hockey [*and*] lawn tennis and is a keen mountaineer. We shall all wish him a long and happy Headmastership.

Reports to the Council 1925 x 1940

☐ *Whatley's reports demonstrate his demanding standards in scholarship, while revealing a sharp eye for administrative detail.*

[67]   January 1925. Head Master's Report to Council
[*HMs Reports. Typescript*]

The Christmas term was very satisfactory. There was much less illness than in the three previous terms, and although there was much bad weather we were very lucky in avoiding interruptions. Scholarships and exhibitions at Oxford and Cambridge have been won this year in the following subjects: Classics 3; Mathematics – 2; History – 2; Science – 2; Music – 1. This is not very good, but is as good as was expected. There may be one or two more to come.

The numbers of the whole School are smaller by ten than last term, though the number of boarders in the Upper School has slightly increased. Many applications for this term were refused, and a considerable number failed in the Entrance Examination. There is thus no sign at present of a general drop in numbers. There is at the moment a slight decline in the demand for places for day boys in the Junior School and for boarders in the Preparatory, but even this may be only temporary.

There has been no serious disciplinary trouble, and the general tone of the School seems to be satisfactory. The recently appointed masters are doing well so far.

The football XV had a very successful season. It will be less good next season, but I do not think we shall have a bad XV for some time. The masters who look after the football do their work extremely well, and are very successful in instilling modesty as well as skill.

The problem which is puzzling me most at the moment is the reorganisation of the work of the School. I am not attempting to make any big change at present, but changes will have to be made before long. The organisation of the top of the

---

[241] Bertrand Leslie Hallward [*HM7*: 1939–48]. He had been recommended by Birdwood, who had just stepped down from the Mastership of Peterhouse. For the the appointment see Winterbottom, *Clifton after Percival*, pp. 119–22, and more generally the same author's *Bertrand Hallward, First Vice-Chancellor of the University of Nottingham 1948–65: A Biography* (Nottingham, 1995).

[242] S.A. Cook, F.E. Adcock and M.P. Charlesworth (eds), *Rome and the Mediterranean 218–133 B.C.* (Cambridge Ancient History, viii, 1930), chapters 1–3 and 15 (on the Punic Wars); the Homer project nodded off, and Hallward wrote only one further scholarly article: *cf.* Winterbottom, *Hallward*, pp. 56–8.

School has never, I think, been quite satisfactorily adapted to the different conditions resulting from the introduction of the School Certificate Examinations.[243] On the Intermediate Side, which is now very popular, the teaching of the more advanced boys is divided up among too many masters who continue the mastership of a form lower in the School with a few hours each week with the more advanced boys. This is very good for the masters, but not so good for the boys. The Modern Language Side is not a success, and is declining in numbers. The Classical Side is prosperous and is understaffed. Young Classical scholars ought not to be placed in forms of nearly thirty boys. I should like to have another form on the Classical Side, and to get hold of a really first class young Classical master, but until there is a complete reorganisation of the whole School – for which I am not yet ready – I do not see my way to reduce the Modern Language staff by one man, though I could reduce it by half a man. I think we must continue to teach advanced modern languages, but at present there are only two or three boys in the advanced classes, and this is a great waste of teaching time.

Before long we ought to provide teaching in Biology. At present boys have to pay for this as an extra, but most schools of our type give it free as part of the ordinary school routine. Perhaps this can be arranged to start with the new labs.

We ought to have another ordained master on the staff, but the supply of chaplains is at present very small and poor.

I am going to ask the Council to allow the Cay scholarship for Mathematics[244] and the two Modern Language scholarships[245] to take the form of money prizes in future. At present they are often won by boys who are leaving, and do not receive any emolument. This causes a good deal of ill-feeling and seems unreasonable. A less satisfactory solution would be to limit them to boys under 17. The examination for entrance scholarships – combined as it is with an examination for various scholarships for boys of all ages already in the School – seems to me to have become too intricate and complicated. I am making it rather more simple this year, but hope to simplify it much more next year. Before doing so, I shall probably have to ask the Council if changes can be made in the conditions attaching to some of the scholarships.

The problem of the honour boards in Big School will come before the Council on the 4th February, and the Finance Committee has asked me to state the problem for members of the Council.

(i) The space for boards will at the present rate be used up in another 10 to 20 years.

(ii) The top row of names – the old ones which are printed large with great waste of space – are getting into very bad condition and something must be done with them. Should they be repainted (a) as they are or (b) in the smaller lettering at present used for the lower row? If (b) were decided on, quite half the space now occupied by

[243] The School and Higher School Certificates were introduced in 1918 by the Secondary Schools Examination Council, in association with the Education Act of that year: G. Sherington, *English Education, Social Change and War, 1911–20* (Manchester, 1981), pp. 89, 98 n. 86. The School and Higher School Certificates were replaced by GCE 'O' and 'A' levels respectively in 1951.

[244] Worth £20 *per annum*; established 1874 in memory of Charles Hope Cay [*M17*: 1865–9], the first of the School's endowed awards: *Clifton College Endowed Scholarships and Prizes* (Oxford, 1914), pp. 11–14.

[245] The Modern Languages Scholarship of £20 *per annum*, founded by Jewish benefactors in 1881 in recognition of the opening of a Jewish boarding house, and the Roquette-Palmer Palmer Scholarship of £20 *per annum* for French and German founded in 1896: *ibid.*, pp. 23–4, 45–6.

the upper row of names could be saved. But there would eventually be difficulty in getting all the boards in one continuing chronological order.

(iii) Should the honours recorded be in future restricted?

(iv) Should the boards at the north end recording public honours (not gained from the School) be altogether removed? To bring the boards up to date is out of the question.

(v) Should a committee be appointed to investigate the problem? The Finance Committee asked me to make this statement, thinking that some members of Council might like to look at the honour boards before the meeting.

26th January, 1925.   N. Whatley.

☐ *In his third year Whatley was asked by the Council to set down his long-term strategy. This gave him the opportunity to develop ideas mentioned in his termly reports, and to outline larger projects.*

[68]   October 1925. Ever onward
[*HM's Report on the Future of the School 1925. Typescript*]

Clifton College.
Report on the future of the School.

At the February meeting of the Council I was instructed to bring before the October meeting my ideas as to the changes and developments which would be required in the future in order to make Clifton the best possible school.[246] I was to say what seemed best for the School without concerning myself whether the suggested changes are financially possible or not. I do not find it easy to make such a report. Much is necessarily hypothetical and indefinite, and educational needs are bound to arise which cannot be foreseen at present but which are bound to affect the development of the School. I have arranged by remarks roughly under headings:

(1) Space.
(2) Buildings and equipment.
(3) Education.
(4) Houses.
(5) Miscellaneous and general.

(1) *Space.*

The greatest material need of the School is undoubtedly the need of more space. The ideal solution is to buy the Zoo.[247] I therefore put that first. It is the only chance of Clifton becoming the best, or equal to the best, school in buildings and design, and all questions of future building depend on this. It is therefore impossible to fill up a detailed picture of future buildings, etc. without a preliminary decision on this point.

In any case I hope we shall slowly acquire the Pembroke Road houses along the Close, even if it is at first only with the idea of letting them out as houses.

---

[246] So resolved instead of appointing a committee to consider the use and development of the College's estate and buildings: Council Minute Book 8, p. 69 (4 Feb. 1925).

[247] Bristol Zoo, on the edge of the Downs, had opened in 1836, and so was well established when the College became its neighbour to the south. Having adapted well to changing circumstances, it has refused to disappear.

Failing the Zoo, and if money were really no object, I think we should acquire Albert Road, get more space round the boarding houses, remove Watson's House altogether and have an open way through from the Memorial Arch to the New Close.[248] A new boarding house would have to be acquired or built to replace Watson's.

Beggar's Bush[249] is a great asset, but it can never be ideal for a public school to have to play most of its games so far off. (See later). If we had the Zoo, Beggar's Bush need not be used for so many boys.

(2) *Buildings*.

The most obvious future needs are:

(a) More class rooms. We are very badly off at the present moment. The old Science rooms[250] will give considerable relief, but as against that we are using one room (24) which is largely underground, and ought not to be used regularly, and there are several other half basement rooms which are very gloomy. Class rooms should be cheerful. For this last reason I hope that in due course all the coloured glass at present in class room windows will be removed.

(b) A proper lecture theatre or hall to seat the whole School, plus visitors, to be used for lectures, concerts, dramatic performances and ceremonies.[251] There are plenty of other uses for Big School. The present system requires constant shifting of chairs into and out of Big School. There is nowhere to stack the chairs, and the system is very expensive both in chairs and labour. The acoustics of Big School are very bad, and it is in many ways not an ideal room for many of the purposes for which it is now used.

One by one the public schools are building new halls of the type I have mentioned.

(c) A smaller lecture room is also required. We ought to have more lectures to boys in the highest forms but there is no suitable place. I hope the Physics Laboratory may be restored as a lecture room when the new laboratories are complete.

(d) The Workshop will one day have to be developed and the instruction given brought up to date. Eventually I think an entirely new building will be necessary.

(e) A new Museum. The old Museum is being gradually ousted by the Library, and this process must inevitably go on. Possibly some of the semi-basement class rooms could be converted into a Museum. School museums are a problem; they attract benefactions, some of which take up much space and are never looked at, but I do not think one can do without a museum altogether. And if a museum is to be any good at all someone must devote a good deal of time to looking after it.

(f) More Fives and Squash Courts. There are not nearly enough for present needs, and the demand increases.

(g) The present Town Rooms are rather small and it would add to the dignity and to the House life of the Towns if they could have larger quarters.[252]

(h) Eventually there must be a new Headmaster's house. This might be built in the Zoo if acquired. Otherwise 24 College Road is probably the most suitable.

---

[248] More usually 'the New Field', 4 acres west of the main site, acquired in 1890: Christie, *History*, pp. 121–2. The vision of a connecting boulevard, worthy of Haussmann or Mussolini, never materialised.

[249] 48-acre site at Abbot's Leigh across the Gorge, acquired in 1910: *ibid.*, pp. 166–7, 174.

[250] Along and above the East Cloister.

[251] The theatre, to become known as the Redgrave, was built in 1965, though on a smaller scale than here envisaged: Winterbottom, *Clifton after Percival*, pp. 251–6.

[252] Achieved with ingenuity in 1974: *ibid.*, p. 283.

(i) Various small things are wanted, e.g. a Headmaster's office not in the School House.

The present Marshal's office should be removed, and the archway between the north and south quadrangles fully opened up. Possibly the Headmaster and the Marshal could both have offices in the old Science buildings, near the Porter's Lodge.

Proper lavatories for the masters. These too might be made in the old Science buildings, near the masters' Common Room.

The general appearance and decoration of the buildings should eventually be improved, especially Big School, Big School stairs and the Chapel Cloisters.

(k) [*sic*] If the Zoo were ever obtained no doubt the haphazard group of buildings round the Gym would be thinned out. But I see no chance of doing this without acquiring the Zoo.

(l) Changes will be required in the boarding houses, but I am dealing with them under a separate heading.

Equipment.

The equipment of the class rooms could be considerably improved, but I do not put this very high on the list of things wanted. It is much more important to give up using those class rooms which are badly lighted, but we must before long provide proper tables for examination purposes, which will involve some expense.

(3) *Education.*

(a) *Subjects taught.* Small changes are constantly necessary but I do not foresee the need of any drastic innovation. Some considerable changes in organisation are necessary and I am at work on them now. The special needs seem to me to be for a general simplification of School organisation and better opportunities for giving special education to the abler boys at the top of the School. The proper arrangement for Modern Languages is also rather perplexing.

We ought, however, in my opinion, to supply teaching in Biology without extra charge. At present boys have to take it as an extra subject. I am also of opinion that the top of the School is understaffed. We want at least one more master at the top of the School who would be a specialist in History, and would be generally in charge of History teaching throughout the School.

(b) *Scholarships.* In my opinion the present eleemosynary system should be given up. More money is required both for scholarships and leaving exhibitions. I am making a separate report to the Council on this subject, but in the distant future I hope we shall have much more money available for these purposes than I have dared to suggest in that report.

(c) *Special Departments.*

(1) *Music* at Clifton is very good; a very large number of boys learn and its success is of great value to us. Boys come to Clifton because of the music. In many ways it would like to expand; in particular it would be a great convenience to have more cells for practising. I do not regard this as an immediate need,[253] but if ever we want to build on the north side of Guthrie Road we ought to remember that later on we may wish to expand the Music School.

(2) *Art* is rather overshadowed by music though as a matter of fact the Art teaching is good and quite a large number of boys do very well. But at present there is very little opportunity for giving general instruction in Art and the History of Art. Nor do

---

[253] These were provided in the 1962 extension.

the surroundings of the class rooms, the class rooms themselves, or even the busts in the Chapel Cloisters encourage artistic appreciation. We are behind many others schools in this and, later on, when there is more time and money, I think we ought to take the advice of experts.

The present Art School is a great improvement, so I gather, on the old, but a larger one will be required one day.

(3) *Workshop* (in so far as it is educational). Amateur carpentering is taught to boys quite adequately. More systematic workshop instruction is given to boys on the Engineering Side. But it is as far as I can judge, of an amateurish type, and we shall before long have to provide something better, though I hope it will never be necessary to develop practical engineering to the extent it has reached at schools like Oundle.[254] But we shall have to face the problem of the Workshop before long, and when we do there will be three main considerations: (a) the building itself, (b) the instruction given, and (c) the work done by the Workshop for the College, Houses etc. (See later).

(d) *The Junior School* is, in my opinion, greatly improved by its transfer to the Pembroke Road site,[255] and I think it is in a prosperous condition. It is also providing the Upper School with the best scholars we get. But my own opinion is that the Junior School ought to be more independent of the Senior School than it is at present. The Junior School suffers through being dependent for many little points of detail on the Headmaster. Eventually the master in charge of the Junior School ought to be given more responsibility and liberty, and be dependent on the Headmaster for general policy only. The more the Junior School can develop its own life, independently of the Upper School, the better for both. This cannot be done while we continue to employ extensively for certain subjects (French and Mathematics) the Senior School staff in teaching the Junior School. Ideally this may be sound. In practice it complicates the time-table very seriously, and I do not think results justify the difficulties involved. I hope that one day all the Junior School buildings can be grouped together. If we ever acquire the Zoo we might transfer the School to the New Close, and use Polack's and other houses in the neighbourhood as its boarding houses, handing the New Close over to the Junior School as its playing field. The present Junior School playing grounds are very inadequate. If we cannot get the Zoo, Hartnell's House and possibly Poole's also should eventually be transferred to the neighbourhood of the new Junior School buildings in Pembroke Road.

(e) *The Preparatory School* is of course on a peculiar footing. Pavey,[256] the Housemaster, has capital in it. When he goes the Council will probably want to re-consider the whole position. I do not believe there is any really valid reason, except space, for a separate Preparatory School. Eventually it should, I believe, be merged in a more independent Junior School.[257] There might be a special boarding house for the younger boys in such a School, but they should not be separated for work.

---

[254] Under F.W. Sanderson (Headmaster 1892–1922) Oundle had become the country's leading school for engineering, an achievement first celebrated by H.G. Wells in *The Story of a Great Schoolmaster* (1924). See also A.C. Percival, 'Some Victorian Headmasters', in Simon and Bradley, *Victorian Public School*, pp. 88–94; C. Freebain, *Sanderson of Oundle* (Oundle, 1992); R. Hansen, 'The technology workshops at Oundle', *International Journal of Technology and Design Education* 9 (1999), pp. 293–303.

[255] 94 Pembroke Road, to which the Junior School moved in 1924 when its existing building (of 1876) was demolished to make way for the new Science School.

[256] Reginald William Juxon Pavey [*5306*: ST 1897–1900; *M228*: 1914–28], Senior Master of the Preparatory School 1920–8.

[257] Effected institutionally in 1930, and physically with the opening of the new Pre School in 1933.

(f) *Gymnasium*. Gymnastics have fallen on evil days in all schools. The O.T.C. has killed them. But at present we cannot entirely dispense with a Gymnasium.

(4) *Houses*.

Two points will need much consideration in the future: (a) the Houses themselves, (b) the system of tenure.

(a) I think the Council know fairly well what the Houses are like. For the present they can go on with patching and small improvements, but a hundred or even fifty years hence, possibly even sooner, some of them will not be tolerated. Watson's may well have to go before the others. I have no definite suggestions to make. Any bold solution would be enormously expensive, and even if finance were no object the detailed solution would depend on the Zoo. More immediately the questions of the numbers in each House and the Waiting House system[258] will have to be reconsidered. Some of the Houses are very full – possibly too full. The Waiting House system is working quite well, but it is a rather hand to mouth arrangement. I do not recommend any immediate changes, but the present system should not be regarded as permanent.

(b) The system by which the Housemaster invests capital in his House and makes what profit he can is, I believe, doomed. The advantages were:

(1) The individual put up capital which could not have been found otherwise.

(2) The possibility of obtaining a lucrative Housemastership made schoolmastering more attractive.

(3) It saved the School from the necessity of arranging feeding, catering, etc.

(4) There was a strong encouragement to economical management.

(5) Losses in bad times did not all fall on the School.

These advantages do not all still hold good:

(1) Most masters now have no, or very little capital. This problem will come before the Council very soon.

(2) The chances of a master obtaining a Housemastership now that the staff is so large, are slight, and I doubt whether the prospect is as strong an attractive force as it was.

(3) The School does not get enough benefit out of good times, and in future I doubt whether Housemasters will stand the loss of bad times.

(4) Separate catering by Houses is not entirely satisfactory. Too much depends on the Housemaster's wife, and modern opinion condemns the system.

Eventually I feel fairly certain that the Housemaster will be paid a fixed salary, while the School takes the risks and the profits, and at least superintends the catering.

As to this last point:

(1) With a central hall this is easy and common even in large schools, but such a central hall seems impossible at Clifton.

(2) Therefore some system is wanted by which the House carries out feeding under School control and finance. The ideal system has not yet been found. Experiments are being tried elsewhere and we may as well await the result.[259]

---

[258] Boys who could not be accommodated in the established Houses were temporarily assigned to 'Small' or 'Waiting Houses'; from time to time these were consolidated for general purposes as the 'United House' (UH).

[259] Wartime exigencies at Bude were to be the catalyst for centralised catering on the return to Clifton. Much consideration was then given to the building of a new hall, but in the end the impossible was achieved by turning Big School into a multi-storey cafeteria.

But the present very complicated financial arrangements between the School and the Housemasters could, I believe, be simplified at once.[260]

Note on the Jews' House.

It is wonderfully patriotic and well behaved, and we get through it some credit for toleration, but it complicates School organisation, and if we were starting fresh I, personally, should not recommend it. But it has been so well conducted and so useful to the School in bad times that I think it would be quite impossible to abolish it now.

But I think it quite possible that we may have to consider this question in a few years time, owing to the lack of support from good class Jews. The latter seem increasingly not to want their sons to be segregated, and the social level of the Jews who come to Clifton tends to decline.[261]

(5) a. *Miscellaneous.*

(1) There is nothing in the School at present playing the part formerly played by the *School Mission*, which is now more or less independent and does not need or receive much actual help.[262] We could start another Mission, but I believe that the old type of Mission has now served its purpose, and that some other way should be found of interesting boys in public service. I have not yet decided exactly what should be done, though I think it possible that it should be something in connection with adult education.

Of course the Officers Training Corps does assist to give boys an idea of public service, and it takes up a fair amount of spare time which used to be free for other social purposes. The Preparatory School have Wolf Cubs, and I am certain that Boy Scout organisation should be started in the Junior School, but I am waiting for the right man and the right moment.[263]

(2) *Day boys.* There is a tendency more than among the boarders for the type to change. I think it will become necessary to limit the distance from the School at which day boys may live, or better, perhaps, to allow boys to attend from beyond a certain distance only if they can show that they are boys who might reasonably expect a public school education and that they cannot afford to come as boarders. The first part of this could not be put in our regulations. The point is that I do not want to exclude the sons of poor persons in south and east Bristol, but I do not see why we should take as day boys the sons of wealthy men who live three miles off.

In any case regular provision of mid-day meals at the School for day boys who want it would be a great advantage.

(3) *The Workshop* carries out School repairs. It is also available to do the work of those Housemasters who wish to employ it. Hardly any Housemasters do employ it because they claim that they can get the work done well much more cheaply by the ordinary tradesmen. Of course there is always a tendency to call official departments like our Workshop, expensive, but I believe it really is true that though the work done by the Workshop is, on the whole, very good, its charges are high, and when there

---

[260] Between 1931 and 1935 Whatley secured this in all the Houses (except in Polack's, with its distinct dietary requirements): Winterbottom, *Clifton after Percival*, pp. 79–80.

[261] Polack's lasted until 2005. It was then closed because of falling numbers, rather than the social considerations which had worried Whatley, and which had contributed to the closure of Cheltenham's Jewish House in 1923: D.O. Winterbottom, *Dynasty*, pp. 195–9; Morgan, *Cheltenham*, pp. 167–8.

[262] See below [117–20].

[263] The man was to be Martin Edward Hardcastle [*M275*: 1924–67], who set up the troop at Whatley's direction, over the head of the Junior School Headmaster: Winterbottom, *Clifton after Percival*, pp. 70, 89.

is an opportunity for re-organising this department (see above), I think the whole question of its system of charges should be thoroughly investigated.

(4) *Acoustics.* I should perhaps have emphasised under the heading of Buildings the badness of the acoustics of Big School and Chapel, especially the latter. It is true that most people, though not all, can learn to be audible in both places. But visiting preachers and lecturers, however carefully we choose them, can often not be heard by many of the boys. This is a very great pity. If ever we build the new lecture hall suggested above the problem of lectures may be solved. But the acoustics of Chapel must in some way be improved. We have tried several experiments which have made little difference, and I hope it will be possible to consult experts and to go on doing so until we find the right solution.

(5) *Transport to Beggar's Bush.* The arrangements by which boys are transported to Beggar's Bush in motor lorries are a constant source of anxiety, and there is without doubt some danger. There have been two accidents this term. We have elaborate rules which are intended to make this transport safe, but sixty boys travel in one lorry, and if the boys have any spirit at all it is obvious that in such crowded conditions there is always some danger. A different type of lorry holding fewer boys would be safer, but the expense would be very great.[264] Personally I shall never be quite happy while the present arrangements go on. Even if it were possible, which it is not, to send several masters out in each lorry there would still be some risk, and it is most undesirable for the general discipline of the School that masters should be used in this way. I have made the Sixth responsible for discipline on the lorries and they do their best.

(6) *Admissions.* On the whole the type of boy who is coming to Clifton, especially the type of those coming to the ordinary boarding houses, is of quite a good type. But we have less than our share of really able boys, and of boys from really interesting homes. It is very desirable in the interests of the other boys in the School that the number of these should be increased. I hope that it may be possible to make our scholarship examination more attractive, but it is also desirable that every means should be employed, except actual advertisement, of attracting such boys to come in the ordinary way without scholarships too.

[5]b. *General.* One of the strongest impressions I have received at Clifton is that it is a School where it has been made as difficult as possible for the individual boy to be criminal or lazy. Everything in and out of School is organised, almost every possible situation is provided for by rules and there is a most elaborate system of marks, orders and reports. The result is that there is probably no school where the average boy is more hard working and law abiding. At the present moment I believe it is especially as a good school for the average boy that Clifton has a reputation.

The danger of this system is that it easily becomes too mechanical and that the products of it may be rather wooden. There is rather a dearth of individuality and initiative among the boys at Clifton now and very few are of outstanding ability or interest. I think initiative should be encouraged rather more, but it will need great care to give it scope without losing the general average which we have at present.

What I mean is well illustrated by the discipline of the School. In the ordinary way this is good and in the ordinary School routine there is very little wrong doing. But when visible authority is absent or on unusual occasions such as the end of term, the boys in bulk seem to me rather unreliable, considering how high their ordinary

---

[264] From the outset the transport had cost £280 p.a.: Christie, *History*, p. 175.

standard is. They seem to me to depend too much on rules and authority and too little on an instinctive standard of their own. The orgy of noise which precedes the Christmas concert seems to me typical of this. I cannot help thinking that this is rather unworthy of the School, but it is widely accepted as a natural thing by many people in the neigbourhood and by many Old Cliftonians, some of whom take a prominent part in it.

In intellectual matters I think there is a little bit the same tendency to depend too much on authority, and the encouragement of marks and promotions and punishments. The work of the average boy is good, but it is not carried out from a very ideal standpoint. Here it is perhaps typical that much the commonest crime at Clifton is 'cribbing' and other forms of unfair work.

The manners of the School show the same thing. The ordinary Clifton boy is easy to deal with, and if there is a rule for his behaving in a particular way in a particular situation he probably obeys the rule quite satisfactorily. He is apt to be gauche in an unexpected situation. In Clifton as in all public schools there are now many sons of newly enriched families. It is not possible to rely on the homes for teaching manners.

I have mentioned this in order to show the Council where I think there is room for improvement in the ideal Clifton of the future. But I fully realise that these are matters in which the Council cannot be expected to help, and where improvement can only be carried out gradually through the influence of the staff.

[69]   March 1928. Head Master's Report to the Council
[*HMs Reports. Typescript*]

The death of Lord Haig made a very deep impression on the School.[265] There is a general feeling that something should be done to perpetuate his name here. The question which was discussed at the last Council meeting of making provision for visible memorials to distinguished Old Cliftonians is brought before us again by Lord Haig's death. I think Mr Whitehead will suggest that the Council should obtain a report from an expert on the possibility of converting the Chapel Cloister into a memorial cloister, which might be named after Lord Haig even if the work cannot be completed at once. There is also a general feeling that something might be done in memory of Lord Haig to assist officers who cannot otherwise afford to send their sons to Clifton. I am afraid that the chances of raising a considerable sum of money for this purpose are very slight, but it has struck me that the Council might be willing to admit one or two boys each year at reduced fees, such boys to be called Haig Exhibitioners. The School has sent £100 to the Haig Memorial Fund.

We have had a satisfactory term on the whole. There have been some cases of measles in the Junior School, and there was a short epidemic of influenza in the Upper School. But no one, so far, has been seriously ill except Dr Williams himself.[266] He has been in poor health all the term, and is now in a nursing home. I have made temporary arrangements for carrying on his work this term. I very much hope that he will be fit to return next term. If he is not, some fresh arrangement will have to be made. I hope to know about this more definitely by the date of the Council meeting.

---

[265] Haig died on 29 January 1928. Clifton's memorial to its greatest son would actually be the bronze statue on the Parapet, unveiled in 1932: below **[445–52]**.
[266] Dr E. Cecil Williams, one of the College Medical Officers from 1921 to 1934.

I have appointed as Mr Pavey's successor E.G. Sharp,[267] who is at present teaching at Temple Grove, Eastbourne. He is an attractive person with a very good record, and a wife who will, I think, be a great asset. Mr Sharp is coming down to see me before the Council meeting and I think he will wish to propose certain alterations in the House. I will bring these if possible before the meeting of the Finance Committee on Wednesday, the 21st. Also the question of Mr Sharp's salary.

Major Muirhead,[268] who is in command of the Officers' Training Corps, has been in poor health for some time. I think he is attempting too much, and I have told him that he must resign the command of the Officers' Training Corps at the end of the present term. He will be succeeded by Major Crawford.[269] Major Crawford is House Tutor of North Town. He has done most valuable work in that capacity and it is most desirable that he should continue to do this work as far as possible. But North Town now has one hundred members, which is really too many for one Housemaster and one Tutor to look after adequately. I ask the Council to approve of an out-House Tutor being appointed when a Town House contains more than 80 boys, at a salary of £25 per annum.

The general report on the day boys which the Council asked me to make will be circulated before the meeting.

A few years ago the Council appointed a sub-committee to examine all boarding houses. The committee made a thorough examination of each house accompanied by the Housemaster. But of that committee, unfortunately, only Mr Tribe[270] is still on the Council. The boarding houses are not good, and they will provide the Council with constant problems in the future. It seems desirable that the Council should know all about them. May I suggest that a fresh sub-committee be appointed, consisting of Mr Loveday,[271] Mr Eberle,[272] and, if he is elected at the general meeting, Mr Abbot?

Of ordinary School news there is not very much, but I think that the School is at this moment in a very healthy and happy condition. The general interest in intellectual matters is certainly increasing, though there is at present no increase in the number of outstandingly able boys. We managed to come out equal first in an inter-school boxing meeting which was held at Clifton this term. But this success was due more to spirit than to skill, and I hope we shall be able to improve the technical skill of our boxing in the future.

N. Whatley.

☐ *Whatley was seriously ill throughout the first term of 1933 and the Second Master F.L. Carter*[273] *took command*

[70]   Lent Term 1933. Acting Head Master's Report to the Council
[*HMs Reports. Typescript*]

[267] Edmund Godfrey Sharp [*M288*: 1928–46] became first Headmaster of the new Pre (the amalgamated Junior and Preparatory Schools) in 1930; from 1946 to 1952 he was Bursar and Secretary to the Council.
[268] James Alexander Orrock Muirhead [*M231*: 1914–49].
[269] John Kenneth Bulfin Crawford [*M262*: 1921–61]; see below **[206]**.
[270] F.N. Tribe, as above **[64]**.
[271] Dr Thomas Loveday, Council 1926–39; Vice–Chancellor of Bristol University 1922–44.
[272] Victor Fuller Eberle [*5499*: NT 1899–1905], Council 1927–74.
[273] Frank Lutton Carter [*M167*: 1900–36].

General.

A year ago the Headmaster warned the Council that we could not hope to be so successful in the ensuing year in the matter of university scholarships; his forecast was correct, as last term we only gained three, but it must be remembered that several boys who would normally have gone up for scholarships last December, were, thanks to their ability, able to obtain them a year earlier. If we did not gain scholarships, we were unusually successful in the examination for the Services, eleven out of twelve candidates obtaining admission to one or other branch of the Services, and amongst them the first two in the Cranwell list, the first boy getting higher marks than the top boy into Woolwich. So far as other School activities are concerned, a good standard was maintained.

I cannot better illustrate the satisfactory tone which, I think, exists in the School than by reference to the influenza outbreak in the first ten days of this term. At the peak three hundred boys and twelve masters were out at once. The behaviour of the boys was wholly admirable: if a master did not turn up to take a form, a boy reported to the Marshal, or the form went on quietly with what work they could. There was no ragging or disorder of any kind. As it was in the School, so too it was in the two Sanatoria. The Matron and nurses could not have spoken more highly of the conduct of the boys, particularly during one twenty-four hours, when nurses and House staff were all ill together, and charwomen were unavailable.

Expulsion.

I regret to report that Edie (Wa.H)[274] was expelled last term for gross misbehaviour.

The Staff and municipal elections.

I think it advisable to ask the Council to pass a resolution with regard to masters standing as candidates in the municipal elections for the Town Council. For some years past one man has been standing in the Labour interest; in the last six months another has put up twice for the Conservative party.[275] The work of the Town Council is done mainly by committees, and the demands upon the time of a man would render it impossible for him to give of his best to the School – and the latter must come first. Apart from that a good deal of heat is engendered in local politics, and it seems to me undesirable for men on our teaching staff to be mixed up publicly in such matters. There are other ways in which they can help, if they wish to, in the social life of the City.

Revival of Big Side Levée.

Old Cliftonian members of the Council may be interested to learn that Big Side Levée, which had fallen into abeyance for the last fifteen years, was re-started last term on modified lines, at the instance of the boys themselves. It exists rather in the nature of a club, membership of which is strictly confined to boys in the Upper part of the School, who are prominent in work or games. A certain number of boys

---

[274] Thomas Ker Edie [*10409*: WaH 1930–2].

[275] The Labour candidate was Robert Francis St John Reade [*M259*: 1921–34]. Council had already curbed his larger ambitions by ruling (Oct. 1925) that a master could not stand for Parliament, but Reade's local campaigning remained an embarrassment. When R.W.B. Garrett [*M239*: 1919–40] stood against Labour in the City elections of 1932, Carter was able to recommend this ostensibly impartial ban on all politicking by masters, which the Council endorsed (24 Mar. 1933). Reade appealed vigorously, but succeeded only in manoeuvring himself into resignation. Two years later he was at last elected to the City Council: RS2/304. Winterbottom, *Clifton after Percival*, pp. 107–9.

become members automatically, others on the proposal of the Head of the School. It can act in a consultative capacity, and membership carries with it certain privileges. It promises to be a useful body, by means of which the Head of the School can enforce discipline amongst the more prominent boys, as membership is considered an honour, and expulsion a disgrace.

Preparatory School.

Part of the Preparatory School has been in use since the beginning of the term. The arrangements for the opening are in course of preparation.[276] I hope that we shall be able, by a judicious use of the press and the local secretaries of the Overseas Branch of the Old Cliftonian Society, to make known to prospective parents overseas the opportunity which it offers them of getting their sons settled at a public school at an early age.

Preparation of boys for Commercial Careers and the Consular Service.

Numbers, I regret to say, have continued to decrease, though the fall at the beginning of this term was accentuated by the unusual number of Service entries. In this connection and in view of the great competition now existing amongst the public schools, it has seemed to me wise to try and make known the curriculum of a form in the top block of the School which is admirably suited for the consular services and the higher posts in the commercial world. With this end in view I drew up a circular which I sent with a letter to certain business houses with which I have been in touch, and to Old Cliftonians prominent in business. I quote from the reply of one of them:

'It would not take long to make known to big business that Clifton was *the* place to look for likely recruits. You are on the right lines, and I am delighted to see Clifton going ahead in this direction.'

I am at present trying to get into touch with some of the big foreign banking corporations, who recruit their staffs in England, and to whom, I think, the type of boy we produce at Clifton should be of value.

Conclusion.

The position of Acting Headmaster might not be an easy one, and I should like to close this report with a tribute to the great help I have received from all my colleagues.

F.L. Carter.

☐ *It will nevertheless be noted that Carter took some decisive action during his regency.*

[71]   29 March 1940. Chairman of Council's report to the Governors
[*Council Minute Book 13, pp. 121–4. Typescript*]

I am glad to welcome these [*recte* those] Governors who have been able to come in these difficult times[277]; their presence is the best possible indication of the real interest which they take in the School.

I will deal first with the most important business, the accounts of the School for the year ending December 31st, 1939. The loss is in fact nearly the same as for the year 1938, viz. £5668. While last year the accounts showed an adverse balance of

---

[276] The opening on 6 May was performed by the Duchess of Atholl (wife of the 8th Duke), who had been Parliamentary Secretary to the Board of Education from 1924 to 1929.
[277] There were 21 present including Council members.

£5397, of that £3862 was in the form of non-recurring expenditure as is the case this year.

A large portion of this loss is accounted for by a drop in the profits made upon the boarding houses, a drop necessarily caused by a reduction in the number of boarders. This item accounts for about £2000. This year too there has been considerable expenditure on the repair of buildings which we hope will not recur, and of course there has also been a large reduction in tuition fees.

To meet the deficit several drastic economies have been introduced. Some reductions have been made in the number of the staff, though only by not filling vacancies as they occur. Watson's House has been closed, mainly as a measure of war time economy. We closed the House with reluctance, in view of the associations it must have for so many Old Cliftonians, and hope it may be possible to reopen it again later on. Meanwhile the boys have been welcomed in other Houses, which of course they help to fill, and Mr Beachcroft[278] who had Watson's has taken Mr Gee's place at Dakyns', Mr Gee having joined the Army.[279] We are letting the House to the British Broadcasting Corporation at a rental,[280] which will make a considerable contribution to our finances, and are also relieved of the rates upon it.

We are now, therefore, in a better position to face a further drop in the number of boarders, if such occurs, as some think is inevitable.

As was the case during the Great War, the Housemasters and masters have most generously agreed to a cut in their salaries, which amounts to more than £1300. The capitation fee per boy in the Houses in both Schools, payable to the Housemasters, has also been reduced. But that we should have to accept so great a sacrifice from a staff which is facing the present difficult times with so much courage is a matter of great regret.

The effect of these economies should be a saving of at least £5000, part of which may, of course, be counteracted by a rise in prices or a further reduction in numbers.

Our large overdraft at the bank, which of course represents a debt for which provision must be made, and which also involves a heavy charge for bank interest, has been increased over the last 4 years by reason of the capital expenditure of about £10,000 involved in modernising and equipping the Houses. We are most anxious to clear off a portion of this debt in order to improve the financial position of the School.

In January, 1940 the numbers of the School were 627 as compared with 650 in January, 1939. They have been as high as 781 in 1931; and may I again remind you that our financial position depends largely upon a steady supply of boys, and ask you to leave no stone unturned to help us in this matter. The School has now a large body of Governors – we have actually about 100. If every Governor could bring one boy to the School within the next two years, our troubles would be halved during the difficult years which face us. As you can see from the report, no one can have any possible hesitation in recommending a school with such an educational record: the recent achievements of Old Cliftonians, too, suggest that our essential standards do not alter. We all tend to look back to the greatness of our own day, but if we ask

---

[278] Samuel Porten Beachcroft [*7249*: NT, WaH 1911–19; *M277*: 1925–65]; House Master of Watson's since 1935, and of Dakyns' from this time till 1960.

[279] Charles Hilton Rodney Gee [*M267*: 1922–68], who had fought with distinction in the Great War; House Master of Dakyns' since 1935; after returning to his Regiment in the Second War, he resumed charge of Watson's from 1946 to 1955.

[280] The Variety Department and the BBC Symphony Orchestra were evacuated to Bristol.

ourselves the question 'Is Clifton's record in any way less distinguished today than formerly?' the answer must inevitably be 'No'.

By an oversight the resignation of Sir Rowland Whitehead from the Council was not referred to in the Annual Report, but while expressing your regret at his resignation, which is only due to ill-health, I am glad to place upon record the indebtedness of the School to Sir Rowland. He joined the Council as long ago as 1901 and became its Chairman in 1930. Members of the Council will confirm how wisely he presided over their deliberations and what a keen and constant interest he took in the affairs of the School. However much he was suffering he never spared himself in its service.

We have also lost the help of Dr Loveday, well known everywhere as Vice-Chancellor of Bristol University; he too had served upon the Council for many years[281] and his sound advice and humanistic outlook were always gladly offered and warmly welcomed.

We are glad to welcome to the Council Mr Christopher Cox,[282] Fellow of New College, Oxford, himself an Old Cliftonian, who is doing most responsible work in the Colonial Office as Adviser in Education. He will bring with him a knowledge of the School itself and of wider spheres of education.

In the past year I regret to say that several Old Cliftonians who were Governors of the School have died. Mr R.E. Bush, one of the oldest living Old Cliftonians, his name a household word in the annals of the School:[283] also Colonel W.J. Gaitskell[284] and I would particularly mention Colonel W.P. Hewett,[285] for many years Secretary of the Old Cliftonian Society, who devoted so much time and enthusiasm to the School he loved so well. On March 21st, 1939, Dr J.E. King, Headmaster during the difficult years of the Great War, died in his 81st year, beloved by Cliftonians of his own period at School and by hundreds of boys during the period of his Headmastership.

The only work of importance done in the boarding houses has been the practical completion of the studies in School House. These studies are now really attractive and a great addition to the House.

A new roof to the Workshop has been built by our own staff and the interior renovated and redecorated. Arts and crafts of various kinds are now taught there with increasing success.

You will remember that last year I spoke of the need of a new Swimming Bath. In the present circumstances we have decided to recondition the existing Bath and to make it water-tight at a cost of about £600. The Headmaster has had offers of substantial help in finding the necessary capital sum to cover the cost, offers with which other Old Cliftonians might like to be associated.

I am happy to be able to report that the new changing rooms for Town boys and the modernised Gymnasium were ready in September, 1939, and I am glad to refer again to the generosity of Mr Melville Wills[286] which made this work possible. The Gymnasium is now a fine building, excellently lighted and equipped and the

---

[281] Since 1927; he was Vice-Chancellor from 1922 until 1944.
[282] Sir Christopher William Machell Cox [*7573*: WaH 1913–18]; member of the Council 1939–75; knighted 1950.
[283] Robert Edwin Bush [*333*: ST 1865–75]; born in 1855; he had been captain of the XI, and had played for Gloucestershire while still at School; President of the OCS 1930–1: *Centenary Essays*, pp. 33, 152.
[284] Walter James Gaitskell [*1358*: SH 1873–6].
[285] Walter Pearse Hewett [*3602*: PHP, OH 1886–94], Hon. Secretary of the OCS 1919–35, and Hon. Treasurer from 1936 until his death in 1939.
[286] Walter Melville Wills [*1168*: NT 1872–9]; also a benefactor to Bristol University.

changing-rooms have made the lives of many Town boys far easier than those of their predecessors.

It is indeed with a great debt of gratitude that we owe to so many benefactors in the past, whose generosity has equipped their School so magnificently with new buildings. The Preparatory School, the Science School and the Pavilion all bear witness to their public spirit. That the School has shown itself specially worthy of the Science School is shown by the results at Cambridge this year where seven first class Honours in Science were obtained, including the top place in Part II.

The work of the School during the past year has been fully abreast of those which preceded it. 48 Higher Certificates and 118 School Certificates were gained. In the Higher Certificate there were 29 distinctions: in itself evidence of the high standard of education maintained.

One very welcome piece of news is that the Merchant Venturers' Society of Bristol have undertaken to provide the School with a sum of money to provide bursaries for boys from the age of 13, a generous gift from a Society which has for years interested itself in the education of this City. We are glad to think that we may thus be brought into closer connection with this great fellowship of which Bristol is so justly proud, and we look forward to electing to the Council Mr Gerald Beloe, the Treasurer of the Society.[287] Mr Victor Fuller Eberle has played a notable part in the matter which I should like to record. And in close connection with this benefaction is that of the bursary offered by Mr E. Fuller Eberle in memory of Mr J. Fuller Eberle,[288] also bursaries from Lt Colonel F.G. Robinson, Mr Foster Robinson, for many years a member of the Council, and Mr F.C. Burgess.[289] The total capital sum represented is considerable and we are indeed grateful for this further evidence of Bristol's interest in the School.

The important and responsible part played by Old Cliftonians in the war is at least suggested, though by no means represented, by the list of appointments appearing in the Report. For the first time in the history of the School an Old Cliftonian and a member of our Council, Lord Caldecote, sits with dignity and authority on the Wool Sack.[290]

You will also have in mind that the late Secretary of State for War, Mr Hore Belisha, is an Old Cliftonian.[291] As also Air Marshal Barrett [*recte* Barratt], Air Officer Commanding in Chief the British Air Forces in France.[292]

□ *Sir Robert Witt concluded by assuring the Governors that they would not wish him to repeat what he had said 'at some length' the previous year about Whatley's resignation* **[66]**, *and by inviting them to meet the new Head Master at lunch.*

---

[287] McGrath, *Merch. Venturers*, p. 484. Gerald Harry Beloe was a member of the Society from 1906, Master 1922–3, and Treasurer from 1930 to his death in 1944; member of College Council 1940–4: *ibid.*, pp. 452 & n. 55, 559, and *passim*.

[288] Victor Fuller Eberle [*5499*: NT 1899–1905] and Ellison Fuller Eberle [*4881*: NT 1894–9] were sons of James Fuller Eberle [*252*: Town 1864].

[289] Norman Francis Clifford Burgess [*7979*: ST 1916–18].

[290] Thomas Walter Hobart Inskip, Viscount Caldecote of Bristol [*3603*: 1886–94]; former MP for Central Bristol and Secretary of State for the Dominions; ennobled on his appointment as Lord Chancellor at the start of the War, but in May 1940 he briefly returned to his former ministerial post; thereafter Lord Chief Justice 1940–6.

[291] Isaac Leslie Hore-Belisha, Baron Hore-Belisha (1954) [*6673*: PH 1907–12], Secretary of State for War since 1937, had been sacked by Chamberlain in January 1940 after falling out with most of the high command and many of his Cabinet colleagues. Though Belisha's political career was turbulent, the eponymous beacon is a benign legacy of his time as Minister of Transport (1934–7).

[292] Sir Arthur Sheridan Barratt [*6337*: NT 1905–9]; knighted July 1940, retired as Air Chief Marshal.

SECTION V: NOTICES AND REGULATIONS

[72] 13 February 1863. Notice of opening a Preparatory School
[*Guard Book 1860–77. Printed*]

Clifton College,
February 13th, 1863.

My dear Sir,

I beg to inform you that arrangements have been made for commencing a Preparatory School, in connection with the College, after Easter.

It will be opened on Wednesday, the 15th of April, and will be under the immediate supervision of the Head Master, but with separate schoolrooms, boarding-house, and playground.

Boys will be admissible to it at the age of six years; and will be moved up into the College as they are found fit for promotion; but none will be allowed to stay in it after the age of thirteen.

The tuition fees are fixed at £12 per annum, for boys under eight, and at £16 for boys over eight and under eleven years of age, if they are nominated by a shareholder of the College; if not so nominated, there is in each case an extra charge of £4 per annum.

For boys over eleven the fees are the same as in the College.

The charge for board is fixed at £42 per annum; for day boarders at £12. No extras.

Our object in opening this School is to secure that boys shall come into the College thoroughly grounded in the rudiments of English, Latin, and French.

Special attention will be paid to Spelling and Writing, Latin and French grammar, Geography, English History, and Arithmetic; and Greek will be taught to all who may be ready to begin it.

By this means we hope that boys will escape the discomfort and loss of time, which they inevitably suffer in changing from one system of teaching to another, or on coming into a school imperfectly prepared or badly grounded.

Thinking that you may perhaps feel an interest in this scheme, I have taken the liberty of thus announcing it to you.

If you wish to send any boys, I shall be glad of an early intimation.

I am, my dear Sir, yours faithfully,
J. Percival, Head Master.

☐ *Confusingly this became known as the Junior School, and from 1874 a separate Preparatory School was established for boys under eleven. The two elements merged in 1930.*

[73]   April 1867. Pocket money
[Guard Book 1860–77. Printed]

Clifton College,
April, 1867.

Dear Sir,

I wish to draw your attention to a change which I have found it desirable to make with regard to weekly pocket money. Hitherto every boarder in the College has been allowed a shilling a week by his House Master, unless his parent preferred a different arrangement. From this date every boy will be allowed a shilling a week, and no exceptions made.

As I have observed that some boys seem to bring too much money with them from home, I should feel obliged if you will limit your son's allowance to a moderate sum.

The Boarding House Master will gladly pay all subscriptions to games and charge them in the account, if you instruct him to do so. This I should recommend, especially in the case of younger boys.

I am, dear Sir, your obedient servant,
J. Percival.

P.S. I do not intend the above change to apply to the Junior School.

[74]   July 1867. General and boarders' rules
[Guard Book 1860–77. Printed]

Clifton College.
Rules &c.

1. No boy shall enter or return to the College from a house in which there has been any infectious disease within the three preceding months, without giving previous notice, and obtaining permission.

2. No boy allowed to be absent from the College unless detained at home by illness.

3. All coats must be either black or dark mixture; all neckties black; black hats are worn on Sundays by all boys above the Junior School, those in the Junior School wearing caps; on other days all wear caps made for the College, or straw hats with a peculiar[293] ribbon. These can be purchased in Clifton.

4. Every boy must acquaint himself with the bounds, as described in the map fixed up in the College Cloisters. Any boy going beyond these bounds must take with him a note from his parents, justifying his doing so.

5. There is a calling over in the large School-room on every half-holiday. Attendance at this is compulsory on all extra half-holidays, and on Thursdays, unless a note be obtained previously from the Form Master, and countersigned by the Head Master. For absence on Saturdays a note must be previously obtained from the Form Master.

---

[293] Meaning of specific design (not jocular).

6. There is a certain hour in the evening (varying with the season) after which no boy must be out of his own home without the express sanction of his parents given for some special purpose. Any boy met by a master after this hour will be required to produce that sanction.

7. Every boy must attend the afternoon service in the College Chapel on Sundays. The morning service is excused, if the parents express a wish in writing to that effect.

J. Percival,
Head Master.

Rules &c., for boarders

1. [*beginning as no. 1 above*] without giving previous notice to the master of the boarding house, and obtaining permission.

2. On the admission of any boy into the College, a certificate of good conduct and character is required from his former master or tutor.

3. A weekly allowance of one shilling is given to each boy for pocket money, and charged in the account at the end of the term, unless the parent should desire a different arrangement. This allowance is liable to be taxed for wilful damage or mischief, or for replacing books lost or destroyed through carelessness.

4. [*as no. 3 above*].

5. Every article of clothing must be distinctly marked with the owner's name in full, and an exact list should be sent in his box. Every boy brings six towels.

Every boy should have a brass label attached to his keys, with his name engraved on it.

J. Percival.

[75]   25 October 1869. Hampers
[*Guard Book 1860–77. Printed*]

Clifton College,
October 25, 1869.

Dear Sir,

We sent a Notice last term about hampers, which seems to have been interpreted by many parents as more stringent than it was intended to be.

I now wish to state that the experience of the present term has, in the opinion of the masters, proved that it is better for boys in regard to health not to have hampers sent, but that rather than make a permanent rule on the subject I leave it to the discretion of parents, whether they send anything of the kind now and then or not, it being clearly understood that no wine or drink of any kind be ever sent, either with a boy or to him, unless it be through the House Master, and by doctor's order.

I am, dear Sir, yours faithfully,
J. Percival.

[76]   Lent Term 1872. Dress code and money supply
[*Guard Book 1860–77. Printed*]

Notice to Parents.

As I find that our rules about dress are very frequently forgotten, I wish all parents kindly to observe that we expect every boy to wear *black coat or jacket and black tie*. We prefer young boys wearing the black jacket and the Eton collar.

I have also observed that many parents neglect our rule, which says that no money should be *sent to boys in the course of the term except through the House Master*. I cannot but think that every parent who sends money to a boy privately does harm both to him and to others, and on that account I should feel obliged if it were never done.

J. Percival,
Head Master.

[77] Michaelmas Term 1872. Rules for the Junior School
[*Guard Book 1860–77. Printed*]

Clifton College
Special rules for the Junior School

1. Wheeler's shop is out of bounds before dinner, except during the break.[294]

2. Day boys who do not intend to play any game must go home directly after school; and, if they play, they must go home when the game is over, unless they remain on the Junior School ground.

3. Boarders (unless they have special leave from their House Master) must be either in their Houses, on their own ground or Fives Courts, or on the way to or fro, except when the Upper boys are in School.

4. Games are compulsory for boarders on all half holidays, unless they have leave from their House Master to be absent.

5. Junior School boys may watch Big Side matches from the slope immediately in front of the School House garden, but no nearer to the Chapel, and from no other part of the Close.

6. The punishment for breaking any of the above rules is, for the first offence, 150 lines of Latin for the Fourths, 100 lines of English for the Third, 75 lines of English for the Upper Second, and 40 lines of English for the Lower Second and First; and, for the second offence, boys will be sent up to the Head Master.[295] The above impositions are to be written in round hand upon double-lined paper.

7. Any boy going beyond the Close, except on his way to or from School, must take with him a note from his parents or House Master justifying his doing so, and stating where he is going.

8. There is a calling over in the Junior School shed in the Close on every half holiday, at three o'clock. Attendance at this is compulsory on all half holidays, for the three highest forms, unless a note be obtained previously from the Form Master; or unless a boy is detained at home for some special reason, which must be specified in a note to the form master the next morning. Day boys in the three lowest forms may be excused altogether if parents express a wish in writing to that effect to the form master at the beginning of each term.

9. There is a certain hour in the evening (varying with the season) after which no boy must be out of his own home without the express permission of his parents, or, in the case of a boarder, of his House Master for some special purpose. Any boy met by a master after this hour will be required to produce that sanction.

---

[294] Charles Wheeler was a bread and biscuit baker living in Portland Place: *Directory* (1872), p. 247. The booth he ran in the College grounds was the first known ancestor of what is called the 'Grubber': Christie, *History*, pp. 79–81, quoting various dissatisfied customers (from 1872: 'to go into it is enough to take away one's appetite'; from 1874: 'the worst possible stuff is sold at the highest possible price').

[295] That is to say, for a beating.

[78]   19 November 1872. Advance booking
[*Guard Book 1860–77. Printed*]

Clifton College,
Nov. 19, 1872.
Dear Sir,
    I take this opportunity[296] of mentioning that, as our boarding houses are at present quite full, and it seems probable that we shall be obliged to disappoint some applicants for admission, it would be well, in case any of your friends wish their boys to come to us, that they should enter their names with the master whom they would wish to take them some time beforehand. I have been led to mention this by the difficulty I have lately experienced on several occasions in accommodating the brothers and other relatives of boys who are here or have been here.
                    I am, dear Sir, yours very faithfully,
                                    J. Percival.

☐ *The following regulations were re-issued with minor modifications throughout the period covered by this volume.*

[79]   6 June 1882. Bye-Laws.
[*Printed booklet*]

Bye-Laws and Regulations,
For the Government of Clifton College, made and passed by the Council of the said College.

Nominations and conditions of admission and dismissal of boys.
    1. Every nomination of a boy by a Governor or donor shall be made in writing under his or her hand and be delivered to the Secretary, who shall present the same to the Council at the next meeting after receiving the same, and enter the same in the minutes of the proceedings.
    2. Nominations by the Council shall be recorded in the minutes of the meeting at which such nominations shall be made.
    3. Subject to the provisions in the Charter all boys nominated by the Council or of whose nomination by Governors the Council shall have received notice, shall be admitted in order of priority of nomination, except that scholars and exhibitioners shall have priority of admission.
    4. Fourteen days before the admission of any boy to the College, a declaration, as nearly as circumstances will admit, in the form set forth in the schedule hereto,[297] and signed by the parent or guardian of such boy or by some other person whose declaration shall be satisfactory to the Council, shall be sent to the Secretary, together with a certificate of good conduct and character from the former master or tutor, if any, of the boy, which shall state the length of time that he has been with such master or tutor.
    5. Every candidate for admission shall be required to pass such an examination as the Council may from time to time determine. Such examination shall be conducted

---

[296] Misprinted 'opportuuity'.
[297] Here omitted; to same effect and in much the same words as Form D in the schedule to the Articles of Association **[7]**.

by the Head and Assistant Masters in such mannner as the Head Master shall direct.

6. No boy shall be admitted whose character shall not be satisfactory to the Head Master or who shall fail to pass the examination required by the Council.

7. Except by special permission of the Head Master no boy shall remain in the Preparatory School after the end of the term or holiday in which he shall attain the age of 11 years, nor in the Third Form of the Junior School after the end of the term or holiday in which he shall attain the age of 13 years; nor in the Junior School after the end of the term or holiday in which he shall attain the age of 14 years; nor in the Lower Third Form of the College after the end of the term or holiday in which he shall attain the age of 15 years; nor in the Upper Third Form after the end of the term or holiday in which he shall attain the age of 16 years; nor in the Fourth Form after the end of the term or holiday in which he shall attain the age of 17 years; nor in the Fifth Form after the end of the term or holiday in which he shall attain the age of 18 years.

8. Except by special permission of the Head Master no boy shall remain in the School after the end of term or holiday in which he shall attain the age of 19 years; or if by reason of misconduct or want of diligence he shall have remained in the same form for four terms.

9. No boy shall attend the School as a day boy unless he reside with a relative, or if an orphan with his guardian, or other person, who in the judgment of the Head Master stands to him in loco parentis.

10. No boy shall attend the School as a boarder unless he board with some person who has a license [*sic, ter*] from the Head Master to take boarders.

11. No boy shall be admitted to the College, either originally or after any vacation, if afflicted with any disease or infirmity which, in the opinion of the medical attendant of the College, may render it inexpedient to receive him. The payment in advance, for a boy so refused, shall be returned. In case an infectious disorder shall affect a boy, or any inhabitant of the house where he may be or may have been resident, immediate notice thereof shall be given to the Head Master; and such boy shall not be allowed to return or be admitted to the College until the Head Master shall be satisfied, either by the certificate of a medical man or otherwise, that there is no risk of infection.

12. If any boy shall at any time fail to attend at the commencement of any term or be taken or kept away from the College during term (except with the Head Master's sanction), he shall not be admitted, or re-admitted as the case may be, without the permission of the Head Master.

Boarders.

13. Licenses to keep boarding-houses, or to take boarders, shall be granted by the Head Master, subject to the approval of the Council. Such licenses shall be revocable by him with the consent of the Council. No payment on account of goodwill shall be made directly or indirectly on the succession to a boarding-house.

Facilities for day boys.

14. Day boys shall be required to sleep at home, but with the consent of the Head master may have their meals at any place previously approved by him.

Terms and holidays.

15. There shall be three terms in each year, a Spring term, a Summer term, and an Autumn term; and three corresponding periods of holiday.

The Spring holiday shall begin about the middle of April, and shall not exceed three weeks. The Summer holiday shall begin in July, and shall not exceed seven weeks and two days. The Christmas holiday shall begin in December, and shall not exceed four weeks and two days. The precise days of the commencement and end of the terms and holidays shall be as the Head Master shall appoint. The Council may from time to time increase or diminish the length of the holidays.

Payments for nomination, tuition, boarding, and otherwise.

16. The fee for nomination of each by the Council shall be £5 per annum.

The School fees for each boy shall be – £25 per annum.

The charges for boarding in the ordinary boarding houses shall be as follows:

For each boy of the age of 13 years and upwards – £72 per annum.

For each boy under the age of 13 years – £60 per annum.

Sanatorium fee for each boarder – £1 1s. per annum.

Charge for dinner in a master's House for a day boy:

In Junior School – £5 0 0 per term.

In College – 6 0 0 per term.

Special rates are to be arranged for as to delicate boys and for boys waiting for vacancies in the ordinary boarding houses.

In addition to the above the following fees are to be paid:

Laboratory fee for private instruction for each boy using both the Chemical and Physical Laboratories – 4 0 0 per term.

Using only one – 2 16 0 per term.

Class instruction in Physical or Chemical Laboratory including use of apparatus and chemicals each boy – £0 10 10 per term.

Workshop fee for each boy using the Workshop – 1 5 0 per term.

Gymnasium – 0 10 6 per term.

Swimming baths and instruction in swimming, Summer term – 0 10 0 per term.

Spring and Autumn terms – 0 5 0 per term.

The boys in the Preparatory School will have the use of the Baths and Gymnasium without payment.

No extra fees shall be charged except such as may be allowed by the Head Master with the approval of the Council for extra instruction applied for by the parent or guardian of the boy, or person standing to him in loco parentis, and required for some special purpose; and no other charges than those above mentioned shall be made except for books and other materials supplied in the College with the sanction of the Head Master and requisites supplied to boarders by or under the order of their House Masters, whose charges and accounts shall all be subject to the supervision of the Head Master.

All fees and charges shall be paid to the Treasurer of the College. The fees and charges payable per annum shall be paid in three equal parts, one part in respect of each term. The nomination, boarding and school fees shall be paid in advance one week previously to each term; but the boarding fees of boys at present in the School may be arranged to be paid otherwise if desired. All other payments shall be made one week previously to the commencement of the ensuing term.

17. One term's notice, at least, in writing of the intention to remove a boy shall be given to the Secretary, and one term's payment of the tuition and nomination fees and one half of the boarding fees shall be due and made for every boy removed without such notice.

18. No boy shall be entitled to enter or return to the College until his term's payment has been made as before required; and if such payment shall remain in arrear for one month after the appointed time for payment, the boy if admitted may

be removed from the College and shall not be admitted again unless by permission of the Council.

Regulations.

19. Each boy whether a day boy or boarder shall conform to the regulations of the Head Master in respect to the bounds within which he must keep, attendance on holidays, discipline, dress, and other like matters.

20. Any boy may be expelled by the Head Master in accordance with the provisions of the Charter.[298]

Chapel Services.

21. Divine Service according to the usage of the Church of England shall be held in the School Chapel at least twice on every Sunday during term, and on such other days as the Head Master shall direct; and once at least on every such Sunday a sermon shall be preached therein by the Head Master or some person appointed by him.

22. Subject to the provisions of the Charter,[299] all boys, unless prevented by sickness, shall regularly attend Divine Service in the Chapel and the religious instruction of the School. Every boy received into a licensed boarding house as a boarder shall attend such religious instruction, and such religious services as may be provided by the Head Master for the boarders in that House.

23. A short service taken from the Book of Common Prayer shall be read on week days as the Head Master may direct.

Sanitary investigations.

24. An investigation into the sanitary conditions of the School buildings and of every House licensed to take boarders shall be made as often and in such manner as the Council may direct.

Sanatorium.

25. The admission to the Sanatorium shall be by order of the Medical Superintendent only, save that in case of emergency any master shall have power to order any boy under his care to be admitted, but he shall forthwith report the fact to the Head Master and Medical Superintendent.

Studies.

26. The School course shall comprise instruction in Holy Scripture, Latin, Greek, and other subjects necessary to prepare boys for the Universities, including Modern Languages, Mathematics, Physical Science, English History, Language, Literature, Composition, and Drawing. It shall also comprise such instructions as may be necessary for boys intended for the Indian Civil Service, the Royal Military Academy, Woolwich, the Indian Civil Engineering College, Cooper's Hill, the profession of civil engineering, or a commission in the Army. The course of study for each boy shall be determined by the Head Master.

27. No change shall be made in the general course of instruction in the School without the previous approval of the Council.

28. The general examination of the School shall be held in the latter portion of the Summer term by examiners not connected with the College, appointed as the Council may from time to time direct, and their reports shall be laid before the Council. The exhibitions to the Universities shall be awarded by the Head Master according to the result of the examinations.

---

[298] Above [**36**], section 70.
[299] *Ibid.*, section 5.

Scholarships and exhibitions to the Universities.

29. The examination for the scholarships and entrance exhibitions shall be held at such times as the Head Master shall determine, and shall be conducted as the Head Master shall direct.

Powers of Head Master.

30. The Head Master, subject to the regulations of the Charter and Bye-Laws, shall have full authority over the boarding houses and the whole organization, instruction, and discipline of the School.

31. The Head Master and assistant masters shall hold meetings on days to be fixed by the Head Master not less than twice in every term, under the title of masters' meetings, to consider and discuss any matter which may be brought before them by the Head Master, or with his consent, by any assistant master. Due notice shall be given of any subject to be considered thereat.

32. No assistant master shall during any term undertake any duties, whether remunerated or otherwise, besides his duties in the School, without the consent of the Head Master.

Given under the common seal of Clifton College, this sixth day of June, one thousand eight hundred and eighty-two.

[80]   26 January 1883. Memorandum from the Head Master to the Finance Committee: payment of boarding fees on removal without notice
[*Council Minute Book 2, inserted loose at p. 135. Holograph*]

Clifton College,

Clifton, Bristol.

Finance Committee. Surplus boarding fees.

When a boy leaves without due notice he may be called on, if a boarder, to pay the whole or any portion of the boarding fees.

Our custom has hitherto been as follows. If a master has been unable to fill the vacancy, the boy would be charged half the fees, which would be paid to the Boarding House Master. If the vacancy has been filled no charge would be made.

The circumstances are now different as the boarding fees are paid to the Council. I should propose:

(1) That when a vacancy in a House is caused by such want of notice, half the boarding fees shall be paid as hitherto to the master.

(2) That the remaining half, or when no vacancy is caused, the whole of the fees be paid to a fund for meeting *bad debts*.

(3) That excess boarding fees, arising from a master's taking, under special circumstances, with the H.M.'s sanction, more boys than he may receive fees for, be paid into the same fund.

I am sure that some systematic way of meeting the losses arising from bad debts should be arrived at, now that the masters are not individually responsible for the collection of the debts.[300]

Jan 26/83.   J.M. Wilson.

---

[300] Wilson's proposal was accepted by the Council on 3 February, save that the proportion of the excess payable to the House Master was raised from half to three-quarters: Council Minute Book 2, p. 135.

[81]   Lent Term 1891. No girls allowed
[*Truscott Miscellanea Box 2 item 1. Typescript*]

Copy of newspaper cutting taken from the collection of C.D. Ruding Bryan.[301]

Mr M.G. Glazebrook writes from Clifton College:
'My attention has been drawn to a paragraph in your issue of February 21st referring to me. I am not concerned to correct false statements about myself; but your intimation that "photographs of actresses," &c., have been customary decorations in Clifton boys' studies, is a libel upon my predecessor, Archdeacon Wilson,[302] to which it is my duty to give the most emphatic contradiction. You owe an ample apology to him and to them.'
Mr Glazebrook misses the point. If he will refer to the paragraph which offends him, he will perceive we do not assert that photographs of actresses have been customary decorations in the Clifton boys' studies, but that the Head Master – no doubt in his enthusiasm for art – confiscated all he found. This, we maintain, was the case. Moreover, we do not think it probable that the Clifton boys are so much pained at our insinuation as to require an apology. They have doubtless perceived that the laugh is not so much against them for harbouring pretty pictures as against the Head Master for running foul of them.[303]
Clifton College has got its bristles up this time with a vengeance. It has been touched in its tenderest part – its Sixth Form. No words of ours can add to the thrill of horror which every public-school boy will experience when he hears that a Clifton Sixth Form boy has been – not reprimanded, not 'lined' but flogged! No wonder Mr Glazebrook is regarded with [*the*] pious abhorrence which good Royalists felt for the miscreants who dared to lay hands on the sacred person of Charles I.

[*MS*] Clifton Society 1891.

---

[301] A temporary member of the teaching staff during the First World War (not allowed a place in the *Register*); he was the scribe of the Roll of Honour: Christie, *History*, p. 204 n. 9.
[302] On leaving Clifton Wilson had become Archdeacon of Manchester.
[303] The problem did not go away and indeed became more severe; in 1984 a marketing committee chaired by Brian Worthington [*M514*], charged with giving Clifton a better image, was worried by the profusion of 'naked ladies' in the studies.

SECTION VI: FABRIC

[82]   1860. Invitation to architects
[Guard Book 1860–77. MS]

Proposed College at Clifton
Instructions to architects and conditions of competition.

The plan which accompanies these instructions shews the land purchased for the College.

The high level sewer is constructed through the sand, and its course with the levels of the ground, the nature of the foundation and the proposed new roads are shewn thereon.

The building is to be either in the Gothic or Elizabethan style of architecture.

The total amount to be expended on the buildings exclusive of Racket and Fives Courts, boundary, fixtures, architect's commission and salary of clerk of works not to exceed £10,000 – the term fixtures to include chimney pieces, grates, warming and ventilating apparatus, gas fittings, bell and paper hanging, and ornamental painting.

The following are considered to be requisite for the collegiate buildings but it is not intended absolutely to bind the competitors, as their experience may enable them to offer better suggestions.

The building is to be for educational purposes only, with suitable offices, and to be constructed for the accommodation of 500 boys, but to be so arranged as to be easily capable of extension if increased accommodation should be required.

It must comprise a Classical and a Modern department: each department consisting of one large school room, with not less than six class rooms to each department, each class room to be capable of accommodating from 35 to 40 boys. One of the large school rooms will be used for the distribution of prizes and must therefore be capable of holding at least 800 persons sitting.

The buildings must also comprise a room for Drawing of good dimensions (say 40 x 20 feet), a Laboratory and a small Lecture room, a Library and Board-room (the same room may answer both purposes), a private room for the Head Master, a Common Room for the other masters, and rooms for the Secretary and his clerk.

A Porter's residence must also be provided.

The outbuildings must comprize two Racket Courts, Fives Courts and all other necessary erections, and it would be desirable if the plan embraced a Cloister or some provision for play in wet weather.

A thorough system of drainage and ventilation must be adopted, and the buildings adapted to the most approved warming apparatus, but it is intended to have open fireplaces in all rooms, and in each of the large rooms two fireplaces.

In laying out the ground, space must be appropriated for a Chapel and for a house and garden for the Head Master. With regard to the Head Master's house and Chapel no plan or drawings are required, but their proposed position must be shewn on the ground plan and they should be so arranged as to form part of the general design, and the Head Master's house may be either attached or not to the School buildings as the architects may consider best. It is not intended to include the Master's house or Chapel in the £10,000.

These several buildings must be so arranged as to afford the greatest possible space for the play ground.

The play ground, except where bounded by the buildings, will be fenced in by iron railings.

The architects to furnish the drawings to the same scale, namely one eighth of an inch to a foot, but details may be on a larger scale.

The plans and sections may be tinted but no color [*sic*] to be applied to any elevation drawing – perspective drawing not considered necessary, but admissible if in pencil only untinted – No plan will be accepted that transgresses this rule.

The architects to provide with the drawings general specifications and estimates.

The drawings and specifications to be so detailed as to enable a contractor appointed by the Council to ascertain the general correctness of the estimates furnished by the architects.

Should the actual cost of the selected plan, when contracted for, exceed the architect's estimate by ten per cent, the Council shall be at liberty to reject the plan and adopt any other design, without rendering themselves liable to any charge of the said architect for any services he may have rendered or be said to have rendered to the Council in the preparation of the said plans. The substituted plan to be subject to the same ordeal and the like conditions and not to be entitled to any premium if rejected on the above mentioned grounds.

Each architect must send in his plan with a sealed letter, such letter to be indorsed 'competitor's name' and must contain his name and address. *No motto or other distinctive mark nor the architect's name or initials to be appended to either plans or letter.*

Each parcel sent will be numbered differently by the Council at the time of opening them, and the number attached to each parcel will be affixed to every plan or document it contains. The letter likewise numbered being laid aside until the period of adjudication.

The letters shall not be opened until after the Committee shall have finally decided upon the plans to which they intend to adjudge the premiums when the letters shall be opened.

All plans &c. to be addressed and sent to the office of the College, Albion Chambers, Bristol on or before the <21st> day of <November> next.

Any plans sent after that date will be laid aside until applied for by the owners.

The author of the adopted design will be employed as architect of the building with the usual percentage, and the architects producing the 2nd, 3rd and 4th best plans shall receive respectively the premiums of £50, £30 and £20.

The Council will, if they think fit, be assisted in the selection by the opinion of an eminent London architect. After the adjudication the selected and premiated plans will be retained for a short time for exhibition together with such of the other plans as their authors may desire to be exhibited.

The Council do not bind themselves to accept or premiate any of the plans which may be submitted, nor do they hold themselves liable to any charge of the architects whose designs shall be rejected for any services they may have rendered.

It is proposed at first to carry out a portion only of the building sufficient for 250 boys.

In sending in the plans therefore the part recommended by the architect to be first built must be indicated with specifications and estimates for that portion. Competitors requiring any information with regard to the work or in reference to these instructions will apply by letter to the Secretary, Albion Chambers, Bristol, and all letters so addressed with the replies will be open to the inspection of the several competitors.

[83]   26 February 1890. Completion and naming of the Wilson Tower
[*Council Minute Book 3, p. 262. MS*]

The Secretary having reported that Mr Wilson had handed to him a cheque for £500, the balance of his gift of £2000 towards the erection of the Tower, it was resolved:

That in recognition of Mr Wilson's munificent gift to the College, the Tower now nearing its completion be called the Wilson Tower.

The Chapel

[84]   24 September 1863. Estimate for Chapel furnishings
[*Works file. MS*]

21 Old Market St.
Septr. 24th 1863.

C. Hansom, Esqr.

Sir,

Our estimate for stalls, floor and joist, skeleton frame, baize, cornice, altar rail &c. as per specification and drawings stained and twice varnished is the sum of ninety one pounds – £91. 0. 0.

[*Over this Hansom has written*] This amount should be £81 – in virtue of the reduction of £10 in Altar Rails. C.H.

Second estimate for curtains, iron standards and iron rail is the sum of ten pounds ten shillings – £10. 10. 0.

Third estimate for desk in 6 compartments is the sum of three pounds four shillings – £3. 4. 0.

Your obedient servants,
Marquiss and Munro.

Estimate no. 1 in detail:

	[£]	[s]	[d]
1. No. 12 stalls 6 on each side	43.	10.	0.
2. No. 2 do. 1 on each side	11.	0.	0.
3. Skeleton frame & moulding covered with baize	10.	0.	0.
4. Altar platform covered with baize	6.	10.	0.
5. Communion railing and iron work	20.	0.	0.
	£91.	0.	0.

[85]   6 June 1867. Notice of Chapel opening
[*Guard Book 1860–77. Printed*]

Clifton College,
6th June, 1867.

Dear Sir,
    The Guthrie Memorial Chapel is to be opened on Saturday, 15th instant. The service will commence at eleven o'clock. The Lord Bishop of the Diocese[304] will preach the inaugural sermon, which will be followed by the celebration of the Holy Communion.
    I am instructed to ask whether you wish to be present at the ceremony. The available space being very limited the Council regret that they can only offer you one ticket.
                 I am, dear Sir, your obedient servant,
                         W.D.L. Macpherson.
An early answer is requested.

The Holman Hunt Mosaic

□ *A distinctive feature of the Chapel was a mosaic retable erected in 1890 to the design of W. Holman Hunt.*[305]

[86]   17 May 1889. Memorandum from the Head Master
[*RS3/185. Holograph*]

                         The Chapel Mosaic
It will be remembered that with the sanction of the Council Mr Holman Hunt has prepared a design for a mosaic to be placed over the Communion table in the Chapel. This mosaic is now approaching completion, and it is necessary to prepare for its being placed in our Chapel.
    The accompanying sketch was prepared at the request of Mr E.J. Hansom,[306] after full consideration. I send also a photograph of the Chapel that the nature of the proposed change may be seen. The framework that surrounds the mosaic will be of alabaster, or some other marble.

---

[304] Charles John Ellicott, Bishop of Gloucester and Bristol 1863–97.
[305] Co-founder of the Pre-Raphaelite Brotherhood (d. 1910). For this mosaic see *Cliftonian* XI (1889–91), pp. 211, 260, 316, and *Clifton Magazine* (2010), pp. 7–10.
[306] Edward Joseph Hansom (d. 1900), son and partner of the original architect; from 1871 at Newcastle-upon-Tyne in partnership with A.M. Dunn.

I am purposely making it of the simplest character in accordance both with the architecture of the Chapel, and the spirit of our services and teaching. I hope the general design will be considered <satisfactory>. I should myself wish it to be even further simplified in certain points.

The arcading on the N. side of the chancel is shewn in the sketch. That in the bays must necessarily be altered eventually but I do not propose to do this at once. I should like however to have the plan approved of as a whole, and to be authorised to carry it out as I can afford it.

May 17/89. J.M. Wilson.

[87]   [17] February [1890]. Memorandum from the Head Master
[RS3/185. Holograph]

The Chancel

I understand that the design for the frame of the mosaic in the Chapel which was submitted to the Council has been accepted, and that permission is therefore given for it to be put up. It is in course of construction, and will be put up during the Easter holidays. Permission was also given for mosaic to replace the tiles on the floor, and that marble steps should replace the Bath stone steps inside the rails. I should like [this *deleted*] to have this permission definitely extended so as to include the steps at the rails, which ought at the same time to be replaced by marble.

Some time ago Mr Wiseman[307] made an offer to replace our present Communion table, which is extremely plain, and is covered by a cloth and frontal, with a handsome table, with open front, like that in the Cathedral. It will be of oak, ungilt, and with no figures, no reliefs, no design. I spoke to the Bishop about it, and he approves. It is necessary to have his permission in such a case. I had hoped to be able to lay the final design before the Council, but I am not sure that I shall receive it in time. I should be glad to know their wish about it. I hope that all these additions will be completed by Commem.

Feb. J.M.W.

[88]   19 February 1890. E.J. Hansom to the Head Master
[RS3/185. Holograph]

23, Eldon Square,
Newcastle-upon-Tyne.
Febry 19th 1890.

Dear Mr Wilson,

I have urged Messrs Burke & Co. to send the new design and estimate, for mosaic panel 'The Jewel'. I trust there will be no difficulty in getting it for the meeting, on the 26th inst.

With regard to the glass in the windows of Tower, I advise that whatever is done now, should be considered as temporary. Do you think it worthwhile to put in leaded cathedral glass above the transoms? I will get a design for treating these parts with stained glass (heraldry) and it should not take long to fill up the spaces.

Believe me, yours faithfully,
Edward J. Hansom.

---

[307] Henry John Wiseman [*M43*: 1869–1903].

[89]   26 February 1890. Council minutes
[*Council Minute Book 3, p. 263. MS*]

Decorations in Chapel Chancel.

Mr Hansom's plan for the decoration of the floor by mosaic at the east end of the Chapel, being part of the decoration proposed to be done by the Head Master as previously approved, was passed and, in accordance with a memorandum from the Head Master dated the 17th of February 1890 **[87]**, authority was given to replace the Bath stone steps at the Communion rails as well as those within the rails with marble.

By the same memorandum an offer from Mr Wiseman was reported to replace the present Communion table with a handsome table, and Mr Hansom's design for it both open and with carved panels was submitted.

It was resolved to accept Mr Wiseman's offer of the Communion table with the best thanks of the Council and to approve both designs, leaving it to Mr Wiseman to adopt which he should prefer.

[90]   17 March 1890. Memorandum from the Head Master
[*RS3/185. Holograph*]

Inscription below the mosaic

When I offered to the Council, I think in the year 1886, to give a mosaic to the Chapel from a painting made for the purpose by Holman Hunt entitled 'Christ among the Doctors' I asked and obtained permission to associate it in some unobtrusive way with the memory of my son, who was killed by a fall from the rocks in the spring of that year.[308] I wish now to obtain the sanction of the Council to my putting up the enclosed inscription in a panel in the alabaster slab below the mosaic in such a position that it cannot be seen when the table is in its usual place. It will be both below and behind the table.

The framework and tablet will be put in their place at Easter, and it would be a convenience to have the inscription sanctioned soon.

March 17/90.   J.M.W.

Inscription

vobis pueri,
qui in hoc sacello Deum colitis
hanc tabellam
quo magis corde teneatis
Jesum Christum
Dominum nostrum atque exemplar
inter Doctores
pie verecunde diligenter
rebus divinis incumbentem
in memoriam filioli dilectissimi
D.D.
Jacobus M. Wilson
M.DCCCXC.

---

[308] Maurice Temple Wilson. T.E. Brown's epitaph (repr. in Winterbotttom, *Brown*, p. 206) suggests the cause of the misadventure: 'Hard by the nest of some celestial merle / We yet shall see you when the morning dawns'.

[G. *then* Gul. Holman Hunt del. / In mosaicā fecit *then* Fecit mosaicā Pow- *all deleted*] Tabella a Gul. Holman Hunt delineata est, [in officinā Powell- *corrected to*] apud officinam Powelliorum mosaicā expressa.[309]

[91]   26 March 1890. Council approval for the inscription
[*Council Minute Book 3, p. 277. MS*]

The Head Master submitted a draft of the inscription which he wishes to place under the mosaic he was about to put up in the Chapel in memory of his son, as given in his memorandum of the 17th instant.

It was resolved that the inscription be approved and placed where proposed by Mr Wilson as shewn in Mr Hansom's drawing submitted.

☐ *Eight years later Hunt responded to a Clifton's boy's request for his autograph.*

[92]   16 August 1898. Holman Hunt to Dudley Kingdon-Allen[310]
[*P5126 Album. Holograph*]

Draycott Lodge,
Fulham,
Aug 16. 1898
Dear Sir,

I am a rebel to the powers that be established in our profession, and not R.A. but such as I am it is a pleasure to me to have this opportunity of satisfying you with proof that I know how to write my own name.[311]
Yours faithfully,
W. Holman Hunt.

☐ *By the 1960s the mosaic had fallen out of artistic and liturgical fashion, and it was moved to the gloom of the south choir aisle where it is barely visible.*

---

[309] 'In memory of his most beloved young son, James M. Wilson gives this tablet to you, boys, who worship God in this Chapel, that you may be more mindful of Jesus Christ our Lord and exemplar, devoting himself among the Doctors dutifully, modestly, and diligently to God's work. 1890. The tablet drawn by William Holman Hunt, set in mosaic at the workshop of the Powells' (translation kindly provided by Mr G.V. Hardyman [*12249/M405*]). The tablet is now placed adjacent to the mosaic. The text as was printed in *Register* (1925), p. lii. (omitting the final line, which as incised ends 'apud officinam Powelliorum arte mosaicā expressa'). James Powell & Sons of Whitefriars were prominent in the design and manufacture of glassware.

[310] Dudley Attwood Kingdon-Allen (plain Allen at school) [*5126*: ST 1896–9] solicited autographs from all manner of celebrities and between 1897 and 1902 received over fifty replies, many in the form of letters. All were pasted into an album which, at his death in 1952, was donated to the College by his executors. The album also contains the letter from Jowett to J.M. Wilson printed below **[129]**, though how Allen came by it is unknown.

[311] Evidently Allen thought Hunt must be a Royal Academician.

Enlargement of the Chapel 1911

[93]   18 January 1911. Total cost presented to Finance Committee
[*Council Minute Book 6, p. 112. MS*]

Chapel Enlargement.
The statement of the Chapel Enlargement Account received from the architect dated January 10th 1911 was as follows:

Contract				8227.	6.	8
Extra excavations	108.	1.	8			
” drainage	55.	7.	10			
	163.	9.	6			
Net saving on the provision for contingencies	[–]86.	7.	3	77.	2.	3
Net total of Enlargement a/c				8304.	8.	11
Chapel Repairs a/c						
Replacing old boarded floors with wood blocks additional to the work included in the contract				105.	3.	2
Organ a/c						
Portion of the work to organ loft included in the Architect's estimate of £80 given to the Headmaster 29–8–10				32.	10.	0
Total				£8442.	2.	1

The burial of Percival

☐ *When the Chapel enlargement was proposed, Percival conceived the desire to be buried there, as Arnold was at Rugby.*[312] *Clifton Chapel was not licensed for burials, and recent legislation appeared to have created further obstacles. A prolonged legal argument ensued.*

[94]   12 November 1908. Sir Lewis Dibdin[313] **to Percival**
[*RS3/143. Holograph*]

Morton's Tower,
Lambeth Palace. S.E.
Nov. 12 1908

My dear Bishop,
I am under the impression that the difficulty really consists in this, that no doubt an order forbidding interments in [the *corrected to*] an area which includes the site of Clifton College Chapel has been made. If this be so consecration of the Chapel would not affect the matter and the P[*ublic*] H[*ealth*] Act 1875 sec. 343 sched. V pt iii does

---

[312] Potter, *Headmaster*, p. 124.
[313] Sir Lewis Tonna Dibdin (d. 1938), prominent ecclesiastical lawyer; Dean of Arches 1903–34 and First Church Estates Commissioner 1905–30.

not seem to apply because the Chapel is not for public worship and is not a 'church'.[314]

My impression is that the Home Office, or rather now the Local Government Board can make orders allowing particular burials in areas which are closed. Bishop Thorold got such an order for burial in the close of Winchester Cathedral.[315] I have not looked into the matter minutely, but would it not be worth while your seeing somebody at the L.G.B. about it?

Your Lordship's very sincerely,
Lewis T. Dibdin.

[95]   13 November 1908. Percival to the Head Master
[*RS3/143. Holograph*]

The Palace,
Hereford.
Novr. 13. '08.

Dear David,

I enclose Abbott's [*recte* Abbot's] letter and Sir Lewis Dibdin's reply to me after reading it.

The illustration he gives I fear may not apply, and the Act, if [*I*] remember right, deals specifically with churches consecrated or to be consecrated after a certain date.

I think Abbott [*recte* Abbot] would know best how to approach the Local Government Board's *legal adviser* – it would, I expect, be nevertheless simpler to ask a clerk's opinion at L.G.B.

Yours sincerely,
J. Hereford.

[96]   14 November 1908. H.N. Abbot to the Head Master
[*RS3/143. Holograph*]

Abbot, Pope, Brown & Abbot, Solicitors

Shannon Court,
Bristol,
14th Nov. 1908

Dear Mr David,

I return the Bishop of Hereford's letter and Sir Lewis Dibdin's.

The best way now will be for the Council (Finance Committee) to instruct Mr Doggett[316] to approach the Local Government Board.

There is a meeting on Wednesday next, at which please ask Mr Macpherson to bring the matter forward. I cannot be there, but will write a letter recommending the course I suggest.

Yours very truly,
H.N. Abbot.

---

[314] 38 & 39 Vict *c.* 55; the schedule recited the relevant provision of the Public Health Act 1848 (11 & 12 Vict. *c.* 63 sect. 83): 'No vault or grave shall be constructed or made within the walls of or underneath any church or place of public worship built in any urban district after the thirty-first day of August one thousand eight hundred and forty eight' with penalty of £50 for each contravention.

[315] Anthony Thorold, Bishop of Winchester from 1891 to his death in 1895.

[316] Hugh Greenfield Doggett, of Richmond Terrace, solicitor, father of E.B. [*5913*: WiH 1902–4]; died 1914: *Directory* (1890), p. 200.

[97] 14 November [1908]. The Head Master to the College Secretary
[*RS3/143. Holograph*]

Memorandum from the Headmaster.
Chapel. Possible use for interment.
The enclosed correspondence arose out of a conversation between the Bishop[317] and myself.
He left it to me to make preliminary enquiry with the help of Mr Abbot whose advice is here given.
Will you kindly bring the matter before the Council.
14 Nov.   A.A.D.

[98] 3 March 1909. H.G. Doggett to the College Secretary
[*RS3/143. Typescript*]

Stanley, Wasbrough & Doggett, Solicitors
18, Clare Street,
Bristol.
3rd March 1909.
Dear Mr Macpherson,
    With reference to the question of a possible burial in the College Chapel, I took the opportunity, some short while ago, when I was in town, of calling at the Local Government Board Offices and the gentlemen whom I interviewed there referred me to schedule 3, part 2 of the Public Health Act 1875, which, so far as he knew, would govern the position. The provision in question is as follows: [*recited as in note to* **94** *above with the penalty clause*].
    In the first place I suppose the Chapel was built in an urban district after the 31st August 1848. Assuming this to be the case, then would the Chapel be held to be a

'church' or 'other place of public worship'? As to this the Local Government Board official said his department would not offer an opinion.
    I have searched in many directories for definitions of the above expressions with the result that I feel a little uncertain whether the Chapel might not be caught by one or other of them. It has occurred to me that possibly the Ecclesiastical Commission might be able to give some advice and I am proposing, when next in town, to call at that office to see if they can help us in the matter. Should I fail to obtain a definite opinion from that source, we might then, if the Council thought fit, lay a case before Counsel versed in this branch of the law for his opinion and advice.
                              Yours very truly,
                              Hugh G. Doggett.

[99] 19 March 1909. Percival to the College Secretary
[*RS3/143. Holograph*]

The Palace,
Hereford.
March 19. '09.

---

[317] George Forrest Browne, Bishop of Bristol 1897–1914.

Dear Mr Macpherson,

Best thanks for your letter and sight of Mr Doggett's which I return. I feel obliged to him for his kind efforts.

My impression is that he will probably not get much help from the Secretary of the Ecclesiastical Commission, but if he were to write to Sir Lewis Dibdin, as Chief Commissioner, telling him why he wants the information, I think Sir Lewis would probably look into the matter and give his opinion.

Yours sincerely,

J. Hereford.

Failing the above I should be for following Mr Doggett's advice.

[100]   6 July 1909. The Local Government Board to Messrs Stanley, Wasbrough & Doggett.

[RS3/143. Typescript copy]

Local Government Board,

Whitehall. S.W.

6th July 1909.

Gentlemen,

I am directed by the Local Government Board to advert to your letter of the 24th of May last inquiring whether any legal impediment exists to an interment being carried out within the Clifton College Chapel, and <I> am to state that, if the School is an endowed school within the meaning of the Endowed Schools Act, 1869, section 53 of that Act, in combination with section 83 of the Public Health Act, 1848, as re-enacted in the third part of schedule V to the Public Health Act 1875, would appear to have the effect of prohibiting the burial of a corpse or coffin in the School Chapel.

I am, Gentlemen, your obedient servant,

John Lesterley, Assistant Secretary.

[101]   14 July 1909. Stanley, Wasbrough & Doggett to the Secretary of the Local Government Board

[RS3/143. Typesecript copy]

18 Clare Street,

Bristol,

14th July 1909.

Sir,

Clifton College Chapel.

We duly received yours of 6th instant, for which we are obliged. We have referred to the Endowed Schools Act 1869 and are inclined to think it does not apply to Clifton College. The College has no endowment in the ordinary sense of the term other than the College lands and buildings, Museum and Library, furniture and fittings, Chapel and fittings, masters' houses, Sanatorium, Baths, Gymnasium and Workshop. There are of course certain exhibitions and scholarships belonging to the College, but under section 6 of the Act the School is not by reason of this fact to be deemed to be an endowed school.[318] The income of the College is derived entirely

---

[318] This allowed that 'a school belonging to any person or body corporate shall not by reason only that exhibitions are attached to such school be deemed to be an endowed school'; sect. 7 explained that 'exhibitions' comprehended scholarships and the like.

from tuition fees and other payments, including the rents of the masters' houses. The College Charter was granted in 1877 when it took over the property and undertaking of the Clifton College Company Limited which had been in existence since 1860. Section 8, subsection 2,[319] therefore, of the Act would seem to specifically render the Act inapplicable.

We should be much obliged if the Board would kindly consider the above circumstances and favour us with their views as we infer that, but for the possibility of the Act applying the Board might be of opinion that a burial in the College Chapel would be legally permissible.

We are, Sir, your obedient servants,
Stanley, Wasbrough & Doggett.

[102]   12 January 1910. Counsel's Opinion
[*RS3/143. Typescript*]

re Clifton College Chapel
OPINION
of Mr A.B. Kempe[320] upon case submitted to him.

I. It is of course desirable to speak with caution in view of the opinion expressed by Sir L. Dibden [*recte* Dibdin] in his letter of May 6th last, that he does 'not think the Public Health Act 1875 affects the question so far as the Chapel of Clifton College is concerned'; but as unfortunately Sir Lewis does not give any reasons for his view, or indicate how far he had seriously considered the matter before expressing it, it is necessary to form an independent judgment on the point.

On a careful consideration I am unable to come to the conclusion that it can safely be assumed that the Public Health Act 1875 (38 & 39 Vic: cap 55) does not affect the matter. Section 343 and schedule V Part 3 of that Act re-enact sec: 83 of 11 & 12 Vic: cap 63 which provides that [*as quoted in note to* **94** *above*] and imposes a penalty of £50 for any burial in such a vault or grave.

Now no doubt the Chapel of Clifton College is a private Chapel to which neither the general public nor the parishoners [*sic*] of the parish in which it is situate have any right of access. Moreover, as I gather from the further instructions that [*though*] the clergymen who officiate in it are licensed to do so under the provisions of the *Private Chapels Acts 1871*,[321] the services held in it are not under the control of the incumbent of the parish, as they otherwise would be. But, though the Chapel is a private one, as the services held in it are attended not only by the masters and scholars, but also by the masters' families, and by other persons who have orders of admission, it appears to me that the worship therein is 'public worship', and the Chapel itself is a 'place of public worship'. In the case of *Freeland v Neale, 1. Robertson's Ecclesiastical Cases p. 651*, decided in 1848 by Sir H. Jenner Fust[322] with reference to the services in the private unconsecrated Chapel of Sackville College, it was said by the learned Judge that, even assuming that the members of the College could be regarded as a family, still as strangers were admitted occasionally as visitors to attend the services, it was

---

[319] Excluding from the provisions of the Act any school which on 1 Jan. 1869 'was maintained wholly or partly out of annual voluntary subscriptions, and had no endowment except school buildings and teachers [*sic*] residences, or playground or gardens attached to such buildings and residences'.

[320] Alfred Bray Kempe, KC.

[321] 34 & 35 Vict. *c*. 66.

[322] Sir Herbert Jenner-Fust, Dean of the Arches 1834–62.

impossible to say that those present were a mere assemblage of a private family, and held that 'where two or three are gathered together who do not strictly form part of a family, there is a congregation, and the reading to them the service of the church is a reading *in public*'.[323]

This decision was followed and approved by Sir A. Charles in 1901 in *Nesbitt v Wallace (1901) p. 366* who added 'as I understand it does not matter how the congregation got there, whether by invitation or otherwise'. The fact that services such as those in Clifton College were thus determined to be public services, and as such would be liable to the control of the incumbent of the parish in which they were held, [was the reason why they were held *deleted*] was the reason which led to the passing to 31 & 32 Vic: cap: 118, sec: 31,[324] as to chapels attached to public schools, of 32 & 33 Vic: cap: 86, sec: 33, as to chapels attached to endowed schools[325] and the Private Chapels Act 1871 (34 & 35 Vic: cap: 66) as to chapels attached to colleges, schools, hospitals, asylums and other public or charitable institutions and to the provisions therein that the services in such chapels shall not be under the control of the incumbent of the parish. These Statutes do not however proceed to enact that the services dealt with shall not be regarded as public worship, or [*recte* on] the contrary, the two first mentioned Statutes both in terms say that the chapels shall be 'deemed to be allowed by law for the performance of public worship', and the Private Chapels Act 1871, though not using these words, because it adopts the somewhat different procedure of authorising the licensing of the officiating minister instead of the chapel itself, as in the other Acts, says nothing whatever which would indicate that it made any difference in the public character of the worship authorised. As the ecclesiastical and statute law thus clearly regard the services in these chapels as public services, I do not see how it could be maintained that the places in which they are held are not 'places of public worship' within the meaning of a Statute the object of which is obviously to put a complete stop in urban districts to the practice of burial in places in which it has been usual but unsanitary to bury, viz. churches and other places attended by a number of persons for public worship.

I could not therefore advise that it would not be a violation of the Public Health Act to have the proposed burial in the Chapel.

II. I do not think that Clifton College is an 'endowed school' within the meaning of the Endowed Schools Act 1869, but this point does not appear to me to affect the question. No doubt sec: 53 of the Act specifically states that the chapel of an endowed school 'shall be deemed to be allowed by law for the performance of public worship', and thereby recognizes that the worship therein is 'public worship', but in view of the considerations to which I have referred in my first answer, it would not in my opinion be possible to maintain that the worship in Clifton College Chapel is

---

[323] The issue was access not ownership. Had the College turned the Chapel into a lumber-room (*cf.* **[190]**) Counsel might have found some support from *Duke of Norfolk v. Arbuthnot (1879)*. In his judgment there Coleridge C.J. observed that 'a stronger assertion of an absolute right of property in a patron of an ecclesiastical building than to exclude every one from it, to treat it as a store-place for tools and ladders, and to suffer it to become almost a ruin, can hardly be conceived.': M.T. Elvins, *Arundel Priory 1380–1980: The College of the Holy Trinity* (Chichester, 1981), p. 96.

[324] The Public Schools Act 1868.

[325] The Statute cited is not material; Counsel meant *c.* 56 (the Endowed Schools Act) sect. 53, which provided that in schools subject to the Act chapels already consecrated or which should be licensed by the diocesan 'to be used as a chapel for such school' should be 'deemed to be allowed by law for the performance of public worship', and should be exempt from the jurisdiction of the incumbent in whose parish they lay.

not equally 'public worship' authorized by law, and that a distinction can be drawn between the worship in the chapel of a school coming under the Endowed Schools Act, and that authorized in the chapel of a school or college by the Private Chapels Act 1871. The worship in both cases is 'public worship'; and the chapel in each case appears to me to be a 'place of public worship', protected by the Public Health Act from the possible danger of interments therein.

III. The question whether burial in the Chapel [*is prohibited*] by Order in Council under the Burial Acts as well as by the Public Health Act 1875, depends upon whether the Chapel lies within any area in which burial has by Order in Council been ordered to be discontinued.

Section 1 of the Burial Act of 1858[326] has provisions (1) as to Orders in Council forbidding the opening of '*new burial grounds*', and (2) as to Orders in Council ordering the discontinuance of burials in '*any burial grounds or places of burial*'. Orders of the first species are only authorised and enforced (sec: 6) in the case of new burial grounds, and not in the case of other new places such as vaults or graves in churches or chapels in which burials have not previously taken place; possibly because the provisions of the Public Health Act, to which I have referred, were considered to sufficiently deal with this matter. But Orders as to the discontinuance of burials prevent (sec: 3) all burials within the area to which the Order applies whether in burial grounds or any church, chapel, churchyard or other place. The question therefore becomes one as to whether any Order in Council exists which orders the discontinuance of burials within an area in which the Chapel stands.

The Order in Council of April 7th 1854 referred to in the memorandum contained in the further instructions, which orders 'that burials in the said City (i.e. the City of Bristol) be discontinued', with certain modifications, would, as I gather that Clifton has been within the City of Bristol since 1832, appear to settle the matter. But as it does not seem to have been regarded as effecting a discontinuance of the burials in the parish church or churchyard of Clifton and the other places referred to in the subsequent Orders in Council specified in the memorandum, and as I do not understand that these places are included in the modifications of the Order of April 7th 1854 referred to therein, there must be some reason why the Order was not supposed to apply to Clifton.

The Order of February 3rd 1858 is ambiguous, and might I think be properly regarded as ordering the discontinuance of all burials in Clifton parish with the exception that burials may be continued in the parish churchyard so far as is compatible with the regulations for new burial grounds. But here again the subsequent Orders given in the memorandum forbidding further burials, not only in the parish churchyard but also in certain other places, assumes that the previous Order of February 3rd 1858 did not stop burials in the latter and was not therefore general.

Under these circumstances I think that probably neither the Order of April 7th 1854 nor that of February 3rd 1858, the only two referred to which could affect the Chapel, have any application, but if it were necessary to pronounce a definite opinion on this, it would I think be necessary to see the Orders *in extenso*, and to make some enquiries <of the Sanitary Authorities> as to why it was not considered that those Orders were general, and applied to Clifton.

IV. The question whether a burial in the College Chapel would be illegal as a nuisance, is one of fact; and if the burial took place under proper precautions I do not

---

[326] 16 & 17 Vict. *c*. 134.

see how it could be said to be a nuisance at all.

V. The conclusions at which I arrive at [*sic*] are therefore that the burial proposed would not be a nuisance if properly effected, that it is probably not forbidden by any Order in Council under the Burial Acts, but is forbidden by sec: 83 of 11 & 12 Vic: cap: 63 which is reenacted by sec: 343 & schedule V part 3 of the Public Health Act 1875 and no vault or grave can lawfully be made for the purpose of such burial.

A.B. Kempe,
Inner Temple, Jan. 13th 1910.

□ *Despite this clear warning of illegality, Percival was not to be deflected from his purpose. Eventually the College felt able to commission the building of the burial chamber.*[327]

[103]   7 August 1914. Walter S. Paul & James[328] **to the College Secretary**
[*RS3/143. Holograph*]

Walter S. Paul & James, Architects and Surveyors
Eagle Insurance Buildings,
Baldwin Street (and 31 Nicholas Street),
Bristol,
August 7th 1914.
Clifton College. Proposed Vault below Chapel.

Dear Sir,

Herewith we forward drawing for the proposed vault beneath the Chancel of the Chapel.

You will notice that it is suggested that a doorway should be formed in the east wall, [that *deleted*], the present openings in the side and end walls closed up, the floor levelled and concreted, the ceiling arch rendered in plaster, and a grave excavated. A mortuary chamber, accessible from the outside would thus be formed. We estimate the cost at about £100.

Should it be decided to merely brick up the present openings, draw a 'temporary' doorway in the east wall and form the grave as shown, <u>the cost would be about £35</u>. [*Underlined thus by Secretrary and marked* X]

We consider that it would be undesirable to cut through the floor of the Choir, with its supporting arch, in order to lower the coffin to the Vault level, and the cost would exceed the last named sum.

Yours faithfully,
Walter S. Paul and James.

[*Minuted by the Secretary*] X [Accepted *deleted*] Approved. W.J.L.

---

[327] Potter (*Headmaster*, pp. 124, 277) says 'officialdom was finally harassed into submission and surrendered', but this can be no more than inference from the source cited (Archive file RS3/143), where there is nothing between Counsel's warning that the vault would be illegal [102] and the architects' letter about its design [103]. There is a clue in Warren's casual reference to the 'kindness' of Bishop Nickson in this regard [437]. Nickson had only arrived in Bristol in 1914, was doubtles much in awe of his brother of Hereford.

[328] The firm founded by W.S. Paul [*102*], member of Council.

[104]   4 December 1918. The Bishop of Hereford[329] to the Head Master
[*RB1/27. Holograph*]

The Palace,
Hereford.
December 4th 1918.

Dear Sir,
    I regret to find that the trains from Hereford to Bristol are so inconvenient that, without great [inconvenience *deleted*] dislocation of engagements I cannot get to the Funeral service on Friday. In these circumstances I have requested Prebendary Wynne Willson[330] to represent me, and I shall myself attend the Memorial service in the Cathedral.

Believe me, yours v. faithfully,
H.H. Hereford.

[105]   6 December 1918. Draft Order of Service for Percival's funeral
[*RB1/27. MS*]

IN MEMORIAM
The Right Reverend Bishop Percival, Headmaster 1862–1878
– Sentences.
– Psalm XV *Dominus refugium* (printed in full).
– Lesson 1 Cor. xv.20.
– Hymn: *For all the Saints* (printed in full).[331]
– The service will continue as in the Order for the Burial of the Dead, except that the Sentence of Committal (Forasmuch as it hath pleased Almighty God) shall not be said in the Chapel.
– While the bier is leaving the Chapel, the Choir shall sing *Nunc dimittis*.
Clifton College
6 Decr. 1918.

[106]   11 December 1918. Formal record Percival's death and burial
[*Council Minute Book 7, p. 102. MS*]

It was reported that the death of the Right Revd Bishop Percival had taken place on the 3rd December and that [the interment *corrected to*] he had been interred in the Vault prepared in the crypt of the College Chapel.

---

[329] Herbert Hensley Henson, Bishop of Hereford 1917–20 then of Durham 1920–39; died 1947.
[330] Archdall Beaumont Wynne Willson, Canon of Hereford and Prebendary of Moreton Magna in Hereford Cathedral; Percival's Domestic Chaplain 1897–1901: *Crockford* (1918–19).
[331] The tune would not have been the stirring *Sine nomine* by Vaughan Williams (1904), but the older *For all the Saints* by Barnby retained in the Clifton Hymn Book.

The pulpit memorial to Glazebrook

[107]   **15 June 1928. Sir Charles Nicholson to the College Secretary**
[*RS3/196. Typescript*]

2, New Square, Lincoln's Inn
15.6.28.

Dear Sir,

Clifton College Chapel.

I shall be much pleased to undertake the pulpit. I designed one some years ago for the Harrow chapel in memory of Dr Butler.[332]

I will come and have another look at the Chapel as soon as I can manage as I should like to refresh my memory.

Yours very truly,
Charles Nicholson.

[108]   **29 July 1928. The Chairman of Council to the College Secretary**
[*RS3/196. Holgraph*]

Magdalen College,
Oxford.
July 20 1928

Dear Mr Lewis,

I am returning herewith the sketch plans for the Glazebrook memorial pulpit.

Speaking generally I think favourably of it and consider that it would do very well in itself and in its surroundings.

I do not feel sure how much heraldry i.e. [shields *deleted*] how many shields are intended. I should be against a double row. My brother-in-law[333] did not belonging [*sic*] to any great family. I should think (1) Dulwich (2) Balliol (3) Harrow (4) Manchester (5) Clifton (6) Ely.[334] (1) His own coat was the outside. Are the shields intended to go round or only to be on the front? Many thanks for sending the papers.

Yours sincerely,
Herbert Warren.

[109]   **17 September 1928. Nicholson to the College Secretary**
[*RS3/196. Holograph*]

2, New Square,
Lincoln's Inn.
17.9.28

---

[332] Henry Montagu Butler, Headmaster of Harrow 1860–85, then Dean of Gloucester and Master of Trinity College, Cambridge (d. 1918).

[333] Glazebrook and Warren had married respectively the fourth and fifth daughters of Sir Benjamin Collins Brodie, Bt, Fellow of Magdalen and Waynflete Professor of Chemistry (d. 1880); they were therefore not strictly brothers-in-law.

[334] He had been educated at (1) and (2), Assistant Master at (3), High Master of (4), Head Master of (5) and Canon of (6).

Dear Sir,

I enclose preliminary sketch for pulpit which I understand is to cost not more than £350; I think it can be done quite well for that amount.

It will be seen that no seating need be disturbed and that there is room for a pulpit 3 ft internal diameter with a convenient stair 2 ft clear width.

I have suggested a sounding board as part of the work, and which should improve the acoustics.

The suggested decoration involving the use of heraldry may or may not commend itself; if not it is quite easy to substitute some other treatments of the panels.

The material would be English oak.

The decoration in colour would in my opinion be advantageous but I do not regard it as essential to the design except that if heraldic panels are used they should be emblazoned – if the emblazoning were disapproved I should advise a different treatment of panels omitting the heraldry because I think that plain carved shields are ineffective; they should be both carved and coloured if used at all.

I have shown 10 shields but there could be 5 if preferred.

Yours faithfully,
Charles Nicholson.

☐ *Nicholson's letter and designs were sent by the Secretary to the OC Secretary and by him to the OC President.*

[110] 22 October 1928. The President of the OCS to the College Secretary
[*RS3/196. Holograph*]

St James's Palace, S.W.
October 22. 1928

Dear Lewis,

I enclose, to save time, the plan and sketch of the Glazebrook pulpit together with Sir Charles Nicholson's covering letter.

Colonel Hewitt [*recte* Hewett] is sending a letter of explanation <re difficulties arising from holidays and accounting for delay> and criticisms he has collected, by the same post as this. You ought therefore to be armed with all the material you require for Wednesday's Council meeting by to-morrow morning's first post.

Yours sincerely,
L.J. Percival.

[111] 22 October 1928. The Secretary of the OCS to the College Secretary
[*RS3/196. Typescript*]

38, Old Jewry,
London, E.C.2.
22nd October, 1928.

Dear Mr Lewis,

Old Cliftonian Society
Glazebrook Memorial

Referring to my letter of the 19th inst. I understand from L.J. Percival that he has sent Sir Charles Nicholson's sketch for the pulpit together with his covering letter direct to you as he thought this would save time and prevent any chance of the sketch reaching you too late for the Council meeting. I had the opportunity after writing my letter of the 19th inst. of showing the sketch and letter to Sir Robert Witt. Both his opinion and that of Preb. Percival is that the pulpit is too elaborate for our Chapel, the whole tone of which is simple, and they are both afraid that it would 'hit one in the eye'. Sir Robert Witt does not like the heraldic treatment of the panels, especially if the shields are to be heraldically coloured as they should be if they are to be used at all. He thinks the heraldic colours which are of course hard and striking will be far too glaring. Preb. Percival would like to see the panels without any heraldic treatment at all, and he, looking at it from the parson's point of view, is also afraid that <the pulpit> if too elaborate, will have a distinct effect in taking the attention of the congregation from the preacher and the sermon to the pulpit itself, and he gave me an instance in this connection very much in point. I must say that my own opinion – so far as it is worth anything in a matter of this kind – is the same as theirs, and that a far simpler design is what is wanted to tone in with the rest of the Chapel.

These of course cannot be taken as the general opinion of the Committee of the Society, to which it has not been possible to submit the design, but I thought the Council would certainly like to have before them the opinion of the President and of Sir Robert Witt.

Yours sincerely,
W.P. Hewett.

[112]   26 October 1928. The Secretary of the OCS to the College Secretary
[*RS3/196. Typescript*]

38, Old Jewry,
London, E.C.2.
26th October, 1928.

Dear Mr Lewis,

Old Cliftonian Society
Glazebrook Memorial

Thank you for your letter of yesterday. The Glazebrook Memorial Sub-Committee, which consisted of Sir Geoffrey Butler,[335] Sir Lawrence Weaver[336] and H. Gardiner[337] has ceased to function, their terms of reference having been that they were to organise the appeal for the funds. The money having been collected and a report made to the Committee, the Sub-Committee [are *corrected to*] is *functus officio*.

The total amount of money available for the pulpit including the architect's fees is from £300 to £325 not £350. The original instructions given by my Committee were that the total cost including architect's fees should not exceed £300, but the Treasurer reported that after paying the expenses of the appeal a sum of £325 would be available for the purposes of the memorial.

Yours sincerely,
W.P. Hewett.

---

[335] Sir George Geoffrey Gilbert Butler [*5750*: HHP, SH 1900–6], historian Fellow of Corpus Christi College, Cambridge; nephew of H.M. Butler, Master of Trinity: above **[107]**.
[336] Weaver [*4232*: NT 1890–2], knighted for public service, was also prominent as an architectural critic; Architectural Director of *Country Life* 1910–16.
[337] Hubert Gardiner [*4102*: NT 1889–1900]; Chartered Accountant and Hon. Treasurer of the OCS.

[113]   19 February 1929. The Chairman of Council to the College Secretary
[*RS3/196. Holograph*]

74 Woodstock Road,
Oxford.
February 19 1929.

Dear Mr Lewis,
    I am returning the two designs for the Glazebrook pulpit. I am very glad to have seen them and obliged by your for sending them.
    I prefer the new design without the heraldic ornamentation. I should not mind 2 shields Balliol and Ely if the Council want to keep any, but I think the new design will look very well. I much prefer the new motto or legend *Emitte lucem tuam* &c.[338]
    It was a pleasure seeing the H.M. on Saturday week.

Yours sincerely,
Herbert Warren.

[114]   15 May 1929. Nicholson to the College Secretary
[*RS3/196. Typescript*]

15.5.29

Dear Mr Lewis,
    Regarding your letter, I think one could easily work in a legible inscription of about 100 letters in one line round the pulpit. I could easily modify the design so as to get two lines of inscription, in which case the letters might be rather smaller, and probably an inscription of 200 letters would be possible, but if it is too long people are not likely to take the trouble to read it.

Yours very truly,
Charles Nicholson.

[115]   30 September 1929. Nicholson to the College Secretary
[*RS3/196. Typescript*]

30.9.29

Dear Mr Lewis,
Clifton College.
    I am very sorry I overlooked to send you the cost of the pulpit. The oakwork will cost £200 and the architect's fees on this should be £30 so that the total cost will be £250. As this was within the figure of £300 which was mentioned to me I have had the work put in hand and I hope to see it on Thursday when I go down to Messrs Bowman, the carvers at Stamford.

Yours very truly,
Charles Nicholson.

---

[338] Psalm 42 v. 3: *Emitte lucem tuam et veritatem tuam.*

[116]   20 December 1930. The contractors to the Head Master
[*RS3/196. Typescript*]

E. Bowman & Sons,
Builders and Contractors, Gothic Carvers and Church Fitters
Stamford,
December 20th 1929.

Dear Sir,

New Pulpit for Chapel

We shall be glad to know if it will be convenient for us to fix the new pulpit between the dates Monday, January 6th mid afternoon, and Saturday the 11th. If this is not convenient we can fix in any week later to suit your convenience.

Your obedient servants,
(for) E. Bowman & Sons, [*signed*] E.S. Bowman.

SECTION VII: THE COLLEGE
MISSION: HEARING BRISTOL

☐ *Many public schools set up missions in the poorest areas of adjacent towns and cities. Clifton was among the first to do so, since this was work to which Percival attached great importance. He wanted Clifton to 'hear Bristol' and then to enter into dialogue. After some unsuccessful ventures a new start was made in 1875 in the parish of St Barnabas. From this developed the separate parish of St Agnes, with its own church and various recreational rooms.*

[117]   19 October 1888. Building the boys' and girls' clubs
[*A10a, Mission Committee Book 1888–1913. MS*]

19 Oct. 1888.

Present: the Headmaster, Mr Macpherson [*Secretary*], Mr Bartholomew [*M44*], Mr Watson [*M46*], Mr Tait [*M57*], Mr Moberly [*M65*], Mr Vaughan [*M92*]; Mr F. Gilmore Barnett [*4*], Rev. E.H. Firth [*2167*]: OC[*s*]; H.J. Boas [*3312*], E. Bonham Carter [*3100*], H.B. Mayor [*3329/M151*], H. Clissold [*3375/M148*]: members of the School.

The Treasurer presented an abstract of expenditure for 1888: the probable balance at the end of the year was estimated at £31.

The plans furnished by the architect for [a *deleted*] boys' and girls' clubrooms, a gymnasium and a church room were exhibited and explained by the Headmaster. A rough estimate of cost gave £800 or £900 for the boys' and girls' clubrooms alone. Of this amount £225 was in hand, and some discussion took place on the question whether an attempt should be made to raise more money in the School, either by subscriptions in the Houses or by an appeal at Christmas, and whether an appeal should be made to Old Cliftonians for aid in the work.

The Headmaster stated that rather more than £100 [pounds *deleted*] per annum [had been *corrected to*] would probably be assigned to St Agnes parish from funds in the possession of the parish of St James; this would serve as a sustentation fund for the work being carried on. It was resolved that, until the Ecclesiastical Commissioners should raise Mr Harvey's salary, an additional £50 per annum should be paid to him from the Mission funds.[339]

---

[339] Thomas William Harvey, Mission Curate 1881 to 1883, when he became Vicar of the new parish of St Agnes. Wilson recalls that at first 'we did not much like him'; but he subsequently showed his mettle and married Wilson's half-sister Annie: Wilson, *Autobiography*, pp. 139, 140–1; *Crockford* (1890).

The next meeting was fixed for Oct. 29.

J.M.W[*ilson*] Oct. 29/88

[118]   29 October 1888. The College buildings given priority over the club room, but the Head Master helps pay for the church room
[*A10a, Mission Committee Book 1888–1913. MS*]

29 Oct. 1888.

Present [*as above less Macpherson and Barnett; with* Mr Fairbanks (*704/M75*)]
A letter of thanks from Mr Harvey was read.

With regard to the proposed boys' and girls' club, the Sixth had resolved that a collection should be made in the Houses at the beginning of the Spring term, but as the resolution had apparently been passed under the impression that nothing could be done to the interior of the Chapel at present, the question was referred back to the Sixth for re-consideration. No appeal to Bristol seemed possible at present, nor to Old Cliftonians, as it was desirable to appeal to them for the completion of the College buildings. As the church room was urgently needed, and £100 (possibly £125) out of £225 in hand could be transferred to that object, and as the Headmaster was willing to be responsible for the expense in excess of £200, it was determined to proceed with the building of the church room and staircase at once, and it was resolved 'That the Mission Committee make itself responsible for any sum not exceeding £100 towards the expense of building the church room.'

The question of building the boys' and girls' club [sho(*uld*) *deleted*] was postponed until the fund should have reached a larger amount.

J.M.W.

[119]   9 May 1890. Balancing the books
[*A10a, Mission Committee Book 1888–1913. MS*]

9 May 1890.

Present: the Headmaster, Mr Macpherson, Mr Wiseman [*M43*], Mr Wollaston [*M60*], Mr Moberly, Mr C.P. Wilson [*M119*], Mr Gray [*M202*], Mr Cook [*M132*]; Mr F.G. Barnett O.C.; H.B. Mayor, H.A. Prichard [*3428*], C.E. Crawford [*3505*], H.D.J. Lyon [*3786*], members of the School.

The Headmaster announced that the full endowment of St Agnes' parish would be paid by the Ecclesiastical Commissioners from May 1.

The statement of accounts up to May 9 was presented and showed on the general fund account a favourable balance of £61. 19. 7; while on the church room account a balance remained to be provided of £63. 8. 8. The Headmaster gave a subscription of £10 to the building fund of the church room, in addition to his present of the furniture. Thus, on combining the two accounts, a balance of £8. 10. 11 remained in favour of the Mission; and it was suggested that part of this sum should be expended in printing and circulating a final report.

It was resolved: 'That it is desirable that some opportunity should be given for workers in the Mission district to meet and bid farewell to the Mission Committee on July 5, or some other date which [should *corrected to*] may prove more convenient.' The Headmaster, Mr Macpherson, Mr Moberly and Mr Cook were appointed a committee to make arrangements for such a meeting.

It was resolved to recommend:

1. That during the year from Trinity Sunday 1890 to Trinity Sunday 1891 the payment of £60 for clerical assistance should be continued.

2. That, in consideration of Mr Corfield's long and valuable services, a grant of £25 per annum should be paid towards the current expenses, as long as Mr Corfield[340] should remain in charge of the Mission buildings and should need assistance.

3. That, in order to keep up some connexion with St Agnes' parish, one or two offertories each year should be devoted to giving grants towards the expenses of the Sunday School children's outing and of the boys' gymnasium,

It was thought desirable to hold another Committee meeting before the general meeting, which would be held to decide on future work; and Wednesday May 14 was named as the day on which it would take place.

James M. Wilson.

[120]   12 February 1909. Reaching beyond St Agnes' Parish
[*A10a, Mission Committee Book 1888–1913. MS*]

Feb. 12. 1909.

Present: the Headmaster, Mr Macpherson, Mr Moberly, Mr Laxton [*M89*], Mr Palmer [*M162*], Mr Wordsworth [*M188*]; Rev. A.S. Rashleigh,[341] Mr Pilkington [*3095*], R.B.G. Birtill [*4794*], [*OCs*]; L.E. Atkinson [*6252*], K.W. Tribe [*6175*].

The purchase by the Headmaster, at a cost of £10. 9. 0, of tea apparatus to be hired out to those wishing to use it was accepted by the Committee.

The Committee were of opinion that the Christmas term was more suitable than the Summer term for the entertainment of St Agnes Club at the College, though it was hoped that the cricket matches (2 teams) would still take place.

It was reported that the attempt to assist a boys' club <in St Werbergh's> had not been successful.

The following resolutions were carried:

1. That after the present year (Sept. 1908 – Sept. 1909) the Committee will reduce the grant of £85 per annum to St Agnes boys' club to £75 per annum, with the view of covering the ground rent, rates, taxes, repairs and expenses of caretaking. The grants of £25 for the Sunday School outing and of £25 for the junior camp will be discontinued.

2. That a new club for working boys shall be established by the College in a neighbouring poor district, and that it is desirable that this club should not be connected with any single parish.

3. That the Committee desire to do all in their power to maintain and even to strengthen the ties at present existing between the College and St Agnes parish.

4. That the Warden, while undertaking the management of the new club, shall continue to be in charge of the St Agnes club as at present.

The Headmaster and Messrs Palmer, Pilkington and Birtill were appointed as a committee to prepare a detailed scheme for this work.

A.A. David, 25 Oct.

---

340 William Corfield, who lived close by in St Thomas Street: *Directory* (1890), p. 190.
341 Arthur Stanhope Rashleigh [*1584*: SH 1874–9]; Curate of St Agnes' 1890–6.

SECTION VIII: TEACHING AND LEARNING

Examiners' reports

☐ *The first extant scrutiny of the Clifton system shows how rapidly the School had attained a high academic standard.*

[121]   July 1864. External examiners' report.
[*Examination Reports, vol. 1. MS*]

Clifton College. Midsummer 1864

Examination Report
To the Council of Clifton College

Gentlemen,

We have examined the first five forms of the College in Divinity, Classics, Mathematics, History and Modern Languages, the examination lasting from Wednesday the 13th to Monday the 25th of July; and we are glad to be able to express our great satisfaction at the results. It is abundantly evident that a thorough system of public school education has been established, and that it is being worked with much energy, discretion and diligence. This is shewn not only by the large amount of satisfactory work done in this examination but also by the considerable progress made in the last year both in the range of subjects and in the quality of the papers. We have therefore no hesitation in speaking very highly of the present state of the School, especially considering the recent date of its foundation; and we are fully confident that before long it will make its name honourably known by successes both at the universities and elsewhere.

I. The Sixth Form contains 6 boys unusually young for the highest class, and they all shewed by their papers that they had been so taught as to take a keen interest in their work, that they had well mastered their subjects, and were able effectively to produce their knowledge. Their papers in Divinity were particularly good, as indeed was the case in every form which we examined. We would specially mention the name of Paul[342] for the excellence of all his work, as a boy of great merit and

---

[342] Alfred Wallis Paul [*48*: Town, SH 1862–6], Head of the School 1863–6; he won a scholarship to

promise. We should also commend Wilson[343] for the good style of his translations and composition.

II. The Fifth Form, Classical Remove, and Upper Fourth were examined together. We can speak in similar high terms of their industry and the good work sent in by most of them, especially noticing the names of Snow[344] in the Fifth, Hall minor[345] and Neale[346] in the Remove.

III. In German we commend Paul and Chichester,[347] and in French, Fox major[348] and Tylecote major.[349]

IV. The work of the Modern Remove includes all the studies required for this important department, and their papers in Divinity, History, Latin translation and Euclid were quite satisfactory; but we find, as of course to be expected in so young a school, that all branches of study are not yet equally developed, and among the lower boys of this and of the three forms previously mentioned, we could have desired to see a higher standard of grammatical Latin composition, and a sounder knowledge of elementary Algebra.

We however sincerely think that these are but small exceptions to take to the general goodness of the school work, which is at the same time the best evidence of the conscientious exertions of the masters and all concerned in the work of the College.

We have the honour to be your obedient humble servants,

G.C. Bell, M.A., Fellow & Tutor of Worcester College, late Mathematical Examiner and Moderator in the University of Oxford.[350]

Arthur Sidgwick, B.A., Scholar of Trinity College, Cambridge.[351]

Having examined the Fifth and two Fourth Forms in grammar, composition and the Classical books in which they have been instructed during the term, I have great pleasure in testifying to the general satisfactoriness of the result.

It should especially be remarked that the papers set in the work of the term were in all the forms, and particularly the Fifth Form, extremely well answered, evincing not only considerable industry on the part of the boys, but also proving that they had been very carefully taught.

The average merit of the composition appeared at first sight to be rather low; but on enquiry it proved that many of the boys had been engaged upon it for a very short time (some only since their arrival here), and that the progress made in that short time was generally satisfactory, and in some cases much greater than might have

---

Wadham College, Oxford before making a distinguished career in the Indian Civil Service.

[343] William Bernard Wilson [*122*: SH 1863–6], younger brother of the second Head Master; he won an exhibition to St John's College, Cambridge and entered the Indian Army.

[344] Charles Robert Snow [*60*: SH 1862–5]; he went to Trinity College, Cambridge.

[345] Henry Sinclair Hall [*235*: SH 1864–8; *M59*: 1873–99]; Scholar of Christ's College, Cambridge before becoming the first OC to return to Clifton as a master.

[346] John Alexander Neale [*99*: 1863–8], Head of the School 1866–8; awarded an exhibition at The Queen's College, Oxford.

[347] Charles Winfred Ackerly Chichester [*229*: SH 1864 (this year only)].

[348] Stephen Newcome Fox [*20*: DH 1862–8]; took a first in Law at New College, Oxford; later Professor of Roman Law at Bombay.

[349] Charles Brandon Lea Tylecote [*136*: SH 1863–7]; won an exhibition to The Queen's College, Oxford.

[350] George Charles Bell, later Headmaster of Christ's Hospital, then (1876) Master of Marlborough.

[351] Independent scholar, best known for opposing compulsory Greek at Oxford, and for advocating the admission of women to degrees.

been expected.

The inequality between the highest and lowest boys in the same form – an obstacle to teaching for which allowance must be made – is a difficulty necessarily consequent on the limited numbers and one which, as the School increases, will entirely disappear.

All the other points of interest connected with the examination are to be found in the list containing the order of merit.

A.S.

[122]   25 July 1872. External examiner's report
[*Report Book 1. MS*]

To the Council of Clifton College.

Gentlemen,

I beg to report that during the past week I have minutely examined the work of the Sixth Form in all its branches. I have also set papers which enable me to test the condition of the larger part of the College.

As a result of this examination it is a great pleasure to me to speak in the highest terms of the efficiency and success of the teaching at Clifton, which, coupled with remarkable vigour and industry on the part of the boys, has produced results unsurpassed in any public school with which I am acquainted.

Clifton College has now completed the first decade of its existence, and in this comparatively short period it has secured for itself a position in many respects unique, to which I may perhaps venture to draw your attention.

With regard to the ordinary subjects of School routine it is hardly necessary that I should say much: the remarkable success of the School is sufficiently attested by the high honours obtained by its pupils at the most distinguished colleges of both universities.

It is more important to observe that this success is not purchased by any neglect of those newer lines in which intellectual training must for the future so greatly run.

It is a great thing for a school to obtain two scholarships at Balliol in one year, and to show a standard of excellence so high as that attained by Warren and Cluer,[352] but it is a greater thing still to prove that this elaborate cultivation is thoroughly consistent with all the exigencies of practical modern life.

In evidence of this I would mention the remarkable accuracy and ability with which the English subjects were handled – [and *corrected to*] while at the same time the success of the School in Mathematics, in Physical Science, and in various competitive examinations, evinces a completeness and a judicious coordination of training which leaves little to be desired.

I may add that [while *corrected to*] although the success of the last year seems to be exceptional, and such as cannot often be expected, yet the condition of the lower forms is satisfactory, and gives good promise of future excellence.

I have the leave to remain, gentlemen, your obedient servant,

J.M. Marshall, M.A., Second Master of Dulwich College, late Fellow of Brasenose College, Oxford[353]

July 25, 1872.

---

[352] For Warren see above [38]. Albert Rowland Cluer [*774:* SH 1869–72] actually entered Balliol with an exhibition, but like Warren he took a first in Greats.
[353] Formerly a Clifton master [*M25*], and a contender for Percival's throne in 1878 [22].

[123]   August 1927. Summary Higher Certificate Report
[*Examination Reports. Printed*]

Oxford and Cambridge Schools Examination Board

August, 1927.
To the Chairman of the Governing Body of Clifton College.

Sir,

We are instructed to send you the following report on the Higher Certificate Examination recently held at Clifton College under the authority of the Oxford and Cambridge Schools Examination Board.

Forms VI and V Classical Modern and Intermediate were examined.

The examiners and the subjects of the examination were:

(a) Classics (30 boys). W.A. Pickard-Cambridge, M.A., Worcester College, Oxford.

(b) Ancient History (30 boys). G.H. Stevenson, M.A., University College, Oxford.

(c) French (9 boys). H.E. Berthon, M.A., Wadham College, Oxford.

(d) English (41 boys). H.F.B. Brett-Smith, M.A., Corpus Christi College, Oxford.

(e) History (17 boys). N.B. Dearle, M.A., D.Sc., All Souls College, Oxford.

(f) Mathematics (12 boys). G.N. Watson, Sc.D., Trinity College, Cambridge.

(g) Physics (12 boys). F. Horton, Sc.D., St John's College, Cambridge.

(h) Chemistry (4 boys). D.Ll. Hammick, M.A., Oriel College, Oxford.

(i) Scripture Knowledge (40 boys). A.V. Valentine Richards, M.A., Christ's College, Cambridge.

25 Higher and 93 School Certificates were awarded to candidates from the School.

The substance of the report is taken from the reports of the examiners.

I. General remarks.

(*a*) *Classics*. The examination showed no scholar of clearly first-class merit throughout in either Greek or Latin; but out of the fourteen candidates in *Group I* four reached or approached that standard in either one or two of the three principal papers set in each language, while five others reached between 60 and 50 per cent. of the total marks available, and in individual papers or answers submitted work of high promise; after them comes a rather rapid drop, ending with one candidate who was very distinctly weaker than the rest.

Speaking generally, a comparison of the translations, unseen or prepared, with the compositions seems to show that most of the boys can at present translate the languages considerably better than they can write them, and that some steady work in grammar, and (for those who write verses) in prosody, is required to raise the standard in composition to a wholly satisfactory level. Also, while the answers to general questions, both on the prepared books and in the General paper, showed a background of general knowledge and an interest in classical life and literature that were very creditable, and here and there very remarkable, there was rather an absence (except, perhaps, in some answers on the Greek prepared book) of detailed knowledge wherever questions of criticism and interpretation were involved.

On the whole, the interest of the result of the Group I examination lay, perhaps, rather in the promise it showed for another year than in the actual performance of this year.

The papers of *Group II* in Latin Book and Unprepared Translation were taken by fifteen candidates, but except in one or two cases the work was rather mediocre, particularly in the prepared book, where only three candidates obtained upwards of half marks, and even the translation of a good many showed some very weak places.

(*b*) *Ancient History. Group I.* Both papers on Greek History were answered distinctly well by half of the fourteen candidates, and the younger boys showed promise. It was clear that the boys had been well taught, and knew what points were really important. One or two of them wrote admirably, showing an unusual power of sticking to the point and avoiding irrelevant detail.

Group II. The papers in Group II presented a great contrast. Some mistakes were made which suggested an almost incredible ignorance of the way in which Rome ruled Italy and the provinces under the Republic. Most of the candidates wrote in a very slipshod style. A good many seemed to be reproducing notes which they had not understood.

(*c*) *French.* In *Unprepared Translation* the majority gave very fair versions of the first passage, but their command of vocabulary was not quite adequate for the harder ones. In *Composition* one boy showed a very good command of French, but most of the work was very inaccurate as regards grammar.

(*d*) *English.* Most of the candidates did very creditable work on their English *Books* and *Period*, and had evidently studied them with appreciation. Those who took the paper on the *Growth and Structure of the English Language* wrote interested and intelligent answers. The English *Essays*, however, were commonplace and below the standard of the other work; candidates made no use of their general reading, and wrote without much attention to style.

(*e*) *History.* The work varied to a considerable extent. Some of it was definitely good; at its best it was better than last year, but some of it was rather commonplace. Whilst there was more first-rate work than last year, there seemed less of a good second-rate type. The answers were generally well-expressed and, as a rule, accurate; but there was some tendency in all three papers, not to wander entirely from the subject, but to fail to give the exact answers required. The facts, on the whole, seemed to have been fairly well grasped, but there was not always sufficient detailed knowledge shown in the *English History, Special Period*, in which paper the results were the least good. Possibly more detailed study was required. The *European History* paper was the best answered of the three. A sound knowledge was, as a rule, displayed, with, except on one or two matters, quite a fair grasp of the period.

(*f*) *Mathematics.* Eight candidates took the Group III papers and four took the Group IV papers. The general level of the work of the Group III candidates was distinctly good, and the answers submitted by the best candidate were excellent. The Group IV candidates showed, on the whole, that they had an adequate acquaintance with the subject with a view to its application.

(*g*) *Physics.* The descriptive work was well done, and several boys were particularly good in their answers to questions requiring mathematical treatment. The average standard of the candidates was very satisfactory.

(*h*) *Chemistry.* The four candidates gave a very satisfactory impression, the physical questions producing, on the whole, the best answers.

The quantitative problem in the *Practical* paper was done well by all the candidates; general weakness was shown, however, over the qualitative exercise.

(*i*) *Scripture.* There were some good sets of answers sent up, particularly by Form VI, but not a few of the other boys seemed to find the set books (*Isaiah* and *St John's*

Gospel) too hard, and often gave rambling answers which were off the point. But evidence of good and careful teaching came out again and again, as also did evidence of real thought on the part of individual boys.

Hebrew. The candidate who offered Hebrew produced a very poor and disappointing set of answers: the candidate who offered *Daniel* and 1 *Maccabees* had a fair knowledge of the content of these books.

II. Further Reports (not printed) containing the remarks of the examiners on the details of the work done in the Higher Certificate, as well as a report on the whole of the work done in the School Certificate, are being sent to the Head Master.

We are, Sir, your obedient servants,

T.G. Bedford, C.H. Wilkinson,

Secretaries to the Board.

Syllabus and scholarship

[124]   Summer Term 1867. Physics syllabus
[*Guard Book 1877. Printed*]

Clifton College.
Syllabus of lectures in Physical Science.
Second term, 1867.

MECHANICS

§1.   Definitions of matter and force – Qualities of matter, primary and secondary – The object of Physical Sciences.

§2.   Primary qualities – Extension – Measures of length, area and volume – Force.

§3.   Secondary qualities – Divisibility – Porosity – Crystallisation – Compressibility and extensibility – Elasticity – Hardness – Toughness – Tenacity – Malleability and ductility – Inertia.

§4.   Force – Measurement of force – Measures of weight – Representation of force by straight lines.

§5.   Assumptions – Principles derived from experiment.

§6.   Definitions – Composition and resolution of forces – Couples.

§7.   Centre of gravity – Equilibrium of a heavy body.

§8.   Simple machines – Mechanical advantage – Lever – Wheel and axle – Pulley – Systems of pulleys – Inclined plane – Wedge – Screw.

§9.   Compound machines – Balance – Steelyard – Weighing machines.

§10.   Friction.

§11.   Virtual velocities.

Motion – Velocity – Acceleration

§1.   Dynamics – Laws of motion – Measure of mass.

§2.   Attwood's machine[354] – Determination of the accelerating effect of the force of gravity.

§3.   Pendulum – Motion of a particle in a circle.

§4.   Motion of a rigid body.

---

[354] Devised by George Attwood (1784) to demonstrate the counter-balancing effects of a pulley.

§5.   Projectiles.
§6.   Impact of bodies.

HYDROMECHANICS

§1.   Definition of perfectly fluid matter – Liquids and gases – Definition of pressure at a Point – Transmission of pressure – Hydrostatic paradox.
§2.   Specific gravity – Density.
§3.   Equilibrium of fluids – Equilibrium under the force of gravity – Whole pressure – Centre of pressure – Resultant pressure.
§4.   Bodies immersed in fluids – Equilibrium of a floating body – Metacentre.
§5.   Determination of specific gravities.
§6.   Capillarity – Diffusion.
§7.   Elasticity of fluids – Gases – Pressure of gases – Boyle's Law – Mixture of gases.
§8.   Weight of gases – Pressure of the atmosphere – Barometers – Determination of heights by the barometer.
§9.   Siphon – Air pump – Condenser – Water pumps – Manometers – Diving bell.
§10. Rotating liquid.
§11. Motion of fluids.

[125]   6 January 1868. Notice from the Head Master
[*Guard Book 1860–77. Printed*]

Clifton College.
Scholarships.

In April next one or more scholarships, value £25 a-year, will be open to competition to boys under 14 on the 1st of January whether previously in the College or not. The scholarships are tenable for four years, if the holders remain as long at the College. They may be gained by proficiency either in Classics or Mathematics.

Candidates will be examined in Latin and Greek grammar; Latin and Greek composition; Translations from Latin and Greek authors into English; also in Euclid, Arithmetic, Algebra, easy Trigonometry.

The examination will commence on Tuesday, the 7th of April at 9 a.m.

Names of candidates to be sent to the Head Master not later than the 31st of March,
J. Percival, Head Master.
Clifton College,
6th January, 1868.

[126]   June [1868]. Whitworth scholarships
[*Guard Book 1860–77. Printed*]

Whitworth scholarships
for the promotion of
engineering and mechanical industry.

Mr Whitworth[355] having placed one of his preliminary exhibitions at the disposal of the Clifton College, the Council have determined to throw it open to public

---

[355] Sir Joseph Whitworth, Bt (so created 1869), FRS, inventor and President of the Institute of Mechanical Engineers, had in this year 1868 established the scholarship fund which bears his name.

competition. The exhibition is of the value of £25 for one year. Candidates must not exceed 25 years of age, and must be either students at the College or youths who have obtained Certificates held by the Universities of Oxford and Cambridge, or the Science and Art Department, or the Society of Arts.[356] The only condition required of the successful competitor will be that he proceed to qualify himself for the competition for the scholarships of £100, to be conducted in May 1869, and satisfy the Council that he will present himself as a candidate at that competition.

The subjects of examination will be: (1) Mathematics; (2) Mechanics, theoretical and applied; (3) Practical, plane, and descriptive Geometry, mechanical and freehand Drawing; (5) Physics; (6) Chemistry, including Metallurgy.

The examination will be held in the last week of June, at Clifton College. The exact times will shortly be published.

Candidates are requested to send certificates of age and qualification to the Headmaster, Clifton College, by Saturday, June 13th.

[127] June 1872. Scholarships
[Guard Book 1860–77. Printed]

Clifton College.
Scholarships.
The following will be open for competition in June 1872:

1. One or more entrance scholarships, tenable during the holder's stay at the College, of the value of £90 a year (which is equivalent to both board and tuition free).

2. The Heyworth[357] and Council scholarships of £75 a year for two years, open to boys of 17 on the 24th of June, to be given in one scholarship, if the best cannot attend the College without becoming a boarder, or in three scholarships of £30, £25 and £20, if the best candidate be able to attend as a day boy.

3. One or more House Master's scholarships of £65 a year, for two years or till election to another scholarship, open to boys under 16 on the 24th of June, 1872.

4. One or more Council scholarships of £25 a year, for two years or till election to another scholarship, open to boys under 15 on the 24th of June, 1872.

The examination will commence on Wednesday, June 19th, at 9 a.m. For the entrance and Council scholarships an allowance for age is made in favour of young boys.

The holders of the entrance and House Masters' scholarships must board where they are placed by the Head Master; the other scholarships can be held by either day boys or boarders without restriction.

Any scholarship may be gained by proficiency, either in (1) Classics; or (2) Mathematics, with some branch of Natural Science; or (3) Mathematics, with French or German and English.

Names of candidates, with certificates of age and good conduct, should be sent to the Head Master at least one week before the examination begins.

No election will be made to any scholarship if the candidates are not considered sufficiently advanced.

J. Percival, Head Master.

---

[356] Became Royal Society of Arts in 1908.
[357] Given by James Heyworth in the previous year: Christie, *History*, p. 234.

It is intended to offer the following scholarships for competition in 1873:

1. One or more entrance scholarships, tenable during the holder's stay at the College, of the value of £90 a year.

2. The Guthrie scholarship of £70 a year for two years, open to boys under 17 on the 24th of June, 1873.

3. One or more scholarships of £65 a year for two years, or till election to another scholarship, open to boys under 16 on the 24th June, 1873.

4. One or more Council scholarships of £24 a year for two years, or till election to another scholarship, open to boys under 15 on the 24th June, 1873.

[128] December 1873. Classics syllabus
[Guard Book 1860–77. Printed]

Clifton College.
Classical Side.
Entrance examination.

1. Boys of 16 are expected to qualify for admission to the Fourth Form, the work of which is as follows:

Latin: Accidence, Syntax, Prosody; Virgil or Ovid, Cæsar or Livy, and easy prose composition.

Greek: Accidence, including chief irregular verbs; Xenophon, and Greek play; and easy exercises.

2. Boys of 15 are expected to qualify for admission to the Upper Third Form, the work of which is as follows:

Latin: Accidence, elementary rules of Syntax and Prosody; Kennedy's *Palæstra*,[358] Ovid; easy prose competition.

3. Boys of 14 and under are expected to qualify for admission to [*the*] Lower Third Form, the work of which is as follows:

Latin: Grammar; Accidence, and a few of the most important Syntax rules.

Henry's Exercises:[359] Ex. 1–47.

Latin: Construing; Prose in Kennedy's *Palæstra* and easy Ovid.

Greek Grammar: to the end of the active voice of τύπτω.

Arnold's first Greek book:[360] Exercises 1–6.

Note: *All boys should be able to write and spell satisfactorily, to do the elements of Arithmetic, and to have a fair elementary knowledge of English, Geography, English History, and French; and also the elder boys are expected to know something of elementary Algebra and Geometry.*

Excellence in one subject may, to some extent, compensate for deficiency in another.

J. Percival, Head Master.
December, 1873.

---

[358] Benjamin Hall Kennedy, *Palæstra Latina: or, a Second Latin Reading Book* (1850).
[359] Thomas Kerchever Arnold, *Henry's First Latin Book* (1839). The author was unrelated to Arnold of Rugby.
[360] T.K. Arnold, *The First Greek Book: On the Plan of Henry's First Latin Book* (1849).

[129]   26 November 1880. The Master of Balliol[361] to the Head Master
[P5126 Album. Holograph]

Oxford Nov. 26 *[1880]*

Dear Mr Wilson,
   I congratulate you and Clifton upon obtaining a success which I believe that no other school has ever obtained: a scholarship and two exhibitions. We were very much pleased with your boys: Jose[362] did well throughout and showed real ability; Boas[363] is rough in scholarship but he did an exceedingly good English essay; and Nash[364] though inferior to them showed that he had taken great pains and was a good scholar.
   We shall be happy to give rooms to either of your two other boys who did themselves credit: Burd[365] wrote a very good essay, though he fell behind in other parts of the examination; Newbolt[366] was not so good in any single subject but more equal throughout.
   Will you kindly tell them to write to me and say whether they wish to accept the offer of rooms and when they would like to reside.
Believe me, yours very truly,
B. Jowett.
The scholar and exhibitioners are required by the Ordinances of the Commission to enter into residence not later than next October.

[130]   23 December 1895. Deed establishing Hugh Lucas scholarships
[Trusts Deeds Box. Original instrument; bound volume of vellum leaves, signed and sealed. The minimal punctuation of the original has been followed]

This indenture made the twenty third day of December one thousand eight hundred and ninety five between Isabel Olga Lucas of 5 Westbourne Terrace Hyde Park London widow William Louis Lucas[367] of the same place Esquire Lionel Edward Pyke of 19 Phillimore Gardens Campden Hill, W. one of Her Majesty's Counsel Mary Rachel Pyke wife of the said Lionel Edward Pyke and Ruth Lucas of Westbourne Terrace aforesaid spinster hereinafter called 'the donors' of the one part and the Clifton College hereinafter called 'the College' of the other part;
   Whereas the donors are the mother, brother, brother-in-law and sisters of Hugh Nathaniel Lucas deceased[368] who was a member of the College from 1885 to 1890 and who was afterwards an undergraduate of New College Oxford and who was

---

[361] Benjamin Jowett, Master of Balliol 1870–93, and a towering figure in high Victorian Oxford; also prominent, with Percival, in setting up Bristol's University College.

[362] Arthur Wilberforce Jose [*1410*: NT, SH 1874–81] taught in Australia and India, later achieving distinction as a military historian and editor.

[363] Frederick Samuel Boas [*2079*: BH 1877–81] became an authority on early modern English drama.

[364] Spencer Hampden Nash [*1416*: ST 1874–81]; Head of the School 1879–81; took a First in Mods but died before achieving further distinction.

[365] Lawrence Arthur Burd [*1835*: PHP, DH 1876–81] was to be a master at Repton and a Machiavelli scholar.

[366] Newbolt was let down by his essay on the the the technique of biography. He stayed on at Clifton and won a scholarship to Corpus in the following January: Newbolt, *My World*, pp. 81–2 (and for his schooldays generally, pp. 45–81; also Chitty, *Newbolt*, pp. 35–58).

[367] *2715*: PH 1881–5.

[368] *3386*: PH 1885–90.

killed by an accident on the Tnesch-horn[369] mountain near Zermatt Switzerland on the 17th August 1893 and the donors are desirous of founding a scholarship or scholarships at the College in memory of the said Hugh Nathaniel Lucas;

And whereas in pursuance of such desire and in order to carry the same into effect the donors have prior to the execution hereof transferred into the name of the College £123. 0. 0 (one hundred and twenty three pounds) East Indian Railway Annuity class B the same being now of the estimated value of three thousand eight hundred and thirteen pounds as the College do hereby acknowledge;

Now this indenture witnesseth and it is hereby covenanted agreed and declared by the College with the privity and assent of the donors testified by their execution hereof that the College will stand possessed of the aforesaid security hereinafter called 'the trust fund' upon trust either to continue the same in its present state of investment or to realize and reinvest the same in manner hereinafter prescribed and to stand possessed of the investments and the dividends and income thereof as the endowment of two scholarships to be called the '*Hugh Lucas scholarships*' to the intent that the College shall from time to time dispense the benefit of the said scholarships and administer the affairs thereof and stand possessed of the trust fund and the income thereof upon the terms and conditions in accordance with the directions upon the trusts and with and subject to the powers provisions and declarations given expressed declared and contained of and concerning the same in the scheme set forth in the schedule hereto.

And it is hereby declared that the College should be at liberty from time to time to reinvest the trust fund in any security for the time being authorized sanctioned or approved by Statute as an investment of trust funds or in any investment for the time being authorized for the investment of cash under the control or subject to the order of the High Court of Justice with power from time to time to vary any such investment for others of the like nature.

In witness whereof the donors have hereunto set their hands and seals and the College has caused the common seal to be hereto affixed the day and year first above written.

The schedule above referred to containing the scheme for the regulation and management of the Hugh Lucas scholarships.

1. The scholarships are to be known as the 'Hugh Lucas scholarships' being `founded in memory of Hugh Nathaniel Lucas a member of the School from 1885 to 1890.

There shall be two scholarships one to be first awarded in 1895 and the other to be first awarded in 1897.

2. The scholarships are to be open to members of the College (with certain restrictions hereinafter mentioned) who are about to leave the School and intend to matriculate and enter into residence at any College at Oxford or Cambridge University and are to be tenable with any other School scholarship but shall be vacated unless such intention (except in the case of illness or other unavoidable accident) is carried into effect within 18 months after the awarding thereof <retrospectively>.

3. Each scholarship to be of the value of £50 (fifty pounds) per annum provided that the income of the trust fund is sufficient to provide for the same and if at any time such income be insufficient to provide for the payment of both scholarships at the full value of £50 then each scholarship shall be of the value of one half of the

---

[369] *Sic* for Taschhorn.

actual income arising from the trust fund after payment of the examiners' fees. Each scholarship shall be tenable for four years (commencing at the date of the scholar's residence at the university) provided that the scholar reside so long at the university. The amount shall be paid to the scholar by two equal half yearly payments on the 1st of November and the 1st of May in each year the first payment of the scholarship awarded in 1895 shall be made on the 1st of May 1896 and the first payment of the scholarship awarded in 1897 shall be made on the 1st of May 1898.

4. The scholarship shall be awarded to the successful candidate in a special competitive examination to be held every alternate year at the School at some time during the Summer term of the School to be fixed by the Head Master for the time being.

5. Candidates must be not under 17 years of age on the first day of the examination nor over 19 years and 6 months of age on the last day of the Summer term of the School year in which the examination is held. They must also have been members of the School for at least 2 years immediately preceding the date of the commencement of the examination.

6. The examiners shall be at least two in number. They shall be Masters of Arts either of Oxford or Cambridge and shall be elected by the Council. No master for the time being of the College shall be eligible as an examiner.

The fees of the examiners shall be regulated by the Council but such fees shall not exceed £20 between them for each examination.

7. Each successful candidate shall undertake in writing to read for an Honours School.

The payment of each scholarship in each year shall be contingent on the receipt by the Council of a report from the Head Master that the scholar's progress and conduct at the university appear to be satisfactory failing which report the amount of the scholarship shall lapse into the reserve fund mentioned in clause 10.

8. (a) The exact days and hours for the examination shall be from time to time fixed by the Head Master in consultation with the examiners.

(b) The examination shall include separate papers in the following subjects.

Group A.

I. Latin prose.

II. Greek prose.

III. Dialogues of Plato. A selection to be prescribed each year to contain one or more complete Dialogues or complete portions of longer Dialogues. Questions to be set involving the matter as well as the language of the Dialogues.

Group B.

I. A period of English literature to be prescribed each year.

II. One or more authors or complete works of authors belonging to the period so prescribed.

III. A paper on the history and development of the English language with some attention to provincial and archaic words and also to include questions on general history so far as it bears on the history of the language.

Note. As regards this last paper it is understood that it will not be necessary for the College to provide any teaching in respect of its subject matter and that certain limits may be annually prescribed within which the subject is to be dealt with and that only such knowledge of the subject will be expected from the candidates as may be attained by a boy of good ability working at the subject without prejudice to the studies prescribed in the School examination.

(c) The special subjects and limits (if any) within which they are to be dealt with shall be prescribed for the first year by the Head Master and afterwards each year for the next year after the examination has been concluded by the examiners of the year in consultation with the Head Master.

(d) The Council with the consent of the Head Master shall have power from time to time to alter or modify the subjects for examination provided that the main object of the founders of the scholarships be kept in view, vizt. the encouragement of the study of literature and history of language.

9. A candidate to be successful must satisfy the examiners in all the subjects in both groups and must also shew real excellence in at least one paper in each group.

10. In the event of there being no successful candidate in a given year the scholarship shall be again competed for in the following year. Should there again be no successful candidate the amount of the scholarship for that year and the three succeeding years shall be divided equally into 2 parts of which one part shall be reinvested and form a reserve fund the other part shall be divided equally between the Library of New College Oxford and the School Library of Clifton College. The reserve fund shall be reinvested and the income thereof shall be added to the income derived from the original donation so as to increase the value of the scholarships until they shall reach the annual value of £70 each – after the happening of that event the reserve fund shall [*word repeated*] be reinvested and accumulated for such period as the Council may think fit and may from time to time decide and when they consider that a sufficient fund has been raised the income thereof shall be applied in or towards founding or endowing an additional scholarship or scholarships to be described as 'Hugh Lucas scholarship' or scholarships and to be of such amount tenable upon such terms payable in such manner and generally to be subject to such conditions regulations and provisions as the Council may determine.

11. Any surplus income derived from the trust fund after providing for the payment of the scholarships and the expenses thereof shall fall into and form part of the reserve fund hereinbefore mentioned and shall be dealt with accordingly.

Signed sealed and delivered by the before named Isabel Olga Lucas, Mary Rachel Pyke and Ruth Lucas in the presence of Edgar R. Everington, 114 Queen Victoria St, London E.C., solicitor.

Signed sealed and delivered by the before named Lionel Edward Pyke in the presence of Edgar R. Everington.

Signed sealed and delivered by the before named William Louis Lucas in the presence of Edgar R. Everington.

[*Signed against seals*] Isabel O. Lucas, W.L. Lucas, L.R. Pyke, Mary R. Pyke, R. Lucas.

The seal of Clifton College was hereunto affixed in the presence of [*signatures*] J.C. Chetwood Aiken; H.N. Abbot: two members of the Council of the College [*Seal*].

**[131]		18 November 1914. Foundation of Moberly Prize**
[*Council Minute Book 6, p. 303. MS*]

Moberly Prize.

The Headmaster having reported that Mrs Moberly proposed to found a prize in memory of her husband, the late Mr W.O. Moberly,[370] the prize to be of the annual

---

[370] William Octavius Moberly [*M65*: 1874–1913] had died on 2 February 1914, two months after retiring; memoir by Canon Glazebrook in *Endowed Scholarships and Prizes*, pp. 76–83.

value of five guineas and to be awarded for Latin prose, and that she had bought on behalf of the College £105 five % consolidated preference stock of the Great Western Railway Company for the endowment of the said prize, it was resolved that the proposal be accepted with the best thanks of the Council and that the seal of the College be affixed to the form of transfer of stock.

[132]   23 March 1929. The Head Master's confidence in the enduring value of a Classical education
[*HM6/Interview Book 1929–30, f. 10, MS*]

Saturday 23rd March 1929.
    Professor Earp, the father of T.C.F. Earp in Watson's House,[371] came to see me about his son's future. The boy wishes to go into colonial administrative service. When he leaves he is to go to King's, Cambridge. The father asked whether there would be anything to be gained by his reading for some subject other than Classics. I said that I thought not, but that I did not know enough of his work to be able to say whether he is likely to do well in Classics at Cambridge.

Record Sheets

☐ *The individual pupil's academic progress was entered on a 'Record Sheet', never more than a single page, with brief comments added each term. These are extant from 1879 to 1919. The following samples are rather more fulsome than the majority. The most prominent figure covered by these records is the future commander of ANZAC, later President of the College.*[372]

[133]   December 1882. Lord Birdwood's Record Sheet
[*K2/1882.3. MS on printed form; printed elements here bold*]

PRIVATE
CLIFTON COLLEGE

Town S.   **Name** Birdwood ma W.R.
Born Sep./65 **Entered** May 1877. **Left** Dec. 1882
Previous School Junior

Form	Date	Reports
IVβ	Oct. 79	25–30. Not satisfactory. Idle. H.J.W[*iseman*]. Not v. strenuous. T[*ait*] 'Never care at home'.
	Nov. 79	Still not satisfactory. If he does not do a fair exam he had better go down next term into IIIα.
	Dec.	Better.
	Feb. [*80*]	Began well. Falls off in attention & [*illegible*]. 'Not quite sat[*isfactory*] but better than last term.'
	Apr.	Much improved.

---

[371] Terence Claud Francis Earp [*9610*: WaH 1925–9]; from King's went straight into the RAFVR, won the DFC, and died on active service 1944. His father Prof. Frank Russell Earp published *The Way of the Greeks* (1929) and other works of Classical scholarship.
[372] See above **[42]**. Birdwood was realistic about his schooldays: 'I usually kept a steady pace near the bottom of whatever form I happened to be in': *Khaki and Gown*, p. 27.

	Jun.	13–19. Unsteady. July better but v. bad blunders. Hopeful, must take great pains.
	Oct.	Better – doing well.
	Dec.	9–1. Very good work – good term.
	Apr. [*81*]	9. A little upset by sports.
	July	Works well – talk comp[*letely*] heedless.
	Dec	1–9.
Remβ	82. Feb.	Latin Greek English bad.
	Apr.	G[*reek*]. I hope he has not really suffered from his run.
	May 82	L[*atin*] and G[*reek*] very weak. He must do his utmost if he is to [*get into*] Sandhurst.
	July	Work suffered much from absence. Conduct v.g.
Vβ	Oct.	He ought to get into Sandhurst eventually and pass the preliminary at once; every care is being taken to secure this. For the final he will have to compete with about 450 candidates up to the age of 20 for 70 vacancies and it is not likely he will succeed very early, perhaps not for 2 yrs. I think his leaving is somewhat premature and unnecessary.
	Dec.	Very careless blunders but industrious.

☐ *The historian of the ANZAC campaign was also at Clifton.*

[134]   July 1898. Record Sheet for Charles Bean[373]
[*K2/1898.2. MS on printed form; printed elements here bold*]

<u>PRIVATE</u>
CLIFTON COLLEGE

                                                              Name Bean, C.E.W.
Born 18th Nov. 1879 **Entered** Sept. 1894
Previous School Sir Anthony Browne's School, Brentwood, Essex (Edwin Bean – father of boy – Headmaster)[374]

Form	**Date**	**Reports**
		Son of an O.C. who is a schoolmaster. Is said to have a taste for art.
IVβ	94.1	Satisfactory. Shows promise.
[IV]α	2	Work & health irregular. Sat[*isfactory*].
	3	Doing very well.
Vγ	95.2	Work very poor.
[V]β	3	Quite sat.
[V]α	96.1	Ab[*sent*].
	2	English bad otherwise sat.
VI	3	Working well but rather childish in mind.
	97.1	Had come on a good deal.
	97.2	Feeble.

---

[373] Charles Edward Woodrow Bean [4775: *BH* 1894–8]; official War Correspondent with Australian forces 1914–19, General Editor of the Australian history of the war, and one of the most influential historians of his adopted country; founder of the Australian War Memorial.

[374] Bean snr [*6*: SH 1862–9] had been assistant master at Geelong and Sydney Grammar Schools, and Headmaster of All Saints' Bathurst NSW before taking charge of Brentwood School in 1891.

97.3	Very feeble. Poor health. Seems to have no mind.
98.1	Slack. S.A.
98.2	Improved all round, but not good.

□ *A more remarkable improvement is found in the record of a Head Master's son.*

[135]   July 1902. Record Sheet for Sir Arnold Wilson[375]
[*K2/1902.2. MS on printed form; printed elements here bold*]

PRIVATE
CLIFTON COLLEGE

B.H.   **Name** Wilson, A.T.

Born 18th July 1884 **Entered** 17th Sept. 1881
Previous School A.G. Grenfell,[376] Mostyn House School, Parkgate

Form	Date	Reports
4b	98.3	Careless and conceited but has wits.
4y	99.1	Work slipshod & casual – manners a shade better.
4z	99.2	Very poor work on the whole.
5z	99.3	Doing very badly all round.
5y	00.1	Working well and behaving much better.
5y	00.2	Working fairly good – thoroughly bad in the House, insubordinate – foul mouthed & a notorious liar.
5z	00.3	Working well except Science.
5z	01.2	Much improved – got the Navy League prize.
VI	01.3	Good on the whole – but still slippery.
	02.2	Has steadily improved, & now seems quite satisfactory. Works well and shows public spirit.

□ *Not all products of Victorian Clifton were soldiers and proconsuls.*

[136]   December 1884. Record Sheet for Roger Fry[377]
[*K2/1884.3. MS on printed form; printed elements here bold*]

PRIVATE
CLIFTON COLLEGE

Tait. S.H.   **Name** Fry, R.E.

Born 14th Dec 1866 **Entered** 22nd Feb. 1881. Left Dec 1884
Previous School [*blank*]

Form	Date	Reports
4α	June	1–9 all his work intelligent.

---

[375] Sir Arnold Talbot Wilson [*5461*: BH 1898–1902], son of HM2; senior diplomat in Persian Gulf, and General Manager of Anglo-Persian Oil Co.; knighted 1919; joined RAFVR aged 55 in 1939, serving as aircrew gunner; killed in action when shot down 1940.

[376] Algernon George Grenfell [*2750*: SH 1881–2], so one of Wilson's father's pupils; see also below **[222]**.

[377] Roger Elliot Fry [*2706*: SH 1881–4]; artist, critic, and member of the Bloomsbury group; Curator of Paintings at the New York Metropolitan Museum of Art 1906–9. His father Sir Edward was a member of the Council 1895–1902. Fry's schooldays are discussed in Potter, *Headmaster*, pp. 93–5. See also below **[162]**.

Dec.		Knows little Greek yet will do – I almost fear he will go up. Very intelligent.
Vγ	Feb.	Begun well.
	Apr.	Much absent. Satisfactory.
	May 82	Good.
	July	V. good.
	Oct.	V. good.
	Dec.	Doing very well in every way.
Vα	Feb.	A quiet blunderer.
	Apr. 83	Good.
	June 83	Construing improving – composition & grammar weak.
	July 83	Classics poor. Taking great pains. I think he ought to have a better report for his Classics. Surely some of these bad mistakes are avoidable by a boy of his intelligence.

[137]   July 1885. Record Sheet for John Ellis McTaggart[378]
[K2/1899.2. MS on printed form; printed elements here bold]

PRIVATE
CLIFTON COLLEGE

H.J.W[*iseman*].   **Name** McTaggart, J.E.
Born 7th Dec. '67. **Entered** Jan. '82
Previous School W.B. Ward, B.A. of Keble College, Oxford; H.A. Haines, Pine Cottage, Weybridge

Form	**Date**	**Reports**
IIIα	Feb. [*82*]	Places very low; if he is intelligent he ought to work at his grammar and get up the School.
IIIα	April	Doing very well.
	May	F[*air*] only; places low.
	July/82	English subjects good.
IIIα(F)	Oct.	Intelligent but very inaccurate; does not work enough.
	Dec.	Does not know what work means; very unpunctual.
	Ap./83	'Good' (Fairbanks).[379] 'Terribly unpunctual, slovenly and untidy' (Moberly and Wiseman),
	June/83	Absent.
	July 83	Absent.
	Oct. 83	Work very unsatisfactory.
	Dec. 83	Not a good term.
	Ap. 84	Better.
IVα	June 84	V. Fair.
	July	Unpunctual; rather sluggish.

---

[378] John Ellis McTaggart, FBA [*2867*: WiH 1887–5]; eminent academic philosopher (authority on Hegel) and Fellow of Trinity College, Cambridge; member of Council from 1913 until his death in 1925. Fry and McTaggart were close friends, united in aversion to Cliftonian orthodoxy: Potter, *Headmaster*, pp. 92–7. See also Christie, *Clifton School Days*, pp. 75–6. ('one very intellectual boy in the School ... quite hopeless at games and yet was very much liked'), and Newbolt's recollection of his School loyalty: *Later Life*, pp. 15–16.
[379] Walter Fairbanks [*704*: SH 1869–71; *M75*: 1875–96]; taught Classics.

Vγ   Oct/.84   Associates with little boys – 2nd report.

        Dec./84   Fair – health weak.

[138]   **July 1899. Record Sheet for Thoby Stephen**[380]

[K2/1899.2. MS on printed form; printed elements here bold]

PRIVATE
CLIFTON COLLEGE

                                                  Name Stephen J.T.

Born 8th Sept. '80. **Entered** Sept. 1894

Previous School G.T. Worsley Esq., Evelyns, Hellingdon, Uxbridge

Form	**Date**	**Reports**
Vγ	94.3	Seems to have a good deal of power but is very shy – nobody has made much of him yet.
[V]β	95.2	Works well, & has wits (lost his mother early in the term).[381]
[V]α	3	Rather slack in Classics.
	96.1	Working well except Science.
	2	Good on the whole but rather slack.
VI	96.3	Slack – overgrown.
	97.1	Much improved – working very fairly.
	97.2	Quarrelled with Pearson[382] in a childish way.
	97.3	Working very fairly & improving.
	98.1	Some improvement.
	98.2	Doing well – much more manly.[383]
	98.3	Good – Exhibition at Trinity.
	99.1	Improving in work & in manners.
	99.2	[A little better – has *deleted*] Some very good work – much broken by illness.

---

[380] Julian Thoby Stephen [*4870*: BH 1894–9]; son of the writer Sir Leslie Stephen, and brother of Virginia Woolf and Vanessa Bell; after Cambridge was expected to have a similarly dazzling career but died of typhoid at the age of 26.

[381] Julia Prinsep Stephen (*née* Jackson) had died on 5 May, from complications after influenza; she was a great beauty who had modelled for the Pre-Raphaelites.

[382] James Edward Pearson [*526*: Town 1867–70; *M69*: 1874–7, 1881–1909]; taught Physics.

[383] A characteristic which gave particular delight to his friend Lytton Strachey.

SECTION IX: SCIENCE

☐ *From the earliest days Clifton was distinguished by the extent and quality of its science teaching, for which Percival secured facilities and staff of the highest order.*[384] *Complementing the curricular instruction was the Scientific Society, which from modest beginnings flourished notably. Less successful were the related institutions of Museum and Botanic Garden. The new Science School of 1927 enhanced a tradition of laboratory teaching which had begun sixty years earlier.*

[139]   July 1867. Opening of the Laboratory
[*Guard Book 1860–77. Printed*]

Clifton College   July 1867
Notice to parents
1. The Lord Bishop of the Diocese is expected to take a Confirmation at the College in the Autumn.
2. The new Laboratory will be open for use when the School meets again in September. Any boy can work in it under the guidance of our Natural Science masters by paying the Laboratory fee of £4 4s. each term. This fee includes the cost of all materials used.
3. The new Gymnasium will be opened for use when the School meets again in September.

Fees, 15s. per term, or £2 2s. per annum.
The instructor is always in attendance when the Gymnasium is open.

[140]   September 1870. Establishment of Museum
[*Guard book 1860–77. Printed*][385]

[*Minuted in MS*] Mem[*orandum*]. Issued without previous authority at the Council.

---

[384] See particularly Sir A.B. Pippard [*10478*], 'Schoolmaster-Fellows and the campaign for science education', *Notes and Records of the Royal Society* 56 (2002), pp. 63–81, and N.R. Ingram [*M642*], 'All that you can't leave behind', *ibid.* 57 (2003), pp. 177–84.
[385] Reprinted in *Transactions*, [i], II, pp. ix–xi.

Clifton College Museum.

For some time past a small collection of Natural History specimens has been in course of formation at Clifton College, intended as the nucleus of a School Museum. The want of a suitable apartment for their reception has, however, prevented any proper arrangement of these contributions being made, and they are almost wholly inaccessible to the pupils of the College, and may be said to be at present practically useless.

The Head Master has, however, recently built and presented to the College an extensive Library and Museum, so that a most favourable opportunity now exists for the full development of a long projected and highly desirable plan. A considerable sum of money will be required to fit up the Museum properly, to purchase certain specimens which are not likely to be procurable from private donors, and to form an endowment fund for its maintenance and management. Unfortunately there are at present no funds available for this purpose, and aid must be sought from the generosity of relatives and friends of the pupils, for whose instruction and gratification the Museum is about to be established.

It may, perhaps, be well to state here the objects and limits of the proposed Museum, and the method to be adopted in its arrangement. A school museum, to be a thoroughly useful one, should be typical and complete, yet, unless some definite plan be formed at the very outset, to procure what is really wanted, *and nothing else*, there is great danger of a collection of sundry miscellaneous objects being formed, interesting enough, perhaps, in themselves, but valueless for all scientific or educational purposes. The experience of other such institutions has shown that, unless a free right of accepting or declining donations of specimens be granted to the curators, it is impossible to make a good museum. Moreover, the amount of space for the disposal of the collection will necessarily be somewhat limited, and it must be turned to the best account. For these and other reasons it has been decided, with the approval of the Head Master, that the Museum shall be essentially a British one, and shall illustrate the Natural History and antiquities of our land by good specimens, systematically arranged, under the departments of Zoology, Botany, Geology, Mineralogy, and Archæology. In addition to this there will be a collection of rare and curious objects, derived from all sources, which may be considered useful for the purposes of scientific teaching, and a large typical series to be used at the lectures and demonstrations given in the College on Comparative Anatomy, and other branches of Natural History.

The Committee of Management will only accept of such specimens as can be classed under some one of these heads. All the various collections will be available, under proper regulations, for the use of the boys, and every assistance will be given to those whose inclinations and tastes lead them to the special study of any particular branch of Physical Science. Mr Barrington-Ward, Natural History master in the College,[386] has been appointed Curator of the Museum, and the charge of its several sections will be placed in the hands of Sub-curators, for the most part, from members of the College Scientific Society who may have given special attention to the study of particular branches of Science. The general administration of the Museum and its funds will be vested in a Committee of Management, to consist of the Curator, Sub-curators, and some other persons nominated by the Head Master.

---

[386] Mark James Barrington-Ward, FRGS, FLA [*M45*: 1870–2], though eminently qualified for the task, left after only a year to become an Inspector of Schools.

A Museum founded with these objects, and energetically conducted, can hardly fail to be of real service in a large public school, and, apart from the interest it will give to all the boys, it will do much to foster habits of observation, and encourage many to give their attention to some of the most delightful branches of study.

The Committee earnestly request assistance in their undertaking, and more especially solicit donations and annual subscriptions in money. As already mentioned the expense of fitting up suitable cases and drawers will be very considerable, while many purchases must be made from time to time so as to render the Museum complete, and it will most likely soon be necessary to procure some paid assistance in preparing and duly preserving the specimens. The Head Master will allow any small sum which parents or guardians may wish their boys to contribute to be entered terminally in the School accounts.

Contributions of objects of interest, in any of the departments of the Museum, will also be gladly received. Communications respecting these should be addressed to M. J. Barrington-Ward, Esq., Clifton College, who will give every information to intending donors. Named specimens of *British* fossils, minerals, stuffed animals, shells, crustacea, insects, dried plants, coins, and antiquities: all skeletons and bones of vertebrata, and good animal preparations in spirit, etc., will be highly acceptable. Any collector or curator of a museum who can spare some duplicate specimens will greatly oblige the Committee and materially help them in their efforts. Gifts of live plants are also solicited for the Botanic Garden, which is now in course of formation, and will (when completed) be under the charge of the Museum Committee.

Subscriptions to the Museum fund will be received by M.J. Barrington-Ward, Esq., Clifton College, Rev. Joseph Greene,[387] Apsley Road, Clifton, and T.H. Warren, Esq., Naseby House, Pembroke Road, Clifton; or they may be sent to the Committee through any master.

Clifton College, September, 1870.

☐ *A further circular issued in the following month most unusually targeted exclusively female benefactors, presumably thought particularly sympathetic to the garden scheme.*

[141]   October 1870. Formation of the Botanic Garden and Museum
[*Guard book 1860–77. Printed*]

[*Minuted in MS*] Mem[*orandum*]. Issued without previous authority at the Council.
                                                                Clifton College, October 1870.
Dear Madam,

We beg to call your attention to the effort now being made for the formation of a Museum and Botanic Garden in this College, and we hope that you will kindly assist in an undertaking so important. There are no funds available for the purpose, and the large outlay necessary at the outset, as well as the annual expenses, must be entirely defrayed by voluntary donations and subscriptions. If, therefore, the enterprise should unhappily fail to meet with sufficient public support it will be necessary to abandon it. The plan is, however, so desirable that we feel sure there are few of those interested in the College who will not contribute something towards its successful development.

---

[387] Father of Alan Douglas [*826*: NT 1870–6] and Walter Lighton [*1361*: NT 1873–9].

To give some idea of the probable sum required for the formation and maintenance of the Garden and Museum it may be well here to state briefly a few particulars respecting them. The Museum will be placed in the large hall recently presented to the College by the Head Master, and estimates have been obtained for the necessary cases and cabinets. We find that not less than two hundred pounds will be needed to carry out this part of the plan fully, while the partial erection, which it is proposed to commence now, will cost over one hundred pounds. The purchase of desirable specimens will also entail a large expenditure, especially at first.

For the Botanic Garden, a large piece of ground, adjoining the Chapel and Laboratory, has been granted by the Council, and workmen are at present engaged in preparing it for the reception of plants. Grants of specimens have been most kindly made by several public institutions, including the University Botanic Gardens of Oxford, Edinburgh, and Dublin, the Royal Botanic Society's Garden in Regent's Park, London, and the Royal Dublin Society's Garden at Glasnevin. To prepare and lay out the ground properly for the growth of these valuable plants, a considerable sum is absolutely necessary, especially as the site given, though excellent in position, is one on which much money will have to be expended before it can be rendered fully available for a Botanic Garden.

The sum annually required for the permanent maintenance of both Museum and Garden could scarcely be estimated at less than one hundred pounds. For this we must rely entirely on subscriptions, and we hope therefore that you will kindly allow us to enter your name as an annual or terminal subscriber, even for a small amount. To the parents and friends of the pupils the appeal is especially directed, as both of the contemplated institutions are to be founded solely for the instruction and gratification of their boys, and on the combined efforts of masters and boys the success of the whole scheme is dependent. A few shillings each term *for every boy in the School* (in addition to contributions from others interested in the College) would form a fund quite sufficient for all our wants.

We have already issued a circular stating the aim and scope of our Museum. If you have not received a copy of it, we shall be glad to send you one. Cheques and Post Office Orders should be made payable to M.J. Barrington-Ward, Treasurer of the Museum Fund, and crossed 'National Provincial Bank of England'. All contributions will be publicly announced from time to time, and a receipt given for each.

We remain, dear Madam, yours faithfully,

Bedford Hartnell, M.A. (Secretary), Rodborough House, Clifton College,[388]
Joseph Greene, M.A., M.E.S., Apsley Road, Clifton,
M.J. Barrington-Ward, B.A., F.L.S. (Treasurer), College Lodge, Clifton College,
G.F. Rodwell, F.C.S., Clifton College,[389]
T.H. Warren, Pembroke Road, Clifton,
W. Claxton, Apsley Road, Clifton,
R.F. Brunskill, Rev. T.E. Brown's, Clifton College,[390]
J. Stone, School House, Clifton College,[391]

Museum and Garden Committee.

---

[388] *M11*: 1863–97.
[389] George Farrer Rodwell [*M48*: 1870–1], Chemistry Master, later Science Master at Marlborough; among his many works *A Dictionary of Science* (1871) was published during his time at Clifton.
[390] Richard Fothergill Brunskill [*435*: BH 1866–71].
[391] John Frederick Matthias Harris Stone [*673*: SH 1868–72], later Fellow of the Linnaean and Chemical Societies. It is notable that two current pupils were members of the Committee.

[142]   1870–1. First Museum donations
[*Museum List of Donations and Specimens 1870–2. MS notebook. Arranged under headings (here omitted) Name of Donor; Address; Where and when acknowledged (no entries at first and all omitted here); Date of Gift (beginning 1870); Donation of; Description*]

R. Bamford [*765*]; Harris's; Sept. 24; coins; (gold, silver, copper & bronze).

H.N. Bawtree [*843*]; Town; [*Sept. 24*]; miscellaneous; 8 shells, 3 coins & 3 fossils &c.

A.E. Batchelor [*373*]; Brown; [*Sept.*] 23; [*miscellaneous*]; 2 fossils & 2 ores.

W.B.S. Mills [*646*]; Town; [*Sept.*] 22; dried plants; illustrating the Botany of Kirkmichael parish, Scotland, about 100 specimens.

[*W.J.P.*] Wood [*793*]; Town; [*Sept. 22*]; dried ferns; a portfolio, principally from Devon.

P. Mordaunt [*760*]; Hartnell; [*Sept.*] 28; dried plants; an old collection (in 2 books), Linnaean arrangement.

A. & M. Duncan [*471, 472*]; Town; [*Sept.*] 29; miscellaneous; sea weeds, locust, larvae, shells.

H.P. Luckman, Esq. [*M9*]; Rodboro' House; [*Sept. 29*]; coins; (about 12, bronze & copper).

[*H.R.*] Leach (ma) [*260*]; School; [*Sept. 29*]; fossils; ammonites &c. from Whitby.

Mr Edwards; Stoke Bishop;[392] Oct. 4; rocks; two pieces of sandstone, containing crystals.

'Masters Gill'; Barbados' [*Oct.*] 7; rocks; a large collection of objects in Natural History from Barbados, including snakes, shells, insects, and plants &c.

E. Fentone Elwin, Esq.; Booton, Norwich; 1st October; greensand fossils; a small box of about 15 specimens, mostly named.

Rev. F. Armitage;[393] Clifton College; 6th [*October*]; echidna; a fine specimen, stuffed.

J.P. Bush;[394] Town; 11th [*October*]; fossils; about 5 – Kentish chalk & corals from the corraline.

H. Wallace Mort, Esq. [*193*]; 9th November; siliceous sponge; '*euplectelle*' from the Philippine Islands.

A. & G Money; 1st. Feb. 1871; 2 'flying foxes' (*pteropus*); stuffed skins from India.

Col. Channer [*father of 374 & 469*]; Pembroke Rd.; Jan.; fossil ferns; from Kingswood.

S.G. Perceval, Esq.; Henbury; [*Jan.*]; minerals.

W.P. Hierne, Esq.; Richmond; [*Jan.*] dried plants.

[*A.W.*] Woodburn [*545*]; Hartnell's House; [*Jan.*]; box of eggs.

F. Cruttwell, Esq., O.C.; Frome;[395] [*Jan.*]; [*box of*] shells.

---

[392] George William Edwards of Sneyd Park: *Directory* (1871), p. 165; above **[8]**.

[393] Frederick Armitage [*M33*: 1867–71]; former Headmaster of King's School, Parramatta, later founding Headmaster of Neuenheim College, Heildelberg; author of *A French Grammar: for the use of Public Schools* (1873) and *Sermons du XIIe Siècles en vieux Provençal* (1886).

[394] James Paul Bush [*723*: ST 1869–76]; born in Australia; see Whitfield, *Victorian Doctors*, pp. 83–7.

[395] A mistaken initial for one of three OC Cruttwell brothers from Frome, P.W.D. [*128*], W.H.W. [*145*], and A.C. [*300*].

Gen. McLeod;[396] Bengal; Oct. 1870; Indian bird skins.

C.B. Dunn, Esq., F.R.H.S.; Clifton; Nov.; British mosses; a case, mounted.

Edinburgh Botanic Garden (per Prof. Balfour[397]); Dec. 1870; living plants for garden; about 170.

Glasnevin [*Botanic Garden*] ([*per*] Dr Moore[398]); Feb. 10, 1871; [*living plants for garden*]; [*about*] 140.

C.B. Dunn, Esq., F.R.H.S.; Clifton; Jan. 1871; rare Br[*itish*] dried plants; *paeonia officinalis, linnea borealis, aquilegia vulgaris, helianthemum polifolium.*

H. Mogg, Esq., O.C. [*263*]; Pemb. Coll. Cantab; [*Jan.*] Br. dried plants & tobacco leaves.

E.L. Maisey [*539*]; Brown's House; 18 March; 2 insects; 'bamboo' & 'walking leaf' – India.

Trin. Coll. Dublin. Bot. Garden; per Prof. Wright;[399] 23 [*March*]; 231 living plants for garden.

F. Morse, Esq.; Shanklin I.W.; 18 Sept; shells & fossils; one large hamper – some named (many useless).

M.J. Barrington-Ward [*M45*]; Clift. Coll; 29 [*Sept.*]; mud from Atlantic bottom; brought from Dr Carpenter's dredging expedition 1870.[400]

J. Gibbons [*1037*]; [Clift. Coll.]; [*29 Sept.*]; petrified stem of cabbage palm; brought from a Trinidad lake.[401]

H.M. Niblett [*632*]; [Clift. Coll.] [*29 Sept.*]; box of British eggs; several new to the collection.

Genl. Younghusband;[402] Pembroke Rd., Clifton; 2 claws of tiger, 2 claws of wild boar; from India.

General McLeod; (Ragatz?) care of Messrs King & Co, Cornhill; July; elephant's skull; from India.

□ *Despite good intentions and some valuable accessions, it proved impossible to adhere to the shrewd principles set out in the first prospectus. The collection soon degenerated into a mouldering clutter; in 1922 it was merged with the Library, and the contents were gradually dispersed.*[403]

---

[396] Gen. W.C. McLeod of Bath, father of N.F. [*732*] and R.G.McQ. [*812*].
[397] John Hutton Balfour, Professor of Botany at Edinburgh University; Regius Keeper of the Royal Botanic Garden, Edinburgh, and HM Botanist in Scotland 1845–79.
[398] David Moore, Director of the National Botanic Gardens, Glasnevin, Dublin 1838–79.
[399] Edward Percival Wright, Professor of Botany at Trinity College 1869–1905.
[400] Philip Herbert Carpenter, FRS (d. 1891), who undertook much scientific exploration of the seabed.
[401] John Abel Gibbons [*1037*: DH 1871–2] was from Barbados.
[402] Gen. R.R. Younghusband, father of A.D. [*1074*], G.W. [*1075*], R.E. [*1076*], A. [*1096*], E.R. [*2692*] and O. [*2850*].
[403] Christie, *History*, pp. 227–8, quoting withering reports in *The Cliftonian* (from 1895: 'On entering it, one is met with a faint odour of putrefaction, and if one has the courage to proceed farther, one finds that disorder reigns on every side'; from 1912: 'long an eyesore').

[143]   12 December 1918. The Head Master to the Head of Physics[404]
[*RS3/80. Holograph*]

Clifton College, Bristol
Dec. 12. 1918

Dear Mr Rintoul,

The expenses of the new Practical Mathematical Laboratory should be part of the Physical Laboratory grant account. The orders should be made by the Head of the Physics Department and the bills go in to him. To start with the Practical Mathematical Laboratory will have a grant of £20 to £30 for apparatus and after that a grant not exceeding £10 per term.

Masters in the new Laboratory wanting fresh apparatus will send in their requests to the Head of the Physical Department who will see that the new Laboratory is kept in order.

Yours sincerely,
J.E. King

[*Postscript at head*] If this will do kindly return and I will have it typed. J.E.K.

[*Minuted*] Dear Headmaster, I think that this is quite clear.
Yours very truly,
D. Rintoul.

[*Minuted*] Mr Rintoul should have a copy and another for reference. J.E.K.

Science Committee

[144]   November 1910. The Science Committee arranges the syllabus
[*Science Committee Minute Book 1905–1918, ff. 1–2. MS*]

November [*blank*] 1910. A meeting was held in Rintoul's House. Present: D.R., H.C.,[405] E.B.L.,[406] K.F.,[407] A.H.F.,[408] P.N.P.,[409] W.C.B.[410]

J.S. and Moderns 3rds Science. It was decided that a two-year cycle should be adopted in the J.S. Thirds. That there should be no cycle in the J.S. Seconds, but that copies of Mr Fish's suggestions for this work should be kept for reference. That in 3b and 3c the subjects taught should be chosen from Astronomy, Physical Geography, Botany and combined 'Physiology and Anatomy of animals'.

That each laboratory should contribute [10/- *corrected to*] up to 10/- terminally for the purchase of apparatus etc. needed for the above work. Mr Clissold consented to be administrator of this fund.

The two-year cycle of the J.S. [and Modern 3rds *corrected to*] 3rds is:

1st term: Formation, shape, revolution and rotation of the Earth, measurement of time.

---

[404] David Rintoul [*M121*: 1886–1919†]; Head of Physics and Science, and author of *An Introduction to Practical Physics* (1898). See J.R. Mozley, *Clifton Memories* (1927), pp. 139–52.
[405] Harry Clissold [*M148*].
[406] Ernest Bowman Ludlam [*M201*: 1908–14]; Head of Chemistry.
[407] Kenneth Fisher [*M210*: 1909–19]; Head of Chemistry from 1914 and briefly Head of Science 1919; later Headmaster of Oundle.
[408] Arthur Henry Fish [*M207*: 1909–13, 1914–18]; Chaplain, and taught Mathematics and Science.
[409] Philip Noël Pocock [*M211*: 1910–14]; taught general Science.
[410] William Cornish Badcock [*M266*: 1922–45]; Head of Physics 1922–40, Head of Science 1940–5.

2nd term: Astronomy of the solar system etc.

3rd term: Formation of the earth's crust, mountains etc., distinction between common kinds of rock.

4th term: Winds, rain, currents, tides and glaciers.

5th term: Denudation of earth's crust, formation of soil, effects of denudation on contour and coast line, effects of climate on vegetation.

6th term: Growth of a plant, respiration, nutrition, description of and distinction between common flowers and leaves.

D. Rintoul, 4/3/11

[145]   28 February 1914. Science Committee meeting
[*Science Committee Minute Book 1905–1918. MS*]

February 28th 1914. The meeting was held in Mr Clissold's House. Present: D.R., H.C., E.B.L., K.F., P.N.P., and E.I.A.P.[411]

J.S. Science. Mr Pocock suggested that Botany should appear twice in the two year cycle, in each of the Summer terms, instead of once as at present. Agreed.

Mil. 3 syllabus (Physics). Mr Pocock pointed out the difficulty in getting through the syllabus for this set, due, in his opinion, to the reduced age at which boys entered the Military Side.

Higher Certificate. There was a general consensus of opinion that it would be of advantage for the Classical Side boys to drop one subject and spend the four hours on the other, doing practical work as well as theoretical, with a view of taking the Higher Certificate Examination.

Museum. The question of the Museum was discussed.

D. Rintoul, 6/6/14.

[146]   6 June 1914. Science Committee meeting
[*Science Committee Minute Book 1905–1918. MS*]

June 6th 1914. The meeting was held at the Hotel Como, Portishead; present D.R., H.C., E.B.L., K.F., P.N.P. and E.I.A.P.

Scientific books suitable for prizes. The list of books from which boys chose their prizes was revised.

Conversazione. In view of the decision arrived at at the meeting held on Feb. 27th 1913, H.C. proposed and K.F. seconded that a Conversazione be held next term. This was carried. A discussion then arose as to who should be invited. It was decided that parents of boys in the Scientific Society should be asked and others individually by members of the Committee. H.C. and K.F. were delegated to make the arrangements.[412]

J.S. Science. D.R. invited opinions about the new arrangements; the various members of the Committee thought the changes made had helped the teaching and it was decided to continue under the present arrangements.

D. Rintoul, 17.10.14.

---

[411] Egbert Ivor Allen Phillips [*M215*: 1911–32]; taught Mathematics and Science on the Military Side.
[412] This became a regular event, and a sample programme is printed below [**187**].

The Science School

[147]   17 March 1924. A.E. Munby[413] **to the Head Master**
[*Science School box/Building. Typescript*]

REPORT.
Proposed re-construction of the Science Department at Clifton College.

Dear Headmaster,

You have been good enough to ask me to advise you as to the provision for the adequate teaching of Natural Science at Clifton based on the confidential report of Mr Dufton and Mr Stead of the Board of Education.

I made last week an inspection of the present accommodation for such teaching and you have placed at my disposal for the purposes of this report three alternative sites for consideration.

1. The site occupied by the stables and garden adjoining the Music Rooms on the other side of Guthrie Road.

2. The site of the present Chemistry Block and adjoining Gymnasium and Courts.

3. The site now occupied by the Junior School.

1. Stables site.

This site besides having the disadvantage of being outside the School close is too small to admit of the erection of suitable buildings. Adequate accommodation would require a three-storey building and I dismiss this situation without further comment.

2. Chemistry and surrounding buildings.

I consider that a very workable scheme could be produced by re-modelling of the Chemistry Block, the utilization of the Gymnasium as laboratories on two floors, the demolition of the three north Fives Courts (one at present out of commission) and in place of the east court the erection of a wing extending within a few feet of the north wall of the Tepid Bath. This would leave the Racquet Court to be entered through the Science Block, and Science Library and Common Room wing intact.

The whole of the present accommodation for Physics in the main building would be discarded.

Scheme I.

These proposals are shown on the accompanying drawings (Scheme I), which must be regarded merely as a sketch plan upon which dimensions are only approximations.

The buildings would form three sides of a court some 50 by 40 feet with a projecting staircase block.

On the ground floor devoted to Physics there would be:

Lecture Room for 35, small Advanced Laboratory for about 6, and Preparation and Store Room with good entrance lobby under the present Chemical Laboratory,

Two Physical Laboratories for about 28 each in the old Gymnasium suitably windowed to the road.

---

[413] Alan Edward Munby, a former teacher of science who became an architect, particularly of scientific and educational buildings.

Lecture Room for 35, small Preparation and Master's Room in the new wing.

A corridor would lead to the old Science Library through the present small rooms, where a workshop might be provided.

On the first floor devoted to Chemistry (and Biology) there would be a Chemical Laboratory for about 28, Balance and Store Room in place of the large Chemical Laboratory which is too large for one class and very wastefully arranged due to insufficient sinks. The floor would be entirely removed and a 'fireproof' floor, arranged for drainage, substituted.

A Chemical Laboratory for about 30, and small Biology and Advanced Chemical Laboratories with a Balance Room would form a floor in the Gymnasium windowed to the road.

The new wing would provide a Lecture Room for 35, small Preparation Room and Master's Room as below.

Probably some storage could be arranged under the Gymnasium roof over the two small Laboratories which might be 9 or 10 feet high. The large rooms would not be less than 12 feet high.

This scheme would involve the provision of a new Gymnasium and Fives Courts elsewhere, and the removal of at least the roof of the covered passage from the Engineering Shops along the Swimming Bath.

Some difficulties might have to be got over in connection with the discharge of necessary drainage on the road side of the buildings.[414]

No great outlay would be necessary upon the elevations of the building in this situation.

The scheme could be carried through without cessation of the School work by building the new wing and converting the Gymnasium before the old Chemical Laboratory was interfered with.

The provision is below the requirements suggested by the Board of Education for advanced work but otherwise conforms roughly to the minimum and no doubt might be brought into nearer conformity; for example, the present Library and small Advanced Physics Laboratory might be interchanged.

Scheme II.

Scheme II is intended to give you an idea of what the provision of entirely new buildings would involve placed on the site now occupied by the Junior School and its forecourt.

Arranged as before on two floors for Physics and Chemistry, the plan indicates the space required in relation to the Junior School, which would be pulled down, and is shown by dotted lines.

Ground Floor. The Physical Department has two large Laboratories for 28 each, flanking a central entrance on the south front leading to stairs and a corridor 6 feet wide, off which are two Lecture Rooms for 35 each, Preparation Room, Master's Room, Store 10 by 19 feet, with further space under the stairs, and Advanced Laboratory for 14.

First Floor. The Chemical Department above has two similar Laboratories with Balance Rooms on the frontage and like accommodation at the rear, except that a Biology Laboratory and Library take the place of the second Lecture Room.

This block would be about 95 feet long on the frontage, 130 feet long at the rear

---

[414] A line of emphasis has been pencilled alongside the last two paragraphs.

and be some 50 feet deep. As placed it would extend about 32 feet in front of the present Junior School entrance and its nearest corner would be some 40 feet from the apse of the Chapel, while on the east it would line with the rear buildings adjoining the Swimming Bath.

This building would call for suitable architectural treatment on the frontage necessary to harmonize with its surroundings. Gothic architecture is not best suited to Science buildings, which require large unobstructed windows, but a satisfactory compromise might be effected by adopting a late Gothic style.

It would leave the present Chemical as well as the Physical Rooms to be utilized, but possibly the large Chemical Laboratory might form the Lecture Hall of intermediate size needed by the College.

Cost.

It will be evident that no accurate forecast of cost can be given on the rough approximations considered in this report, but as a guide I am of opinion that a builder's tender for Scheme I would be likely to amount to about £9000 and for Scheme II about £18,000.

To these the cost of joinery fittings, gas and water services, drainage and ventilation would have to be added, a matter difficult to estimate as requirements vary much, but were all fittings new, which should hardly be necessary, these would probably involve a further outlay of between three and four thousand pounds.

Further, under Scheme I the cost of a new Gymnasium and Fives Courts has to be added, and under Scheme II outlay in installing the Junior School in premises already acquired.

I am, yours faithfully,
Alan E. Munby.

9, Old Square,
Lincoln's Inn, W.C.
March 17th, 1924.

[148]   18 March 1924. The Head of Science[415] gives his immediate reaction to the proposals
[*Science School box/Building. Holograph*]

Clifton College,
18 March, 1924.

Dear Headmaster,

As you desire, I am sending you my comments upon Mr Munby's proposals and suggestions.

1. After due consideration of the alternatives, I am in favour of that which involves re-arrangement of and addition to the present Chemical Laboratories.

2. In the first place, this scheme means an expenditure of some £7000 (at least) less than the other, and I do not think that the possible advantages of a new Science Block on the site of the Junior School would justify this additional and by no means negligible expense.

---

[415] Eric John Holmyard [*M243*: 1919–40]; Head of Chemistry and of Science.

3. There are certain features of the present building which I should be sorry to give up. The Science Library, for example, is eminently sited for its purpose and will allow very considerable expansion, especially when it is remembered that many Science text books become out of date after 10–15 years, and these would therefore presumably be got rid of as occasion arose. I regard the close proximity of the Chemical rooms to the main School buildings as of distinct importance; with ¾ hour periods the time taken in changing over cannot be neglected, and my experience of sets coming from the new house in College Road has not rendered me optimistic. Again, the present Chemical Laboratory has a sentimental attraction for me and, I have no doubt, for many Old Cliftonians, by reason of the celebrated work which Shenstone[416] carried out in it; I believe that tradition counts for much in the Science Department at Clifton, and if we could incorporate the old Lab in the new building I should be much happier.

4. The scheme I favour would not involve the loss of the present Common Room. While the staff would, of course, readily acquiesce in any change for the good of the School as a whole, I understand that the feeling is general that a change of Common Room to, for example, the main block of School buildings is undesirable. I do not know what your ideas would be about the C.R. if the new Science buildings were put up on the Junior School site.

5. As far as I am able to judge, after thinking the matter over very carefully, the 'alteration' plan – if properly carried out – should simply suffice for all the desirable Science teaching for as far ahead as one can see. The Third Forms would be able to get at least one laboratory period each per week. With an intelligent interpretation I do not see why the re-arranged and improved block should in any way lack dignity, and it will certainly have convenience.

6. On points of detail, the following remarks may be made:

(a) Entrance to the Racquet Court through the Science Block, which at first sight appeared very undesirable to me, [would *corrected to*] could be made unobjectionable by a simple arrangement of doors, which will no doubt occur to you when you look at the plans.

(b) The lecture rooms are designed for 35, but there is plenty of room to enlarge at least one to hold 50–60.

(c) If the proposed scheme is accepted I should like to retain Room 15.

(d) The Physical Laboratory, on the [sight *corrected to*] site of the present Gymnasium, would be lighted on one wall only. The windows would therefore have to be large, especially as unfortunately they face north, but for many purposes it is an advantage to have one side of a Physical Laboratory rather dark (e.g. experiments in optics).

Yours sincerely,

E.J. Holmyard.

☐ *Despite this initial preference for retaining the core of the original laboratories, Munby's second scheme was chosen in principle, though its details were then much debated. One modification would have retained the shell of the Junior School building. The architect duly made plans for this option, while recommending instead a completely new structure developed from his original Scheme II.*

---

[416] William Ashwell Shenstone, FRS [*M101*: 1880–1908†]; see below [**160, 165, 171**].

[149]   10 October 1924. Further report from the architect to the Head Master
[*Science School box/Building. Typescript*]

Clifton College Science Buildings.
Fourth Report on Schemes 5 and 6.
October 1924.

Dear Headmaster,

You have asked me to report further on your proposed Science buildings following a conference with yourself and the senior Chemistry and Physics masters as the result of certain criticisms of Scheme no. 4 last submitted for the utilization of the Junior School. These criticisms are in the nature of further demands for space. It appears that four lecture rooms are requisite in place of three, each able to accommodate sixty boys, that the elementary laboratories must be increased in area by some 25 per cent, that more storage is requisite, and provision must be made for a small electric plant, steam boiler, and other minor additions.

As I understand that it is desired to see how these provisions can be met by still retaining the Junior School buildings, I submit a new Scheme no. 5 on these lines, but as I cannot recommend this scheme I also submit a further Scheme no. 6 so that you can compare their respective merits.

Scheme no. 5.

This resembles Scheme no. 4, the main difference being increased depth of new frontage rooms, destruction of large School Room roof with the formation of another room over, and enlargement of the proposed basement.

[*Details here omitted.*]

Cost. This scheme is likely to cost £18,000 on the basis of prices adopted for Scheme 4, apart from fittings and furniture.

Scheme no. 6.

This scheme shows a reversion to the type of Scheme 2 but with material differences and additions. It assumes the complete removal of the Junior School with a road 10 feet wide at its narrowest position behind a new block of buildings which are designed to skirt round the existing boundaries. This enables the actual encroachment on the Close to be made less than that involved in Scheme 5.

[*Details here omitted.*]

Style and Construction. The style of the building – very late Gothic – will follow that approved for Scheme 4 and construction generally will be as described for that scheme. If the Junior School proves to be built in lime mortar, as is likely, the stone should be capable of profitable use in the new building and the slates could be partly used for roofing.

Cost. Priced as before, Scheme 6 is likely to cost about £21,000, apart from fittings and furniture.

Conclusions. The increased demands for accommodation which have not [*recte* now] been brought to my notice since my previous report appear to be necessitated by the working needs of the College, and though the space provided in former schemes was based on the recommendations of the Board of Education's Inspector's report, they were the minimum of a somewhat elastic proposal. For a school of eight hundred boys the provisions made in Scheme 6 cannot be called extravagant. The area per head in the Elementary Laboratories to be provided is now 42 square feet, and as these are the main rooms it may be of guidance to give one or two similar figures for other institutions of recent date. Bristol University has 50 sq. ft., Harrow School 52 sq. ft., Oxford University 72 sq. ft. in recent Chemical laboratories. Some encouragement for research by provision of Masters' rooms is undoubtedly an asset which is of great, if indirect, benefit to the pupils, while adequate storage enables purchases to be made on favourable terms.

If funds are available for the accommodation now proposed there is no question as to which of the schemes now presented should be adopted. I consider that the utility limit of the Junior School site has been fully reached in Scheme 4 previously put before you, and a very cursory inspection of Scheme 5 will show how little of the old walls can remain. Further details can be discussed at your Committee meeting on the 13th instant, which I am to have the privilege of attending.

I am, sincerely yours,

(Signed) Alan E. Munby,

10.10.24.

[150]   7 April 1925. Presentation of tenders
[Science School box/Building. Typescript]

Clifton College.
Proposed Science Buildings.

The following are the tenders for the above:

Messrs Holland, Hannen & Cubitts	£36,290
James Carmichael, Ltd	35,700
Hayward & Wooster	35,400
W. Moss & Sons	35,200
R.F. Ridd & Sons	34,950
W. Cowlin & Son	34,500
Foster & Dicksee	34,483
Willcock & Co.	33,975

All these tenders, except that of Messrs Cowlin & Son, contain a statement that they are based upon present building prices and are subject to variations in the cost of labour and materials.

Messrs Willcock's extra price for maple over pitch pine flooring is £280.

Presented to the Council of Clifton College, April 7th, 1925.

Alan E. Munby.

☐ *Willcock's tender was duly accepted, and the cost of the project was met thanks to generous donations from OCs. The principal benefactors were commemorated by tablets in particular rooms; oversight of these features and of the heraldic decoration of the building was committed to Sir Henry Newbolt and Mr Speaker Whitley.*

[151]   23 October 1926. The Speaker to the College Secretary
[*Science School box/Building. Holograph*]

23.x.26.

Dear Mr Lewis,

Thank you for your letter of the 22nd. Mr Munby came to see me yesterday evening and discussed the questions of (a) the name tablets and (b) the arms.

(a) He will prepare a drawing of a sample tablet to be submitted to Sir Henry Newbolt and myself; it appears that bronze with incised letters filled with white enamel will make the best job.

(b) He is in favour of colouring the arms over the Science School doorway, and will take the loan of my coloured copy. As to the gateway, he thinks that Mr Holden[417] should carry out the colouring; so will you advise him of the Council's decisions, and ask him to put this work in hand for completion, say, in April.

Yours truly,
J.H. Whitley.

[152]   30 January 1929. The Head Master interviews the Head of Science
[*HM6/Interview Book 1929–30, ff. 1–2, 6. MS*]

Wednesday, 3rd January, 1929.

I had an interview with Dr Holmyard on Wednesday, 30th January. We discussed the following points.

1. Teaching of Biology. He expressed his willingness to be paid less than the present rate of six guineas per boy for boys taking special instruction in Biology in preparation for the First M.B. He suggested that if he could be paid a fixed salary for this purpose of £50 a year, the School could charge these boys say four guineas each per term, with the present average numbers taking this course; the School would pay expenses.

2. He said that he thought it would be necessary to introduce a course in general Science as an alternative to Physics and Chemistry in the middle block of the School, and that this would, to a certain extent, meet the growing demand for general Biology instruction in schools. He said that he thought it would not be necessary to engage a specialist Biologist for this. He and Muirhead[418] knew enough Biology for this purpose. At the same time he asked if the Science staff could possibly be increased from 6 to 7. The course could then be made much more adaptable and it would be possible for Science specialists to teach Science in the Junior School. He suggested that when Finter[419] returns, Philbrick[420] should be kept on <on> the permanent staff.

I said that this was a point on which I should ask the Inspectors next term for their views.

2. Grace term. He said that at the end of the coming summer he would have completed 10 years, and would like to apply for a grace term. He asked how much of his salary he would be paid in this case, and whether he would lose for that term

---

[417] Charles Holden, designer of the Memorial Arch: see below **[428]** and *passim*.
[418] James Alexander Orrock Muirhead [*M231*: 1914–49], Head of Chemistry 1916–19.
[419] Francis Boyne Finter [*M269*: 1923–54]; Head of Chemistry 1941–54, and author of *An Introduction to Physical Chemistry* (1933).
[420] Frederick Arthur Philbrick [*M293*: 1928–41]; co-author with Holmyard of *A Text Book of Theoretical and Inorganic Chemistry* (1932); later Head of Chemistry at Rugby.

both his salary as Head of Department and the fees. I told him that this probably is the case, but that I should have to make inquiries and would do so.

* * *

Wednesday, 13th February, 1929.
I interviewed E.J. Holmyard with further reference to his proposed grace term. I had written to him to say that if he went on a grace term he could not possibly receive any of the fees for extra Biology that term, but that he would receive his salary as Head of Department except in so far as part of it was needed to pay whoever did the work for him. He said that he thought that Muirhead would look after the Chemistry without any extra payment, but that Badcock[421] ought to be paid something extra for taking general charge of all the Science. With regard to Biology, he suggested that either no Biology should be taught in the Christmas term and that more should be taught in the two following terms to make up, or, that a lady (? Mrs Henderson) of Bristol University[422] should be asked to take the Biology in the Christmas term. She has experience of teaching boys. I said that I would go into this.

Scientific Society

☐ *The Society was founded in June 1869, and met fortnightly. For some periods its proceedings can be followed in printed* Transactions.[423] *The Minute Books on which these are based are extant only from 1871, at which time the printed versions are often much fuller than the MSS. For the present purpose samples have mostly been taken which do not duplicate the published texts.*

[153]   10 February 1871. Scientific Society
[*Scientific Soc. Minute Book 1, p. 1. MS*][424]

First term 1871.
The first meeting for the term and year was held on Feb. 10th in the Physical Lecture Room, at which 59 members and visitors were present.
The minutes having been read by the Secretary[425] and passed, the President opened the business of the evening with an address, the chief heads of which were:
the progress of the Museum,
the state of the Botanical Garden,
the working of the Society by sections,
the numerous advantages the neighbourhood affords for scientific pursuits.
After which R.F. Brunskill[426] proposed a vote of thanks to the President for his <able> address, which was carried by acclamation.

---

[421] W.C. Badcock [*M266*]; see above **[144]**.
[422] Isabel Jean Henderson: *Reg. Univ.*, p. 104.
[423] *Transactions of the Clifton College Scientific Society* (2 vols, 1871–87); each volume contains four separately paginated parts; a new series ran from 1908 to 1914 (6 vols); after the war there was an *Annual Report*.
[424] Much fuller report in *Transactions*, [i], II, pp. 1–5.
[425] J.M.F.H. Stone [*673*].
[426] R.F. Brunskill [*435*], Treasurer of the Society.

J. Duncuft[427] and J. Stone next delivered a lecture on the steam-engine. Stone opened the subject by tracing the history of the steam-engine from its invention to the time of [Stevenson *corrected to*] Stephenson. Duncuft then explained the working of the locomotive engine and Watt's double acting cylinder. The lecture was illustrated throughout with diagrams and working models, and was received with much applause.

(signed) M.J. Barrington-Ward, President.

[154]   1 March 1872. Adam Sedgwick[428] to the Secretary of the Scientific Society
[Scientific Soc. Minute Book 1, p. 111 MS][429]

Trinity Coll, Cambridge,
March 1st. 1872.
Dear Sir,
I have received a copy of the *Transactions of the Clifton College Scientific Society*, Part II,[430] for which I return you my best thanks. I am suffering [from *corrected to*] by such an infirmity of sight that I scarcely can read anything now, except what relates to actual business; but I trust my eyes will become a little less irritable than they are at present and that I may be able to make myself acquainted with the proceedings of your Scientific Society. I ever have felt a great interest in Clifton, since I began my life as a practical geologist, for there I received my first lessons from my friend and fellow labourer, the late Dean Conybeare[431] in the years 1819 & 20. The beautiful scenery which surrounds Clifton still is a living picture in my mind's eye, and never can I forget the happy days I spent with Canon Guthrie and his admirable wife, the Foundress of your Chapel. May God continue to prosper your College, which has flourished so nobly, through the years of its early life.
        I remain, dear Sir, very kindly and gratefully yours,
                A. Sedgwick.
P.S. My present infirmity has compelled me to dictate this to an amanuensis.

☐ *This was read at the meeting on 8 March and ordered to be entered into the Minutes.*

[155]   24 February 1876. Unresolved disagreement on the origins of civilisation
[Scientific Soc. Minute Book 1. MS][432]

24th February 1876.
        The second meeting of the term was held in Mr Grenfell's[433] room on Feb. 24th. There were 29 members present. The minutes of the last meeting were first read

---

[427] John Duncuft [*555*: WaH 1867–73].
[428] FRS; Woodwardian Professor of Geology at Cambridge from 1818 to his death in 1873, and a pioneering eminence in his field.
[429] Referred to and printed in *Transactions*, [I], iv, pp. 79–80.
[430] Published 1872, covering meetings for the first two terms of 1871.
[431] William Daniel Conybeare, FRS, Dean of Llandaff from 1845 to his death in 1855; eminent geologist and palaeontologist.
[432] *Transactions*, ii, II, pp. 29–37 prints the paper in full but adds merely that an 'animated conversation' followed between Wollaston, Tilden, and the speaker.
[433] John Granville Grenfell [*M51*: 1871–89], Vice-President of the Society; taught Physics and Chemistry.

and passed. Mr Wollaston then called on R. Fitz-Gibbon[434] to read his paper on the 'Origin of Civilisation'.

After the paper had been read, Mr Wollaston[435] asked if any member had any observations to make. Dr Tilden[436] then got up and made a few observations. 'He failed', he said, 'to see the point of some of R. Fitz-Gibbon's arguments.' R. Fitz-Gibbon got up and explained. Dr Tilden still objected. Mr Wollaston gave his opinion, and drew a figure on the board to explain his views, which caused much merriment. Dr Tilden however still objected, and an animated conversation ensued between him and Mr Wollaston, and in which R. Fitz-Gibbon joined. Dr Tilden however did not feel inclined to give in, and as it was getting late, Mr Wollaston proposed a vote of thanks to R. Fitz-Gibbon for his interesting paper, which was passed unanimously. The meeting was then adjourned.

G.H.W.

[156]   8 November 1877. A rare failure of Clifton science
[*Scientific Soc. Minute Book 1. MS*]

Corrected copy of Minutes. Thursday Nov. 8.

The fourth meeting of the term was held in the Chemical Lecture Room on Thurs. Nov. 8. 86 members and visitors were present. The President in the chair. The minutes of the last meeting were read <[in a most unconstitutional manner *deleted*] by the President> and passed. The President then called upon E.G. Marks (O.C.)[437] to read his paper on the 'History and manufacture of Coal Gas'. The paper was brought to an abrupt close by the failure of the main experiment, which was intended to show the method of producing tar from coal.

The lecturer then begged to be allowed to say a few words upon another subject. This proposition was received with applause. He then proceeded to call forth the latent energy of the Society and to reprove its members for their cowardice in not reading papers. At the close of this discourse [*several words deleted*], the President put a few questions to the reader touching the subject of his paper.

[*All struck through*] Dr Tilden then rose to express his disappointment [firstly for having heard not, as he had expected, a lecture on coal gas, but only a dissertation on the dormant state of <the> Society, and secondly *deleted*] at seeing so much apparatus on the table which had not been used. E.G. Marks pleaded as excuse that he had prepared his experiment subsequently to the writing of the paper. However, after expressing his thanks to Dr Tilden for reminding him of his neglect and his willingness to continue, [he *corrected to*] E.G. Marks in continuation endeavoured to explain the explosibility of a mixture of coal gas and air, and the method of measuring the intensity of light. [Here he was found at fault and corrected by J.S.W. Chitty[438] *inserted then deleted*]. The lecturer then apologised for the interrupted nature of his paper. After a few words from Dr Tilden, the President declared the meeting

---

[434] Robert FitzGibbon [*1194*: DH 1872–6]; career as mechanical engineer in Montreal.

[435] George Hyde Wollaston [*M60*: 1873–99]; Natural History Curator of the Museum and Botanic Garden, and taught Biology and Zoology. See Mozley, *Memories*, pp. 165–78.

[436] Sir William Augustus Tilden [*M56*: 1872–80]; FRS 1880, Professor of Chemistry, Mason College, Birmingham from 1880–94, then at the Royal College of Science, Kensington, to 1909; knighted 1909.

[437] Edward George Marks [*587*: 1868–76], no buffoon but a Doctor of Medicine; his father the Revd Robert Marks [*M28*] had given private coaching to Haig: De Groot, *Haig*, p. 16.

[438] John Shaw Willes Chitty [*876*: HHP, WiH 1870–8]; took a 1st class in Chemistry at London University.

adjourned. L.G. Watkins[439] rose to propose a vote of thanks to Marks, which C.C.H. Milles [*recte* Millar][440] was about to second, when the President declared the meeting was <already> closed.[441]

**[157]	28 March 1878. Explosives**
[*Scientific Soc. Minute Book 1. MS*][442]

The last meeting of the Easter term was held on March 28th, the President[443] in the chair. Over 100 members and visitors were present. R. Threlfall[444] read a paper on 'Modern Explosives' illustrated by many successful experiments. Among the subjects treated were the explosions of dynamite, picric acid, the manufacture of gun-cotton and nitroglycerin, Noble's[445] blasting oil, &c. &c. A unanimous vote of thanks was passed to Threlfall for his paper. [This was then p(assed) *deleted*].

H.H. Turner (for Secretary).[446]

**[158]	13 November 1879. The night of the meteors**
[*Scientific Soc. Minute Book 1. MS*][447]

The fourth meeting of the term was held on Thursday Nov. 13th in Mr Grenfell's school. There were 71 members present. The minutes of the previous meeting were read and passed after undergoing a slight alteration. There were no exhibitions so the President proceeded at once to lecture on the November meteors.[448] He began by giving a list of the dates on which great showers have taken place, and from these data shewed that every year there is a slight shower on the thirteenth of November, and every thirty third year there is a much greater display of meteors.

From an accurate series of observations the orbit of the meteors was calculated by Professor Adams,[449] and found really to occupy a period of 33 years. The relation of meteors to comets, the physical properties of meteors, and their source of heat were then dwelt upon at some length, and the lecture was hardly ended by eight o'clock; and consequently no vote of thanks was passed to the President. The fact that the meeting was held on Nov. 13th lent additional interest to the subject, and altogether the lecture was most instructive.

J.M.W.

---

[439]	Leonard George Watkins [*1327*: WiH 1873–8]; Director of Ordnance Stores, Indian Army.
[440]	Charles Christian Hoyer Millar [*1374*: SH 1873–9]; author of two books on the phosphates of North America.
[441]	The *Transactions* (ii, III, p. 7) ignore the fiasco and merely record the reading of a paper by 'R.G.' Marks.
[442]	Similar entry in *Transactions*, ii, III, p. 15.
[443]	The Head Master.
[444]	Sir Richard Threlfall [*1301*: PHP, SH, WaH 1873–80]; FRS, Professor of Physics, University of Sydney and pyrotechnical adviser to the armed forces; knighted 1917.
[445]	This word deleted in a later hand and the term omitted from the printed account, doubtless to correct the miswritten name and the tautology ('blasting oil' being the original name for Nobel's nitroglycerine).
[446]	Herbert Hall Turner [*1594*: DH 1874–9]; FRS; Savilian Professor of Astronomy at Oxford and Hon. Secretary of the British Association.
[447]	Entry in *Transactions* (ii, III, p. 38) of similar extent but differently phrased.
[448]	Sir Francis Newbolt [*1918*] found the Head Master's lecture 'exciting': *Diary of a Fag*, p. 169; evidently so much so that he mistook the date.
[449]	John Couch Adams, Lowndean Professor of Astronomy and Geometry at Cambridge (d. 1892).

[159]   27 November 1879. Exhibitions
[*Scientific Soc. Minute Book 1. MS*][450]

Fourth [*recte* Fifth] meeting Nov. 27.[451]
Some specimens of Celestine were exhibited by Black.[452] Mr Grenfell explained the formation of crystallised minerals and gave a short account of the occurrence of the different modifications of Celestine at Clifton. It appears that Clifton has been noted for Celestine since the beginning of the century,[453] and is one of the few localities in which Baryta Celestine is found. This mineral as it occurs at Clifton does not admit of any formulae: it appears to be an amorphous and varying mixture of the Sulphates of Barium and Strontium.

A most perfect bronze [*implement*] was then exhibited by Mr Grenfell. The original was found in a cave in France, and is now in the British Museum. The copy exhibited was one of several which were made when the bronze first came to England.

M. Henri Cathélan at the invitation of the President then exhibited and sold[454] several pocket lenses and microscopes.

The President then called upon Bolton (Wa.H)[455] to read and explain his solution of the 'Challenge Problem'. The inventor then made a drawing and explained the principle of his solution. The temperature was to be registered by a Breguet[456] expansion bar in connection with a revolving drum and a series of levers.

The President devoted the remainder of the hour to the explanation of Perrin's [457] solution of the 'Challenge Problem'. In this case an air [pyrometer, or rather *deleted by Head Master*] thermometer was employed to give motion to an index moving on a dial. The great feature of the solution was the ingenious way in which the alarm was to be sounded on a 'sudden' fall of temperature.

The meeting was then adjourned; there were sixty eight members and visitors present.

J.M.W.

[160]   4 November 1880. Phosphorescence
[*Scientific Soc. Minute Book 1. MS*][458]

One of the most successful meetings of the Society was held on Thursday Nov. 4th in the Physical Lecture Room, when Messrs Jupp[459] and Shenstone[460] exhibited some most interesting experiments on Phosphorescence.

---

[450] Entry in *Transactions*, ii, III, pp. 38–41 prints full texts of what were evidently the two best solutions to the problem set by the Head Master. The 'Challenge' was not a regular feature of the meetings.
[451] Attended by Sir Francis Newbolt, who recalls (*Diary of a Fag*, p. 175) 'a very ingenious machine for detecting icebergs in the Atlantic.' Had this worked it might have saved the life of Thomas Clinton Pears [*5103*: WaH 1896–1901], who was to drown in the *Titanic*.
[452] Claude Black [*1489*: HHP, SH 1874–83]; FGS, and professionally qualified as mining engineer.
[453] It was discovered at Paradise Bottom at the north of Leigh Woods.
[454] *Sic*, but 'and sold' does not appear in the printed account.
[455] Lyndon Bolton [*1341*: WaH 1873–80]; taught at Wellington then Senior Examiner in the Patent Office.
[456] From Abraham-Louis Breguet (d. 1823), French watchmaker and jeweller.
[457] Edward Pearce Perrin [*2115*: NT, WaH 1877–9].
[458] Text in *Transactions* (ii, IV, p. 9) supplies *lacunae* but otherwise as MS.
[459] Herbert Basil Jupp [*M96*: 1879–97†]; taught Physics and Mathematics.
[460] William Ashwell Shenstone [*M101*: 1880–1908†]; first at Clifton as assistant to Sir W. Tilden (*q.v.*) 1874–5, succeeding him as Senior Chemistry Master 1880; FRS 1898; author of *Elements of Inorganic Chemistry* (1900), *Methods of Glass Blowing* (1902) and *The New Physics and Chemistry* (1906) &c.

After the minutes of the last meeting had been read and passed, Mr Jupp [*began*] with explaining that by phosphorescence is meant the power with [*recte* which] certain bodies have of absorbing rays of light, and slowly emitting them in a dark room; the rays absorbed being the chemically active ones, which are of a violet colour. Among such bodies is Calcium Sulphide, with which the following experiments were shown. The paint formed by mixing the Sulphide with turpentine was excited by the light of Magnesium wire and when exposed in the dark gave a magnificent violet phosphorescence. Plates of glass of various colours were then placed on the surface of the paint and it was shown that they only allowed light of their own colour to pass through, and hence under all but violet plates the paint was not excited. The effects of heat and cold on the paint was also shown. The chief practical use of this light at present is for lighting warehouses and powder magazines, and for buoys at sea.

Mr Shenstone then illustrated the phosphorescence of dry Phosphorus in [dry *deleted*] air by the following experiments. By passing a current of air over Phosphorus it becomes phosphorescent, burning to form Phosphorus Bioxide. Strange to say this effect is almost entirely destroyed by passing a current of Oxygen gas, unless the temperature of the Oxygen is raised, or its density decreased, which practically comes to the same thing. The presence of vapour of turpentine has a similar power of destroying entirely the phosphorescence of Phosphorus. The chief use made of this phosphorescence is to discover the presence of Phosphorus in poisons. The suspected poison is boiled with Sulphuric acid and the presence of the least trace of phosphorescent vapour indicates the presence of Phosphorus.

After the President had expressed the thanks of the Society to the lecturers, Southby[461] exhibited a megalethescope [*recte* megalethoscope], an instrument for [*showing*] the appearance of a place when lighted up by night.

The large number of members present made it impossible to count the numbers, but the room was completely filled.

The meeting then adjourned.

G.H.W.

[161]   23 February 1882. Boring under the Severn
[*Scientific Soc. Minute Book 2, pp. 31–3. MS*][462]

The third meeting of the term was held on Feb. 23rd in Mr Grenfell's school. Mr Wollaston was in the chair.

[*After other business*] Mr Wollaston then exhibited an apparatus to be fastened to a wheel, which it was proposed to use in measuring the Long Penpole course.

Mr Grenfell also exhibited some humming birds and nests.

After this H.A. Garratt[463] read a paper on the Severn Tunnel. Garratt fully described the locality of the tunnel with the aid of some diagrams which were provided. He then went into the boring of the tunnel and explained the difficulties which occurred owing to the repeated breaking out of water in the tunnel.[464] An original method

---

[461] One of the brothers Richard Edward [*1858*: ST 1876–83], William Philip [*2017*: ST 1877–81] and Francis Fretz [*2158*: ST 1878–87].

[462] Text as *Transactions*, ii, IV, p. 18.

[463] Herbert Alfred Garratt [*2418*: SH 1879–83]; engineer and author of works on mechanics; Principal of London County Council School of Engineering and Navigation.

[464] Work had begun in 1873 and the main problems with flooding were resolved by the end of 1880; the tunnel was completed in 1885 but did not open for traffic until the following year.

was adopted in the laying out of the tunnel and with such success that when the two borings met [the *corrected to*] under the middle of the river, there was a fault of only three inches. The immense pumping engines which were in constant use were described and Garratt ended his most interesting paper.

After Mr Stuart[465] had made a few remarks, a vote of thanks was unanimously passed to the lecturer, and the proceedings ended.

G.H. Dolby, Sec.[466]

[162]   27 November 1884. An artist's study of moss
[*Scientific Soc. Minute Book 2, pp. 103–5. MS.*][467]

The fifth meeting of term was held on Thursday November 27th at 7 p.m. in the Physical Lecture Room.

[*After other business*] R.E. Fry[468] was then called upon to read his paper on 'Mosses'. The lecturer began with a definition of a moss. He took plants with and without flowers and of the 2nd class he said there were two subdivisions: those with and those without woody fibres. Those without woody fibre were divided into 2 classes, some having stems and leaves and some without. Mosses are of the former class, having no real roots. This put shorter may be worded thus. Mosses are cryptograms with no woody fibres and no real roots, but possessing stems and leaves. He then passed on to their process of generation and described their method of growth. The classification and distribution of mosses was then described. The extraordinary way in which mosses are distributed is accounted for by the varying fertility of the soils on which the spores settle.

At the close of the lecture Mr Wollaston complimented Fry on his extremely lucid and interesting paper. A vote of thanks proposed by Pike[469] was then unanimously carried.

Members present, 27.   A.H. Pott.[470]

[163]   8 October 1885. A future Bishop's enthusiasm for railways
[*Scientific Soc. Minute Book 2, p. 131. MS*][471]

Thursday Oct. 8th
    The first meeting of the term was held in the Physical Lecture Rooms. In the absence of the Vice-President,[472] the chair was taken by Mr Jupp. After the minutes of the last meeting had been read and passed, [the Chairman *deleted*] J.T. Inskip[473] read a paper on the 'Construction of Railways', relating more especially to the formation of embankments and cuttings, and the constructions of tunnels and bridges. The paper was very well illustrated by the aid of limelight, and was [heartily *deleted*] highly appreciated by the audience. On its conclusion, the applause [sufficiently *deleted*]

[465] Charles Maddock Stuart [*M100*: 1880–2]; taught Chemistry; later first Headmaster of St Dunstan's, Catford.
[466] George Herbert Dolby [*2278*: OH 1878–83].
[467] Text as *Transactions*, ii, IV, p. 32–3.
[468] See above [**136**].
[469] Markham John Willoughby Pike [*2875*: ST 1882–5].
[470] Arthur Henry Pott [*2429*: DH 1879–84]; constructional engineer.
[471] Longer abstract on p. 130; corrected text with abstract printed in *Transactions*, ii, IV, p. 51.
[472] Wollaston.
[473] James Theodore Inskip [*2244*: ST 1878–86]; Bishop of Barking 1919–48.

was so hearty that no formal vote of thanks was deemed necessary. The meeting adjourned at 8.0 p.m.

The number of members present was about 110, or nearly double the average of the past few terms.

W.H. Moreland (Sec).[474]

[164]   17 December 1885. Eyes and brains
[*Scientific Soc. Minute Book 2, p. 155. MS*][475]

Dec. 17. 1885.

The last meeting of the term was held in the Physical Lecture Room at 6.30. Over 130 members and visitors were present. In the unavoidable absence of the Head Master, Mr Wollaston took the chair and introduced Dr Richardson Cross,[476] who at once delivered his lecture on 'The Eye'. The lecture was illustrated by the lime light, and also by eyes, brains &c., and was listened to with great pleasure. On its conclusion Mr Grenfell proposed a vote of thanks to Dr Cross, which was carried by acclamation. Dr Cross, in responding, expressed his thanks to Mr Dunscombe of Bristol,[477] and the students who had assisted him in his demonstration. The meeting was then adjourned.

Signed: G.H.Wollaston, V. President
W.H. Moreland, Secretary

☐ *The printing of the Society's minutes as Transactions ends with this term.*

[165]   4 February 1886. Preparation of Oxygen
[*Scientific Soc. Minute Book 2, p. 159. MS*]

The opening meeting of this term was held on Thursday, February 4th, 1886 in the Chemical Lecture Room. After the minutes of the last three meetings had been read and passed, it was unanimously resolved to elect A.P. Marwood[478] as member of the Committee for Wa.H.

Mr Shenstone then gave a most interesting lecture on 'The preparation of Oxygen: A. Commercially. B. Chemically pure'.

The second part of the lecture was illustrated by some very elaborate apparatus for obtaining Oxygen in a state of chemical purity, which the members present inspected at the close of the lecture. At the end Mr Wollaston made a few remarks, and the lecturer was thanked and loudly applauded.

There were 55 members and visitors present.

Signed: J.T. Inskip, Secretary.
G.H. Wollaston, V. President.

[*With abstract here omitted*]

---

[474] William Harrison Moreland [*2808*: OH 1881–6].

[475] Text printed in *Transactions*, ii, IV, p. 55.

[476] Francis Richardson Cross, surgeon, Bristol Royal Infirmary from 1879; opthalmic surgeon 1885–1900; member of the College Council 1900–27: Smith, *History of BRI*, p. 485.

[477] Matthew William Dunscombe, optician and scientific instrument maker, optician to Bristol Royal Infirmary and the General Hospital, and maker of instruments for the University College, the Grammar School, and Clifton College: *Directory* (1886), p. 176.

[478] Arthur Peirson Marwood [*3165*: WaH 1883–7].

[166]   6 October 1887. The Head Master looks to the stars
[*Scientific Soc. Minute Book 2, p. 211. MS*]

The first meeting of the term was held in the Physical Lecture Room on Thursday Oct. 6th when the Head Master delivered a most interesting lecture on *Stars*. Members present 64.

The Hon. President urged on the Society the duty of each member to do his utmost, and not to depend on external aid; that personal research however small was of the greatest importance to the life of the Society.

He then proceeded to point out the various constellations which could and ought to be recognised by everyone; dwelling especially on the form of the Great Bear.[479] He told us of the great use which was now being made of photography in the discovery of new stars and even new planets.[480]

The lecturer further dwelt on double stars and velocity with which the constellations travel through the universe. The whole lecture was illustrated by lantern slides and received with great applause.

The Hon. Vice-President then thanked the Head Master on behalf of the Society, and the meeting [then *deleted*] terminated at 8 p.m.

G.H.W., V. President
W.R. Fry, Acting Secretary[481]

[167]   6 March 1890. Halo over Clifton
[*Scientific Soc. Minute Book 2, p. 275. MS*]

The third meeting of the term was held on March 6th in the Physical Lecture Room; Mr Wollaston presided at first, but on the arrival of the Head Master left the presidential chair which remained vacant until the end of the meeting.

The hour was spent investigating the subject of halos, both lunar and solar; Mr Rintoul delivered a lecture on the subject, and minutely described the cause of the halos; the lecturer more particularly explained the halo which had been seen on March 1st at Clifton, but also gave some interesting accounts of various halos both round the sun and round the moon; the appearance of mock suns was also accounted for.

After the bulk of the lecture was over, a discussion ensued, in which the Head Master and Mr Rintoul took the leading parts, and many interesting facts were given, among which a very simple method of measuring angles without [complicated *deleted*] instruments was not the least conspicuous.

The House adjourned at 8 p.m. There were 40 present, of which more than [half *deleted*] a quarter consisted of masters and visitors.

Signed: G.H.W., President
M. Muspratt, Secretary[482]

---

[479] Wollaston, being large and furry, was affectionately known as 'Woolly Bear'.
[480] Since the discovery of Neptune in 1848 astronomers had been searching for a ninth planet; when this was identified in 1930 the name Pluto (proposed by an Oxford schoolgirl) was successfully recommended to astronomers by Professor H.H. Turner, former Secretary of the Society [157].
[481] Walter Raymond Fry [*3321*: DH 1884–7].
[482] Sir Max Muspratt, Bt [*3641*: 1886–90]; MP, Lord Mayor of Liverpool 1916–17, Chairman of the Association of Chemical Manufacturers and President of the Federation of British Industries; created Baronet 1922.

[168]   12 March 1891. Shedding light on bad drains and jerry-builders
[*Scientific Soc. Minute Book 2, p. 288. MS*]

The 4th meeting of the term was held in the Physical Lecture Room on Thursday March 12th, and seven o'clock. There were 40 members present.
Mr Wollaston took the chair, and called upon V.N. Gilbert[483] to conclude his paper on ventilation. Mr Gilbert then proceeded with his paper, explaining it in a very lucid manner. Before concluding he showed with the lantern some slides lent by Mr Jupp, which illustrated defective drains, [and *corrected to*] explaining the deceitfulness of jerry-builders, and the way in which they work harm to the health. Mr Wollaston, in thanking the lecturer, told some of his own experiences, and some [cases *corrected to*] disastrous cases brought about by defective drainage systems which had come under his own knowledge.
Mr Cook[484] then exhibited with a microscope a 'bacillus tuberculosis', and gave a short summary of our present knowledge of the subject.
The meeting then adjourned.

[169]   28 March 1891. The anatomy of the cockroach
[*Scientific Soc. Minute Book 2, p. 292. MS*]

The fifth meeting of the term was held in the Physical Lecture Room on Thursday March 28th 1891, Mr Wollaston in the chair.
Mr Wollaston immediately called on A.W. Rogers[485] to read his paper on 'The Cockroach'. He began by explaining [the *corrected to*] its history, explaining that it was not a beetle, and also that it was not black. He then went on to describe its anatomy, more especially of its head, nerves and heart, [There not *deleted*] illustrating it thoroughly by numerous lantern slides. There not being time to finish it, the remainder was postponed for a week. There were some sixty members present including two visitors.

R.C. Slater.[486]

[170]   10 November 1898. The electric telegraph
[*Scientific Soc. Minute Book 2, p. 211. MS*]

The third meeting of the Christmas term was held in the Physical Lecture Room on November 10th at 6.15.
N.B. Ellington[487] gave a lecture on 'Telegraphy'. He showed and explained the single needle instrument, the morse sounder and ink writer, and a set of Wheatstone automatic instruments lent by the Post Office.[488] The automatic transmitter is worked

---

[483] Vyner Noel Gilbert [*3039*: HHP, WaH 1882–91]; entered the church.
[484] The Revd Edward Barnwell Cook [*M132*: 1888–92]; taught Chemistry; Curate of St Agnes, Bristol 1890–1, and of All Saints, Clifton 1892–3; latterly Vicar of Wells, Canon of Wells and Prebendary of Ashill in Wells Cathedral: *Crockford* (1947).
[485] Arthur William Rogers [*3411*: PHP, OH 1895–91]; FRS; Director of the Geological Survey of the Union of South Africa.
[486] Robert Charles Slater, later Sclater [*3649*: BH 1886–91], astronomer (FRAS, taking part in expedition to the solar eclipse of 30 Aug. 1905); later master at Charterhouse.
[487] Noel Bayzand Ellington [*4854*: DH 1894–9]; became a professional engineer.
[488] Among the many inventions of Sir Charles Wheatstone (d. 1875). All UK telegraphs were put under the control of the the Post Office in 1870.

by passing strips of paper through the machine on which the messages have been punched by the clerks. He also explained the relay and its uses.

Mr Wollaston proposed that a [vote of *deleted*] letter should be written by the Secretary to thank Mr Tombs, the Postmaster,[489] for the loan of instruments. The proposal was carried unanimously.

Mr Rintoul then read and explained extracts from a description of the Bristol Central Telegraph Office lent by Mr Tombs.

The meeting was then adjourned at 7.15.

Signed: H.C. Playne, Pres.[490]

J.T. Stephen, Sec.[491]

[171]   21 February 1901. Shenstone on silica
[*Scientific Soc. Minute Book 2, p. 377. MS*]

The second meeting of the term was held on February 21st 1901 at 6.15 p.m. in [*the*] Physical Laboratory, when, after the minutes [and *deleted*] of the last meeting had been read and passed, Mr Shenstone gave a very interesting lecture on *Vitrified Silica*.

He began by explaining how Silica is found in nature, and showed several lumps of this substance. He then went on to say that it had long been looked upon as a possible substitute for glass, on account of its standing heat so much better, but no one had discovered how to manipulate it, except to draw it out into long fine needles.

The lecturer however explained that he had at last hit upon a means of working Silica tubes, and this difficult experiment was performed by Mr Lascell[492] so that everyone could see upon the wall the magnified reflection of this operation. By several experiments Mr Shenstone showed that Silica will not splinter like glass even when treated strongly and then plunged into cold water.

At the close of a most interesting lecture, Mr Playne said a few words thanking Mr Shenstone and Mr Lascell for the trouble they had taken.

The meeting was <then> adjourned about 7.15 p.m., there being about 70 members present.

H.C.P., President.

H.A. Prichard, Secretary.[493]

[172]   6 February 1902. Orchids
[*Scientific Soc. Minute Book 2, p. 385. MS*]

The first meeting of the Easter term 1902 was held on February 6th in the Crow's Nest[494] when, after the minutes of the previous meeting had been read and passed, Mr Playne called upon B. Baron[495] for his lecture on the '*Morphology of Orchids*'.

---

[489] Robert Charles Tombs, of the Post and Telegaph Office, Small Street: *Directory* (1898), pp. xvii, 482.
[490] Herbert Clement Playne [*2735*: HHP, SH 1881–9; *M146*: 1893–1906; Head of the Military Side from 1902; co-author with R.C. Fawdry [*M181*] of *Practical Trigonometry* (1906).
[491] Thoby Stephen: see above **[138]**.
[492] Technician.
[493] Harold Adye Prichard [*5162*: 1896–1902]; Canon of St John the Divine, New York.
[494] The top floor of the Wilson Tower, where the main archives are now kept, so home to most of the documents printed in this volume.
[495] Barclay Baron [*4558*: ST 1892–6]; Editorial Secretary, TocH.

The lecturer explained the methods by which orchids are fertilized by bees and other insects, and drew diagrams of the ingenious devices by which the insect is made to pass so as to touch the pollen in his search for honey. Many beautiful hand painted drawings of orchids were passed round, and a few living specimens.

At the conclusion of the lecture questions were asked by the President and C.H.C. Sharpe,[496] and after Mr Playne had thanked Baron for his interesting lecture and the paintings he had handed round, the proceedings terminated at 7.10 p.m.

There were about 40 members present.

H.C.P., President.

H.A. Prichard, Secretary.

[173]   20 February 1906. Wire to wire
[Scientific Soc. Minute Book 3, pp. 66–8. MS]

The first meeting of the Easter term 1906 was held in the Physical Laboratory on Tuesday 20th February at 6.15 p.m.

First a member for South Town was elected: Savory.[497]

No members of North Town or Polack's House in the Fifths were present and these Houses consequently continued without a member of Committee. Then when the minutes of the last meetings had been read and passed the President called on M.N. Perrin[498] to lecture on:

Wireless Telegraphy.

The lecturer started by explaining [with slides *inserted then deleted*] the simple telegraph with a simple circuit and then <with> the double circuit, turning then to morse receivers and relays; all these points were clearly explained with slides. He then explained the various kinds of waves [and *deleted*], their wave lengths and their relations to the spectrum; the wave length of an electric wave used for signalling varies from an inch to 1000 ft. To start one of these long waves in the ether,[499] the ether must be violently disturbed; this is done by an oscillatory spark from a condenser. For signalling long distances an aerial or high wire is attached to the sending apparatus. To detect these waves a coherer is used; the best form of this consists of two terminals of silver in a hollow glass tube with silver and nickel filings between; these filings allow a current to pass when acted on by an electric wave. To show this an interesting experiment was performed. A <D'Arsonval> galvanometer[500] was connected with a cell and such a coherer, a mirror on the coil of the galvanometer reflecting a spot of light onto the wall; when a spark was passed from an induction coil, the wave striking the coherer made it a conductor and [a *corrected to*] the spot of light moved away on the wall; when the coherer was tapped, it ceased to conduct and the spot of light returned to its original position.

---

[496] Colin Hugh Calvert *Sharp [5452*: NT 1898–1904]; Headmaster of Abbotsholme 1927–46.

[497] James Henry Savory *[6028*: ST 1902–6].

[498] Maurice Nasmyth Perrin *[5877*: BH 1901–6]; took a First in Part 1 of the Cambridge Natural Sciences Tripos; killed in a flying accident in 1919.

[499] The entire concept of 'ether' had been dismissed by Einstein in the previous year: *Relativity: The Special and the General Theory* (2004 edn), p. 63; *cf.* A.P. French (ed.), *Einstein: A Centenary Volume* (1979), p. 249. I am grateful to Mr A.W. Hasthorpe for noting this.

[500] Invented by the French physicists Jacques-Arsène d'Arsonval and Marcel Deprez in 1882, featuring a stationary magnet and a moving coil.

After the circuit used for wireless telegraphy had been explained, the lecturer [concluded *corrected to*] continued by showing <and demonstrating> the apparatus which had been provided and which worked perfectly, concluding with some slides of stations and famous men.

Mr Clissold[501] then rose and pointed out that the time necessarily spent in preparing <such> a lecture was certainly well spent and was appreciated by the Society. He then gave some facts about directing messages and judging the distance from which they had come, especially as intended for lighthouses.

As the meeting was about to adjourn, Mr Rintoul pointed out a very interesting fact; when Marconi was lecturing in Big School in 1898,[502] he had part of his apparatus in the gallery and part on the platform; but a Wimshurst machine[503] was being worked in the room underneath and this made his experiments wrong. He, however, sent up balloons in the room attached to copper wires and this enabled him to receive only the waves from his sending apparatus in the gallery. This was probably the first instance of any attempt at tuning.

After applauding heartily the meeting was adjourned at 7.16 p.m. About 80 members were present.

Signed: President: F.B.S.[504] Secretary: A. Christie.[505]

[174]   29 November 1908. Birds and their calls
[Scientific Soc. Minute Book 3, pp. 105–6. MS]

The fourth meeting of the term was held at 6.15 p.m. in the Physical Laboratory on Thursday Nov. 29th. The President[506] observed that the Committee thought it desirable to raise the subscription to 1/- per term including the Summer term with a view to publishing a small annual report containing a list of members and notes of the lectures: the motion was carried by 32–29.

The President then called upon D'O.D.E. Miller[507] to give his paper on 'Birds of the Neighbourhood'. The lecturer gave an account of the various birds to be found including notes on their habits and the times at which they are to be seen, and illustrated his remarks with lantern slides. Jacob[508] then gave a lecture on shrikes and nightingales, giving many observations of his own on their habitats and habits. He also mentioned that there were four nightingale nests in Leigh Woods last summer and he also found a shrike's storeroom in the neighbourhood, a slowworm from which was exhibited.

[501] Harry Clissold [*3375*: WaH 1885–9; *M148*: 1894–1917]; at this time House Tutor WaH and OC of the Corps. Later House Master WiH; served with distinction in the War (DSO) and killed 1917.
[502] No direct record of this occasion has yet been found. It is not featured in the Society's minutes, perhaps because the lecture was to the whole School and so was not reckoned a meeting of the Society. In the previous year Marconi had conducted his famous experiments across the Bristol Channel from Brean Down to Lavernock Point.
[503] For generating a spark by turning wheels; invented by James Wimshurst in 1883.
[504] Francis Bernard Stead [*3360*: ST 1884–91; *M172*: 1901–8] taught Chemistry.
[505] Archibald Christie [*5892*: NT, PHP, SH 1901–7]; first husband of the writer Agatha Christie.
[506] E. Cuthbert Anderson [*M189*: 1907–12]; taught Science and Mathematics.
[507] Douglas Owen d'Elboux Miller [*5621*: ST 1900–10]; the Secretary was evidently hazy about his forenames.
[508] Lancelot George Jacob [*6153*: ST 1903–19] or John Reginald [*6184*: ST 1903–11].

MacLellan[509] then gave a short paper on call notes and songs which he had intended to illustrate, but some apparatus sent for had not arrived. Some questions having been aired and answered, the meeting adjourned at 7.15.

(signed) L.M. Milne-Thomson (Secretary).[510]

E.C.A. (President).

[175]   9 November 1909. The shadow on the glass
[Scientific Soc. Minute Book 3, pp. 119–20. MS]

The third meeting of the term was held on Tuesday November 9th when Mr Rintoul gave the first part of his lecture on 'Electrons'.

The lecturer began by mentioning that electrons and the theory of ionization play a very important part in modern science. He then showed some experiments to illustrate the way in which air can be ionized, the ionization being detected by the conducting power which it confers on the air. A charged electroscope was shown to be discharged by the passage of a current of hot gases from a Bunsen flame. It was also discharged by X-rays, which were at first shielded from the electroscope by a metal plate, when the electroscope was unaffected. On removing this plate, the electroscope was at once discharged. A small tube containing a little Radium produced the same effect.

A description followed of an experiment in which a cloud is formed in dust-free <air> which has been ionized – the ions acting as nuclei.

Next, experiments <were shown> illustrating the effect of passing a current from an induction coil through tubes containing gases at low pressures. As the pressure decreases a flashing light appears which gradually fills the whole tube. At very low pressures, the end of the tube opposite the kathode begins to glow, and a metal plate, placed in the path of the rays, casts a sharp shadow on the glass.

These effects are due to kathode rays, which possess the property of making a small wheel with vanes rotate, and are deflected by a magnet.

The lecture concluded the first part of his subject by indicating how these and other experiments furnish an estimate of the mass, velocity, and charge of an ion.

The meeting adjourned at 7.15.

P.D. Sturge, Secretary.[511]

E.C.A., President.

[176]   11 March 1920. The science of sport
[Scientific Soc. Minute Book 3, pp. 250–3. MS]

The third meeting of the term was held on Thursday March 11th. Owing to the absence of the Secretary, the minutes of the previous meeting were not read. Mr Holmyard took the chair and immediately called upon Mr Muirhead[512] to deliver his

---

[509] George Aikman MacLellan [*6390*: OH 1905–8].

[510] Louis Melville Milne-Thomson [*6535*: SH 1906–9]; FRS (Edin); Professor of Mathematics at RNC Greenwich; 1921–56; author of *The Calculus of Finite Differences* (1933) and many other works, and commemorated in the Milne-Thomson Circle theorem.

[511] Paul Dudley Sturge [*6191*: NT 1904–10]; took a First in Part I of the Cambridge Natural Sciences Tripos.

[512] James Alexander Orrock Muirhead [*M231*: 1914–49]; represented Cambridge at athletics in 1911 and 1912; at Clifton in charge of athletics 1916–43, and at various times in charge of football, swimming, boxing and shooting; President of the Scientific Society 1917–25.

lecture on 'The Application of Scientific Principles to Athletics'.

Mr Muirhead first explained the meaning of scientific methods and the way in which scientific observation can be used for the improvement of athletics, and the difference between inductive and deductive methods. He next explained Lamark's law of the use and disuse of members.[513] Tissues worn out by exercise are repaired by means of the blood, the repairs usually exceeding the loss, thus producing growth of muscle. This points to the use of training, but their [*sic*] is a danger of overtraining, a feeling of staleness being the result.

Suppleness and quickness are more important than mere strength. The village blacksmith type of athlete is no more – the blacksmith being beaten by the scientifically trained athlete at his own game of throwing the hammer. Dumbells [*sic*] and weightlifting tend to produce muscle at the expense of agility, and are therefore to be avoided, skipping and boxing being recommended instead. Quickness is attained by the practice of short sprints and starts. Greater ease and speed are obtained by running on the toes even in long events. The lecturer showed on a slide the skeletons of a man and horse, to point out the metatarsal bone of the horse greatly developed by toe running. He then spoke of the importance of the start of a race; observations show that the first stride in the hundred [*yards*] is usually little more than 3 ft, increasing to the full stride of 9 or 10 feet at the tenth stride, the head being raised from the all-fours position gradually. The finish is nearly as important as the start. There is a great temptation to look behind, and to begin to slow up before reaching the tape.

The next point was the effect of corners. Methods of running the quarter [*mile*] were discussed. There is no hard and fast rule, except to avoid, in the mile, half and quarter, trying to overtake at the corners, where the man outside has further to go, and at the same time to avoid being shut in by a clump of runners: and, conversely, to avoid being overtaken in the straight.

In the high jump, much unnecessary work is done: the excess is estimated at 50%. Mr Muirhead showed slides of the American style of jumping, in which the unnecessary work is a minimum,[514] and the Clifton style. The next slide showed energy wasted in hurdling, and a race lost by looking round. The least wasteful method is with straight legs. In the long jump it is important to jump high. Mr Muirhead showed a diagram illustrating the [real *corrected to*] relative distances jumped with the same impetus but different heights. He showed several slides illustrating the bad and good points; and explained the best way to practise the steps and take-off.

He lastly dealt with putting the weight, explaining the best way, of beginning the motion with a hop, and showing the weakness of the style in which there is no body work, and the calm leverage obtained by a change of steps.

After a few questions raised by members of the audience had been discussed, the meeting concluded with a vote of thanks to the lecturer.

J.A.O. Muirhead, President.
M.F. Proctor,[515] Secretary.
June 28th 1920.

---

[513] Jean-Baptiste Pierre Antoine de Monet, Chevalier de la Marck, commonly called *Lamarck* (d. 1829), who in his *Philosophie Zoologique* (1809) showed that body parts grow with use and decrease by disuse.
[514] The 'Eastern cut-off', pioneered by Michael Sweeney, flattened the back to achieve a more efficient jump than the older 'Scissors' method.
[515] Maurice Faraday Proctor [*7116*: NT 1910–20].

[177]   16 March 1922. The military use of Meteorology
[*Scientific Soc. Minute Book 4, pp. 32–6. MS*]

On Thursday March 16th the Scientific Society held a reception in the Chemical Laboratory to meet Lt Col. E. Gold, D.S.O., F.R.S.,[516] who afterwards gave an account of his work as Chief of the Meteorological Staff at G.H.Q. France from 1915 till the end of the war. About 170 members and visitors were present.

Colonel Gold first drew attention to the decisive influence of weather in the campaigns of the past. Incidentally most of us discovered for the first time that a preliminary east wind was responsible for the success of the Norman invasion in 1066. At the beginning of the war, weather reports were issued to G.H.Q. from London, but the introduction of gas made it essential to have the weather reports on the spot. The first big test of their efficiency came at Loos three months later.[517] We were shown a couple of isobaric charts of the previous day, and a copy of the forecast. In view of the immense issues at stake, we were struck by the boldness of the forecast, and perhaps for the first time realised the enormous responsibilities of Col. Gold and his staff. The Commander-in-Chief[518] paid tribute to the soldierly way in which the elements had carried out the orders. The part played by the weather forecast in other big battles was also described. The cold air rolling down the slopes of hills may produce a 'gravitational' current near the surface of the ground, directly opposed to the direction of the general wind. Use was frequently made of this current to the consternation of the enemy, who complained in their reports that we were using gas when the conditions did not justify it.

Forecast was not the only function of the Meteorological Unit. Col. Gold went on to describe the effect of wind, especially upper currents, on the flight of artillery shells. It was the duty of his department to discover the velocity of these currents, and to calculate the allowance to be made, especially when conditions only allowed of map ranging. The methods of computing velocities were outlined. We believe very few of our members could have followed Col. Gold through the mazes of calculation, and feel grateful he did not put us to the test.

Finally we were given a short account of the work of the Meteorological Office under peace conditions in connection with civil aviation.

Colonel Raymer[519] proposed vote of thanks to the lecturer, which was heartily endorsed.

President, J.A.O.M.
B.E. Berry, Secretary.[520]

---

[516] Ernest Gold was an official of the civilian Meteorological Department, appointed Captain in the Royal Flying Corps and attached to Haig's First Army HQ: Charteris, *Haig*, pp. 170–1; Terraine, *Haig*, pp. 158, 348.

[517] Gold had played a crucial part in timing the attack. In the early hours of 25 September 1915, Haig waited in the meteorological hut until Gold forecast a change of wind that would carry chlorine gas towards the German trenches. Haig then took his cue from the rustle of leaves in the poplars, as the wind began to rise: Haig, *Private Papers*, p. 104; Charteris, *Haig*, pp. 171–2.

[518] Sir John French, C-in-C of the British Expeditionary Force.

[519] Col the Revd Robert Richmond Raymer [*M221*: 1913–20], Commandant of the Corps 1913–20; served with great distinction in both wars (CMG, DSO, and Greek Order of George I).

[520] Brian Exley Berry [*8499*: NT, WaH 1919–22].

[178]   20 July 1926. Expeditions: aeroplanes attract more interest than soap
[*Scientific Soc. Minute Book 4, pp. 150–8. MS*]

The last day for expeditions in the Summer term, 1926, was on Tuesday, July 20th. There were six expeditions arranged by the Society: (a) a second visit to the G.P.O.; (b) to the Bristol Aeroplane Co.'s Aero-engine Works at Filton; (c) to Messrs Christopher Thomas' Soap Works, (d) to the Bristol Tramways & Carriage Co.'s Motor Constructional Works, Brislington; (e) to the *Western Daily Press* Printing Offices in Baldwin Street, and (f) to Messrs Stothert & Pitt, Engineers, Bath.

12 members went to the Post Office, in charge of P.C. Matthew,[521] arriving there at 2.30 p.m. They were conducted round on the same tour as the party on the previous occasion.

About 40 members went on the expedition to the Filton Aeroplane Works in charge of the President, arriving there at 3.15 p.m. This was by far the most interesting and attractive expedition of the whole term. They were shown all round the 'shops', and also were shown various engines 'on test'. Several aeroplanes were inspected, and finally free ices and lemonade were provided at the Works canteen. Our thanks are due to Mr C.H.R. [*recte* A.H.R.] Fedden,[522] of the Bristol Aeroplane Company, for the manner in which we were received.

5 members went to Messrs Christopher Thomas' Soap Works, Broad Plain, Bristol, in charge of D.D. Lindsay,[523] arriving there at 3.0 p.m. The party was shown the processes in the manufacture of soap, and its by-products. This expedition was unable to compete in popularity with the others.

The expedition to the Bristol Tramways' Works at Brislington consisted of about 15 members, in charge of J.N. Malcolm.[524] They arrived at the works at 3.15 p.m. and were shown all the stages in the construction of 'Bristol' buses and lorries. This expedition was very instructive, and would have been much more fully attended in the absence of the Aeroplane Works expedition.

About 12 members went on the expedition to the *Western Daily Press* Offices, in charge of J.M. Hooper,[525] arriving there at 3.0 p.m. They were shown all over the Printing Works, and, on leaving, were each presented with a copy of the *Bristol Evening News*, which had just been printed there.

The party going to Messrs Stothert & Pitt's Works at Bath numbered about 25, and was in charge of the Secretary. About 12 boys from the 'Pre'[526] came in cars with two masters, Mr Heath and Mr Pavey.[527] The members of the Society travelled by train, meeting at Bath (G.W.) Station at 2.55 p.m.

---

[521] Patrick Crichton Matthew [*9063*: ST, OH 1922–6].

[522] Sir (Alfred Hubert) Roy Fedden [*5057*: NT, BH 1895–1904]; Designer and Chief Engineer, Engine Dept BAC, 1920–42; among many honours and appointments President of the Royal Aeronautical Soc. 1938–9, and knighted 1942. See B. Gunston, *By Jupiter: The Life of Sir Roy Fedden* (Royal Aeronautical Soc. 1978, repr. as *Fedden* (Rolls-Royce Heritage Trust Historical Series, no. 26: Derby, 1998), esp. (for his schooldays) pp. 15–19.

[523] Donald Dunrod Lindsay [*9416*: WaH 1924–9]; Headmaster of Portsmouth Grammar School 1942–53, and of Malvern College 1953–71.

[524] John Neill Malcolm [*9119*: BH 1922–7].

[525] John Maurice Hooper [*9289*: BH 1923–7].

[526] At this point the 'Pre' still meant the separate establishment for boys up to 11, distinct from the Junior School.

[527] Newton Heath [*M260*: 1921–6] and Reginald William Juxon Pavey [*5306*: ST 1897–1900; *M228*: 1914–28].

On arriving at the main Works, the Society and the 'Pre' boys with their masters formed two parties, and each was conducted round separately by its own guide from the Works. The most interesting things of note were an 80-ton crane for Bermuda; several 2-ton level-luffing cranes[528] for Calcutta; and numberless pumps of all sorts, concrete-mixers, etc. In addition all the 'shops' necessary to a constructional engineering works were inspected. Members returned separately, some remaining in Bath for tea.

The Natural History Section arranged an expedition to the grounds of Blaise Castle.

The Archaeological Section arranged an expedition to Nailsea Court.

This year the expeditions arranged by the Engineering Section were merged into the Society expeditions.

P.N.D. Porter, Hon. Sec.[529]

F.B. Finter, President.[530]

[179]　　17 February 1927. Oil
[Scientific Soc. Minute Book 4, p. 176. MS]

A meeting was held on Thursday, Feb. 17th, at 6.0 p.m. in the Chemical Lecture Room. About 40 persons were present.

We were fortunate in getting Prof. A.W. Nash, M.Sc., M.Inst.P.T., M.I.Mech.E., F.C.S., of Birmingham University,[531] to give a lecture on 'Oil Engineering'. He spoke about oil engineering as a profession, and also explained how oil is actually obtained from the vast underground supplies. He illustrated his remarks with lantern slides showing diagrams and views taken from oilfields all over the world. The lecture was clear and interesting, if rather technical for some of the younger members of the audience,[532] and at the end a hearty vote of thanks was accorded to the lecturer.

The meeting adjourned at 7.10 p.m.

P.N.D. Porter, Hon. Sec.

[180]　　8 December 1927. Fedden foresees career prospects in aero-engineering
[Scientific Soc. Minute Book 4, p. 214. MS]

A general meeting was held on Tuesday, Dec. 8th at 6.0 p.m. in Room J. About 60 members were present.

Mr A.H.R. Fedden (O.C.)[533] read an extremely interesting paper on 'Aircraft Power Plant'. The subject was divided into sections dealing with past, present and future developments in aero-engine construction, and was profusely illustrated [with *corrected to*] by slides. At the close of the lecture, specimens were displayed to

---

[528] In which the jib remains horizontal while lifting; Stothert & Pitt's own 'Toplis' design of 1914 was a significant development.

[529] Patrick Nixon Dick Porter [*9134*: BH 1922–7].

[530] See above **[152]**.

[531] Alfred William Nash, Professor of Oil Engineering and Refining 1922–42, and head of a newly established research centre within the Department of Chemical Engineering.

[532] But not for the Hon. Secretary, who went on to study under Nash at Birmingham, graduating with honours in Oil Engineering and Refining, and then began a successful career in the oil industry.

[533] See above **[178]**.

show the high standard of workmanship necessary in aero-engine parts. The lecturer referred to the opportunities awaiting the keen and intelligent boy in this branch of engineering. He warned his audience that the openings were limited in number at present, but would probably grow rapidly during the next 20 or 30 years.

After several questions had been replied to, a hearty vote of thanks was passed to the lecturer, and the meeting adjourned at 7.30 p.m.

P.N.D. Porter, Hon. Sec.

[181]   17 March 1932. Soap and bubbles
[Scientific Soc. Minute Book 5, p. 62. MS]

The third meeting of the term was held on Thursday March 17th at 6 p.m. in Room J.

Mr Finter and 55 members of the Society were present.

Mr Penny of the Broad Plain Soap Works lectured on 'The Art of Soap Making'. He brought with him Mr Lewis, the chief chemist, to assist with the demonstrations.

He first mentioned the underlying principle of soap manufacture, the condensation of a fatty acid with caustic soda. He then told us of the two tests used, the iodine test and the titre test, and explained how by means of iodine values the soaps could be blended to the right hardness, illustrating the theory with some large bars of soap. He then discussed some of the technical points of manufacture such as salting out and removing glycerine, showing slides of the actual operations.

He then performed some glorious experiments with soap film and bubbles. He played ping-pong with a bubble, blew one inside another, and filled one with smoke. He also dropped lead shot through a bubble.

The lecture was much appreciated, as was shown by the applause, and the meeting adjourned about 7.20 p.m.

P.M. Thomas, Hon. Sec.[534]

N.L. Ross-Kane, President.[535]

[182]   24 March 1932. Talkies
[Scientific Soc. Minute Book 5, p. 64. MS]

The fourth meeting of the term was held on Thursday, March 24th in Room J at 6 p.m.

Mr Finter, Mr Graham[536] and 61 members of the Society were present.

Mr J.F. Tilney O.C.[537] spoke on 'The Production and Reproduction of Talking Film'.

He first of all discussed the underlying theories of the two methods used, the disc method and the film method, but as the disc method is practically obsolete now except for interval music, he dealt chiefly with the film method.

He then dealt shortly with the production of the sound films, showing a few slides of the apparatus used.

He then dealt much more fully with the reproduction of the film in the cinema theatre, discussing the apparatus and safety devices in great detail, and succeeded in showing us how foolproof it has been made.

---

[534] Patrick Muirhead Thomas [*9963*: WiH 1927–32].
[535] Noël Lindsay Ross-Kane [*M305*: 1931–5]; taught Science before joining ICI.
[536] Alan Philps Graham [*M301*: 1931–40]; taught Science.
[537] James Frederick Tilney [*9499*: UH, OH 1924–8]; by profession an electrical and mechanical engineer.

He ended by showing us a few [slides *corrected to*] pictures on the epidiascope of projectors.

The lecturer was applauded and the meeting adjourned about 7.10 p.m.

P.M. Thomas, Hon. Sec.

N.L. Ross-Kane, President.

[183]   24 May 1934. Expeditions
[*Scientific Soc. Minute Book 5, 140. MS*]

The first series of expeditions was held on May 24. We visited the following factories:
(a) D.C.L. Yeast Works[538] (55); (b) *Evening World* (10); (c) Bristol Tramways
(45); (d) Bristol Gas Works (30); (e) Georges' Brewery[539] (63); (f) Peckett's Loco.
Works[540] (30); (g) Portishead Radio Station (25).

Few members of the Society put their names down for D.C.L. Yeast Works, but
those who went found the visit exceedingly interesting. Tea was served in the canteen afterwards.

Mr Wilson[541] took a party to the *Evening World* Printing Works, and the visit
proved of absorbing interest. The only difficulty was that the party had to be small.

45 members visited Bristol Tramways Co.'s Works at Brislington, and saw the
engine fitting shops etc. Tea was served afterwards.

Those who went to the Gas Works were presented with copies of 'The Romance of
a Lump of Coal'. An interesting, if odourous [*sic*], afternoon was spent by everyone.

Those who visited Georges' Brewery managed to obtain half a glass of beer each,
chiefly owing to the absence of any masters.

Peckett's Locomotive Works as usual gave their visitors a pleasant and instructive
afternoon, showing them all stages of locomotive construction etc.

The newly formed Wireless Section visited Portishead Radio Station, and the more
technically minded of them enjoyed the trip very much. The station transmits on as
many as six or seven wavelengths to ships in all parts of the world. The actual operators
and the receiving station are situated at a distance of fifteen miles from Portishead.

J.C. Kendrew, Hon Sec.[542]

N.L. Ross-Kane (President).

[184]   23 May 1935. Visit to Bristol Cathedral and other sites
[*Scientific Society, Archaeological Section, Minute Book 1931–9, pp. 137–41. MS*]

Summer term 1935

On Thursday May 23rd the Society visited Bristol Cathedral. The Dean[543] had very
kindly offered to show us round. We visited first the famous Chapter-House and saw
from a door the ruins of the Bishop's Palace, burnt down in the Reform Bill riots. Mr

---

[538] The Distillers Company Ltd, in Cheese Lane: *Directory* (1934), p. 596.

[539] In Victoria Street, Temple: *Directory* (1947), p. 642.

[540] The Atlas Locomotive Works in Fishponds: *Directory* (1947), p. 838.

[541] Kenneth Gledhill Wilson [*M286*: 1927–43]; Modern Languages Dept; played Water Polo for England.

[542] Sir John Cowdery Kendrew [*10423*: WaH 1930–6]; FRS; Nobel Prize for Chemistry 1962; knighted 1974.

[543] Harry William Blackburne, DSO, MC, Dean 1934–51; member of Council 1937–51, and Hon. OC (one of very few other than former masters): *Register* (1947), p. lxviii. As an army chaplain he had been well regarded by Haig: N. Cave, 'Haig and religion', in Bond and Cave, *Haig*, p. 249.

Billingham,[544] Mr Ruding-Bryan,[545] and the Dean had a very elucidating discussion, the former pointing out the curious division between two types of diaper work which covered the roof. We then returned to the South Transept through the Cloisters. The Dean showed us a Saxon grave stone with a harrowing carving on it; he put forward a theory of his own that such stones were used for teaching children by example.[546]

The complete roof of the transepts and crossing has been restored to its original colours by the expert [*marked* ?] hand of Professor Tristram[547] and on the initiative of the Dean. We spent a long time in examining the beautiful bosses, of which the Dean is rightly very proud. He took us next into the Lady Chapel, a lovely piece of architecture but difficult to appreciate because of its darkness. We walked round the Ambulatory into the Choir and Presbytery, then into the Lady Chapel, the east wall of which is a marvelous [*sic*] stone screen. We came out past the [Warwick *deleted*] Berkeley Chapel, and after thanking the Dean profusely hurried to St Mary Redcliffe's. We did not go into the church, but just opposite it is the 'Shot Tower', the oldest in the world, in fact the place where the method of manufacturing shot was discovered.[548] The owner, an O.C. [*minuted* E.W. Thomas.[549] The Office is in Cheese Lane] kindly showed us round and told us how shot was made by dropping <molten> lead through a sieve into a tank of cold water. He also told us about the dream through which this method was discovered.

From the shot factory we walked to a hermit's cave in a school playground nearbye [*sic, and marked* ?]. There was little to see; in fact members seemed far more interested in the gravestones of Quakers who were buried there.[550] They all seemed to have lived to phenomenal ages. [*Minuted* The cave is through the end of Jones Lane. For the key, apply 3, Freshford Lane. Canynge's House is at 97, Redcliffe St.]

This first expedition was well attended by members as well as a large number of masters and their wives.

[*Signed*] L.M. Munby (Hon. Sec.),[551] E.P. Bury.[552]

---

[544] Philip Henry Billingham, FRHistS [*M292*: 1928–41].

[545] See above **[81]**.

[546] A misunderstanding of the title of the 'Harrowing of Hell' carving, found beneath the Chapter House during 19th-century excavation. Although it had been used as a coffin lid, it is doubtful that this was its original purpose, and it is more likely to be 12th century than Anglo-Saxon: C. Oaksey, 'Romanesque architecture and sculpture', in J. Rogan (ed.), *Bristol Cathedral: History & Architecture* (Stroud, 2000), pp. 64–78.

[547] Ernest William Tristram (d. 1952), art historian and pioneering conservator of wall paintings and other medieval decoration; some of his techniques were flawed (especially the use of wax as a sealant), but Bristol remains in his debt: *ibid*., p. 112.

[548] The tower was built by William Watts in 1782.

[549] Edward Wilson Thomas, JP [*7073*: ST 1910–17].

[550] The burial ground at the foot of Redcliffe Hill was given to the Quakers by Charles II in 1665. The cave, known as St John's Hermitage, was first occupied in 1346 by John Sparkes, a recluse employed by Lord Berkeley to pray for himself and his family.

[551] Lionel Maxwell Munby [*10590*: OH 1931–6]; took a first in History at Oxford and wrote widely on local history.

[552] Eric Pryse Bury [*M253*: 1920–47].

[185]   26 March 1936. The Science Library
[*Scientific Soc. Minute Book 5, pp. 190–2. MS*]

On Thursday March 26, at 6.30 p.m., in Room J, Dr E.J. Holmyard lectured on 'Exploring the Science Library'. The President, Secretary, and about 40 members were present.

The lecture took the form of a series of exhibits of books, <etc>, shown on the epidiascope, accompanied by an extremely entertaining and instructive commentary. Most of the books, autographs, pictures and medals had, of course, been collected by the lecturer himself. His diffidence in acknowledging practically all the specimens to be rare or scarce was perhaps excusable; the fact remains that they *are* rare, and that at Clifton we are surrounded by such rarities that we become too blasé.

The main part of the lecture concerned Chemistry, the history of which was traced from Avicenna through Gelor [*recte* Galen] and the Alchemicals (many of whose works were shown; also pictures of alchemical labs) to the beginning of modern Chemistry, with [Dalton *deleted*], Boyle, Black, Priestly and Rouelle[553] – then on to more modern times, with Dalton, Avogadro,[554] Cannizzaro,[555] Stas,[556] Haber[557] and many others. Especially full and interesting exhibits dealt with Priestley, Rouelle and Lavoisier.

The lecture was concluded by [a *deleted*] short exhibits in Physics and Biology – dealing with Newton, Pascal, Torricelli,[558] Galvani,[559] Faraday, Darwin, Jenner, Huxley and Pasteur.

The meeting broke up with much applause at 7.35 p.m. The small size of the audience was due to the proximity of the end of term, but those who did go spend [*recte* spent] an extremely enjoyable evening.

J.C. Kendrew, Hon. Secretary.
A.P. Graham, President.

[186]   2 November 1939. Wartime science
[*Scientific Society Diary 1937–9. MS*]

Michaelmas term 1939.
On Thursday Nov. 2 we held our first meeting 'under war conditions'. I distributed five tickets per House, giving them to House representatives; they were instructed to make a list of all those members who wanted to attend the lecture, and then distribute the tickets to the first five in the order of preference applying to the lecture. (We propose to vary this order, to give everyone a fair chance of attending a lecture, and so that we can confine the more specialised lectures to specialists, and open the more 'popular' ones to the lower forms). House representatives should be told to write the names of applicants on the tickets, and impress on them that they should

---

[553] Guillaume François Rouelle (d. 1770), who identified the base.
[554] Lorenzo Romano Amedeo Carol Avogadro, Count of Quarenga and Cerreto (d. 1856); formulator of 'Avogadro's Constant' defining relationship between masses of gases and their molecular weights.
[555] Stanislao Cannizaro (d. 1910); developed Avogadro's work.
[556] Jean Servais Stas (d. 1891); refined the atomic mass scale.
[557] Fritz Haber (d. 1934), Nobel Laureate and pioneer in chemical warfare.
[558] Evangelisto Torricelli (d. 1647), who invented the barometer.
[559] Luigi Aloisio Galvani (d. 1748), pioneer of electrophysiology (originally 'galvanism', hence 'to galvanise').

attend the lecture once they have received a ticket; if they do not, it means that some other people [are *corrected to*] lower down who want to go, could have gone, and that altogether it is very inconsiderate not to use the ticket, or not to return it to the House representative if it cannot be used. After this lecture we decided that House representatives need not have any tickets for admission, and that they should be allowed to attend any lecture, whether they [were *corrected to*] are included in the order of preference or not. Hence only four tickets per House are required. This makes a total of 45 members attending, assuming all House representatives attend. The maximum is 50; hence this leaves five for any House or Houses who happen to have more than five applicants per tickets.

Tickets should be collected at the door, for each lecture; it is then possible to find out if some of the quota from any House did not turn up; if the tickets collected at the door are less in number than those given out to that House, transmit a 'raspberry' via House representatives to the offenders; (if, however, the tickets collected are greater in number than those given out, get a water-marked paper for the tickets!)

The above-mentioned maximum attendance of 50 is fixed by black-out restrictions. It must be remembered that no windows can be open in any of the Science School lecture rooms when the blinds are pulled up; more that 50 members (+ the President, lecturer, masters and any guests) in a hermetically sealed lecture-room tend to make the atmosphere a trifle fuggy.

About the war-time system of subscriptions, and marking them up in the Register. For this term I have put a tick in the 1939^3 columns; I suggest that a tick should be placed in each successive column for the duration of these war modifications of the system, and that no lines should be drawn. Mark off when a member has left the School; while this war affair is on, it automatically follows (see typed sheet in Minute Book) that no one will leave the Society, except when he leaves the School altogether. Further, always put the initials of entries in the Register; it makes identification so much easier. 'Davis', for instance, is apt to be a rather vague identification when there are as many as seven of that clan in the School.

About fixing dates for lectures – remember that Dr Fox[560] has a treble and alto practice on Thursdays at 5; i.e. the same time as S.S. lecture. The choir *always* has priority over S.S. lectures, and so be very careful not to admit any songster to a Thursday meeting at this time; if you <do>, the Director of Music will be annoyed, to say the least of it!

Conversation piece

[187]   22 March 1934. Scientifc Society Conversazione programme
[*Science Box. Printed; with MS comments and markings by the President of the Society, N.L. Ross-Kane, here printed* **bold**]

The Clifton College Scientific Society
CONVERSAZIONE
the twenty second of March, 1934
Refreshments will be served in the Council Room

---

[560] Douglas Gerard Arthur Fox [*6057*: ST 1903–10; *M302*: 1931–57], Director of Music. The vigour with which he defended his territory is recalled by John Thorn [*M366*] in his *Road to Winchester*, p. 55. See also below [**289**].

PROGRAMME.

Ground Floor: Demonstrations in the Physics Lecture Rooms and Laboratories.
Exhibition by the Archaeological Section.
Exhibition of records of the Scientific Society.

First Floor: Demonstrations in the Chemical Lecture Rooms and Laboratories.
Demonstrations in the Biological Laboratory.

Second Floor: The Science Library.
Demonstrations in the Biological Laboratory.
Exhibition by the Natural History Section.

GROUND FLOOR.

Room A. (The Tait Room).
The discharge of electricity through gases.
The Philips 'Philora' sodium lamp for road lighting,[561] kindly lent by Messrs
Philips Lamps Ltd. W.J.M. Scott [*10224*], H.G. Liversidge [*10371*].

Room D. (Photographic Dark Room).
All members of the Society may use the dark room.

Room G. (The Gotch Robinson Room).
1. A ripple tank to illustrate the reflection, refraction and interference of waves.
E.A. Nahum [*10591*], R.M. Burton [*10492*].

2. Glass conducting an electric current. F.L.J. Cary [*recte* F.J.L.: *10521*], H. Bird
[*10334*].

3. The peculiar behaviour of rotating bodies. F.H.E. Anthony [*10243*], R.F. Evans
[*9395*].

4. Water boiling and freezing simultaneously. I.D.H. Anderson [*10397*], D.C. Hill
[*10577*].

5. An application of a photo-cell relay (apparatus kindly lent by the General
Electric Co. Ltd.). J.M. Tyndall [*10291*], P. Morcom [*9562*].

Room H.
Some lights on portraiture. J.M. Pinkerton [*10720*], R.C. Williams [*10878*].

Room J. (The Heath Room).
A cathode-ray oscillograph. For this demonstration the beam of electrons is made
to oscillate both horizontally and vertically by two valve oscillators. The frequency
of the horizontal oscillation is varied, and when the ratio of the two frequencies is a
simple one the pattern on the screen is simple. The patterns are Lissajous figures.[562]
J.P.H. Green [*recte* P.J.H: *10215*], D.S. Wilson [*10604*].

Room L. (The Percival Room).
1. A phantom lamp. A.J. Burton [*10491*].

2. A solid steel ball floating on glycerol. P.R. Levy.[563] **Not convincing because one
could not touch the ball.**

3. A soap bubble. J.L. Braithwaite [*10823*], C.D. Walker [*10916*].

4. Some effects of surface tension. G.A. Gibbs [*10315*], P.D. Mort [*10861*].

5. More effects of surface tension. A.M.G. Trower [*10876*], H.P.B. Whitty [*10756*].

6. Detecting radiation with a thermopile. K. Chitty, A. Couper.[564] *α+*

---

[561] Invented in 1931; the first commercial sodium vapour lamp.

[562] From the French mathematician Jules Antoine Lissajous (d. 1880).

[563] Percy Reginald Levy [*10583*: PH 1931–5]; professional engineer and sometime director of a firm of
steelfounders.

[564] Keith Chitty [*9988*: ST 1927–38] became Senior Registrar at Bristol Royal Infirmary; Aitkin Couper
[*10829*: ST 1933–8] was Senior Lecturer in Physical and Inorganic Chemistry at Bristol University.

Plate 1   The Wilson Tower, completed in 1890.

Plate 2   Councillors: *top left* H.S. Wasbrough (served 1860–92); *top right* Canon H. Moseley (1865–72; Chairman of Council 1865–8); *bottom left* Sir Henry Newbolt (1919–37); *bottom right* Sir Herbert Warren (1882–1930; Chairman 1917–30).

Plate 3   Head Masters: *top left* John Percival (1862–79); *top right* J.M. Wilson (1879–91); *bottom* The first five Head Masters at the College's Golden Jubilee 1912 *left to right, standing* M.G. Glazebrook (1891–1905); A.A. David (1905–10); *seated* Percival; J.E. King (1910–23); Wilson.

Plate 4   Masters: *top left* T.E. Brown; *top right* G.H. Wollaston; *bottom left* M.R. Ridley; *bottom right* J.A.O. Muirhead.

Plate 5   Music: *above* Douglas Fox, Director of Music 1931–57, at Clifton, and as a master sketched by Katie Rintoul (daughter of the Head of Science); *below* Sir Hubert Parry's MS score of the School Song; A.H. Peppin, first Director of Music, to whom the song is dedicated.

Plate 6   The Sixth Form Room, on the second floor of the Wilson Tower.

Plate 7 Nonconformity: *top left* J.H. Whitley became Speaker of the Commons but refused a peerage on retirement (see Documents **40–6**); *top right* J.E. McTaggart, who refused to play games and became an eminent philosopher (see Document **137**); *bottom* Letter from the Corps Commander to the Head Master, returning the .22 round found in the pockets a boy in 1918 (Document **275**).

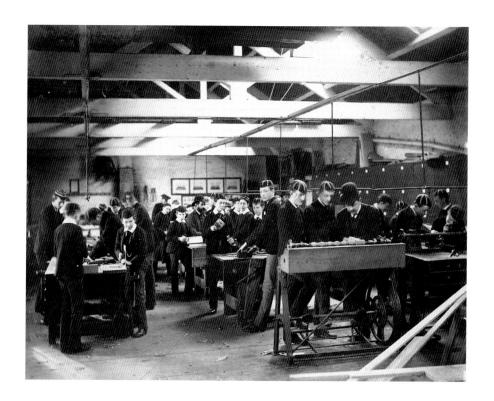

Plate 8   Practical work *c*. 1900: *above* The Workshop; *below* The Chemical Laboratory.

Plate 9   The Engineer Corps *c*. 1900: *above* Ready for anything; *below* Building bridges in the Close (see Documents **200–1**).

Plate 10   Sportsmen: *above* Boxers (unidentified, *c*. 1900); *below left* A.E.J. Collins, whose 1899 innings of 628* remains a world record (see Document **285**); *below right* R.J. Potter, rackets pair and Head of the School (see Documents **289–90**).

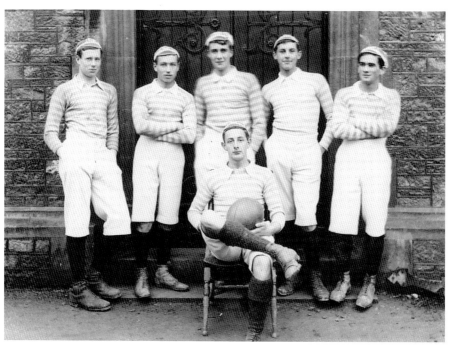

Plate 11   Sportsmen: *above, left to right* G.W.E. Whitehead, Captain of the XI of 1914, A.A.E. Chitty, and D.S.H. Woodward, photographed in 1912 (see Documents **423–4**); *bottom* North Town caps of 1897 *standing, left to right* H. Lecky, A.C. McWatters, P.G. Robinson, G.S.J. Fuller Eberle, H.S. Hall; *seated* G.D. Barne (see Document **408**).

Plate 12   Chapel: *above* The Holman Hunt mosaic of 1899 (see Documents **86–92**); *below* The Glazebrook memorial pulpit of 1930 (see Documents **107–16**).

Plate 13   Michael Redgrave as Captain Absolute in the 1926 production of *The Rivals* (see Document **363**).

Plate 14   Royalty: *above* King George V and Queen Mary leaving after their visit in 1912; the Head Master (J.E. King) stands beside Their Majesties' carriage; Percival, in episcopal habit, is in front of the other spectators (see Documents **382–4**); *below* The opening of the Science School in 1927; *left to right* The Head of the School (R.H.T. Whitty), The Head Master (N. Whatley), The Prince of Wales, the President (Earl Haig).

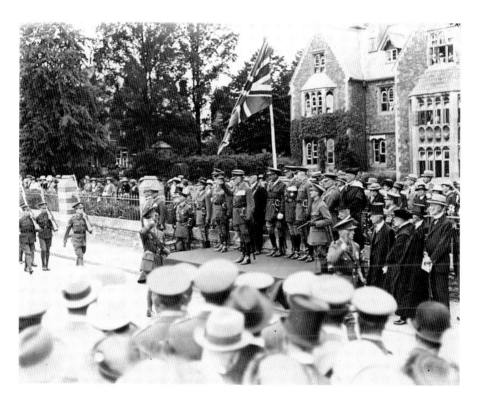

Plate 15 Memorials: *above* Haig taking the salute at the dedication of the Memorial Arch 1922; *below left* Haig with the Head Master, J.E. King (see Documents **428–44**); *below right* Lady Alexandra Haig at the unveiling of her father's statute in 1932 (see Documents **445–52**); the statute stands at the point from which Haig took the salute in 1922.

Plate 16   Big School interior, before partition, with the pipes of the Father Willis organ left and right of the far window (see Document **301**).

7. Mixing coloured lights. P.S. Steen [*10597*], A.J. Middleton.[565] *a+*

8. A lesson in optics. The prism and the telescope. D.F. Kerr [*10711*], D. Malcolm [*10531*].

9. Another lesson in optics. Pinholes and a lens. D.T.Piper,[566] E.C. de Chazal [*10703*].

10. The Rainbow Cup. The colours are produced by interference between the light reflected from the upper, and that reflected from the lower, surface of a soap film. The colours change as the film becomes thinner. It is thinnest at the centre. T.B.N. Caws [*10403*], C.G. Silcocks [*10051*].

11. Comparison of the light from a Neon sign with that from an ordinary electric lamp. B.V. Jacob [*10580*], V.M. Halsted [*10367*].

12. Which colour is it really? G. Hellings [*10018*], R.C. Blackney [*10489*]. *The red lamp that looks green. a+*

13. The batsman's nightmare. A real image formed by a concave mirror. A.J. Bath [*10399*], J.L. Savignon [*10308*].

Room M. (The Whitehead Room).

1. Testing fuse wires. Melting knitting needles. W.M. Barber [*10488*], P.A. Wilson [*10486*].

2. Just in a few moments, please. W.D.L. Filson-Young [*10705*], R.H.H. Kingdon [*9907*].

3. Boyle's Law. Inflating and deflating a balloon. N.L. Griffiths [*10573*]. Cartesian divers. P. A. Holloway [*10844*].

4. Circular motion as a result of two vibrations with a suitable difference of phase. Can you do this simple trick? C.E.H. Martin [*10856*], D.J.O. Brandt [*10824*].

5. A model of a hot-water supply system for a small house. J.A.D. Wedd [*10733*], R.B. Lorraine [*10637*].

6. The behaviour of an 'Osglim' lamp on an A.C. circuit. R.H. Graham [*10141*], J. Macfarlane [*10585*].

7. A disc receiving set for television. M.W. Peters [*9529*], P.H. Peirano [*10274*].

8. Waves in a string. They are produced by the electric light current. L.J. Page [*10050*], R.G. Pilkington [*10719*]. *Not very convincing.*

9. Demonstration of the fact that the air exerts a pressure of 14lb. wt. per sq. inch. I.G.P. Fraser [*10522*], D.J. Mathias [*10498*], H.V.H. Gorton [*10414*].

10. A baby eletromagnet for weightlifting. Its weight is less than 2lb., and it will lift half a hundredweight with a current of one tenth of an ampere. A.J.P. Deacon [*10761*], J.W. Marshall [*10787*].

11. Pins and a magnet. W.F. Gibb.[567] G.P. Knowles [*10851*].

FIRST FLOOR.

Room N. (The Shenstone Room).

At 8.45 p.m. and 9.30 p.m., a lecture on Liquid Oxygen (with experiments) will be given by L.J. Aspland [*10208*] (8.45) and [*word repeated*] C.E.B. White [*10455*] (9.30). *N.B. The doors will be shut during the lectures, so that visitors are requested to be in their seats by the times stated above. a+*

---

[565] Anthony John Middleton [*10499*: BH 1931–6]; great-uncle of HRH The Duchess of Cambridge.

[566] Sir David Towry Piper [*10721*: NT 1932–7]; art historian, Director successively of the National Portrait Gallery, the Fitzwilliam Museum, Cambridge, and the Ashmolean Museum, Oxford.

[567] Walter Frame Gibb [*10785*: DH 1933–6]; DSO, DFC; Chief Test Pilot, BAC 1955–6.

Room W. (The Wilson Room).

At 8.45 p.m. and 9.30 p.m. a lecture on chemical warfare (with experiments) will be given by G.E. Coates,[568] assisted by D.B. Gardiner [*10708*]. [*Note as above.*] *α+* Demonstration of a micro-projector used in practical biological work. The demonstration will take place between and after the lectures on chemical warfare. J.L. Phillips [*10435*], E.L. Houghton [*10304*].

Room S. (The Sumner Room).

1. Experiments with Carbon dioxide. J.C. Kendrew [*10423*]. *No good.*[569]
A chemical cocktail bar. J.R. Wilkins [*10380*], R.G. McFall [*10653*].

2. Attempted preparation of Heavy Water. A specimen of Heavy Water will be exhibited, kindly lent by Balliol College Laboratory, Oxford. G.E. Coates, R.M. Lodge.[570] *(α+)*

3. Plastics. R.M. Lodge, C.P. Hanna [*10416*]. *α*

4. Carbon and some of its products. H.G. Stack,[571] D.N. Whatley.[572] *α*

5. Perfumes and cosmetics. C.A.U. Craven [*9837*], A.C. Turner [*10599*]. *More emphasis on the cosmetic side. α*

6. Weighing signatures, A. Hewitt [*10843*], D.B. Gardiner. *β-*

7. What to do in times of drought. H.G. Stack, R.M. Lodge. *(α)*

Room Z. (The Leonard Room).

1. A Common Scents Competition, for which a prize is offered, will be conducted by R.G. Hamilton [*9432*] and S.S. Hart [*10341*]. Entry forms may be obtained at the bench, and should be completed and handed to Hamilton or Hart before 9.30 p.m. The result will be announced at 9.45 p.m. in Room Z. *Perhaps too difficult. α++*

2. Soap making. J.F. Rigden [*10116*], A.B. Logan [*10584*].

3. A collection of the elements. J.P.T. Pearman [*10673*], B.A.C. Yandell [*9726*]. *α-*

4. Some basic substances of chemical industry. A.J. Bailey [*10133*], J.S. Perry [*10674*].

5. Various methods of distillation. F.G. Dickie [*10833*], C. Griffiths [*10839*].

6. Drugs and poisons, including the preparation of Aspirin. J.R.E. Hamilton-Baillie [*9876*], A.J.R. Hudson [*10156*]. *α*

7. The effect of disinfectants on bacteria, and the sterilising of swimming baths. L.F. Rigden [*10502*], P.S. Jones [*10233*].

8. Some very sensitive tests. D.M. Sladen [*10444*], M.W. Stead [*10503*]. *Not very good.*

9. Chemical gardens. Liquid diffusion and osmosis. M. Rutherford [*10442*], D.J. Dunn [*10056*].

10. An alarm to prevent the milk boiling over. A.T. Holmes [*10845*], R.G. Baggott [10818]. *Should have several lots of milk because it cools so slowly.*

11. Electric wiring. H.A. Lucas [*10672*], J.M. Davis-Brooks [*10783*].

12. Electroplating. R.B. Joly [*9996 or 10771*], N.L. Snell [*10327*]. *α*

13. Active carbon. S.H.V. Durell [*10408*], G.B. Mitchell [*10789*].

---

[568] Geoffrey Edward Coates [*10299*: HHP, UH, OH 1929–34]; Professor of Chemistry at Durham then Wyoming.

[569] Was to do better (Nobel Prize for Chemistry 1962).

[570] Reginald Montague Lodge [*10426*: UH, OH 1930–5]; Tutor and Lecturer in Chemistry at Exeter College, Oxford; during the war engaged in Chemical Defence research.

[571] Hugh Graham Stack [*9357*: ST 1924–34]; Senior Orthopaedic Registrar, Middlesex Hospital.

[572] David Norman Whatley [*9694*: NT 1925–37], the Head Master's eldest son and himself a schoolmaster.

Room Y. (The Wills Room).

1. The analytical chemist at work. J.S. Hellier [*10574*], D.O.C. Hall [*10526*].

2. More analysis. A.M. Champion [*10297*], J.M. Corrie [*10760*].

3. Gas fires, their use and abuse. G.C. Playne [*10593*], P.M. Black [*10518*].

4. The corrosion of metals and its prevention. M.C. Davis [*10702*], D.P. Cowan [*10700*].

5. Chemistry in the home. Cleaning materials and the removal of grease and stains. E.F. Henderson [*10575*], F.A. Cousins [*10563*].

6. Reviving 'Old Masters'. D.W. Abbott [*recte* Abbot: *10693*], D.S. Goldfoot [*10302*].

7. Artificial silk. P.D. Simon [*10726*], J. Josephs [*10710*]. *α*

8. Hardness in water: its cause and consequences. Methods of softening hard water. R.C. Lorraine [*10496*], I.G. Curtis [*9725*].

9. A few fireworks. M.J. Riddell [*10620*], T.A. Braithwaite [*9590*].

10. Chemical magic. A.P. Cornwell [*9989*], J.M. Cook [*10828*].

11. The diffusion of gases. D.V. Buchanan [*10520*], G.T. Gray [*10525*].

12. Silvering mirrors. P.H. Woodward [*10735*], L. Molyneux-Berry [*10305*]. *α*

13. Glass blowers at work. A.I. Merrit [*recte* Merritt: *9593*], R.D. Vacha [*10601*].

Dispensary (between Room Y and Room Z).

Medieval alchemists in their laboratory. K.H. Salomon [*10307*], E.R.T. Shaerf [*10537*]. *α++*

Room R. (Biological Laboratory).

1. Cultures of bacteria. R.B. Walker [*9835*], M.H. Anderson [*10398*].

2. The fermentation of yeast. P.W.C. Maxwell [*10429*], J.B. Squire [*10448*].

3. Exhibit of elvers. A. Skene [*10596*].

4. Respiration of seeds. J.R. de Chazal [*10338*].

5. Dissection of the lizard. J.R. de Chazal.

6. Some interesting members of a freshwater fauna. R.G. Boyd [*10401*].

7. Motile spores of horsetails. D.N. White [*9399*].

8. Measurement of blood pressure. D.N. White.

9. Photosynthesis by the green plant, and starch prints. R.J. Sansom [*10536*], F.G. Wellstood [*10505*].

10. Demonstration of the presence of conducting channels in the plant stem. R.W. Orton [*10433*], J.R. Sidgwick [*10376*].

11. Some physiological experiments on the frog. J.A.S. Green [*10415*], N.R. Fallon [*10240*].

12. Experiments on plant transpiration. J.A.S. Green, N.R. Fallon. *Not much interest taken in 12.*

SECOND FLOOR.

The Wollaston Room (Biological Laboratory).

1. An exhibit illustrating the effect of different kinds of food on the shape and size of teeth. J.A. Wyatt [*recte* J.H.: *10294*].

2. How a cell divides. E.F.W. Truscott [*10598*].

3. Dissection of the earthworm. T.C. Carter.[573]

Demonstration of parasites within the earthworm, D.V. Peters [*recte* D.U.: *10792*].

4. Dissection of the frog. J.H.L. Rogers [*10148*].

---

[573] Thomas Christopher Carter [*10559*: UH, OH 1931–6]; FRS (Edin), prominent in field of animal genetics, and latterly Director, ARC Poultry Research Centre.

5. Demonstration of living larvæ and pupæ of British mosquitoes. Microscopic preparations and microstereographs of different species of British mosquitoes. N. Ambache [*10556*].

6. Palæontological evidence for organic evolution. A.D. Lees.[574]

7. Dissection of the crayfish. A.D. Lees.

Collection of photographs and reports arranged by the Natural History Section.

Must have more indicators – people didn't seem to realise that there was a 2nd floor.

THE STONE MEMORIAL SCIENCE LIBRARY.
Assistant Librarian – J.H. Glover [*10255*].

At 8.30 p.m., 9.0 p.m. and 9.45 p.m., Glover will give a short talk on the chief features of interest in the library.

1. Collection of books to illustrate the development of Chemistry from the earliest times.

2. Some classics of Physics.

3. Autograph letters and manuscripts of celebrated men of science.[575]

4. Exhibition of the original quartz glass, invented by William Shenstone, F.R.S., formerly Head of the Chemical Department, Clifton College [*M101*].

Flying Machines

[188]   30 April 1918. The Head Master to Col. C.D. Breene, Director of Training, Air Ministry
[*RS1/70. Typescript copy*]

30th April 1918.

Sir,

G.9/6415/1918.

In answer to your letters of March 18 and April 27, I write to say that we shall be glad to accept the offer of an aero-engine, for the purpose of instructing pupils upon the conditions laid down.

I am Sir, your obedient servant,

[*blank for signature*], Headmaster.

P.S. Delay in answer is due to the intervention of the holidays, which prevented consultation of masters, for which I wish to express my regret.

[189]   30 May 1918. The Head Master to C.L. Tireman
[*RS1/70. Typescript copy*]

30th May, 1918.

Dear Mr Tireman,

Aeroplane Engine.

This engine has now arrived and been put upon a stand by the Workshop. Mr Fawdry[576] will be responsible for the care of it, whilst it is here. You kindly offered at

---

[574] Anthony David Lees [*10424*: ST 1930–5]; FRS, Professor of Insect Physiology, Imperial College, London.

[575] See above **[185]**.

[576] Reginald Charles Fawdry [*M181*: 1903–33], Head of the Military and Engineering Side 1911–33.

a masters' meeting to help in showing its working to boys. I shall be glad, therefore, if you will arrange with Mr Fawdry as to suitable times and conditions of showing the engine and its parts. Anything that involves extra expense will have to be referred to the Secretary at the Office.

Yours very truly,

[*blank for signature*], Headmaster.

[190]   1918. Memorandum by R.C. Fawdry
[*RS1/70. Holograph*]

Aeroplane Engine

A suitable place is a recess under the Chapel – now occupied by some furniture discarded from the Chapel. It has a stone floor and no woodwork. An improvement in the lighting would be necessary.

R.C.F.

Mr Thomas[577] would require your sanction for the removal of the furniture.

☐ *The School already had an entire aeroplane.*

[191]   9 January 1935. Memorandum by the former College Secretary
[*RS1/71. Holograph*]

The Bat Aeroplane.

Presented by D.G. Gilmour (O.C.)[578] in 1912 – on the day of his death (Feb.17th).

It [was *corrected to*] is believed to be the aeroplane in which he flew the Channel and was modelled on Bleriot's monoplane.

His fiancée <Madame Marcia de Belle Roche> wrote after his death to the H.M. saying that the machine was at Brooklands and, if we would still care to have it, she would send it at her own expense.

This was accepted and the machine was put in the Gym.

9:1:35.   per W.J.L[*ewis*].

☐ *The plane was suspended from the rafters until it was decided that the City Museum would be a better place for it.*

[192]   21 February 1935. The Director of the Bristol Museum and Art Gallery to the College Secretary
[*RS1/71. Typescript*]

City and County of Bristol
The Museum and Art Gallery
Queen's Road, Bristol 8
21 February 1935

---

[577] Major A.D. Thomas, Superintendent of the Workshops 1883–1926.
[578] Douglas Graham Gilmour [*5486*: SH 1899–1902] was a pioneer aviator who performed many famous stunts, including flying low over the 1911 University Boat Race. He was killed while testing a new monoplane on a flight from Brooklands to Richmond.

Dear Sir,

I reported to my Committee the offer conveyed by Mr Victor Eberle to present to this Museum the aeroplane used by the late Mr Gilmour.

I am instructed to say that they will be very glad to accept this for the Transport section. The Bristol Aeroplane Company has kindly agreed to remove the aeroplane from the Gymnasium, to repair it and to deliver it here, and I have asked them to be good enough to consult you as to a suitable time for the removal.

Yours truly,
H.W. Maxwell.

☐ *On 18 July 1935 the Museum formally acknowledged the gift of the 'Bat'. The machine was destroyed by an air raid in November 1941; its engine was however salvaged and was formerly displayed in the Club Room of the Society of Bristol Savages at Red Lodge in Park Row, itself a branch of the City Museum.*[579]

---

[579] Further letters in file RS1/71.

SECTION X: CADET CORPS

[193]   11 December 1875. The Clerk to the Lieutenancy to the College Secretary: foundation of the Corps
[*RS1/158. Holograph*]

Lieutenancy Office,
Gloucester.
11 December 1875

Dear Sir,
    By a letter received by the Earl of Ducie (Lord Lieutenant) from the Secretary of State for War [authorising *deleted*] the formation of a Cadet Corps at Clifton College is [to consist *deleted*] authorised to consist of one Company and one Sub-Division with a maximum strength of 159 and a minimum strength of 90, to be attached to the 2nd Gloucestershire Engineer Volunteer Corps and to form part of the 1st Administrative Battalion of Gloucestershire Engineer Volunteers.
    The Corps will be entitled to one Commanding Officer who must be an adult and will bear the Honorary rank of Captain and whose name should be submitted for Her Majesty's approval through the General Officer Commanding the District.
    Captain Irwin[580] of Bedminster the Adjutant of the Battalion will no doubt communicate with you upon the further steps needed.
                    Yours truly,
                    Geo. Riddiford,
                    Clerk to the Lieutenancy.

[194]   23 / 26 February 1877. Resolutions by the Sixth
[*Registers 1–2 (1866–84), ff. 124–5. MS*]

23 Feby 1877 [*after other business*].
    With reference to the shooting Eleven it was resolved:
    That colours be given up at the end of each year.
    That at the beginning of each Summer term Officers and N.C. Officers elect three members of the Eleven.
    That with this exception all colours be given by the Colours.

---

[580] Capt Francis George Irwin.

That the Colour senior in rank be at all times Captain of the Eleven.

That all shooting details, including the right of sending and [receiving *corrected to*] accepting challenges, be left to the Captain of the Eleven, subject to the approval of the School Captain of the Corps.

C. Cannan.[581]

Feb. 26.

Mr Plant[582] having offered a prize for a Rifle Corps race at the Athletics, it was resolved that Mr Plant be thanked for the offer, and the question of the introduction of such a race be referred to the Stewards.

C. Cannan

[195]   8 October 1886. The Commanding Officer to the Head Master
[*RB2/36. Holograph*]

Subject. Cadet Corps Finance

From: Colonel E.C. Plant, Hon. Capt. Clift: Coll Engineer Corps.
To: The Head Master, Clifton College.

Clifton College,
Oct. 8. 1886.

Sir,

Owing to the new arrangement for supply of equipment to Cadets, particulars of which are contained in your circular letter to parents, dated July 15/86 (copy attached), it will be necessary for the funds of the Corps to incur an outlay of something like £100 in Decr. next for the purchase of belts, helmets, caps, pouches, &c. which are at present the property of members of the Corps. The great increase in the strength of the Corps this term will involve an additional outlay of about 50£ for thirty new sets of equipment: (capes, water bottles, haversacks, helmets, caps, belts and pouches). The fittings of the new Armoury will involve a further considerable outlay, which added to the deficit of £71. 7. at Decr. last will have to be met to the extent of about £300 by Decr. 1886.

I beg to ask if you could bring the subject under the notice of the Council with a view to their being asked to kindly advance <this sum £300> to the Cadet Corps of the School. With the increased rate of subscription which comes into force this term, there is a good prospect of the amount being repaid in about six yearly instalments of 50£ each.

Mr Thomas the head of the Workshop, and myself estimate the cost of fitting up the new Armoury and Clothing Store at about £50. As the Corps bore the whole expense of fitting up the old Armoury, now demolished, I venture to ask if the Council could <now> assist the Cadet Corps by a special grant towards meeting this charge.

I have the honour to be, Sir,
Your obedient servant,
Edmd. C. Plant, Col.,
Hon. Capt. Clift. Coll. Engineer Corps.

---

[581] Head of the School [*897*].
[582] Edmund Carter Plant [*M32*: 1867–1902]; taught Mechanical and Engineering Drawing; CO of the Corps until 1893 and CB in the Diamond Jubilee honours. After his death it was reported that he had maintained a second life (and wife) as Edmund Hall, a Dorset accountant and apiarist: *The Star* [Canterbury NZ], 7560 (18 Nov. 1902), p. 2. (With thanks to Margaret Davis for drawing attention to this story, and to the NZ Government for providing an excellent online newspaper archive.)

[196]   13 October 1886. The Head Master to the Council
[*RS1/158. Holograph*]

Memorandum from the Headmaster.
Engineers Corps.
I beg to send herewith a memorandum and request from Col. Plant [*above*].
He asks in the first place for a loan of £300 to be paid off in annual instalments.
The Council have similarly made loans to the Chapel Fund which are now paid off,
and to the Fives Courts. I hope they will see their way to granting this.
In the second place he asks for a grant of £50 towards the fitting of the Armoury.
We have now a large Cadet Company, of 150 boys, and it forms an important element
in the life and work of the School. It is in excellent working order. Col. Plant devotes
much energy and enthusiasm to his work, and I think this recognition of the value of
the Engineers Corps and of his services would be rightly given and much appreciated.
13 Oct/86.   J.M.W.

☐ *On 15 October the Council agreed to these payments.*[583]

**[197]   31 July 1901. Choosing the form of the South African War
Memorial**[584]
[*RS3/243. Printed*]

14, Old Square,
Lincoln's Inn, London, W.C.
July 31st, 1901.
Old Cliftonian Memorial
Dear Sir,
    The Committee appointed at the meeting of Old Cliftonians on May 10th have
considered the various suggestions, made at the meeting and subsequently, as to
the form which the Memorial should take, and are of opinion that the following
proposals may be feasible, viz.:
    1. A separate architectural monument on the Terrace overlooking the Close.
    2. A gatehouse or gateway at the entrance in College Road.
    3. A monumental loggia or antechapel along the west front of the Chapel and open
towards the Quadrangle.
    Before obtaining designs the Committee wish to ascertain the opinion of Old
Cliftonians as between these three proposals, and also to know approximately
what funds are likely to be available, as the precise form of the Memorial must be
influenced by this consideration. They will therefore be obliged if you will kindly let
me know on the enclosed slip of paper what is your opinion and what amount you
are willing to contribute. If that amount would vary according as one or other of the
proposals is adopted, please indicate this.
    After sufficient time has elapsed for replies to be received from abroad, the
Committee will submit plans for a further meeting of Old Cliftonians.
    Those who have already subscribed, or promised definite amounts, will understand
that the inquiry on that point does not apply to them.

---

[583] Council Minute Book 3, p. 42.
[584] The creation of the Memorial is described in *Register* (1925), pp. cxvii–cxxii.

It will be convenient if those who intend to subscribe will now send in their contributions.

> Yours truly,
> Rowland Whitehead,
> *Hon. Sec. O.C. Memorial Committee.*

[198]   22 June 1904. Unveiling the Memorial: invitation from the College Secretary
[RS3/293. Holograph]

> The College, Clifton,
> Secretary's Office.
> 22nd June 1904

Dear Sir,

In case you may not already have received any intimation with regard to the erection at the College of a Memorial to the Old Cliftonians who fell in the recent war in South Africa I am requested to inform you, in case you should wish to attend, that it will be unveiled by General Lord Methuen G.C.B. on Saturday next the 25th inst. at 3.30 p.m.[585]

> I am, dear Sir,
> Yours faithfully,
> W.D.L. Macpherson, Secretary.

[199]   12 May 1906. Inspection by Field Marshal Lord Roberts:[586] instructions from the Head Master
[CCF. Printed]

> Clifton College.
> Visit of Lord Roberts.
> 12th May, 1906.

Arrival and inspection   11.30   Lord Roberts arrives at Guthrie Road entrance, and inspects the Engineer Corps in the Close.

The School will stand along the Parapet, visitors along the iron railings west of the Memorial.

Address in Big School about 12. At the conclusion of the inspection the School will be seated (not by Forms) in Big School. The Junior and Preparatory Schools will enter by the old Sixth Room staircase. The Corps having piled arms in the Quad will

---

[585] Paul Sanford Methuen, 3rd Baron Methuen (d. 1932), commander of the 1st Division during the war and despite a chequered career, highly regarded. Details of the ceremony, with the text of the preceding Commem Sermon by Percival are in *Cliftonian* XVIII (1903–5), pp. 236–40, 260–7 (also in a separate pamphlet included in bound sets of the magazine).

[586] Frederick Sleigh Roberts, 1st Earl Roberts of Kandahar, Pretoria and Waterford (d. 1914), one of the greatest military figures of the age, having won the VC during the Indian Mutiny and commanded British forces at the start of the Second Boer War. When sending his autograph to Dudley Kingdon-Allen, he explained: 'I was a little boy at Clifton for many years before the College which you attend was built' (P5126 Album, 1 Sept. 1898). His father had lived in Royal York Crescent. Roberts himself was brought up by relations in Clifton, and between the ages of 8 and 10 he attended the private school of a Monsieur Desprez; in 1904 he became an honorary member of the Society of Merchant Venturers: E.F. Sellar, *The Story of Lord Roberts* (1906), pp. 1–2; Jones, *Clifton*, p. 147; McGrath, *Merch. Venturers*, p. 558.

occupy the front rows. Visitors will be seated after and behind the Corps and the rest of the School.

Departure about 12.40. At the conclusion of the address the remainder of the audience will keep their places until the Corps has left Big School. The Corps will be followed by the School and then by the visitors. The Corps will line the road between School House and the Close on the School House side. Lord Roberts will leave by the College Road entrance.

Visitors will be admitted without ticket to the Close for the inspection.

Admission to Big School will be by ticket only, except for Old Cliftonians.

A limited number of tickets will be issued to relatives of members of the Towns in the Sixths and Fifths.

A.A.D.

☐ *The Engineers' main activity was building bridges, and if necessary digging holes over which bridges could then be built; their enthusiasm sometimes exceeded their authority.*

[200]   19 December 1910. The Commanding Officer to the Chairman of the Ground Committee, W.O. Moberly[587]
[*RS1/158. Holograph*]

Clifton College Engineer Corps.
O.T.C.
Engineering   19/12/10

Dear Moberly,

The change from New Field to Close and from two days a week to one involves the construction of a new bridging pit.

I enclose a sketch and detail of the work proposed to be done during next term.

If the Ground Committee will sanction it, I should greatly like to have their authorization at least a fortnight before the beginning of term so that I can get the turf professionally cut and sand.

Yours very truly,
H. Clissold, Capt. Cmdg. C.C.E.C.[588]

[201]   6 March 1911. W.O. Moberly to the Secretary and Bursar
[*RS1/158. Holograph*]

1, Worcester Crescent,
Clifton.
6 March 1911

Bridging pit

Dear Macpherson,

I enclose a letter from Capt. Clissold with reference to the above, received on Dec. 19 last [*above*]. The work is an extension of the bridging pit previously constructed and used for a good many years.

---

[587] William Octavius Moberly [*M65*: 1874–1913].
[588] Clissold [*M148*] had commanded the Corps since 1905.

The Ground Committee inspected the proposed work, and decided that the work would not in their opinion interfere with the existing grounds for cricket and football. I wrote to Capt. Clissold during the holidays in this sense.

I feel sure that the Ground Committee will wish me to express their regret, if an irregularity has been committed through ignorance. No such question has come up since I have been on the Ground Committee: and I was unaware that the leave of the Council was required before such work was undertaken.

Yours sincerely,
W.O. Moberly.

☐ *A few days before the outbreak of the First World War a Clifton Cadet sent this despatch home from camp.*

[202]   29 July 1914. Sydney Barratt[589] to his parents
[P6578 file. Holograph]

Clifton College O.T.C.
Mychett [recte Mytchett] Camp, Frimley.
Wed. 29/7/14.

Dear _____ <parents ? mother & father ? père et mère ? pater et mater>,

I am sorry that I have not had an opportunity to write before, but we have been exceedingly busy preparing the camp and looking round.

We arrived at [the *deleted*] North Camp station at 6 pm. – travelling by way of Chipping Sodbury, Badminton and Reading. On the way I saw Huntley & Palmer's biscuit manufactury[590] and various other well-known companies' works. The camp itself lies about ¾ mile from either of the two 'North Camp' stations, both of which we have used already. All the chief roads here are tarred! At the camp itself, in a large field, there are some 30 rows of 17 tents apiece, all of which are now filled. The camp is bound on one side by a canal, which is used by the public for canoeing, but not by us. The other three sides are bounded by plantations of fir trees, and along one of the long sides are the refreshment rooms, the post office, the clock, the barbers and the general stores, also the 'recreation' tent where the sing songs etc. take place. The wash up place and the cookery establishment, for our part of the camp, are at the end of the camp away from the entrance. The tents are about 10 ft high and 3 yds diameter at the bottom. The floor-boards are two in. thick. Each boy has a water proof sheet, a palliasse, a pillow (both filled with straw) and two blankets. The mattress or palliasse is 5 ft long, but only about 9 in. wide at the bottom, and the whole rather resembles the roof of a house in its 'draining' propensities. We have to pack the kit-bag on one side and the great-coat on the other, to stay on at all. No one slept much the first night. Sutton[591] practised his bugle calls in his sleep, and Crawford[592] attempted a successful imitation. We were talking about the war crisis[593] at 3.30 and

---

[589] Sir Sydney Barratt [*6578*: NT 1906–16]; member of the Council from 1956 until his death in 1975 (Chairman 1958–67, President 1967–72); academic chemist and industrial magnate, knighted 1961. The document was kindly given to the archives by Mr B. Worthington.

[590] A vast complex outside Reading.

[591] Douglas Empson Sutton [*7217*: NT 1910–15]; served in the war as 2nd Lt, Royal Welch Fusiliers.

[592] The future Lt-Gen Sir Kenneth Noël Crawford [*7008*: WiH, NT 1909–14] or his younger brother Victor Raymond Wallen [*7292*: NT 1911–15], later Brigadier; the elder left the School at the end of the Summer term, but might still have gone to camp.

[593] On the previous day Austria-Hungary had declared war on Serbia, starting the chain reaction which brought Britain into the war on 4 August.

got up willingly at 5.30. – Reveille goes at 6 am. Prayers parade 6.30. Breakfast 7.30. Final parade 9.15. Dinner when we get back. Afternoon parade 3 pm for 1 or 2 hrs. Tea 5.30. Lights out 10. We have Irish neighbours, from Belfast, and at 10.30 they sang all through the death of Cock Robin. Everybody slept well on Tuesday night, however, after all the masters had been serenaded.

On Tuesday morning we proceeded to Lord's. London is an hour's ride from Aldershot. From the train we saw the Veriton Mantle works[594] [and *deleted*] the Doulton Pottery works[595] and the Houses of Parliament in the distance. London, after all, is much like Bristol, except for the Tubes, in which we travelled from Waterloo to the Great Central.[596] The fresh air in these railways is marvellous, for they are so far below the ground that lifts are used to reach them.

Lord's is in the middle of residential London, and is surrounded by shops and houses. We won – as you know, very easily[597] – and thereby lost a free tea from Mrs Whitehead,[598] as it was over by 3 o'clock instead of 5. We went back the same way and got back in time for tea.

This morning we had some tactical exercises a short distance from the camp. The chief amusement was watching Mr Burbey[599] on his 'ors[600] – and listening to the bag pipe band of Campbell College, Belfast, who played exceedingly well.

It was not 'sweaty' at all and was only followed by ½ hour drill at 3 o'clock. We are 'company-in-waiting' today, and have to stay in uniform all day.

Tea Monday & Tuesday   Poloney, ham, tea, bread, & butter
Breakfast Tues & Wednesday   Bacon (salt), bread, butter, tea, jam (strawberry)
Dinner [*Tuesday* deleted] *Wednesday*   meat (sort ?), potatoes, peas, spotted dog,[601] jam

General Notes
The Corps gave each man 6^d 'for drinks' – apparently a present.
This went in 2^d lemonades at Lord's, ½^d elsewhere.
There is a place outside London called Goodwood, which proudly calls itself the 'London Necropolis'.[602] It is run by a 'Necropolis Company'.
Eton boys wear a grey instead of a brown uniform, as does another school.
There is a contingent from Liverpool.
Mr Burbey tripped over a tent rope and swore like a trooper.

---

[594] Clock factory.
[595] The original factory of the Royal Doulton Company at Vauxhall Walk in Lambeth.
[596] Marylebone, the terminus of the Great Central Railway.
[597] Clifton beat Tonbridge by 9 wickets. The next time the match was played at Lord's (1919) Tonbridge won by the same margin: *Cliftonian* XXIII (1913–15), pp. 381–3; XXVII (1919–21), pp. 69–71.
[598] The then Mrs George Whitehead, wife of George Hugh [*1881*: SH 1876–80], who succeeded to a Baronetcy 1917; their sons James Hugh Edendale [*6291*: SH 1904–9] and George William Edendale [*7052*: SH 1909–14] were two of Clifton's most celebrated cricketers; see below **[423–4]**.
[599] Major John Leonard Burbey [*2608*: NT 1880–7; *M145*: 1893–1930], twice Commandant of the Corps; served in the war as 2nd in command, 11th Bn The Loyal Regt and with the 51st King's Royal Rifle Corps.
[600] Presumably this represents the Major's way of describing his mount.
[601] An alternative name for 'spotted dick'.
[602] *recte* Brookwood Cemetery, established in 1849, which was indeed so known and was run by the London Necropolis Company. There was a dedicated rail link from a station in Westminster Bridge Road.

Edelston[603] & one other boy have already stopped away from a parade.
Two boys fainted in Clifton Corps at 6.30 Tuesday morning (hunger?).
I have not seen a hospital yet (hurrah!)
The refreshment rooms are very good. Hot coffee 2^d per cup is excellent at night.
Each tent has a box containing plates, knifes and forks, stores, ropes, salt, pepper, mustard, boracic acid, and a zinc cover to keep away flies.
Every morning each boy has to make a pile of his belongings outside the tent. Two boys are told off [604]each day to procure food, wash up, and tidy up generally – called the 'orderlies'.
On the first night Raymer[605] went into Presses'[606] tent at 4 a.m. to tell him to stop talking – they were having an excited discussion on Pythagoras' theorem.
Kippers were served for tea on Wednesday, and two bands then gave an exhibition concert. I have seen Clifford Lewis and Johnnie Ludlow, or whatever his name is.[607]

> Written under difficulties, by,
>
> S. Barratt.

P.S. Five including myself have not b ____!!! out of our seven, so far as I can tell. Arrangements excellent.

> [*Sketch map*]

Cannot write again for some days, except post-card, – in all probability.
Every afternoon we all are going to Aldershot to see the Regulars drill.

> With love,
> And hoping all – including Dick – are well
> TAKING PILL TONIGHT.

☐ *On 1 August the War Office gave orders that all OTC Summer camps were to be prematurely disbanded.[608]*

[203]   10 October 1914. Major Clissold to the Secretary
[*RS1/158. Holograph*]

> South Midland R.E.

> Head Quarters,
> Park Row,
> Bristol.
> 20.10.14

Dear Mr Lewis,
I am in receipt of your letter with regard to the return which the School is now making to this Corps for the forty years of assistance which the Corps has given to the School.

---

[603] Roger Heathcott Edelston [*7577*: SH 1913–16]; served in the war as Lt, Royal Flying Corps, and was taken prisoner. See further below **[256–73]**.
[604] In the sense of 'deputed', not 'reprimanded'.
[605] Commander of the Corps: see above **[177]**.
[606] Edward Press [*7192*: NT 1910–15], Head of the School 1914–15; served as Lt in the South Midland Royal Engineers, winning the MC and the Italian *Croce al Merito di Guerra*.
[607] A John Ludlow [*2658*] was in ST for a term in 1880, and Clifford Michael Lewis [*5589*] was in BH 1899–1903.
[608] Parker, *Old Lie*, p. 31 (noting that the Mytchett camp had been especially rife with 'gloomy rumours').

I understand from Capt. Burbey[609] that he had been authorized to deal with this question and that it was not necessary for me to obtain permissions from anyone else. I may say that I have not as yet asked for or made any use of the class rooms – nor of Big School – for my men, the only occasion on which I have used the latter being to do some signalling with a few Old Cliftonians. I should not of course hesitate to ask for its use if I considered it essential to the training of my units.

Yours very truly,

H. Clissold, Major (T.F.).

[204]   13 January 1915. The Commanding Officer[610] to the Secretary
[*RS1/158. Holograph*]

Officers Training Corps,
Clifton College,
Bristol.
13.1.15

Dear Mr Lewis,

The Officer commanding the Black Watch Battalion of the 77th Brigade[611] has asked me to send him some bridging material for the instruction of his officers. I have told him that we shall be using it this term, but that if he can arrange to carry out his training over our bridging pit at times convenient to us, I shall be glad to give him the use of the material and any other assistance in my power.

I therefore write to ask if you will obtain permission for this Battalion to use the ground *at times convenient for us* but more than 25 could not use it at a time, and they could come in by the Sanatorium entrance and thus not interfere with the Close.

I am, very sincerely yours,

D. Rintoul.

[205]   June 1917. Memorandum by the Head Master
[*RS1/158. Holograph*]

June 1917.

During the period of the war the members of the Officers Training Corps have increased and the result has been a substantial balance for the years 1915, 1916, 1917 amounting to a total of about £2000.

After consultation with the O.T.C. Committee I therefore recommend that the subscription per boy be reduced from £1. 1. 0 per term to 15/- per term.

As the Sanatorium fee of £1. 1. 0 is not sufficient to meet the expenses of the Sanatorium I recommend that the fee be raised to £1. 5. 0 per term for each boy.

J.E. King

---

[609] J.L. Burbey [*M145*]; see above [**202**].

[610] David Rintoul [*M121*] commanded from 1894–1904 and again (after Clissold had gone to the war) 1915–18.

[611] This was the newly-formed 10th Bn The Black Watch, in training on Salisbury Plain though at first lacking most equipment; they embarked for France in September, though were then transferred to Salonika.

[206]   June 1929. The Head Master proposes appointment of Adjutant
[*HM6/Interview Book 1929–30, ff. 16–17. MS*]

Friday, 7th June.

I interviewed Crawford.[612] I had decided that he is the most suitable person to succeed Matthews[613] as Master of North Town after this term, but I did not want Crawford to give up his command of the Officers' Training Corps yet if it can be avoided. I asked whether he can combine the two if another officer of the Officers' Training Corps acted as Adjutant, and relieved him of some of the work, especially of interviews during the break. Of course, in that case, a portion of the salary paid to the Commanding Officer out of O.T.C. funds would have to be paid to this other officer instead. I asked Crawford to think this out. He wrote a few days later to say that he thought it would be possible. I told him that I would send him a formal letter before long.

---

[612] John Kenneth Bulfin ('Jock') Crawford [*M262*: 1921–61], Commandant of the Corps 1938–33, House Master NT 1929–33.

[613] Harry Norton Matthews [*M196*: NT 1908–29].

SECTION XI: HEALTH

[207]   January 1870. The Head Master to parents
[*Guard Book1860–77. Printed*]

Clifton College.
18th January, 1870.

Dear Sir,

I beg to inform you that the Sanatorium can now be used by day boys as well as boarders, provided that the parents subscribe regularly to the Sanatorium fund 7s. per term for each boy, just as the parents of boarders do.

For this subscription, room and ordinary nursing are provided, but medical attendance, food and washing are not included.

A building is now being erected for the reception of boys who may be suffering from diseases which are not infectious. As soon as this building is finished, day boys whose parents subscribe to the Sanatorium fund will be admitted to lodge them there under the circumstances described as case 3 in our rules relating to infectious diseases.

It will be understood that a parent who wishes his son to be received into the Sanatorium, if necessary, must be a regular subscriber, as the offer to subscribe only when a boy required the Sanatorium, would not be accepted.

Hoping that this arrangement will prove a convenience to many parents and save them from some anxiety,

I am, dear Sir, your obedient servant,
J. Percival, Head Master.

P.S. Should you wish to subscribe to this fund on behalf of your son for the term now commencing, please to inform the Secretary not later than Saturday next by filling up and returning the enclosed form.

□ *A further circular dated 27 December announced that the second building had been completed.*

[208]   24 April 1876. The Head Master to parents
[*Guard Book 1860–77. Printed*]

Clifton College, Clifton, Bristol.
April 24th, 1876.

Dear Sir,

I have to inform you that I have resolved to defer the assembling of the College till *Tuesday, May 9th*, on which day, by 9.30 p.m., all boarders will be expected to be in their Houses. Day boys must be in their places in Chapel by 9 a.m. on Wednesday, the 10th.

I have made this change because our doctors tell me that there are still some remains of scarlatina in some parts of Clifton, and also some cases of measles, and they are of opinion that on the whole it would be better to wait for another week.

As I am informed that some exaggerated rumours have got abroad with regard to the health of the College last term, I take advantage of this opportunity to mention that out of our 375 boarders there were only 16 cases of scarlatina, and that the epidemic did not become in any sense general in the School, as the boys in the five largest boarding houses, 260 in number, were entirely free from it, and also the Preparatory School.

I desire in conclusion to ask your attention to the enclosed rules, as we have on one or two occasions suffered in consequence of the neglect or carelessness of parents in regard to their observance.

I am, dear Sir, yours faithfully,
J. Percival.

P.S. [*at the head of the letter*] The entrance examination for new boys is also deferred till Thursday, May 9th, at 1 p.m.

[209]   February 1885. The Head Master's proposal to appoint a Medical Officer
[*Health file. Duplicated holograph*]

Memorandum from the Headmaster on the appointment of a Medical Officer.

Three years ago I asked the Council to consider the appointment of a Medical Officer, and they did not at that time see the necessity of doing so.[614] I wish to re-open the question and I trust that the interval will not be considered too short. In that interval the question of the health of schools have [*recte* has] made much progress, and much more attention is paid to it by the public.

A great institution like Clifton College needs more than a physician to attend in cases of illness; it needs an Officer of Health to share with the Headmaster the responsibility of all sanitary arrangements; to have charge of the Sanatorium; of the disinfection of Houses after infectious diseases; to arrange for nursing special cases, and for convalescence after infectious illnesses; to keep an eye on all matters, games, diet, clothing, dormitories, baths, school-hours, that affect the health of the School; to make it his object to keep the boys in a maximum amount of health.

It is also very desirable that he should examine every new boy and report on his fitness for games &c., or other exceptional circumstances.

---

[614] Council Minute Book 2, p. 81 (22 June 1882): 'After hearing the views of the Council the Head Master withdrew his proposal for the present.'

It may be said we have hitherto done without such an officer. But to this there is a complete reply. First that Doctor Fox[615] to some extent, and to a still larger extent Doctor Fyffe,[616] has discharged gratuitously and incidentally with very great kindness some of the duties of the Medical Officer, and secondly that the non-discharge of others is not only a perpetual source of danger, but have [recte has] involved us in great blunders and expense. The fatal case of typhoid last year would never have occurred had the Houses been under proper medical inspection.[617] I suppose that outbreak cost the Council £1000, and the masters not short of £500 to put it at the lowest figures. Every term mistakes are made by masters who are unwilling to incur a charge of a fee for a boy whom they suspect of incipient illness. I myself made a terrible and possibly fatal mistake last term. The boy is absent this term, and it is still doubtful whether he will recover.[618] Had there been a Medical Officer seeing boys gratuitously, I should unquestionably have sent this boy to him, but I accepted his repeated assurance that he was perfectly well.

I will not go into details as to the duties or fees and arrangements with Mr Prichard[619] and the homœopathic doctor[620] untill [sic] the principle has been accepted that the boarders should all pay a terminal fee for medical supervision and care in illness. I earnestly request the Council to accept this principle by a resolution, and to appoint a Committee to prepare and submit detailed proposals at the next meeting of the Council.

Feb. 85.

J.M. Wilson

☐ Discussion was deferred at the Council meetings of 19 February and 28 May,[621] and further representations were made.

[210]   8 June 1885. Council's rejection of the Head Master's proposal
[Council Minute Book 2, p. 402. MS]

The Head Master attended.

The Head Master's Memorandum dated May as to the appointment of a Medical Officer was read, with a Memorandum enclosed from Dr Fyffe.

The question was discussed, and it was unanimously resolved that the Council do not see their way at present to taking any steps in the matter.

It was also resolved that the Head Master, according to the provisions of 73 and 74 of the Charter,[622] be requested to require from the House Masters such periodical reports as may seem to him to be necessary as to the sanitary condition of their Houses.

---

[615] Edward Long Fox, Medical Officer (as retrospectively designated) 1862–82; see below [217].

[616] William Johnstone Fyffe, MD, Medical Officer 1882–97.

[617] The dead boy was A.J. Curtis [2856: BH 1882–4†], who had just reached the Modern Upper Fourth. See Brown, Newly Discovered Letters, i, p. 101 (Brown to H.G. Dakyns, 13 May 1884: 'four cases of Typhoid in my house at the end of last term ... One of my poor fellows died'). Brown describes the awkwardness of the funeral and the hideous features of the sanitary engineer who reconstructed the drainage in all the Houses.

[618] No further deaths occurred in the School until 1890: below [212].

[619] Augustin Prichard, MD, Medical Officer 1862–91.

[620] Not Francis Black [1], who had moved to London in 1881: Whitfield, Victorian Doctors, p. 16.

[621] Council Minute Book 2, pp. 356, 397.

[622] Text as [7] above, nos 82–3 of the Articles of Association.

[211]   18 October 1889. Dr Fyffe's sanitary report.
[*Health file. MS*]

Sanitary Report
Third term 1889

The term inspection has been made during the past week.

Mr Moberly's.[623] In good working order and well looked after.

Mr Heymann's.[624] Working well.

Mr Wiseman's. Very satisfactory.

Mr Hartnell's. There as [*recte* is] a dry area at the back door near the ashpit which contains a good deal of refuse, rotten wood &c. I think it should be cleared out.

Mr Tait's.[625] The new drainage in this House works admirably, and can be inspected at any time through the chamber.

Mr Bartholomew's.[626] In perfect order.

Mr Watson's.[627] The terminal closet in the boys' W.C. became clogged in the holidays. Mr Thomas thinks it arises from the faulty way in which the closet communicates with the House sewer. The area between this House and College Gate should be re-asphalted so as to keep the gullies clear.

Mr Brown. The soil pipes have been better ventilated and have been carried up in their full size to the roof. The new W.C. for use at night by the boys works well and there is no mess. All the new drainage of the House is working admirably.

Mr Carter's.[628] The wastes of the lavatory do not work well, and are frequently clogged owing to a faulty construction which could be easily remedied.

School House. The smoke machine has been applied and all found working well. The boys' closets should be white limed; also the scullery and the urinals should be scrubbed in the holidays with spirits of salts.

Mr Laxton's.[629] Working very well.

Mr Luckman's.[630] There is some rotten wood work in the seats of the boys' W.C. which should be removed and [the *deleted*] mended.

Mr Martin's.[631] In very good order.

Sanatorium. I am happy to be able to state that I think the Sanatorium drainage has been brought up to the highest point of excellence. The whole sewerage has been renewed on the system introduced by Mr Rogers Field.[632] Five brick ventilated inspection chambers have been constructed along the line of the sewerage. Any fault can now be detected and remedied at once. A current of air passes from the fresh air inlet at the termination of the system through the chambers and up the soil pipes to the roof of the house. This work is one of the greatest value to the Sanatorium

---

[623] W.O. Moberly [*M65*] at this time had a 'Small' or 'Waiting House' from 1883–92.

[624] The Jewish House, later Polack's.

[625] Later Oakeley's.

[626] Later Dakyns', run from 1881 to 1892 by Francis Medley Bartholomew [*M44*: 1869–93†].

[627] Henry Charles Watson [*M46*: 1870–1900], first master of the House which was to take his name, 1878–93.

[628] A House in the Junior School run by Reuben Thomas Carter [*M74*: 1874–1923].

[629] The House in the Junior School later called Poole's, run from 1885 to 1897 by William Holden Scott Laxton [*M89*: 1877–1913, 1915–19].

[630] The South Town in the Junior School, run from 1880 to 1898 by Horace Pope Luckman [*M9*: 1863–98†].

[631] A House in the Junior School run from 1885 to 1892 by Alfred Trice Martin [*M97*: 1879–1910].

[632] A syphon employing air pressure to induce a surge of effluent as a self-cleansing mechanism.

and has been admirably done by Messrs Thomas & Son,[633] under the direction of Mr Macpherson, who warmly approved of my suggestions when the necessity was pointed out to him. I have now every reason to believe that there will be no further trouble with the Sanatorium drainage.

October 18th 1889.   W. Johnstone Fyffe.

[212]   1889–90. Head Master's notes on health and sanitation
[*Health file, Notebook titled 'Sanitary Regulation', pp. 25–30. MS (Head Master's holograph except inserted receipt and final section)*]

Feb./89.

Feb. 20/89. Dr Fyffe called my attention to a grave defect in the drainage of *Mr Grenfell's House:*[634] details given in the Sanitary Report of this term. I wrote Feb. 26 enclosing report to Mr Grenfell 'Please therefore to obtain without loss of time from Mr Thomas, the sanitary inspector who has now replaced Sainsbury[635] in working with Dr Fyffe the necessary designs, and get them approved of by Dr Fyffe, and send me note that they have been so approved. Also please to see that the work is begun at once as soon as the Easter holidays begin i.e. on Ap. 11. It will be for you, not for me, to arrange with Mr Oakeley[636] as to payments. But it is for me to say that the licence to take boarders will be withdrawn from your house unless this matter is attended to according to my instructions .... [*writer's dots*] Also please ask Dr Fyffe to send me a certificate that the house is safe not less than 3 full days before the end of the holidays.'

On March 10 I signed an estimate and specification supplied by Thomas of 16 Berkeley Place to carry out the work, as approved by Dr Fyffe, for £22. In May Mr Tait [637] assured me that this was thoroughly effected.

May/89.

In consequence of a case of typhoid – Prideaux,[638] at Mr Brown's House, early in the term a careful examination was made. There was a temporary stoppage in one of the water closets; but the drains were clear and clean, and there was no fouling or stoppage. Certain alterations were ordered as an improvement; the moving of a W.C. outside the House and the making inspection chambers. (*Vide* correspondence of this term.)

May/89.

Some cases of otitis after measles in the Sanatorium, which suggested blood poisoning occurred, and an examination of drains was made. The smoke test shewed that some of the drains leaked in many places, though the ventilators were working well. Some temporary cementing was done, but a more thorough relaying of the drains was recommended. See Dr Fyffe, May 3/89.

---

[633] L. Thomas and Son of Berkeley Place: *Directory* (1890), p. 451.
[634] The House later called Oakeley's; John Granville Grenfell [*M51*: 1871–8] had been the master since 1884; later in 1884 he handed it over to C.W.A. Tait.
[635] J.D.N. Sainsbury, builder and contractor, of Oakfield Grove: *Directory* (1889), p. 298.
[636] E.M. Oakeley [*M31*], Grenfell's predecessor (1877–83).
[637] Charles William Adam Tait [*M57*: 1873–1904].
[638] Philip Edward Prideaux [*3794*: BH 1887–91].

[*Insertion in Fyffe's hand*] Received from the Rev. J.M. Wilson, Head Master of Clifton College, the sum of twenty two pounds one shilling being fees for sanitary inspection of the masters' houses during the year ending June 1889.

£22–1–0.   [*over stamp*] Wm. J. Fyffe, M.D, July 13/89.

In Feb. and Mar./90 there was an outbreak of influenza in the School, and the term was brought to an end a week before the proper time in order that masters and boys might have a longer time in which to recruit.[639]

Only one death occurred[640] – and no lasting bad effects seem to have been produced by the illness in those who suffered from it. The symptoms were high temperature, pain in the limbs and shivering. Bronchitis, congestion or inflammation of the lungs was a frequent sequel, but this was only severe in 3 or 4 cases.

Influenza.

The real danger from influenza arises from exposure after convalescence. This danger is great. It is therefore necessary to make the following regulations:

I. No boy who has had influenza, whether at home or at school, may strip for games, i.e. runs, fives, football etc, or for the School bath, till *three* weeks have elapsed after convalescence.

II. He must then moreover get a certificate from Dr Fyffe that he is fit for games; the certificate to be brought to the House-master.

III. A list of the boys affected by these rules in each House must be posted in the matron's room, giving the dates.

Feb/90. (signed) J.M. Wilson, Headmaster

Influenza 1890

[213]   13 February 1890. Dr Fyffe to the Head Master
[*Health file. Holograph*]

2, Rodney Place,
Clifton.
Feb. 13/90.

Dear Mr Wilson,

With reference to the proposition which I understand has been made that the boarders should rise an hour later in the morning during the prevalence of this present cold weather,[641] I write to say that I entirely approve of the step – I think that at present the School is in a weak physical condition and the additional rest proposed will help to raise the standard of health.

Very sincerely yours,
W.J. Fyffe.

---

[639] One of four national epidemics of Russian 'flu between 1889 and 1894; at Clifton it lasted five weeks and affected almost a quarter of the boys. Dr Fyffe gave a full report in *The Cliftonian*, XI (1890), pp. 256–8. His statistics were used by Bristol's MOH in his report to the Local Government Board: D. Large, *The Municipal Government of Bristol, 1851–1901* (BRS L, 1999), p. 148.

[640] Graham Duncan Wright [*3874*: WiH 1888–90†].

[641] The day normally began with prayers at 7 a.m.

[214]   20 March 1890. Circular from the Head Master
[*Health file. Printed*]

Clifton College,
March 26, 1890.

Dear Sir,

At a Council meeting held this day a memorandum from our School Medical Officer was read, in which he urged, on purely medical grounds, the need of an extension of our Easter holidays, in the interests of boys, masters and College servants, in order to restore full health and efficiency at the close of a very exhausting term.

The influenza epidemic has now abated, but there are still fresh cases in Clifton and relapses. More that 160 boys have had it during the term, and 34 of the boarding-house servants, and several masters; and these have not generally recovered their full strength. There are besides evidences of weakness and liability to illnesses in those who have not had the influenza.

I should not have proposed any extension of holidays myself, nor would the Housemasters whom I have consulted, but the Council naturally attach great importance to the opinion of Dr Fyffe; and I must admit that we are below par. I am not sorry to be obliged to postpone our athletic sports, for which the School is not very fit, till next term; and the days of examination, which the boys will lose at the end of this term, are of less importance than usual, as the term has been so much broken up by illness.

The Council having these facts before them resolved unanimously that the School shall break up on April 2, and that boarders shall reassemble on the evening of Wednesday, April 30, thus lengthening the holidays by 4 days.

I am, yours faithfully,
James M. Wilson.

Dental anaesthesia

[215]   [*c.* 1890]. Dr Fyffe to the Head Master
[*Health file. Holograph*]

2 Rodney Place,
Clifton.
17 July.

Dear Mr Wilson,

I had a talk with Coker[642] a few days ago on the subject of gas. The present arrangement is this – Arthur Prichard[643] calls every day at Coker's house at 2.30 to administer gas to any boy who comes for tooth extraction. This has worked very well for the last few years. But I confess I do *not* think boys ought to have gas without the knowledge of their *House* Masters.

I can understand that it would not always be easy to obtain the sanction of parents – it might occupy a good deal of time and it would be hard to keep a boy in the misery of toothache until leave from his parents was obtained. It might be done

---

[642] T.V. Coker, dental surgeon, of Chesterfield Place, Queen's Road: *Directory* (1890), p. 186.
[643] Arthur William Prichard, surgeon, Bristol Royal Infirmary 1878–1906; one of the College Medical Officers 1892–1914: Smith, *History of BRI*, p. 485.

by telegram, of course, but I should think the leave of the House Master is all that would be necessary – every boy is examined before gas is administered, and Prichard is particularly good in giving anaesthetics. The risk is probably *nil*. The accidents amount to about 1 in 22,000. At the same time I am quite sure that no boy should be permitted to have gas given to him without the knowledge of his House Master. I have until lately been under the impression that this was always done.

I think you should make a rule that the boy must bring a written authority to Mr Coker for gas to be given – or if you like the boy to come to me, I will take the responsibility and give Coker the order for gas to be given. But the House Master should know in any case.

Yours very truly,

W.J. Fyffe.

Typhoid 1897

☐ *Clifton experienced a severe and highly localised outbreak, which was traced to the supply of contaminated milk from a farm in Long Ashton.*[644]

[216]   18 November 1897. Complaint from the mother of an infected boy
[*Council Minute Book 4, pp. 288–9. MS*]

A letter from Mrs. Williams dated [*blank*] was read with regard to the treatment of her son[645] who was a patient at the Sanatorium with typhoid fever and her visits to him.

Letters were also read from Major General Henderson[646] dated the 4th and 17th of November with regard to the recent outbreak of fever and the mode of treating it.

The Secretary was instructed to inform Mrs. Williams that her letter and accompanying statements were laid before the Council and were receiving their careful consideration. That with regard to the point raised as to the remission of fees, it should also have their attention. That the Council are glad to hear that her son is making satisfactory progress and that he may suffer no permanent harm from his illness.

[217]   16 December 1897. Report on typhoid outbreak
[*Council Minute Book 4, inserted between pp. 293–4. MS*]

The College, Clifton,

Secretary's Office.

The Council of the College, after having on the 18th of November and the 7th of December considered a letter and narrative from Mrs. Williams respecting certain circumstances attending the late outbreak of typhoid, and the necessary inquiries

---

[644] The MOH's report gives full details of the infection in the College and other schools: Large, *Municipal Government of Bristol*, pp. 135–6.
[645] Vivian Pericles Barrow Williams [*5033*: WaH 1895–7].
[646] P.D. Henderson, father of Harry Esmond [*4858*: WiH 1894–7].

having been made, hereby instruct the Secretary to send the following reply to the various allegations made by her.

1. It is true that the doctors did not discover any symptoms indicating typhoid till the end of the second week, but this was owing to the fact that none of the patients either at the College or in Clifton exhibited the characteristic signs of typhoid. The whole of the medical profession in Clifton was in fact misled by the entire absence of these symptoms.

2. Dr Edward Long Fox was properly consulted. He was himself the College Physician from 1863 to 1882;[647] and since his retirement, which was due to the claims of his large practice, he has held the position of Consulting Physician to the College, and his distinguished professional abilities need no indorsement by the Council. The innuendo suggested by Mrs. Williams is one which the Council cannot pass over without an expression of regret that it should have been made.

3. Having regard to the large and sudden call upon the resources of the Sanatorium at the onset, the Council are satisfied that its establishment and management proved adequate to deal with the patients both while the character of the attack was misunderstood and also as soon as it was known, and they are thankful that all the patients [have made *corrected to*] are making a satisfactory recovery.

4. The first portion of this complaint the Council decline to take notice of; but with respect to the question of access to patients (which in the case of treatment in wards is necessarily subject to certain rules and regulations) the Council point out: (a) that Mrs. Williams was not denied access on her first visit; (b) that the bad effect of that visit on the condition of the patients made it the duty of the Medical Officer to prohibit a repetition of the visit under similar circumstances in the interests of the other boys in the ward; (c) that the Head Master therefore only acted on the express and responsible advice of the Medical Officer in enforcing the printed rules of the Sanatorium; and (d) that arrangements to facilitate her access under different conditions were forthwith devised, and she then enjoyed free access to her son during her stay.

5. The Council accept the withdrawal of Mrs. William's elder son[648] at the end of this term without further notice, and without payment of fees in lieu of notice, in accordance with her request.

W.D.L. Macpherson, Secretary.

16th December 1897.

---

[647] Physician at Bristol Royal Infirmary and Lecturer at the Bristol Medical School 1869–74: Smith, *History of BRI*, pp. 478–9; father of Ernest Long [*1262*: DH 1873–8].

[648] Demetrius George Cecil Williams [*4826*: WaH 1894–7].

Weights and Measures 1910

[218]   7 July 1910. Dr J.M. Fortescue-Brickdale[649] to the Head Master
[*RS3/74. Holograph*]

52 Pembroke Road,
Clifton, Bristol.
July 7th 1910.

Dear Headmaster,
I enclose a draft scheme for weighing and measuring the boys, and notes as to probable cost, apparatus required &c.
Yours very truly,
J.M. Fortescue-Brickdale.

Scheme for weighing and measurement of boys at Clifton College.
1. Each boy is to be measured &c. as soon after his entry into the School as is practicable; the schedule in the right hand top corner with a figure denoting the term of entry (1, 2 or 3) and the subsequent measurements &c. will always be made during the same term once a year.
2. The measurements and tests will consist of:
(a) Determining acuity of vision for each eye after method adopted at Oxford in the University Laboratory.
(b) Determining the height both sitting and standing (without boots). Measurement to be made in centimetres.
(c) Determination of weight in gymnasium clothes, without boots or coat. Weight to be expressed in kilograms.
(d) Determination of chest measurement (in centimetres) for maximum inspiration and expiration, and of chest capacity by means of spirometer (as at Oxford).
(e) Recording colour of hair and eyes. Form on entering and leaving, games, prizes and scholarships.
(f) References to any relations at the School of whom measurements &c. have been taken.
3. The files of schedules will be kept alphabetically arranged, one for boys still at School, another for boys who have left.
4. All boys who are going on to the Universities of Oxford or Cambridge will be given a card directing them to present themselves for measurement at the Anthropometric Departments of the [University *corrected to*] Universities.
5. This scheme has been drawn up so as to obtain records capable of continuous comparison with those at the Universities. Hence the methods of measurement and the instruments recommended.
6. A copy of the proposed schedule and a list of the apparatus required are appended.

List of Apparatus
1. A weighing machine – cost would be about £3 to £4.
2. A spirometer – cost about £4.
3. A <weight> measuring scale. This and the seat, which must be fixed with a

---

[649] John Matthew Fortescue-Brickdale, DM (Oxon), one of the College Medical Officers, from 1910 to his death in 1921. Co-author of *A Manual of Infectious Diseases occurring in Schools* (Bristol, 1912), and of other standard works.

hinge to the scale will have to be fastened to the wall. An estimate of cost would have to be obtained.

4. A steel measure, and a set of set types (cost about 5/-).

5. Files and schedules for records.

This could all be installed at the end of one of the galleries at the Gymnasium but in order to protect the apparatus from misuse, there would have to be a gate or door put up across the gallery shutting off the portion containing it. An estimate of the entire cost could be obtained from Messrs Ferris & Co.[650]

[*Minuted in pencil*] Memorandum: Table accompanying this returned to Dr F.B. 30 July.

The Pollard case 1914–15

[219]   18 November 1914. Notice of claim for medical negligence
[*Council Minute Book 6, p. 305. MS*]

Pollard: Son's illness.

A letter was received from Dr R. Pollard[651] to the Chairman of the Council dated the 21st of September 1914 giving notice that he intended to hold the College responsible for his expenses in connection with the illness of his son;[652] and the Headmaster having submitted a report on the case, it was resolved that the Chairman be requested to write to Dr Pollard in reply to his letter, and to inform him that the Council having made enquiry must disclaim any legal responsibility in the matter, but would nevertheless wish to deal with the case with sympathy and that if he will tell them what expense has been incurred the Council will give the matter further consideration.

[220]   17 February 1915. Legal advice taken
[*Council Minute Book 6, p. 320. MS*]

Mr Doggett[653] attended and Messrs Le Brasseur and Oakley's letter of the 2nd inst. to the Secretary was read and considered, and Mr Doggett was instructed to obtain opinion of Counsel – if possible Mr H.E. Duke K.C.[654] – in order that the case might be fully considered by the Council at their meeting on 3rd proximo.

[221]   3 March 1915. A sum claimed
[*Council Minute Book 6, pp. 323–4. MS*]

Mr Doggett attended and the Chairman's letter to Dr Pollard dated November 20th 1914 and a letter from Messrs Le Brasseur and Oakley to the Secretary dated the

---

[650] Pharmaceutical Chemists and Surgical Instrument Makers of Union St: *Directory* (1910), p. 452.

[651] Reginald Pollard, MB, DPH [*1476*: PHP, SH 1874–9]; held appointments at the Western Hospital for Consumption, Torquay, the Chelsea Hospital for Women, and elsewhere.

[652] Reginald Graham Pollard [*7242*: SH 1911–13]; died 1914.

[653] The College Solicitor, who died in the course of these proceedings: Council Minute Book 6, p. 338.

[654] Henry Edward Duke, at this time MP for Exeter and Recorder of Devonport; later a Lord Justice of Appeal, created Baron Merrivale 1925.

2nd February 1915 demanding £750 for expenses stated to have been incurred by Dr Pollard in connection with the illness and death of his son having been read and considered, the Council approved the Chairman's letter and resolved to disclaim any legal liability and to decline to make the payment demanded by Messrs Le Brasseur and Oakley and to instruct their solicitors to inform Messrs Le Brasseur & Oakley accordingly; and that the further conduct of the matter be left in the hands of Mr Rowland Whitehead K.C., Mr H.N. Abbot and the Headmaster to deal with, it being understood that they will report to the Council for further instructions when pleadings have been delivered and discovery has been obtained.

[222]   7 March 1915. A.G. Grenfell[655] to the Head Master
[*HM5 Correspondence/Pollard. Holograph*]

> Mostyn House School,
> Parkgate,
> Cheshire.
> 7 March 1915.

Dear King,

Mrs. Irvine[656] declares that so far as she knows the *man* who had the impudence to crab[657] the S.H. to her never knew or heard of anyone called Pollard. I couldn't ask her the man's *name*: I wish I could get him by the throat!

I have discussed the Pollard case (without name) with my doctor, a *very* good man – a Scotty, first of his year at Edinburgh: been our M.O. for 20 years.

He says the action would be hopeless and ridiculous: no decent lawyer would touch it: no decent specialist would back it.

The boy must have had sarcoma (ordinary melanotic)[658] *before* the blow or strain: probably the pain felt was *due to* the *sarcoma* and not to the blow or strain at all: the latter only drew attention to it. He cites an exactly parallel case: a woman supposed to have severe *sciatica*: surgeon cut down and stretched the sciatic nerve – result, femur instantly snapped. Tried for maltreatment: case laughed out of court: femur broke *because* rotted by sarcoma; no-one could diagnose the thing properly beforehand.

Anyway, boys at Public Schools are supposed to be *normally* healthy and are therefore treated in normal ways: no-one ever heard of sarcoma, or anything else malignant, being *caused* by a blow or strain, except in sense of introductory cause.

Does Pollard suggest Prichard[659] should have cut the boy's leg off the moment he thought he had a blow or strain? Really it's too absurd.

If I were you I should 'devancer' Mr P. by an action for libel: you'd win *that* easily enough, if you could prove she had deterred a parent from sending a boy to Clifton unless 'in answer to a question'.

The Public Schools should all combine to jump on cantankerous people of this class, and put the fear of death into them.

---

[655] Algernon George Grenfell [*2750*: SH 1881–2]; Assistant Master at Westminster 1887–90 before becoming Headmaster of Mostyn House.
[656] Widow of J.W. Irvine of Neston, Cheshire: *Register* (1925), p. 491.
[657] Meaning 'complain (of)'.
[658] Skin cancer.
[659] A.W. Prichard: above **[215]**. At the Council meeting when the Pollard case was first mentioned (18 Nov. 1914), the Head Master reported that Prichard had resigned his appointment as Surgeon because of a worsening cataract in his eyes: Council Minute Book 6, p. 306.

Mrs. Irvine is *more* than satisfied; she is exceedingly grateful that you'll take her boy – a very tall overgrown weed, owing to his many illnesses in the past. He has been as fit as a flea here: the air seems to suit him, and it will at Clifton too.[660]

Y[*ours*] v[*ery*] s[*incerely*],

A.G. Grenfell.

[223]   21 July 1915. Proposal for Out of Court settlement
[*Council Minute Book 6, pp. 344–5. MS*]

A letter from the College Solicitors dated 20th July 1915 stating that there was a prospect of disposing of the Pollard case 'during the next few days at the proposed figures i.e. three hundred guineas damages and forty guineas costs' was read and authority was given to any two members of the Committee to sign a cheque for the amount when required.

[224]   17 November 1915. Settlement
[*Council Minute Book 6, pp. 354–5. MS*]

The settlement of the Pollard case was reported, and in connection therewith the following letters were read:

18 Clare St, Bristol.
4th August 1915.

Messrs Le Brasseur & Oakley,
Solicitors, 40 Carey St, W.C.

Dear Sirs,

Clifton College ats Pollard

We have taken the instructions of the Council of Clifton College on the suggestion that a sum of three hundred guineas and costs should be paid by the Council to your clients towards the expenses incurred by them in consequence of the illness and death of their son.

The amount so proposed to be paid appears to be a fair estimate of the expenses incurred and the Council having regard to the letter of their Chairman to Dr Pollard of the 20th November last are prepared to make the payment. We have therefore the pleasure to enclose our cheque for £367.

Yours faithfully,
(signed) Stanley, Wasbrough, Doggett and Baker.

40 Carey Street, Lincoln's Inn W.C.
August 4th 1915

Dear Sirs

Pollard v. Clifton College

We have received your letter of to-day's date enclosing cheque in our favour for £367 which is accepted by our clients in satisfaction of all claims by our clients arising out of the illness and death of their son and in settlement of the pending action against Clifton College.

---

[660] Ian Robert Thornewill Irvine [*7824*: SH 1915]; duly came to Clifton in May 1915 and left at Christmas.

Our clients have asked us to express their true appreciation of the way your clients have met them in this very sad and unfortunate matter.

Yours faithfully,

(signed) Le Brasseur and Oakely <1d. stamp. 4.8.16>.

Messrs Stanley, Wasbrough,

Doggett & Baker, Solicitors, 18 Clare St, Bristol.

Meningitis 1915–16

[225]   29 December 1915. The Head Master to School House parents
[*RS3/111. Typescript*]

School House,

Clifton College,

Bristol,

29th November 1915.

Dear Sir,

I regret to say that, since going away for the holidays, a School House boy[661] has developed cerebro-spinal meningitis. I write to inform you of this in order that you may consult your medical attendant as to precautionary measures against this disease.

The recommendation of Dr Davies, Medical Officer of Health for Bristol,[662] is that all 'contacts' should have the nasal cavity as well as the throat sprayed twice daily for 14 days with the following:

Iodine 4 grains; Menthol 8 grains; Parolein 1 ounce.

Yours sincerely,

J.E. King,

Headmaster.

[226]   [January 1916]. Notice from the Head Master to all parents
[*RS3/111. Typescript*]

Meningitis.

All boys should be sprayed 14 days before return to School, and forms should be collected. Boys whose spraying is not complete, or who do not bring forms, should be reported at once to Dr Shingleton Smith.[663]

Spraying should be continued night and morning under supervision for all boys for a week.

The back of the throat – soft palate should be sprayed, and each nostril, pointing spray backwards along floor of nose, head leaning a little back till spray is felt coming into throat.

---

[661] See below **[227–8]**.

[662] David Samuel Davies, Medical Inspector from 1865 to 1886, whose appointment has been described as 'crucial': D. Large (ed.), 'Records of the Bristol Local Board of Health, 1851–1872', *A Bristol Miscellany*, ed. P. McGrath (BRS XXXVII, 1985), pp. 133, 177 n. 34; he lived in Lansdown Place: *Directory* (1915), p. 453.

[663] Robert Shingleton Smith, Physician, Bristol Royal Infirmary 1873–1905; Professor of Medicine, University College 1893–5: Smith, *History of BRI*, p. 484; *Reg. Univ.*, p. 235.

One spray should be used for each boy, or, if used for more than one boy, dipped into boiling water before use in each case. All sprays should be dipped in boiling water after use. Any case of soreness in throat or symptoms of cold should be noted and referred at once to doctor.

Masters must remember that they and their households can be carriers as well as boys.

J.E. King.

[227]   31 December 1915/29 February 1916. Report by the Head Master to the Council
[*RS3/111. Holograph*]

Report to Council, Clifton College.

On Monday Dec. 13th a boy (Bredin mi)[664] in Mr Rintoul's House[665] was taken ill and sent to the Sick Room. On Friday Dec. 17th his illness was diagnosed as cerebro-spinal meningitis and he was removed to the Sanatorium. The case was notified to the Medical Officer of Health whom I saw with Dr Shingleton Smith to consider what was to be done with reference to the rest of the School who were due to go home on Monday Dec. 20th. It was decided to keep back all boys [who *deleted*] in Mr Rintoul's House who were near 'contacts' from sleeping in the same dormitory or using the same study, and have them bacteriologically examined. The rest were allowed to go home, but the parents of all boys in Mr Rintoul's House were notified of the illness. As the bacteriological examination showed no trace of the disease the rest of Mr Rintoul's boys went home by Thursday 23rd.

On Dec. 26th a letter was written to me to say that a [boy in the School House *corrected to*] School House boy named Maxwell[666] had been taken ill within 24 hours of [arriving *corrected to*] reaching home on Monday Dec. 20th and that the illness had been diagnosed as cerebro-spinal meningitis on Friday Dec. 24th. On Monday morning the 27th this boy died.

[On Thursday *deleted*] I saw the Medical Officer of Health and Dr Shingleton Smith upon hearing of Maxwell's illness and sent out a circular to the parents of boys in the School House **[225]** telling them of this case of illness and recommending spraying.

On Wednesday Dec. 29th there came news that Prichard mi of Mr Rintoul's House[667] had been taken ill, and after consultation with the medical authorities it was decided to notify the parents of all boys in the School recommending precautions. It was also decided in order to save time for precautions to be taken at the School and in boys' homes to put off the beginning of term from Sat. Jan. 15 to Sat. Jan. 22.

J.E. King,
Dec 31. 1915.

Notice was sent to all parents that boys should have their throats sprayed – as recommended by Dr Davies – for a fortnight before the beginning of term **[226]**. This spraying was continued for a week after the boys returned. Since the beginning of term the boys, masters and staff of the boarding houses have been bacteriologically

---

[664] Guy Howard Bredin [*7727*: OH 1914–16†].
[665] Rintoul [*M121*] was master of the House later called Oakeley's 1904–18.
[666] Frank Philip Maxwell [*7868*: SH 1915†].
[667] Basil Stennett Prichard [*7756*: OH 1914–17].

examined by Dr Walker Hall[668] at the University. All cases of suspect throats have been isolated. At present 3 boys, one master and Miss Clissold are isolated and will not return to school until they are pronounced clear. The Secretary has the certificates of the holiday spraying and the results of Dr Walker Hall's examination, and has seen him with reference to the question of payment. Parents have not been told that they will have to pay the fee of 10/6 nor told that they will not have to pay <only that the examination was necessary>. Whether as a result of the throat spraying or not, the health of the School this term has so far been very much better than usual.[669] There is for instance a remarkable absence of coughing in Chapel, and it may be well in future always to spray boys for a week at the beginning of the Lent term.

J.E. King,
Feb. 29. 1916.

[228]   18 March 1916. Professor I. Walker Hall to the Head Master
[*RS3/111. Typescript*]

University of Bristol.
18th March, 1916.

Dear Dr King,

As an introduction to a short summary of the results of the examinations upon the members of Clifton College, I may recite the fact that your outbreak of cerebrospinal fever last December was manifested by three definite cases of meningitis. Of these three cases the distribution was, I believe, as follows.

1. Bredin, Modern IVa, Mr Rintoul's House. Died January 24th, 1916.
2. Prichard, [Modern IVa *corrected to*] Classical IVβ, Rintoul's House. Recovered.
3. Maxwell, Modern IVa, The School House. Died December 23rd, 1915.[670]

At the close of term, some sixteen boys in Mr Rintoul's House were examined for meningococci. They yielded negative results and went to their homes.

During the holidays, all the boys were expected to spray their naso-pharynges at least once a day. Before returning to school some of the boys were examined for the presence of meningococcus and in two instances they were found to be 'positive'. These boys did not come back until they were quite free, and the findings are not included in the following figures.

The occurrence of these positive results suggests that if the entire School had been examined during the vacation, evidence of a wider spread might have been obtained. As, however, the meningococcus does not easily exist for many weeks in the pharynges of healthy individuals and is less likely to retain its hold when fresh air and daily spraying are resorted to, it was anticipated that very few of the boys would harbour <the> meningococcus upon their return to School. An examination at this time should, therefore, demonstrate the value of the precautions already taken, and also indicate the necessity of any further treatment in particular cases.

---

[668] Isaac Walker Hall, Professor of Pathology and Morbid Anatomy, University College, and Professor of Pathology, Bristol University 1909–33: *Univ. Reg.*, pp. 9, 234. See Council Minute Book 9, pp. 1–2.
[669] The Head Master fails to mention that Bredin had died on 24 January.
[670] The date (27 Dec.) given in the Head Master's more circumstantial report is likely to be the correct one.

In response to your wish, I commenced such an examination of the boys and staff of the College on January 24th, and am now in a position to submit the following statements for your consideration.

First, the number of positive contacts is below the average. This is probably due to the intervention of the holidays and the medical and general treatment adopted.

Next, as you will note from the following figures, the boys directly associated with those boys who suffered from the infection, viz. the contacts, have provided the larger number of 'carriers'.

		Positives	*Per-cent*
Total number of individuals examined	657	7	1.06*
Total contacts: boys 84, masters 48	132	4	3.08
Total non-contacts	525	3	0.56

[* *corrected from* 0.938]

If the findings among the non-contacts are applied to the various parts of the School, they show the following percentages:

	Number examined	*Positives*	*Percent*
House staffs 120, less 19 masters§	101	2	1.98
Town boys	205	1	0.487
Non-contact House boys	219	0	0

When we enquire into the distribution of the positive contacts in the various Houses we at once note the freedom from carriers of the 'non-contact' Houses so far as the scholars are concerned. This is evident from the following table:

Contacts	*Number of boys examined*	*Positives*
Mr Rintouls's House	21	1
Form IVa	14	1
The School House	<u>49</u>	<u>1</u>
	84	3
Masters	<u>48</u>	<u>1</u>
	132	4

Non-contacts	Number of boys examined	Positives	Number of staff examined	Positives
Mr Rintoul's & School House	–	–	31	–
Mr Barff's[671]	35	–	11	–
Rev. Polack's [*sic*]	40	–	14	–
Mr Russell's[672]	32	–	15	–
Mr Clissold's[673]	39	–	14	2
Mr Mayor's[674]	39	–	12	–
Mr Barlow's[675]	9	–	13	–
Mr de Gex's[676]	25	–	10	1§
Town boys	127	1		
Preparatory Sch.	78			
	424	1	120	3
Less 19 masters			19	
			101	

§ One positive master included under contacts on page 2 [*first table above*]

As it is now permissible by means of recently devised methods to assign a type or place to the strains of meningococci present in cerebro-spinal fever, investigations were carried out in the case of the boys with C.S.F. who remained in the Sanatorium during December and January. The results showed that the infecting organism belonged to the No. 1 type, namely to that organism which occurred in the early part of the 1915 epidemic.

Similar methods were applied to the cocci isolated from the 7 carriers found during this investigation. Six of these yielded meningococci identical with the organism obtained from the December case, that is to say, they belonged to the No. 1 type; one gave results which enabled its identification with a No. 2 type.

It is therefore fair to infer that six of these positive contacts, at the least, were carriers of the same meningococcus which was present in the School during December last.

The evidence which has been brought forward, however, does not afford any clear insight into the manner in which the School became infected. That is to say, the findings do not point to this or to that positive contact as the immediate cause of the outbreak, although it is possible that one of the contacts may have been responsible for the initial spread. On the other hand, it is probable that had the origin of the cases arisen in this way, there would have been manifestations during the earlier weeks, or months, of the term; it would be unusual, though not impossible, for the carrier to

---

[671] The former and later Dakyns', run 1907–18 by Edward James Barff [*2266*: DH 1878–83; *M126*: 1887–1927].

[672] The former and later Brown's, run 1907–18 by Cecil Henry St Leger Russell [*M128*: 1887–1928].

[673] The former and later Wiseman's, run 1912–14 by H. Clissold [*3375/M148*].

[674] The former and later Watson's, run 1916–26 by Henry Bickersteth Mayor [*3329*: WiH 1884–90; *M151*: 1895–1926].

[675] The Junior School House later Hartnell's, run 1902–18 by Harry Grimshaw Barlow [*M134*: 1889–1927].

[676] The Junior School House later Poole's, run 1915–30 by Ralph Octavius de Gex [*4374*: SH 1891–5; *M173*:1901–30].

remain dormant for so long a period. In my own mind, although I cannot offer any tangible support for the impression, I have come to regard the outbreak as due to an extra-mural origin.

As you are aware, the positive contacts have been isolated and treated and re-examined, and finally removed to the country for 'mountain air'. It is satisfactory to find that they are now all practically free from meningococci and will be able to return to work next term.

I may be allowed to express my appreciation of the excellence of the various necessary arrangements you have made and for the facilities you have so freely placed at my disposal during the course of the examination.

Yours very truly,

I. Walker Hall.

[229]   21 March 1916. The University Registrar[677] to the College Secretary: expenses of the examination
[*RS3/111. Typescript*]

University of Bristol.
21st March 1916.

Dear Sir,

I enclose accounts for fees in connection with the cerebrospinal fever investigations. I may state that the normal fee for the naso-pharyngeal examination is one guinea. In consideration of the numbers examined, a fee of half a guinea has been charged and various items, amounting to about 100 examinations, have been deducted owing to special circumstances such as previous certification, repeat examinations of Mr Clissold's House and Mr de Gex's House and some of the masters.

Yours faithfully,

James Rafter.

Diphtheria 1930

[230]   Summer Term 1930. Expense sheet
[*RB3/16. Typescript*]

Expenses to College in connection with diphtheria outbreak in Brown's House in 2nd term, 1930.

	£	s	d
Pilkington's[678] fees for 1930/3 remitted	22	13	4
Swabbings	20	14	0
Mr Philbrick's[679] board 1 term	36	0	0

---

[677] James Rafter, Registrar of University College, Bristol 1902–9, first Registrar of the University 1909–24: *Univ. Reg.*, pp. 4, 232. One so named (presumably this man or his father) had been Clerk to the College Secretary from 1875 to 1888.

[678] Robin Pilkington [*10010*: BH 1928–32].

[679] F.A. Philbrick [*M293*]; see above [**152**].

Payable to Mr Imlay[680]	67	18	0
Gait (3 mo[*nth*]s @10/- a week)	6	0	0
Redecoration[681] of dormitories in Brown's	12	7	0
New slop sink in Brown's	37	0	0
	£202	12	4
R.K. Jones[682]		10	5

[231]   30 September 1930. Diphtheria vaccination: notice to Housemasters
[*RB3/16. Typescript*]

Clifton College,
30 September, 1930.

To all Boarding Housemasters.

Last term each House rendered a list of boys who had not been immunized to diptheria [*sic*], but whose parents were willing for this to be done. For various reasons this was not possible last term, but it would be well to carry this out as early as possible this term, if your boys could be sent along any afternoon next week, the earlier the better, at a time most convenient for School hours.

H.J. Orr Ewing.[683]

---

[680] Alan Durant Imlay [*5233*: ST 1897–1904; *M194*: 1907–45]; House Master BH 1918–33; Bursar 1939–45.

[681] Mistyped 'Redocration'.

[682] Richard Keith Jones, later Keith-Jones [*9940*: BH 1927–32].

[683] One of the Medical Officers 1934–46.

SECTION XII:
LEAVING UNDER CLOUDS

The boy who could not be taught

[232]   7 March 1891. F. Harvey to the Head Master
[*HM3 Correspondence/Harvey. MS copy*]

Glanmôr,
Hayle, [*Cornwall*]
7 Mar: 1891.

Dear Sir,

I am in receipt of my son's[684] mid-term report in which you strongly advise that he should be taken away at the end of this term and add 'He is so much behind the form that it is impossible to teach him'. Mr Jupp[685] also speaks of his ignorance as 'extreme'. He entered the Preparatory School in June 1885 (mid-term) so that he has been almost six years at Clifton and practically received the whole of his education there. Of course if it is impossible for you to teach him I must remove him, but for reasons of my own I desire that you should give me formal notice to that effect. You say that no stigma is incurred by a boy who is superannuated. I differ from you altogether. And what am I to do with him now? What other school will take him, ignorant as [you *corrected to*] the report says he is, and at his age of 15, and superannuated? If all his education (!) had not been received at Clifton, the case would have been different. As it is I consider I have reason to complain most strongly and bitterly of time wasted, opportunity lost, and a large sum of money misspent. If he be so utterly ignorant I ought to have had notice before that he could not be taught at Clifton, when I could have made arrangements to have prevented the waste of valuable years of his life; for if he be physically not robust and of a very nervous temperament, yet I know full well he is not altogether deficient of brains. I am of opinion that superannuation is not just in such a case as mine where the boy has had all his training with you. I do not think it could be supported on equitable grounds, for if the conduct is good, it would have to be shown that the School on its part has done its duty to the full, and this probably would not be an easy matter if, as I believe for one thing, for instance, it is a fact that a considerable proportion of the

---

[684] Frank Stewart Harvey [*3457*: HHP, SH 1885–91].

[685] H.B. Jupp [*M96*], who taught Mathematics and Physics; see above [**160**].

boys entering the Preparatory School disappear early, presumably superannuated. It cannot be all the fault of the boys. I did not appreciate this fact so keenly until it has [*sic*] been brought home to me so forcibly though my son's case, although my wife and I have frequently commented on the disappearance of names known to our boys as schoolfellows.

Doubtless a school desires to keep up its intellectual tone as stated in your circular but it should not be done at the expense of boys who cannot attain the highest pitch. As in all other [business *deleted*] human affairs the 'bitter must be taken with the sweet'. Parents have their claims and rights equally as well as schools their aspirations.

I reserve the right to send a copy of this letter and further correspondence if any to the Council.

(signed) Frank Harvey.

P.S. An elder brother left last term after being 9 years at Clifton, having entered the Preparatory School also.[686]

[233]   11 March 1891. The Head Master to F. Harvey
[*HM3 Correspondence/Harvey. MS copy*]

Clifton College, Bristol.
March 11th 1891.

Dear Sir,

I am sorry that you should have taken offence at a piece of advice which was offered simply in the interest of your boy. I am not personally responsible for his past education, but I have to deal with the facts as I find them. According to the School rules, he ought to have been superannuated in July 1889,[687] but he was allowed to stay on for four terms in the hope that he might be brought up to the standard for his age. Then, without being fit for it, he was put into the lowest form of the College, having already stayed in the Junior School six months beyond the maximum age. His Form Master, who is a man of great experience and skill in teaching dull boys, pronounces him not only backward but quite extraordinarily stupid, and my own observation confirms that opinion. Next term he will again fall under the superannuation rule and must certainly leave in July. But if he returns to School after Easter it will only be to waste three months, since he is a boy who cannot be taught with a class, but requires a master to himself. That he may be saved that waste of time and disappointment, I advise you to remove him at Easter; but if you do not choose to do so I do not think it right to insist. It is natural that you should hold a different opinion about your son's intelligence, and prefer to throw the blame of his backwardness upon the teaching he has received. I come to the question without prejudice and I can only say that the teaching of our Junior School is successful in all ordinary cases, and I believe that you will find it very difficult to get better teaching at any other school. It was a great mistake to allow your boy to remain after July 1889; but that was due to kindliness and not to want of skill. His case will be a warning to me for the future of the need of observing the rule more strictly. I must ask you to excuse me from discussing the general principle of the superannuation rule. It has for 20 years been part of the

---

[686] William Francis Trevithick Harvey [*2957*: HHP, SH 1882–90]; he served in the South African War and remained in that country as a businessman.

[687] He was 14 in July 1890, thus reaching the maximum age for the Junior School: above **[79]** section 7.

constitution of Clifton College, and of every school of high repute.[688] I have of course the power to relax it where I think it desirable in the interest of the boy and of the School. But in your boy's case I should be doing an injury to both.

I do not object to your sending the correspondence to the Council. But I do not quite see what you can gain by it. They can only tell you that by the constitution of the School such questions are entirely in the hands of the Head Master.[689]

Believe me, dear Sir,

Yours faithfully

(signed) M.G. Glazebrook.

☐ *The substance of Mr Harvey's reply, occupying six sides of foolscap, is evident from the Head Master's briefer response.*

[234]   16 March 1891. The Head Master to F. Harvey
[*HM3 Correspondence/Harvey. MS copy*]

Clifton College, Bristol.

March 16th 1891.

My Dear Sir,

You letter interests me very much and I should like to reply to it at length, but I have not the time. May I just jot down the points that strike me most in the order which your letter suggests them?

I have reason to believe that, on the average, boys who have been in our Preparatory School do *better* than the others. What I said of the Junior School was meant to include the Preparatory.

I quite agree with you that many boys who are not good at learning gain much from a Public School. But that would cease to be the case if they were in the majority. It is only because the average tone of work and thought is above them that they gain. That is why, for every mistake, it is necessary to keep down the number of such boys.

Clifton boys were overworked to some extent ten years ago, and the reputation of a School is always ten years behind the facts.[690] At present I see no sign of overwork. In the upper part of the School they have less work than at Harrow.[691]

You don't appear to be aware that Clifton goes farther than any other other school in the kingdom in the way of 'letting boys follow their particular bent'.

I think the reason why Clifton boys have not yet attained distinction as men is the fact that on the whole its pupils have been below the average of the Public Schools in ability. Good teaching has made up for that defect in earlier life, but it takes good material as well as good teaching to make distinguished men, and you must remember that no Clifton boy taught all through at Clifton is yet over forty.

---

[688] With the notable exception of Eton; but the principle was enshrined in the 25th General Recommendation of the Clarendon Commission of 1864: Bamford, *Public Schools*, p. 69.

[689] See above **[36]** clause 68 and 70.

[690] Harvey had been told by 'a present and very eminent dignitary of the Church' that 'The boys are worked too hard at Clifton; you don't hear that they do well after they leave. Their brain power is exhausted by overpressure too early in life'.

[691] Where Glazebrook had been an assistant master.

As to the food I can only speak particularly of the School House. It did exactly answer to your description, and the first thing I did here was to make a complete change; for I entirely agree with your view of what school feeding ought to be.[692]

I am really glad for your boy's sake that you will take him away at Easter. I will give notice to the Secretary myself. He is a good little boy, and I heartily wish him well in his new life wherever it may be.

Yours sincerely,

(signed) M.G. Glazebrook.

☐ *Mr Harvey was not mollified by this, and on 28 March he informed the Head Master that he would appeal to the Council, in the belief that the fees and other payments he had made gave him the legal right to maintain his son at the School so long as his conduct was good.*

[235]　28 March 1891. The Head Master to F. Harvey
[*HM3 Correspondence/Harvey. MS copy*]

Clifton College, Bristol.

March 28th 1891.

My dear Sir,

I am obliged to you for giving me notice of your intention. But I am sorry you should give yourself the trouble of challenging a rule which all the great Public Schools have found it necessary to make for themselves.

As you refer again to the legal aspect of the question, I may tell you that I have already submitted the case to an eminent barrister, and received his assurance that your legal claim is quite imaginary.

Believe me,

Yours faithfully,

(signed) M.G. Glazebrook.

☐ *Harvey's father wrote to the Council on 30 March reiterating his case, but as the Head Master had warned this was a wasted effort.*

[236]　3 April 1891. Decision of the Finance Committee
[*Council Minute Book 3, p. 347. MS*]

Superannuation. F.S. Harvey

A letter was read from Mr F. Harvey with regard to the superannuation of his son and enclosing a correspondence that had passed between him and the Head Master on the subject.

The Secretary was instructed to reply that having regard to rule no. 16 the question of the superannuation of Mr Harvey's son was one which was wholly with the Head Master, and to enclose a copy of the Rules.[693]

---

[692] Harvey had called for 'good wholesome food, dressed in an appetising way. Plain it may be. But joints wretchedly cooked, vegetables not good, bread and butter of inferior quality, ought not to be imposed on boys whose parents pay the price asked'.

[693] The rule on superannuation, originally no. 7: above **[79]**.

☐ *Frank Harvey went to the Royal Indian Engineering College, Cooper's Hill, obtaining a Diploma in Civil Engineering, then qualifying as AMICE, and joining the Admiralty Works Department.*

The boy who broke down

☐ *The following papers are collected in a printed memorandum submitted to the Council by a father who considered his son to have been punished unfairly and had withdrawn him from the School. The material has been adjusted to the format of the present volume, omitting some linking passages.*

[237]   16 July 1900. Memorandum from W.D. Scott-Moncrieff
[*HM3 Correspondence/Scott-Moncrieff. Printed copy*]

Mr Scott-Moncrieff is prepared to make a statutory declaration to the following effect:

That his son[694] who is 14 years and 4 months of age, was educated first at Mr Blunt's, St Salvator's School, St Andrews, N.B.,[695] and that he went from there with an excellent character to Mr C.D. Olive, at Wimbledon,[696] who also gave him an excellent character. That on the strong recommendation of Mr Olive, who is an Old Cliftonian, his son's name was put down for Clifton College, where he passed a creditable entrance examination.

In his first report the Head Master spoke of him as 'a good little boy and should do well' or words to that effect. In a report received in the beginning of March last year, Mr Scott-Moncrieff was greatly astonished and grieved by the following statement by the Head Master: 'I have had to punish him for idleness and worse than that he has been found cheating at his work, for which I have had to punish him as well'.

On receiving this report Mr Scott-Moncrieff immediately telegraphed for particulars, and on the second of March the Head Master addressed the following letter to the boy's mother.

[238]   2 March 1900. The Head Master to Mrs W.D. Scott-Moncrieff
[*HM3 Correspondence/Scott-Moncrieff. Printed copy*]

Clifton College,
Bristol,
March 2nd, 1900.

Dear Mrs. Scott-Moncrieff,

I am obliged to be brief in answer to your telegram for I have gout in both arms.

As to your boy's idleness the report speaks for itself; and you will remember that I wrote to you about it not long ago. The other matter is perhaps more serious. He was caught by Mr Watson prompting his neighbour while a Euclid lesson was being

---

[694] William Walter Scott-Moncrieff [*5599*: SH 1899–1900].
[695] St Salvator's (borrowing its dedication from a College of the University) opened in 1882; its premises overlooking the first tee of the Old Course are now Scores Hotel. 'N.B.' (North Britain) enjoyed brief currency as a euphemism for 'Scotland'.
[696] Charles Daniel Olive [*401*: SH 1866–70]; Headmaster of Rokeby Preparatory School, Wimbledon from 1879 to 1909.

said. It is not the worst form of cheating, and was only punished by an imposition. But such an offence is very rare at Clifton,, and I regard it as a serious matter. I hope you will be here tomorrow, and will talk to him about it.

Yours very truly,

(signed) M.G. Glazebrook.

Note: The other punishment was a caning for alleged idleness, about which the boy made no complaint of any kind.

[239]   3 March 1900. W.D. Scott-Moncrieff to the Head Master
[*HM3 Correspondence/Scott-Moncrieff. Printed copy*]

4, Adelaide Crescent,

Hove,

March 3rd, 1900.

Dear Canon Glazebrook,

It was I who sent the telegram from London and was glad to have your letter this morning.

I quite understand that you cannot tolerate anything like an infringement of the rules that are essential to the work of the School being carried on fairly. Your short report alarmed us very much indeed, because though we believed our boy incapable of any meanness, we feared both his fault and his punishment might have been worse than they were. I do not think it likely to happen again.

Mrs. Scott-Moncrieff intends going to Clifton on Tuesday next and hopes she may be able to see Billy on Wednesday. We are both very sorry indeed to hear of your suffering from gout. I had one bad attack many years ago, and can the better sympathise with you. With kind regards.

I am yours sincerely,

(signed) W.D. Scott-Moncrieff.

[240]   12 March 1900. W.D. Scott-Moncrieff to the Head Master
[*HM3 Correspondence/Scott-Moncrieff. Printed copy*]

15, Edwardes Square,

Kensington, W.,

March 12th, 1900.

Dear Canon Glazebrook,

Mrs. Scott-Moncrieff returned yesterday evening and has informed me of what passed in her interview with you last Friday morning. I am sorry you should have formed so poor an opinion of my son, and the more so as I am sure that a better acquaintance with his character would quite alter your present impressions. I have been greatly upset by what has taken place, but will reserve my further judgment in the matter until I have seen him myself. In the mean time I fully confirm the decision that he is not to be pressed for the Navy, and I hope that in future, corporal punishment will be not even thought of as an incentive to work. I understand that for idleness and incompetence there is an automatic remedy in superannuation. I shall see you myself I hope and discuss matters at the beginning of next term as to what line of work should be followed later on.

I am, your truly,

(signed) W.D. Scott-Moncrieff.

[241]   17 March/12 June 1900. Summary of further exchanges
[*HM3 Correspondence/Scott-Moncrieff. Printed*]

In reply to this letter Canon Glazebrook stated that he is responsible to the Council of the College for the discipline of the School and that this included corporal punishment for idleness.

On the 17th March Mr Scott-Moncrieff wrote to the Head Master giving several reasons why the boy should not be overpressed in his work. Two severe accidents (a scalding and a double fracture of the wrist), also a surgical operation recently performed on his throat were mentioned in the letter. At the same time there was no wish to interfere with the discipline of the School, and Mr Scott-Moncrieff said that after the explanations that had been made, he was sure that his son was quite safe in the Head Master's hands.

During the last holidays the boy brought the infection of mumps back from the School with him and had a rather severe attack. Going back several days after the commencement of the term, he naturally made rather a bad start. A report came in on the 9th June, in which reference is made to 'want of energy and determination'. On the forenoon of the 12th June the boy fell down in a dead faint. This led to the loss of two days' work and was referred to in the following letter from Miss Thomas the Matron.

[242]   15 June 1900. The School House Matron to Mrs. Scott-Moncrieff
[*HM3 Correspondence/Scott-Moncrieff. Printed copy*]

The School House,
Clifton College,
June 15th, 1900.
Dear Mrs. Scott-Moncrieff,
    You were naturally alarmed about your son having fainted, but I hope your mind will be quite easy about it as it was only caused through indigestion. The Doctor saw him afterwards and gave him a tonic which soon put him to rights. Now he is looking very well again, and has promised me to tell me at once should he feel seedy. I must say he is a plucky boy, for after getting an hour's sleep he wanted to go into afternoon school, he is so anxious not to miss any of his work this term. I hope you are well and that your family are not causing you any anxiety as to health. You know how very glad I shall be to look after Moncrieff at any time, so please do not worry over him.
                I am,
                    Yours sincerely,
                    (signed) M.E. Thomas.

[243]   [16 June 1900]. Scott-Moncrieff to his mother
[*HM34 Correspondence/Scott-Moncrieff. Printed copy*]

School House,
Clifton College, Bristol.
Saturday night.
My dearest Mother,
    Thank you very much for your letter and Daddy's. I am sorry to hear my spelling is so bad. I am staying out for most of this week because I fainted. I fell slap across

the floor. I am all right now so don't worry. You seem to have forgotten all about my request for turkeys' eggs. But it does not matter if it is too much trouble. I am awfully glad Daddy is coming down for Commem. I am sure he would like it. Can you on one of the days take two of my small friends, namely Knox[697] and Lapage[698]. If this could be managed it would be rattling. Or perhaps you would take us and have an ice, etc. On Friday last we had a whole holl commemorating the relief of Pretoria and Mafeking.[699] We all broke up in parties of 16 and went to all parts of the country. My party went to Tintern in Wales. We went through the Severn Tunnel and got to Tintern at about 12 o'clock. We then had lunch and went over the Abbey. After that we took boats and went on the Wye – we bathed about six times and altogether we had a glorious time. I am glad Bertie is getting on well at Olive's! I am sure to get out of my form this quarter. I am now afraid my news has run short.

I remain,

Your affectionate son,

(signed) Billy Scott-Moncrieff.

P.S. Please thank Daddy for his letter.

[244]   [26 June 1900]. Scott-Moncrieff to his mother.
[*HM3 Correspondence/Scott-Moncrieff. Printed copy*]

School House,

Clifton College, Bristol.

Tuesday morning.

My dearest Mother,

I have delayed my letter until now because I was waiting for a certain event to come off and that event is that last night at 7.30 I was again caned by the H.M. This is the whole story. My places are in form:

7th. 19th (absent). 11th. 8th. 20th (absent). 8th. 18th.

These places bring me to an average place of 12th, and considering 20 get out I do not think I have done so badly. However one day he told me I had got a bad report and that I should have to bring a report from Mr Moberly to him. This I did. The first week I got 'Improved, set work good'. The second week I got 'Latin poor and one English lesson'. He then told me he was going to cane me, which was duly done, and for which little performance you will have to pay 2/6d. The reason why I am so low is because there are two or three new boys who ought to have been put in the next form above. Another is because the two times I have been low is because as you know I fainted and was not well. However I am perfectly happy. But I should like Dad to see the H.M. himself. What grieves me is that there are some boys far worse than me but who do not receive so much as a talking to.

[245]   [26 June 1900]. Summary of further exchanges
[*HM3 Correspondence/Scott-Moncrieff. Printed*]

This letter was unfinished as above.

---

[697] Utred Arthur Frederick Knox [*5586*: SH 1899–1903].

[698] Charles Herbert Swaine Lapage [*5587*: SH 1899–1900].

[699] The relief of the siege of Mafeking on 17 May 1900 occasioned widespread celebration at home. When Pretoria was taken by Lord Roberts on 5 June it seemed that the South African War had been won.

Note: The places in the form do not correspond with those in the report of the 9th of June but the boy says he got them from 'the board'. He is about 8 months below the average age of the form.

The only remark made by the Head Master upon the report of the 9th of June is 'He must do better than this'. Mr Scott-Moncrieff was so much annoyed by the pressure which was apparently being put on the boy when he was evidently not fit for it that he went to see Mr Olive, his son's former master, who expressed himself strongly on the subject and kindly wrote to his Form Master, Mr Moberly, a letter on the boy's behalf. Mr Scott-Moncrieff hoped that the effect of this letter would be to relieve the pressure at any rate for the present term.

On hearing that the boy had again been thrashed by the Head Master, Mr Scott-Moncrieff was very indignant, and having arranged to go to the Commemoration ceremony on the 29th June, he wrote to Canon Glazebrook saying that he was sorry to hear of what had happened and asked for an interview. On reaching Clifton he received the following note.

[246]   28 June 1900. The Head Master to W.D. Scott-Moncrieff
[*HM3 Correspondence/Scott-Moncrieff. Printed copy*]

Clifton College,
June 28th.

Dear Mr Scott-Moncrieff,

I have given your boy leave to dine with you to-morrow, returning at 9.0. I am sorry to say it is quite impossible for me to make an appointment with you either on Friday evening or on Saturday, for I am not master of my time, having so many hundreds of guests, but I shall be happy to make an appointment for a later day.

Yours very truly,
(signed) M.G. Glazebrook.

[247]   29 June 1900. W.D. Scott-Moncrieff to the Head Master
[*HM3 Correspondence/Scott-Moncrieff. Printed copy*]

Glendower Private Hotel,
Clifton Down,
June 28th, 1900.

Dear Canon Glazebrook,

I am obliged by your note and am sorry that I cannot have an interview, although I quite understand the difficulty of arranging one this week. If I had been able to see you I do not suppose it would have modified my determination to take my boy away *at once*. I shall give my reasons to the Governing Body of the College.

I have written to Miss Thomas asking her to have his things packed and ready for Monday morning.

Yours truly,
[*signed*] W.D. Scott-Moncrieff.

[248]   30 June 1900. The Head Master to W.D. Scott-Moncrieff
[*HM3 Correspondence/Scott-Moncrieff. Printed copy*]

Clifton College,
June 30th, 1900.
Dear Mr Scott-Moncrieff,
Your note, which I received this morning, surprises me greatly. In your letter of March 17th, which is in my possession, you say you have no wish to interfere with the tradition of discipline of the School, and in reply to a letter of mine you expressly left the whole question of corporal punishment in my hands. I had refused to keep Billy on any other terms.
It seems to me a pity that by a precipitate action now you should contradict yourself and do the boy a serious injury.
Yours faithfully,
(signed) M.G. Glazebrook.

[249]   30 June 1900. W.D. Scott-Moncrieff to the Head Master
[*HM3 Correspondence/Scott-Moncrieff. Printed copy*]

Glendower Private Hotel,
Clifton Down,
June 30th, 1900.
Dear Canon Glazebrook,
I am in receipt of your letter by hand this morning.
Referring to my letter to you of 17th March last, on the evidence before me, I am forced to the conclusion that the confidence I then reposed in you has not been justified by your subsequent treatment of my son, and the only course open to me is to remove him from the School at once. I shall come for him myself on Monday morning.
I am yours truly,
(signed) W.D. Scott-Moncrieff.

[250]   [16 July 1900]. Conclusion of submission.
[*HM3 Correspondence/Scott-Moncrieff. Printed*]

Mr Scott-Moncrieff submits that the foregoing correspondence speaks for itself. In the last interview, the evening before he was taken away, the boy states that the Head Master told him that his besetting sin was idleness and that he had tried to cure him of it. The boy says it is not true that he was idle – 'he had to work' and was most anxious to get on.
Mr Scott-Moncrieff was quite satisfied with his son's place in the School. He thinks that the expression 'cheating' is not a fair use of the word, and should not have been sent to a parent as an explanation in one sentence of what actually occurred. The boy was not in a fit state of health to receive corporal punishment on the 25th June last, and the letter of the Matron of the 15th June, is good evidence of the boy's anxiety about his work.[700]

---

[700] Misprinted 'wotk'.

[251]   16 July 1900. W.D. Moncrieff to the Chairman of Council
[*HM3 Correspondence/Scott-Moncrieff. Printed copy*]

14, Victoria Street,
Westminster,
July 16th, 1900.

My Lord,
I have the honour to inform you that on the morning of the 2nd inst. I took away my son William Walter Scott-Moncrieff from Clifton College. It appeared evident to me that, in spite of the boy's own efforts to disguise the fact, he was breaking down under the strain to which he was being subjected from too much being required of him in the way of work.

I enclose a Memorandum [*rearranged above*] giving the greater part of the evidence upon which I came to the conclusion that the boy should be taken away. It has never been suggested that the corporal punishment complained of was administered for any reasons but those set forth in the reports.

I have the honour to remain,
My Lord,
Your obedient servant,
(signed) W.D. Scott-Moncrieff.

[252]   17 October 1900. Report to the Finance Committee
[*Council Minute Book 5, p. 37. MS*]

The Secretary reported that he had received a letter from Mr Scott-Moncrieff's solicitors declining to pay the fees of the present term in lieu of notice of his son's removal.
The matter was referred to the Council.

[253]   2 November 1900. Claim for fees in lieu of notice waived by Council
[*Council Minute Book 5, p. 39. MS*]

Scott-Moncrieff Account.
The correspondence with Mr Scott-Moncrieff having been read, it was resolved that whilst the Council are unable to accept as proved the charges made by Mr Scott-Moncrieff in respect of his son's treatment in the School they are willing to abandon their pecuniary claim against him and thus to put an end to any further controversy on the subject, and the Secretary was instructed to send a copy of this resolution to Mr Scott-Moncrieff's solicitors Messrs James Sinnott & Son in reply to their letter of the 14th of August regarding the claim of the College.

☐ *Billy Scott-Moncrieff qualified as an architect, and served in the Great War as a Captain in the Royal Engineers, winning the Military Cross.*

The Percival Boy and the sausage incident

[254]   **7 October 1917. L.J. Percival[701] to the Head Master**
[*HM5 Correspondence/Percival. Holograph*]

St Mary's Rectory,
36 Gloucester Place, W.
Oct. 7. 1917.

My dear King,

It is difficult indeed to write. But now that my Sunday work is my own I feel I must try and send you a line as you naturally will expect to hear by tomorrow. Your letter addressed to Reay has not yet reached me. With regard to Jack's[702] future I fear there is only one conclusion that we can come to and that is that his Clifton career is finished. It is quite impossible that you should wish him to try again. Anyhow I know now that I could never persuade him to go back even though he went as a day boy as was once suggested in Ridley's House.[703] So ends this sad catastrophe. We are broken hearted about it. I don't know how to break the news to my dear old father. It is a terrible blow to me as I was so proud to have him at the old School and I loved going down to see the dear old place. But the boy was miserable – always has been and begged to be taken away many a time. I hate saying anything which may hurt but I feel it only right to say that we feel that the boy had good [reason to *corrected to*] reasons.

Before ever he went to the School House several friends gave us warnings about the boys in S.H. but I refused to believe them and perhaps was vain enough to think that the boy with my help would pull through and help to make the House what it used to be. Then came that awful first term from which he never recovered, as it appears that they made a dead set against him and everybody who had the name of Percival. His games I hoped might save him but it is evident that success in games counts for little in S.H.

These were all facts which were confirmed by my own experience and by many friends at Clifton. I only hope that all will come well and that the School House will soon be taking its proper position in the great School. It is my earnest wish that one of my boys may yet go to Clifton and be as happy as I was.

It is a sad and bewildering calamity and I know full well that you feel it as much as I do. What to do with the boy now is a problem. But I have hopes that we may with your kind help get him into some other Public School. On this point I shall of course be writing to you again. I have been down to see Percy Christopherson[704] and we have together talked over various places. No school would we think care to have him new this term but some might take him after Christmas. Meanwhile I must try and find someone I can send him to where he will have hard work and a nice home.

We shall be glad if his things can be packed up and sent by passenger train to this address.

Besides all his clothing and books there are his pictures, racquets (2) and a press for the racquets. I presume too that his chair could be sent.

---

[701] The Bishop of Hereford's fourth son, at this time Rector of St Mary's, Bryanston Square: above **[44]**.
[702] John Douglas Percival [*7912*: SH 1916–17], the writer's son.
[703] M.R. Ridley [*M230*] was the House Tutor in School House.
[704] A master at Wellington College; also as a rugby international and Kent cricketer (d. 1921).

With regard to the question about the money, Jack tells me that Roxburgh[705] *gave* him the money. I see the point and can only hope that you will be lenient to Roxburgh. Evidently the plan was made to shield the boy Roxburgh by giving out that Jack *took* the money. Butler[706] knows that Jack was given the money. I have examined Jack very closely and am quite sure that his story is the true version. I have spoken to Mr Evans on the point and what Jack told him agrees in every detail with what he told me. Whatever Jack's faults may be I am quite sure that he is a thoroughly straightforward and guileless boy. But once again I pray that Roxburgh may not get into trouble. His position was difficult – his actions were meant kindly but thoughtless – the blame must rest on Jack.

His answer to the question about the 'unsocial' attitude seems to me quite good – the Fifth table made life at school worse than ever. Because he was on the Fifth table they went for him – sometimes in considerable numbers. This they didn't do when he was on the Fags' table. They made mischief whenever they could. The sausage incident was one of them. He had been waiting longer than anyone for his sausage and was overlooked by the Lady Butler. He naturally stood on his rights and secured his sausage, but in no mean manner.

It is a small point but it proves his case, namely that the Fifth table – or some of them, meant to give him a hot time.

The food that went to Miss Thomas's room[707] was I believe taken there when he was away.

It appears that many boys do hand on some of their belongings to Miss Thomas as there is much pilfering.

I myself saw a boy breaking into the pantry to get food while another boy kept the small pantry boy busy in another part of the House. I mention this because I knew not who the boys were but one of the boys seemed to think it a good joke and told me about it. I said nothing but I thought a good deal!

I fear this is a long letter but I am glad to have written it as it takes a load off my mind. It has been written with sincere affection towards you and Clifton College, but with a sad heart.

> Yours very truly,
> L.J. Percival

[255]   14 October 1917. Percival to the Head Master
[*HM5 Correspondence/Percival. Holograph*]

> St Mary's Rectory,
> 36 Gloucester Place, W.
> Sunday night, Oct: 14. 1917.

My dear King,

Many thanks for your letter of Oct. 8 and please excuse me for not answering your letter of the 9th, asking for names, more promptly. I went to Hereford and stayed there longer than I had intended. My father is far too unwell for any bad news at the present time so I said nothing about Jack. You will ∴ I hope not write to the father. He goes to Oxford on Oct. 22 and may improve a little in health when the break is

---

[705] George Pearson Roxburgh [*8024*: SH 1916–19].
[706] Leonard Douglas Butler [*8126*: SH 1917–19]; unless meaning the Lady Butler referred to later.
[707] The SH Matron: see above **[242]**.

made and he has settled in.[708] Later of course I shall have to tell him the sad news. Is it too much of a digression to say now that I am sure the father will never be able to attend another Council meeting? I believe Mrs. Percival suggests that the resignation of all his positions on Committees &c. shall be sent in when the next notice of those various meetings reach him. Would it not be well to get the notice of the next Council meeting to be sent in as soon as possible? This would give longer notice on the new Chairman.[709]

But to return to your question, I have now had time to think over what Jack has told me. It is not a nice thing to have to do but I feel in justice to Jack and the School House and the College *the* boy who is at the bottom of all the misery caused is *Fawcett.*[710] The name is only too familiar as it was mentioned very frequently in all the trouble that took place in Jack's first term. He is the ring leader and there are others who are only too ready to follow.

I need not mention more than what has happened in this very term. On the very first night in the dormitory all his things were hurled out of the drawers under the beds &c. He was set upon and Fawcett as usual was the leader. I understand that a good deal of horseplay, what Jack calls bullying, took place in the dormitory between first bell and second bell when the Sixth appears and all is quiet. He speaks nicely of Sankey[711] who he looked upon as a friend. It was Fawcett and two or three others who thought it a fine thing to come into Jack's study and make disgusting smells. It was Fawcett who was always doing what he could to get others to make Jack miserable.

Then I think the sausage incident is a good example of what goes on at the Fifth table. The reason why there is often a shortage is that Fawcett and several others put their sausage in their pockets and then pretend that they have not had one. Sometimes a boy in this way gets *three*! That is what happened on that particular Sunday without a doubt. I gather than Swanboro' [*7890*], Bennetts [*7268*], Fowlds [*recte* Folds: *7821*], Tosh [*7769 or 7784*], Liebert [*7749*] and Miller mi [*7827*] could, if they would, speak the truth, give evidence as to this point. They seemed to be all guilty of the trick, and these were the boys who were in the study into which Jack was forced to go. Whether they all took part in the mock trial and punishment I cannot of course say – Fowlds, Bennetts, Swanborough, Tosh and Miller were I believe present. But *Fawcett* was the ring leader and the whole thing took place in Wilding's[712] study. Wilding, Jack says, is better than he used to be but still of a very rough class of boy.

I am sorry about Miller, Jack's old study companion, but he was persuaded by Ingolby[713] to leave Jack, and Ingolby for some reason or another has always been beastly to Jack, finally setting to work to get Miller away into his study.

I need not say any more – it is evident that Fawcett is the black spot and that he has some evil power which enables him to make others like himself.

With regard to Jack's future nothing is as yet settled, but I ought to say that I have hopes that Kindersley of Eton[714] may take him after Christmas. Kindersley said he would be writing to you.

---

[708] On resigning his see Percival retired to a rented house in Banbury Road: Potter, *Headmaster*, p. 254.

[709] On 7 November a letter from Percival was read to the Council resigning the Chairmanship but retaining membership of the body, and Sir Herbert Warren was elected in his place on 5 December: above **[37]**.

[710] Roland Norris Fawcett [*7855*: SH 1915–19]; passed to Sandhurst and commissioned in the 16th Lancers; died in an accident in 1933.

[711] George Ronald Sankey [*8028*: SH 1916–18].

[712] Leslie Armstrong Wilding [*7892*: SH 1915–19].

[713] Geoffrey *Ingoldby* [*7861*: SH 1915–19].

[714] Richard Stephen Kindersley had a House at Eton from 1900 to 1920: *ex inform.* Eton College Archives.

I am much obliged to you for sending on Jack's things; everything arrived safely. The only things missing are all his books, Chapel books and music.

Yours ever,

L.J. Percival.

☐ *Jack Percival went in fact to Radley, and then to Westminster, before proceeding to his grandfather's old College at Oxford.*

Private side

[256]   20 December 1915. Dormitory prefect's deposition
[*HM5 Correspondence/Edelston, Kay & Bryant. MS (text in Head Master's hand)*]

On Monday morning Dec. 20th 1915 I was in No. 7 dormitory, of which I was in charge. I woke about 5 a.m. I believe and soon after got up. Before I got up Bryant[715] came into the dormitory. It was light enough to see. I saw him go to Edelston's[716] bed where he sat on the end of the bed talking. I went round the other dormitories to wake up boys going by early trains. When I came back to No. 7 I found that Bryant was in bed with Edelston – inside and under the clothes lying down flat, with their heads on the pillow. They were talking to one another. There were two beds between Edelston's bed and mine. A few boys had got up – others were in bed asleep. I did not say anything to Bryant or Edelston. I knew that they ought not to be in bed together, and that I ought to have stopped it, but I did not like to take Bryant to account. I left the dormitory soon after coming back, and went out leaving the two in bed together.

Signed Friday March 17th 1916:

Francis Kinloch Middleton Hunter.[717]

Witnesses to signature:

John Edward King.

Maurice Roy Ridley.[718]

☐ *On the basis of other evidence the Head Master had already corresponded with the parents of the accused boys, his initial and subsequent letters phrased in identical terms.*

[257]   8 March 1916. The Head Master to Bryant's father
[*HM5 Correspondence/Edelston, Kay & Bryant. MS file copy*]

School House,

Clifton College, Bristol,

March 8 1916.

Dear Bryant,

Owing to the discovery of moral trouble in this House I have had to make inquiry and I found that your son has been guilty of immoral conduct with another boy, and

---

[715] Cecil Musgrave Beadon Bryant [*7519*: SH 1913–16]; went straight into the Royal Engineers.

[716] Roger Heathcott Edelston [*7577*: SH 1913–16]; went straight into the Royal Flying Corps and was taken prisoner; after the war he became a solicitor.

[717] *7743*: SH 1914–19.

[718] *M230*: 1914–20; House Tutor of SH.

this has become notorious in the House. I am very sorry to say that this leaves me no alternative except to say that I cannot have him here any longer and so I have sent him home. I wish sincerely that I could have dealt with the matter in any other way but I cannot.

Yours very truly,
(signed) J.E. King.

[258]   9 March 1916, J.B. Bryant to the Head Master
[*HM5 Correspondence/Edelston, Kay & Bryant. Holograph*]

Rydens,
Walton-on-Thames.
9/3/16.

Dear King,

My boy has arrived home and I have received your note of March 8th stating that the boy has been guilty of immoral conduct with another. This can bear but one interpretation I suppose, viz. 'sodomy' and I shall be obliged if you will inform me what proof you have of his being guilty of such a serious offence. I would also request the name and address of the boy with whom he is accused of misconducting himself.

Cecil has always been an upright and well behaved lad. He seems to have had no opportunity of answering the charge made against him.

Am I to understand that he has been expelled from the College [and *deleted*]? Such a verdict will very seriously affect his future and render him ineligible for any of the Services.

Yours sincerely,
J.B. Bryant.

[259]   10 March 1916. The Head Master to J.B. Bryant
[*HM5 Correspondence/Edelston, Kay & Bryant. Holograph duplicate*]

Clifton College,
March 10.

Dear Bryant,

I very much regret the sorrow this has caused you but I cannot entertain the request you make me to give you the proofs upon which I thought fit to exercise the duty confided to me by my office.

As to the offence itself, I can only refer you to the terms of my previous letter.

Yours sincerely,
J.E. King.

[260]   13 March 1916, J.B. Bryant to the Head Master
[*HM5 Correspondence/Edelston, Kay & Bryant. Holograph*]

Rydens,
Walton-on-Thames.
13/3/16.

Dear King,

Your letter of the 10th in no way satisfies me, and I cannot acquiesce in the present position. I consider it my right as a parent to be told the exact circumstances which led you to suddenly send my boy away, without giving him any opportunity of defending himself.

As you refuse to answer the enquiries made in my letter, I now ask you for an interview, to be held with my son present. If you will give me an appointment on Thursday or Friday next at about 2.30 p.m., I will come down and see you.

Yours sincerely,
J. Beadon Bryant.

[261]   14 March 1916. The Head Master to J.B. Bryant
[*HM5 Correspondence/Edelston, Kay & Bryant. Holograph duplicate*]

Memorandum from the Headmaster

March 14. 1916

Dear Bryant,

I shall be quite ready to see you about 2.30 p.m. on Friday next. It will however be better for you to see me without the boy.

Yours sincerely,
J.E. King.

☐ *Friday 17 March was the day on which King secured the deposition from the Dormitory Prefect* **[256]**.

[262]   19 March 1916, J.B. Bryant to the Head Master
[*HM5 Correspondence/Edelston, Kay & Bryant. Holograph*]

Rydens,
Walton-on-Thames.
19/3/16.

Dear King,

Following our discussion concerning my son, I write to say I am willing to remove him from the College – it being understood that the charge made against him of immoral conduct with another boy has not been proved, and that this will not prevent his obtaining the character to which his previous good behaviour [entitles *deleted*] and reports entitle him – and I would ask you to write me a letter to this effect.

Whilst in no way admitting the boy's guilt, I fully appreciate, and thank you for, your action in allowing the matter to be settled in this way. Of course a much more satisfactory solution for the boy's future would be if you could see your way to let him come back again, if only to the end of this term. He has had a very severe lesson, and I am sure he would behave himself well. He has always been a good and manly fellow, and I feel certain has not been guilty of anything beyond indiscretion. If he does not return most of the School will think he has been expelled, and the stain will remain with him all his life. He has always been so proud of the School House and done all he could for it, and the deputation of the boys asking that he should not be sent away seems to me a strong point in his favour – and so I must leave the decision to you. If you can see your way to give him the benefit of the doubt and take him back, I shall indeed by very grateful.

Yours sincerely,
J.B. Bryant.

[263]   20 March 1916. The Head Master to J.B. Bryant
[*HM5 Correspondence/Edelston, Kay & Bryant. Holograph duplicate*]

Clifton College,
Bristol.
March 20. 1916

Dear Bryant,
    Though I consider your son behaved improperly – as proved to my mind by the evidence of different boys – if you now remove him from the College I will not report his going or enter him in our records as sent away. I have no wish to injure his future and will – when he comes to need it – give him the certificate for his School career to which his reports entitle him. I am very sorry to say, however, that in view of the circumstances I cannot as Headmaster consent to his coming back to School to finish the term.

Yours sincerely,
J.E. King.

P.S. For the next year or two he should not come to the School but eventually he will be able to return as an O.C.

[264]   March 1916. Head Master's notes on the case
[*HM5 Correspondence/Edelston, Kay & Bryant. Holograph*]

Account.

Early in March Mr Ridley came to tell me that a boy in the School House – Arnold ma[719] – had consulted a master (Mr Lutton Carter)[720] to whom he went this term for private tuition. Arnold said that there was a good deal of filthy talk and also misconduct going on in the School House. He was leaving in the summer and leaving his younger brother[721] behind and a young relation of his was to come to the School House in September. Arnold thought that he ought to speak to his people about the state of things in the House, because as things were he did not like the idea of his young relation coming.
    Mr Ridley saw Arnold at Mr Carter's house and questioned him.
    On the night of Mr Pollen's lecture to the School before Christmas Mr Ridley had just before 9 p.m. looked across the court in the School House into a study – the blind being up – and had seen a boy called Kay[722] and Edelston holding a third boy between them, and was convinced that something indecent was going on. Unfortunately he did not go round to the study. He saw the boys concerned about the matter <afterwards> but they denied that anything was going on except 'ragging', and Edelston and Kay denied being in the study at the time.
    Arnold told Mr Ridley that <from what he had heard he believed that> something had been going on and that the boys concerned had been much frightened about the inquiry.
    Arnold also stated that Bryant was understood to have got into Edelston's bed on the morning of Monday Dec. 20th, the last day of the Christmas term.

---

[719] Reginald Percy Arnold [*7559:* SH 1913–16].
[720] F.L. Carter [*M167*] was later House Tutor SH (1917–18).
[721] Frederick William Arnold [*7560:* SH 1913–17].
[722] George Leonard Kay [*7524:* SH 1913–16].

He also stated that some of the younger boys in the House were corrupted and he mentioned Bennetts.[723]

On March 7th I had different boys out of school and examined them.

As to Bryant and Edelston two [older *inserted then deleted*] Gwatkin and Waugh[724] said there was no doubt about what happened on Dec. 20th, that Edelston and Bryant had been in bed together in no. 7 dormitory. But being in another dormitory they could not give direct evidence. Two boys Ferguson and Wigley[725] said that Bryant came into no. 7 early. They knew he was there but did not see what he did.

Bennetts, when he was getting up in no. 7, dropped a stud or something and was turning up the light when someone said 'Don't turn up the light, [Bennetts *corrected to*] Bryant is here'.

Arnold and Gwatkin say that a boy came into no. 3 dormitory saying 'Come to no. 7 and see Bryant and Edelston in bed together.'

Hunter, the Monitor or Sixth Power in charge of no. 7, when examined, said that on the last day of term he had got up about 5 a.m. and left the dormitory and could tell me nothing about Bryant and Edeleston.

Edeleston and Bennetts. A boy called Waugh, seen first by Mr Ridley and then by me, said that on Tuesday Feb. 8th (as far as could be made out) Edelston had said in his presence that he had 'had' (he could not remember the exact phrase but understood something indecent to be meant) Bennetts in a study. I saw Bennetts – told him what I had heard, and on being questioned he said Edelston had come into the study – got on top of him 'all over him' and attacked him in the region of his parts.

In the evening of March 7th I saw the House Sixth and spoke to them. On being questioned they admitted that the House was not what it ought to be and that they had not been doing enough to stop things, especially filthy talking.

On Tuesday March [*7th*] I asked Edelston about the conduct in the study on the night of Mr Pollen's lecture, and he again denied that there had been anything wrong.

On Wednesday March 8th at 11.15 a.m. I saw Bryant and Edelston. I [told *corrected to*] saw Bryant first and told him he would have to go. 'You have been guilty of immoral conduct' – 'Not so much since my Confirmation' – 'But you have been guilty of it since', and he dissented without saying anything articulate.

I saw Edelston and told him he would have to go. He said 'Why?' – I said there are three things against you – the conduct in the study on the night of Mr Pollen's lecture – what happened on the morning of Dec. 20 in no. 7 – and your conduct with Bennetts. He said 'What did I do to him?'

I gave the boys journey money and sent them off before 12. Sent telegrams to their parents to say they were coming home, and wrote letters to their parents to say why they were coming home.

Before the boys left Mr Ridley saw them and said goodbye. Bryant said nothing.

Mr Ridley said to Edelston – 'I'm sorry about this' – Edeleston said – 'I'm not sorry for myself: it's my own silly fault and I deserve it. I'm sorry for my people.'

Four older boys in the House, on hearing of what had happened, came to appeal for a lighter punishment – a licking or made to leave at the end of term.

---

[723] John Messer Bennetts [*7268*: HHP, SH 1911–18]; at 15 years and 7 months not significantly younger than the others involved (Edelston was a few days short of his 17th birthday).

[724] Norman Wilmshurst Gwatkin [*7497*: SH 1913–16] and James Lister Waugh [*7335*: PHP, SH 1912–17].

[725] Malcolm Hewit Ferguson [*7736*: SH 1914–18] and James Percival Wigley [*7808*: SH 1915–17].

On Wednesday March 15 Mr Edelston[726] called with his brother-in-law Sir G. Toulmin.[727] He discussed the various charges against his son. As to the 20th of December he said that, according to his son, Hunter the Sixth Power had been in the dormitory whilst Bryant was there. I said I would examine Hunter again about this. He said that Bryant had only sat on the end of the bed and talked to [him *corrected to*] Edelston with a rug over him. The rest of the evidence was not enough to hang a cat on.

He asked for leave to examine Bennetts in my presence, as his son could give an account of the way he had spent the afternoon <named>. I declined to allow him to examine Bennetts – but said I would question [him *corrected to*] the boy again. <Mr Edelston said there was 'rottenness' in the House> and I was responsible. I said 'of course I was and had to deal with it'.

Mr Ridley came down to give an account of what he had seen in the study on the night of Mr Pollen's lecture, and was asked why he had not at once gone to the study.

The interview (which lasted about 3 hours) ended in my saying that after I had seen Mr Bryant I would write to Mr Edelston.

I saw Hunter that evening and told him that Edelston said that he <(Hunter)> had been in no. 7 on Dec. 20 all the time that Bryant was there. After a good deal of pressing he said that he was 'practically certain' that Bryant had been in Edelston's bed. Pressed as to how he knew, he eventually admitted that he had been in the dormitory and had seen what had happened. Asked why he had not said so before, he replied that he had not liked 'to give them away'. I told him what his duty was and he admitted he had not done it. He was in the sick room next day with a high temperature, but on Friday he was better and I took down from him the statement enclosed **[257]**. He has not been in charge of a dormitory since.

I saw Bennetts and asked him again about the incident of Feb. 8th with Edelston. He was much confused. Eventually he said 'I don't think it was Edelston' – I said he must know – he had made a serious charge, quite definite – what did he mean? He said 'it was not Edelston it was another boy – on a different day' and he described a different set of circumstances. I could get nothing <else> from <him> but tears and he had to be left as he was stopping out and seemed to be quite unwell. His mother was coming next day and he promised to tell her the truth. He told her, as he had told me, that it was not Edelston as he had first said but another boy. He thought Edelston was condemned for another charge and that to put something else upon him would make no difference.

His father was sent for and it was arranged that the boy – who seemed wholly confused and frightened – should be left alone for the present and should be asked later about things when he had recovered himself in the holidays.

On Friday March 19th I saw Mr Bryant. I went into the evidence about Dec. 20th – including all that Hunter had said. He would not admit the correctness of the evidence. He asked me to examine his boy – who was outside – in his presence. This I did. I asked [him *corrected to*] the boy if he had not admitted being guilty of immoral conduct when questioned on March 8th. He said 'Yes' but said he thought I meant self-abuse. He denied having been in Edelston's bed. I asked him if Hunter had been in the dormitory or not and he said he did not know. I told Mr Bryant when the boy had gone that I could not have the boy back. He said he did not want him to come back. He wanted to take him away himself. I said if he would do so that I

---

[726]   W.S. Edelston of Preston (Lancs.): *Register* (1925), p. 478.

[727]   Sir George Toulmin, Liberal MP for Bury, and a prominent newspaper magnate in Lancashire.

would not report it to the Council as a case of expulsion. He said he would write, and I enclose his letter and my answer [262–3]. I told him it was not necessary to prove the commission of an act of immorality. For two boys to be in bed together was sufficient to justify expulsion.

I wrote to Mr Edelston to tell him what Mr Bryant had asked, and requested him to say if he were ready to do the same. The letter and his answer and another of mine are enclosed.[728]

On Wednesday March 22 Mr Edelston came to see me again with his brother-in-law. The interview was directed to what happened on Dec. 20th. They argued that <it was the last day of term>, there was so much openness in what was done, that vice could not have been intended. There was no daylight at 5 a.m. on Dec. 20th.

Then they endeavoured to separate the case of Bryant from that of Edelston. Bryant was a strong boy with athletic prestige. Hunter was afraid of him. The case of Edelston and Bryant could not be on the same footing. Eventually I said 'What do you ask for?' – 'For Edelston to come back for the Summer term – and his mother will be in Clifton a good deal to look after him'. He also said 'I should not ask for my son to return for next term if I knew that Bryant was going to be here' – I said 'Do you ask for an answer now?' He said 'Yes' – I said I could not give an answer then. My impulse was to meet him if I could but I must have time to consider. I had to consider Bryant's case as well as his son's. I would consider the matter carefully and write to him as soon as I could. As Mr Edelston was leaving he said 'Can I trust you?' – and I said 'Yes'.

I considered the matter for a day and wrote to him next afternoon – letter enclosed.

I have not mentioned the case of the boy Kay who was sent home at the same time as Bryant and Edelston but for different reasons. I have allowed Kay to finish out the term here, because immediately after he had gone, I found out that there was no charge against him supported by direct evidence. Mr Edelston, who knows Mr Kay,[729] asked me on March 22 if Kay's case had been settled. I told him I had seen Mr Kay but it had not been settled. It has not, for I have not yet told Mr Kay whether the boy is to leave at the end of term or not. This is what Mr Edelston may refer to when he speaks about my 'personal honour'.

I add a letter from a clergyman in Exeter acting as tutor to a boy called Row[730] absent for this term whom I should have examined – had he been here. The father consented to his boy's being questioned as his letter shows.

[265]   6 April 1916. S.E. Baker to the Head Master
[*HM5 Correspondence/Edelston, Kay & Bryant. Holograph*]

Stanley, Wasbrough, Doggett and Baker, Solicitors
18 Clare Street,
Bristol,
April 6. 1916.
Dear Dr King,

I am enclosing the draft of the letter to Mr Edelston for your approval. I think he ought to have a reply as soon as possible, so should be much obliged if you

---

[728] The other letters King refers to are retained in the same file.
[729] W.P. Kay of Lower Darwen (Lancs.): *Register* (1925), p. 475.
[730] James Elswood Row [*7761*: SH 1914–19]; the father was John Row of Powderham Crescent, Exeter [*Register* (1925), p. 488] and the tutor was J.H. Prince, Vicar of St Thomas's, Exeter.

would return it to me with your comments by next post, or at any rate by Monday, if you can. When I was thinking over the position after our conferences it occurred to me whether a possible solution of the position might be to let the boy return for next term as a day boy living in Bristol. If this were consented to by you it would I suppose be necessary for his mother to take a house or rooms for the time being in Bristol. I expect you have already considered the possibility of this being done and decided that it would not do, but I thought I would mention it as I was writing as the only possibility that I can think of to help the father and in order that no chance of solving the problem may be overlooked.

With kind regards,

Yours faithfully,

Sidney E. Baker.

[266]   7 April 1916. The Head Master to Baker
[*HM5 Correspondence/Edelston, Kay & Bryant. Holograph file copy*]

April 7. 1916
Say's Hotel,
Aldeburgh.

Dear Mr Baker,

I return the enclosed of which I quite approve. The suggestion that Edelston should come back to Clifton for a term and live with his mother had occurred to me but I have not mentioned it to the father. I think it might be accepted on the ground that Edelston is the less guilty perhaps of the two concerned in the incident of Dec. 20th. Would it do if you added to your letter that you were prepared to suggest to me that, though you knew that I could not consent to the boy's returning as a boarder, I should allow the boy to remain at the College for a term as a day boy under the care of his mother. I should prefer that the boy left altogether but there would be less harm in his presence as a day boy under a parent's care.

Yours faithfully,

J.E. King.

[267]   10 April 1916. Telegram from Baker to the Head Master
[*HM5 Correspondence/Edelston, Kay & Bryant. MS on Post Office form*]

To Dr King Says Hotel Aldeburgh

Letter received. Difficulty as to Bryant [*recte* Edelston] suggests itself. If he were accepted as day boy would not Bryant claim same treatment? How would that affect your view? Please wire reply early tomorrow so that I can see Abbot at eleven.

Baker c/o Stanleys Bristol.

[268]   [11 April 1916]. Telegram from the Head Master to Baker
[*HM5 Correspondence/Edelston, Kay & Bryant. Holograph file copy*]

Baker c/o Stanley's, Bristol.

If risk of having Bryant back better not make offer to other. Have sent letter from Kay.

King.

[269]   11 April 1916. Baker to the Head Master
[*HM5 Correspondence/Edelston, Kay & Bryant. Holograph*]

Stanley, Wasbrough, Doggett and Baker, Solicitors
18 Clare Street,
Bristol,
April 11. 1916.

Dear Dr King,
I received your telegram this morning and subsequently your letter with its enclosures. Since receiving these I have talked the position over again with Mr Abbot and he agrees with me that under the circumstances it would not do to make any offer of the nature of allowing Edelston to return as a day boy.

I am consequently writing to Mr Edelston to-night in accordance with the draft letter I sent to you saying that you cannot re-consider the case.

It looks as though Mr Kay, Mr Edelston and perhaps also Mr Bryant are working together, and I should therefore strongly advise you not to write any letters to them without first conferring with Mr Abbot or myself.

I am sorry to have had to trouble you during your vacation.

With kind regards,
Yours sincerely,
S.E. Baker.

[270]   17 April 1916. Baker to the Head Master
[*HM5 Correspondence/Edelston, Kay & Bryant. Holograph*]

Stanley, Wasbrough, Doggett and Baker, Solicitors
18 Clare Street,
Bristol,
April 17. 1916.

Dear Dr King,
Thanks for your two letters. I see no need for you to return to Clifton.

I am enclosing a copy of a letter of the 14th inst. which we have received from Mr Edelston and of the reply which I have sent today after consultation with Mr Abbot.

We should like to have your views as to what further reply should be sent to Mr Edelston and in particular dealing with the passages of his letter which I have marked in pencil.

It is of course possible that Mr Edelston may contemplate taking some sort of proceedings against Mr Ridley, and you may think therefore that Mr Ridley should know what is going on.

I have no knowledge of what sort of certificate e.g. the Army would require, but we must of course be careful not to promise what we may later on find ourselves unable to fulfil.

Please excuse the rather rough copying of letters, due to war time and diminished staff.

Yours faithfully,
S.E. Baker.

[271]   17 April 1916. The Chairman of Council to the Head Master
[*HM5 Correspondence/Edelston, Kay & Bryant. Holograph*]

The Palace,
Hereford.
April 17.1916.

Dear King,

First of all I must ask your indulgence – I made a mistake and sent my reply to David, and he has just returned it.[731]

I am sorry for this new trouble, and I hope you may be able to insist on the withdrawal of those 2 boys.

If there is any evidence against them of bad tone, lewd talk or anything of that sort, their being in bed together should be conclusive.

Under such circumstances a father would be mad to take you into court, and by so doing inflict a public stain on his son which would cling to him through life.

So far as I understand the matter I think your duty to the moral life of the School justifies you, and indeed this necessitates your taking a certain amount of legal risk, if a parent proves to be a madman who to punish the School does not hesitate to inflict such a stain on his own son.

Yours sincerely,
J. Hereford.

[272]   20 April 1916. H.N. Abbot to the Head Master (at Say's Hotel, Aldeburgh)
[*HM5 Correspondence/Edelston, Kay & Bryant. Holograph*]

Shannon Court
20/4/16.

Dear H.M.,

Mr Baker has gone for a short holiday so his clerk brought me your letter, and the Bishop's [*above*], before sending it after him. I write therefore without having had the advantage of consulting with him.

The Bishop's letter is on the right note, and shows you will have his support if need be, and I am very pleased you wished me to see it, tho' it is amusingly provoking that he sent it to David by mistake.

I think the Edelston situation is improving; but whether it does or it doesn't, after all the only thing that really matters is the good of the School, irrespective of any threat of litigation and its consequences, financial and such like; and one cannot justify (at least so it seems to me) allowing a boy such as the original three, or such as this fourth boy,[732] of whom I now hear for the first time, to come back.

But here I an encroaching on Mr Baker's province, as you ask his advice; so you are welcome to discount my opinion, which is determined not by considerations of the legal aspect of any particular line of treatment, but of how a School like ours ought to be carried on, cost what it may.

Yours sincerely,
H.N. Abbot

---

[731] David had departed for Rugby six years before.
[732] Bennetts.

[273]   20 April 1916. The Chairman of Council to the Head Master
[HM5 Correspondence/Edelston, Kay & Bryant. Holograph]

The Palace,
Hereford.
April 20.1916

Dear King,

I have been reading over your letter and thinking about the case of the 2 boys you sent home, and of the risk if the parent takes you into court.

I think the fact of the 2 boys being in bed together, if admittedly boys of bad tone or lewd language, should be sufficient to make you quite safe, but I see you say you withdrew the charges as to misconduct this term. This withdrawal would I fear rather weaken your case; but I suppose you only meant that the evidence, though establishing bad tone and bad influence, was perhaps too weak to satisfy you as to immediate expulsion, if it had not been accompanied by the evidence of last term's misconduct. Anyhow I don't see what you can do but take any risk there may be and present a firm front to this parent.

If a man of any sense, he will be shy of publicly branding his own son with a mark that will stick to him through life.

If you took these boys back all your other parents would feel that you were not protecting their boys, and others would be deterred from sending boys. The result of a trial might even do the School good, in shewing that you insist on keeping up the moral standard.

Yours sincerely,
J. Hereford.

☐ *Bryant, Edelston and Kay left immediately but were not formally expelled. All went straight into the forces: Bryant to the Royal Engineers, Edelston to the Royal Flying Corps and Kay to the London Scottish. After the war Edelston and Kay became solicitors. Bennetts completed his schooldays, and was accepted into Sandhurst in 1918.*

The boy with a bullet in his pocket

[274]   21 November 1918. The Head Master to F.S. Philpott[733]
[HM5 Correspondence/Philpott. Typescript copy]

21 November 1918.

Dear Mr Philpott,

I am very sorry I was out when you called last Tuesday. I have however since then been making further enquiry. On Saturday evening, November 2 the keys of Mr Titcombe and a model engine were taken from the Drawing Room. On [Saturday *corrected to*] Sunday morning it was found that 3 bunches of keys and 2 loose keys were missing from the Porter's Lodge. Damage was done to the scientific apparatus in the inner quadrangle and two cupboards were opened in the Town Rooms. The engine and the keys, but not all, have since then been found about the premises. Your

---

[733] In the address the initials were incorrectly inverted.

son[734] came to his Town Room at 8 p.m. <or before> on November 2nd, but on the ground of headache and sickness obtained leave to go home. If he had felt ill there is no reason why he should have come; he could have brought a note on Monday. Your son tells me that after leaving the Town Room he went to the lavatories, and was there for ¼ of an hour and then went home.

On the evidence of another boy, however, your son went with him to the Drawing Room and they took away the engine. They afterwards went to the Town Rooms, unlocked the doors, and opened the cupboards. A cup which they took out was found in the room on Sunday morning. About 9 p.m. they met two boys and told them what they had done in the Drawing Room. On the evidence of the three boys your son produced a revolver. One of these boys states that your son said he had taken cartridges from the Armoury and said the revolver was loaded. Another boy stated that your son did the damage to the scientific apparatus in the inner Quadrangle in the presence of other boys. Two other boys tell me that your son showed them about a fortnight ago a master's key and said that he had a stroke of luck in getting <it>. These two boys state that your son said to them that he had been in the Drawing Room when the model engine was taken.

I have seen your son twice. He denies the statements of these five boys. He denies going to the Drawing Room on November 2nd, having a revolver, opening the Town Rooms, seeing the other boys and the statements they have made about him. When I saw him on Tuesday I told him to turn out his pockets. He had a cartridge which Colonel Rintoul tells me [275] is the same as that used for miniature rifle practice by the O.T.C. Your son declined to tell me how he got it.

He was absent last Monday afternoon. In the evening it is admitted that he went to the house of the boy called Newman, who states that he was with your son in the Drawing School on November 2nd. Your son went with a boy called Hall (now absent from School) and a Midshipman called Davies, and they pressed Newman to give himself up as the boy who took the engine.[735]

I shall be glad to see you about this matter when you are well enough. Any evening will I think suit me. It is difficult to believe that all these five witnesses are to be discredited as well as other statements which have been made to me.

Yours very truly,

[*blank for signature*], Headmaster.

[275]   21 November 1918. D. Rintoul to the Head Master
[*HM5 Correspondence/Philpott. MS*]

Engineer Contingent Officers' Training Corps.
Clifton College
Nov. 21st 1918.

Memo. from O.C. *to* The Headmaster.

The enclosed cartridge[736] is the same as we use for miniature rifle practice in Big Bath.

D. Rintoul, Lt Col.

Found on Philpott by me on Tuesday Nov. 19.

J.E.K.

---

[734]   Clifford Sydney Philpott [*8271*: ST Jan–Dec 1918].

[735]   There were too many of these names in the School for identification to be made.

[736]   The live .22 round was found still enclosed with Rintoul's note in 2011. It has now been de-activated.

[276]   29 November 1918. F.S. Philpott to the Head Master
[*HM5 Correspondence/Philpott. MS*]

67, Pembroke Road,
Clifton, Bristol,
Nov. 29/18.

Dear Sir,
I am deeply overwhelmed with the misdeeds of my son which have come to my knowledge since seeing you. He has confessed to having participated in all you mentioned in your letters, and I am sure he is penitent. I am thoroughly convinced that Pauli[737] has been the cause of all the trouble and apparently the master mind to plan and carry out with the assistance of boys younger than himself all the arrangements which have led to my son's undoing. The bag of tools mentioned is a motor-cycle set which was given to him; the jemmy a carpet-tack lifter; the revolver belongs to my elder boy and is not in working order, and [that *deleted*] my son's statement that it was loaded was mere bombast on his part. The removable board in his bedroom was known to his mother, but not suspected by her as a receptacle for articles he wished to hide. He has never taken anything from the home. I thank you for Mr Newman's address, and called there last evening, but he was from home. I desire to express my deepest regret to him, and endeavour to make good any loss he may have suffered.

I note it is your wish that my son should not return to School.

I cannot close without expressing how deeply sensible I am of the kindly consideration you have given this regrettable matter and trust it may prove a turning point for the better in his further career.

I am, dear Sir, yours faithfully,
F.S. Philpott.

☐ *Clifford Philpott served as Major with the Cheshire Regiment in the Second World War and was killed on active service in 1946.*

---

[737] Kenneth Roger Pauli [*7712*: NT 1914–18].

SECTION XIII:
PLAYING THE GAMES

[277]   15 February 1864. Introduction of gymnastics: circular to parents
[*Guard Book 1860–77. Printed*]

February 15th, 1864.

Dear Sir,
As many representations have been made to the Council of the desirability of introducing into the College a system of gymnastic training, it is proposed to build a Gymnasium if a wish for one is expressed by such a number of parents as would warrant the expenditure. But, gymnastic apparatus without supervision and direction in its use being both dangerous and detrimental to the majority of boys, it would be necessary to have a qualified instructor always on the spot.

The Council, therefore, propose to engage Mr Maclaren of Oxford,[738] the most accomplished and scientific gymnastic trainer in England; the benefits of his system being incalculable, especially to delicate boys. For his services and those of an assistant, he would require an annual fee of three guineas for each pupil. The Council consider the advantages so great that they are willing to build the Gymnasium, if as many as 100 parents wish their boys to avail themselves of it, paying the fee above-mentioned.

I enclose a short sketch of Mr Maclaren's system in his own words.

If you wish your son to become a pupil in the event of the proposed plan being carried out, I shall feel obliged by an early answer.

I am, dear Sir, yours faithfully,
J. Percival, Head Master.

☐ *The Gymnasium was built in 1867.*

[278]   1866. Big Side Levée. First rules
[*VI/Big Side Levée Register vols. 1–2 (1866–84), ff. 1–2. MS*][739]

---

[738] Archibald MacLaren opened a gym in Oxford in 1856 and published *A System of Physical Education: Theoretical and Practical* (1869) and other guides to his system, which was taken up by the Army and many public schools. He also founded the prep school in Summertown now called Summer Fields: *ODNB*.
[739] The early Sixth/BSL Books have been bound into groups with single foliations for each bound volume.

General Rules.

1. The Head of the School shall be President of Big Side Levée, and also of the School Levée; and he shall enter the proceedings in a book, which he shall keep for that purpose, and for which he is responsible to Big Side.

2. Caps and members of the XI are members of Big Side, as are all who are not fags. Any member of Big Side may call a Levée.

Foot-ball Rules.

1. That, when there is an extra half-holiday, there [shall] be two Big Sides, (weather permitting), and also, when there is not, unless a Big Side Levée shall determine to the contrary; provided that, if there be only one, it shall be played on Thursday.

N.B. The Head-Master will be judge as to weather.

2. All boys who play on Big Side shall be bound to attend, unless they obtain a note signed by the Head of their House, and countersigned by masters appointed for the purpose.

N.B. Here and elsewhere the Head of the Town is spoken of as a Head of a House.

3. There shall be a compulsory Little Side on Thursday for boys below Big Side; their match shall be arranged for them by the Head of the School-House and the Head of the Town or by deputies appointed by them; leave of absence being given in the same <way> as in Big Side.

4. Caps shall be given by the Heads of Houses with the con[sent] of the praepostors in the House. If there be a disagreement the majority shall decide.

5. Praepostors may take caps if they choose without leave from any one.

6. Praepostors may exempt themselves from Big Side.

7. No punt-about shall be allowed before 11 a.m.

8. No one shall be allowed to drop or place kick on Big Side under penalty of a fine of 6d. for each offence.

9. Hacking in a scrummage shall not be allowed; except [accidently *corrected to*] accidentally in kicking the ball.

10. The Rugby rules shall be adopted except in any case in which they may clash with the preceding.[740]

These rules are not to be altered without the sanction of the Head-Master.

[279]   21 December 1868. Introduction of swimming: circular to parents
[*Guard Book 1860–77. Printed*]

The College, Clifton,
21st December, 1868.

Dear Sir,

I beg to inform you that we have now added to the College two Swimming Baths, one a large open bath for Summer use, the other a smaller covered and Tepid Bath for the Winter.[741]

As the expenses of these Baths will be considerable, and as it will be part of the duty of the Swimming Master, who will be in attendance whenever they are open, to see that every boy who goes there learns to swim, it is proposed to charge every

---

[740] *The Laws of Football as played at Rugby School* (1845), which duly formed the basis of *The Rugby Laws of Football as played at Clifton College* (1869); *cf.* Dunning, 'Origins of football', pp. 173–5.
[741] Use was already made of various public baths: Christie, *History*, p. 318, quoting SH boy's letter of 1867 printed in *Cliftonian* XXIII (1913–15), pp. 32–3 (misdated 1866, as evident from report of Chapel opening).

boy at the rate of £1 a year for bathing and instruction in swimming. The Boarding House Master will pay 5s. of this sum, so that the annual charge to the parent will be only 15s.

If I do not hear from you to the contrary I shall assume that you wish your son to avail himself of the opportunities thus offered; and the following charges will be made to you in future: for the Summer term 10s., for each of the other two terms 2s. 6d.

I am, dear Sir, your obedient servant,

J. Percival.

[280]   30 May 1874. Perils of cricket
[CC Company Minute Book 3, p. 305. MS]

Damage by cricket balls.

A letter was read from Mr C.C. Prichard of Worcester Lodge complaining [*of*] the damage done to his greenhouses by cricket balls and the Secretary was instructed to see that steps were taken to prevent the balls from going over.

[281]   15 October 1877. Reporting matches and removing buckles
[VI/Big Side Levée Registers vols 1–2 (1866–84), f. 132. MS]

Monday Oct. 16th. 1877.

It was resolved:

That House matches be begun on Thursday October 18th.

Vidal[742] and Richardson ma[743] were appointed to send up accounts of matches to the *Field* &c.

It was also resolved:

That in all matches the forwards wear their jerseys over their trousers to prevent scratches from buckles &c., and that if possible the latter be cut off, as well as brace-buttons.

J.W. Cawston.[744]

[282]   19 October 1877. Shortening the game
[VI/Big Side Levée Registers vols 1–2 (1866–84), f. 133. MS]

Oct. 19th. 1877.

It was resolved:

(1) That no football-game last more than an hour and a quarter in future.

(2) That all passing back of the ball from the scrimmage be abolished, and that umpires be requested to treat it as any other case of off-side play.

(3) That the two lower Fifth Forms <taken together> have for the future two representatives instead of one in Big-Side Levée.

[283]   25 October / 9 December 1895. The Sixth instructs the Head Master in the value of discipline, and the Head Master responds
[VI/Big Side Levée Registers 1–4, (1871–1906), ff. 202–3. MS]

[742] William Sealy Vidal [*1392*: BH 1873–7].
[743] Ernest Lamont Richardson [*1115*: ST 1872–8].
[744] Sir John Westerman Cawston [*1182*: SH 1872–8], Head of the School 1877–8; knighted 1919.

Friday Oct. 25th 1895.

The Head of the School[745] addressed the Sixth on the subject of an occurrence which had taken place on the day before and had been brought to their notice by a master.

The following motion was passed:

The Sixth, having heard that licking is considered by the authorities an unconstitutional penalty for cutting a School game, think it right not to conceal from the Head Master their impression that the penalty is the customary one for that offence in all Houses but one. (The Sixth in this House said that the custom had fallen into disuse within the last two years, but that they seriously thought it necessary to revert to the old order.) The Sixth would also represent to the Headmaster their fear that a change in this custom which they believe to be well-known throughout the School might possibly be attended by grave consequences.

A vote of censure was passed upon two members of the Sixth for kicking a football against the Chapel.

The School Captain of the Rifle Corps resigned his post.

[signed] L.B. Fyffe,
[counter-signed] M.G.G.

[Minuted by the Head Master] I must make two comments upon the above.

The last item is entered in error. As the Captain of the Rifle Corps is not appointed by the Sixth, it is not to the Sixth that his resignation can be offered. Any such action on his part is therefore void of effect.

With reference to the punishment for cutting games, as there was evidently a discrepancy between the ancient constitution and the modern practice, I have had a conference with the Heads of Houses. As it seems that the present practice, as described in the above minute, is working well, I am willing to confirm it, but with two small qualifications: (1) Very strict proof should be forthcoming that any such offence was intentional; (2) In the case of young boys the extreme penalty should generally be waived for a first offence. These points are not new, for they have been recognized by the good sense of the Sixth for some time past; but it is just as well to put them formally on record.

Dec. 9th 1895.   M.G.G.

[284]   19 May 1899. Summary of rules and customs
[VI/Big Side Levée Sixth Register IV, 1899–1906. MS]

The following statement of rules and customs has been drawn up by a representative Committee of the Sixth, and is correct up to the present time <1899>.

Fagging

All members of the Third and Fourth Forms are fags except Caps, Colours, shooting Eights, [Gymnasium Eights *deleted*], and School representatives for boxing and racquets.

Generally any fag may be ordered by any Sixth, or Sixth power of his House, to perform any service (within reason).

The *particular* duties of a fag may be divided into School and House duties.

(1) School duties are net-fagging and roller fagging in the Summer term.

---

[745] Laurence Bruce Fyffe [*3986*: ST 1888–96], Head of the School 1895–6.

(2) House duties. In all Houses except N.T. and S.T. a certain number of fags are allotted to each Sixth and are on special duty for one week at a time. The fag on duty must fetch his Sixth's tea and boots, clean his study if necessary and perform other necessary offices as his Sixth requires.

In all Houses the fags must tear scent for any members of the House going hare, and keep the Library or Town Room in order.

In return for their services the Sixth is supposed to exercise a certain friendly supervision over his special fag's work and deportment generally.[746]

Library

The School Library is open to all above the Fourth Forms every whole school day from 12.15 – 1.15, and from 2 – 5 (on Sundays 2 – 4); and on half holidays from 2 – 3, and if wet from 3 – 4. It is also open for those not in form during other school hours. Those below the Fifths are permitted to use the Library if they give in their names at the beginning of each term, and attend at least four times a fortnight. All entering the Library must enter their names in a book kept for that purpose.

The Sixth furnishes eight librarians, to each of whom is allotted one hour a week in which his presence in the Library is required. These librarians to be volunteers if possible, but in the case of volunteers falling short, the old compulsory system to be re-instated.

The duties of librarians are:

(1) To see that absolute silence is maintained in the Library.

(2) To give help as to finding books etc.

(3) To keep their hours regularly, and in case of unavoidable absence to provide a substitute.

The Library is also used once a fortnight for School debates.

Cricket

The cricket of the School is organized officially by the Captain of the School XI, who [may or may not be *corrected to* is generally *then to*] must be a member of the Sixth, and the cricket of the House by the Captain of the House XI, who will be the senior Colour in the House. If there be no Colours in a House, the oldest member of the House XI takes the captaincy. In the case of two members of equal standing in the House XI, of whom one is in the VI and the other not, the VI has superior claim to the captaincy.

A. School cricket.

(i) All School matches and XIs to represent the School are arranged by the Captain of the XI, with the sanction of the Head Master.

(ii) With the exception of Big Side, which is managed by the Captain of the XI, the School play on half holidays according to their forms. These are divided into two groups, one consisting of the VIth and Vths, and the other of the IVths and IIIrds, every form playing every form in their respective groups as arranged by the Head of the School. Each form has its own cricket materials and is entirely under the management of the form captain, who also arranges about form 2nd XI matches, if there are any. The 2nd XI of the VI counts as a first XI. (In 1898 two equal XIs were played).[747]

---

[746] *Cf.* Newbolt, *Diary of a Fag*, pp. 48–50 ('the chief privilege of a fag was to get out of his master [i.e. Sixth] as many "cons.," or helps in construing, as might be necessary').

[747] The two latter sentences struck through.

(iii) A bat is presented to any player who scores 50 runs in a School match.

(iv) All colours are given by the Captain of the School XI. The colours given are a first XI and a XXII of which the upper half has the additional distinction of a 2nd XI coat. XI colours and XXII colours are retained always, when once gained; but 2nd XI colours are given up at the end of each year.[748]

(v) The XI and XXII net practices are arranged by the Captain of the XI, who also arranges about fagging at those nets.

B. House cricket.

(i) The Houses play in House matches according to a 3-round scheme, arranged and drawn by Big Side Levée, and each House providing a first and second XI, [P.H. counting as a 2nd XI *deleted*].

(ii) House games take place on the evenings of all whole school days at 6.30 and last till 7.25. Each House plays by itself, and these games are looked after by the captains of the House XIs.

(iii) On all whole school days at 2 o'clock and on all half holidays at 6.15 there are House nets. The North Town are permitted to have their nets on whole school days at 12.15 instead of 2 p.m.

(iv) Choice of grounds for nets and evening games depends on the order in the previous year's House matches.

Football

Two main principles underlie all Clifton football:

(i) Its management is *entirely* in the hands of the Sixth.

(ii) All the distinctions are House and not School distinctions, and thus the House football is the vital part of all Clifton football.

Football is compulsory for all who can play. The games are organized as follows:

(i) School games. There are 9 School games, Big Side, Second Big Side, Middle Side, and six Little Sides, in which players are placed according to merit at a meeting of the Heads of Houses at the beginning of each football term. The Head of the School is ex officio Captain of Big Side, and should therefore take his cap, if not already possessing it,[749] and the captain of every game must be a Sixth. The captains of games are responsible for picking up sides every half holiday and it is their duty to see that all attend and play hard.

(ii) House Little Sides are played twice a week on the mornings of whole school days. Two Houses play together, the backs of one playing with the forwards of the other. The Houses play in Little Sides according to a scheme lasting for seven years, at the end of which each House will have played with every other; the scheme is then made out anew from the first round of House matches in the last year of the seven. 1897 was the beginning of such a series. The fifteens are made up by the House captain who is the senior Cap in the House Sixth or – if there is no Cap in the House Sixth – the Head of the House . <Not necessary as long as he is a VI or VI Power>.

(iii) House matches for 1st and 2nd XVs are played on the league system, every House playing every other (P.H. counting as a 2nd XV). Caps are House distinctions

---

[748] This custom, which required the physical removal of light blue trimmings on white blazers, was recalled along with related lore by Sir Francis Newbolt in *Diary of a Fag*, pp. 116–17.

[749] An embarrassing exception was Spencer Hampden Nash [*1416*: ST 1874–81], Head of the School 1879–81, a brilliant scholar but deemed incapable of playing in any game above the first Little Side. He did not take his cap until his second year as Head, and then delegated the captaincy: *ibid.*, pp. 140–3.

given by the House Sixth. It is usual to consult the Head of the School before giving a cap, but his consent is not necessary. The number of caps in the School is generally about 22 but there is no fixed limit, unwillingness to lower the value of a House cap being sufficient security that caps will not be given to players beneath a certain standard.

(iv) School matches are arranged by the Head of the School, who is ex officio Captain of the School XV. If he is physically unfit to play football or not good enough to play for the School, the senior Cap in the Sixth playing is captain on the field.

Fifteens to represent the School are chosen by the Head of the School, subject to the Head Master's consent.

The oldest remaining Cap is considered the football representative, and is a member of Big Side Levée (ex officio), besides being a steward at the Concert; but, unless a Sixth, he has no right to captain a side in any School game.

Runs

Every boy in the School, save those who have obtained a doctor's leave of exemption, is compelled to run in one of four packs. Each pack is composed, as far as possible, of boys of the same age and strength, so that no member may be injured by continually straining himself to keep up with better runners than himself.

The four packs are known by the names of 'Upper'. 'Lower', 'Third' and 'Fourth' packs. The leaders of the Third and Fourth packs (two for each) volunteer their services at the first Sixth meeting of the Easter term. The leaders of the Upper and Lower packs are elected at the same meeting. The leader of the Lower pack is generally the Head of the School. The leader of the Upper pack, otherwise known as the 'Huntsman' or 'Holder of Big Side Bags' is generally the member of the Sixth who came in highest in the previous year's Long Penpole. These leaders, besides actually leading the packs or providing substitutes to do so, have to post notices of runs in the Cloisters, and in the case of the Upper and Lower packs, have to provide 'hares'.

The hares, before they start, must indicate to the leader of the pack the general direction of the course they intend to take, so that if the scent is lost at one point, it may be found at another. The hares are supposed to lay the scent so clearly as possible without stoppages or feints; to avoid crossing hedges or forbidden land, and to provide water-jumps whenever possible.

The 'whips' are chosen by the leaders of the first two packs from among the Sixth, the Caps, and successful runners of the previous years. There are twelve whips for each of the packs, running in three sets of four each on appointed days. The duties of the whips are to keep the pack as near the leader as possible, to prevent shirking of jumps, and to let the leaders [*recte* leader] know when he is setting too fast a pace.

The fourth pack comprises the smallest and weakest runners in the School. Its pace is little more than a walk; in fact at least half of the 'run', which is never more than about four or five miles, is walked. The leader of this pack should always be in the rear.

The third pack goes somewhat faster and somewhat further than the fourth.

The third and fourth packs have no regular whips, but their leaders generally ask some of the bigger members to act as whips.

The only difference between the Lower and Upper packs is that the Upper generally runs a little further and faster than the Lower. The length of the runs depends upon the hares; the average length of Upper pack runs is about ten miles. Both the packs follow scent.

Towards the end of the running term – the first term of the year – two cross-country races are held. The 'Long Penpole', a race of about ten miles, is open to those *over* sixteen years old who have run in not less than eight runs in the Upper pack, or six runs if members of the Cadet Corps. The 'Short Penpole', between seven and eight miles, is for those under sixteen who have run in a similar number of Lower pack runs. These runs count as part of the Athletic Sports held about a fortnight later, and those who arrive within ten minutes of the winner of the Long, or five minutes of the winner of the Short, score a certain number of marks for their House. Besides these races some Houses have separate races for those under sixteen.

Fives and Racquets

The subscription of the 'Fives' Courts in the School is either 21/- for life or 5/- per term – after 5 payments the subscriber becoming a life member. There are in all nine courts, two of which are for bat fives and the remainder for hand fives. These courts are obtained by anyone through the Heads of their Houses, who meet every day at 11 o'clock in the Sixth Room for that purpose. The choice of courts is in the callover order, beginning with that Head of House who stands highest on the callover list; on the second day the first choice rests with that Head of House who is next in callover order, and so on throughout the term. A notice is published every morning in the 'break' on the School notice board, shewing which Houses have the various courts. If [*word repeated*] any court is left unoccupied for a quarter of an hour after the time at which it is nominally engaged anyone is at liberty to take it for the rest of the hour.[750] On half holidays courts occupied from 3 – 4 may be retained until 5.

House matches in fives are played in the Lent term. Each House is represented by three pairs, and that House which wins two out of these three sets of games wins the match. School doubles and singles in hand fives and School singles in bat fives are played, the two latter in the Lent term, the first in the Xmas term. The prizes are provided from the School funds.

The Racquet Court is open to all members of the School without subscription, and they have the free use of the services of the Racquet Professional. The court is secured by application at break on the day for which it is wanted, for which purpose a book is kept at the Professional's shop. In racquets also House matches are played. Foreign matches are played with other schools and clubs, the first player being allowed to choose his partner. There is a competition in the Christmas and Lent terms for the right to be in the first 'Six'. The racquet representative is a member of the Sixth elected by them to arrange School matches etc. in racquets.

May 19th 1899   [*signed*] M.G. Glazebrook.

☐ *The greatest sporting event (and for many people the greatest event of all) in Clifton's history was a Junior School cricket match played over six days in June 1899, when the 13 year-old Arthur Collins amassed 628 not out, which has stood ever since as the highest individual score in any form of cricket.*[751]

---

[750] Sir Francis Newbolt (*Diary of a Fag*, pp. 62–3) explains the etiquette.
[751] The match generated worldwide interest as news of Collins's mounting score was flashed round the Empire, and its story has been retold many times: see particularly John Arlott, *The Boy Collins* (1959); D.O. Winterbottom, *A Season's Fame* (Bristol Branch of the Historical Association pamphlet 77, 1991); A.J.A. de Sybel, 'The Soldier Cricketer', *Clifton Magazine* (2007), pp. 7–11.

[285]   22–27 June 1899. Collins 628*

[*Cricket Scorebooks. MS on printed scoresheet; printed matter here bold, omitting some headings and all sections not used.[752] This is a fair copy version made at the end of the season. The match scorebook survives but the figures for Collins' score cannot now be read with certainty; those in the copy here transcribed make a total of 631. Other inaccuracies will also be noted*]

Match played at Clifton College **between** Clark's House and North Town **on** June 22nd & 23rd 1899

FIRST INNINGS

1	Collins, A.E.J.	2 2 2 1 2 5 2 2 3 2 4 1 3 2 4 2 2 4 4 1 2 5 2 2 3 2 5 2 5	
		2 2 2 2 1 3 2 4 2 2 3 2 1 3 2 2 2 2 2 3 2 2 2 1 2 2 2 2 2	
		4 4 4 2 2 2 2 2 4 3 1 2 2 3 2 4 2 1 3 2 3 4 3 4 2 2 2 5 2	
		2 2 2 2 2 2 2 2 1 4 4 2 1 1 3 3 2 2 2 1 4 3 2 2 2 2 2 1 3	
		2 4 2 4 4 1 3 2 2 3 3 4 2 2 1 2 2 2 1 2 2 4 3 3 2 2 2 1 1	
		1 1 2 2 1 2 1 1 4 2 2 1 1 2 2 2 2 4 2 2 2 2 1 2 4 1 2 3 3	
		2 2 2 2 2 2 4 4 1 2 2 3 2 1 3 1 1 2 2 2 4 2 2 3 4 2 4 1 2	
		1 3 1 1 2 3 2 1 6 2 3 2 2 2 4 2 2 1 2 1 2 2 2 2 2 2 2 1	
		1 2 4 3 2 2 3 2 1 2 2 1 1 1 1 4 4 2 2 1 2 3 2 1 2 1 2 1 2	
		1 2 2 3 2 2 1 2 3 1 1 2 2 2 3 4 1 1 2 2 1 2 1	
		not out	628
2	Champion, A.M.	2 2 1 2 2 2 2 1 1 2 2 2 3 3	
		caught Monteath [*bowled*] Rendall	27
3	Gilbert, H.P.	1 1 2 2 3	
		bowled Crew	9
4	Studdy, H.A.	1 1 2 1 3	
		caught Davies [*bowled*] Sainsbury	8
5	Shirreff, C.M.	1 1 2 2	
		bowled Crew	6
6	Galwey, A.W.	1 1 1 2 2 4	
		caught & bowled Crew	11
7	Whitty, N.I.	2 2 2 3 2 2 2 2 2 2 2 2 2 3 3 2 2 1	
		caught & bowled Monteath	42 [*sic*]

[752] The teams: *Clark's*. [1] Arthur Edward Jeune Collins [*5327*: PHP, NT 1987–1902], XI of 1901–2, Lt, Royal Engineers, killed in action 1914; posthumously gazetted Capt and mentioned in Despatches; [2] Arthur Mortimer Champion [*5183*: NT, PHP, NT 1896–1904]; [3] Hugh Porter Gilbert [*5232*: NT, PHP, DH: 1897–1900]; [4] Henry Allix Studdy [*5342*: PHP, WiH 1898–1902]; [5] Cecil Murray-Shirreff [*5205*: PHP 1897–1901]; [6] Arthur William Galwey [*4990*: PHP 1895–9]; [7] Noel Irwine Whitty [*5410*: PHP, OH 1898–1904]; [8] Ronald Alix Spooner [*5092*: PHP, WaH 1896–1902], killed in action 1916; [9] Gordon Lea Leake [*5190*: PHP 1897–9]; [10] Robert Cecil Raine [*5237*: PHP, BH 1897–1902]; [11] Thomas Archibald Redfern [*5406*: PHP, DH 1898–1901].

North Town. [1] Sir David Taylor Monteath [*4946*: NT 1895–1906], Head of the School 1905–6, XI of 1906, Permanent Under-Secretary of State for India and Burma, knighted 1942; [2] Archibald Hibbard Crew [*5184*: NT 1896–1905], Captain of the XI 1905; [3] Sir (Alfred Hubert) Roy Fedden [*5057*: NT, BH 1895–1904], XI of 1904, aeronautical engineer, knighted 1942; [4] Edward Alfred Sainsbury [*4630*: NT 1892–1901], XI of 1901; [5] Walter Agar Thomas Barstow [*4986*: NT 1895–9]; [6] Victor Fuller Eberle [*5499*: NT 1899–1905]; Captain of the XI 1905; member of the Council from 1927 to his death in 1974; [7] Thomas Shuttleworth Rendall [*5062*: NT, BH 1896–1903]; [8] Cyril James Lindrea [*5375*: NT 1898–1900†]; [9] Cecil Wentworth Gordon Ratcliffe [*5405*: NT 1898–1903]; [10] Sir Edward Stanley Gotch Robinson [*5407*: NT 1898–1906], eminent numismatist, knighted 1972; [11] Harold Arthur Davies [*5398*: PHP, NT 1898–1902].

8	Spooner, R.A.	bowled Monteath	0
9	Leake, G.L.	2 3 1 2 2 2 1 3 2 3 1 3 1 2 2 2	
		bowled Monteath	32
10	Raine, R.C.	4 2 1 1 1 3 1 1	
		bowled Sainsbury	14
11	Redfern, T.A.	1 2 2 2 1 1 2 1	
		caught Eberle [*bowled*] Crew	13

Byes 2 1 2 2 2 2 2 2 2 2 2 2 2 2 2 1 2   **Leg Byes** 1
Wide Balls 1 1 1 1 1 1 1 1 1 1   **No Balls** 1   [*Total Extras*] 46
                                        Total First Innings 836

| **1 for** 127 | **2 for** 169 | **3 for** 226 | **4 for** 268 | **5 for** 311 |
| **6 for** 436 | **7 for** 451 | **8 for** [*blank*] | **9 for** 698 | **10 for** 836 |

[*The Bowling analysis was not filled in on the fair copy; the original gives*
  Lindrea: 50 overs, 5 maidens, 0 for 218
  Sainsbury: 32 overs, 7 maidens, 2 for 166
  Crew: 42.3 overs, 5 maidens, 4 for 165
  Rendall: 10 overs, 3 maidens, 1 for 44
  Davies: 14 overs, 0 maidens, 0 for 79
  Monteath: 17 overs, 2 maidens, 3 for 113
With the 46 extras this is 5 short of the stated total.]

FIRST INNINGS

1	Monteath, D.T.	2 2	
		run out [*bowler*] Gilbert[752]	4
2	Crew, A.H.	2 2 1 1 2 2	
		bowled Collins	10
3	Fedden, A.H.R.	2 1 2 3 1 1	
		bowled Collins	10
4	Sainsbury, C	lbw Collins	0
5	Barstow, W.A.T.	2 4 3 2 2 2 1 2 3 2 2 1 2 2	
		bowled Shirreff	32
6	Eberle, V.	2 2 2 2	
		caught Galway [*bowled*] Collins	8
7	Rendall, J.S.	2 2 1 2 1 1	8 [*sic*]
		bowled [Collins *deleted*] Studdy	
8	Lindrea, C.J.	1	
		bowled Collins	1
9	Ratcliffe, C.W.G.	2 2 2	
		not out	6
10	Robinson, E.S.G.	bowled Collins	0
11	Davies, H.A.	2 2	
		bowled Collins	4

---

[753] Bowler wrongly credited with the wicket here and in the analysis.

Byes 2	Leg Byes [–]	Wide Balls 1	No Balls [–]	[*Total Extras*] 3
				Total First Innings 91
1 for 12	**2 for** 27	**3 for** 27	**4 for** 42	**5 for** 60
6 for 80	**7 for** 87	**8 for** 87	**9 for** 87	**10 for** 91

BOWLING ANALYSIS

[*Collins' figures first entered as for Gilbert, and Studdy's as for Collins, then deleted*]

	Balls	Runs	Maiden Overs	Wickets	Wide Balls	No Balls
Collins	102	35	8	7	–	–
Whitty	48	11	5	0	–	–
Studdy	30	9	2	1	–	–
Shirreff	35	10	3	1	–	–
Gilbert	50	19	3	1	–	–

SECOND INNINGS

1	Monteath, D.T.	2 2	
		caught & bowled Gilbert	4
2	Crew, A.H.	2 2	
		caught Champion [*bowled*] Gilbert	4
3	Fedden, A.H.R.	1	
		lbw Collins	1
4	Sainsbury, C.	2 2 2 2 2 2 1	
		lbw Collins	13
5	Barstow, W.A.T.	bowled Collins	0
6	Eberle, V.	1 2 2 2 2 1 4 1	
		bowled Shirreff	15
7	Rendall, J.S.	2 2 2 2	
		bowled Collins	8
8	Lindrea, C.J.	2 3 1 1 1 2 1	
		bowled Shirreff	11
9	Ratcliffe, C.W.G.	caught Champion [*bowled*] Shirreff	0
10	Robinson, E.S.G.	caught Raine [*bowled*] Shirreff	0
11	Davies, H.A.	not out	0

Byes 2 2	Leg Byes [–]	Wide Balls 1	No Balls 1	[*Total Extras*] 5 [*sic*]
				Total First Innings 61
1 for 4	**2 for** 9	**3 for** 9	**4 for** 19	**5 for** 32
6 for 40	**7 for** 60	**8 for** 60	**9 for** 60	**10 for** 61

BOWLING ANALYSIS

	Balls	Runs	Maiden Overs	Wickets	Wide Balls	No Balls
Gilbert	70	18	6	2	–	1
Collins	90	36	6	4	–	–
Whitty	5	2	0	0	–	–
Studdy	5	1	0	0	–	–
Shirreff	21	1	3	4	–	–

☐ *The result is not recorded: Clark's won by an innings and 684 runs.*

[286]   26 November [1911]. Football, haircuts and chess
[*VI/Big Side Levée Registers 5–7 (1907–22), f. 81. MS*]

Friday, Nov. 26th.
The Head of the School[754] read a letter from Canon Maud in reply to that sent by the Sixth Form on Nov. 12th.[755]
It was resolved that:
There should be no football during the Easter term. [*Minuted by the Head Master*: As the general standard of football throughout the School and knowledge of the game is not what it ought to be, it would be an advantage to have some Big Side practice games for the first few weeks of the Easter term.]
Those not in the Corps should not be allowed to play hockey on the days of Corps parades. [*HM*: I do not think the Corps need propping up in this way. One run a week is enough.]
Cock House v. School House match should be played as of old on a large sized ground consisting of Big Side, First Little Side and the intervening space; if this were thought impossible, the whole of the New Field should be used. [*HM*: To be referred to Games Committee.]
The Head Master be asked to appoint Chest [*as*] School barber as well as Bennett, and to make it possible for boys to have their hair cut there (as at present at Bennett's) without paying out of their own pocket.
The Sixth Form desire to express their disapproval of Mr Fowler's[756] action in refusing to allow chess to be played in the Library except on Wednesdays from two to three o'clock and Saturday evenings, and they would like the question submitted to the Library Committee.
If it should be determined that the Library must not be used except at the above times, play should be allowed in the Old Sixth Room during all hours when there are no regular lessons. [*HM*: Must be passed in different form before it can be brought up before Library Committee. J.E.K.]

F.N. Tribe.

---

[754] Sir Frank Newton Tribe [*6304*: NT 1904–12], Head of the School 1911–12; a senior Civil Servant knighted in 1941; member of the Council from 1944, and Chairman from 1951 to his death in 1958.
[755] This (at f. 79) congratulated John Primatt Maud, Vicar of St Mary Redcliffe, on being appointed Suffragan Bishop of Kensington, and expressed the hope that his association with Clifton would continue.
[756] John Henry Fowler [*M149*: 1894–1920], Librarian; author and editor of many literary works, including *School Libraries* (1915).

[287]   21 January 1920. Football, runs, Gym and God
[*VI/Big Side Levée Registers 5–7 (1907–22), ff. 209–11, MS*]

January 21. 1920. Wednesday.
A meeting of the Upper Sixth was held. The proposal that we should make overtures to the Bristol Grammar School for the purpose of arranging a match between our Colts and theirs was discussed. After considerable argument [it was deci(*ded*) *deleted*] the motion that we should play the Grammar School was defeated.

It was resolved that, apart from the 'soccer' XI from each House on Tuesday and Thursday, there should be games for a second XI from each House composed of boys under 16½ who are not [in *deleted*] playing rugby at Beggar's Bush. It was also decided that [one or two so(*ccer*) *corrected to*] once or twice during the term a soccer Big Side <game> be arranged on Saturdays for the best players in the School.

After some discussion the Sixth fixed the date of the Long Penpole for March 2 Tuesday, considering it advisable to leave three clear weeks before the Sports. It was also decided to fix the Sports for Tuesday March 23 and Wednesday March 24, and to begin the heats on Friday March 19. The Head of the School[757] informed the Sixth that the Headmaster considered soccer games impossible as qualifications for the Long Penpole. The number of necessary qualifying runs was then discussed. Having fixed the Long Pen date for March 2 it was impossible to have Corps parades as qualifications. It was suggested that the number be 'six', or else [5 *deleted*], if this were considered too few, '6' and [three *corrected to*] two Engineering parades. The Head of the School said he would ask the Headmaster which of the two it had better be. [*Minuted*: Qualifications for Long Pen fixed at 6 Upper pack runs + 2 Engineering runs].

The Head of the School said that the Games Committee had decided that train runs were feasible so far as expense was concerned.[758] The difficulty was the obtaining of permission from the farmers. It was decided that Mr Mayor[759] should be asked to assist the Holder of Big Side Bags in selecting the courses and obtaining the necessary leave. It was resolved that these runs should be limited to thirty boys.

Attention was drawn to neglected apparatus in the Gym. It was stated that the punching ball has not been replaced by a new one, and that it was believed that Franklin[760] had bought a new one, but that the School had refused to buy it. Also the boxing gloves were in bad repair, and new ones were needed. It was asked if these things might not be seen to. Further, it was suggested that a master be asked to be in charge of the Gym [and *deleted*] to be responsible for the upkeep of the apparatus. The Head of the School said he would ask the Headmaster if a master might be appointed.

Before the meeting adjourned the Head of the School spoke a few words about the branch of the Public Schools Scripture Union that was being re-established at Clifton. He detailed the proposed scheme, and said that he hoped that Clifton would not lie behind the other Public Schools in giving its support. He had a letter from Dr David[761] to Mr Inskip[762] in which our former Headmaster expressed the hope that the movement would meet with success. The Head of the School said that he hoped that

---

[757] Kingsley Sargent Storey [*7233*: NT 1911–20], Head of the School 1920.
[758] This meant taking a train from Clifton Down (usually to Sea Mills) and running home.
[759] Henry Bickersteth Mayor [*3329*: WiH 1884–90; *M151*: 1895–1926].
[760] There was a boy of this name in the School [*8075*] but this may mean a Gym assistant, unidentified.
[761] Still Headmaster of Rugby, but shortly to become Bishop of St Edmundsbury and Ipswich.
[762] The future Lord Caldecote [*3603*], for whom see above [**71**]; at this time MP for Bristol Central.

the influential members of the Sixth would give their support, and encourage people in their Houses to do the same.

[288]   20 March 1921. Clapping and coughing
[*VI/Big Side Levée Registers 5–7 (1907–22), f. 239, MS*]

Sunday March 20th. At a meeting of Praepostors:
It was decided that the [cricket *deleted*] games scheme for 1920 should be retained for 1921 with the following alterations.
That school on Fridays should be 3.0 – 5.15, and that there should be thus time for a practice game 1½ hours, instead of the short fielding out as last year.
That House matches should not be played on Commemoration Friday, but that the School be allowed a free day.
That the Sec. for Cycling have power to eject undesirable members.
It was further decided:
That fixture cards be printed this summer.
That the Headmaster be asked to [explain *corrected to*] say whether clapping was desirable at 'Lusty Juventus'[763] and if so at what points.
That the object of the book in which those who <play racquets in the holidays> write their names be enquired into, and [that *deleted*] if the book is necessary, that it should be kept at the Porter's [Office *corrected to*] Room not at the Secretary's office. [*Minuted by Head Master*: Reserved. J.E.K.]
That those who have coughs should instead of going to Chapel or to lectures be compelled to do work during those times (e.g. O.T. or N.T.) in order to do away with coughing in Chapel, which would then become a punishable offence for not reporting [a *corrected to*] the cough. [*Minuted by HM*: Reserved till Mich. term. J.E.K.]
A notice recently posted on the School Board was enquired into, and the Head of the School[764] said he would see about it.

R.N. Birley, 20/3/21.
[*Counter-signed*] J.E.K.

☐ *A tradition had developed for the outgoing Head of the School to give his designated successor a formal and highly confidential briefing. These letters were written into a notebook kept by the successive Heads. On this occasion the message had an especially apocalyptic tone.*

[289]   27 June 1940. R.M. Jenkins,[765] Head of the School, to his successor
[*Head of the School Letters 1932–41. MS*]

June 27th, 1940.
Dear Potter,[766]
There is not a great deal for me to say beyond what I have already told you, and I will confine myself to emphasising what I consider is most important. It seems

[763] Poem by Robert Weever (1565), included in *The Oxford Book of English Verse*, ed. Sir A.T. Quiller-Couch [*2666*: DH 1880–2].
[764] Robert Neville Birley [*7934*: OH 1916–21]; Head of the School 1920–1.
[765] Richard Mowbray Jenkins [*10158/11067*: NTP, WiH 1929–31, 1935–40], Head of the School 1939–40; killed in a flying accident while serving with the RAFVR 1942.
[766] See [**290**].

very probable at present that the School will have to be evacuated before next term, and even with adequate air-raid shelters – which we have not at the moment – this continual bombing every night makes normal daytime routine impossible. It will depend to a certain extent on the nature of the bombing during the next few weeks, but the scales seem weighted heavily in favour of evacuation. In that event there is little in which I can help you, as your actions will depend entirely upon circumstances, which are likely to be very different from those I have known.

Masters. You will have a very difficult and, I am afraid, rather thankless job in the event of evacuation, and you will more than ever need the help and support of masters. It pays every time, even in the comparatively smooth run of life here, to be on good terms with every master in the School [wh(*om*) *deleted*] with whom you come into contact, as nearly all of them are only too willing to help you in any way they can, and you will find that life is very difficult indeed without that help. I need not tell you how to deal with individual masters, as you have probably had as much experience in dealing with them as I have, and you know that each likes to be treated differently; in general, however, it is always best to let the master feel that he is the superior and that you are asking a great favour or receiving reliable advice, and if you are clever you will give this impression while actually getting the master to do exactly what *you* want him to do, and to all intents and purposes take advice from you. It is, I know, extraordinarily difficult to keep on good terms with some masters, especially those who have a point of view different from your own, but it is worth the effort to do so.

Games. Secondly, if the School is evacuated, it will be even more important than at present to provide exercise or some occupation for everyone on every half-holiday afternoon, with an occasional exception. Not only does this greatly help the general discipline of the School, but in the strain of these days it helps to keep it cheerful and reduces to a certain extent the inevitable feeling of the futility and artificiality of School life at present – in other words it keeps people from thinking too much. Whether here or elsewhere you will find this the most onerous of your duties, but do it as conscientiously as possible. Personally I feel that it is best to devote as much of games time as possible to some work of national value, though that again depends on circumstances, and rugger does at least keep one fit for cannon fodder. It is much better if people can feel that they are doing something for their country, even if it is actually of small value.

The Headmaster. There are one or two points for me to mention in case you are still here and life going on more or less normally. You probably know better than I do how to deal with the H.M., but be careful on such subjects as drink, breaking out, and lack of discipline generally, as he has very strong views on these, and would be shocked by any light-hearted view of them. Provided things are comparatively normal he is only too glad to hear your views, information and ideas on any subject connected with the School, however small, but *he will make unscrupulous use of any information you may give him.* He will use you as a meter, so to speak, of School opinion, and will expect you to know the reaction of the School to any action, and to be continually '*au courant*' in such matters. He will ask your opinion on the most divergent things, from House food to whether a certain Housemaster is inefficient at his job, and will normally take good note of your answer. [767] He will often have a

---

[767] Hallward ran a widespread espionage network, encouraging boys to denounce errant or incompetent masters: Winterbottom, *Hallward*, pp. 99–100.

sudden vague idea and ask you to organise it or see if it is practicable, and in such cases he will almost invariably ask you *the next day* whether it is possible etc., so you must be quick on the job, as efficiency is a demi-god to him. In actual fact nine out of ten of these schemes will be impracticable and fall through. I think you will get on with him better if you are rather freer and more intimate with him than I have been – always remembering to respect his strictness of conscience – and you will, by your nature, be less restrained than I. He expects a lot of you, but if you are prepared to give a lot, you will find him an excellent man to work with. You will soon realise his faults, but he is a strong man, and Clifton needs one at the moment. On any matter on which you need advice more practical than the H.M.'s, which is usually theoretical, go to C.F.T.[768] – I do not need to tell you what an excellent man he is.

Praepostors' and B.S.L. Meetings. As regards Praepostors' and B.S.L. meetings, except for the first meeting of the term, when it is impossible, always try and circulate an agenda to Heads of Houses several days before the meeting so that people can form an opinion beforehand, and not have to make up their minds at very short notice. If anything important is to come up at the meeting, make sure of the right decision by careful canvassing beforehand – careful, because boys of this age hate to think they are being dictated to. (See Steiger on this.[769]) Do not forget to [allott *corrected to*] allot House game pitches and times at your first Praepostor's [*sic*] meeting and give a list immediately to D.G.A.F.[770] Also ask Heads of Houses to collect 1/- for Worcester College for the Blind and hand the money to C.F.T. when you have received it all. Ask also for the numbers in each House, as this is invaluable information in making out games etc.

Committees. The committee for considering the constitution of B.S.L. has never met, so if circumstances permit appoint a new one and try to arrive at some decision on the subject. The H.M. has some ideas on it which I think are impracticable – he wants it limited to a certain proportion of the XV and XI. The committee for considering the new boxing scheme has not met either. Personally I do not think any alteration in the present system is practicable or necessary, but then I do not know a great deal about it, and it would be better to have a committee to decide the question. The committee should consist of yourself, the Captain of Boxing and one other praepostor to represent other School interests apart from boxing.

While on the subject of committees, if things are more or less normal you are on the Chapel, Social Service, Boxing, Swimming and Sports Committees. In the case of Boxing and Swimming you are there not, as you may suspect, because of your deep knowledge of the sports, but merely to see that the interests, traditions and rules of the School are not threatened in any way; indeed you will be little more than a bored spectator at their meetings.

Easter term. In the Easter term get on to the Pen and the Sports – especially the Sports – some time before they actually take place. Some of the Sports notices (see special envelope) have to go up 4 weeks before the beginning of School heats. Remember that you are responsible for all prizes, cups and programmes in the Sports, and that as something normally goes wrong, it is better to start on them as soon as possible.

---

[768] Cecil Francis Taylor [*M217*: 1912–48], Second Master 1938–48.
[769] Thomas Theodore Steiger, later T.T.S. Hayley [*9519*: PHP, UH, DH 1924–32], Head of the School 1932; i.e. his farewell letter earlier in the book.
[770] Douglas Fox [*M302*]; the Director of Music was alert to any encroachments on music time *cf.* above **[186]**.

Summer term. Remember to make sure that Gibbs'[771] mistake is not repeated next summer, and that Townsend's[772] is run by a boy and not a master. If you leave before then, make sure your successor sees to this. If you have league games in the Summer term, get them started as soon as possible. Most of these last remarks, of course, will only apply if you remain here under fairly normal conditions, which I sincerely hope will be the case, but the beginning of what I have said will apply wherever you are.

I fully intended to write very little, but something more always just came into my mind, as things do. However, I hope you will find it all of some value to you. Read, too, and inwardly digest Steiger at the beginning of this book, especially [that *deleted*] on the first few days of term, before you come back to School. You will find being H. of S. hard work, but very interesting work, and training more valuable than the rest of your School career put together. I wish you the best of luck – and your good sense should make life as smooth as circumstances will permit.

May good fortune attend you!

R.M. Jenkins.

P.S. Garden[773] would profit little by these remarks, as he will have little to do for the rest of this term, so I will hand this book over straight to you. The rest of the stuff I will give to Garden, who will leave it with J.K.B.C.[774] for you at the end of term. You should have a master-key, but one of my predecessors lost it, so see the Marshal about getting a new one.

[290]   10 September 1940. Jumps, tugs and trunks
[*Big Side Levée Minutes II (1939³–1946²). MS*]

Tuesday 10th Sept.

A meeting of Big Side Levée was held in the New Sixth at 12.15. The rules and constitution were read.

2nd & 3rd House Matches. The draw for 1st XV House matches then took place, but those for 2nds and 3rds were postponed owing to the uncertainty of exact numbers in Houses and to doubt as to whether it was better for Houses with 42 members, for instance, to produce a full 3rd XV, [or 12 *deleted*] arrange for a 12-aside game or [not *deleted*] only to put out two teams. It was generally agreed that the last course was the worst.

Relay Jumps. The Head of the School[775] then said that there had been some controversy about the manner in which points were allotted in the Sports for relay jumps. Taking the average of every House's team meant measuring every jump, and this apparently took far too long. It had therefore been decided that last year's system of grades was to be continued, but now, to make things fairer, 4 grades were to be used in each event instead of 3. This seemed to meet with approval.

Tug-of-War. A tug-of-war was next suggested, and a resolution was passed that a tug-of-war, with perhaps a few points [in the *deleted*] towards the House Shield going with it, would be a welcome addition to the Sports.

---

[771] Nigel Gibbs [*10316*: PHP, SH 1930–41], the incumbent Captain of the XI.

[772] A cricket game for the Colts of the previous year; named like its pitch from Charles Lucas Townsend [*4507*: NT 1892–4], of Gloucestershire and England, generally considered Clifton's greatest cricketer; *cf.* Christie, *History*, p. 271 n. 21.

[773] Neil Ramsay Garden [*10313*: ST 1929–40].

[774] J.K.B. Crawford [*M262*]: see above **[69]**, **[206]**.

[775] Ronald Jeremy Potter [*11130*: WiH 1935–41]; champion of Richard III and author of, among much else, *Headmaster: The Life of John Percival, Radical Autocrat* (1998).

Soccer. The Head of the School then said that a few games of soccer for those lower in the School who were quite useless at Sports had been suggested. This did not meet with any particular approval or disapproval; the general feeling seemed to be that there were other things that could be done [by *deleted*] besides soccer.

Colts' boxing. Mr Wilson's[776] suggestion for Colts' boxing in the Winter term as a separate competition from the open boxing comp. in the Easter term was then discussed. The Capt. of Rugger[777] said that he thought it would interfere with rugger, in particular with 4th XV matches. Another criticism was that the School was not sufficiently interested in boxing to warrant the extension. [Finally *deleted*] Rudman,[778] the prospective Sec. of Boxing, was asked his views, and he said that he thought there were few enough entries for the Easter term competition as it was without excluding more by holding another competition. It was also mentioned that the case as had happened recently with Whitty,[779] of an [*recte* a] small senior boy fighting [junior *deleted*] boys considerably younger than himself was exceptional. The [mot(*ion*) *corrected to*] suggestion was therefore deplored [*sic*] without opposition.

Bathing Costumes. [A *corrected to*] The resolution passed on 13th May, which had apparently never come to the notice of the Headmaster, had never accordingly been legalized and had never come into use, was then very strongly endorsed: the resolution was to the effect that bathing costumes and trunks of a reasonable nature [should *corrected to*] might be allowed in the baths as an alternative to slips, which are considered unsatisfactory. [*Minuted by the Head Master*: I am prepared to agree to the introduction of trunks as an *alternative* (not compulsory) to slips, but only of a *regulation pattern* to be obtained from the Games Shop. I suggest that this should start next Summer term. B.L.H.]

Grubber. This was followed by [another *corrected to*] a unanimous resolution 'that the Grubber be open on Sundays, if necessary under the charge of a master, and that regulation hours (which should be as long as is reasonable) be posted'. Dissatisfaction was expressed at the Grubber's odd hours of business, and it was felt that if it were open on Sundays, much of the money that now finds its way into the pocket of the so-called 'Chocolate Man' might be diverted into channels more beneficial to the School. It was known that Mr Brook[780] was in favour of the Grubber being open on Sundays, and that, if the scheme did materialize, he might be willing to help. [*Minuted by HM*: This seems to me hardly a matter for B.S.L. – see next page – but I will give it consideration.]

Bicycles. Finally, the view was expressed that, since bicycles had been brought back and since many were paying for keeping them, it was not unreasonable for boys to use them for their own needs or pleasure. The Head of the School promised to ask the Headmaster about the matter. [*Minuted by HM*: This hardly seems to me business within the competence of B.S.L. whose function it is to deal with games matters. It might be referred to Praepostors. B.L.H.]

There was no further business.

R.J. Potter, 10.ix.40.
[*Counter-signed*] B.L.H.

---

[776] Kenneth Gledhill Wilson [*M286*: 1927–43]; i/c boxing and swimming.
[777] Charles Peter Lewis-Smith [*10615*: MHP, HHP, DH 1931–41].
[778] John Harold Rudman [*10390*: MHP, PHP, OH: 1930–40].
[779] David Hugh Noel Whitty [*11135*: OH 1935–40]; he had left in the previous term.
[780] Peter Watts Pitt Brook [*M317*: 1936–71], Senior Chaplain.

SECTION XIV: DEBATES

☐ *The School Debating Society was founded in 1865 by J.A. Neale. Its Minute Books are extant from 1867 to 1915 but there is then a gap until 1946. For the intervening period there are, however, the records of several House societies.*

[291]   27 September 1879. Clifton supports the invasion of Afghanistan
[*Debating Society Minute Book 2 (1878–95). MS*]

Saturday, September 27th 1879
A Government had been formed consisting of:
President, R.F. Blakiston.[781]
Vice-President, H.J. Newbolt.[782]
Secretary, L.H. Bennett.[783]
Leader of Opposition, A. Baker.[784]

They brought forward the motion:
That this House strongly disapproves of the policy of Her Majesty's Government in Afghanistan.[785]
The speakers were: For the motion: Against:
                      R.F. Blakiston.   A. Baker.
                      H.J. Newbolt.   F.S. Boas.[786]
                      C. Cannan (O.C.).[787] E.L. Fox (O.C.).[788]

---

[781] Rochfort Folliott Blakiston [*1328*: PHP, SH 1873–9].

[782] Newbolt recalled school and university debates as 'the scenes which created in so many of us the ambition of a political career': *Later Life*, p. 17.

[783] Lawrence Henry Bennett [*1972*: ST, SH 1877–80].

[784] Arthur Baker [*1629*: BH 1875–80].

[785] The Second Afghan War (1878–80) was provoked by the spread of Russian influence and the Amir's rejection of a British diplomatic mission. Britain invaded and established a measure of control; following an uprising in September 1879 a larger force was despatched under Sir Frederick Roberts, which succeeded in occupying Kabul.

[786] Frederick Samuel Boas [*2079*: BH 1877–81]; distinguished literary scholar: see above **[129]**.

[787] Charles Cannan [*897*: BH 1870–7], Head of the School 1876–7; at this time an undergraduate at Corpus Christi College, Oxford.

[788] Ernest Long Fox [*1262*: DH 1873–8]; at this time a Balliol undergraduate.

On a division the numbers were:

Ayes 18.   Noes 27.

The motion was therefore lost by 9.

On the House going into committee on private business the Government tendered their resignation but, on a vote of confidence being passed, retracted it. The minutes of the last two debates having been read and approved the House then adjourned.

A. Baker, Secretary.

[292]   13 October [1900]. Clifton votes to keep the death penalty
[Debating Society Minute Book 3 (1896–1915). MS]

The second meeting of the term was held on October 13th, when the motion before the House was: 'That in the opinion of this House, capital punishment should not be abolished'. The speakers were:

For the motion: President, C.M. Dunn.[789]
                      Vice-President, W.H. Jordan.[790]
                      Secretary, H.A. Prichard.[791]

Against the motion: Leader, A.G. Macpherson.[792]
                      Supporter, L.J. Coates.[793]

R.P. Keigwin[794] also spoke against the motion.

The speeches of the Opposition were remarkable for the scarcity of points or arguments they contained, and the Leader of the Opposition, with truly Gaelic pathos, painted vivid but slightly imaginative pictures of murderers being let out of prison, and by their estimable conduct being things of beauty and joy for ever to their fellow countrymen. We hope that the crushing defeat, which silenced their well meant efforts at philanthropy, may shew them the error of their ways and lead them back to the paths of righteousness.

On a division the votes were: for 27, against 4. The motion was therefore [lost *corrected in another hand, with three exclamation marks, to*] won by 23 votes.

On entering into a committee for private business, the minutes of the last debate were read and passed.

Mr Jordan, whose asthmatic wheeze had already <much> alarmed the House, then arose and feelingly told the House that he had a bad cold. He therefore proposed that a glass of water be provided for the refreshment of speakers. Mr Keigwin then arose and was heard to imply that he wanted something stronger than water, but did not think he could get it. Some discussion followed, and it was at last decided that the Head of School House should provide a glass of water. Mr Prichard then proposed a vote of thanks to the Hon. Speaker for his excellent services as Secretary. Mr Cole[795] seconded and the vote was carried unanimously, and as there was no more business the House was adjourned at 8.40 p.m.

H.A. Prichard, Hon. Sec.

---

[789] Charles Marshman Dunn [*5004*: DH 1895–1901].

[790] William Henry Jordan [*4833*: PHP, WiH 1894–1901].

[791] Henry Adye Prichard [*5162*: ST 1896–1902].

[792] Alexander Geldart Macpherson [*4325*: NT 1891–1901]; son of the College Secretary.

[793] Sir Leonard James Coates [*4972*: NT 1897–1902]; accountant and civil servant; knighted 1924.

[794] Richard Prescott Keigwin [*5297*: WaH 1897–1902; *M246*: 1919–35].

[795] Assumed to be Arthur Frederick Andrew Cole [*5133*: DH 1896–1901], later a Bencher of Lincoln's Inn; the other Cole then at School, Kenneth Preston [*5430*: DH 1898–1902] did not progress beyond the Fourth Form.

[293]   15 February 1902. North Town debates legal ethics
[*NT Debating Society Minute Book 1902–7. MS*]

The first debate of the term was held on Saturday February 15th, when the motion before the House was that 'In the opinion of this House a lawyer is justified in defending a client whom he knows to be guilty'. The speakers were:

For the motion   President: B. Wyman.[796]
                             Vice-President: E.B. Reed.[797]
                             Secretary: W.F. Waite.[798]
Against the motion   Leader of the Opposition: A.F. Richards.[799]
                             Supporter of Opposition: E.A. Harris.[800]

Mr Wyman opened the debate with a singularly dull and uninteresting speech; he was followed by Mr Richards, who tried to bring his hearers over to his views by quoting some poetry of the lowest possible description, but he failed in his endeavours, as his speech was merely a remarkable example of what a lot can be said about nothing, as he brought forward no arguments whatever.

Mr Reed then rose and delivered an harangue which appeared to have been copied from the President's speech; such however he denied to be the case. For the Opposition then followed Mr Harris, who said he had tried to skate that afternoon, with the result that what little brain he had was completely addled, with which opinion the House unanimously agreed.

Mr Waite then made some remarks, which were all more or less off the point. Then followed short speeches from all the members of the ministerial table and from a few other gentlemen, amongst others Mr Coates (O.N.T.),[801] who deigned to shed the light of his countenance on the House; for which side he spoke, however, was not quite clear, though it is believed that he sided with the Government.

On the House dividing at 8.47 p.m. the votes were for the motion 11, against 2; the motion was therefore carried by 9 votes.

The House then entered into committee for private business; the minutes of the last meeting were not read owing to the late Secretary having absconded with the book.

A lengthy debate then took place about the House papers, but was terminated by the Speaker saying that they could not be changed.

Mr Wyman and Mr Mills[802] were elected Serjeants-at-Arms; and soon after Mr Mills was ejected from the room for making a general nuisance of himself; after he had been expelled, peace and order were restored to the general relief of the House.

A vote of censure was passed on Mr Richards and Mr Waite for addressing people by name in their speeches.

---

[796] Bernard Wyman [*5397*: NT 1898–1902].
[797] Edward Baines Reed [*5087*: NT 1896–1902].
[798] Wilfrid Fabian Waite [*5199*: HHP, BH, NT 1896–1903]; Bencher of Lincoln's Inn and member of the Bar Council.
[799] Arthur Frederick Richards, 1st Baron Milverton [*5536*: NT 1899–1904]; from 1930 to 1947 Governor successively of North Borneo, Gambia, Fiji, Jamaica and Nigeria; ennobled 1947.
[800] Edward Alfred Harris [*4796*: NT 1894–1902]; for several years President of the Bristol and West of England Society of Chartered Accountants.
[801] The later Sir L.J. Coates, as in [**292**].
[802] Forster Mills [*4994*: 1895–1904; killed in action 1917] or his brother Herbert John [*5272*: NT 1897–1902].

The House then proceeded to chose [*sic*] a subject for the next debate; but no one had any sensible subject to suggest, so the House adjourned at 9.30 p.m.

B. Wyman
Hon. Sec.

[294]   20 October 1906. North Town considers a German invasion to be a realistic threat
[*NT Debating Society Minute Book 1902–7. MS*]

The first debate of this term was held on October 20th, when the subject before the House was: 'That in the opinion of this House a German invasion of Great Britain is practically impossible'.[803]
    The speakers were:

For the Government: For the Opposition:
Pres: T.W. Nott.[804]   Leader: M.R. Ridley.[805]
Vice-Pres; F. Gee.[806]   A.S. Barratt.[807]
Sec: F.E. Waite.[808]

Mr Nott opened the debate, straightway plunging the House into an atmosphere of politics and naval statistics, interspersed with stray scraps of geography. He earned the undying gratitude of the House by delivering his speech in an audible voice, as contrasted with the three remaining ornaments of the ministerial table; three I say, because Mr Barratt is hardly fit to be described as ornamental. He explained the condition of the English Navy, and after drawing attention to the difficulties of transport, including sea-sickness on the part of the drinkers of sauer kraut, he called upon all members who had not taken leave of their senses to support the Government.
    Mr Ridley succeeded Mr Nott, but was incoherent and incomprehensible, partly on account of the din from the lower part of the House, and partly because of his total ignorance of the subject in hand. He contributed something to the debate, however, by suggesting that the Germans had sent across lighters of coal to test the feasibility of the plan. Then he said he hoped he had said enough, which statement evoked a volley of applause from his delighted hearers.
    Mr Gee responded, and immediately let the cat out of the bag by admitting that he did not agree with his President. Unfortunately the remainder of his speech was thrown away in the uproar which still issued from various portions of the House, where childish games were apparently in progress. He was observed to look at his watch, and then collapsed, upon which the unfortunate House had to submit to a speech by *Mr Barratt*. The hon. gentleman cast a timid glance at the Speaker, and encouraged by that gentleman's smile of approval and encouragement (for Mr Barratt is still somewhat young, and unused to the searching gaze of the public) he said 'Er'. This monosyllable, it may be said, was the only audible word which issued from Mr

---

[803] Doubtless prompted by William Le Queux's *The Invasion of 1910*, first published from March 1906 in the *Daily Mail*. In the wave of popular 'invasion scare' stories, *The Riddle of the Sands* by Erskine Childers (1903) had been particularly influential in identifying Germany as the enemy. The Liberal Government responded to these fears expressed through fiction by substantially increasing the army reserve.
[804] Thomas Walker Nott [*5657*: NT 1900–6]; killed in action 1917.
[805] Maurice Roy Ridley [*5624/M230*]; see above **[64, 256]**.
[806] Frank Gee [*5504*: NT 1899–1908].
[807] Air Chief Marshal Sir Arthur Sheridan Barratt [*6337*: NT 1905–9], AOC British Forces in France 1940; see above **[71]**.
[808] Fabian Evans Waite [*6103*: NT 1903–7].

Barratt's lips till towards the close of his monologue. He should do well as an infant prodigy in recitation. The bland innocent expression on his cherubic countenance would beguile the most wary observer into thinking he was a good little boy – till he knew him better. However the House had just given up in despair any hopes it had entertained of discovering if Mr Barratt knew what the motion was, when their horrified ears caught the words 'German sausage'. Mr Barratt could not be persuaded to realise the crass idiocy of his remark, and after repeating it, as he evidently thought it highly humorous, he subsided.

Mr Waite was uproariously greeted, possibly as being the last speaker. He was heard to allude to the School Militia, and after referring to Mr Barratt's facial peculiarities, sat down. Then followed a mixed argument, in which Mr Nott complained of Mr Ridley's use of the word 'lighter', and Mr Barratt complained of the aspersions cast on his face. Mr Nott then requested to be told the numbers of the respective armies of Germany, France and England, and so Mr Barratt, as a member of the mysterious community known as the Military Side, felt himself competent to answer. It appeared from his responses that the German army comprised 1,300,000 men, the French army 2,000,000 men, and the unfortunate English army only 19,000 men!

After this a period of deep silence ensued, broken only by the Speaker's pathetic appeal for someone to speak. As no one offered to do so, he put the question to the House, and announced the motion lost. Votes for 14. Votes against 17. Opposition majority 3.

Then the rules were read, and the minutes of the last debate read and carried, though the customary objections were made. A vote of censure was passed on Mr Barratt, and another proposed against Mr Ridley, but was not carried. The Speaker thought the subjects for the next debate too futile to be put to the vote, and adjourned the House at 9.25 p.m.

H.G. Dennehy,[809]
Hon. Sec.

[295]   16 March 1918. Polack's accepts that the grass is not greener on the other side
[*Polack Centre, PH Debating Society Minute Book 1917–21. MS*]

The 2nd meeting of the Easter term 1918 was held on March 16th when the subject for debate was that in the opinion of this House 'The School should be taken to Beggar's Bush'.

Mover of the motion: C.E. Benzecry.[810]   Leader of Opposition: L.C. Cook.[811]
Supporter: L.B. Prince.[812]   Supporter: S. Foster.[813]

Mr Benzecry, the first speaker, said we must omit the question of money, and pick out the real advantages of such a move. It was difficult now to make any enlargements at School, but Beggar's Bush offers [much *corrected to*] plenty of building accommodation. The School, by living in the country instead of town,

---

[809] Sir Harold George Dennehy [*6182*: ST, NT 1903–9]; Chief Secretary to the Government of Assam; knighted 1946.
[810] Charles Elias Benzecry [*7673*: PH 1914–19].
[811] Leslie Colin Cook [*7732*: PH 1914–18].
[812] Leslie Barnett Prince [*7878*: PH 1915–19]; Chairman of the OCS Executive Committee 1938–48; Sheriff of the City of London 1954–5.
[813] Samuel Foster [*7636*: PH 1913–19].

would become much more healthy and less prone to contract the illnesses which are caught in Bristol. In addition there is more room for games, and he concluded it was a shame for us not to use Beggar's Bush after we have payed [*sic*] so much for it.[814]

Mr Cook declared that, as the scheme had been rejected long ago by the authorities, [it *corrected to* that there *then to*] there was an end of the matter. There would be great difficulties to overcome during removal and the standard of the School would go down. Particularly the old familiar sights of the School would go, and at Beggar's Bush there is no cricket field at all. He denied that shops could be built there as all the ground was private.

Mr Prince considered the football at Beggar's Bush had been a great success (doubtless he belongs to the small party who enjoy being collared among the thistles!) and that a ground could be purchased for cricket for the good people to play, [while *deleted*] entirely neglecting the fact that the young people who want good ground and coaching would be unable to obtain this. He had hopes of tennis courts,[815] and longer Corps parades, since we could begin operations at once without our accustomed march over the Bridge. Boys were to have bicycles and so School life would become much brighter.

Mr Foster said the cost was most important. It would [*be*] rather unfortunate [on *corrected to*] for the Town Boys who form a great part of the School, while the Old Cliftonians would not welcome a break with [the old *corrected to*] traditions.

Mr Wolf[816] thought Town Boys a nuisance, and said a new School would encourage [new and *corrected to*] more boys. The obvious advantages at Beggar's Bush would be new and better buildings, especially a good Sanatorium. The levelling of the field would not [so *corrected to*] be difficult. Harrow for example levelled a field worse than Beggar's Bush. He decided we could have a piquet of masters at the Bridge to catch people going out of bounds.

Mr Constad[817] thought if we moved we should be called Beggar's Bush High School.

Mr Hillman[818] who spoke next, said that he was not intelligent, and this statement was greeted with loud and prolonged cheering; [and *corrected to*] he was quite right in saying the School was too large to carry [bodily across *corrected to*] across bodily.

Mr Benjamin[819] said the House system would give way to School system owing to feeding [together *corrected to*] difficulties. Previous debate had shown the former to be the better, especially from [P.H. *corrected to*] our point of view, [School system would not be good *deleted*] as we might lose our Jewish feeling, which is now so strong in the House.

Mr Frank[820] talked a lot about 'cacti', being obviously very pleased with the word.

Mr H.L. Cohen,[821] who made his maiden speech <and> was welcomed with terrific

---

[814] The contract price for the 48 acres had been £12,000, though £13,781 was eventually paid: Christie, *History*, p. 166.

[815] These duly arrived; and since 1997 Cliftonians have been able to play not only the low game of spharistike but also *Real* Tennis, in the court on the site run by the Bristol and Bath Tennis Club.

[816] Edward Lionel Saville Wolf [*7957*: PH 1916–18]. He was a Londoner.

[817] Victor Constad [*8164*: PH 1917–21].

[818] Maurice Hillman [*7775*: PH 1914–20]; actor, dramatist and theatrical impressario.

[819] Ernest Frank Benjamin [*7561*: PH 1913–18].

[820] Sydney Frank [*7327*: PH 1912–18].

[821] Harold Lionel Cohen [*7819*: PH 1915–19]; grandson of the House Master, which no doubt accounts for the warmth of his reception.

applause, [and told us Mr Imlay said *corrected to*] quoted Mr Imlay as saying that Beggar's Bush would never be satisfactory for cricket.[822]

Mr [*Mendelsohn* corrected to] *Mendelssohn*[823] [rose also and *deleted*] might have been heard by those sitting on each side of him, but that was rather improbable.

The following also spoke: Messrs Quas-Cohen [*8107*], Cohen [*7679 or 7710*], Rosenburg [*recte* Rosenberg *7966*], Stern I [*8057*], Levy [*8003*], Grossman [*8261*], Salinger [*8110*], Sassoon I [*7697*] , Davis [*8073*], Salaman [*8027*], Polack [*8015*].

Mr *Cook* was very emphatic on the necessity for all to play cricket properly and not only the XI.

Mr *Benzecry* concluding showed surprising lack of knowledge of Beggar's Bush ground although he had visited it often in the capacity of a Sapper in the O.T.C.

The House then divided after an interesting debate and the motion was lost by 8 to 15. House adjourned at 9.10.

Signed: J. Polack, *President*[824]

H.D. Barnard, *Secretary*.[825]

[296]   20 March 1920. Wiseman's fags vote for the Navy and against cats
[*Clissold's House Fags' Debating Society Minute Book 1917–35. MS*]

The second debate of the term was held on Saturday March 20th at 8.5 p.m., when the motion for debate was:

'That in the opinion of this House the Navy should be fostered, even at the expense of the Army'.

President of the Government	C.H.M. Bowen[826]
Vice-President	H.M. Brodhurst[827]
Secretary	W.S. Field[828]
Leader of the Opposition	T.C. Toogood[829]

The speakers were:

For the motion	*Against*
C.H.M. Bowen	T.C. Toogood
H.M. Brodhurst	K.R. Boulton[830]
W.S. Field	J.D. Brown[831]
J.K. Norman[832]	St G.A. Galfin[833]

On division the voting was as follows:

For the motion 18.	*Against* 5.

The motion was therefore carried by 13 votes.

---

[822] With great effort the ground was levelled, and by 1931 there were eight pitches. Imlay [*M194*], who had kept wicket for Cambridge, directed the operation.

[823] Gerald Mendelssohn [*7825*: PH 1915–20].

[824] Joseph Polack [*M139*: 1890–1923], House Master.

[825] Henry Dan Barnard [*7724*: PH 1914–19].

[826] Charles Herbert Minshull Bowen [*8123*: WiH 1917–21].

[827] Hugh Maynard Brodhurst [*7961*: HHP, WiH 1916–21].

[828] Walter Strickland Field [*8131*: WiH 1917–20].

[829] Thomas Cecil Toogood [*8094*: WiH 1917–20].

[830] Kenneth Roy Boulton [*8299*: WiH 1918–21].

[831] John Duncan Brown [*8414*: PHP, WiH 1918–22].

[832] John Kenneth Norman [*8586*: NT, WiH 1919–21].

[833] Almeric St Gall (so ordered in Register) [*8230*: PHP, WiH 1917–22].

The House then went into committee for private business. Mr Brodhurst rose and made the fatuous proposal that the mustard-pots should be filled. Mr Toogood opposed on the grounds that the mustard had gone up in price.

Then Mr Toogood proposed a vote of censure on Mr Brodhurst for using the word 'snag' in his speech. After some discussion the motion was passed, and Mr Brodhurst had to apologise.

After that Mr Cooke II[834] tried to pass a vote of censure [of *otiose*] on Mr St G.A. Galfin. The motion was lost.

Mr Toogood rose to propose that bee's-wax should be used on the wooden flooring of the changing-room, as so many splinters were coming off it and hurting people's feet. The motion was passed unanimously. Mr Speaker said he would put the matter before the Head of the House.

Mr Field proposed a vote of censure on Mr Brodhurst for standing at the same time as the Speaker. The motion was quashed.

Mr Slater then rose and proposed that both the top ends of the fags' table should be served first. The motion was carried unanimously.

Then Mr Boulton passed a vote of censure on Mr Brodhurst for emitting wind through his hands. Mr Brodhurst apologised.

Mr Slater[835] then rose to pass a vote of censure on Mr Cooke II for being mentally deficient. The motion was approved by the House. So Mr Cooke had to apologise.

After that Mr Brodhurst proposed a vote of censure on Messrs Cooke II and Seldon for talking during the debate. After some discussion the motion was carried.

Mr Toogood then proposed with great gusto that active measures should be taken against the cats, since they were becoming a general nuisance, and beyond a joke. Then there was some rather one-sided discussions [*sic*] in matter to do with their suppression. At length it was passed that the fags should take their own measures in the matter at their responsibility.

Mr Samways[836] then made a proposal that members of Vth Forms should not be allowed to come into any debate of the Society. The motion was quashed.

Mr Cooke II tried to pass a vote of censure on Messrs Boulton and Toogood, but he was severally ticked off.

Mr Brodhurst made some proposals about the House soap and the sweeping of the 'Fugger',[837] but his proposals were passed over.

Mr Toogood rose to propose that those fags who did toast fagging before breakfast should not spoil the fire by raking it out. The motion was carried.

Mr Cooke II tried to pass a vote of censure on Mr Toogood for upsetting a glass of water. But Mr Cooke's motion was again opposed with great vigour, his efforts being of no avail. Mr Toogood was not censured.

There being no more business of importance the House adjourned at 9.14 p.m.

D. Slater. Hon. Sec.: 24:III:'20

[297]   21 October 1933. Polack's votes to fight.
[*Polack Centre, PH Debating Society Minute Book 1932–7. MS*]

---

834 Gordon Grenside Cooke [*8165*: WiH 1917–21].
835 Maurice David Slater [*7543*: HHP, WiH 1917–1920].
836 George Swithin Samways [*8321*: WiH 1918–22].
837 Room next to changing-rooms with heated rails for drying clothes. (With thanks to Mr G.V. Hardyman for this explanation.)

The second meeting of the Winter term was held in Hall on Saturday October 21st. The rules were read, and the minutes were read and duly signed. There was no private business and the House proceeded to debate that: 'This House will under no circumstances fight for the country'.[838]

For the motion: Mr H.J. Collins.[839] Against the motion: Mr C.H.R. Gee.[840]

Mr V.M. Halsted.[841] Mr A.M. Jacob.[842]

Mr Collins opened the debate with an extract from the *Bloody Traffic*.[843] He then went on to say how much we having [*recte* have] advanced since the time of the Canaanites who offered up human sacrifices; we offer millions for sacrifice to the god of Patriotism. He then quoted Marie Antoinette on going to the guillotine. The sufferings caused by war are dreadful; we are still tottering from them. Democracy is losing ground everywhere. The last war <was> fought to make <the> world safe for democracy.[844] He went on to say that civilization is based on the dictum of the sacredness of human life. Mr Waley-Cohen[845] objected. Unperturbed, Mr Collins continued, and said that V.C.s were obtained for murder. He then gave us some facts about a future war – incendiary bombs reaching temp. of 2000°C, bacteria, gas, luisite and mustard. Then followed more quotations from the *Bloody Traffic*, and six charges against arms manufacturers. He wound up with more quotations, a lengthy recitation, and some more quotations.

Mr Gee opened the case for the Opposition with a very interesting description of the Blundell's match.[846] He then started the debate proper by [so(*me*) *deleted*] making some very rude remarks about the hon. mover of the motion. He then maintained that Mr Collins appealed entirely to sentiment, that killing an enemy is not murder. Pacifism is founded on two or three false issues. People are apt to get war out of proportion; there are more casualties through influenza than through war. Peace is not an ideal; the real ideals are justice, liberty etc., and these are often obtained through war. War pays in the long run, and the Great War was the most pleasant war that ever happened. We were relieved to hear that the object of war, according to Mr Gee, was not to kill the other side, but merely to starve them. He told us to beware of [the *deleted*] logic founded on sentimentality.

Mr Halsted rose hazily to support the motion. He hoped we would not be 'missled'[847] by the hon. opposer's speech. The British anti-war movement is international and can

---

[838] Prompted by the infamous debate in the Oxford Union on 27 February, when the motion 'That this House will under no circumstances fight for its King and Country' was passed by 275 votes to 153.

[839] Henry Joseph Collins [*10562*: PH 1931–6]; served during the war in the Royal Army Ordnance Corps.

[840] Charles Hilton Rodney Gee [*M267*: 1922–68]; served in the First World War as Captain in the Durham Light Infantry (Despatches, MC); commanded the Cadet Corps with rank of Major 1932–5 (TD); rejoined his Regiment 1939 and was again mentioned in Despatches before being taken prisoner.

[841] Victor Michaelis Halsted [*10367*: PH 1930–5]; served during the war as Paymaster Sub Lt RNVR.

[842] Alexander Michael Jacob [*10421*: PH 1930–4]; served with the County of London Yeomanry, attached to British Liaison HQ, Polish Forces.

[843] Fenner Brockway, *The Bloody Traffic: A Study in Worldwide Armament Combinations* (1933). The author was a prominent pacifist campaigner.

[844] The phrase used by President Woodrow Wilson before a joint session of Congress on 2 April 1917, when proposing a declaration of war on Germany.

[845] Sir Bernard Nathaniel Waley-Cohen [*10378*: PH 1930–2]; property developer, knighted 1957; Lord Mayor of London 1960–1 (and as such created Baronet 1961); member of the Clifton College Council 1952–81.

[846] Played at Tiverton earlier in the day; 'very fast and exciting', ending in a 16–16 draw: *Cliftonian* XXXV (1933–4), pp. 146–7.

[847] Deliberate mistake; *cf.* Kanter's speech below.

stop war. The next war will be fought against civilian population. The results of war are blindness, cripples etc. This war there were comparatively few deaths. Next war will be much worse. The capitalist press is to blame. The opposers exhort us to fight for Krupps, Thyson [*recte* Thyssen] etc. This was Mr Halsted's maiden speech from the table; his points were quite sound, but he must try and improve his delivery.

Mr Jacob concluded the speeches from the table. He thought that the British navy was the greatest peace machine the world has ever known. We seem to have heard that before somewhere.[848] We would all fight on account of patriotism and common sense. Hitler[849] will not refuse to fight simply because we do. Why should we disobey Parl[*iament*] when they decide to fight? This was Mr Jacob's maiden speech from the table; his arguments were not very convincing.

Mr Myer[850] opened the debate from the House. He wished to know if we would stand like weeds if attacked.

Mr Burton II[851] though patriotism was sloppy.

Mr Waley-Cohen demanded whether we would like our country to be flooded with German troops. The income-tax would certainly go up. Victory cannot be obtained without fighting.

Mr Burton I[852] thought it quite easy to prevent war by having a decently organized force to start with.

Mr Kanter[853] maintained we must do everything to stop war. He implored us to forgive Halsted for his pronunciation of the word 'misled'. He accused Mr Collins of being a hypocrite.

Mr Simmons[854] announced bombastically that it [would *corrected to*] takes two to make a quarrel.

Mr Emanuel[855] maintained that the mover of the motion was not sincere. He wants a wholesale slaughter of capitalists. Not fighting is no use in stopping war.

Mr Levy I[856] maintained that the masses were used as gun-fodder.

The Hon. Sec. brought some comic relief into the debate by a dissertation [of *corrected to*] on what would happen in an invasion by cannibals. Even pacifists would not allow themselves to be made into ham sandwiches.

[*The President* corrected to] *Mr Saloman* [*recte* Salomon][857] weighed up the pros and cons of the case, and decided that other generations should not say we were soft.

The President read a speech from the Vice-President[858] who was on a bed of sickness. He lives in a country where personal liberty is paramount; he hoped his children would receive this too in spite of Mr Collins. We must not allow black and yellow races to control the country, nor must we allow a dictator or a bully to

---

[848] Probably an allusion to Admiral of the Fleet Lord Fisher, First Sea Lord 1904–10, 1914–15 ('The supremacy of the British navy is the best guarantee for peace in the world').
[849] Hitler had become Chancellor of Germany on 30 January.
[850] Roger Graham Myer [*10500*: PH 1931–4]; served during the war as Lt RNVR.
[851] Raymond Montague Burton [*10492*: PH 1931–5]; during the war rose from the ranks to be Major in the Royal Artillery.
[852] Arnold James Burton [*10491*: PH 1931–5], twin brother of II; served during the war in the RAF.
[853] Victor Ben Kanter [*10530*: PH 1931–6]; served during the war as Sub Lt RNVR.
[854] Basil Simeon Simmons [*10595*: PH 1931–5]; served as Territorial then during the war as Lt in the Royal Artillery.
[855] Charles Ansell Emanuel [*10171*: PH 1929–33]; barrister, who served during the war as Lt in the Hampshire Regiment and then (1945–6) as permanent President of the British Military Court at Lüneburg.
[856] Nissim Joseph Neville Levy [*10495*: PH 1931–4]; served in the Middle East, and killed in action 1941.
[857] Kenneth Henry Salomon [*10307*: PH 1929–35]; served as 2nd Lt in the Royal Artillery.
[858] Unidentified.

dominate matters. Countries that go mad can only be resisted by fighting. Man sees the world through the glasses of the editor of the newspaper, whether they be blue or red. He maintained that armament firms should be controlled, but if it became necessary to fight, we must fight. It was a very good speech, and we only wished he could have been able to deliver it himself.

Mr Gee then summed up. He said that if one thought one's country definitely in the wrong, one should fight for the enemy. He asked if we were going to watch our families being beaten up.

Mr Collins then summed up his case at great length. He declared that war was nothing more nor less than mass murder. He made some references to the British anti-war movement. On the whole, his summing-up speech was rather better than his original one.

The motion was then put to the vote and lost by 12 votes to 29. The House then adjourned.

The debate proved quite interesting, and while extending cordial thanks to our visitor Mr Gee, we hope he enjoyed the debate as much as we did his speech.

N. Lermon (Hon. Sec.)[859]
A.I. Polack (Hon. Pres.)[860]

---

[859] Norman Lermon [*10347:* PH 1930–4]; served during the war as Major in the South Wales Borderers, and mentioned in Despatches.

[860] Albert Isaac Polack [*5972:* PH 1902–11; *M270:* 1923–49]; House Master throughout his time on the staff, in succession to his father Joseph [*M139*].

SECTION XV: MUSIC

☐ *Music, as an academic discipline and an extra-curricular activity, is notably well documented, and is therefore prominetly featured here.*[861]

Organists and Organs

☐ *For the first five years Big School also served as the College Chapel.*

[298]   27 January 1864. Appointment of first Organist and Choir Master
[*CC Company Minute Book 1, p. 299. MS*]

Resolved that Canon Guthrie be empowered to engage Mr Trimnell[862] as Organist and Choir Master for the College Chapel at a salary not exceeding £30 a year.

[299]   23 February 1864. Hire of first organ
[*CC Company Minute Book 1, p. 302. MS*]

Resolved that an organ be hired for the Chapel and that Mr Trimnell be authorized to hire the organ lately in St Andrew's Church,[863] and that the Council agrees to make up the £20 for hire, of which the Revd J. Percival has promised to contribute £10.

[300]   21 December 1870. Memorandum from the Choir Master to the Head Master
[*Guard Book 1860–77. MS*]

Clifton College
Decr 21. 1870

The Headmaster having complained of the large amount charged to the members of the Choral Society for music, and requested me to state the cause of so large an

---

[861] See J.I. Birley, 'The organs in Clifton College', *The Organ*, no. 137 (July 1955), pp. 34–40; D.G.A. Fox and Y.P. Lidell, 'Music at Clifton', in *Centenary Essays*, pp. 95–127.

[862] William Frederick Trimnell [*M14*: 1864–96]; Deputy Organist of the Cathedral and Organist of Stoke Bishop Church.

[863] An early 19th-century building which replaced Clifton's medieval parish church; it was destroyed in the Blitz; only the churchyard remains.

outlay being required, I beg to inform you, that the music lately obtained has been of a higher class, and consequently more expensive than that formerly practised and also that the charge includes music required for the next term in addition to that which is now required for the concert.

W.F. Trimnell,
Choir Master.

☐ *When services were transferred to the new Chapel in 1867 a new organ was given by the Head Master, and the hired instrument was no longer needed in Big School. However the newly formed Choral Society soon began to use that venue for large-scale works which needed the support of an organ. The Society therefore raised funds to buy one of its own, and this was installed in 1873. Although this was the work of the greatest craftsman of the age, its first concert performance was a fiasco, as stops failed to open or retracted of their own accord.[864] The Society set out its terms in a letter to the Chairman of the Council.*

[301]   3 March 1874. Council Minutes: letter to the Chairman of the Council setting rules for the Big School Organ[865]
[*CC Company Minute Book 3, p. 267. MS*]

Olden Lodge,
Clifton College, Bristol.

Dear Sir,

The Choral Society beg to offer for the acceptance of the Council the organ recently erected by them in Big School and hope that the Council will agree to receive it on the following conditions:[866]

I. That the organ shall be for the use of the School and those connected with it only, preference being given to the requirements of the Choral Society in regard to such use of it.

II. That the Council will in future keep it insured and in tune and repair.[867]

III. That the care of it and the arrangements for its use be rested in the Organist and Choir Master of the College for the time being, subject to the approval of the Head Master.

The total cost of the organ has been £715, and it is entirely paid for. I have handed Mr Willis's[868] receipt to the Secretary of the College.

I am, dear Sir, yours faithfully,
Robert B. Poole,[869] on behalf of the Choral Society.

---

[864] See the scathing review of the December 1873 concert in *Cliftonian* III (1872–4), p. 339.

[865] See Birley, 'Organs', pp. 34–6. The Big School organ was removed when the building was comparted in 1968, restored in 1972, but thereafter again dismantled. In 2004 it was sold to St Mary Magdalene, Bridgnorth: J.L. Turnock, *The Organs at St Mary Magdalene, Bridgnorth* (Bridgnorth, 2009); R.C. Massey, 'A Willis resurrected at Bridgnorth', *Organists' Review* (Nov. 2009), pp. 23–7.

[866] The Council had on 12 Dec. 1871 given leave to the Organ Fund Committee to erect an organ in Big School according to plans submitted: CC Company Minute Book 3, p. 80.

[867] On 23 Dec. 1873 it was agreed to insure the organ for £700 or £800, and on 8 Dec. 1875 a tuning contract was agreed with Messrs Vowles for £7 a year: CC Company Minute Book 3, pp. 237, 348.

[868] Henry Willis (d. 1901), known as 'Father Willis', the doyen of Victorian organ builders.

[869] Robert Burton Poole [*M16*: 1864–77], first master of the Junior School House established in 1867 at Olden Lodge (the original location of Dakyns' House): *Register* (1925), p. lxxviii.

☐ *Not until 1890 was the Chapel organ completed. Willis was again the builder.*

[302]   30 September 1890. Completion of Chapel Organ
[*Council Minute Book 3, pp. 306–7. MS*]

A memorandum from the Head Master dated the 23rd Sept. 1890 was read asking the permission of the Council to complete the Chapel organ for which donations had been given by friends of the School. It was resolved to authorize the work on the condition that it be carried out by Mr Willis the builder of the organ.[870]

☐ *When the Chapel was extended to its present size in 1909–11, a new instrument was built by Harrison and Harrison of Durham.*[871]

[303]   3 October 1908. A.H. Peppin[872] **to Messrs Harrison & Harrison**
[*Archives of Harrison & Harrison, Durham. Holograph*]

[32, College Road *corrected to*]
40 Clifton Park Road,
Clifton, Bristol.
Oct. 3. 08.

Dear Sirs,

It is possible, tho' not certain, that the organ in Clifton College Chapel may be rebuilt into a practically new instrument within the next two years or so.

I have lately seen and examined your new instrument at Ely Cathedral and I like it so much that I should like to consider the possibility of asking you to send us an estimate for the work.

The organ at present is in a very bad condition and wants cleaning very soon, and if we are able to find the money for the rebuilding we should like the same builder to clean it now who is to undertake the [job *deleted*] complete job later on.

I am asking for estimates from two other builders and shall have to lay all three before the Headmaster and Council of the College, who will probably allow me to have a voice in the selection.

Under these circumstances would you care to look at the Chapel and organ and give two estimates – one for cleaning as at present needed, and one for the complete rebuilding? It would be necessary to have this estimate by the end of October, or Nov. 1st.

---

[870] On 16 February 1891 Willis's firm informed Trimnell that they would undertake no further work in the Chapel organ because it had already been altered by another builder: Council Minute Book 3, p. 355 (meeting of 2 June).

[871] The firm, founded in 1861, had since 1896 been run by the brothers Arthur and Harry Harrison. For the instrument see Birley, 'Organs', pp. 36–40.

[872] Arthur Hamilton Peppin [*M152*: 1896–1915], Organist and first Director of Music; formerly secretary to Sir George Grove, Director of the Royal College of Music; left to become Director of Music at Rugby.

I may say that both Dr Davis of Wells Cathedral[873] and Mr Basil Johnson of Rugby[874] have advised me to write to you.

Yours truly,

Arthur H. Peppin.

(Organist and Director of Music at Clifton College).

☐ *Arthur Harrison visited Clifton on 16 October; he subsequently reported that immediate repairs would cost £105, and provided an estimate for a new four-manual organ within a £2000 budget, with provision for a smaller machine if the budget could not meet that sum.*

[304]   21 July 1909. Peppin to Harrison

[*Archives of Harrison & Harrison, Durham. Holograph*]

40 Clifton Park Road,
Clifton, Bristol.
July 21.09.

Dear Mr Harrison,

We have decided to ask you to undertake the Chapel organ.

The pecuniary situation is as follows:

We can see our way to £1400 and I am therefore able definitely to ask you to let us have that amount of work by Sept. 1910.

But we want to have the complete £2000 organ eventually. The £600 may take some time to collect; on the other hand it may come in soon.

I therefore propose that you should plan the organ according to the specification which we have discussed, and let us have for certain as much as you can for £1400. If in the meantime the rest of the money comes in I will let you know immediately.

What I should like to have to start with is the work which will give the greatest amount of [to(*ne*) *deleted*] variety and tone for accompanying a simple congregational service. The suggestions I made in my last letter[875] may serve as a basis. I should very much like the Tuba if that can be got in.

The Headmaster suggests that when the time comes for erection you should confer with Sir Charles Nicholson as to the arrangement of pipes with a view to an organ-case at some future date.

The builders take possession of the Chapel on August 9th. Can you arrange to take out the old organ as soon as possible after that date?

Yours very truly,

Arthur H. Peppin.

---

[873] Thomas Henry Davis, DMus, Organist and Master of the Choristers at Wells 1900–33 (later Canon and Precentor): L.S. Colchester, rev. R.D. Bowers and A. Crossland, *The Organs and Organists of Wells Cathedral* (Wells, 1974), p. 24.

[874] Organist of Rugby School 1886–1912, then Precentor of Eton: J.E. West, *Cathedral Organists, Past and Present* (2nd edn, 1921), p. 132.

[875] Letter of 3 July in Harrison & Harrison Archives, suggesting omission of 15 stops.

[305]   24 July 1909. Peppin to Harrison
[*Archives of Harrison & Harrison, Durham, Holograph on postcard*]

40 Clifton Park Road,
Clifton, Bristol.
July 24

Since writing we have had a conditional offer of a gift of £2000 complete from a friend. I shall probably know by tomorrow if the gift can be accepted, and will write at once. Could you let me have the contract by Tuesday morning? I go away on Tuesday at midday.

Yours,
A.H. Peppin.

[306]   24 July 1909. Peppin to Harrison: the mystery donor revealed
[*Archives of Harrison & Harrison, Durham. Holograph*]

40 Clifton Park Road
Clifton, Bristol
July 24.09

Dear Mr Harrison,
    I am very glad to tell you that we have been given the lump sum of £2000 for our organ (exclusive of case) and I am empowered to ask you to undertake the work. The Chapel is to be rebuilt, and the contractors hope to have it finished by next June. The date however is not to be relied on, and we shall [*be*] more likely to have the opening in Sept. or Oct. 1910, and we should like the organ to be ready by then.
    The donor of the organ is Mr H.H. Wills,[876] and he wishes to pay the money himself direct to you, and he wishes the contract to be made out and sent to him, and not to me or the Headmaster.
    I enclose his cheque for £500, dated Aug. 15th, the day before you propose to dismantle the present organ.
    Mr Wills has made one or two very reasonable conditions, which I will state.
    1. He wishes the specification to be inspected and passed by Sir Walter Parratt.[877]
    2. He would like a clause in the contract stating that the organ, after completion, is to be passed by an expert appointed by the Headmaster. We hope to ask Sir W. Parratt to open the organ, so he would naturally be the expert chosen.
    3. He suggests that the case should be plain. We are to pay for it, and we have sufficient money up to (say) £200. Will you kindly consult Sir C. Nicholson about it?
    It is very important that the sum of £2000 should not be exceeded. Mr Wills wishes the gift to be his complete, and we cannot ask him for a penny more. In saying this I have noted things in the specification which are not included in the £2000 – that is all right – it is merely that the actual organ must not exceed £2000.

---

[876] Herbert Henry Wills [*1156*: Town 1872–4], one of four sons of Henry Overton Wills III to attend Clifton, and member of Council from 1917 until his death in 1922. The organ was donated in memory of his brother Maitland [*1071*: NT 1871–7], killed in a climbing accident in 1885. H.H. was a Director of the Imperial Tobacco Co., JP (Somerset) and High Sheriff 1910; he and his brother George (not at Clifton) gave the Wills Memorial Building to the University in memory of their father.
[877] Organist of St George's Chapel, Windsor from 1882 until his death in 1924, and from 1893 Master of the Queen's, and later of the King's, Musick.

If you could manage to arrange that the front row of the gallery (except of course where the console comes) could still be used for seating, so much the better; but this is not absolutely necessary.

Mr Wills's address up to Aug 1st is: H.H. Wills Esq., Barley Wood, Wrington, Somerset. After Aug 1st.: Tulchan Lodge, nr. Alyth, Forfarshire, N.B.

We have every confidence in asking you to undertake the work, and are sure that you will give us a worthy instrument.

My address after next Tuesday is: Nanjulian, St Just R.S.O. [*Railway Sub Office*], Cornwall (till Aug. 11th). After that I shall be in Scotland, and will send you my address.

Yours very truly,

Arthur H. Peppin.

[307]   27 July 1909. H.H. Wills to Harrison & Harrison
[*Archives of Harrison & Harrison, Durham. Typescript*]

Barley Wood,

Wrington, R.S.O.,

Somerset,

July 27th, 1909.

Dear Sirs,

I have your letter of 26th July enclosing specification and agreement in duplicate for Clifton College Chapel organ.

I return the three latter with a few suggested pencil corrections which you will, I believe, approve and agree to sign before I sign. I cannot but think that, if the specification is to go to Sir Walter Parratt for his approval, that until he has replied and signified his agreement therewith it is a little premature for me to sign the agreement, for he may possibly suggest some alteration. I shall, however, be prepared to sign as soon as he has approved the specification and you have agreed to my pencil alterations.

Thank you for suggesting that Mr Harrison might come to see me at Alyth before August 8th. I do not expect to be there before 9th or 10th, so that would be too late for him and I hardly think that there is any real necessity for him to take this trouble, as, with the exception of these few points, the matter seems to be in order.

I am not sure whether there are to be three swell boxes or two, and some date for completion should be inserted. As to the latter point, the Headmaster is, I believe, hoping that you will be able to complete in time for the Commemoration services next summer. [*Added in MS*] Is this possible?

Yours faithfully,

H.H. Wills.

☐ *Detailed and sometimes animated discussion followed between Peppin and Harrison, with Wills and Parratt adding their voices to the mixture. Peppin was concerned to avoid what he felt to be unnecessary elaboration.*

[308]   30 September 1909. Peppin to Harrison
[*Archives of Harrison & Harrison, Durham. Holograph*]

40, Clifton Park Road,
Clifton, Bristol.
Sept. 30. 09.

Dear Mr Harrison,

The Headmaster wrote to Mr Wills about three days ago, saying that we were having some difficulty with Sir W.P. on certain comparatively small matters, and asking if he would consent to you and me fixing up the details between us. The answer has not come as yet, and I don't know what it may be, but Mr Wills is very reasonable and kind about it all, so I have some hopes about it.

In case matters should be so arranged, I will state my own views.

1. The Clarinet – I agree with you.

2. The Swell Mixture – on this point I can't really see your objection. The Swell 15th is often delightful without the Principal and 12th. With the Sw[*ell*] Diapason and nothing else it forms a delightful accompaniment to a little solo on the Orchestral Oboe or Clarinet in a verse of the Psalms. Also with the Sw. Oboe alone it forms a delightful combination for the same sort of purpose – in all such cases the addition of the other two ranks would quite spoil the effect. On the other hand the 12th and 22nd would *never* be used without the 15th, and so what's the odds? Whatever and wherever the break, the 15th would exist throughout, and I can't for the life of me see what is the harm of being able to use the one rank (15th) separately if one wants to for a special effect. Your offer to add the other rank is very generous and is quite in keeping with the spirit in which I know your work is done, but I really can't see why?

3. *The Contrafagotto.* It would be a great disappointment to me to go without this stop, especially the sort I know you would make. Every single organist I have consulted has agreed with me and Sir W.P. that it is what we should all prefer. But if it would really break your heart to go without the Double Trumpet I suppose I must reluctantly give way!

I believe you agree with me as to the need for keeping the Mixture, 15th and Principal on the Great pretty quiet. If the Great Organ has any weak point it seems to me it is in paucity of 8 ft work in proportion. I am anxious that this should not result in a lack of *dignity* which I fear might be the case unless the Mixtures and mutation are kept in their proper place. If I consulted merely my own ideas I would willingly sacrifice the 12th and Mixture for another 8 ft stop – particularly as we are to have a Clarion with harmonic trebles. However I daresay you will not mind having my views in mind in avoiding any tendency to shrillness in the Mixture.

I agree with you as to the Geigen – particularly as a change would involve difficulties with the Pedal Organ.

I will let you know as soon as we hear from Mr Wills. He is at present in Scotland and will not be back for 2 or 3 weeks. Probably the best plan would be for the Headmaster and me to see him personally and talk it over. He is interested in organs, and has a big old Willis in his house, and I daresay a personal interview would make it all straight. But this might involve a delay of 3 weeks – how would this matter to you?

Yours very truly,
Arthur H. Peppin.

P.S. I hope nothing in this letter suggests any lack of confidence in you. Please be assured that I am quite certain we have gone to the right man, and have said so to everybody,

I am coming to the conclusion that there are two different points of view about certain matters – that of the player and the builder. Sometimes these may be difficult to [*illegible word corrected to*] reconcile – the more so when the builder is an artist and not a tradesman, and so is keener upon his own ideas. I recognise the fact that we must be willing to meet each other half way in certain points.

□ *The organ was eventually installed in the spring of 1911, having reached Bristol by train.*[878]

[309]   27 January 1911. Harrison and Harrison to H.H. Wills
[*Archives of Harrison & Harrison, Durham. Typescript on printed form*]

Durham,
27th Januaruy 1911.

Dear Sir,

We beg to inform you that your organ will be consigned to [you *deleted*] Clifton on [the (*blank*) inst., *deleted*] Thursday next, railway carriage paid, and that our men will leave here at once to erect and complete it in the [Church *deleted*] Chapel.

[It is our custom to receive, according to contract, about two thirds of the cost on delivery of the work to our clients' agents *deleted*]. We shall [therefore *deleted*] be pleased if you will kindly send us a cheque in the course of a post or two for £1000 according to contract.

We are, your obedient servants,
Harrison & Harrison.

[*Minuted by Wills*] Acknowledged Jan 30th saying cheque sent to Mr Peppin to forward to the organ builders when the organ has arrived in Clifton Coll: Chapel. H.H.W.

[310]   21 March 1911. Harrisons' foreman to his employers: finishing touches
[*Archives of Harrison & Harrison, Durham. Holograph*]

Clifton College,
Bristol.
March 21st 1911.

Dear Sirs,

The men have come to stain the case work before the scaffold is taken down and the joiners are not quite finished yet. They expect to be done this week. They had orders from the College that they had [*to*] finish and get the scaffold down before Saturday first, as there is a Confirmation service in the Chapel. We are having some trouble with the coupler chests. The sw[*ell*] [*h*]as been to pieces and we are now putting back the choir. These were both running. This [*h*]as thrown us back two days.

---

[878] Sea transport might have been an option: in 1843 a London builder sent a new organ to St Davids by schooner: G. Bowen, *The Organs of St Davids Cathedral* (St Davids, 2001), p. 6.

The Choir will be back tonight.
Yours truly,
F. Oddy.
Please send us some silvering for touching up front pipes.

[311] 22 May 1911. The Head Master to Harrison
[*Archives of Harrison & Harrison, Durham. Holograph*]

School House,
Clifton College,
Bristol.
May 22. 1911.
Dear Mr Harrison,
On April 21 last I had a letter from Mr Wills, who is now abroad, in reference to the balance of price for the organ which was to be paid as soon as the organ was completed to the entire satisfaction of the expert appointed by the Headmaster. Dr David and I have agreed to appoint Dr Alcock[879] and he has handed me a letter expressing his satisfaction with the organ in the terms of the contract, and I accordingly enclose Mr Wills's cheque for £500.

I most heartily congratulate you on the successful completion of your labours. Not only Dr Alcock but all who have heard the organ are delighted with the result. It will be a valuable and permanent possession of the School for the happiness and benefit of many generations, and I am glad that you are yourself content that it is housed in a building which will do justice to its sweetness and power. Again thanking you on behalf of the whole School,
I am, yours very truly,
J.E. King.

☐ *Unfortunately the blowing mechanism was soon found to be inadequate, and scientific advice was sought.*

[312] 11 October 1915. Report by the Head of Physics on failure of the organ motor
[*RS3/147. Holograph*]

Memorandum on motor used for blowing the Chapel organ.
This motor was made by a Doncaster firm which has I believe recently come to an end. It has caused a great deal of trouble since it was installed, mainly on account of bad workmanship in one particular part. It so happens that the electric supply being alternating current, and alternating current motors being more difficult to manage than direct current, the motor was probably as good as could be obtained at the time so far as its design is concerned. (A great cause of the trouble is that the motor is required to start on practically full load.)

I am informed that alternating current motors can now be obtained of much better design and I am of opinion that it would be more economical to obtain a new motor than to continue to 'nurse' the old one.

---

[879] Sir Walter Galpin Alcock (knighted 1933), Organist of the Chapel Royals 1902–16, and thereafter of Salisbury Cathedral. Having certified that the organ answered contract, he then gave the inaugural recital, including ('by special request') the march *Floreat Cliftona* by E.M. Oakeley [*M31*].

If I may be permitted to do so I would like to suggest that unless a fair sum can be obtained for the present motor, it would be worth while to retain it as a 'stand by' in case of anything happening to the new motor, because I believe that the present one can be made to run satisfactorily for a few weeks. But three years' experience of it leads me to believe that it will be a constant source of trouble.

D. Rintoul.

I shall be pleased to go into further particulars orally if desired. There are several points which it would take a good deal of writing to explain.

D.R

Oct. 11th 1915.

□ *A new motor was bought for £16 in January 1916, though a year later this needed a new rotor which cost more than the motor itself. The more general problem of over-heating remained.*

[313]   24 March 1924. Harrison and Harrison to the College Secretary
[*RS3/147. Typescript*]

Harrison & Harrison, Organ Builders

Durham, 24th. March 1924

Dear Sir,

Our men at Clifton have reported to us the state of the organ in the College Chapel, and say that they have also reported it to you. The organ appears to have been 'baked', and they say that the trouble is due to nothing but excessive heat. Can nothing be done to keep the temperature more even, for it is really a thousand pities that such a fine organ should suffer as it does?

[*With arrangements for immediate attention.*]

Yours faithfully,

Arthur Harrison.

[314]   27 March 1924. Harrison and Harrison to the College Secretary
[*RS3/147. Typescript*]

Harrison & Harrison, Organ Builders

Durham, 27th. March 1924

Dear Sir,

We thank you for your letter of the 25th. inst. We think there can be no doubt as to the cause of the trouble, and Gavey says he has reported it before. We would point out that great variations of temperature also are bad for the organ. The air gets very much hotter in the organ gallery and in the upper portion of the organ than it does on the floor of the Chapel where the other wood work is situated.

The question of ventilation is really an expert one for an architect, and, although we cannot of course now say definitely what happened 14 or 15 years ago, we have for many years made a practice of pointing out to every architect with whom we are brought into contact the vital importance of ventilation in an organ chamber.

Mr Harrison[880] will gladly call and see you when next he is in Bristol, but unfortunately he is not likely to be in your district again for some time. If you would

---

[880] The writer's brother Harry Shaw Harrison, who was the principal designer.

like to see our Mr Wood[881] who is doing the work, he will be at the organ all next week.

Yours faithfully,

Arthur Harrison.

The School Song

☐ *Clifton's song 'The Best School of All' has words by the OC poet Sir Henry Newbolt. The music was supplied by Sir Hubert Parry at the prompting of his son-in-law baritone Harry Plunket Greene, also an OC.[882] Parry composed in the mornings before going off to his official duties as Director of the Royal College of Music. He worked quickly: 'Jerusalem' occupied him just one morning, the Clifton song a little longer.*

[315]   25–27 February 1908. Extracts from Sir Hubert Parry's Diary
[*Shulbrede Priory, Parry Archive*]

[*25th*] Worked on the school song Harry wants me to write for Clifton. To Coll. at 1.
[*26th*] Wet. Clifton song.
[*27th*] Last touches to Clifton song. Harry came in. To Coll.

Shortly before the first scheduled performance Clifton's Director of Music was still fussing over the details

[316]   9 November 1908. A.H. Peppin to Parry
[*Shulbrede Priory, Parry Archive*]

40 Clifton Park Road,

Clifton,
Bristol.
Nov. 9. 08.

My dear Sir Hubert,
    We are hoping to have 'The Best School of All' sung at the School Concert on Dec. 21st. I suppose it will fall in with your views that each verse should be sung by the choir in unison, the whole School and the mass of Old Cliftonians joining in the chorus, *unless* Plunket Greene can come and sing the solo, or some other soloist who could do it justice. I take it that in any case the whole assembly should join in the chorus. In that case would you have any objection to the chorus accompaniment being arranged for organ and strings? I think the piano, however vigorously thumped, would not be enough to support the assembled multitude.
    I was discussing it yesterday with the Headmaster and he was saying how delightful it would be if you could be present. I wonder if there is any chance of that? I feel sure that it would be pleasant to you – so many of the boys know of you through 'Blest

---

[881] Herbert Wood, jnr, 'fair bellows hand', employed 1923–30; with thanks to Mrs Radford of Harrison and Harrison for providing this information from the firm's archives.
[882] Harry Plunket Greene [*2059*: NT, OH 1877–81], Irish baritone, renowned for interpretation of his father-in-law's works; also much associated with Elgar (a soloist in the première of *The Dream of Gerontius* alongside Edward Lloyd [**407**]).

Pair of Sirens',[883] and you may be well assured of a hearty welcome from the School, and I think that their youthful enthusiasm would be pleasant to witness. I need not say what a real delight it would be to me to see you here. I wouldn't propose it if it involved any work, you would just be present in order that we might express our gratitude for the song, which would at any rate give *us* much pleasure.

I hope you are well. I hear that you are going strong at the College. I *should* awfully like you to hear our youngsters sing and play.

Yours most truly,

Arthur H. Peppin.

☐ *Parry did not come to the first performance, which was (perhaps because of the uncertainties mentioned here) deferred to the following term. Eight years later Newbolt hoped to meet Parry to discuss arrangements for commercial publication.*

[317]   11 June 1916. Sir Henry Newbolt to the Head Master
[*RB3/63*]

Netherhampton House, Salisbury
June 11. 1916.

My dear King

I do not know quite how things stand about the Song, and I shall be grateful if you will tell me. The facts as I know them are these: Sir H. Parry has instructed the Year Book Press, and I have instructed my Agents, Wate & Son, to arrange for publication of the Song. The Year Book Press have raised two points. First they object to the Song being labelled for Clifton only, as that would defeat the only object of general publication. This difficulty I think could easily be met by heading the Song 'The Best School of All' and placing a note beneath to say that it was written and composed for Clifton and first published in the *Cliftonian*.

Secondly, they say that the Song has already been printed and sold at 1d by Arrowsmiths, and they ask that this form of publication may cease. This I think seems reasonable, and I imagine you would not object. The price of the Song will now be 3d.

---

[883] This much admired piece for chorus and orchestra was written for Queen Victoria's Golden Jubilee in 1887. The text (from Milton) was suggested to the composer by Peppin's former employer, Sir George Grove. Peppin had directed a performance at Clifton in 1907, and although Parry could not be present he sent a message, to which Peppin replied: 'You are really awfully kind! That you should have thought of writing at all whilst you are ill and overworked, and should have borne this small matter in mind, has, I assure you, touched me deeply. I shall read out your letter to my young people at rehearsal tomorrow, and they will be very much pleased and much honoured. You will quite understand the kind of affection which one gets to feel for a lot of youngsters from the ages of 10 to 18 with whom one is doing happy and enjoyable work; they and I are bound together by a strong tie, and that tie has been much strengthened and vitalized lately by our common love and admiration of your glorious work. It would have given me intense pleasure if you could have seen for yourself how their young faces regularly glow even at the bare mention of 'Blest Pair of Sirens'; and whatever the merits of their performance may be they will not fail for lack of enthusiasm. You will, perhaps, think of us tomorrow evening when we shall just be beginning the work ... You will know that there is a gang of 70 or 80 children here who will tomorrow be thinking of you with very warm feelings of gratitude and admiration and who would have been awfully pleased if you could have come.': Peppin to Parry, 5 April 1917: Shulbrede Priory Archive.

I understand that Parry is keen on 'Clifton' being included in the title, but probably the above suggestion would satisfy him.

I am going to London on Thursday and may be able to see Parry. Perhaps you could let me have a note of your views at: 9 Atherstone Terrace S.W.

Yours sincerely,
Henry Newbolt.

☐ *Parry and Newbolt did not meet at this time, and no evidence has been found that they ever did.*

Douglas Fox: the early years

☐ *One of Parry's star pupils was Douglas Fox, who had entered the School in 1903.[884] His talent was immediately evident to Peppin, who had high musical connexions including Sir Walter Parratt, Master of the King's Musick. Parratt was due to be in Bristol on 2 June 1895 to inaugurate the organ in Colston Hall, and Peppin persuaded him to hear young Fox play. The Bristol visit was cancelled but Parratt then invited the boy to Windsor.*

[318]   [May 1905]. Arthur Peppin to Gerard Elsey Fox, father of Douglas
[*Keble College Archives AD 330. Holograph*]

Dear Mr Fox,
    Parratt is not coming after all; some Royal function has cropped up to interfere.
    But he is very willing to hear Douglas. He suggests a Saturday at Windsor – what do you say? I shall have to get leave from the H.M. both for him and myself.

Yours most truly,
Arthur H. Peppin.

[319]   4 June [1905]. Sir Walter Parratt to Peppin
[*Keble College Archives AD 330. Holograph*]

Windsor Castle
June 4

My dear Peppin,
    Forgive me. I have been sore driven [*?*] in the last week – two Courts with their rehearsals – Ascension Day services and rehearsals – endless correspondence about the Royal Wedding.[885]
    The little boy Fox interested me greatly. He possesses a keen musical organization, enough technique, good taste and considerable power of expression. His prospects of success as a professional musician are excellent.
    There is in these days a great and increasing demand for educated musicians and I should not like to recommend any course that would interfere with his mental development but if he is to be of any good as a musician he must have more time to his art than that allowed to the ordinary public school boy. I suggest a graduated

---

[884]   Douglas Gerard Arthur Fox [*6057*: ST 1903–10; *M302*: 1931–57 (Director of Music)].
[885]   The King's niece Princess Margaret of Connaught married Prince Gustav Adolf of Sweden (later King Gustav VI Adolf) in St George's on 15 June 1905.

specialization and I think at first he should be allowed about 3 or 4 hours in the week in addition to his present time. Also I advise that he should begin to learn the organ at once. He would be almost sure of gaining one of the many organ scholarships in Oxford and Cambridge. Also there is no more sure way of finding a musical career than that of the organist.

> Yours ever,
> Walter Parratt.

☐ *Peppin acted immediately, obtaining Glazebrook's agreement to Parratt's advice and starting Fox at the organ*

[320]   [5 June 1905]. Peppin to Gerard Fox
[*Keble College Archives AD 330. Holograph*]

> College Gate
> Monday

Dear Mr Fox,
    Parratt has written me at last. He says 'the boy ... excellent' [*as above, omitting* 'Fox'].
    He then recommends just what I suggested – a remission of 3 or 4 hours a week for musical study, and strongly advises beginning the organ at once. I have sent the letter to the H.M. with a strong case, and have hopes that he will consent. You shall see Parratt's letter when I get it back. He spoke to me most favourably of Douglas, and was evidently really struck with his ability. The letter only reached me this morning.

> Yours very truly,
> Arthur H. Peppin.

[321]   5 June 1905. Peppin to Gerard Fox
[*Keble College Archives AD 330. Holograph*]

> College Gate
> [May *deleted*] June 5/05

Dear Mr Fox,
    The Head Master gives his consent, quite willingly, to the remission of:
    1 hour form work
    1 " French
    1 " Science
    1 " Drawing
    I enclose Parratt's letter **[319]**. If you wish Douglas to begin the organ at once will you ask him to come and see me tomorrow at 2.30?
    I have told him nothing. This will be rather an epoch in his life, so I thought it right that you should have the telling of him.

> Yours very truly,
> Arthur H. Peppin.

☐ *After that year's Christmas concert, in celebration of the centenary of Trafalgar, Sir Charles Stanford conducted his own* Songs of the Sea, *with words by Sir Henry Newbolt and sung by Harry Plunket Greene. Also on the programme was Georg Goltermann's* Romanze *from the Grand Duo Op. 15, performed by J.C. Davies*

('Pop'),[886] *'cello, with Fox playing the piano and Sir Charles turning the pages for him.*[887]

[322]   [19 December 1905]. Peppin to Fox
[*Keble College Archives AD 330. Holograph*]

College Gate
Tuesday

My dear Douglas,
Thank you so much for your kind and beautiful present. I value it very much indeed, and the kind and affectionate feeling which made you send it.
I thought you got on splendidly at the concert, both you and Pop, and Sir Charles Stanford was very much pleased with you both. Best Xmas wishes to you all.
Your affectionate,
Arthur H. Peppin.

☐ *Fox's Form Master also sent congratulations.*

[323]   19 December 1905. T.S. Peppin[888] **to Fox**
[*Keble College Archives AD 330. Holograph*]

1 Percival Road
Clifton
Bristol
Dec 19. 1905

My dear Douglas,
I must write at once and thank you for your delightful gift. It is fortunately one that will *last*, and it will remind me always of the giver.
I have another thing to thank you for, and that is your playing in the concert so well last night.
You and 'Pop' performed excellently. I quite understand the reasons of your being able to play, and not being able to do all your exams. I knew all about it and fully approved. The only thing that I am sorry about is that your absence unluckily robbed you of your Class Prize which would have been a certainty.
You came top, all right, in the Latin prose exam. We obtained a very good result – in short a great victory!
In that 'classical exam' which I spoke of, i.e. the exams on unseens and proses (Greek and Latin) IIIγ acquitted themselves nobly: in fact we were 2nd best form in the whole School, which is not bad considering that 5 were absent. I have placed you top, in accordance with your term's order so you get your remove all right.
James[889] is 2nd and Turner[890] 3rd. Turner got a class prize.
IIIγ beat all the other 3rds easily on the history paper, so on the whole we have done pretty well, and you and your merry little companions have helped to give me a very jolly holiday.

---

[886] Jenner Conway Davies [*6181*: ST 1903–11].
[887] *The Cliftonian* XIX (1905–7), pp. 153–4; Fox, *Douglas Fox*, p. 12. Sir Charles Villiers Stanford (d. 1924) was Professor at Music at Cambridge.
[888] Talbot Sydenham Peppin [*M157*: 1897–1918†]; brother of A.H.
[889] Walter Amyas James [*6297*: ST 1904–8].
[890] Thomas Henry Lockley Turner [*6244*: NT 1904–9].

Thomas[891] got a 2nd class in English!

A-hem.

Mind you get all right soon, and enjoy yourself at Xmas. Mr Hemsley[892] is very pleased with your Greek! He told me about it specially.

Goodbye now.

Thanking you once again for your delightful present, I remain,
Yours ever,
T.S. Peppin.

□ *Sir Walter Parratt continued to take an interest in Fox's progress.*

[324]   6 July 1909. Parratt to A.H. Peppin
[*Keble College Archives AD 330. Holograph*]

Windsor
July 6. 1909

My dear Peppin,

Such an account *coming from you* gives me pause, and I could not send a hasty answer. Such a boy ought to go to the university and I am inclined to think that he should stay at School until he has gained his Certificate, then come to the Royal College until he is of age for a College organ scholarship. Keble will be vacant in about three years I suppose, and that would bring him to the proper age. But I would send him in for the R.C.M. scholarship next January anyhow. The preliminary should *not* be taken at Bristol. At present he could not be in better hands. Armitage[893] is *very* slow, and a great anxiety to me, but it would be a pity to separate him from his most wholesome bent. He still spells out every bar.
Ever yours,
W.P.

□ *From the RCM Fox went up to Keble College, Oxford in 1912. At the start of the War he sought leave to enlist; this was at first refused. Peppin, who in September 1915 had just moved to Rugby as Director of Music, tried to discourage his continuing wish to serve.*

[325]   26 September [1915]. Peppin to Fox
[*Keble College Archives AD 330. Holograph*]

2 Vicarage Road,
Rugby
Sun. Sept. 26

My dear Douglas,

I haven't heard much of you lately, but I am thinking that you will soon have to make up your mind finally as to the question of military service. Since you have previously consulted me I think that there can be no harm in my saying that the more I think about it the more do I adhere to my opinion – that you will really be of more

---

[891] Wyndham Wakeham Thomas [*6117*: HHP, WaH 1903–6].

[892] William James Hemsley [*M185*: 1904–15].

[893] Perhaps Frederick Clifford Armitage [*6218*: OH 1904–8], who went on to the RCM before becoming a piano and pianola maker.

use to the community by staying as you are. I think that the same applies to a good many others, and this practice of hounding all sorts of people into the army, whether they have any aptitude for it or not, is a dangerous one. I am afraid that, whichever way you decide, you will have qualms, but I think that on the whole you will be happier if you decide against military service. If you come to the conclusion that this view is right you will need a good deal of moral courage to stick to it – probably more than if you follow popular opinion, which is the line of least resistance; but all your friends will know and understand, and none of them will think the worse of you. That is my view.

Yours affectionately,
A.H.P.

☐ *Fox enlisted in the 4th Bn the Gloucestershire Regiment and was sent to the Western Front in 1916. On 27 August 1917 he was severely wounded in the right arm, which was amputated the following day.*[894] *Among the many who wrote letters of sympathy were Parry and Stanford, though in strikingly different styles.*

[326] 9 September 1917. Parry to Fox
[*Keble College Archives AD 330. Holograph*]

Highnam Court,
Gloucester.
Sept. 9 1917

My dear Fox,
   Your father and Peppin have both written to tell me of the really dreadful tragedy that has happened to you – and to us all – to me it is one of the most cruel things that has happened in the war. I daresay you may think I am exaggerating: but then I can't help setting such a great value on the things you were capable of doing that it represented something quite irreplaceable – You may be sure that everyone who knows you will be stirred to their very deepest sympathy. I am afraid I am in such a bitter humour about it that I can't say anything that will be the least helpful. It's one of the severest trials that I have ever heard of being put on anyone. No doubt your devotion and courage will bring you through. I can only trust that it may be so. My loving sympathy is beyond my powers of expression – and with your father too.
   I hope I shall hear more news of you somehow.

Your old friend,
C. Hubert H. Parry.

[327] 13 September 1917. Sir Charles Stanford to Fox
[*Keble College Archives AD 330. Holograph*]

Walmer Lodge
Abbey Road,
Malvern.
Sept 13. 17

---

[894] Fox wrote to Peppin on 4 September: 'I was wounded on the 27th, and on the 28th they took my arm (right) off just above the elbow. Apparently they consulted very carefully before doing it, but it seems to have been hopelessly shattered, and they thought I probably shouldn't have lived if they had left it': full letter in Fox, *Douglas Fox*, p. 25.

My dear Fox,

You father (and also our friend Lang)[895] was good enough to write to me and tell me about your troubles. It grieves us all as you know: but there is a certain relief that it is only a wing, however valuable, and that you are now comparable to Nelson. You'll find that, bar the five finger exercises in the right hand, you'll adapt yourself to things quicker than you imagine. Anyhow you've got a jolly good brain, and it may do quite as much for you minus an arm as plus one: and you can always make other people play the wrong notes and not be responsible! When you come back, be sure and come and see me (9 Lower Berkeley St, Portman Sq.). I'll cut up your dinner for you. We go back to term on the 20th. I perceive in my mind's eye that you will take to writing things and conducting them (like that confounded young Richard II of Bayreuth) with the *mano sinistra*.[896] Cheer up. The Fox has not lost his brush anyhow.

Yours always,
C.V. Stanford.

[328]   11 September 1917. A.A. David (Headmaster of Rugby) to Fox
[Keble College Archives AD 330. Holograph]

School House,
Rugby
11 Sep. 1917.

My dear Fox,

I was in Clifton and saw your father just after the Chaplain's letter came to say that you had been wounded. It was a blow, and one could enter into their anxiety, but there was comfort in it. Now comes the much more grievous news. Short of life no heavier sacrifice could have been asked of you. I know how bravely you will make it, and of course there will be consolations more and better than you can judge of now. The enjoyment of your dear music will remain, and even her service will not I believe be wholly denied to you. But I think I know what the first bitterness must be, and I want to tell you that I am sharing it with all your friends, and thinking of you continually. I pray that Christ may comfort you. Meanwhile *that* warfare of yours is ended, and I thank God for it.

I hope to see you when you come home.

Yours ever,
A.A. David.

[329]   13 October 1917. Mabel Clissold to Fox
[Keble College Archives AD 330. Holograph]

1, Albert Road,
Clifton, Bristol.
13.10.17

Dear Mr Fox,

A month ago nearly I received a letter from my brother containing this message for you 'if I saw you'.

---

[895] Craig Sellar Lang (known as Robin) [*6185*: ST, BH 1903–10; *M257*: 1921–9 (Assistant Music Master)], Fox's contemporary and close friend at school and the RCM; by the time Fox did return to Clifton, Lang had moved to Christ's Hospital as Director.

[896] Wagner was one of the first conductors to employ the left hand as well as the right.

'I am exceeding sorry to hear of Douglas Fox's lost arm. It is a costly gift he has given his country. I expect he is secretly proud that he has given so great a thing. I should be I think but I fear my limbs can't claim to be specially valuable! If you see him tell him I have been thinking of him [and *deleted*]'.

You will have heard that he has now given himself.[897] Today there is a Memorial service in the School Chapel.

Yours sincerely,
Mabel E. Clissold.

[330] 6 December 1917. Michael Glazebrook (Canon of Ely) to Fox
[*Keble College Archives AD 330. Holograph*]

The College, Ely.
Dec 6 1917.

My dear Fox.

I was at Clifton some six weeks ago, taking the Memorial service for Clissold, and I then heard of your wound. Ever since then Mrs Glazebrook and I have been wanting to send some expression of our sympathy, but we have only just got your address from Mr Peppin.

We feel it very acutely as a personal loss that the talent, whose beginnings we watched with so much pleasure, is robbed of its best instrument. We remember so well the first time you came to play for the one of the newly-invented 'stars'[898] – a little boy in the Pre, who sat so straight and played with such delightful seriousness: and we have always looked forward to your being a famous pianist. Well! You have given a nobler gift to your country than all the music would have been. I thank God for all the sacrifices my old boys have made, and for yours among the greatest.

And yet we can't help hoping. You will see that on the Xmas card Mrs. Glazebrook has written Browning's line 'So may a glory from defect arise'.[899] Sometimes what seems misfortune really turns a man's life into the channel which is best and highest for him. There is one thing better than a great pianist, and that is a great composer. The two [powers *corrected to*] lines run so close together that I believe it is often an accident which a man takes.

We unite in affectionate regards.

Yours most truly,
M.G. Glazebrook.

[331] 5 April 1918. Testimonial by Parry on behalf of Fox
[*M302 file. Holograph*]

Royal College of Music
April 5. 1918

I have the honour to state that Mr Douglas G.A. Fox was, before the war, one of the finest performers on the organ in the United Kingdom, if not in the world, and would, without doubt, have risen to one of the very foremost positions in the country, as his general musical outfit and his sterling character both fitted him for great

---

[897] Harry Clissold was killed on 28 September.
[898] Stars were originally for schoolwork only; Fox was the first to be awarded one for a musical performance (of a Bach two-part invention in C major): Fox, *Douglas Fox*, p. 10.
[899] From *Deaf and Dumb*.

responsibilities; and that the truly tragic wound which entailed the amputation of his right arm has entirely shut him out from doing the exceptional services to his country which his great abilities would have fitted him for, and from the honour he would have brought to himself and the nation if his unselfish devotion to duty had not made him set aside all personal consideration and subject himself to the same risks as men with no special individual gifts – and I venture to suggest that the truly tragic outcome merits the favourable consideration of the authorities in considering the amount to be granted him in some compensation for the entire ruin of very exceptional prospects.

C. Hubert H. Parry,

Director of the Royal College of Music.

McKie appointed Director of Music 1926

□ *Fox adjusted to his disability with remarkable speed, and in 1918 he was appointed Director of Music at Bradfield College. Peppin took orders and became Vicar of Shepton Montague in Somerset. From there he urged Fox to apply for the Directorship at Clifton in 1926.*

[332]   25 May [1926]. Peppin to Fox
[*Keble College Archives AD 330. Holograph*]

Shepton Montague,

Wincanton.

Somt.

May 25.

My dear Douglas,

Your family have been over here and we discussed you, and I promised to write.

Unless you really don't want to go to Clifton I think you are really mistaken in not applying.

I don't think that Robin[900] will get it anyhow. He says that he could work under you there but nobody else. You and he would be a strong combination and would help each other out and work well together, like the Kings of Barataria.[901] So if you don't go the School may lose him as well as you, which would be a pity. If you don't apply there seems to me some risk that the sort of man may get it whom I at least don't want to see there. If you are not qualified then no one is – and, as I say, Robin's position need be no obstacle. You had better apply soon, or it may be too late – now, my dear old boy, don't let your silly old diffidence keep you back! Hang it all, if you are not suitable and qualified who the Dickens is? Go in and win, is my advice! If you want me to write a testimonial I'll do so, tho' I have already told Whatley what I think of your qualifications.

In haste – your affectionate,

A.H.P.

---

[900] C.S. Lang [*6185/M257*]; above **[327]**.
[901] The co-regent gondoliers imagined by Gilbert and Sullivan.

[333]   26 May 1926. Peppin to Fox.
[*Keble College Archives AD 330. Holograph*]

Shepton Montague,
Wincanton,
Somt.
May 26.26.

My dear Douglas,
Thanks for your card which was brought by the same postman who carried away my letter to you.

I repeat that I am almost certain that Whatley won't appoint Robin! I myself don't think Robin would do. With all his conspicuous virtues and merits he is not *big* enough, and a man whose sole interests are absolutely confined to music would never dominate the abler boys in the School, nor masters. On the other hand he is so chivalrous and large-hearted that he would (as he has said) work cheerfully and loyally under you, and would be an immensely valuable 'Chief of Staff'. I think the two of you would be a very strong combination.

It is also not unreasonable to take into account that he has money of his own and need never be absolutely dependent on what he earns.

I may say, *in strict confidence*, that Whatley spoke to me about Robin long ago in this connection, and consulted me quite seriously. He did not commit himself, but we both agreed substantially with the views I have stated above. He said 'I don't think he would do'. But you must not mention this. I believe Robin would like you to get it.

Your affectionate,
A.H.P.

[*Postscript at head*] To apply would not necessarily bind you to take it, even if it was offered to you.

☐ *Fox did not apply, and the front runner was a young Australian, William McKie,*[902] *whose candidature Peppin had already promoted. Michael Glazebrook and the Precentor of Eton wrote in support. Despite doing his best to talk himself down, McKie was appointed.*

[334]   14 April 1926. Canon Glazebrook to Whatley
[*RS2/386. MS*]

The College,
Ely.
April 14th.

My dear Whatley,
A letter from Peppin, received this morning, tells me that Beachcroft[903] is leaving you, and that he <(Peppin)> is suggesting among others the name of W.N. McKie. As I know McKie very well and am much interested in him, I venture to write a few lines for your consideration.

---

[902] Sir William Neil McKie [*M284*: 1926–30 (Director of Music)]; Organist and Informator Choristarum at Magdalen College, Oxford 1938–41; Organist and Master of the Choristers of Westminster Abbey 1941–63 (knighted for directing the music at the 1953 Coronation); see H. Hollis, The *Best of Both Worlds: The Life of Sir William McKie* (Melbourne, 1991).

[903] Richard Owen Beachcroft [*M160*: 1897–1926]; had succeeded Peppin as Director of Music in 1915.

Five years ago he came to take our organist's place for a month. He was just then going from the Royal College, as their most brilliant pupil, to be organist at Worcester.[904] He was a charming boy, full of life and interest. We had him for our guest, and from that time onward he had been frequently with us, almost on the footing of a son of the house. My wife,[905] who is no mean judge of young men, formed a very high opinion of him. In one respect he has disappointed us: with his great talent, we wanted to see him organist in a great cathedral. But various causes have turned him to teaching, for which he undoubtedly has a great gift. At Oxford he made a mark. He rowed in the boat, was head of the College club, and was twice President of the <Oxford> Musical Society – which has never happened to an undergraduate before.

I gather that he is doing well at Radley: but he is hampered by being second to a man who is very much his inferior. I know the latter quite well.

By my advice he refused a tempting offer to go to Toronto last year – to Upper Canada College. I felt he would be wasted there. For he is a real musician. He has a fine taste, is a rapid and brilliant composer, and has (like Peppin) a sense of the place of music in general culture. Of course he is popular with boys, and indeed with people in general. All my friends who have met him at my house have invited him to stay with them. Popularity, as I tell him, is his temptation. He is a little too willing to oblige by taking up extra jobs which don't belong to him. But he has, *au fond*, a very strong and fine character. His parents, a Melbourne clergyman and his wife, are admirable people, if I may judge by their letters and by what he tells me.

If it were not for that I should hesitate to recommend so young a man. But I believe he would rise to the position.

You will of course take this with a grain of salt, as coming from one who has a real affection for him. But I hope you will give him an interview, and notice his eyes and his chin as indications of character.

My dear wife would gladly have endorsed all this. But she lies at death's door. For five weeks she has been unconscious, and the end must come before long. I have been ill in consequence of the long strain. I am spending a few days at Hunstanton in order to gain a little strength to meet what is to come.[906]

Yours very sincerely,

M.G. Glazebrook.

[335]   19 May 1926. H.G. Ley[907] to the Head Master
[*RS2/386*]

Private

Savile House,
Eton College, Windsor.
May 19. 26.

---

[904] Worcester College, Oxford, where McKie was Organ Scholar.

[905] Ethel Glazebrook (d. 1926), fifth daughter of Sir Benjamin Collins Brodie, Bt, Waynflete Professor of Chemistry.

[906] The door opened first for Glazebrook himself, on 1 May; his wife followed him a fortnight later: Christie, *History*, p. 160.

[907] Henry George Ley (d. 1962), Precentor of Eton 1926–46; Fox's predecessor as Organ Scholar of Keble. He had already recommended McKie to R.O. Beachcroft by letter of 4 May [*RS2/386*].

Dear Headmaster,

On musical grounds, I should say McKie was the most gifted. He and Huggins[908] were both pupils of mine. Ross[909] is also *very* gifted, but he is a curious personality, and not easy to make friends with. Of the three, I think I should choose McKie, though I find it very difficult to choose between him and Huggins, as the latter has had more experience of English public schools. McKie, as you know, was brought up in Australia, and was awarded a scholarship at the Royal College.

We are just getting settled, and everyone is most kind here.

Yours sincerely,

Henry G. Ley.

Has Douglas Fox applied?

[336]   1 June [1926]. McKie to the Head Master
[*RS2/386. Holograph*]

Radley College,
Abingdon,
Berks.
June 1.

Dear Mr Whatley,

As Huggins [*sic*] has withdrawn his name, I should like to give mine as a provisional candidate for the Directorship of Music at Clifton: but obviously I can't stand definitely until I know something more about the position and the conditions of appointment.

Sincerely yours,

W.N. McKie.

[337]   11 June [1926]. McKie to the Head Master
[*RS2/386. Holograph*]

Radley College,
Abingdon,
Berks.
June 11.

Dear Mr Whatley,

Thank you for a very pleasant day yesterday. One or two things have come into my mind since. I came down yesterday not quite knowing whether I wanted to apply. If I had complete confidence that I could walk in and run the job magnificently, I shouldn't hesitate. Of course I know I'm not big enough for the job now – that could hardly be expected, and it would be ludicrous to compare me with a man like Dr Beachcroft – but I wonder whether I should grow to it. When I first heard Huggins was applying I was very glad, because if he had been appointed, I should have stayed here, and I know I could run Radley quite well – the boys know me, and I think trust me. But as I have not had a great deal <of> experience [of *corrected to*] in dealing

---

[908] Geoffrey Joseph Higgins [*8573*: NT 1919–24; *M295A*: 1929–34]; Music Master at Harrow. Ley was evidently vague about names (writing to Beachcroft on 4 May as 'My dear Beechcroft').
[909] Hugh Cuthbert Melville Ross [*7334*: HHP, NT 1912–16]; won an organ scholarship to the RCM, and Organist of Holy Trinity, Winnipeg, and Director of the New York Schola Cantorum.

with large masses of people, nor of running things, I feel rather afraid of Clifton – especially as there is no retreat possible!

Please don't think I'm hedging and want to withdraw: on the contrary, having seen everything, I'm quite decided I do want to apply. I think it's really a wonderful job. Perhaps you may have thought of all these things already, and I needn't have mentioned them; but I think it only common honesty to point them out, and also that, if you appoint me, it will be quite a gamble, and I can't guarantee how it will turn out! I need hardly say that I should do my best, but whether it would be a good enough best is for you to decide.

My expenses yesterday came to about 32/-.

With kind regards, sincerely yours,
W.N. McKie.

[338]   15 June 1926. McKie to the Head Master
RS2/386. Holograph]

Radley College,
Abingdon,
Berks.
June 15

Dear Mr Whatley,

Thank you very much for your letter, and for the honour you have done me. It's a big thing to succeed to such a tradition. I think it's very adventurous of you to appoint me, and I hope you won't regret it; for my part I shall do all that I can to see that you don't.

I should very much like to come down during this term, for a week-end if possible. I think you told me that there would be House music competitions this term; perhaps you would let me come for those.

Sincerely yours,
W.N. McKie.

Fox appointed Director of Music 1930

☐ *But after just four years the gamble had failed. McKie was suffering from home-sickness and, when this was not accommodated, severe depression.*

[339]   12 January 1930. McKie to the Head Master
[RS2/386. Holograph]

Avonswick [*recte* Avonwick], S. Brent
Devon
Jan. 12: 1930

Dear Headmaster,

I talked to you some months ago about a job in Melbourne.[910] The City Council are at last doing something about it, and I have just had particulars sent me.

---

[910] City Organist and Musical Adviser.

The curious thing about it is that they will not at first elect permanently, but want someone to go out for 12 months (including time spent in travelling both ways). There is a note that during these 12 months the question of appointing a permanent organist will be considered: but no guarantee can be given that the organist appointed under these conditions will be appointed permanently. From unofficial information I think it very likely that they will try several people and not appoint permanently for two or three years.

So there is no question of my going there permanently. It is obviously impossible for me to go out even on these conditions (if appointed): I can't resign Clifton and go for a year on the chance of getting a job when I come back here; and I can't ask for a year's leave of absence from Clifton.

Is there any possibility of just giving me leave off for a shorter period, two terms if possible? (1930.2 – 1930.3 or 1931.1 – 1931.2) I know that I am asking a lot, and I can see many difficulties, so I shall quite understand if you just say no at once; but I should be most grateful if you would consider it. If it were not for family reasons I should have put this out of my mind long ago: but family reasons are rather pressing. I have <not> been home for four years (and actually have only spent five weeks at home in the last 11 years) and I see no chance of going in the next four or five years, for financial reasons with which I won't bother you now. My father is not likely to live long. I mention this is in self-justification, for I don't want you to think that I want to rush away from Clifton or to ask leave to go off on a pleasure jaunt.

If I do apply, I must do so by Feb. 14. Of course it's quite possible that, if I state in my application that I can't go for the full time that they ask, I should be disqualified at once.

Please don't bother to answer this; I'm going to Ross on Monday, and am back at Clifton on Thursday.

I've had a very good time here; this is an excellent inn and very good country. The local squire is the father of Cornish-Bowden:[911] we met the family at church this morning, where we had an uncommonly good sermon.

I hope you are all well. Best wishes to Mrs. Whatley.

Yours sincerely,
W.N. McKie.

[340] 2 June [1930]. McKie to the Head Master
[*RS2/386. Holograph*]

46 College Road
Clifton, Bristol
June 2.

Dear Headmaster,

I'm very sorry to be staying out so long; at present things are stationary – I can't throw this thing off, and feel completely useless, and don't seem to get either better or worse.

This is the climax of six unpleasant months: for I have felt out of sorts ever since December and increasingly so lately. It seems to me that I must take drastic steps (if necessary) to get fit again – give up all outside activities and cut down work to bare essentials for a time – or else give up altogether. The latter I naturally don't want

---

[911] James Hubert Cornish-Bowden [*9699*: DH 1926–30], of Black Hall, Avonwick. The inn was doubtless the Avon Arms at Avonwick, which displays the Cornish-Bowden arms.

to do, for a great many reasons: but it's not fair to the School music to try to carry on like this, for I know that I'm not doing the job properly. One can do things by screwing oneself up to it, but there is a limit to that kind of thing, and I think I have reached it. I've been conscious during the last three months of staleness and lack of guts, and a good many things are not as I should like them.

This is not as you might think, written hastily in a fit of depression; but it has been vaguely in my mind for some time now and I should like to discuss it frankly with you.

Yours sincerely,

W.N. McKie.

☐ *In the event McKie secured the appointment as City Organist in Melbourne, and his post at Clifton was immediately advertised.*

[341]   30 June 1930. Notice of vacancy
[*RS2/201. Typescript*]

June 30th, 1930.

Directorship of Music

The post of Director of Music will be vacant at the end of the Autumn term.

The duties of the Director are (1) to supervise and organise the whole musical life of the School, including private lessons in music and the School orchestral and choral societies; (2) to act as organist and choir master; (3) to give instruction to not less than 20 private pupils.

The Director of Music is under the same general conditions of employment as other members of the staff. He is paid according to the School salary scale with the addition of £100 per annum, paid to him as Head of the Music Department. He would be required, after five years' service, to join the School pension scheme.

The salary scale starts at £300 per annum, non-resident, rising by £10 per annum to £350, and subsequently by £20 per annum to £670. Allowance may be made for previous experience up to a maximum of ten years.

The pension scheme, which is partly contributory, provides for a pension of £300 per annum at the retiring age of 60. A capital sum may be taken in lieu of the pension, or in case of retirement before the age of 60.

☐ *This time Fox did apply and was successful.*

[342]   5 August 1930. Fox to the Head Master
[*RS2/201. Holograph*]

Grand Hotel Kronenhof-Bellavista
Pontresina (Engadine)
Aug. 5. 1930

Dear Mr Whatley,

Many thanks for your letter. I shall be very glad to accept your offer and the generous terms you mention, and I have written to Mr Whitworth[912] to obtain his

---

[912] E.J. Whitworth, Headmaster of Bradfield; on 2 August he had informed Whatley that he had given Fox leave to apply for the Clifton post: 'I am quite certain that we shall not get a better man. He has been here twelve years and the reward of going to his own school is indeed deserved and our loss with be your gain'; RS2/101.

formal acceptance of my resignation. I will write to you again directly I hear from him.

There is a non-contributory pension scheme at Bradfield, and I think I am entitled to carry on the policy at my own expense unless some other <and better> arrangement is made. I will send you further particulars as soon as I receive them.

I should like to come and see you one day before the end of the holidays, if convenient.

Yours sincerely,
D.G.A. Fox.

[343] 12 August 1930. Fox to the Head Master
[*RS2/201. Holograph*]

Grand Hotel Kronenhof-Bellavista
Pontresina (Engadine)
Aug. 12. 1930

Dear Mr Whatley,

I heard from Mr Whitworth yesterday and he has accepted my resignation. I shall therefore be able to accept your offer definitely, and shall look forward to coming to Clifton after Christmas. I would have written to you immediately on receipt of Mr Whitworth's letter, but I had to start at 4.30 this morning for a long walk.

I much appreciate your having offered me this appointment, and I realise the difficulty and responsibility of maintaining the high standard of music at Clifton. I have obtained particulars of my Bradfield pension and can show them to you when convenient for you to consider the matter.

Yours sincerely,
D.G.A. Fox.

☐ *Before Fox left Bradfield he was asked to contribute to accessories for the Clifton Chapel Organ.*

[344] 30 September 1930. McKie to Arthur Harrison
[*Archives of Harrison & Harrison, Durham. Typescript*]

Clifton College
Bristol
Sept. 30, 1930

Dear Mr Harrison,

I am leaving here after Christmas to take up an appointment in Australia, and am being succeeded here by Douglas Fox, of Bradfield. I don't know whether you know him – but anyhow you may know that he lost his right arm in the war. He wants to know if two things can be added to the organ:

I. A Swell sub-octave coupler; II. A zero piston or pedal, to put all stops in.

Could you tell me: I. Whether these things could be put in without difficulty; II. What the cost would be; III. Whether it could be done in the Christmas holidays?

The ideal arrangement would be to have it done when the organ is cleaned next summer; but Fox depends very much on these two things, and would like it done before he comes, if it is possible.

I hope I may be in the north before I go, and in that case I shall hope to pay the visit to your works which I have so long promised myself.

With all good wishes to Mrs Harrison and yourself,

I am, yours truly,

W.N. McKie.

[345]   2 October 1930. Harrison to McKie
[*RS3/147. Typescript*]

Harrison & Harrison, Organ Builders

Durham, 2nd. October, 1930.

Dear Mr McKie,

Clifton College organ

Thank you for your letter of the 30th ult. There would be no difficulty in putting in the two proposed additions to the organ, but, as there is no provision or preparation for them of any sort whatever, you will understand that they would cost more than if they had formed part of the original scheme.

We estimate that the Swell sub-octave coupler, to act though the existing unison manual couplers, i.e. 'Swell to Great' and 'Choir to Swell', would cost ninety-two pounds (£92).

A zero piston or pedal to put in all stops would cost sixty-five pounds (£65). I think perhaps a pedal would be more useful for Mr Douglas Fox for this purpose than a piston.

They could be done during the Christmas holidays if an order were given at once, so that we could put in the new work immediately. I quite see that these additions would be specially useful to Mr Fox, and they would also, of course, prove a valuable and lasting improvement to the organ.

Yours sincerely,

Arthur Harrison.

[346]   6 October 1930. The Head Master to Fox
[*RS2/201. Typescript file copy*]

6 October, 1930.

Dear Fox,

We have now received estimates from Harrisons for the additions to the organ. The Swell sub octave coupler would cost £92, and the zero piston or pedal (they recommend a pedal) would cost £65. The Council meets towards the end of this month and I will bring these estimates before them. They come at a rather unfortunate moment as the Council has this year to spend a large sum on cleaning the organ.

McKie says that he thinks you are willing to contribute something towards the cost. I do not know if that is really so, but if it is, could you tell me what sort of amount you had in mind?

Yours sincerely,

[*minuted*] N.W.

[347]   7 October 1930. Fox to the Head Master
[*RS3/147. Holograph*]

Bradfield, Berks.

Oct. [*6 corrected to*] 7.30

Dear Mr Whatley,
    Many thanks for your letter about the organ. I am rather appalled at the cost of these additions and would not have asked for them if I had realised what they would charge.
    I think I can manage without the zero pedal, especially if a boy can be in the organ loft to help me.[913] The Swell sub octave would certainly be very useful and I feel I ought to contribute at any rate half the cost (£46), but if this is not considered enough I would increase this by whatever you and the Council think necessary. The one compensation of the organ here is that it contains a sub-octave and this stop happens to be more useful to me than to other organists.
    I hope to come down for the week-end on November 8th.

Yours sincerely,

D.G.A. Fox.

I am most grateful that any alteration or addition to the organ should be considered at all, and hope I am not asking for too much.

[348]   22 October 1930. Council's approval
[*Council Minute Book 9, pp. 31–2. MS*]

Additions to Chapel organ.
    The Headmaster reported that additions to the Chapel organ had been recommended by Messrs Harrison and Harrison, particularly in view of the appointment of Mr D.G.A. Fox to succeed Mr McKie as Director of Music, and that Mr Fox had offered to pay £46, being half the cost of the installation of a Swell sub octave coupler.
    On the motion of Mr Tribe, seconded by Mr Coles, it was decided that the College would contribute £46 towards the cost of the Swell sub octave coupler, but that no further action should be taken in regard to the installation of the zero piston or pedal.

☐ *On 24 October the Head Master conveyed the Council's approval to Fox, who duly undertook to pay half the cost of the coupler.*

Fox as Director of Music

[349]   16 March 1937. The Bursar[914] to Fox
[*RS3/147. Typescript*]

Subject. Tunint [*sic*] of the organs in the Chapel and Big School

16th March, 1937

---

[913] A toe piston cancelling the pedal stops was subsequently installed specifically to assist Fox: Birley, 'Organs in Clifton College', p. 40.
[914] Col. Gerald Eliot Badcock, Bursar 1936–9, whose regime was described by Whatley as 'an orgy of sham efficiency': Winterbottom, *Clifton after Percival*, p. 114.

Dear Douglas,

Do give me your help and advice, in regard to the possibility of making a reduction in the charges made by Harrison for tuning the organs in the Chapel and the Big School. Their charge for the Chapel organ is £30 a year, a figure, I understand, agreed upon in May, 1919. Whilst that for the Big School comes to sixteen guineas a year and this latter arrangement was made in May, 1923. In other words, we pay for these two organs £46. 16. 0 a year.

Do you think we could get a lesser price or, if we do, do you think it is likely to affect the organ to its detriment?

You would know better than I do, of course, the number of times these organs are tuned each year, but, from what Gough[915] tells me, I understand that they send to do it any time within reason when we ask them to do it.

Yours sincerely,
G.E. Badcock.

Copy to the Chairman of the Finance Committee.

[350]   17 March 1937. Fox to the Bursar
[*RS3/147. Holograph*]

March 17 37

Dear Badcock,

I will find out if Harrisons will do the tuning for any less, but I much doubt it. The contract is for 6 times in the year, and occasionally, in the very hot or extremely cold weather, before Commem, etc. he has to go over it again. Harrisons' man, Chapman, knows our organs very well, and I should never consent myself to one of the local firms doing it. In fact, it could eventually damage both organs very seriously. There is a tuner in Bristol belonging to Rushworth & Draper, a very good builder, and I can ask them for an estimate, though I suspect it may be even more than Harrison charges at present.

(The cost of tuning, say, York Minster organ is probably about £200 a year, but that is neither here nor there.)

I will in any case make enquiries.

Yours sincerely,
D.G.A. Fox.

(Considering the skill [and *deleted*], labour, and time involved in tuning, I think the charge is really [quite *inserted*] reasonable.)

[351]   17 March 1937. Fox to H.S. Harrison
[*Archives of Messrs Harrison & Harrison, Durham. Holograph*]

Clifton College
March 17.37

Dear Mr Harrison,

The School Council have asked me to find out if there is possibility of your being able to reduce the tuning charges (for which a contract was made in 1919) £30. 0. 0. for Chapel, £16. 0. 0. for Big School. They want to save something here and I wonder if you can help us at all. I must have them done twice a term, as this

---

[915] E.N. Gough, the Bursar's Clerk.

is an ordinary minimum, which can hardly be reduced. The Head Master also is worried about the matter and asks if it cannot be done by a local firm, to which I replied 'certainly not'; I said I would do what I could to get you if possible to reduce the charge somewhat.

With regard to the Big School organ, can it be done before October next?

When you most kindly called a few weeks ago, I could not tell you on that occasion that I had <previously> got Rushworths to look at the organ; since then they have sent in their scheme and are prepared to do it before October, though for a slightly larger estimate. I think the situation (as a distinguished organist said) is so very awkward for me that I must hope you will realise and sympathise [*deletion*], and I am therefore putting all my cards on the table.

I have the greatest possible dislike of offending you or Simon, who I asked to come down, having virtually decided that we would employ him. He knew nothing whatever about the organ beforehand, nor of course did he tender for it in any way. I was advised thus by a quite indifferent authority, while other equally good authorities said afterwards 'Stick to Harrison!' So you understand how I have become entangled in this muddle.

Is it quite final that you cannot do the work before next Christmas holidays? I hope in any case to make a decision before the end of next month, and that it will be the right one. The matter has really been a great worry to me.

Yours sincerely,
D.G.A. Fox.

[352]   24 March 1937. Harrison to Fox
[*RS3/147. Typescript*]

Harrison & Harrison, Organ Builders
Durham, March 24th, 1937.
Dear Mr Fox,
Clifton College & Big School organs.
Thank you for your letter of the 17th. and for writing so frankly. It would never do to let your organ into local hands. I am relieved, and grateful, that you have pointed out the danger of this to the Head Master, and I am prepared to reduce our fee to thirty-five guineas per annum for the two organs if this will meet the call for economy. You may be assured of the same attention as heretofore.

With regard to the overhauling of the Big School organ, since I saw you I have been trying to bring about a re-arrangement of time (to which we are committed) for the overhauling of a large organ in Birmingham so that we might have suitable men free for your organ, and I hear this morning that the church authorities agree to my suggestion. The work to the Big School organ can therefore be completed by October, and I do hope this will free you from worry.[916] We have looked after the organ for the past 14 years, we know just what you want and you may be sure the work will be carried out in the best manner.

With kind regards,
Yours sincerely,
Harry S. Harrison.

---

[916] By March 1938 the Willis organ in Big School had been restored and retuned for performance with an orchestra: *Centenary Essays* p. 124.

[353]   2 April 1937. Fox to Badcock
[*RS3/147. Holograph*]

Clifton College,
Bristol.
[March *corrected to*] April 2 37

Dear Colonel Badcock,
   I enclose a letter from Harrisons [*above*] (which I am acknowledging today). I do not know when the reduced charge for tuning will come into operation. I think this is now a very fair charge for the two organs, and we must keep the Big School one in order as it gets a lot of use.
   I will come and see you about the lights in Big School when I come back.
Yours sincerely,
D.G.A. Fox.

☐ *One of Fox's pupils was a future Director of the Royal College of Music, Sir David Willcocks, who in 1938 won the organ scholarship at King's College, Cambridge with the help of this recommendation.*

[354]   [1938]. Draft testimonial from Fox
[*Keble College Archives AD 330. Corrected holograph*]

as from Clifton College, Bristol

D.V. Willcocks[917] has been my pupil in organ and piano since January 1934, having held a Music scholarship at Clifton for the last four years.
   He has considerable natural ability, and especially during the last two years, his work and progress have been unusually satisfactory. He passed the F.R.C.O. in January last, and his piano playing has also reached a high standard (Beethoven, 4th Concerto; Ravel, 'Jeux d'Eaux'). In July last he passed the H[*igher*] C[*ertificate*] in M[*usic*] with dist[*inction*]. He is a [very *deleted*] reliable and tactful accompanist [so far as his experience in School Chapel services has shown, which has included congregational and choir singing, and his general musicianship, though his opportunities confined hitherto to *corrected to*] of both choir and congregational singing. He has absolute pitch and an alert and critical ear. His general musicianship is developing well, and he shows patience and common sense when taking a choir practice. His executive and written work shows thoroughness and power of application; [since in the *deleted*] in the latter he is approaching the standard of Cambridge 1st Mus. Bac.
   [His knowledge of Music is not particularly wide as yet, but he *deleted*; *MS breaks off.*]

☐ *After Willcocks had secured the King's scholarship, Fox received this letter from his predecessor.*

---

[917] Sir David Valentine Willcocks [*10917*: WaH 1934–8]; Organist of Salisbury Cathedral 1947–50, of Worcester Cathedral 1950–7, Director of Music at King's 1957–73; Director of the RCM 1974–84.

[355]   21 December 1938. William McKie to Fox
[*Keble Archives AD 330. Holograph*]

Magdalen College,
Oxford.
21.xij.1938

Dear Douglas,

Congratulations – it really was a darn good concert. Both choral society and orchestra of a quality we should not have thought possible 10 years ago. I hope you are pleased with them and proud of yourself. You ought to be.

Congrats also on Willcocks, though this does not give me any particular thrill, as I never had the least doubt of his getting the schol. I think he will do you proud.

Happy Christmas,
As ever,
W.

☐ *When Fox was revising the Clifton Hymn Book, the recently retired Norman Whatley encouraged him to maintain the Clifton tradition.*

[356]   27 April 1939. Whatley to Fox.
[*Keble College Archives AD 330. Holograph*]

The Elms,
Amberley, Stroud, Glos.
(till 5th May)
27. April 1939

Dear Fox,

Many thanks for your letter. I am so glad that you enjoyed Italy. I was afraid Musso.[918] might drive you back.

Don't alter the hymn book to oblige Ley. You are a better judge than he, and it is Clifton's book, not Eton's.

I shall be delighted to see the proposed new buildings if I am in or near Clifton at the right time.

I hope I may sometimes be allowed to come and hear concerts (not Bach) and send my best wishes for your future at Clifton, with very sincere congratulations on what you have already done.

May I thank you very much not only for the delightful book (in which I have written an inscription) but also for so kindly contributing to the masters' magnificent present to me.

Yours sincerely,
N. Whatley.

---

[918] Benito Mussolini, Head of the Italian government 1922–43.

[357]   10 February 1940. Whatley to Fox
[Keble College Archives AD 330. Holograph]

10, Staverton Road,
Oxford.
10. February 1940.

Dear Fox,

The Hymn Book is delightful and I am very grateful for it. The mixture of old pages and new does not give at all a bad impression and I suspect that it is as good a collection of hymns and tunes as has ever been put together. I hope you feel that your labours are rewarded.

I rather like the general appearance of the cover: it is certainly an improvement on the old brown. I think you may find that the binding is not so strong as the Psalter's and that the copies of your choirboys become a bit untidy. I rather wish we had changed the title-page with its dreadful variety of type. But it is an interesting museum piece.

John has made a wonderfully rapid recovery and is now at home on sick-leave.[919]

I wrote to congratulate Prentice[920] on his A.R.C.O. and he told me you were down with Flu. I do hope you are really recovered now. I have been enjoying the same foul complaint, but am now up again and beginning to get about.

I rather doubt whether we shall get to Clifton this term, but I must manage it some time and hear the new Hymn Book in action.

My love to everyone.

Yours sincerely,
N. Whatley.

---

[919] John Whatley [*9987*: NT 1937–34]; returned to serve in 4 Commando, and was killed at Dieppe. Another of Whatley's sons William Denham [*10061*: PHP, NT 1928–39] was also killed in 1942.

[920] Evan Ridley Prentice [*11237*: WiH 1936–40; *M351*: 1947–66†]; succeeded Fox as Director of Music in 1957.

SECTION XVI: DRAMA

☐ *Acting was not encouraged by the first two Head Masters, and the dramatic tradition took some while to evolve. Its origins can be traced to art exhibitions in Big School to raise money for the College Mission. In 1895 these shows were brought to life.*

[358]   15 February 1895. Living sculpture
[*Council Minute Book 4, p. 127. MS*]

Use of Big School. Entertainment.

On the application of the Head Master for the use of Big School in May next for *Tableaux Vivants* to be arranged by Mr Glazebrook in order to raise a fund for the boys' club in St Agnes, it was resolved to empower the Finance Committee to accede to the application subject to the Head Master ascertaining what magisterial licence (if any) might be required, and the terms upon which it would be granted being satisfactory to the Finance Committee.

[359]   22 July 1908. The first 'dramatic entertainment'
[*Council Minute Book 5, pp. 409–10. MS*]

Use of Big School. Entertainment.

The Head Master by Memorandum dated the 18th of July asked that the use of Big School might be granted next term for a dramatic entertainment for which admission will be charged [in connection with *corrected to*] for the benefit of the St Agnes girls' club.

It was resolved that the request be granted on the understanding that the connection of the School with the St Agnes club is the ground upon which the request is made and subject to the College Solicitor advising that the charge for admission does not render the College liable to taxation.

[360]   4 November 1908. Anxiety over taxation resolved
[*Council Minute Book 5, pp. 421–2. MS*]

Use of College for entertainment and assessment [*of*] Income Tax.

The Secretary reported upon his communications with the Surveyor of Taxes as to the use of the College for an entertainment for which payment is made for the benefit of a charity, the correspondence regarding it being as follows:

[First the College Secretary's letter of 24 September to the Surveyor regarding the use of Big School for an entertainment, at which the admission charge was solely for the use of the St Agnes girls' Club]

(1st District)
Telephone Avenue,
Baldwin Street, Bristol
26th Sept. 1908

Dear Sir,

I have your letter of the 24th Sep. as to the use of the School Hall for a concert.

Provided the proceeds are devoted entirely to charitable purposes no steps will be taken to charge the buildings on that account on this occasion. Please however note that this does not refer to any future use of the buildings, but solely to the present occasion mentioned in your letter.

Yours faithfully,
(signed) A. Hook, Surveyor of Taxes.

☐ *With the taxation issue settled at least for the time being, the players presented a popular work by Sir Arthur Wing Pinero.*

[361]   24/25 November 1908. Play bill
[Theatre file. Printed]

Amateur Dramatic Performances of A.W. Pinero's celebrated comedy in three acts enititled:

'Sweet Lavender'
Kindly arranged by Mr Frank Morris and Mr Norton Matthews.[921]
In aid of S. Agnes' Mission.
Big School, Clifton College,
Tuesday afternoon, Nov. 24, and Wednesday evening, Nov. 25, 1908.

'Sweet Lavender'   Programme

Mr Geoffrey Wedderburn (of Wedderburn,	
Green & Hoskett, Bankers, Barchester)	Mr Vincent Fedden, O.C.[922]
Clement Hale (his adopted son)	Mr Cuthbert Hicks, O.C.[923]
Dr Delaney (a fashionable physician)	Mr W.J. Hemsley[924]
Dick Phenyl (a barrister)	Mr Frank Morris, O.C.
Horace Bream (a young American)	Mr H. Norton Matthews

---

[921] Henry Frank Morris [*217*: Town 1864–9] and Harry Norton Matthews [*M196*: 1908–29].

[922] Harry Vincent Fedden [*2741*: NT 1881–90].

[923] Cuthbert Crowden Hicks [*4690*: NT 1893–6].

[924] W.J. Hemsley [*M185*: 1904–15].

Mr Maw (a solicitor)	Mr E.A. Belcher[925]
Mr Bulger (a hair dresser)	Mr A. Champion, O.C.[926]
Mrs. Gilfillian (Wedderburn's sister)	Miss Ethel Parr
Minne (her daughter)	Miss Ida Prichard
Ruth Rolt (housekeeper)	Miss Mary Parr
Lavender (her daughter)	Miss Sylvia Heaven

Stage Manager: Mr Frank Morris, O.C.

Act I. – Morning.	Nobody's Business.
Act II. – Evening of the next day.	Somebody's Business.
Act III A week afterwards.	Everybody's Business.

Scene. – Chambers of Mr Phenyl and Mr Hale, The Temple.

MISS FYFFE'S BAND
Overture ... Suite in G ... *St George.*

———

I. Prelude. II. Allemande. III. Bourrée. IV. Gigue.
Chanson de Matin ... *Edward Elgar.*
Three Dances (by request) ... *Edward German.*

———

Pilgrim's March .... *Mendelssohn.*
Swedish Melody .... *Svendsen.*
Bridal March .... *Söderman.* (*Arranged by M.A. Fyffe.*)[927]

□ *But these innocent amusements were generating awkward financial problems, which led to a frosty edict from the Head Master.*

[362]   December 1910. Head Master to Norton Matthews
[*Theatre file*, Waterloo/David Garrick *Album 1914*. *Typescript*]

Clifton College, Bristol.
16th December, 1910.

Dear Mr Matthews,
    The Finance Committee have felt unable to grant the request for the use of the College for the proposed dramatic entertainment next term. They consider that it is too great a disturbance to the work of the School: it involves nice questions with regard to taxation which they are unwilling to raise: and they have a general objection to such a use of the College.

Yours very truly,
J.E. King.

---

[925] Ernest Albert Belcher [*M200*: 1908–12]; author of *Rambles among the Cotswolds* (1892) and duller works; also dedicatee of Agatha Christie's *The Man in the Brown Suit* (1924), where he is caricatured as the master criminal Sir Eustace Pedler. He had taught the novelist's first husband Archibald Christie [173], with whom he later worked in preparing for the Empire Exhibition of 1924. The editor is obliged to Dr P. la Hausse de Lalouvière for alerting him to the Christie connexion.
[926] Arthur Mortimer Champion [*5183*: NT, PHP, NT 1896–1904].
[927] Daughter of the Medical Officer Dr W.J. Fyffe.

□ *In 1913 the Committee reversed its decision subject to confirmation that such use would not invalidate College's exemption from payment of Income Tax Schedule A. So the plays resumed, but only after the First World War was a College Dramatic Society formed. Its first decade was graced by the emerging talent of Michael Redgrave.*[928]

[363]   June 1926. Programme for 'The Rivals'
[*Theatre file. Printed*]

Clifton College.
The Amateur Dramatic Society
June 1926.
'THE RIVALS'
by Richard Brinsley Sheridan
(*First produced at Covent Garden Theatre in 1775*)

Characters.
(*In the order of their appearance*).

Mr Fag (Captain Absolute's 'Gentleman')	P.C. Bartrum [*8924*]
Thomas (Sir Anthony's Coachman)	P.B. Greenway [*9106*]
Lydia Languish (niece of Mrs Malaprop)	D.C. Mandeville [*8903*]
Lucy (her maid)	G.H. Bird [*9604*]
Julia Melville (ward of Sir Anthony)	M.B. Hollway [*9570*]
Mrs Malaprop	A.W. Anstey [*8724*]
Sir Anthony Absolute	H.W. Hawkins [*9190*]
Captain Absolute (his son)	M.S. Redgrave [*9027*]
Faulkland (in love with Julia)	E.B. Gammell [*8940*]
Bob Acres (a suitor of Lydia's)	W.J.L. Drapkin [*9010*]
Sir Lucius O'Trigger	R.W. Nevin [*8819*]
David (servant of Acres)	G.C. Ehlers [*9011*]
	or E.G.I. Lousada [*9240*]

[*Synopsis and list of scenes here omitted*]
The Orchestra: F.L. Hetley (Conductor) [*8777*], P.H. Gent [*9104*], E.T. Worsley [*8972*], M.W. de la P. Beresford [*9181*], R.C. Symonds [*9039*], J.F. Tilney [*9499*], W.H.T. Luce [*8950*], Mr C. Eyles.
President of the Dramatic Society: J.H. Barrington [*8746*].
Property Master: H.L. Pryce [*8961*].
Electricians: A.V. Stephens [*9139*], G.E.M. Jones [*9467*].
Stage Hands: J.N. Malcolm (chief) [*9119*], P.N.D. Porter [*9134*], S.E. Naish [*8818*], G.I. Watson [*8543*], D.R. Bell [*9180*], C.M. White [*8969*], J.M. Hooper [*9289*], O.P. Haig [*9189*].
Prompter: Mr H.J. Webb.
Scenery by Messrs J.H. Wilson & W.J. Cox.
Costumes & Wigs by Messrs B.J. Simmons & Co., Covent Garden.
Furniture by Messrs Chilcott & Co.

---

[928] Sir Michael Scudamore Redgrave [*9027*: DH 1922–6]; knighted 1959.

The Society has performed the following plays:

1921   'The School for Scandal'.
1922   'The Critic'.
1923   'The Admirable Crichton'.
1924   'She Stoops to Conquer'.
1925   'Macbeth'.

The acoustic properties of Big School are not good, but the audience will find that it can hear if perfect silence is maintained till the ear gets accustomed to the peculiarities of the room.[929]

☐ *A press cutting enclosed in a copy of the programme included this perceptive comment:*
   'In a company where all did well and there were no 'star' parts, it seems invidious to mention a few. Yet there was no doubt that an outstanding performance was given by M.S. Redgrave as Captain Absolute. He has always scored his successes in the past in girl's parts [*sic*], notably, Lady Mary in 'The Admirable Crichton' and Lady Macbeth. But as the gay young lover of Lydia Languish he showed the same intelligence, grace of movement and vivid expression, interpreting every thought to the audience as before.'

Polack's Reading Society

☐ *The annual House Drama competition in the Spring term, now a distinctive feature of the Clifton stage, only began in the 1940s when the School was at Bude. There were however House dramatic societies of various kinds; in Polack's this involved text readings and theatre visits.*

[364]   10 March 1924. Outing to the theatre
[*Polack Centre, PH Reading Society Minutes 1923–31. MS*]

The Green Goddess
On March 10th the Society visited the Prince's Theatre, Bristol,[930] in accordance with rule 7(b).[931] The play produced was a drama by William Archer;[932] it was, according to a critic in the *Observer*, 'all that a drama should be' and had had already 500 performances in London; the provincial company who came down to Bristol was equal <to>, if not better than that of the metropolis (complaints should be forwarded to the member who has seen both productions and is therefore fit to judge). In choosing the play, the members who did not vote for *The Green Goddess* were inclined to object to the choice, but after the performance all were unanimous in its praise. The President[933] was unfortunately ill and was therefore unable to take part

---

[929] This discouraging rubric was printed every year. Redgrave recalled Big School as being 'totally unsuited for the presentation of plays of any period': *In my Mind's Eye: An Autobiography* (1983), p. 35.
[930] In Park Row; destroyed in the Blitz.
[931] 'The Society shall, in the Easter term go, at members' own expense, to see a play at the theatre. A record of these events shall be kept in the record book'.
[932] First produced 1921 and enjoying much success.
[933] The House Master A.I. Polack [*M270*].

in the expedition, much to our disappointment; however Mr Gee [*M267*] came with us instead and played an excellent game as 'sub', providing so much enjoyment for us without sharing in it himself. To Mr Gee for his excellent chaperonage and to Mr Polack for his welcome to the home-coming revellers [*thanks are due*].

J.H.E. Nahum, Hon. Sec.[934]

[365]   28 September 1927. Selection process
[*Polack Centre, PH Reading Society Minutes 1923–31. MS*]

The Society held its first meeting of the term on Sunday Sept. 28th. After they had got over the first shock of seeing one another they proceeded to elect a new Secretary in the person of Mr Lousada.[935] Mr Gollin's[936] keeness [*sic*] in resigning his duties was quite amazing. He has a nasty sneering laugh that is most annoying to a new Secretary. We then elected Messrs Manasseh[937] and Simon[938] who entered, the one supported by a *Grand* magazine[939] to mark the importance of the occasion; the other cheering the Society with his charming smile. The next problem was [a *corrected to*] the Shakespeare play to be [selected *corrected to*] read. Everybody shouted out a different play, each of which was seconded by the genial Secretary. At length *Julius <Caesar>* beat *Henry IV* on points. The next discussion was concerning the other plays to be read. Suggestions sprouted from all parts of the room. Several arm-chairs were heard to mumble names of plays, while the sofa gave quite a large contribution. We particularly remember a chair in the neighbourhood of the fireplace that murmured *The Good-Natured Man*[940] at intervals. The sofa by the way was distinctly Shavian. The Secretary was of the opinion that *Hay Fever*[941] would do the Society some good, while *Ambrose Applejohn's Adventure*[942] was favoured by those of buccaneering [tendencies *corrected to*] temperament. At length after a great deal of heated argument, and not a little [unnecessary *deleted*] rudeness, in addition to *Julius Caesar*, *Ambrose Applejohn*, *And So To Bed*,[943] *The Skin Game*,[944] and *Hay Fever* were chosen.

[366]   10 February 1939. *Hay Fever* strikes again
[*Polack Centre, PH Reading Society Minutes 1939–45. MS*]

Intellectually the play was not up to much, but [for *corrected to*] in providing a good evening's entertainment it definitely succeeded. Everyone thought that Mr [Noel's *corrected to*] Noel Coward's dialogue was, in parts, very funny, but Mr Myer's[945] interpretation of it was even funnier. There were several disturbances to the play; concentration was not all it might have been and some members seemed to find it

---

[934] Jack M.E.di V. Nahum [*8787*: PH 1920–4].
[935] Eric George Isidore Lousada [*9240*: PH 1923–8].
[936] Edward Marcus Gollin [*9409*: PH 1924–8].
[937] Philip Joseph Manasseh [*9298*: PH 1923–8].
[938] Leonard Joshua Simon [*9497*: PH 1924–8].
[939] *The Grand Magazine*, published from 1905 to 1940, a pioneering venture in fashionable ephemera.
[940] By Oliver Goldsmith (1768).
[941] By Noël Coward (1925).
[942] By Walter C. Hackett (1920).
[943] By J.B. Fagan (1926), about Samuel Pepys and taking its title from his familiar phrase.
[944] By John Galsworthy (1920).
[945] Richard Henry Myer [*11165*: PH 1936–40].

hard to follow the place; Mr H.I. Cohen[946] suddenly found out that he was a woman, [and *corrected to*] while the aforementioned Mr Myer's French pronunciation caused some amusement. Some members expressed their dissatisfaction with the play but all were agreed that they had spent an enjoyable evening reading it.

At the beginning of the meeting the Society decided to go and see *The Last Trump* by James Bridie on Tuesday March 14th; this decision being left to alteration.

J.M. Cohen, Hon. Sec.[947]

J.B. Evans, [*President*].[948]

17/2/39.

[*No.*] 320	*Hay Fever*	Noel Coward

Hon. Pres.: David Bliss.

Hon Sec.: Sorel Bliss.

Mr Samuels [*11008*]: Myra Arundel.

Mr Toeg [*10755*]: Clara.

Mr Raperport:[949] Richard Greatham.

Mr Dent [*10983 or 11103*]: Simon Bliss.

Mr Myer: Judith Bliss.

Mr Cohen H.I.: Jackie Coryton.

Mr Panto [*11070*]: Sandy Tyrell.

10.2.39.

[367]   6 February 1940. Chorus lines
[*Polack Centre, PH Reading Society Minutes 1939–45. MS*]

As usual *Of Thee I Sing*[950] provided a hilarious evening although its contribution towards the elevation of the intellect of the Society can but have been very small. There being a superabundance of parts, Mr R.E. Jacobs[951] was invited as a substitute for Mr J.M. Cohen and to help matters out. Anxious to impress the Society, Mr Jacobs gave us many varied interpretations of how the parts he had should be read, such as in an accent which can only be described as a cross between those heard in the hearts of Whitechapel and Somerset or in a tremulous falsetto or in an unintelligible fog of nasal sound produced by speaking while holding the nose between forefinger and thumb, an action which [neither *deleted*] enhanced neither Mr Jacobs' general appearance nor his vocal production. Mr Jaffé[952] in the part of Mary Turner was too charming while Mr Goodenday[953] in his part as Diana was devastating, or was it Devereaux? The reading generally was up to standard but not brilliant, although the play did not call for great dictorial [*sic*] effort. Though humorous, this play is hardly likely to go down to 'oomposterity'.[954]

G. Raperport, Hon. Sec.

J.B. Evans, Hon. Pres.

15/4/40.

---

946 Harry Isaac Cohen [*11208*: PH 1936–41].
947 John Moss Cohen [*11098*: PH 1935–40]; killed on active service 1941.
948 John Brereton Evans [*M322*: 1938–77]; House Tutor PH 1938–40, 1946–50.
949 Gerald Raperport [*11239*: PH 1936–40]; the next Hon. Secretary.
950 Libretto for the Gershwins' musical lampoon on American politics (1931).
951 Ralph Eric Jacobs [*10809*: NTP, STP, PH 1933–41].
952 Gabriel Vivian Jaffé [*11297*: PH 1937–41].
953 David John Goodenday [*11147*: PH 1036–40].
954 From the refrain of one of the numbers: 'Posterity is just around the corner'.

344   *Of Thee I Sing*   by George S. Kaufman
                                                        and Morrie Ryskind
Hon. Pres.: Lyons. Judges. Photographers. Clerk. Secretary.
Hon. Sec.: Wintergreen. Narrator.
Mr R.H. Myer: Lippman. Sightseer. Senator(s). Reporters.
Mr H.I. Cohen: Throttlebottom. Miss Benson. Flunkies.
Mr I.T.H. Rossdale [*11316*]: Gilhooley. Jenkins. Committee. Doctor.
Mr G.V. Jaffé: Chambermaid. Mary Turner. French Ambassador.
Mr D.J.A. Goodenday: Fulton. Diana Devereaux. Scrub woman.
(Mr R.E. Jacobs: Jones. Girls. One of girls. Guide. Loudspeaker.)
6.2.40.

[368]   13 and 16 February 1940. A duck too far
[*Polack Centre, PH Reading Society Minutes 1939–45. MS*]

On the whole these two meetings were not a success. After *Of Thee I Sing* the
Society felt that something serious should be read but *The Wild Duck* went too
far and might almost be called morbid. It did not improve matters that the Society
should be in frivolous humour at the second meeting for this made appreciation well
nigh impossible. We were deprived of Mr Goodenday's harmonious articulations at
meeting 346 but Mr Myer graciously condescended to take over his part as he (Mr
Myer) had no more to say in his original part. Mr Jaffé rather wallowed in the heavily
scored part of Hjalmar but the reading all round was poor. Mr J.M. Cohen, to whom
no doubt the two words mean the same thing, <once> interpreted 'birthday' as 'bath
day', while Mr Jaffé's 'flirting' caused some amusement. As [for *corrected to*] to the
pronunciation of the word spelt W-E-R-L-E, it caused general consternation, but no
solution was forthcoming. At the end of the second meeting the Society indulged
in a sort of bacchanalia, the cause of which was the imminence of meeting 350 and
the celebration thereof, but no outcome of any import was apparent, although the
suggestion of *Les Folies Superbes* was <only> reluctantly rejected.

345 and 346   *The Wild Duck*   by Henrik Ibsen
               Hon. Pres: Relling. Pettersen.
               Hon. Sec.: Werle. Molvik.
               Mr J.M. Cohen: Gina Ekdal. Thin-haired guest.
               Mr R.H. Myer: Ekdal. Graaberg. Short-sighted guest.
               Mr H.I. Cohen: Hedvig. Flabby guest.
               Mr I.T.H. Rossdale: Gregers. Werle.
               Mr G.V. Jaffé: Hjalmar. Jensen.
               Mr D.J.A, Goodenday: Mrs. Sörby. Waiter.
13.2.40 and 16.2.40
                                                    G. Raperport, Hon. Sec.
                                                    J.B. Evans, Hon. Pres.
                                                    20/2/40.

SECTION XVII:
TRIBUTES TO MASTERS

Death in harness

☐ *The first Clifton master to die in post was Edward Miller,[955] who collapsed while playing golf on Durdham Down on 14 May 1889. A memorial book was compiled from the letters of condolence sent to his family. Among the contributors were the current and past Head Masters, and a passer-by who had descended from her Bath chair to assist the stricken man.*

[369]   15 May 1889. The Head Master of Rugby to Miller's brother
[*M55 file. MS copy*]

School House,
Rugby.
May 15 1889.

Dear Mr Miller,
    I cannot refrain from sending you a line to express my sorrow and my sympathy with you in your brother Edward's death.
    The sudden breaking of such ties of friendship as he represented is a great shock, though a painless summons whilst in the midst of duty and with powers unabated is not an unhappy lot.
    He leaves many friends who will miss him and mourn his loss.

Yours sincerely,
J. Percival.

☐ *Clifton's Second Master was a more expansive letter-writer.*

---

[955] *M55:* 1872–1889†; at first he taught Classics, then French and Mathematics; known to the boys as 'Sambo' and remembered as 'a quiet, kindly man'; Newbolt, *Diary of a Fag*, p. 56. He lies buried in Redland churchyard, close by T.E. Brown.

[370]   15 May 1889. T.E. Brown to J.D. Miller (nephew)[956]
[*M55 file. MS copy*]

Clifton
May 15./89.

My dear Miller,
I must write you a word about your dear old uncle. I can't tell you how much I shall miss him. Indeed we all shall, but by the 'old hands' like myself the loss will be more acutely felt, all the more perhaps because it brings so forcibly before us the breaking up of the old lot which must come sooner or later. I lose in him a very kind and faithful friend, and the College one of the most loyal and public-spirited of its masters. To me he was always most genial and sympathetic, knowing well how to hold his own and more than hold it; he never met me otherwise than in the spirit of thorough good feeling and mutual regard. I did like him very much, and though this place did not perhaps furnish him with the opportunity of producing all the power that I knew to be in him, still it is a melancholy pleasure to me to think that it did yield him a life of much interest, and a happiness very special and peculiarly his own.

He was amongst us emphatically a representation of 'the grand old name of gentleman'; the type seems to be dying out; all the more did I prize his unfailing courtesy, his social brightness, his unspotted honour, and the good nature which with him amounted to a Christian grace.

I loved the man, and shall always cherish his memory. Sturdy and strong, yet so gentle, so patient, so free from the most distant taint of envy – I assure you we can never replace him, for men like that are *sui generis* and cannot be replaced.

I write to you as knowing how you loved and respected him, but I also desire to include in my deep sympathy all the family who must feel their ranks so sadly broken by the withdrawal of a man of such genuine worth.

As a very old friend I may be permitted to say this much.

Ever yours,
T.E. Brown.

Parting gift

☐ *This exchange concerns the appropriate way of marking the retirement of a long-serving master C.W.A. Tait.*[957]

[371]   1 April 1904. The Chairman of Council to the College Secretary
[*RS3/282. Holograph*]

The Palace,
Hereford,
Good Friday 1904.

Dear Mr Macpherson,

---

[956] John Day Miller [*336:* SH 1865–74].
[957] Charles William Adam Tait [*M57:* 1873–1904]; taught on the Modern Side; first House Master ST 1875–80, ran a Waiting House 1880–5, again in charge of ST 1885–9 and of OH 1889–1904; member of Council from 1907 to his death in 1913, the first to be appointed as nominee of the assistant masters. A leaving scholarship was founded in his memory: *Endowed Scholarships and Prizes*, pp. 72–5.

I return the enclosures and my first thought is that we should offer Tait (a) some memento in the shape of plate or books, and (b) ask him privately whether it would be agreeable to him to have £500 handed to him, or whether he would prefer its being given towards an <entrance> scholarship for a town boy, and bearing his name, thus immortalising his work as the man who did most for our unique town boy system.

My impression is that he does not care for money except to make some good use of it.

It is, however, possible that he may have something on his mind which he would like to do with £500, if it were given, and so I am rather in favour of consulting him privately, if it were decided to put some such sum at his disposal.

I know him well enough to discuss anything with him *provided* that the Council desire it.

> Yours sincerely,
> J. Hereford.

[372] 5 April 1904. Tait to the College Secretary
[*RS3/282. Holograph*]

> 26, College Road,
> Clifton, Bristol.
> 5.IV.1904

My dear Macpherson,
The kindness and generosity of the Council has touched me very much. About that however this is hardly the time to speak. But as they have been good enough to wish to give me a mark of their confidence and to leave the form of their gift to me, I should rather have some smaller pieces than one larger one.

I would rather not face Commemoration but if the Council wished I would gladly come to a Council Meeting and thank them personally for all that I owe them.

> Yours very sincerely,
> C.W.A. Tait.

[373] 3 June 1904. The Chairman of Council to the College Secretary
[*RS3/282. Holograph*]

> Lollards Tower,
> Lambeth S.E.
> June 3. 1904.

Dear Mr Macpherson,
Overleaf I have put down a few words by way of suggestion. You, and Mr Abbot and the other members of Council will probably have improvements to suggest.

> Yours sincerely,
> J. Hereford.

To C...W...W.... Tait (name in full),[958] from the Council of Clifton College in grateful recognition of his devoted service to the College and his many acts of generosity and kindness during his mastership of .... [*filled in* 31] years.
May 1904.

---

[958] It will be noted that Percival did not know the first name, or even the correct initials, of a master whom he had appointed and who had remained in the School for a generation.

Vale in tempore belli

☐ *When the first Director of Music moved to Rugby during the First World War, he felt it inappropriate to accept a farewell gift; instead he was presented with this address, elegantly inscribed and bound.*

[374]   29 March 1915. Valedictory address to A.H. Peppin
[*M152 file. Illuminated MS on vellum, bound in calf*]

Arturo H. Peppin,
Musarum et Sanctae Ceciliae fido cultori,
Temporis, studii, laborum, semper prodigo,
Nunc, pro patria et vulneratis in bello militibus,
Donum oblatum deprecanti,
Gratiae pignus et amicitiae,
Magistro discipuli Collegii Cliftoniensis,
Fidem, studium, observantiam praestantes,
A.D. IV. Kal. Apr. MCMXV.
Hunc librum d.d.d.

Scripsit C.R.S. Harris 1915.[959]   Fecit Mark van Oss 1915.[960]

To Arthur H. Peppin, a loyal follower of the Muses and Saint Cecilia, always generous with his time, his support, and his industry, who on behalf of our country and soldiers wounded in the war begs to decline the gift he was offered, the pupils of Clifton College now as a pledge of gratitude and affection, offering their loyalty, enthusiasm, and respect, present and dedicate this book to their teacher, 29 March 1915.[961]

Written by C.R.S. Harris 1915.   *Made by Mark van Oss 1915.*

[*There follow 115 signatures.*]

---

[959] Charles Reginald Schiller Harris [*7174*: OH 1910–15]; who went on to a First in Greats at Magdalen College, Oxford and a Fellowship of All Souls.
[960] Mark Dunbar van Oss [*7323*: OH 1911–16]; also took a First in Greats at Magdalen and became a Fellow there.
[961] Translation kindly made (2011) by Mr G.V. Hardyman [*12249/M405*].

Queen Victoria's Golden Jubilee 1887

☐ *By virtue of its Charter the College may claim to be of royal foundation. This status does not carry any privilege beyond that of addressing the Sovereign in a filial way. The first opportunity for this came when Queen Victoria celebrated her Golden Jubilee, which coincided with the College's twenty-fifth anniversary.*

[375]   20 June 1887. Address to Queen Victoria
[Selecta. MS on vellum, illuminated and bound, covered in a purple velvet chemise]

We, the representatives of the Council, masters and boys of Clifton College, wish to express to your Majesty our congratulations on the completion of the fiftieth year of your Majesty's happy reign; our loyalty to your Majesty; our desire to serve our country faithfully at home, and in all parts of your Majesty's dominions; and our prayers that Almighty God will continue to bless your Majesty with the love of your children, the devotion of your subjects, and the peace and prosperity of the Empire.

20th June, 1887.
F.N. Budd, Chairman of Council.
James M. Wilson, Headmaster.
C.A. Hooper, Head of the School.[962]

The Duke of Clarence and Avondale 1888

☐ *Clifton's first royal visit was something of an embarrassment. Prince Albert Victor, Duke of Clarence and Avondale, second in line to the throne, visited Bristol on 25 July 1888 to unveil the statue of his grandmother Queen Victoria on College Green. A cousin of the Head Master who had known the Prince at Cambridge persuaded him to pass by Clifton and receive a deputation at the College gates. Only two days' notice was given, which is doubtless why the Head Master did not have the Council's*

---

[962] Charles Alexander Hooper [2576: PHP, WiH 1880–8], Head of the School 1886–8.

authority for the preparations. These were in fact considerable, including a triumphal
arch decorated with Latin verses which had come to the Head Master as he slept. In
the event it poured with rain and the Prince arrived very late; he then moved on after
hearing only the start of the formal welcome being read to him.[963]

[376]   27 July 1888. Application to Finance Committee for reimbursement of costs
[*Council Minute Book 3, p. 165*]

Visit of Prince Albert Victor.
The Head Master by a Memorandum dated the 26 of July 1888 reported that on the occasion of the visit of Prince Albert Victor to Bristol it was arranged in accordance with the Prince's request for him to pass by the College and that the Prince had consented to receive an address from the School. That with all possible despatch he the Head Master had made suitable arrangements for the event by the preparation of an address, the erection and decoration of an arch by the College gates, and he the Head Master asked that <the> expense should be borne by the Finance Committee or that they should make some substantial grant towards it.
It was decided to leave the consideration of the question until the cost could be ascertained.

[377]   15 November 1888. The Council grudgingly authorises payment
[*Council Minute Book 3, p. 181. MS*]

Visit. Prince Albert Victor.
A memorandum from the Head Master dated 25 Sept 1888 relative to the reception of Prince Albert Victor with accounts and memoranda of expenses shewing a total of £62. 8. 2 referred to the Council by the Finance Committee were laid before the Council.
The Secretary was instructed to reply, that although the Council felt a difficulty in recognising expenditure not authorized by them, yet in the special circumstances of the case they resolve to pay the amount.

Queen Victoria's Diamond Jubilee 1897

□ *This second expression of loyalty to the Fundatrix was more ponderous in tone than the Address of 1887.*

[378]   20 June 1897. Address to Queen Victoria
[*Selecta. MS on stiffened card, illuminated and solidly bound*]

To Her Most Gracious Majesty The Queen.
On behalf of the Council, masters and boys of Clifton College, we humbly offer to your most gracious Majesty our loyal congratulations on the completion of the sixtieth year of your Majesty's happy reign, and we desire to renew the profession of our devoted attachment to your Majesty's person.

---

[963] Wilson, *Autobiography*, pp. 148–50; Christie, *History*, pp. 131–3.

Ever grateful for your Majesty's gracious gift of a Royal Charter to our School, we pledge ourselves always to remember that the chief aim of a public school is to train up faithful men to serve their Queen and country in church and state, at home and abroad, in peace and in war.

And we pray that Almighty God may long spare your Majesty in the enjoyment of all public and private blessings to rule over a prosperous, loyal and united Empire.

Chairman of the Council: J. Hereford.

Head Master: M.G. Glazebrook.

Clifton. June 20th 1897.   Head of the School, S.V. Williams.[964]

Princess Louise 1899

☐ *A Clifton boy fearlessly flouts protocol by asking for the autograph of the Queen's daughter.*[965]

[379]   27 January 1899. The Princess's Secretary to Dudley Kingdon-Allen[966] [*P5126 Album. Holograph*]

Kensington Palace, W.

27 Jan. 99

Dear Master Allen,

Members of the Royal Family do not give their autographs to strangers. However H.R.H. the Princess Louise has kindly made an exception in your favour and allows me to send you the enclosed. Please do not tell your schoolfellows the Princess has given it you, or I may receive other applications which I should only be obliged to refuse.

Yours sincerely,

Arthur Collins, Colonel.

☐ *The autograph is not retained in the book.*

Edward VII and Queen Alexandra 1908

☐ *In July 1908 King Edward VII and Queen Alexandra came to open the Royal Edward Dock at Avonmouth. Although the King and Queen did not visit Clifton, the Corps was in attendance and the School sent a delegation with their formal compliments.*

[380]   17 June 1908. Request from the Head Master for additional funds [*RS2/66. MS*]

Memorandum from the Headmaster

to Finance Committee

Grant for illuminations [at *corrected to*] on day of King's visit.

---

[964] Sidney Vivian Williams [*4748*: BH 1893–7], Head of the School 1896–7.
[965] Princess Louise, Marchioness of Lorne (later Duchess of Argyll), Queen Victoria's fourth daughter; she was noted for her liberal views and informality.
[966] See above **[92]**.

I asked originally for £25, but it is now evident that this will not be sufficient to do what we consider ought to be done. Will the Committee kindly make it 'not to exceed £40'?

We do not propose to *decorate* but only to *illuminate* the buildings.

17.vi.8   A.A.D.

☐ *The Committee, meeting later that day, set a maximum expenditure of £30.*[967]

[381]   9 July 1908. Address to the King and Queen and His Majesty's response
[*Printed and framed*]

Address presented to His Majesty King Edward VII and to Her Majesty The Queen on their visit to Bristol and Avonmouth, 9th July 1908.

To the King's Most Excellent Majesty and to Her Majesty The Queen.

May it please Your Majesties,

On behalf of the Council, Masters, and Boys of Clifton College, we humbly desire to express our share in the gratitude of the Citizens of Bristol for Your Majesties' most welcome visit to our City. We cherish thankfully the memory of the Royal Charter granted to our School by Her late Majesty Queen Victoria in 1877, under which we have striven and shall ever strive to send forth faithful servants of their Sovereign, brought up in loyal attachment to Your Majesty's Throne and Person, and prepared to serve their King and Country in Church and State, in peace and war, at home and abroad.

And we pray that it may please Almighty God to bless Your Majesty with a long and prosperous reign, and with the ever increasing love of the people of this Land and Empire.

Given under the common seal of the College this 9th day of July, 1908.

J. Hereford	Chairman of the Council.
A.A. David	Head Master.
O.M. Tweedy	Head of the School.[968]

His Majesty was graciously pleased to reply:

The Queen and I are very glad to receive your loyal and dutiful Address from the Council, Masters and Boys of Clifton College.

Since a Charter was granted to your School by my beloved Mother in the year 1877, Clifton College has made its mark amongst the Public Schools of this Country. Its name is famous alike for patriotism, scholarship and sport, and it has developed in a high degree the public spirit, the sense of good comradeship and the splendid rivalry in all honour and manliness and good feeling which is the finest tradition of our great Schools. I am specially gratified to learn that Clifton maintains a modern and efficient system of instruction in science and modern languages. These branches of education are of great importance to a boy's career whatever profession he may adopt, and the thoroughness of the preparation which Clifton gives is shown by the success of her sons alike in examination and practical life.

I am struck by the interesting feature of your curriculum which is colloquially

---

[967] Council Minute Book 5, p. 408.
[968] Owen Meredith Tweedy [*5419*: PHP, WiH 1898–1908].

termed 'Civics', a study of existing English institutions.[969] This branch of general information is rarely, I think, imparted at our public schools, but it seems to me a most useful element of education.

I am well aware that many Old Cliftonians have entered my Army, and have distinguished themselves in all parts of the world. Many have fallen on active service, leaving you proud memories of names and deeds, unfading examples to stir the spirit of those that follow. So long as men of their stamp, men of honour and courage, of energy and intelligence come from Clifton and our other great Schools to serve their Country alike in peace and war, so long we need have no fears whatever dangers threaten.[970]

George V and Queen Mary 1912

☐ *The King and Queen visited the College as part of its Golden Jubilee celebrations. There are photographs of Their Majesties in their carriage being greeted in the South Quad, but there is very little surviving documentation.*

[382]   28 June 1912. Expenses of the visit
[*RS2/66. MS (layout adjusted)*]

Visit of H.M. The King
28th June 1912
Expenses

	[£]	[s]	[d]
Putting up stands and providing seating			
accommodation for visitors	34	7	11
less cash received	3	7	0
	31	0	11
Address to The King	10	10	0
C.C. Souvenir Book	1	1	0
Flags and decorations	5	0	0
Bunting for stands &c.	2	0	0
Printing	1	8	6
Alterations to entrance	8	1	1
Removing and replacing gate pillars	18	3	2
	77	4	8

[383]   19 July 1912. G.H. Clark[971] to H. N. Abbot, Chairman of the Finance Committee
[*RS2/66. MS*]

42 College Rd.
Clifton
July 19th 1912

Dear Mr Napier Abbott [*sic*],

---

[969] That is to say national and local politics, introduced into the classroom by David in the previous year: Christie, *History*, p. 164.

[970] Copied into the minutes of the Finance Committee 17 June (Council Minute Book 5, pp. 411–12), with (pp. 412–13) resolution to spend no more than £20 on printing the Address, deferring 'how to deal with the King's reply' to the next Council.

[971] George Herbert Clark [*M125*: 1887–1924].

I have been asked to lay the following suggestion before the College authorities. Mr C. Wasbrough,[972] to whom I mentioned it today, asked me to write to you as Chairman of the Finance Committee of the Clifton College Council.

The suggestion came from Mr Savory of the Vandyck Printers, Park Row,[973] whom I have seen a good deal about the Jubilee book of Clifton College pictures.[974] It is that Mr Will. Hatherell R.I.[975] should be asked to paint in oils a picture of the King and Queen receiving the address from Clifton College in the Quadrangle. Mr Savory thinks he could get him to do it for 100 guineas, and to come down to get details of grouping, colours, dress and buildings. It would be a large picture, say five feet long, and would commemorate a historic occasion and [*illegible word corrected to*] be invaluable in after years.

Of course Mr E.W. Savory with an eye to business suggested that the payers of the price could recoup themselves by having 100 artist signed proofs at 2 guineas each, and a thousand others at 5/-.

I am rather doubtful whether these would sell, but the first part of the suggestion seems to me worthy of consideration. I may be acting informally in communicating with you at all except through the Head Master, but I think not, as my own interests are not concerned.

Yours sincerely,
G.H. Clark.

Minuted by recipient: Please lay before Finance Committee. H. Abbot.

[384]   30 October 1912. Approval of Council
[*Council Minute Book 6, p. 210. MS*]

Visit of H.M. the King.
    The Secretary submitted a return of the expenses involved by the visit of H.M. the King in June last and the Finance Committee were authorized to pay the amount of the same, viz. £77. 4. 8.

Suggested Picture. King's visit.
    A letter from Mr G.H. Clark **[383]** was read suggesting that an artist be commissioned to paint a picture of the ceremony on the occasion of the King's visit and it was resolved to reply that the Council would be willing to accept as a gift a good picture of the event.

☐ *Nothing came of this proposal.*

---

[972] See above **[62]**.

[973] Ernest Wyman Savory, Managing Director of his own firm in Perry Road (by Park Row), and Chairman of the Royal West of England Academy; father of J.H. [*6028*], R.N. [*6548*], E.M. [*6744*] and B.W. [*8206*]. (With thanks to his great-grandson Richard Savory for the identification and details.)

[974] *Clifton College 1862–1912* (priv. pr. 1912), a loose-leaf portfolio.

[975] William Hatherell (d. 1928) was best known as a magazine illustrator.

First visit of the Prince of Wales 1921

☐ *On 10 June 1921 the Prince of Wales, who was in Bristol as the guest of the Society of Merchant Venturers, made a brief visit to Clifton. This was engineered by Sir Herbert Warren, Chairman of the Council, who as President of Magdalen had overseen the Prince's time as an Oxford undergraduate.*

[385]   1 June 1921. The Chairman of Council to the College Secretary
[*RB2/41. Corrected typescript*]

June 1st, 1921

My dear Mr Lewis,

1. *Prince of Wales's Visit.* I am coming down for the luncheon to the Prince of Wales at the Merchant Venturers' Hall,[976] and I propose to come on to the College, to join in the reception of H.R.H. there.

I understood that it was likely that the Council and masters would meet him near the South African Memorial.

What was suggested after the Council meeting was, that the Prince should enter the Close by the corner near Worcester Lodge, and then walk across, perhaps speaking to the XI, and seeing the School on the way, and then, that he should be received by the officials by the South African Memorial, and should, if he was willing, perhaps say a word or two to the boys from the Terrace, and should, if he has time, see the Chapel, and then be picked up by motor, and so on to tea at the Mansion House.

Speaking generally, that seemed to me a good idea.

I think he will like to have the staff presented to him, if there is time <and will say something> but will not want any very formal address.

I was just going to write to the Headmaster about it. Perhaps you will show him this letter.

I hope to come down and stay with Mr W.W. Ward[977] on Thursday night, June 9th.

Doubtless you will let me know if there is any special suggestion or question <to be considered>.

I suppose the Headmaster and staff will wear gowns and hoods.

I am not quite sure whether I had better come in the D.C.L. gown,[978] or <only> in morning dress. There is something to be said for the former.

2. With regard to the draft of the circular, I will think it over. I think it is perhaps a little curt. I think we said rather more on previous occasions, did we not?

Could you send me a copy of the last one or two notifications?

Yours sincerely,
Herbert Warren.

[*MS postscript*] Is it settled just when H.R.H. will arrive and how long he can give?

---

[976] McGrath, *Merch. Venturers*, pp. 446, 560. Warren himelf had been admitted to honorary membership of the Society in March 1919. The Prince declined to receive an honorary degree from the University, on the rather ungracious grounds that he had already acquired a good many others during the year: BRO, BCC/A/LM/C/LM2/3 (two loose letters in file on 1927 visit).
[977] William Welsford Ward, member of Council, resident in Prince's Buildings: *Directory* (1921), p. 770 and below [387].
[978] Perhaps meaning the festal robe, with which the hood is not worn.

[386]   6 June 1921. Earl Haig to the Head Master
[*RB2/41. Typed file copy*]

Cavalry Club,
127 Piccadilly, W.1.
6th. June, 1921

Dear Head Master,

I cannot allow the visit of H.R.H. the Prince of Wales to Clifton College to pass without sending you a few lines to say how very sorry I am not to be able to be present, and join in the hearty welcome which all connected with the School will wish to give the Prince. Would you very kindly express to H.R.H. on my behalf a very cordial welcome; and please say how very glad I am, in common with all Old Cliftonians, that he should have found time, in the midst of his really hard and busy life, to visit my Old School.

And with kindest remembrance to all old friends,

Believe me, yours most truly,
Haig of Bemersyde.

[387]   7 June 1921. The Chairman of Council to the Head Master
[*RB2/41. Holograph*]

From the President of Magdalen College, Oxford.

June 7 1921.

My dear King,

I asked Lord Haig to send a *message* which we might read when the P. of W. comes. He sends the enclosed [*above*] which I think is very nice. Will you keep it; I will ask you to read it out when we are on the Terrace. It will I think be very effective. I think Whitley is also going to send a message.

I am coming down by train on Thursday, arriving about 6, and shall go to W.W. Ward at 6 Prince's Buildings.

There does not seem to be much to arrange.

Yours ever,
Herbert Warren.

I think I ought to present the Council, and also to present you, and ask you to present the staff. In any case I must present *you*.

Perhaps I could see you on Thursday evening or Friday morning early.

[388]   9 June 1921. W.S. Paul[979] to the Head Master: putting out more flags
[*RB2/41. Holograph*]

Clifton
9th June 1921

Visit of H.R.H. The Prince of Wales

Dear Head Master,

As you know I represent the Council (by request) on the reception committee and therefore consider that I am justified in asking that the sham arch at the S.W. corner of the Close *should be at once removed*. It is most inartistic and a great eyesore.

---

[979] Walter Stuckey Paul [*102*: Town 1863–6], was an architect.

A good sized flag at the top of each pole, with (*perhaps*) a string of smaller flags stretched between the poles would sufficiently mark the entrance.

I am sorry to trouble you, and trust you will not object to my writing somewhat strongly on the matter.

In haste, yours faithfully,
Walter S. Paul.

[389]   10 June 1921. General orders for the day
[*RB2/41. Typescript*]

Clifton College.
Visit of H.R.H. The Prince of Wales on Friday, 10 June 1921.
(Wet or Fine).
The Prince will arrive at the S.W. Corner of the Close in College Road at 3.45 p.m., and be received by the Chairman of the Council, Head Master, etc.

The School will be arranged by Houses under the trees on the west side of the Close: boys will wear flannels, School blazers and straw hats, and will stand up and take off their hats as the Prince passes.

When the Prince has gone past the Houses to the South African War Memorial, the boys will follow (say 50 yards distant) and group at the foot of the steps of the War Memorial – the Head of the School[980] in front. Cricket on Big Side (Masters v. School) will go on until the Prince is near the War Memorial, when play will stop and the players come to the War Memorial steps.

Junior School and Preparatory, wearing flannels, blazers and straw hats, to take their places at 3.45 at the Parapet and steps S.W. of the Chapel.

Members of the Council not receiving the Prince on entrance, and masters not on duty with the boys, will stand on top of the steps of the War Memorial. Masters will wear gowns but not hoods.

Visitors will be placed in the N.W. corner of the Close, and will not be allowed in the roadway or in the Quadrangles, except on the roof outside the Library and Museum. They must be in their places before the arrival of the Prince.

After the Prince has spoken (if he does) from the War Memorial steps, he and his party will get into their cars in the Quadrangle and drive out under the Wilson Tower.

While the party is getting into the cars, the School (not Junior or Preparatory) can make their way to the small Quadrangle to cheer the Prince on departure.

[390]   [10 June 1921]. Instructions from the Head Master
[*RB2/41. Typescript*]

Visit of H.R.H. the Prince of Wales.

1. The Houses will arrange themselves along College Road in order of seniority, the School House nearest to the wicket-gate, the two Towns nearest to the School gates.

2. When the Prince enters the Close, the School will stand. As he passes each House in turn, the Head of each House will call on his House by name for cheers for the Prince. After cheering the School will remain uncovered.

---

[980] Stanley Horace Steadman [*7284*: NT 1911–21; *M327*: 1942–63†].

3. When the Prince has passed on some 50 yards, the School House will fall in behind him, and the other Houses will fall in behind them in turn, and follow the Prince to the Monument. There must be no short cuts.

4. When the Prince has reached the top of the steps, the School without hurrying or disorder will group themselves at the foot of the steps.

5. If opportunity offers, the School will pass to the North Quad, in order to cheer the Prince on his departure. No one must mount the steps until word is given. Ample space must be left for the Prince's and the other cars to pass under the Wilson Tower, though the North Quad, and across Guthrie Road into the Zoological Gardens.

6. It must be remembered that there must be no accosting of the Prince, no autograph-hunting, no crowding round his car. Cameras may be used with discretion.

A. Space will be reserved in the Close immediately west of the Monument for Ladies of the College, who will be entitled to bring two guests each. Ladies and their guests must bring tickets, which can be obtained from the Secretary. Ladies and guests will pass to the enclosure through the School House garden.

B. The School and House staffs and the staffs of masters other than House Masters will be found places in the School House garden, and when the Prince has reached the Monument, they will leave the garden and stand at the west corner of the Quad. Masters should be careful to provide each member of the staffs with a card inscribed 'School House garden'.

C. When the boys have grouped themselves at the foot of the steps, the visitors will be permitted to leave their enclosure and stand behind the boys.

J.E.K.

Second visit of the Prince of Wales 1927

☐ *Six years later the Prince returned to Clifton to open the new Science School. This was a much more substantial occasion, and the sole purpose of the Prince's coming to Bristol. The preparations were correspondingly more prolonged and detailed, as these sample papers show.*

[391]   18 February 1927. The Prince of Wales's Private Secretary[981] to the Head Master
[*Royalty box. Typescript*]

St James's Palace, S.W.
February 18th, 1927.

Dear Sir,

The Speaker's Secretary has forwarded me your letter of the 10th instant regarding The Prince of Wales's promised visit to Clifton College on June 2nd.

---

[981] Sir Godfrey John Vignoles Thomas, Bt, Private Secretary to the Prince since 1919, and Assistant Secretary to him as King.

I should welcome the opportunity of discussing the programme with you, and perhaps you would kindly let me know when you are next coming up to London.

I rather doubt whether The Prince will be prepared to leave London as early as 8.55 a.m., but I think that the greater part of the proposed programme can be carried out even were His Royal Highness to come by a later train. I, of course, agree that no other public functions can possibly be included that day, and am prepared to be quite firm with the Lord Mayor of Bristol on this point.

Yours very truly,
Godfrey Thomas, Private Secretary.

P.S. There is no objection to your making an announcement that HRH is coming on June 2nd.

[392]   19 February 1927. The Head Master to the Lord Mayor of Bristol
[BRO, BCC/A/LM/C/LM2/3 (formerly S5.4.1). Typescript]

Clifton College,
19 February 1927.

My dear Lord Mayor,

The Prince of Wales is paying a visit to this School on June 2nd next, and during his visit will open our new Science School. I am sending you the date at once as we very much hope that you will be able to be present.[982]

I shall shortly be seeing the Prince's Secretary in London, and will let you know as soon as the programme is fixed.

Yours sincerely,
N. Whatley, Headmaster.

[393]   3 March 1927. The Head Master to the Lord Mayor's Secretary.[983]
[BRO, BCC/A/LM/C/LM2/3 (formerly S5.4.2). Typescript]

Clifton College,
3 March 1927.

Dear Mr Woodward,

I had an interview yesterday with the Prince of Wales' Secretary Sir Godfrey Thomas. He says that he will himself write to the Lord Mayor about the arrangements for meeting the Prince and escorting him to the College. The Prince is to arrive at 1.15 at Bristol, and to leave at 5.15.

Now that these times are definitely fixed, we can get to work on making detailed arrangements for the visit to the School. Perhaps I may see you about these when we have got rather further.

Yours sincerely,
N. Whatley.

---

[982] At this time the Lord Mayor took office in November, so the June visit would be within the term of the incumbent Edward Malachi Dyer.
[983] Augustine Hugh Woodward [*2208*: NT 1878–83]; also the Lord Mayor's Swordbearer.

[394]   8 March 1927. The Prince's Secretary to the Lord Mayor
[*BRO, BCC/A/LM/C/LM2/3 (formerly S5.4.4). Typescript*]

St James's Palace, S.W.
March 8th, 1927.

My dear Lord Mayor,

You are probably aware that The Prince of Wales is paying a visit to Clifton College on Thursday, June 2nd, arriving at Bristol by train 1.15 p.m.

I understand that you would like to meet The Prince at the station, and His Royal Highness suggests that you should drive with him to Clifton.

Provided that the summer trains remain the same, His Royal Highness will return to London by the 5.15 train from Temple Meads.

Believe me, yours very truly,
Godfrey Thomas, Private Secretary.

[395]   8 March 1927. The Prince's Secretary to the Head Master
[*Royalty box. Typescript*]

St James's Palace, S.W.
March 8th, 1927.

Dear Mr Whatley,

The Prince of Wales entirely approves of the suggested programme for his visit to Clifton College on June 2nd, but for the time being, would like to leave the question of whether he actually plays squash in the afternoon at the conclusion of the opening of the Science School. The programme would then run:-

1.15 p.m. Arrive Temple Meads: Met by Lord Mayor of Bristol with whom H.R.H. will drive to Clifton College.

1.30 p.m. (about). Arrive Clifton College: Guard of Honour of O.T.C., Lunch at School House.

2.15 p.m. Opening of Science School (short speech).

2.45 p.m. Possibility of a game of squash. Walk round cricket ground and see boys swimming [*sic*].

4.30 p.m. Tea in School House garden.

4.55 p.m.. Leave Clifton College.

5.15 p.m. Train leaves Temple Meads.

I have written to the Lord Mayor of Bristol [*above*] telling him that The Prince would like him to meet His Royal Highness at the station and drive with him to the College.

Will you arrange with the Lord Mayor for two open cars to be supplied?

Yours very truly,
Godfrey Thomas, Private Secretary.

[396]   6 April 1927. The Prince's Secretary to the Head Master
[*Royalty box. Typescript*]

St James's Palace, S.W.
April 6th, 1927

Dear Sir,

Thank you for your letter of the 5th instant.

The Prince of Wales will wear a lounge suit and a bowler hat on June 2nd, so there is no need for top hats and morning dress.

Yours faithfully,

Godfrey Thomas, Private Secretary.

[397] 20 May 1927. The Prince's Secretary to the Head Master
[*Royalty box. Typescript*]

St James's Palace, S.W.

May 20th, 1927.

Dear Mr Whatley,

After I saw you yesterday, I talked to The Prince of Wales about the visit to Clifton on June 2nd, and he entirely approves the suggested programme of which you kindly said you would let me have a copy in its final form.

His Royal Highness does not think he will want to play squash, but would like to leave this open for the time being. Perhaps you could warn the boy you were thinking of to stand by,[984] and will telegraph to you, anyhow the day before, to say whether H.R.H. is bringing his squash-kit with him.

I will also send you, in good time, a Prince of Wales' Standard, medium size, which you can post back to me after the visit.

Yours sincerely,

Godfrey Thomas.

☐ *Meanwhile the Lord Mayor had got wind of the bowler hat business, and instructed his Secretary to enquire if it applied even to him.*

[398] 27 May. The Lord Mayor's Secretary to the Prince's Secretary
[*BRO, BCC/A/LM/C/LM2/3 (formerly S5.4.9). File copy*]

27th May.

Dear Sir,

In reference to the visit of His Royal Highness The Prince of Wales to Bristol on Thursday next, the Lord Mayor understands that it is the wish of The Prince that there shall be no formality whatsoever, and the College authorities have intimated that lounge suits are to be the order of the day. The Lord Mayor desires me, however, to ask you if you will be good enough to inform him if he should in these circumstances follow the usual procedure of welcoming royalty in his official dress, or whether His Royal Highness would prefer him to be in morning dress.

The Lord Mayor only desires to carry out the wishes of His Royal Highness, but is anxious that he shall not in any way fail to show the respect and loyalty of the citizens of Bristol.

Yours faithfully,

[*blank*], Lord Mayor's Secretary.

---

[984] John Henry Walters [*9326:* DH 1923–8], one of the rackets pair, was selected for this duty, and did indeed hit a few balls with HRH.

[399]   28 May 1927. The Prince's Secretary to the Lord Mayor's Secretary
[*BRO, BCC/A/LM/C/LM2/3 (formerly S5.4.10). Typescript*]

St James's Palace, S.W.
May 28, 1927.

Dear Mr Woodward,
    In reply to your letter of the 27th instant, The Prince of Wales will be in a lounge suit and bowler hat for the visit to Clifton College on June 2nd. In view of the fact that there is on this occasion nothing in the nature of a civic welcome, His Royal Highness hopes that the Lord Mayor will follow suit.

Yours truly,
Godfrey Thomas, Private Secretary.

[400]   30 May 1927. The Lord Mayor's Secretary to the Prince's Secretary
[*BRO, BCC/A/LM/C/LM2/3 (formerly S5.4.11). File copy*]

30th May.

Dear Sir Geoffrey,
    Thank you very much for your letter of the 28th instant. The Lord Mayor will be pleased to fall in with the wishes of His Royal Highness.

Yours very truly,
[*blank*], Lord Mayor's Secretary.

[401]   [1927]. Proposal for electrically-operated doors[985]
[*Royalty box. Typescript*]

Actual opening of the building.

The ordinary procedure is of course to unlock the door with an ornamental key.

This is rather common-place and in these circumstances would not be very dignified. There is no flight of steps up to the door and the Prince would have to descend from the dais, turn his back to the company and insert the key and turn it, and as he is somewhat short the ceremony would only be seen by very few.

Would it be possible to have on the dais a pedestal (quite small) carrying an electric switch preferably of the 'knife' or 'rocker' variety made in silver and suitably ornamented and engraved and mounted on an ebony base?

This could quite easily be ornamented with an arrangement inside the building which would release weights which, by a suitable arrangement of pulleys, would slowly open the doors when the switch was depressed.

The President of the College would ask the Prince to formally open [*sic*] the buildings; he would then depress the key, the doors would swing open (it is to be hoped!!) and the Prince, accompanied by those on the dais, would enter the building.

If this can be arranged easily there can be no doubt that the opening would be much more impressive and as it is a Science building the opening might well be something new with a scientific basis.

☐ *Evidently this was judged too risky, and the Prince was entrusted with a simple key.*

---

[985] This is presumably from the Head of Science E.J. Holmyard [*M243*].

[402]   2 June 1927. General orders for the day
[*Royalty box. Typescript*]

Orders for Thursday 2nd June.
Senior School.
Dress – (all day) as for cricket with straw hats.
June 2nd will be a holiday. Two hours preparation will be set for Friday. One hour will be done on Wednesday and the other on Thursday night. There will be no early preparation on Thursday or Friday.
Arrangements for Thursday.
9.   Prayers in Big School. Immediately after prayers there will be a rehearsal of the part to be played by the School in receiving the Prince.
9.45.   House matches,
12.   Play stops.
12.30.   Dinner in Houses (except School House).
1.0.   Boys admitted to the Close. Day boys to be back at the School by this time and enter by the Memorial Arch or the Armoury Gate. School House will take up a position on the footpath along the School House garden. Junior and Preparatory Schools on the footpath opposite. Remainder to line the fence along College Road to welcome the Prince in the following order starting from the right: B.H., D.H., O.H., Wi.H., Wa.H., N.T., S.T., P.H., U.H. When the Prince has passed a particular House that House may go up to the Parapet facing School House, but must not climb on the Parapet or come inside it. Cheering must stop while the Prince is placing wreaths in the Memorial Arch and while he is being presented to members of the Council. Cheering may start again as soon as these ceremonies are over.

When the Prince has entered the School House garden the School House will pass through the South Quad round Big School and enter the Dining Hall.

Other Houses will go to their seats for the opening ceremony. School House will take their seats later.
2.15.   Boys will stand as the Prince approaches the Science School for the opening ceremony.

After the opening ceremony as soon as the Prince enters the Science buildings boys will leave their seats and start cricket (Big Side and House games). A few boys will play squash. Those playing in the New Field will go straight there through the Armoury Gate and by Cecil Road. Each House will have to make arrangements to have bats, pads, etc. available without returning to Houses for them. Boys not playing will watch their own House games.

Cricket on the New Field will stop at 4.30. Boys will return via Cecil Road and the Armoury Gate to the Close.

Cricket on the Close will stop at 4.45.

For the departure of the Prince (4.55) boys will line the fence along College Road.

SECTION XIX:
AROUND THE HOUSES

☐ *It has long been customary for the Houses and Towns to chronicle their activities
and achievements in volumes variously called 'Annals' or 'Records' – collectively
the 'House Books'. The format has varied from one society to another, and from
time to time: in some cases a bare list of academic honours and sporting results, in
others a detailed journal, supplemented with photographs and other memorabilia.
This selection is biased in favour of the fullest of the surviving records. It begins with
Brown's, which is richly documented from its early days until its demise in 1993. The
first extant volume begins in 1875, with a term when there was only one topic.*

[403]   Michaelmas Term 1875. Brown's House
[*BH Annals 1875–96. MS*]

1875.

Football.   House Twenty.
    C. Cannan [*897*], A.G. Haines [*1040*], E.O. Curtler [*1188*], P. Mordaunt [*760*].
    W.D. Thomson [*1390*], W.S. Vidal [*1392*], W.J. Haines [*1041*], H.G. Wells [*1228*],
C.A. Browne [*933*], C.A. Wedderburn [*1463*], H. Hadden [*1363*], H.L. Spence
[*1653*], E.A. Brown [*1079*], P. Evershed [*1353*], E.E. Haines [*1265*], W.H. Barrett
[*1743*], G.L. Morris,[986] S.H. Evershed,[987] M.C. Cattley [*1557*], H. Haines [*1749*].

House Matches.
    Brown's were drawn with Harris';[988] and after three days' play the sides remained
so equal that the umpires gave an extra day. Brown's then proved superior and got
a try.
    The umpires gave Brown's the match.
    Brown's were next drawn with Dakyns'. We were heavier forward but Dakyns'
were much superior behind the scrimmage: for the first two days however the game
was nearly equal; on the third day we had decidedly the best of it and got a try. The

---

[986] Sir George Lockwood Morris, Bt [*1762*: BH 1875–8]; played rugby for Wales five times; succeeded to
baronetcy 1947 and died later that year.
[987] Sir Sydney Herbert Evershed [*1354*: BH 1873–7]; played rugby for Midlands and cricket for
Derbyshire; knighted 1929.
[988] The House which became Oakeley's; at this time still under its original Master, Edward Harris [*M26*:
1865–76].

umpires gave an extra day: we were still heavier but Block[989] got the ball and ran for Dakyns' – the try was unsuccessful but afterwards through a mistake of our whole backs they got another touch down from which Block placed a goal. A majority of the umpires refused to give another day.

Thus we were badly beaten by Dakyns' for the third year in succession. It should be mentioned that several of our twenty were unable to play on the last day and owing to a new rule we could not have substitutes except for Caps. There was a good deal of hacking, especially towards the end of the game: the forwards' play was exceedingly good on the third day, and considering the loss of weight they played very pluckily on the last day – the match was lost entirely through the mistake of the two whole backs, and if Dakyns' had not had Block there could have been no doubt of the result.

We had one day against the North Town: we were much the stronger but could only kick one goal out of several tries. Our placing throughout the season was very feeble.

A cup was given by the Caps for the best play below Caps was won by E.E. Haines.

[404]   Michaelmas Term 1877. North Town
[*The Annals of North Town 1875–1905* (Bristol, 1905), pp. 10–11. *Printed*]

Football term, 1877
[*House list, here omitted*]
The boundary between the Towns was altered at the beginning of this term from a line drawn east and west through the Pavilion, to one passing from the Suspension Bridge along Vyvyan Terrace and Oakfield Road.[990]

People who had been more than two years in the South Town did not leave in consequence of this alteration; the remainder of those living north of the new boundary came into the North Town as a body.

The House Caps this year were H.W.R. Gribble[991] and H.W. Priestley.[992] Gribble was disabled early in the term and could not play for the rest of it.

In the First Drawing of House Matches S.T. beat N.T. (W. Fairbanks, Esq., sub. for Gribble).[993]

In the Second Drawing, Dunn's[994] beat N.T. by two points (S.H. Evershed,[995] sub. for Gribble).

Order of Houses: S.H., Brown's or S.T., Oakeley's, Dunn's or Dakyns' or N.T.

---

[989] Sir Adam Samuel James Block [*771*: DH 1869–75], a Cap and member of the XXII; later a diplomat.
[990] The Pavilion was north-east of the present (1923) structure, level with the New Sanatorium (formerly the Old Sanatorium); the boundary change extended North Town's catchment area south by up to 300 yards.
[991] Herbert Willis Reginald Gribble [*1085*: NT 1871–8]; he later played cricket and rugby for Gloucestershire.
[992] Henry Wood Priestley [*1379*: NT 1873–7].
[993] Walter Fairbanks [*704*: NT 1869–71; *M75*: 1875–96]. In the early days it was not unusual for masters and OCs to play as substitutes.
[994] Later Wiseman's, still under its original master T.W. Dunn [*M38*: 1868–78], for whom see J.A. Spender *et al.* (eds), *Thomas William Dunn* (priv. pr. 1934), with (pp. 76–85) a memoir by his pupil Sir Charles Firth [*904*: Town, WiH 1870–5].
[995] Evershed was another outsider, being from Brown's: above **[403]**.

[405]   Summer Term 1893. Polack's House
[*Annals of Hamburg House (Sophie Polack's journal), vol. I, p. 21 MS in posses-sion of Polack family*]

Second Term 93.
In this term there were no entries and owing to the departure of Lousada [*4026*] and Montagu[996] our numbers diminished to ten. Archdeacon and Mrs. Wilson came to Commemoration. The former made a memorial speech in laudation of Mr Brown.[997] His Commemoration sermon was extremely beautiful and the aspect of the Chapel when the Rev. preacher was in the pulpit was impressive in the extreme. The [flowers in *corrected to*] floral decorations of the Chapel were in exquisite taste.

The honours which fell to our boys were very numerous, viz.:
Blume:[998] a £50 Council scholarship, also German composition prize and Form prize; Gubbay:[999] French comp. prize; Stiebel:[1000] Shakespeare prize; Charles Cohen:[1001] Reading prize; Halford:[1002] Form prize.

The fire escape was fitted this term.

Boys this term: Blume, L.; Gubbay, M.M., Stiebel, A., Cohen, R.W. [*4264*], Davis, L.C.J. [*4423*], Haas, F.A. [*4356*], Halford, J.M., Lumley, E.A. [*4359*], Enoch, C.D. [*4266*], Cohen mi C.W.

Arthur Stiebel left at the end of this term to enter the university.

[406]   Lent Term 1894. Polack's House
[*Annals of Hamburg House (Sophie Polack's journal), vol. I, pp. 25–6. MS in pos-session of Polack family*]

First term 94.
This term was <a> remarkably healthy <one>. Dr Fyffe only once called in and for quite a trifling ailment. Gubbay's condition seemed to have greatly improved and the attacks from which he suffered diminished in frequency. He carried off the prize for German composition open to the whole School. Lumley did not return so our numbers were only 13 counting Robert Cohen, who remained at home this term owing to ill health.

Boys this term were [*as above, with Lumley deleted and five newcomers.*]

---

[996] Edwin Samuel Montagu [*4381*: PH 1891–3]; Liberal MP brought into Government by Asquith (whose brother was a Clifton master); entered Cabinet as Chancellor of the Duchy of Lancaster 1915; Minister of Munitions 1916; Secretary of State for India 1917–22.
[997] Brown [*M12*] had left Clifton a year earlier to devote himself to pastoral work on the Isle of Man. From there on 27 June he wrote to S.T. Irwin [*M77*]: 'Well, and so you have had the Guthrie [*Commemoration*]. What a comfort to have it behind you!': Brown, *Letters*, p. 122.
[998] Lionel Blume [*4570*: PH 1892–5]; won an exhibition to Gonville and Caius College, Cambridge.
[999] Moses Mordecai Simeon Gubbay [*4272*: PH 1890–6]; won a scholarship to Caius, and became Financial Secretary to the Government of India.
[1000] Sir Arthur Stiebel [*4039*: PH 1889–93]; went to University College, Oxford; Senior and Chief Registrar in Bankruptcy, High Court of Justice 1936, knighted 1943.
[1001] Charles Waley Cohen [*4573*; PH 1892–7].
[1002] John Montagu Halford [*4586*: PH 1892–4].

In the Gymnasium competition at Aldershot Clifton ranked 4th. Littlejohn[1003] and Bryan[1004] were [champions *corrected to*] our representatives. I was much struck with Littlejohn's good style in the exercises I saw him perform at the Gymnasium.

Enoch, Halford and Cohen went to Aldershot manoevres [*sic*].

Purim happened to fall this year on the eve before Good Friday[1005] so our boys were not obliged to do preparation. We had a very successful evening. Music and reading before supper, a charade afterwards.

James[1006] spent a few days with us.

The Long Penpole was won by Riseley. The Short by Blenkinsopp. [1007] Stiebel came to us the last week. The Sports took place on the <last> Thursday and Friday of term. Two boys were hurt in attempting the high jump, Saville and Hall,[1008] the latter seriously. The School concert was very successful. Davis played a Polish dance which was well received.[1009]

The boys left by a very early train on Tuesday morning the tenth.

[407]   Summer vacation/Michaelmas term 1896. Polack's House
[*Annals of Hamburg House (Sophie Polack's journal), vol. I, pp. 57, 59–60. MS in possession of Polack family*]

[*From the entry for Summer Vacation*] Building operations were being persecuted at Clifton and on our return were in so backward a condition that we felt very anxious as to the possibility of our being able to accommodate our 24 boys. The weather was inclement and rain came pouring in to the dormitories. However, before the opening day matters had improved and the boys were delighted with the alterations.

$$* \quad * \quad *$$

3rd term 96

In this term several important changes took place. We opened with 24 boys. Gubbay [*4272*] stayed with us during the first week of the term and we were very pleased to have him. Mr Clissold[1010] took up his position as House-Tutor and occupied temporarily a small study. He had bedroom accommodation at 13 Canynge Square. The children also were located at Canynge Square with Nurse but as Bennie[1011] soon became unwell I asked Bona[1012] to take him to Weston where he enjoyed fairly good health during the whole term. The children also had very good health but the servants, including Nurse, Sarah and Florence, had bad throats. An epidemic of mumps broke

---

[1003] Beresford Hobbs *Littlejohns* [*4432*: WaH 1891–5]; won the Bronze Medal at Aldershot in the following year.

[1004] Frank Bryan [*4214*: SH 1890–5].

[1005] Good Friday was on 23 March.

[1006] The writer's brother-in-law.

[1007] George Murray Riseley [*3996*: ST 1889–94] and Bernard Arthur *Blenkinsop* [*4635*: ST 1893–8] (who won the Long Pen three times in succession, 1896–8).

[1008] Eustace Claud *Savile* [*4362*: ST 1891–8] or his brother Lawrence Wrey [*4626*: ST 1892–8]; there were several contemporaries called Hall.

[1009] The concert was on 9 April; the programme lists the piece only as Scharwenka's 'Polish Dance': *Cliftonian* XIII (1893–5), p. 248. It is likely to have been no. 1, in E flat minor, most popular of the five in Op. 3.

[1010] Clissold [*M148*] was House Tutor for two years before being given a House of his own.

[1011] The writer's son Benjamin [*5838*], not yet in the School.

[1012] The writer's sister-in-law.

out this term. About 90 cases were nursed at the Sanatorium and in some of the Houses, dormitories were turned into sick wards. We had six cases viz. Lyons [*5014*], Tuck [*5171*], Montagus mi and tert[*iu*]s [*4789, 5158*], Lazarus [*5152*] and Abrahams ma [*4995*]. Four of the boys remained some time at the San. After the end of the term the new Matron <of the Sanatorium> Miss Plum[1013] seemed to give great satisfaction in her management. We had serious trouble this year respecting one of the boys, and the term was an anxious one in some respects. After some weeks the boys were located in the new studies and seemed to like the change. The lavatory arrangements were a difficulty as the space for changing was limited. The new dormitory at the top of the House, though completed, was not used. This term we had Helps as a man-servant. The domestic arrangements seemed satisfactory, so I was surprised when I heard that the cook and parlour-maid had decided to leave. During the last week the kitchen-maid was taken ill, and her mother fetched her away. I [got *corrected to*] engaged a girl by the week to fill her place.

[*List of visitors.*]

Meyer [*4820*] took the Shakespeare prize, and Haas a Science exhibition of £30 at Sydney [*sic*] Sussex Coll. Cambridge.[1014] The term was the best ever known for football. Six matches were played of which three were won by our House. Henriques won the House cup.[1015] Abrahams mi [*5037*] and Abraham [*5178*] were both laid up with severe colds and left <a day> before the other boys. Our numbers at the House Supper were 35, 17 [guests *corrected to*] boys, 7 guests, 8 O.C.s. Guests were Mr Carter [*M74 or M167*] and daughters, Mr and Mrs Harper [*M112*], and Mr & Mrs. Shenstone [*M101*]. O.C.s Lousada [*4026*], Gubbay, Robert Cohen [*4264*], Enoch [*4266*], Halford [*4586*], Stiebel [*4039*] and Herbert Cohen [*3770*]. The supper party was very hilarious and Enoch's songs most successful. The concert in Big School was excellent, the music tasteful and well-selected. During this term the musical festival was held in Bristol. I enjoyed Haydn's *Creation* and had the pleasure of hearing Fraulein Malten, Edward Lloyd, Albani &c.[1016]

We accommodated six O.C.s with beds.

Mr Fairbanks[1017] gave up his House this term. It was carried on temporarily by Mr Clarke.[1018]

No leavers this term.

[408]   Michaelmas Term 1897. North Town
[*North Town Book 1892–1906. MS*]

Cock House. Our House Match against T.H.,[1019] which was really Cock House match, was one of the most exciting games that the Close has ever seen. We scored all our points before half time, and for the last 20 minutes T.H. were always in our 25

[1013] Actually *Plumb*; she served from 1896 to 1898.

[1014] Felix Alfred Haas [*4356*: PH 1891–7].

[1015] Cyril Quixano Henriques [*4780*: PH 1894–8]; co-author of *Report on the Possibilities of Jewish Settlement in Ecuador* (1936).

[1016] This was the 9th Bristol Triennial Festival; the German soprano Therese Malten (d. 1930) was best known for her Wagnerian roles; the English tenor Edward Lloyd (d. 1927) frequently appeared with the Canadian soprano Dame Emma Albani (d. 1930).

[1017] Walter Fairbanks [*704/M75*] had run what had been and was to become Watson's.

[1018] G.H. *Clark* [*M125*].

[1019] Tait's House (formerly and later Oakeley's), then under Charles William Adam Tait [*M57*: 1873–1904].

and seemed as if they were going to score every minute. But our defence was very sure and that saved us. G.D. Barne's place-kicking was magnificent.[1020]

G.S.J. Fuller Eberle[1021] played football in the holidays for Clifton Club, and had some very encouraging remarks made about his play in the papers.

Cock House Supper. In honour of our great success in games during the year, a very large number of Old North Town boys were invited to the House Supper. A number of parents of members of the House, together with the whole House of 83 boys, completed the gathering.

Such a large number could not be accomodated [*sic*] in the Town Room; accordingly we used the Gymnasium for the Supper, which was a great success in spite of the difficulty of hearing speeches in the Gymnasium. We had a piano, and Mrs Wollaston[1022] kindly accompanied several songs. We had the pleasure of hearing speeches from many distinguished Old North Town boys, H.J. Newbolt,[1023] H.C.V. Harrison,[1024] J.H.F Mills[1025] and W.M. Barclay,[1026] who told us of the House in their days and expressed their pleasure at being able once more, if only for one night, to belong to 'The Old North Town'.

[409]   Michaelmas Term 1899. North Town
[*Annals of North Town 1875–1905*, pp. 110–11. *Printed*]

Football term, 1899
[*Lists and results omitted*]
W.W. Vaughan, Esq., became House Master of the North Town this term. [1027]
Presentation to Mr Wollaston.

On December 18th, Mr Wollaston was publicly presented with his portrait by 150 old members of the North Town. The presentation took place in the Council Room, and was attended by the N.T., Old Cliftonians, the Head Master, Mr Vaughan, and several other masters, and several ladies. The picture, which is an excellent likeness, was painted by Mr William Carter.[1028] H.J. Newbolt took the chair, and the picture

---

[1020] George Dunsford Barne [*4705*: NT 1893–8], Bishop of Lahore 1932–4; played golf for Oxford and (once) cricket for Somerset.

[1021] George Strachan John Fuller Eberle [*4616*: NT 1892–1900]; played rugby and water polo for Oxford; see P.J. Casey and R.I. Hale, *For College, Club and Country: A History of Clifton Rugby Football Club* (2009), pp. 172–4 and the Clifton RFC website.

[1022] Wife of the House Master George Hyde Wollaston [*M60*: 1873–99].

[1023] Newbolt recalled the occasion in his richly imitable manner: 'Clifton was perfect ... It's a pure marvel, a School, and the intangible invisible thing we call 'House-feeling' is about the most wonderful thing in it.': *My World*, pp. 335–6.

[1024] Halford Claude Vaughan Harrison [*1909*: NT 1876–80], winner of the Long Pen in 1879; an officer in the Royal Artillery, killed on active service 1916.

[1025] John Harold Francis Mills [*3304*: NT 1884–93], a former Cap and member of the XI.

[1026] William Martin Barclay [*2454*: NT 1879–82], a surgeon at Bristol General Hospital.

[1027] William Wyamar Vaughan [*M138*: 1890–1904]; later Headmaster of Giggleswick, Master of Wellington and finally Headmaster of Rugby (where he succeeded A.A. David); married a daughter of John Addington Symonds Jr: Newsome, *Wellington*, pp. 273–313; Hope Simpson, *Rugby since Arnold*, pp. 188–212.

[1028] A well-reputed portrait, animal and landscape artist (d. 1939) but eclipsed in fame by his brother Howard, the archaeologist.

was formally handed over by F.G. Newbolt.[1029] Mr Wollaston feelingly responded in a few well-chosen words.

In this and succeeding years the House Supper took place in the newly-built Music School. At the suggestion of Mr Wollaston, who joined us late in the evening, a telegram of 'Good wishes from the Old House', was dispatched to the O.N.T.s serving in South Africa.

[410]   Lent Term 1901. Polack's House
[*Annals of Hamburg House (Sophie Polack's journal)*, vol. II. *MS in possession of the Polack family*]

We had a week spent quietly in making our preparations for the boys who arrived Tuesday Jan. 22nd.

Our dear Queen dangerously ill.

First term 1901.

Queen Victoria died.[1030] All the House attended memorial service at the Synagogue, the Cadets being in uniform.

Visitors this term: Mr & Mrs. Myer and Mr & Mrs. Davidson, Mr & Mrs. Solomon, Sir Samuel and Lady Montagu.[1031]

Ezra[1032] celebrated his Barmitzvah March 9th.

Purim was celebrated March 5th. All the boys were present except Montefiore quartus[1033] who was travelling on account of his health. Mr Palmer[1034] and Bennie [*5838*] present. We supped all together at 6.15. The supper was not quite a success as boys had to leave without partaking of dessert.

At the Sports Moss[1035] came in fourth in Short Penpole, Franklin[1036] 5th in Long Penpole. Moss won two prizes at the Sports.

Our House came out first in the House Squad competition.

We gave a House entertainment at which Miss Peck, Miss Miles, Mr Household,[1037] Joseph <Mr Polack> [*M139*], Montefiore ma [*5105*], Montefiore mi [*5313*], Wolff [*recte* Woolf: *5645*] and Montagu [*5158*] took part.

Bennie took mumps March 17th and was removed to Miss Lucas.

Myer ma [*5219*] left this term.

Health of the House excellent.

Albert[1038] took mumps March 31st.

[1029] Sir Francis George Newbolt [*1918*: ST, NT 1876–83], Sir Henry's brother and like him primarily a lawyer; author of *Clifton College Twenty-Five Years Ago: The Diary of a Fag* (1904), and *Clifton College Forty Years Ago: The Diary of a Praepostor* (1927) [concerning 1882–3]; both with much affectionate recollection of Wollaston.

[1030] On 22 January.

[1031] No boys of the first three names had yet entered the House. Montagu (later created Baron Swaythling) was father of Lionel [*5158*] mentioned in this entry and above **[407]**, Gerald Samuel [*4789*] also in **[407]**, and Edwin Samuel [*4381*] mentioned in **[405]**; see also above **[19]**.

[1032] Ellis Ezra [*5753*: PH 1900–5].

[1033] Thomas Henry Sebag-Montefiore [*5737*: PH 1900–4].

[1034] George William Palmer [*M162*: 1899–1911], author of *Arithmetic* (1907); had become second House Tutor PH in 1900: Winterbottom, *Dynasty*, p. 56.

[1035] Henry Nathaniel Moss [*5534*: PH 1899–1903].

[1036] Jacob Arthur Franklin [*5289*: PH 1897–1902].

[1037] Horace West Household [*M158*: 1897–1901].

[1038] Albert Isaac Polack [*5972*: PH 1902–11; *M270*: 1923–49]; succeeded his father as House Master PH.

[411]   Michaelmas Term 1908. Polack's House
[*Annals of Hamburg House (Sophie Polack's journal)*, vol. III. *MS in possession of the Polack family*]

3rd term 1908

Nine new boys entered, namely Joseph [*6864*], Montagu mi [*6870*], Benjamin [*6840*], Birnstingl [*6841*], Isaac [*6862*], Hart [*6860*], Dreyffus [*recte* Dreyfus: *6849*], Shimberg [*6886*], Abrahams [*6893*].

On our return to Clifton Joseph and I went to see Bernard Shaw's *Arms and the Man* which only pleased us moderately.

Bennie was slightly hurt in Big-Side game.

Mr & Mrs. Evans dined with us on Oct. 7th.

On Oct. 10 Joseph, I and boys went to Festival Concert. Plunket Greene [*2059*] sang. 'Ode to the Duke of Wellington'[1039] was given.

Bennie played in 2nd XI match against Bath College.[1040] Clifton won.

Oct. 22. Field day at Cheltenham.

Went with Joseph to see *The Thief*. George Alexander[1041] and Irene Vanburgh.[1042] Interested.

We gave a gentleman's dinner party on Oct. 28th. Our guests were: The Headmaster, Messrs Shettlewell, Clark [*M125*], Rintoul [*M121*], T.S. Peppin [*M157*], Borwick [*M142*], Wollaston [*M60*], Matthews [*M196*], Helmesley [*recte* Hemsley: *M185*], Lamb,[1043] Dr Prichard, Professors Burrell and Herrier.

Bennie played against Bristol Medicals. Clifton won 26–13.[1044]

[*Family details and visitors*.]

The Marlborough match was won by home team. Bennie was asked to play but could not, owing to its taking place on Saturday.[1045]

Went on train for first time since illness Nov 7th.

Saturday Nov. 28th. Mr Smith[1046] gave a lecture to House on Norway.

In a friendly match against Barff's Belisha[1047] and Rossdale mi[1048] were hurt. Both had teeth damaged and Rossdale mi slight concussion.

[*More visitors*.]

Our football was very successful this year. We won every second 15 match in which we played and none of our opponents scored a single point. A great many difficulties arose which finally prevented our playing Russell's 2nd 15, and owing to bad weather and an apparent lack of sportsmanlike qualities in our opponents, the

---

[1039] By Tennyson (1852).

[1040] Established 1878 under the former Clifton House Master T.W. Dunn [*M38*], and closely modelled on Clifton; though a centre of excellence in Classics, the school lacked a broader base and closed in 1909: Spender, *Dunn*, pp. 11–30, 35–7.

[1041] Sir George Alexander (knighted 1911), actor manager.

[1042] Dame Irene *Vanbrugh* (d. 1949), the original Gwendolen in *The Importance of Being Earnest*.

[1043] Sir Walter Rangeley Maidment Lamb [*M191*: 1907–9]; Secretary of the Royal Academy 1913–51.

[1044] On 29 October: *Cliftonian* XX (1907–9), p. 410.

[1045] Played on 14 November; Clifton won 16–13: *ibid*., pp. 412–13.

[1046] Presumably either Edmund Henry Cocks Smith [*M84*: 1877–1922] or Walter Ernest Smith [*M180*: 1902–54].

[1047] Isaac Leslie Hore Belisha, *later* Hore-Belisha [*6673*: PH 1907–12], the future Cabinet Minister: above **[71]**.

[1048] George Harold Rossdale [*6417*: PH 1905–12].

Challenge medal against Russell's first fifteen was not played, which was a great disappointment in our House. Laski[1049] left at the end of this term.

The House supper was a very great success. We mustered 76. The visitors were [*listed*]. Mr Milne sang 'The Clan McTavish' in most amusing Scotch fashion.[1050]

[412]   Michaelmas Term 1915. Brown's House
[*BH Annals 1914–38. MS*]

Christmas term 1915.

As in the last Christmas term football was only played twice a week and the old system of four rounds of House Matches was reverted to.

Unfortunately the House did not seem to have grown any older or bigger than it was last year, which of course was fatal in the House Matches; but all worked together and well for the unattainable success.

In the first round we were beaten by North Town. The score was as much as 35–0 but the impression given is not a true one as the game was hardly contested throughout.

In the second and third rounds we were beaten by South Town and Polack's respectively.

In the fourth round we were a bye.

As it was useless to challenge we were left bottom House.

The House XV were: T.S.W. Brown [*7427*], Capt. XV, M.H. Bates [*7423*], R.J.B. Anderson [*7558*], F.S.D [*recte* F.D.S.] Fripp [*7440*], S.D. Iplikian [*7595*], A. Hutchison [*7444*], G.H.S. Fripp [*7583*], A.J.D. Perkin [*7829*]

C.M. St A. Campbell [*7520*], P.G. Fairhurst [*7735*]

M.E. Nalty [*7803*], F.R. Evershed,[1051] J.G. Williams [*7771*], F.E. Knowles [*7747*]. H.F. Cockill [*7572*].

As last year there were not [*recte* no] festivities and no House supper at the end of this term.

It was during this term that Mr and Mrs. Russell lost their son, an Old Cliftonian, who was killed in October. The House expressed their heartfelt sympathy with them in their loss.[1052]

[413]   Lent Term 1917. The South Town
[*ST Book 1875–1919. MS (This volume is a retrospective compilation)*]

Head of the House: D.C. Prowse[1053]   *Numbers* 66; *in* VIth 8.

G.L. Alexander and R. Avery[1054] received House Sixth power.

[1049] Neville Jonas Laski [*6168*: PH 1904–8], President of the Board of Deputies of Bristish Jews 1933–40; Recorder of Liverpool 1956–63; author of *Jewish Rights and Jewish Wrongs* (1939).

[1050] William Proctor Milne [*M192*: 1907–19] was a genuine Scot, graduating with distinction from Aberdeen University; later Professor of Mathematics at Leeds.

[1051] Francis Raymond Evershed [*7582*: BH 1913–17]; Head of the School 1917; Master of the Rolls 1949–62, created Baron Evershed of Stapenhill 1956, Lord of Appeal in Ordinary 1962; member of the College Council from 1945 (Chairman 1945–51), President of the College from 1951 until his death in 1966.

[1052] C.H. St L. Russell [*M128*] was House Master BH 1907–18; his son Harley Raymond [*5803/6401*: Town 1901, SH 1905–10], Lt, 10th Bn, Gloucestershire Regt, had been killed in France on 13 October.

[1053] David Crawford Prowse [*7215*: ST 1910–17].

[1054] George Laurie Alexander [*7557*: ST 1913–18] and Ronald Avery [*6833*: ST 1908–18].

The arrangements of the term were wrecked by long continued frost and snow and the prevalence of German measles and mumps.

Running. The Short Penpole was abolished. *The Long* was run for the last time. The start was made from the Downs. Only six started, as qualified from last year.[1055] Winner: H. Bagot N.T. *[7723].* S.T. W.E.S. Stone[1056] 5th.

The runs were much curtailed this year, and were mainly arranged as training for the Long, not as a general exercise for the School.

The Sports. Cock House C.H.[1057] Challenge cup E.H. Hurst C.H. *[7590].* S.T. was 4th. E.W. Thomas[1058] won the open hurdles. No prizes were given, as a war economy. As a further economy no School prizes were to be given till the war be over.[1059] The money is to be invested in war savings certificates to be realized[1060] after peace is declared, when books will be purchased for the prize winners.

Football had been arranged for the bulk of the School, but little was played owing to bad weather and illness.

Fives. Cock House: Polack's House. S.T. was beaten in the first round by Rintoul's.[1061]

Racquets. Cock House *[blank].* S.T. did not enter, but A.R. Aslett[1062] was 4th in the racquet six.

Corps. H.F. Sherborne *[7147],* Captain. E.W. Thomas and D.C. Prowse, Serjeants. W.S.B. Freer *[6905]* and R. Avery, Corporals. W.P. Symonds *[7148]* and C.G. Brasher *[7655],* Lce Corporals. S.T. 1st equal with Mayor's[1063] in knotting and lashing.

Digging. During the Xmas holidays levelling of pitches at Beggar's Bush was carried out by N.T. and S.T. During term and in the Easter holidays a good deal of the field was preparing for growing food under the superintendence of Mr Imlay.[1064]

[414]   Summer Term 1918. Brown's House
[Russell's House Annals 1914–24. MS]

Summer 1918.

Although we had a team that might have done quite well we showed great inability to rise to an occasion and were once more bottom House, being beaten by ST and [SH *inserted*].

R.N.B. Cox[1065] *[won]* his 2nd XI colours and also W. [H. *corrected to*] M. Hampton[1066] who played for the Colts, making 55 against Marlborough.

[1055] Not because of the war, but in deference to feeling that the runs were weakening the XV by diverting sprinters from the three-quarter line. In 1918 a shorter cross-country race of six miles was introduced, known for tradition's sake as the Long Pen, though Penpole was no longer on the route: Christie, *History*, p. 299–300.

[1056] Walter Eric Slater Stone *[7110:* ST 1910–17].

[1057] Clissold's House (later Wiseman's).

[1058] Edward Wilson Thomas *[7073:* ST 1910–17].

[1059] *Sic.* The writer has copied from a rubric of the time without adjusting the syntax to his sentence.

[1060] MS. 'realezid'.

[1061] Later Oakeley's.

[1062] Alfred Rimbault Aslett *[6789:* Town, MHP, PHP, SH, ST 1908–18]; England XV 1926 and 1929.

[1063] Later Watson's, then under Henry Bickersteth Mayor *[3329:* WiH 1884–90; *M151:* 1895–1926].

[1064] A.D. Imlay *[5233/M194:* 1907–45]; *cf.* above **[295].**

[1065] Robert Norton Bayliss Cox *[7513:* HHP, BH 1913–18].

[1066] William Marcus Hampton *[8180:* BH 1917–22], Head of the School 1921–2; later played for Worcestershire, and taught at Winchester.

The House XI were: R.N.B. Cox (capt.), W. [H. *corrected to*] M. Hampton, S.L.L. Russell [*7881*], J.G. Williams [*7771*], P.G. Fairhurst [*7735*], F.E. Knowles [*7747*], J.R.T. Morris [*7693*], A.J.D. Perkin [*7829*], F.L. Morris [*7643*] E. Thornton Jones [*8211*], J.J.H. Greer [*7993*].

In the 2nd XI we were [*blank; minuted* ?6th or 7th] House. We were 7th in the competition for the Canada Trophy.[1067]

Towards the middle of the term, the House Tutor, Mr Peppin,[1068] who had not been well for some time, was compelled to give up his work in House and School and go <to> the Sanatorium. When he left to go and live in the country the House made him a presentation. An outbreak of influenza at the end of term prevented [many *corrected to*] some Houses from competing in the swimming Sports and we had no entries.

This was Mr Russell's last term as House Master. The eleven years of his House Mastership have among them some of the most successful terms in the history of the House, and all showed regret at his leaving.

The House musketry competition was put off until next term.

We had every prospect of winning the House Music competition but were unfortunately prevented from competing in the finals owing to some of our team falling victim to influenza.

In the preliminary rounds S.L.L. Russell won the Kadoorie Cup.[1069]

[415]   Summer Term 1926. Dakyns' House
[*DH Book 1909–39. MS with printed matter pasted in*]

Summer term 1926

This term we were 2nd House at *cricket*, losing to School House in the first round and winning all our other matches. We lost to School House by 57 runs, beat North Town by 8 wickets, Wiseman's House by 7 wickets, Polack's House by 7 wickets and Watson's House by 1 wicket.

The House XI were as follows: F.M.S. Tegner (Captain of the School XI) [*9142*], W.C. Carr (XI) [*8836*], G.H. Whittington (XI) [*9329*], R.C. Arendt (XI) [*9085*], R.W. Owen [*9484*], T.W. Lloyd [*9295*], W.H.T. Luce [*8950*], R.E. Peel [*9131*], J.H. Walters [*9326*], J.H.H. Whitty [*9219*], J.M. Lings [*9294*].

We were *Cock House at Music*, the first time since 1906, and M.S. Redgrave[1070] won the Kadoorie Cup for the best individual performance. The following was the programme:

[*Printed insert*]
1. Piano solo. Rhapsody in B minor, Op. 79, No. 1   *Brahms*
       M.S. Redgrave.

[1067] For excellence in the Corps; presented 1903 by William Hamilton Merritt [*1053*: DH 1871–4], Canadian cavalry commander and Air Force Colonel; see *Cliftonian* XXII (1913–15), p. 200 and pl. facing p. 134.

[1068] Talbot Sydenham Peppin [*M157*: 1897–1918†]; remained on the staff, but died next term.

[1069] Given by the Hong Kong magnate Sir Elly Kadoorie (d. 1944), father of Lawrence, Baron Kadoorie [*7523*: 1913–14] and Sir Horace [*7540*: PH 1913–14]. Studley Leslie Russell [*7881*: BH 1915–19] became Organ Scholar of Christ Church and later an Oxford DMus; the second 'L.' initial twice written here is otiose.

[1070] Sir Michael Scudamore Redgrave [*9027*: DH 1922–6].

2. Quartet for two violins, 'Cello and Piano; Golden Sonata, Grave, Allegro   *Purcell*
    F.E.R. Merritt [*9159*], T.W. Lloyd, W.H.T. Luce, M. Lings [*9116*].
3. Duet for two pianos. Variations on a theme of Beethoven, Op. 35   *Saint-Saens*
    M.S. Redgrave, W.H.T. Luce.
    Reserves:
(a) Piano solo. Sonata in E minor, Op. 7 (1st movement)   *Grieg*
    W.H.T. Luce.
(b) Piano solo, Sonata in B *flat*, Op, 22 (1st movement)   *Beethoven*
    M. Lings.
(c) Organ solo. Short Prelude and Fugue in F.   *J.S. Bach*
    P.C. Bartrum [*8924*].

We were 8th House at *shooting* but 3 of our best men were required to play cricket and were unable to shoot. W.L. Lang[1071] won the Younghusband Cup for the highest individual score outside the eight.

    W.L. Lang also represented the school in the Cadet Pair.[1072]

Corps promotions:
To be Sergeant	Cpl. G.H. Whittington
To be Corporal	L/Cpl. R.C. Arendt
	L/Cpl. M.S. Redgrave
	L/Cpl. R.E. Peel
To be Lance-Corporal	Spr. C.E. Whitaker [*8893*].

[416]   Lent Term 1929. Dakyns' House
[*DH Book 1909–39. MS*]

Easter term 1929[1]

In *Colts* rugger we were unfortunate to meet the ultimate winners, Wa.H., in the first round, being beaten after a close and surprisingly skillful [*sic*] game on both sides, by the narrow margin of 8–3. We had more of the game than they had, our forwards, among whom T.W. Howard-Smith[1073] and G.F.K. Morgan[1074] are in School Colts, playing a wonderful combined game. Bainbridge,[1075] however, on the wing was twice too fast even for Minett's[1076] wonderful tackling.

    We easily won our remaining matches against S.T. and O.H.

    The team were as follows:

Full back K.D. Woolley [*9821*].

[1071] William Laurie Lang [*9572*: DH 1925–30]; later shone more as an athlete, representing Oxford, and both universities; killed on active service with the RAFVR, 1941.

[1072] At Bisley.

[1073] Trevor Wallace Howard-Smith [*8995*; PHP, DH 1922–32], known to the world as the actor Trevor Howard. At Clifton he excelled as a sportsman, in the XI, the XV and the School boxing team. It is often said that he never acted at school, but this DH book shows that he performed in a House show. His schooldays are recalled in V. Knight, *Trevor Howard: A Gentleman and a Player* (1986), pp. 7–25. Michael Redgrave left two years before Howard moved to the Upper School, so they were not contemporaries in the House; they acted together only in Anthony Asquith's RAF film *The Way to the Stars* (1945).

[1074] George Frederick Kenneth Morgan [*9585*: HHP, DH 1925–30].

[1075] Emerson Muschamp Bainbridge [*9766*: WaH 1926–41]; Captain of the XV 1930.

[1076] Richard Woodruff Woodruff-Minett [*9165*: PHP, DH 1922–31].

Three quarters W. Minett, A.R. Rigby [*9958*], G.P. Careless [*9081*], J. Waterston [*9968*].

Half backs T.T. Steiger [*9519*], K.H. [*recte* H.K.] Bowring [*8911*].

Forwards T.W. Howard-Smith (Capt.), G.F.K. Morgan, M.B. Brash [*8690*], H.E. Girardet [*10003*], D.P. Howell [*9556*], H.M. Field [*9926*], D.B. Taylor [*9815*].

At *fives* we were runners-up to Oakeley's. We beat N.T. and S.H. in all three pairs with the utmost ease. Oakeley's, however, had tit-for-tat with us for last year, since this time our first pair won easily, while their second pair never let ours begin to play, and the duel for the cup was fought out with desperate keeness [*sic*] in the third pair, which was eventually victorious for Oakeley's. The scores in the Cock House match in games was as follows:

I pair D.H. 2–0, II pair 0–2, II 1–2 (0–15, 19–14, 15–12).

The pairs were: I – R.W. Owen [*9484*], H.G. Greer [*9614*]; II – K.D. Woolley, T.T. Steiger; III – J.G. Harrison [*9786*], T.W. Howard-Smith. Our first House pair also received School first pair colours.

At *racquets* we were defeated in the first round by the ultimate winner, S.H. Our pair on paper did not do themselves a great deal of credit in losing the last two games to love. S.H. undoubtedly played a very fine game and showed the temperament which wins matches.

Our pair was: W.E. Carr (1st string cup; School 1st string at Queen's)[1077]; J.M. Lings [*9294*] (racquets VI).

D.B. Taylor came in 15th in the *Long Pen*, 6 minutes after winner.[1078]

[417]   26 December 1932. Sir Henry Newbolt to J.K.B. Crawford, House Master of North Town
[*P 1917 file. Holograph*]

29, Campden Hill Road, W.8.
26 Dec. 32.

Dear Colonel Crawford,

Many thanks for your letter and for sending the *North Star*.[1079] I am very glad to hear so good an account of the House. The Town system has indeed justified not only itself but also the foundation of Clifton as a school for the west of England, and the new Preparatory will complete the whole scheme. But I hope we shall continue to attract a certain number of recruits from Scotland and the Midlands – Haigs, Tylecotes and Whitleys.[1080]

Yours sincerely,
Henry Newbolt.

[1077] Sir William Emsley Carr [*9774*: DH 1926–31); Golf Blue at Cambridge and founder of the Emsley Carr Mile (annual track event named after his father, long-serving editor of *News of the World*).

[1078] The time limit for a placing (being said to have 'come in').

[1079] The North Town magazine.

[1080] Earl Haig [*1981*], his brother John Alicius [*1039*: SH 1871–5], his nephew Oliver Peter [9189: NT, SH 1923–6] and two others of the name; the Tylecote brothers Charles Brandon Lea [*136*: SH 1863–7], Edward Ferdinando Sutton [*137*: SH 1863–8] and Henry Grey [*425*: SH 1866–73], all great cricketers, especially Edward; Mr Speaker Whitley [*2251*], his brothers Alfred William [*2691*: HHP, WiH 1881–6], Samuel Rinder [*2892*: HHP, WiH 1882–8] and Sir Edward Nathan [*3740*; WiH 1887–92], and other family.

I hope we shall meet in May, at the opening ceremony.

[418]   Lent Term 1934. Brown's House
[*BH Annals 1933–44. MS*]

Easter term.

On the whole we had quite a successful term for although we did not do well in Colts' rugger we had several minor successes and some very good individual performances.

Our Colts' team was definitely disappointing. We had a very good pack for an under 16½ team, and for the most part they played extremely well but unfortunately they were let down by their outsides who, with the exception of two, were rather young and inexperienced. This should mean that our outsides next Easter will be more of Colts' standard than this year.

In running, this term, we did very well to be 3rd in the Cock House for the Long Pen. This position was due to the efforts of White[1081] and Evershed[1082] – White coming in first and Evershed seventh. Running has become much more popular in this House than it was three or four years ago and this is a very good thing to happen, but it is very discouraging to a person who is keen on running to be continually hearing what a terrible form of exercise running is.

During the whole of this term Sergeant Bragge came up every Saturday evening to give instruction to those going in for School boxing and to those who already showed some knowledge of the subject. In School boxing we sent five entrants in but only one was successful; this was Evershed, who beat Crichton of School House[1083] after a very close fight. The other boxers from Brown's who were entered all lost their fights and it must be said that they all fought very pluckily and especially Cunningham[1084] who fought an extremely good fight.

As usual we did not do at all well in the Sports. The weather did not treat us very kindly either, for although it did not rain on the final three days it rained a good deal before that, thus necessitating the elimination of several of the School heats as well as one or two of the House heats.

This term we managed to carry off the Cock House chess shield by dint of careful and studied play. Early in the term there was held a chess tournament to determine the four best players in the House. The most successful victory was that over Polack's in the final when Graham[1085] beat Nabarro[1086] who was already School champion.

[419]   Summer Term 1938. Brown's House
[*BH Annals 1933–44. MS*]

Summer term 1938

Though the weather was extremely unkind, we passed a very pleasant Summer term. As throughout all the past year, our athletic achievements were undistinguished

---

[1081] Christopher Edmund Benson White [*10455*: BH 1930–4].
[1082] Sydney John Anthony Evershed [*10363*: BH 1930–4]; killed in action 1940.
[1083] John Louis Crichton [*10564*: UH, SH 1931–5], in the School boxing team; killed in a flying accident 1942.
[1084] Peter Moresby Cunningham [*10832*: BH 1933–9], Head of the School 1938–9.
[1085] Robert Henry Graham [*10141*: HHP, BH 1928–34].
[1086] Eric John Nunes Nabarro [*10432*: PH 1930–5].

without being mediocre. However, we were Cock House in swimming, our only outstanding success of the year. Also, we had two XIs for the first time since 1932. We were very glad to hear, too, of Cunningham's appointment as Head of the School for next term.[1087]

We should not fail to record in these annals the visit of B.M Steere as exchange scholar from Loomis School, U.S.A.,[1088] which has largely contributed to the pleasantness of life in the past year. His unassuming enthusiasm and readiness to conform to what must sometimes appear rather ludicrous traditions made him immensely popular, and his stay has no doubt been as important to our own education as to his.

[420]   Summer Term 1940. The South Town
[*ST Book 1933–43. MS*]

Summer term 1940

House organsation.

House Sixths: N.R. Garden (Head of the House) [*10313*], D.A. Imlay [*10241*], A.A. Adams [*11090*], E.H.C. Davies [*10311*], P.H.F. Clarke [*10239*].

House Fifths: J.S. Ross (Head Vth) [*11244*], W.N. Hargreaves-Mawdsley (Deputy Head Vth) [*10317*], J.F. Durant (Sec.) [*10647*], E.H. Griffiths [*10744*], A.H. Wood [*11040*], R.C. Greene [*10544*], N.B. Finter [*10804*], R.S. Hignell [*11474*].

Cricket.

In the first round we met N.T., the previous Cock House, and were defeated by an innings and 212 runs. D.M. Evans[1089] took 4 wickets for 35 runs.

In the next round we were playing P.H. and they gained a first innings lead, but owing to intense air activity nearly all the boarders went home and so the game was abandoned.

The 1st XI consisted of: D.A. Imlay (Capt.), R.C. Greene, J. Robertson [*11593*], E.R.F. Weaver [*10817*], D.M. Evans, R.S. Hignell, J.S. Ross, J.B.G. Barnett [*10765*], J.W.V. Palmer [*11489*], G.M. Britton [*10954*] , J.A. Goodchap [*11464*].

Our 2nd XI was soundly beaten by D.H. in the first round, but in the next redeemed itself by winning against B.H., Brown[1090] scoring 51.

[*Team list omitted*]

The 3rd XI match against N.T. ended in a draw.

[*Team list omitted*]

D.A. Imlay won his XXII.

The Fielding Cup[1091] was awarded to R.C. Greene.

[1087] See above **[418]**; he became a Headmaster.

[1088] Bruce Middleton Steere [*11379*: BH 1937–8]; continued his education at Yale and Harvard Business School before a career in the aerospace industry and finance. Loomis Chaffee is a co-ed school at Windsor CT, which has nurtured celebrities as varied as Secretary of State George Schultz and satirist Tom Lehrer.

[1089] David Meiros Evans [*10803*: ST 1933–40].

[1090] Basil Ernest Brown [*11185*: ST 1936–44].

[1091] Presented 1885 by Hugh Cecil Cookson [*1561*: ST 1874–81].

Rowing.

Unfortunately, owing to the fact that the boarding houses had practically ceased to exist by the end of June since most of the boarders had returned home, there could be no House rowing matches.

Rowing IV: A.A. Adams.

Shooting. Swimming. Fencing.

These were likewise affected by the early return of the boarders to their homes. R.H. Wood [*11292*] obtained his swimming colours.

A.A. Adams – Secretary of the Natural History Section.

[421]   Michaelmas Term 1940. Brown's House
[*BH Annals 1933–44. MS*]

Christmas term 1940.

Owing to the premature end of the Summer term, those in authority decided that we must have a longer succeeding term to make up for the lost work caused by air raids. So the Christmas term started in a blaze of sunshine, which resulted in baked pitches on which it was impossible to play rugger without serious injuries. The idea was put forward that the first few weeks should be devoted to sports, and this was received with joy by Major Muirhead,[1092] who hoped that the hot weather would help runners break records. In the open and under 15 relays, we were placed in every event except the 2 mile open, but in the under 13½ relay, we could only obtain 3rd place in the hurdles.

We were fortunate in having Pinkerton[1093] to run our swimming, and his enthusiasm helped us to take 3rd place in the relays.

Rugger was cut down to two half-holidays a week, owing to lumbering activities at Portbury, but, on the whole, this was good, as unrelieved rugger is inclined to pall towards the end of term. Only two rounds were played, as the term was again cut short by blitzes; the first, against Wiseman's, we lost in all three teams, and the second, against Polack's, we won.

The House Fire Brigade dealt effectively with incendiaries which fell during the Clifton blitz, while the First Aid Party, trained by Mr Mounsey,[1094] became very efficient, but, unfortunately for them, had no chance to show their skill.

[1092] J.A.O. Muirhead [*M231*], in charge of athletics 1916–43.
[1093] James Robert Hamilton Pinkerton [*11236*: WaH, BH 1936–40].
[1094] Michael James Mounsey [*M317*: 1936–46].

SECTION XX: FIRST WORLD WAR

[422]   18 November 1914. Status of masters serving in the Forces
[*Council Minute Book 6, p. 304. MS*].

The Headmaster reported that six masters, viz. Messrs Raymer,[1095] Clissold,[1096] Parr,[1097] Langley,[1098] Williams[1099] and Bache[1100] were absent on military service, that he was arranging for their work by temporary appointments and certain rearrangements, and that he had undertaken to reinstate them in the terms of the following circular letter:

'If any assistant master with the Head Master's consent vacates his post at Clifton to serve in war, I shall regard him as being still an assistant master as long as his service in war is necessary, and undertake to reinstate him in his work as soon as the state of the School enables me to do so.

I shall furnish the Council with a list of names of those who have to vacate their posts for purpose of serving in the war in order that if there be any change of Head Master the circumstances may be known to my successor.

10th August 1914.   (signed) J.E. King, Head Master.'

☐ *The writer of the two following letters had been Captain of the XI of 1914.*

[1095] Robert Richmond Raymer [*M221*: 1913–20]; Commandant of the Cadet Corps; served as Colonel, South Staffordshire Regt; CMG, DSO, four times Mentioned in Despatches.

[1096] Harry Clissold [*3375*: WaH 1885–9; *M148*: 1894–1917†]; Major, Royal Engineers; DSO; killed in action.

[1097] Hugh Wharton Myddleton Parr [*4407*: NT 1891–1901; *M206*: 1909–15†]; 5th Bn, South Staffordshire Regt; killed in action.

[1098] Oswald Read Langley [*M179*: 1902–33]; Major, Royal Engineers.

[1099] A.G. Williams [*M229B*: 1914–?], appointed second Chemistry Master for Michaelmas term 1914: Council Minute Book 6, p. 303.

[1100] Harold Godfrey Bache [*M229A*: 1914–16†]; appointed to the Junior School and as House Tutor HHP for Michaelmas term 1914: Council Minute Book 6, p. 304. A prolific sportsman, representing Cambridge at cricket, soccer and lawn tennis, and University lawn tennis champion; then playing cricket for Worcestershire and football for West Bromwich Albion, Corinthian Casuals and as amateur for England; 2nd Lt, Lancashire Fusiliers; killed in action. Like Williams not in the printed *Register* because he enlisted before taking up his appointment to Clifton, though recorded among the war casualties (Christie, *History*, p. 184); in view of King's ruling here both names have now been placed on the register of masters.

[423]   20 March 1915. G.W.E. Whitehead to a friend[1101]
[*P7052 Memorial album. Typescript extract*]

R.M.A., Woolwich,
20th March 1915.

I still think that the School House and Clifton are the most important places in the world though I have enjoyed my last three weeks at the Shop[1102] in a sort of way. But there is no doubt about it Clifton is *the* place ... By Jove, I am glad I was at Clifton and in the School House. I hear we're playing for Cock House at fives which is splendid. Don't despair of winning . . .

It's rather nice to think of cricket again soon, but I don't suppose it will be very much fun at the Shop compared to what it was at Clifton. By Jove, last Summer term *was* the time of my life and the Cheltenham match was the only real hitch.[1103] But I wouldn't have missed last term for much either . . .

I don't know what I value most about Clifton: I think perhaps it's the friends I've had. There's poor old Arthur Chitty,[1104] Woodward [*6980*], Roxburgh,[1105] Williams [*7104*], Hodge,[1106] Jimmy James,[1107] Ealand [*6421*], Barney de Roebeck [*7436*], Montealegre [*7067 or 7068*], Ward,[1108] Streather,[1109] Bertie Petman,[1110] 'Bunny' McLeod [*6449*], Mr Parr,[1111] yourself and a few others. Not an awful lot, perhaps, but as Bertie used to say five good pals are worth 500 of the other sort. Then there's the *Spiritus intus alit* business which is truer about Clifton than most other schools, and there's much less snobbishness about the place than there is about some. Then there's the ripping old – not in the sense of ancient – buildings. Go and stand in the bottom corner of the Close one fine evening next term at about 7.15 when there is fielding out all round; can you imagine anything more perfect? The sun sending great long shadows from behind the School House and the Wilson Tower and the dome of the Chapel, and everything showing up against the skyline. If I was an architect given the job of designing Heaven, I'd make it like Clifton.

[1101] George William Edendale Whitehead [*7052*: SH 1909–14]; XI of 1911–14 (Captain 1913–14; his 259 against Liverpool Club in 1912 was the highest individual score made for the School); went straight into the Royal Artillery, transferring to the Royal Flying Corps and (on its creation in 1918) to the RAF. This entry and the next are taken from a collection of his letters and diaries, and tributes presented to his mother.

[1102] The Royal Military Academy, Woolwich (for the Royal Artillery and Royal Engineers) was called 'the Shop' because it occupied a former workshop of Woolwich Arsenal.

[1103] At Cheltenham on 10 and 11 July 1914: Whitehead made only 23 and 15, and Cheltenham won by 25 runs: *Cliftonian* XXIII (1913–15), pp. 283–5.

[1104] Arthur Alexander Ernest Chitty, later Merlott-Chitty [*6965*: SH 1909–12]; XI of 1912; Capt, Royal West Kent Regt, wounded at the start of the war and then taken prisoner.

[1105] John Hewitt Roxburgh; [*6884*: SH 1908–14]; Major, Machine Gun Corps, killed in action 1918.

[1106] George Cedric Hodgkinson [*7303*: SH 1911–14]; XI of 1914; Lt, 8th Bn, York and Lancashire Regt; killed in action 1916.

[1107] Donald Croft James [*6656*: NT 1907–14]; XI of 1914; 2nd Lt, 4th Bn, Gloucestershire Regt, killed in action 1916.

[1108] Paul Francis Seymour Ward [*6992*: ST 1909–14]; 2nt Lt, Worcestershire Regt, killed in action 1918.

[1109] Edward Harry Parsons Streather [*7394*: SH 1912–16]; 2nd Lt, Royal Flying Corps, killed in action 1917.

[1110] Bertram Hamersley Bevan-Petman [*6963*: NT, OH 1909–14]; XI of 1914.

[1111] H.W.M. Parr [*4407/M206*] mentioned above **[422]**; killed in action earlier in 1915.

[424]   14 September 1915. Whitehead writes on the eve of the Battle of Loos
[*P7052 Memorial album. Typescript extract*]

Sept. 24th, 1915.
There is something of a show on. I think we are to bombard the Germans and their line of approach for about four days – then the advance begins.[1112] Several batteries have been moved up for it like ourselves. We have a couple of eight inch batteries, ¼ mile and ½ mile behind us, another on our right, and a couple of R.F.A.[1113] batteries immediately on our right and on our left. That is only just around us and there are lots more batteries scattered about.

The *general* bombardment begins at daylight and goes on till dusk. Our show begins at 6.0 p.m. and goes on until 7.0 a.m. We have to keep a couple of guns firing one on each of the two roads at the rate of six rounds an hour per gun with irregular intervals between the rounds. In between our fire machine-guns play on the roads. These roads are the two targets that should have been registered by aeroplane. We had to measure them off the map and lay by the compass. I hope we shall hit something but it doesn't seem likely to me.

You'll probably hear of it in the papers before you get this. I shall be perfectly safe. It seems rather a feeble way to go to war, a long way behind the infantry and Sappers who do all the dirty work and get all the danger. This is a well known district for fighting ... there are some colossal shell holes – about twelve feet circumference and six deep – My diary is several days overdue so it'll just have to go hang. Dennison and I are sharing the job. I slept until twelve and am now on duty until seven.

It's 2.30 a.m. now and here I am in the signallers' dug-out thinking of home and Clifton. It's sad to think I've finished with Clifton. I can't help thinking about it: all the old places and corners crop up into my mind ever since I was a fag. No. 18 study in the back passage with Roxburgh – Chitty and Woodward[1114] over the way, Bates[1115] in no. 16, Charlie Russell[1116] who took IVa in no. 22 class room; Otto Siepman who took us in French up in the Crow's Nest;[1117] the Fives Courts, toasting in Hall – I sat next to Roxburgh and Burrell [*6369 or 6802*], Albert Rissik [*6933*] and Arthur Chitty on the other side of the table next the fire. Fags' boxing: I always used to box Johnny Folds.[1118] My first House match and how bucked I was when we were Cock House. Then there were the runs, and how I used to hate them. My second Summer term when I got my XI at Malvern for 92; we'd have lost but for me; I caught Knight and someone else in the slips when they went in to get the runs.[1119] How we used to

---

[1112] The attack which began on 25 September was hampered by the inadequacy of the preceding bombardment, and the battle ended on 14 October with massive casualties and no significant advance. Subsequently Haig, who had directed the operation, replaced Sir John French as Commander of the British Expeditionary Force.
[1113] Royal Field Artillery.
[1114] Brigadier Douglas Stewart Hillersdon Woodward [*6980*: SH 1909–13].
[1115] Lt-Col Austin Graves Bates DSO, MC* [*6424*: SH 1906–9].
[1116] Cecil Henry St Leger Russell [*M128*: 1887–1928]; Form Master, Classical Side.
[1117] *Siepmann* [*M137*: 1890–1921]; first Head of the Modern Language Department (1900) and author of numerous French and German Text Books. The Crow's Nest is the uppermost room of the Wilson Tower.
[1118] John Christopher Folds [*6567*: PHP, SH 1907–12].
[1119] Played at Malvern on 5 and 6 July 1912. Whitehead's 92 dominated Clifton's second innings. D.J. Knight had made 139 in Malvern's first innings; by catching him on 37 in the second Whitehead ensured Clifton's victory. His earlier victim had been G.C. Lucas: *Cliftonian*, XX (1911–13), pp. 58–61.

rot about the Baths and in the House. Arthur Chitty, Roxburgh, Woodward, Dougie McColl [*6696 or 6697*], Puppy, Ponty, Cherry D., Baby,[1120] Bill Dyer[1121] and the others. In Vb taken by Imlay [*M194*] in the room with the glass door at the end of the Cloisters. How we used to stand up and look out of the window before I played for the XI and look at the scores when School matches were on. Then all the old places: the Chapel, I sat under the pulpit nearly all the time. The XI nets just beneath the Chapel and old Tunny[1122] bowling and grousing and bucked as anything when he thought he'd bowled a good one. Stephen Beverley;[1123] poor old Johnny, what a topping bowler he was and how he used to carry us on his shoulders my last year match after match. Old 'Hodge', one of the best chaps I ever met, and Mr Parr and Barney[1124] and how we used to rot about in Mr Parr's room. Sam Coombes' fat old face,[1125] and Miss Thomas and the H.M. and K.F.[1126] and Harry Muggins,[1127] seems a strange mix up, but that's how they come into my mind. Then the new VIth Room, the new Lib, the VIth Room, how I turned it into my study. The lavs downstairs where we used to skip and tug of war before the Sports, and box and play fives. Corps parade days – O Lord. Then there was the old House Lib with all the Cock House photos, the House clock, all those passages, the notice boards, the hatchway, 'Butter please, Joe'. How we sweated to be Cock House at fives and turned big odds against at the beginning of the Footer term into the fives cup at the end of the Easter two years running. Then there was the area outside the House, where all the footballs used to drop and the fire escape and the wall we used to get over when we were late for lock-up; Prayers in Big School; the Marshal's Office; the School notice board; old Discobulus [*sic*] whom we used to dress up in a Jew's house-cap, a pair of pads and a bat; the School Song and the '*Revenge*'.[1128] Standing on the Parapet by the Monument and watching School footer matches – those topping Big-Side goal posts. The Chapel door with lists of casualties; waiting for Phillips[1129] under the School clock to take us in the Phys Lab at 8.0 during second Prep. By Jove when I think of Clifton I feel like Mephistopheles in *Dr Faustus* who says of the mind that it can 'make a heaven of hell, a hell of heaven',[1130] or like poor old Samson 'irrevocably dark, total eclipse, without all hope of day'.[1131] Well, if you substitute Clifton for day and adapt the rest the principle's just the same. Then Bertie P.[1132] and Bunny McLeod and Muffy. I don't believe I shall ever be able to set my mind to any work away from Clifton. When I've got a spare half hour now I always lug out my Latin Anthology or Calverley,[1133] I don't know why – I suppose Latin is a sort of connection with

---

[1120] Bernard Harold Hartley [*6861*: SH 1908–12]; Lt, 26th Bn, Lancashire Fusiliers, killed in action 1916.
[1121] Cecil MacMillan Dyer [*6851*: SH 1908–12]; 2nd Lt, 6th Rifle Brigade, killed in action earlier in 1915.
[1122] John Tunnicliffe, Cricket Professional 1908–22.
[1123] Stephen Beverley Morgan [*7130*: BH 1910–14]; XI of 1913–14; 2nd Lt, Leicestershire Regt, killed in action earlier in 1915.
[1124] Brigadier Bernard de Robeck MC* [*7436*: SH 1912–15].
[1125] SH butler 1899–1917.
[1126] Kenneth Fisher [*M210*: 1909–19]; House Tutor SH 1910–19.
[1127] H.B. Mayor [*3329/M151*] as above **[228]**; taught Classics to the Sixth.
[1128] Stanford's setting of Tennyson's poem, celebrating the heroic action fought by Sir Richard Grenville's *Revenge* at the Battle of Flores (1591); a window in the North Cloister shows Grenville with his ship.
[1129] Egbert Ivor Allen Phillips [*M215*: 1911–32]; Chaplain, and taught Science and Mathematics.
[1130] Actually from *Paradise Lost*, 1.249: 'The mind is its own place, and in itself, can make a heaven of hell, and a hell of Heaven'.
[1131] This is correctly remembered as from Milton (*Samson Agonistes*, 1.80), but should be 'irrecoverably'.
[1132] Bertram Bevan-Petman, as **[423]**.
[1133] Charles Stuart Calverley, prolific translator of Latin verse, e.g. *Verses and Translations* (1862).

Clifton. I daresay one's mind gets narrowed down always being in one place, but if you proved conclusively to me for an hour a day that Clifton wasn't the best place in the world you wouldn't persuade me. It's the best and cleanest school on the face of this earth.

☐ *George Whitehead was killed in action on 17 October 1918.*

[425]   1 December 1917. Sir Herbert Warren to Frank Borwick[1134]
[*Editor's Collection. Typescript*]

Magdalen College,
Oxford.
December 1st, 1917.

My dear Mr Borwick,

I am very much obliged by your sending me the *Cliftonian*. I was specially glad to see my brother-law's sermon on Major Clissold.[1135] He seems to have been really moved, and I think it is a fine and beautiful and touching tribute.

I am interested also to see the number generally.

There is one little slip in the sermon, I think. Thirty years ago it was not an Officers' Training Corps, I suppose, but the Volunteers.[1136] That is unimportant.

I should like to take the *Cliftonian* [in *deleted*] regularly, and sent [*sic*] you subscription for [a year 3/6d *corrected to*] 3 years 10/-.

Yours sincerely,
Herbert Warren.

[426]   24 July 1918. Annual Meeting of the OC Society
[*OCS Minute Book 1918–24, pp. 13–14. MS*]

The twenty-first Annual Meeting of the Society was held on Wednesday July 14th 1918 at Central Buildings, Westminster at 5 o'clock. About twenty members were present. The President the Right Hon. J.H. Whitley took the chair.[1137]

*   *   *

The Chairman in moving the adoption of the [*Annual*] Report referred to the unexpected presence of the Secretary, Col. Arthur Stone,[1138] and congratulated him in the name of the Society on his having received the D.S.O. for courage and coolness in leading a raiding party to the enemy's wire. He referred to Bishop Percival's resignation of the Chairmanship of the College Council and it was unanimously decided to send a message of sympathy to the Bishop, thanking him for his great

---

[1134] Borwick [*M142*: 1892–1926] was Treasurer of *The Cliftonian* from 1909 to 1925.

[1135] Clissold was killed on 28 September; the address at the Memorial Service on 14 October was given by Canon Glazebrook, and was printed in *The Cliftonian* XXV (1917–19), pp. 116–22.

[1136] In 1908 all school Cadet Corps were placed under the direct control of the War Office as the (junior) branch of the OTC; this was part of the reform of the army reserve promoted by R.B. Haldane as Secretary of State for War: Parker, *Old Lie*, p. 63; Christie, *History*, p. 247.

[1137] President of the OCS. He was at this time Chairman of Ways and Means and Deputy Speaker of the House of Commons.

[1138] *4447*: WaH 1891–6; Secretary of the OCS since 1903; serving as Lt-Col, 16th Bn, Lancashire Fusiliers, and had already been twice mentioned in Despatches.

services to the School. He congratulated the Society on the choice of Sir Herbert Warren at the Bishop's successor.

[427]   16 October 1918. OCS Executive Committee Meeting
[*OCS Minute Book 1918–24, pp. 16–17. MS*]

Minutes of Meeting of Executive Committee held in Mr Whitley's room at the House of Commons on Wednesday, October 16th, 1918, at 5 p.m.

*   *   *

The late Lt. Col. A. Stone.

The Committee received with deep regret the news of the death on active service in France of Lt. Col. Arthur Stone, for many years Secretary of the Society. The following resolution was passed.

The members of the Executive Committee of the Old Cliftonian Society desire to place on record the profound grief with which they and all Old Cliftonians have heard of the death on the battlefield of Lt. Col. Arthur Stone, D.S.O., who for so long has been the faithful and enthusiastic Secretary of the Society.

His fall in the hour of victory is a tragedy alike for his old School and for his Country: he served both without stint in life; in death he has given to Clifton and to England a memory that boys and men will treasure. Proposed by Sir S. Finney,[1139] seconded by J.A. Neale[1140] and carried unanimously.

Sir D. Haig.

It was resolved by J.A. Neale, seconded by Sir S. Finney and carried unanimously that the following resolution should be forwarded to Field Marshal Sir Douglas Haig by the Chairman.

Resolved that:

We the Executive Committee of the Old Cliftonian Society do record our profound admiration for the single purpose with which you have so conspicuously served your King and Country in these critical days and assure you of our united warm and affectionate regard.

[1139] Sir Stephen Finney [*599*: DH 1868–71].
[1140] John Alexander Neale [*99*: SH 1863–8].

SECTION XXI:
THE WAR MEMORIAL

[428]   [October 1919]. Report of the OC War Memorial Sub-Committee
[RS3/67. Typescript]

Report of the War Memorial Sub-Committee as to the form of the permanent
memorial to be erected at Clifton.

The Sub-Committee beg to submit the following report and recommendation.

In considering the various forms of permanent memorial, they felt that the
help of some architect experienced in such matters would be of very great help.
They accordingly obtained the assistance of Major Chas. Holden,[1141] who has
been advising on the New College, Oxford, War Memorial, and various other war
memorials in this country, and who is at the head of the war grave scheme in France,
it being understood that there was no guarantee or suggestion whatever that he would
ultimately be employed as architect for the memorial finally selected.

The Sub-Committee met at Clifton on June 28th last, and in company with Major
Holden, inspected the possible sites at Clifton, and discussed with him the various
schemes suggested, and in particular those of a gateway, an obelisk, memorial
cloisters, a companion statue to the South African War Memorial, and the remodelling
of the interior of Big School. Major Holden subsequently submitted a report in which
he strongly recommended the scheme of an arched gateway in College Road for
the following reasons. Firstly, because a gateway is in itself a recognised form of
memorial, perhaps on the whole, the most satisfactory known to history. Secondly,
the main group of College buildings urgently required something in the nature of a
gateway to complete it, and its erection will greatly improve the appearance of the
whole group by giving it a sense of finality and completeness. Thirdly, it alone has
the great advantage as a war memorial of being passed daily by most of the boys in
the College. By setting it back slightly from College Road, there would be ample
space for it, and only a few yards of the Head Master's garden would be affected.
Thus placed, it would not be too close to the house on the opposite side of the road,
and would combine well with the trees on either side.

[1141] Charles Henry Holden (d. 1960) was an architect holding the rank of Major by virtue of his extensive
work for the Imperial War Graves Commission; he was also well known for London Underground
stations. In Bristol he designed the Central Library (1906) and the King Edward VII Extension of the
Royal Infirmary (1911–12). The memorial for New College was not built. See E. Karol, *Charles Holden,
Architect* (Donington, 2007).

His report was accompanied by a design showing a suggested sketch for the gateway. He also recommended that the names of the Fallen, with a suitable inscription, should be inscribed on tablets on the inside walls, and estimated that the total cost of the scheme would not exceed £5000.

The Sub-Committee met on July 30th to consider Major Holden's report, and were unanimously in favour of the gateway scheme, such scheme to include a continuation of the stone balustrade from the South African War Memorial up to the gateway. They were, however, evenly divided on the question whether to record the names on the inside walls of the gateway, or in the New Cloisters, and the chairman decided to submit this point to the Committee.

They accordingly recommend the scheme of an arched gateway in College Road, on the lines put forward by Major Holden, with the continuation of the balustrade above mentioned, and ask for the decision of the Committee as to the recording of the names of the Fallen.

The Executive Committee unanimously accepted the above report, and recommended that the names of the Fallen be recorded on the inside walls of the gateway and a dedicatory inscription placed thereon.

[429]   24 October 1919. Extract from minutes of the Annual Meeting of the Old Cliftonian Society
[*OCS Minute Book 1918–24, pp. 46–7. MS*]

War Memorial.

The next business was the consideration of the report of the Committee as to the form of the permanent war memorial at Clifton, and to the progress of the war memorial scheme. The Rt. Hon. J.H. Whitley moved that the report and recommendations of the Committee be adopted and that the Committee be directed to proceed accordingly in a short speech in which he pointed out the great need for an adequate endowment fund for the School and described the steps by which the Committee had arrived at this recommendation for a gateway as the permanent memorial at Clifton. The resolution was seconded by R.C. Witt[1142] who emphasised that all suggestions put before them as to the form of the visible memorial had received the most careful attention of the Committee. A discussion followed in which Sir F.G. Newbolt described the steps taken by himself and A.G. Little[1143] in the matter of the portraits of Earl Haig and Sir William Birdwood, and R.P. Keigwin [*M246*] voiced the views of the O.C. Masters and others at Clifton who he stated were at present rather against the idea of a gateway and very anxious to see the design, but he did not move any amendment. J.A. Neale, R.E. Whitehead,[1144] W.C. Urwick,[1145] A.T.A. Dobson[1146] and the President also took part in the discussion. The resolution was then put to the meeting and carried unanimously.

☐ *Three designs for the Arch, including Holden's, were submitted to the adjudication of the President of the Royal Academy.*

[1142] The future Chairman of Council.
[1143] Andrew George Little [*2041*: BH 1877–82].
[1144] Another future Chairman of Council.
[1145] Walter Chamberlain Urwick [*2601*: DH 1880–2]; portrait painter and miniaturist.
[1146] Alban Tabor Austin Dobson [*5574*: OH 1899–1904].

[430]   27 July 1920. Sir Aston Webb[1147] to Lt-Col. W.P. Hewett, OC Secretary
[*RS3/67. Typescript copy*]

19 Queen Anne Gate,
Westminster,
London S.W.
27th July 1920.

Dear Sir,

Clifton College War Memorial.

I have made a very careful examination of the three designs submitted for the above, and have also visited the site in the company of the Headmaster.

Each of the designs shew much care and skill in their preparation, but I am of opinion that the best and most suitable is the one submitted by Mr Holden, and I therefore recommend that he be appointed architect for the memorial.

I return the three sets of designs and reports herewith.

I am, dear Sir, yours faithfully,
sgd: Aston Webb.

[431]   27 July 1920. Webb to the OC Secretary
[*RS3/67. Typescript copy*]

19 Queen Anne Gate,
Westminster,
London S.W.
27th July 1920.

Dear Sir,

Clifton College War Memorial.

I enclose herewith my formal award in this competition.

I may say that I consider Mr Holden's an excellent design with much character, and the lofty centre arch would certainly, in my opinion, be a most satisfactory feature.

Having paid a special visit to Clifton and examined the problem very carefully on the spot, the following two points that have occurred to me may be of interest to your architect and the Committee.

Although each of the competitors has recessed his arch back from the road, this appears to me a doubtful arrangement, one of the disadvantages of the site being that the arch can only be seen sideways from the approach road, but if set back as proposed it will not be seen at all from the road until you are close up to it. The question of trees – important as they are – should not be allowed to interfere with the selection of the best <position> possible for a permanent monument of this sort. If the present trees are allowed to remain and the gateway set behind them, the gateway itself would be entirely obscured from the road.

The other point is the placing of the archway, and this certainly, in my opinion, should be placed on the axial line of the Chapel and therefore central with it, which would involve the widening of the road and a new footway on the south side. I would also venture to suggest placing the Boer Memorial on the same axial line facing the

---

[1147] Webb (d. 1930) was a Past President of the RIBA, and President of the Royal Academy 1919–24; his work included the main building of the V&A (1891), the façade of Buckingham Palace (1913) and the setting of the Victoria Memorial (1911), and the new Christ's Hospital at Horsham (1894–1904).

arch, greatly adding to its dignity and that of the entrance, and leaving the steps free and open as access to the playing field. See sketch attached. [*With sketch*]

I am, dear Sir, yours faithfully,

sgd: Aston Webb.

[432]   18 January 1921. The OC Secretary to the College Secretary
[*RS3/67. Typescript copy*]

38, Old Jewry,
London, E.C.2.
18th January, 1921.

Dear Mr Lewis,

Old Cliftonian Society
Proposed Memorial Gateway

Major Holden, the architect, writes me [*sic*] with reference to the proposed gateway that he has made enquiries about the reddish stone used in the School buildings and is informed that this was quarried on the site, and Messrs Cowlin, of whom he has made enquiries, tell him that they do not know of anywhere in the neighbourhood where similar stone can be obtained.

It has occurred to me that when the Chapel was enlarged additional stone of this sort must have been obtained. Can you tell me if this was so, and if so from where the stone was obtained, and whether it would be possible to obtain stone for the gateway from the same source?

It has also occurred to me that a possible source of supply would be Beggars Bush Piece if the stone underlying it is of the same nature. I wonder if you can tell me whether this is so?[1148]

Yours very truly,

W.P. Hewett.

[433]   15 February 1921. The OC Secretary to the College Secretary
[*RS3/67. Typescript copy*]

38, Old Jewry,
London, E.C.2.
15th February, 1921.

Dear Mr Lewis,

Old Cliftonian Society
War Memorial

Thank you for your letter of yesterday. In reply to the second paragraph the question of putting up a full size model, as originally contemplated, was discussed with Mr Holden at the last meeting of the War Memorial Sub-Committee, but Mr Holden estimated that a proper model would cost under present conditions at least £1000 [and *deleted*]. The Committee considered that they would not be justified in going to anything like this expense, while a rough model simply of scaffold poles and canvas would not give any idea of the appearance of the gateway though it would of course give some idea of the bulk, and according to Mr Holden such an erection could not be made either wind or weather proof, and in his opinion would not be worthwhile the trouble and expense of erection. In any case it would hardly be possible to have

---

[1148] In the event enough red sandstone was quarried from the edge of the Close: *Register* (1925), p. cxxiv.

this put up before the 23rd inst. as I gather that Mr Holden would like to supervise any erection of this sort himself.

Yours very truly,

W.P. Hewett.

[434]   29 September 1921. The architect to the College Secretary
[*RS3/67. Holograph*]

9 Knightsbridge,
Hyde Park Corner, London S.W.1.
Sept. 29 1921

Dear Mr Lewis,

Memorial Gateway Clifton College

Colonel Hewett has forwarded to me a copy of your letter of the 23rd inst.

I have compared the working drawing with the original sketch design approved by the Council and find very little variation in the proportions of local stone to ashlar in the two designs.

I shall be visiting the College on Tuesday next October 4th and will call upon you to discuss this matter. I expect to be at your office about 2.45 p.m.

Yours faithfully,

Charles Holden.

[435]   7 March 1922. The Head Master to Earl Haig
[*K48. Typescript file copy*]

7th March, 1922.

My dear Lord Haig,

The Council have formed a small committee to consider the unveiling of the War Memorial here on June 30.

I enclose an account of the unveiling of the South African War Memorial for you to see. It was thought that the form of service might be much the same – that the Chairman of the O.C. Society (Sir F. Younghusband) might hand the key of the gateway to you, and you could give it to the Chairman of the Council (Sir Herbert Warren) who would speak in acknowledgement. After that, you would be asked to unveil the names which are inscribed in the gateway and say what you wished to say. After the 'Last Post' and National Anthem the School O.T.C. could be marched off through the gateway, which would end the proceedings.

I was instructed to ask whether you would be ready to come in uniform and take the salute at the gateway – also whether we should ask O.C. officers, who come, to be in uniform. I shall be glad to know if you think these arrangements will be suitable, and if you have any suggestions or alterations you would like to make.

The afternoon of Friday would probably suit us best for School purposes. In the evening there is a reception in the Library and some speaking and acting, and I am asked to say how glad we shall be if Lady Haig and you can stay over the Friday night. The Commemoration service, at which Canon Storr of Westminster[1149] is to preach, takes place at 10 a.m. on Saturday.

I am, yours sincerely,

[*blank*], Head Master.

[1149] Vernon Faithfull Storr [*3115*: DH 1883–8], Canon of Westminster from 1921 till his death in 1940.

[436]   10 March [1922]. Haig to the Head Master
[*K48. Typescript*]

Eastcott,
Kingston Hill,
Surrey.
March 10.

My dear Head Master,

Many thanks for your letter of 7th March. I think your proposed arrangements for unveiling the War Memorial quite satisfactory.

I shall of course be pleased to wear uniform; and I think all who have uniform should be asked to put it on, but I would suggest that it should be distinctly stated that all are invited to be present whether they have uniform or not, and it is hoped that noone will go to any expense in order to provide himself with uniform for the occasion.

As regards taking the salute, I would suggest that the School O.T.C. should first salute the Memorial and that I should be some little distance beyond it, and take the salute independantly [*sic*] of the gateway.

I shall arrange to arrive with Lady Haig about lunch time on Friday 30th June so as to be in good time for the ceremony, and my wife and I will be very pleased to stay over Friday night and attend the Commemoration service at 10 a.m. on the Saturday. We propose to go to Swansea on that day, so would leave soon after the service is over.

I think that I have answered all your questions, and with kind regards,

Believe me, yrs very sincerely,
Haig.

[437]   24 June 1922. The Chairman of Council to the College Secretary
[*K48. Typescript*]

Magdalen College,
Oxford.
June 24th, 1922.

Dear Mr Lewis,

I am much obliged by your letter, and the lists you send.

I am sorry to see some of the refusals, especially that of Mr and Mrs. Abbot.[1150] On the other hand I think we have got a very good gathering.

Is it proposed to have any service, or ceremony, in regard to the Percival Memorial Chapel? Will that be completed, and will it be open?

I do not see the Bishop of Bristol's[1151] name on either of the lists. Has he not been asked? It seems to me a little odd if that is so, more particularly considering his kindness in regard to the Percival Chapel.[1152]

I see that the Dean[1153] has been asked, but cannot come. I did not know that he was married.

With regard to the procession <from the luncheon>, I think what is suggested will do very well.

[1150] H.N. Abbot had resigned from the Council two years before.
[1151] George Nickson, Bishop 1914–24.
[1152] For overlooking the legal objections to interment in the College Chapel: *cf.* above **[94–106]**.
[1153] Edward Arthur Burroughs, Dean 1922–6, thereafter Bishop of Ripon.

I shall be glad to have the order of ceremony.

I think the menu will do quite well. I do not think there is need for Champagne, but I suppose 'red and white wine' means Bordeaux red or white and also, port and sherry.

There will, I suppose, also be smokes supplied.

Has the question of toasts, or speeches, been considered? We shall, of course, drink the King's health, which the President will propose, and I think the health of the President himself ought to be drunk, either without a speech or with a brief speech. Perhaps, as Chairman of the Council, I ought to do this.

If he would, in replying, propose *Floreat Cliftona* very briefly, to which he would couple the health of the Headmaster, that would, I think, be enough.

As to the order of precedence, I will think it over, and write on Monday.

I suppose the Speaker and Mrs. Whitley, [1154] and Canon and Mrs. Wilson, [1155] ought to be put very high on the list, and also, of course, the Lord Mayor of Bristol, [1156] and Mrs. Cook. Is Mrs. Cook the Lady Mayoress? I imagine so.

I thought we were going to ask the chief military authority of the neighbourhood. I do not see any such name on either list.

Yours sincerely,
Herbert Warren.

☐ *Though Champagne was not appropriate, a decent level of hospitality was offered.*

[438]   27 June 1922. John Harvey & Sons to the Secretary
[*K48. Typescript*]

John Harvey and Sons, Limited.
Denmark Street,
Bristol.
June 27th, 1922.

Dear Sir,

We thank you for your letter of yesterday and will send up in time for the luncheon in your Council Room next Friday 30th inst. @ 1.30 p.m.:

2 dozen white wine, Barsac Superior,
2 dozen claret, Chateau Langos 1914,
[6 *corrected to*] 12 bottles Fine Old Tawny 'Hunting' Port,
6 bottles Merienda Luncheon Sherry,
[2 *corrected to*] 6 bottles Superior Old Scotch Whisky;
which we feel sure will be approved.

We are, dear Sir, your faithful obedient servants,
For John Harvey & Sons, Ltd.,
Saward Harvey, Director.

[1154] In the same file is a telegram from Whitley to the Head Master, 28 July: 'Speaker agrees as to precedence'.

[1155] The former Head Master had since 1905 been a Canon of Worcester.

[1156] Ernest Henry Cook, Lord Mayor 1921–2.

[439]   30 June 1930. Luncheon menu.
[*K48. MS*]

John S. Milton
Confectioner, Baker and Pastrycook.

7ᵃ & 8, Portland Place,
The Mall,
Clifton, (Bristol.)
June 30th, 1922.

Special luncheon for Earl Haig

Mayonnaise of Salmon.
–

Roast Chicken. York Ham.
Ox Tongue: English.
Braised Beef. Galantine of Veal.
Dressed Salads.
New Potatoes.
–

Peache [*sic*] Melba.
Strawberry Cream.
Fruit Jellies.
–

Cheese. Butter. Biscuits.
Coffee.
[*Added in pencil*: for 50. 10/6 per head][1157]

[1157] This was the menu chosen from the tenders of several firms.

SECTION XXII:
DOUGLAS HAIG AND CLIFTON

The education of a soldier

☐ *Haig's time at Clifton is poorly documented. The examination report below shows that a boy who generally struggled with Latin was on this occasion top of the class. Among those placed below him, Lawrence Burd was to take a First in Classics at Balliol.*

[440]   December 1877. Examination report
[P4627 Album 3, p. 31. (Photograph of) MS on printed form, though not wholly adhering to its structure. Printed elements are here in bold, some omitted]

EXAMINER'S REPORT
Date Dec. 1877

Form or Set IVA **Examiners** F.M.B.[1158] W.H.S. Laxton.[1159]
Subject Latin Books   **Teachers of the Subject** H.G.D.[1160] E.M.O.[1161]

N.B.   1. The marks entered on this Report indicate the actual portion of the maximum gained by each Boy.

2. The Master who examines is expected to send this Report without delay to the Teacher of the Subject, who will forward it as soon as convenient to the Head Master.

[1158] Francis Medley Bartholomew [*M44*: 1869–93†].
[1159] William Holden Scott Laxton [*M89*: 1877–1913, 1915–19].
[1160] Henry Graham Dakyns [*M3*: 1862–89].
[1161] Edward Murray Oakeley [*M31*: 1867–87]. Haig later wrote to him: 'I had a very affectionate regard for our friend Dakyns, and if I took interest in Ovid, it was entirely owing to his personality and good taste, which threw a sort of reflected light on to me as one of his pupils and induced in me in a feeble kind of way some appreciation of a few of the passages.': P4627 Album, p. 30 (typed extract). *Cf.* J.R. Mozley, *Clifton Memories* (Bristol, 1927), pp. 53–74.

Names.			Exam. Marks.
Mr Dakyns **Max.** 198			Mr Oakeley Max. 198
		169	Bennett, L.H. [*1972*]
		163	Pringle, J.W. [*1246*]
	·	158	Rogers, Walter [*2119*]
		148	Parker, R.W.E. [*2114*]
(D.) Haig	143		
		141	Moore, H. [*1607*]
		138	Burd, L.A. [*1835*]
		136	Barrow, W.C.D. [*1775*]
		134	Rathbone, H.R. [*1648*]
		130	Wills, A.S. [*1487*]
(C.W.F.) Whyte [*1773*]	128		
(B.) Hedley [*2098*]	125		
[*20 other names*]			[*16 other names*]

Notes.

	D[*akyns*].			O[*akeley*].
Highest mark gained	143	169	**out of Maximum of** 198	
Lowest	65	79		
Average mark	95	181		

Vα D[*akyns*]. Ovid.
  Haig very good.
  Translation fair in many cases.
  Parsing very fair, but only one knew 'redimitor'.[1162]
  Questions inadequate, especially on constructions.
IVA. O[*akeley*]. Ovid.
  A very good paper with one or two exceptions.
Livy.
  Excellently done in IVA.O, with some good papers from IVA.D.
  oratio obliqua: capital in O, poor in D.
  Explanations of subjunctive, not elaborate enough.
  Knowledge of author, quite satisfactory.

[*MS note from the J.E. King attached at head*] Clifton College May 2 1922. The document has gone and has been handed over to IVα who are to frame it and hang it in their room for an heirloom.

J.E.K.

☐ *Haig was devoted to his mother. This letter from Clifton was one of the last he wrote to her.*

[1162] A severe criticism for not recognising this rare passive imperative form of *redimio*.

[441]   [Jan. x March 1879]. Haig to his mother[1163]
[National Library of Scotland, MS 28001, ff. 158–9. Holograph]

School House.

My dear Mamma,

Thank you very much for your letters of Sat: I got one y'day and the other this morning. I enclose one I got from Willie[1164] y'day – J.P. does not think I should go to a coach; neither does my Form Master.[1165] But he advised me to get some of the old Matric: exam papers and he said he would be very happy to go through them with me – which was rather good of him considering how hard the masters are worked here. Percival does not think I should leave till [Easter *corrected to*] Xmas <as> you saw by his letter to Willie. And what he said to me was that one's school time only comes once and when it is over it is gone – They tell me I could easily get in[1166] at Xmas time – No more time – Post time.

Heaps of love to yourself and all with you,

Ever, your very affectionate [brother *corrected to*] son,

Douglas.

Monday.

Later exchanges

☐ *Haig thanks the OC President for the Society's generosity in funding the education of the sons of officers killed in the War.*

[442]   1 December 1916. Haig to Sir Francis Younghusband[1167]
[P1981 file. Typescript]

General Headquarters,
British Armies in France.
1st December, 1916.

My dear Younghusband,

I am very glad to learn from your letter of the work that is being done by Old Cliftonians towards assisting the education at our old School of the sons of fallen officers.

You tell me that enough money has been secured to provide 17 exhibitions of £60 each for this purpose, and it is most gratifying to me to know that so much has already been accomplished. I feel confident that the work so well begun will be carried on by all Old Cliftonians with the same public spirit of which the recent legacy of £2500 left by Lieutenant H.F. Segnitz,[1168] who fell at Loos, is so noble an example.

[1163] Rachel Mackerras (*née* Veitch); she died on 21 March this year, so the letter must be dated between Monday 6 January and Monday 17 March; *cf.* D. Scott (ed.), *Douglas Haig: The Preparatory Prologue 1861–1914, Diaries and Letters* (2006), p. 5. (With thanks to Miss A. Metcalfe of the National Library of Scotland for locating the letter among the Haig MSS.)

[1164] William Henry Haig, Douglas's eldest brother (d. 1884).

[1165] W.W. Asquith [*M78*], whose brother, as Prime Minister in 1915, appointed Haig to command the British forces in France.

[1166] To Oxford; Haig went up to Brasenose in 1880.

[1167] Sir Francis Edward Younghusband [*1849*: PHP, SH 1876–80 (with Haig)]; soldier, diplomat, explorer and author; Council 1905–37; member of a prominent Clifton dynasty.

[1168] Hermann Ferdinand Segnitz [*6551*: WaH 1906–11]; 2nd Lt in the 19th London Regiment.

It is only right that the sons of those who have sacrificed everything for their country should be given the chance of an education such as their fathers would have wished for them, and the knowledge that the chance will be given will bring comfort to the minds of many who are yet serving.

I am sure that your efforts will meet with a very ready response.

Yours very truly,

D. Haig.

□ *Haig was promoted Field Marshal on 1 January 1917*

[443]   21 January 1917. Telegram from Haig to the College
[*P1981 file. MS on printed form*]

[*Telegram timed 1025 received Bristol 1135 on 21 January 1917.*]

To Clifton College Clifton Warmest thanks for the welcome message of congratulations from my old school. Douglas Haig.

[444]   27 October 1926. Haig to the Secretary: authority to display his arms.
[*RS2/48. Holograph*]

Bemersyde
St Boswells
Scotland
27 Oct: 1926

Dear Sir,

In reply to your letter of 21st Oct: I shall be pleased that my Arms should be carved on any shield at Clifton College, and, as requested, I enclose a copy of my Arms. This was drawn by the Lyon Office, but I would suggest that you communicate with the Lyon King of Arms,[1169] Register House, Edinburgh, and ask something less ornate for the shield in question.

Believe me, yours very truly,
Haig, F.M.

The Haig Memorial

[445]   5 February 1929. The Head Master to the OC Secretary
[*RS2/58. Typescript file copy*]

5th February 1929

Dear Hewett,

The Sixth at a recent meeting appears to have discussed the memorial to Lord Haig. They asked the Head of the School[1170] to convey to me the views of the School on this subject. These views are, according to the Head of the School, as follows. They think that the memorial should, in part at any rate, serve some useful purpose.

[1169] The Lord Lyon King of Arms, chief herald of Scotland; the incumbent was Sir John Balfour Paul.
[1170] George Edward Mellersh Jones [*9467*: SH 1924–9].

They suggest either (1) that a bust of Lord Haig should be placed in some public place in the School, e.g. the Library, and that the greater part of the money raised should be devoted to founding scholarships in his memory; or (2) that the memorial should take the form of some architectural feature such as a gateway in Guthrie Road opposite the newly opened Arch which would be designed so as to commemorate Lord Haig, and would at the same time serve a useful purpose. They do not want a statue. I dare say that these views will not carry much weight, but I felt that the Committee ought to know them now rather than find out afterwards. I should perhaps add that this resolution of the Sixth was quite spontaneous. The statue has been a good deal discussed, and I know that the suggestion of a statue in School House garden is not at all popular with the masters, but I do not think any one suggested to the Sixth that they should formally discuss it.

Yours sincerely [blank].

☐ *The Head Master's prediction was correct and the OC Society was not deflected from its intention to raise a statue.*

[446]   2 October 1929. The OC Secretary to the Head Master
[*RS2/58. Typescript*]

38, Old Jewry,
London E.C.2.
2nd October, 1929.

Old Cliftonian Society

My Dear Headmaster,

Thank you for your letter of yesterday. I do not know of any reason why you should not speak to Lady Haig about the Haig Memorial. The present position is as follows: at the general meeting of the Society held at Lord's on the 29th July the joint recommendations of the two Sub-Committees of the Council and the Society, namely that there should be a standing statue of Lord Haig were adopted, and the Committee of the Society was requested to proceed accordingly. I enclose a copy of the recommendations. I am exceedingly sorry that these were not sent to you earlier. They should have been, but I went away almost immediately after the Tonbridge match and this was overlooked. Please accept my sincere apologies.

You will notice that the two Committees by a majority decided in favour of a standing statue and not an equestrian one.

We gathered at the general meeting from two or three Scottish O.C.s who had been in touch with Lady Haig that the idea of a statute at Clifton was acceptable to her and also to other members of the family.

I hope I shall be able to get down to Clifton at the end of the term, especially as I was not able to get down last Commemoration.

Yours sincerely,
W.P. Hewett.

[447]   20 June 1930. The Bursar to Colonel Truscott, Assistant OC Secretary
[*RS2/49. Typescript copy*]

20 June 1930

Dear Colonel Truscott,

I have just heard from Sir Robert Witt, who tells me that Sir Francis Newbolt asks whether Holden is in touch with McMillan[1171] over the Haig Memorial, and Sir Robert suggests that if he is not they should be put in touch with one another, for the sculptor and the architect who designs the base should, of course, be working together. I pass this on to you, in case you would like to take any action.

Yours sincerely,

N.R.U., Secretary and Bursar.[1172]

[448]   18 December 1930. The Head Master to Charles Holden
[*RS2/58. Typescript file copy*]

18 December 1930

Dear Sir,

I have now examined the suggested architectural treatment for the Earl Haig Memorial, and have discussed it with the master who is in charge of School House.[1173] (The Headmaster is no longer in charge of School House.)

On the whole we both prefer the suggested position for the statute to the central position suggested before, which would cut the line of the Hall windows in the view of the School House from the Close and College Road. But we do not like the proposal to make a square platform, which will cut up part of the School House lawn. I have always been told by the Old Cliftonian Society that they proposed to do nothing which would in any way affect the lawn of the School House and that only part of the flower bed would be wanted. When the sculptor came down here to see me he stated that, as far as he was concerned, he thought that it would not be necessary to interfere with the grass at all. Would not a narrow crescent shaped platform be sufficient?

We had rather hoped that the scheme would include the removal of the iron railings all along the garden and of the stone pillars. We discussed this with the sculptor when he came down here.

The School Council does not meet for several weeks and so these plans have not been before them. I gather that you only wish for my private opinion before submitting the design to the Old Cliftonian Society and that if they recommend it, it will come on from the Society to the School Council.

Yours faithfully,

N.W., Headmaster.

P.S. I notice that in the plan a line of trees is marked along the south end of School House garden. These trees were removed shortly after the erection of the War Memorial Arch. I do not suppose that this affect the plans, but I thought that I ought to point it out.

N.W.

[1171] William McMillan (d. 1977), Master of the Sculpture School at the Royal Academy 1929–41; his statuary includes three other great warlords: Beatty in Trafalgar Square (1948), George VI on Carlton House Terrace (1955), and Trenchard on the Victoria Embankment (1961).

[1172] Nicholas Robin Udal, Secretary and Bursar 1930–6, the first with that dual title. He had earned a CBE in the Sudan Civil Service, but found Clifton a tougher territory: Winterbottom, *Clifton after Percival*, pp. 112–13.

[1173] Cecil Francis Taylor [*M217*], House Master SH 1926–38; *cf.* above **[64]**.

[449]   17 August 1931. Countess Haig[1174] to the Chairman of the Council[1175]
[*P4627 Album 3, p. 33. Typescript copy*]

Bemersyde,
St Boswells,
Scotland,
17th August, 1931.

Dear Mr Whitehead,

I am grateful to you for sending me the delightful letter written to you by Douglas so long ago, and I am busy at the material for future publication of my husband's life.[1176] I will certainly add this letter as you give me permission to see it. It shows my husband's concern then also for officers, and his realisation of what it was for them not to be well off, and also his concern for the health of the little boys in the class room and the playing field.

As regards the statue, I am going to confide in you about this. I do not know whether you had heard that I was asked to go and see the artist a long time ago and his beginning of the statue. I expressed my approval of the pose which I thought quite excellent, and very typical of my husband standing in the road with his map (just as I understand he used to do at the front, contemplating his next plan), but I told the artist quite clearly that I thought the likeness was not good enough, and tried to point out certain defects in the chin which I considered at the time overdone as regards prominence. I also thought the head and nose not very good.

I heard from my brother[1177] a few days ago that he had received a photograph of the statue which is now to be erected, and my brother mentioned that he thought the likeness excellent. He asked me, too, whether I had seen a copy of the photograph. From my point of view I was candidly disappointed that the artist had not sent me a further copy of a [*recte* the] photograph, and do you not think it will be better for me to see how the likeness stands, in case I can help in the matter before the statue is finished? Of course I would only be too proud to unveil my husband's statue, particularly at the School where he was a small boy, and I know how much he thought of the School. I had the pleasure of being with my husband when the War Memorial was unveiled, and I know how delighted he was at being allowed to do this. I also visited the School with my husband one day before, and was much amused that he and Younghusband[1178] began recalling their schooldays, and my husband said to me afterwards that he felt quite like a boy again at the time.

Once more I want to thank you a thousand times for sending me the copy of the letter written by Douglas to you. I could not get much information about Clifton for the material, although some of Douglas's school-fellows wrote to me when I appealed for it in the press, but what they did write to me was quite charming, because it showed that, even at that age, my husband had a serious side to his character,[1179] and that he was always contemplating what his future career would be, although

---

[1174]   Dorothy Maud (*née* Vivian), Countess Haig (d. 1939).

[1175]   Sir Rowland Whitehead, who had been in School House with Haig. He had become a Baronet on the death of his brother Sir George on 21 May 1931, but Lady Haig cannot have been aware of this.

[1176]   *The Man I Knew* (Edinburgh and London, 1936). *Cf.* De Groot, *Haig*, p. 2 ('reveals how little she knew').

[1177]   George Crespigny Brabazon Vivian, 4th Baron Vivian (d. 1940).

[1178]   Sir Francis: see above **[64]**.

[1179]   Some unattributed extracts from these letters are printed in *The Man I Knew*, p. 15

he was so young, and of course by his School reports I know that as a little boy he found concentration hard (a good deal due, I think, to his health, as he suffered from asthma). But his mother's wonderful influence and interest in his work, and her guidance, gave that little boy the inspiration to try and work hard, especially at his Latin which was his great stumbling block, and at which his mother begged him to work up. All this is very interesting when one finishes with the wonderful work that my husband was privileged to do for his country, to realise that Clifton School had a great deal to do with that early training and that Mr Percival and the mother's combination gave the boy the beginning seeds of what he was to do later.

After I have said all this, you can imagine that it will be *such a pride to me* to unveil the statue as you ask me. Thank you just a thousand times, and the Council of Clifton College, for such a high honour.

Yours sincerely,

(sgd) Dorothy Haig.

P.S. I enclose a series of photographs which I did receive soon after my visit, I believe, to the artist and my comments. I wonder whether these are the photographs my brother writes about. I shall be glad if you will kindly return the enclosures to me.

[450]   31 May 1932. The Head Master to Colonel Truscott
[*RS2/49. Typescript copy*].

31 May 1932

Dear Truscott,

Imlay, Udal and I had a meeting yesterday about the arrangements for the unveiling, and it was agreed that I should write to you about the following points.

(1) The actual ceremony. We think it would be best if this could be done by Lady Haig pressing or pulling something without leaving the platform from which the speeches will be made. This platform will be on the pathway by the Parapet, and will have the Parapet road between it and the statue. I enclose a very rough sketch plan [*not copied*]. There will be a lot of traffic along the Parapet road up to just before the unveiling, so that any rope, wire or string that has to cross the road would have to be placed in position at the last moment. The platform would have to be just to one side of the statute and not in the direct line in front of it.

I think you said that, if we gave you these particulars, you would find out from the architect and sculptor whether this suggestion is feasible.

(2) The bulk of the spectators will have to stand on the Close. A certain number of chairs can be placed along the path on either side of the Parapet road immediately joining School House garden. We shall have to find chairs here for members of the Council and their wives and certain special guests, and we could easily accommodate a certain number of Old Cliftonians and their wives. They will probably neither see nor hear very well, but they will have chairs to sit on and be out of the crowd. We will send tickets for these reserved seats to any Old Cliftonians of outstanding distinction who inform us that they are coming, If you could tell us of any for whom the Old Cliftonian Society would specially like us to reserve seats, we will do it. It is not easy at present to mention an exact number of seats available. The number of seats we can put down need not be strictly limited but, if we extend it very far, people on the extremities may feel rather out of it. I suggest that you send us the names of say, ten Old Cliftonians. We will, as I have said, see that, if any Old Cliftonian not on your list who obviously ought to have a seat turns up, he is provided for.

(3) Will you find out if the architect is coming, and, if so, with or without his wife[1180] – also the sculptor with or without his wife? It would be a great help if you could also let me know whether, if coming, they wish to be put up for the previous night. (We will deal with the contractor.)

(4) Would you like a poppy wreath to be laid on the statue on behalf of the Old Cliftonian Society? If so, could you nominate a representative to do this? It might be simpler if it was not Birdwood as he will already be occupied, but it could easily be arranged for him to do it if you think it ought to be your President. It is proposed that the Head of the School[1181] should lay one on behalf of the School, and I expect that, if Birdwood does it, I ought to do it rather than the Head of the School, and I would much prefer that the latter did.

I have written to Haig's brother.[1182]

Yours very truly,

N.W.

[451]   [Before July 1932]. Arrangements for unveiling: exchange between the Head Master and Lady Haig

[*RS2/58. Typsecript extracts*]

Extract from the Headmaster's letter to Lady Haig

The Committee is very anxious that, before proceeding any further with the arrangements, I should ask for your views about the nature of the unveiling ceremony. I suppose that, in any case, it would be natural for a representative of the Old Cliftonian Society (I hope Sir William Birdwood) to hand over the statue to Mr Whitley, as President of the School, and for Mr Whitley to ask you to unveil it. What is less easy to decide is how the ceremony should begin and end, and among the members of the Committee two opinions were expressed. One was that there should be a military element with a Guard of Honour from the Officers' Training Corps. The other was that it should be treated rather as a continuation of the service in Chapel, and that the School, not in uniform, should proceed straight from Chapel and draw up near the statue. In either case, there would, of course, be a good many details to work out, which would be submitted to you later on, but it would be a great help to the Committee if you could let me know whether you would prefer that there should be a military element in the proceedings or not.

Extract from Lady Haig's reply

It was most kind of you letting me know the suggested arrangements, but, I hope please that you will realise I will want only to carry out whatever is decided as best by you and your Committee.

You ask rather especially my view as to how the ceremony should begin and end, and you have mentioned to me the two opinions expressed in your Committee [*rehearsing the above*].

Personally I prefer the latter suggestion because of its simplicity and feel certain that Douglas would have preferred the boys in their school kit, and that the military

---

[1180] Holden lived with Margaret Steadman, who had separated from but never divorced her husband James; she was nevertheless acknowledged as Mrs Holden: Karol, *Holden*, pp. 46–7. Had these circumstances been known to the Head Master it is unlikely that an invitation would have been issued.

[1181] Norman Oliver Brown [*9506*: NT 1924–32].

[1182] John Alicius Haig (d. 1933), the only surviving brother.

element be not included in the proceedings. But of course you will know best which suggestion is the best to carry out.

May I just put one suggestion to you that no speech will be expected from me. The speaking will be so much nicer from a Cliftonian, and I will so much prefer doing the actual unveiling.

☐ *In the event Lady Haig was prevented by illness from attending, and the unveiling was performed by her daughter Lady Alexandra (later Lady Dacre of Glanton).*

[452] 1932. Draft of Head Master's speech at the unveiling
[*RS2/58. Corrected MS*]

It is my difficult but pleasant duty to conclude this ceremony by speaking for the School. And first I want to thank Lady Alexandra Haig for coming here today. To us the significance of this statue is <made> very much fuller even than it would otherwise have been, through being unveiled to us by a member of Lord Haig's own family.

Secondly the School would like to echo the [words *corrected to*] thanks already expressed by our President to the Old Cliftonian Society for this further evidence of their unfailing devotion and generosity. And lastly I want to say very briefly what the statue will mean to us. It will remind us of a very great Cliftonian who was here in an age of great Cliftonians. It will make us [reverence *corrected to*] revere the past, but I hope that even more it will [inspire us for the future *corrected to*] inspire our future. It will keep before us the character of a man whose outstanding qualities were endurance and resolution under every kind of strain and difficulty, unfailing <dignity and> courtesy [?] superior [to all *corrected to*] to [*illegible word*] and jealousy [and a care for those under him which *corrected to*] He carried without flinching a heavier responsibility than any other Briton has ever carried. He expected those under him to do their best and reminded them by putting their interests before his own.

No school could wish <for> anything better than to send out into the world boys in whom these qualities prevail. We thank those who have today given to us this fresh inspiration [to *corrected to* towards] acquiring them.

SECTION XXIII:
BLITZ AND EVACUATION

[453]   16 May 1939. Air Raid Precautions: extract from Finance Committee Minutes
[*Council Minute Book 13, pp. 44–5. Typescript*]

A.R.P.

Mr A.D. Imlay reported the conversation he had had that morning with the Superintendent of the Bristol Fire Brigade. The latter had expressed the view that, in the event of an air raid, it was very possible that the pressure of water supply in the street hydrants in the vicinity of the College would be much lowered and that therefore it would be a very wise precaution on the part of the School to have both the large and small Swimming Baths filled to capacity as an alternative source of water supply. He calculated that if this were done there would be sufficient water in the baths to last for seven or eight hours for use with a trailer pump.

He estimated that the cost of purchasing a trailer pump together with the necessary equipment would be about £350. Sir Robert Waley Cohen[1183] suggested that the School insurance company might possibly contribute something towards the purchase of this trailer pump or, alternatively, reduce the annual premium on account of fire.

The Headmaster stated that Auxiliary Fire Brigade courses were being held twice a week, consisting of classes composed of two masters, 18 boys and 7 porters. Whilst, in addition, 40 of the assistant masters were attending an air-raid wardens' course. The Headmaster stated he was anxious to send a communication out to all parents telling them what was being done in regard to A.R.P., and that he felt very strongly that if he could state that the School had their own fire brigade to deal with any emergency fires that might arise, it would create a very favourable effect on the minds of parents. The Headmaster further stated that he was in close contact with the City Engineer in regard to the best method of propping and strutting the basement rooms in boarding houses, and he thought that, with practically no expense to the School, the timber required for props could easily be obtained by a suitably thinning out of some of the trees at Beggar's Bush, which boys could cut down and the struts then be removed in the School lorry to the boarding houses.

The Committee resolved: (1) that the Chairman should approach the manager of the Eagle Star & British Dominions Insurance Company in regard to the suggestion

---

[1183] Sir Robert Cohen [*4264*: PH 1890–6]; member of Council 1931–52.

made above for a reduction of the premium or contribution towards the purchase of a trailer pump, and (2) that all further matters requiring executive action should be left in the hands of the A.R.P. Sub-Committee appointed by the Council on the 28th March, 1939. (Note: Sir John Inskip, Mr C.H. Abbot and Mr C. Meade-King.)[1184]

[454]   19 September 1939. Sir John Inskip to the Bursar
[*RS1/67. Typescript*]

> The Chantry,
> Abbot's Leigh,
> Nr Bristol.
> 29th September, 1939.

Dear Imlay,

I have had a word today with both the City Engineer and Mr Oaten with regard to the A.R.P. shelters. They both confirm what I said at the Committee meeting yesterday about the possibility of our getting these shelters completed before next term, now that a decision has been delayed until the Council meeting. That, however, cannot now be helped. It is all a question of priority and obtaining materials, which at the moment are very difficult to get even for important public shelters.[1185]

Mr Oaten expressed himself with regard to these basements even more strongly than he had done before, and whilst I have no intention of pressing my own views too far, I must be careful to see that the Council has the whole picture before them. I therefore thought it right to acquaint Sir Robert Witt with my views so that he may decide what, if any, further information he would like to have before the Council meeting. I enclose a copy of my letter to Sir Robert and shall be glad if you will take the opportunity of letting the Headmaster see it.

I am not sure that as Sir Hugh Ellis [*recte* Elles][1186] was mentioned during the discussion yesterday and in view of the important position which he occupies here, and especially as he is himself an Old Cliftonian, it might be as well to take him into our confidence and ask him whether he cares to express an opinion for the guidance of the Council in the light of the advice which we have received from the City Engineer and the architect. I feel that in a matter of such importance we want to take every possible step to help the Council come to a right decision. I should be more than glad to find that my fears with regard to the basements are groundless and that the risks of putting the boys into them during an air raid are so small as to make it possible for us to ignore them. Quite frankly, I am nowhere finding myself in that state of mind at present.

> Yours sincerely,
> John H. Inskip.

[455]   20 September 1939. Report on the Air Raid Shelters
[*RS1/67. Typescript*]

Extract from a letter from Mr A.E. Oaten, dated 20th September 1939.

[1184] Sir John Hampden Inskip [*4211*: ST 1890–8]; member of the College Council 1937–59; Lord Mayor of Bristol 1931–2; for Abbot and Meade-King see above **[66]** and **[41]** respectively.

[1185] *Cf.* C.M. MacInnes, *Bristol at War* (1962), pp. 92–5.

[1186] Lt-Gen Sir Hugh Jamieson Elles [*4716*: SH 1893–7]; President of the OCS 1935–6; Regional Commissioner, South-West Region 1939–45; in case of invasion he would have commanded the resistance.

Air Raid Precautions
Clifton College

In company with Mr Drummond of the City Engineer's Department I inspected the provision which had been made for protection from damage by air raid in the School Houses known as 'Matthews'', 'Poole's', 'School House', 'Brown's House', 'Dakyns'', 'Oakeley's', 'Hartnell's', and 'Wiseman's', also the provision made in the Chapel crypt and the basement of the Science Building. The basement of the Sanatorium was also inspected.

'Polack's' and 'Watson's' Houses were not inspected internally.

It would appear that the work which has been carried out was designed in the light of such limited knowledge of air raid precaution as was available some months ago before the present Government data was available and as this is constantly being revised the requirements vary from time to time.

Generally speaking the basement apartments selected are definitely unsuitable for the purpose for the following reasons:

(1) The floor immediately above which forms the ceiling of the shelter is totally inadequate to sustain the debris load, and in most cases the cost of the necessary strengthening would be very considerable and the supports would prohibit the use of the rooms for normal purposes.

(2) The exits are in nearly every case unsuitable. In some cases they necessitate going through an unprotected portion of the building and in other cases where they connect immediately with the external air they are so near the main building (usually three stories [*sic*] high) that they are likely to be blocked by debris.

(3) In several cases the proposed shelters are insufficient in area, especially in view of the fact that they are littered with furniture.

(4) In many instances the proposed shelters contain domestic hot water or heating pipes which cannot be protected and could only be valved at considerable expense and some risk, and in several instances the proposed shelters are near and at the same level as the boilers and calorifiers with the attendant risk of flooding.

(5) In some Houses, passages or corridors are proposed to be used as shelter accommodation. These are definitely unsuitable on account of openings (doors and windows) which would all require to be 'traversed' or baffled and such protection would make the adjoining rooms unusable.

The sandbag protection to many of the windows needs improvement.

The only exceptions to these objections appear to be a part of the Chapel crypt which with additional baffles could be made suitable, and one portion of the Sanatorium, but this latter would require the ceiling of the scullery properly strengthened to provide access to a suitable exit through the window.

It would be possible to provide some accommodation in the basement dressing rooms of School House but the necessary strengthening would seriously interfere with the use of the rooms as dressing rooms and the necessary baffles to the doorways and windows would occupy so much space that the accommodation remaining would be very limited.

[456]   14 July 1940. William Walch to the Bursar: completion of Pre shelters
[*RS1/67. Typescript*]

> *W.H. Watkins, F.R.I.B.A., Chartered Surveyor*
>
> Sun Buildings,
> 1, Clare Street, Bristol.
> 17th July 1940.

Dear Sir,

> *re Air Raid Shelters, Clifton College.*

Please accept my best thanks for your telephone message of today and I now have pleasure in confirming that I have instructed Messrs Stone & Co. (Bristol) Ltd, to proceed with the erection of Hartnell's shelter to accommodate 56 boys, and to place the work in hand immediately.

Will you also kindly note that I have ordered upon your behalf no. 16 Elson chemical closets from Messrs Gardiner Sons & Co. Ltd, at 47/6 each together with no. 8 portable urinals for fitting to these shelters – including Matthews'. The chemical closets should be delivered tomorrow (Thursday) but it may take a week or so to obtain delivery of the portable urinals.

> Yours faithfully,
> Wm. Walch,
> for and on behalf of W.H. Watkins, F.R.I.B.A.

☐ *The shelters were completed just in time. Among their occupants was a Dakyns' boy, whose letters to his mother describe the Clifton Blitz.*

[457]   15 September 1940. Richard Martin[1187] to his mother
[*P11231. Typescript copy*]

> Dakyns' House,
> 28 College Road,
> Clifton, Bristol
> 15th September, 1940

Darling Mummy,

Thank you for sending on my Home Guard uniform. There have been raids every night this last week and every day but they do not really affect us much. At night they usually start as we are going to bed but as we sleep in the shelter they do not worry us unless there is a lot of noise. In daylight when we are working in School and the warning goes, as it does every morning, we take no notice of it even if the guns start firing. We only take cover if there is immediate danger here. All the classroom windows have been painted with transparent anti-splinter paint. If we are playing games near the School we return to our Houses and stay inside, though not in the shelter unless there is bombing. We have watched a German aircraft being fired at as it flew over but so far few bombs have been dropped around here. Two landed near the hotel at which we all had lunch before Edward[1188] went to France.

[1187] Richard Francis Hingston Martin [*11231*: DH 1936–40]. The editor is grateful to the writer for permission to print these letters, and for checking and supplementing the typescripts from the originals in his keeping.

[1188] Richard's elder brother Cyril Edward Hingston Martin [*10856*: BH 1933–7], already serving in the Royal Engineers; killed in action in the Mediterranean 1944.

You said in your letter that the Home Guard were called out on Tuesday the 10th. I think you may have the date wrong; we were called out on Saturday the 7th when the church bells rang – did you hear them? I did not but a lot of people did hear them and we manned our post at Beggar's Bush until the Monday. It is a noisy place when the AA guns fire in our direction. It looks as if the invasion must happen this week or not at all. I have done a Mills bomb course and am now learning the Browning automatic rifle; we have a number out of the first batch from the U.S.A. We had one snag when called out the night of the 7th; the Armoury was locked and the person holding the keys was on duty at Beggar's Bush so we had to wait some time before we were able to get the rifles and ammunition.

London seems to be having a bad time and Lord Haw Haw[1189] says that the German Air Force will deal with Bristol after it has finished with London.

Lots and lots of love,
Richard.

[458]   28 September 1940. Richard Martin to his mother
[P11231. Typescript copy]

Dakyns' House,
28 College Road,
Clifton, Bristol.
28th September, 1940

Darling Mummy,

It has been a very exciting week. First we have had the usual raid at night and two or three warnings a day where one plane usually comes over. However on Wednesday things changed when at 10 a.m. there was a warning that lasted for about 15 minutes and was followed by another at 11.30. We take no notice of these warnings and do nothing until a bugle is blown as a warning of immediate danger. Just after the 11.30 warning we changed classes and I went to Maths, and after about five minutes in the class we heard a low droning sound like bees in the distance and it got louder and louder and suddenly all the AA guns opened up firing a barrage and then the bugle sounded, so we rapidly left the class and went to our shelter in the Chapel crypt. To get to it we had to go outside and so I saw all the shells bursting around a mass of bombers and some parachutes in the sky before getting into the shelter. There was quite a noise with the guns, bombs and aircraft. We have been told that some 90 German bombers came over and that about 26 were shot down. Unfortunately it seems that they hit the target and caused a lot of damage and casualties; the whole thing was over in about 20 minutes and we went back to the Maths class.

On Thursday night I was on Home Guard duty at Beggar's Bush and it was a noisy night with quite a lot of AA fire. We returned to the House in time for breakfast and then went to bed but we were woken up by a warning at 10 a.m. but nothing happened so slept till 11 a.m. and then got up and dressed. I had just finished dressing when the warning went again and after about five minutes there was the roar of aircraft engines. I collected my field glasses and went with the Matron to the top floor, and leaning out of a window I could see a squadron of Spitfires climbing up over the

---

[1189] The nickname of William Joyce, who was employed by the Nazis to broadcast disheartening propaganda to Britain. Although everyone knew his reports of German success were exaggerated when not wholly imaginary, it was widely supposed that they contained unwelcome truths censored by the British government. Joyce, who had British citizenship, was captured and executed for treason in 1946.

House and away from us. Then suddenly out of the clouds over the town appeared a stream of bombers; they seemed to be flying in formation of twelve abreast and there seemed to be a great number of them, more than fifty I should think. The Spitfires climbed up in front and above the bombers and their fighter escort and then turned and dived straight at the leading German bombers. There was no AA fire and a huge dog-fight developed; after a minute or so the Germans turned back and retreated and then the guns started to fire at them. I saw one bomber shot down by our fighters and it dived straight down with its engines going flat out and crashed with a loud explosion behind some houses. It is reported that the Germans were chased all the way back to the Channel and a large number were shot down. This evens things up after what happened on Wednesday and I was very lucky to have been able to watch it all. The noise was not so bad as I had expected but though it seemed to be over us it was in fact about three miles away.

The warning bugle has been abolished as a result of these large daylight raids and we now take shelter on the air raid warning.

I wear a greatcoat, three sweaters, a shirt and a vest while on Home Guard duty; it just keeps me warm. From now on we are no longer going to sleep at the post but in our Section Commander's house half way to Beggar's Bush.

Lots and lots of love,
Richard.

[459]   24 November 1940. Richard Martin to his mother
[*P11231. Typescript copy*]

Dakyns' House,
28 College Road,
Clifton, Bristol.
24th November, 1940

Darling Mummy,

The air raids have been a lot noisier this week with a lot of German planes passing over on their way to the Midlands and only one or two have dropped their bombs here; some fell in Leigh Woods. Most of the noise is caused by our AA guns; at least we are shooting back at them.[1190]

Lord Haw Haw said the other night that Bristol would be next after Coventry and would be dealt with soon; so far nothing much has happened.

Thursday night I was on Home Guard duty at Beggar's Bush and enjoyed it. I think the post is now more comfortable than the House shelter.

On Saturday night to entertain the House, they had to find out who has murdered the House Master!![1191] There were pools of blood all over the House and a number of clues. Once all the clues had been found a suspect was arrested and tried at a mock trial. He was found guilty but was let off 'for doing a good job'.

I am continuing this in the shelter; it is Sunday evening and I went to a film in the Pre-School and a raid started but the film went on as everyone thought that the aircraft were passing over as usual. It turned out that we are the target and became very noisy. We had to wait for a lull in the firing and then run for it back to the House. The sky was full of bursting shells and the middle of Bristol on fire; the church across

---

[1190] *Cf*. J. Penny, *Bristol at War* (Frome, 2002), pp. 66–91.
[1191] S.P. Beachcroft [*7249/M277*]; *cf*. above **[71]**.

the Close[1192] was on fire and shrapnel was bouncing off the railings along the road; as you can imagine I did not waste any time getting back here. All the Home Guard are in uniform and hoping to go out. (Pen has run out.) We are not allowed back into the House. Everyone is very cheerful; most are reading, talking or eating. Two sticks of bombs have just landed very near, I should think about Pembroke Road. It is now 9 p.m. and this has been going on since 6.15 p.m. I hope it is not going on till daylight. I will continue this tomorrow if we are still standing. Another stick of bombs has landed very close, so close that everyone shut up and leant against the wall and hoped for the best. There is a strong smell of cordite and smoke. A hunt is organised for incendiary bombs but none found. The House Tutor[1193] has just told us that the last lot landed close to Polack's and Wiseman's House in Caninge [*recte* Canynge] Square and that several masters live in that area. I will stop now as things are quieter and we are going to try to get some sleep.

Monday.

No mains water this morning so no washing at all. The raid stopped around midnight, which was as well or we might have ended up like Coventry. I have just seen some of the damage. Polack's House is minus a lot of glass and close by all the fronts of the houses have been blown out and everything is in ruins. A small tree that was growing on the pavement is now on the top of what remains of the roof of a house. Large fires are still burning in the town; the lack of water does not help. The School fire brigade rescued most of Dr Rendel [*recte* Rendle] Short's[1194] belongings as the house next to his had been hit and was burning. The A.F.S. were standing there doing nothing because there was no water, so the boys cut their way into the house and flung everything they could into the road. Some of the boys spent the morning clearing debris and we spent this evening carrying water in buckets from the Swimming Pool as there is still no water from the mains. Lord Haw Haw seems to have fulfilled his words after all. A direct hit was scored on your dress shop.

Lots and lots of love,
Richard.

[460]   3 December 1940. Richard Martin to his mother
[*P11231. Typescript copy*]

Dakyns' House,
28 College Road,
Clifton, Bristol.
3rd December, 1940

Darling Mummy,

A heavy raid last night and it seemed to rain incendiary bombs; a number landed on the Close and in School House garden. One hit us and went through the roof into the attic below and was quickly dealt with by the House fire brigade and so did not do much damage. The Pre-School Hall was set on fire but it was put out by the School fire brigade; also several buildings and a church on the other side of the Close were

---

[1192] All Saints in Pembroke Road, directly east of the Close.

[1193] Francis Cyril Gould [*M320*: 1938–45].

[1194] Arthur Rendle Short, one of the College Medical Officers from 1921–49; Professor of Surgery at Bristol University 1932–46; he lived at 69 Pembroke Road, though when the air raid of 24 November began he was out addressing a religious meeting: *Directory* (1940), p. 1082; W.M. Capper and D. Johnson (eds), *The Faith of a Surgeon: Belief and Experience in the Life of Arthur Rendle Short* (Exeter, 1976), esp. p. 100 (reference to raid misdated 1941).

on fire and the School fire brigade helped at the church.[1195] Then came the worst part; a lot of high explosive bombs fell on us. The new Squash Courts were hit and demolished. Wiseman's and Polack's suffered a lot of damage and several bombs fell on the edge of the Close. A lot of the ceilings in the dormitories are down and the place is swimming in water. While all this was going on we were in the House shelter; it was very noisy and got worse as each plane approached and dropped its bombs. Some of the younger boys who were in a separate section of the shelter got rather frightened, so three of us used their bunks while they slept in ours. Nobody got much sleep until about 1 a.m. We had supper in the shelter so some of us had to fetch it from the kitchen in the House. I got there and back with the food but had to stop and lie down on the floor as more bombs fell. We had to sleep in our clothes because of the damage upstairs.

Lots and lots of love,
Richard.

P.S. The whole School is going home tomorrow except for those trying to take the School Cert., so I will stay until that is over. You will be getting a letter from the Headmaster.

[461]   3 December 1940. The Head Master to parents of boarders
[*Bude file. Photocopy of untraced typescript original*]

Clifton College,
Bristol, 8.
December 3, 1940.

Dear Sir or Madam,

I am sorry to say that Bristol received a second very heavy attack last night, and considerable damage was done in the School premises, two of the boarding houses being rendered temporarily uninhabitable owing to breakage of windows and damage to roofs.

In these circumstances I had to decide at once whether or not to continue the term. I have come to the decision that it hardly seemed wise to incur the possible risk of another attack on the same scale simply to complete in a somewhat disorganised condition the thirteenth and fourteenth week of an extra long term. Consequently I am sending home today and tomorrow those boys whose parents I have reason to believe are in a position to receive them. I realise that this may in some cases cause inconvenience, which I greatly regret, but I believe it to be the wisest course in the circumstances. It seemed to me after giving the matter my most anxious consideration that parents would understand my desire to return boys to their homes with the least possible delay rather than await instructions which under present postal conditions could hardly be received for three or four days.

As to the future, you may expect to receive a further letter from me at an early date. I should like to add that I consider that the conduct of the boys has been admirable.

Yours sincerely,
B.L. Hallward, Headmaster.

P.S. You will be glad to learn that no-one connected with the College has been hurt in the recent raid.

[1195] Despite these efforts All Saints was gutted; some of the structure was retained when the church was rebuilt in 1967.

[462]   7 December 1940. Evacuation decision
[Council Minute Book 13, p. 158. Typescript]

A meeting of the Council was held in the Council Room at 1.15 p.m. on Saturday, December 7th 1940.

Present: Field Marshall [*sic*] Lord Birdwood (in the chair); Sir Edgar Bonham-Carter,[1196] Mr C.H. Abbot, the Dean of Bristol, Mr V. Fuller Eberle, Sir John Inskip, Lt. Col. G.A. McWatters,[1197] Mr Cyril Meade-King, Professor H. A. Prichard,[1198] the Headmaster, the Bursar.

General Sir Hugh Elles, the Regional Commissioner, attended the meeting in an advisory capacity.[1199]

After a lengthy discussion, in the course of which Sir Hugh Elles gave it as his opinion that evacuation was now advisable, it was decided that in view of the mass air attacks on Bristol as an industrial target and the evidence that a considerable proportion of the parents of the boarders as well as many of the day boys would not let their sons return to the School it was advisable to move the School to another site. It was also decided to appoint a Sub-Committee consisting of Sir Robert Waley Cohen, Sir John Inskip, Mr V. Fuller Eberle and the Headmaster, to review all possibilities for evacuation sites, the Chairman of the Council to be kept informed of any action taken.

The Council passed a resolution of thanks to the masters and boys who had done such wonderful work in helping to fight the incendiary bombs and in giving assistance in Bristol in many different ways, and also expressed their gratitude to the Headmaster for the resolution he displayed in facing such a formidable crisis.

[Signed] B[*irdwood*]. 21/12.

[463]   8 December 1940. Richard Martin's last letter from Clifton
[P11231. Typescript copy]

Dakyns' House,
28 College Road,
Clifton, Bristol.
8th December, 1940.

Darling Mummy,

The School has gone home except for a few who are doing fire brigade work protecting the buildings and those doing their School Cert. We had another heavy raid mostly aimed at the centre of Bristol. We spend most of our spare time working in salvage parties trying to rescue people's belongings from ruined houses and at night are ready to help fight fires.

I will be coming home on Friday 13th arriving at 6.12 p.m. at Tavistock.

Lots and lots of love,
Richard.

[1196] *3100*: SH 1889–93; diplomat and politician; member of Council from 1931 to 1950 (Vice-Chairman 1934–46).

[1197] George Alfred McWatters [*3208*: NT 1893–92]; member of Council 1938–47; uncle of Stephen John [*HM10*: 1963–75].

[1198] Harold Arthur Prichard [*3428*: OH 1885–90]; member of Council 1931–45; White's Professor of Moral Philosophy and Fellow of Corpus Christi College, Oxford 1925–37.

[1199] He also happened to be an OC: above **[455]**.

☐ *Martin went straight into the RAF, becoming a Flight Lieutenant in Bomber Command.*

The School that stayed

☐ *In January 1941 the Upper School evacuated to Bude, the Pre to Butcombe Court in the Mendips. Nevertheless a small school for Pre day boys was maintained at Clifton. In 2010 one of the surviving inmates wrote a memoir of that time, and deposited it in the Archives; it is here printed, after some editorial revision, with his permission.*

[464]   *1941–44.* 'Clifton at Clifton' by Robert MacEwen[1200]

After the Dunkirk evacuation and the fall of France the summer of 1940 had seen spasmodic 'Battle of Britain' activity; the height of it for us boys in the Pre were the pre-emptive strikes in broad daylight against the Bristol Aeroplane Company's Filton works.

The two raids within one week are described in the book *Double Entendre*; the first raid on the 25th September 1940 was a disaster; the second on the 27th repulsed.[1201]

On the playground at break we heard the loud hum and witnessed the Heinkels and ME110s[1202] fly unhindered across the blue sky over the city; no air-raid sirens had gone off.

The second raid saw us in the air-raid shelter wherein, from a vantage position at the end of the dug-out, we witnessed the dog-fights over Bristol that caused the German rout.

The night raids started on 24th November. This was twelve hour bombardment, 6 p.m. to 6 a.m. A night of extreme concern for those in charge of affairs at Clifton College. A straddle of bombs had dropped across the New Field, one bomb hitting Wiseman's House; luckily the boys and staff were in an overground shelter which saved their lives.

Next day the boarders disappeared to their homes; we day-boys continued classes despite further air raids; but by the start of the Lent term 1941 the School had evacuated to Butcombe and Bude. That part of the School's history is well documented.[1203]

Less well known is the story of those few pupils left behind who became known as 'Clifton at Clifton'. Starting with numbers about 35 maximum, we were accommodated in Matthews' House which had been urgently converted from dormitories to classrooms.

[1200] Robert Kenneth Gillespie MacEwen [*11192*: NTP 1936–42] went on to Bristol Grammar School, Loughborough College and St Catharine's College, Cambridge, and made his career in management consultancy and operational turnaround. He played rugby for Cambridge in 1953 and 1954 and for Scotland from 1954 to 1958, as well as for several county teams and Barbarians RFC (see Casey and Hale, *College, Club and Country*, p. 189 and the Clifton RFC website).

[1201] See R.F.H. Martin's letters above **[457–60]** and the *Memoirs* (2011) of Lord Rees-Mogg [*11331*: MHP, PHP 1937–41], pp. 33–4. The book mentioned has not been traced.

[1202] Messerschmitt Bf 110s.

[1203] Principally in *Clifton at Bude and Butcombe: The Story of a School in Evacuation* (Bristol, 1945), edited (if not wholly written) by James Charles Harrison Tompkins [*M353*], a temporary assistant at Bude, awarded his 'M' number on the strength of that publication: *Register* (1947), p. lxvii.

There were three forms: Forms I, II and III. I myself started in Form II which was situated on the ground floor, but was soon moved up to Form III, high up on the 1st floor.

We had a class of about 12–15 pupils; there was much fluctuation as, owing to the bombing uncertainties, families were moving away and then re-appearing, with the occasional new boy making an entrance; and/or, like myself, promotion from Form II as we grew older.

To my memory the more stable class III list was as follows:

Hearn	Hadley	Lennard	Price	MacEwen
[*11804*]	[*11515*]	[*11031*]	[*11756*]	[*11192*]
	Parker	Anderson	Breddy	Stradling
	[*11283*]	[*11749*]	[*11720*]	[*11740*]
	Harding	Stirling	Wellings	Whyte
	[*11753*]	[*11562*]	[*11742*]	[*11449*]

These were the sitting positions (5 rows of 3) facing the master's desk.

The masters were:	H.D. Gawne[1204]	English Language; Latin
	H.R. Dodds[1205]	Greek
	J.B. Hope Simpson[1206]	English Literature; French
	S.P.T. Wells[1207]	Mathematics

[Some details of the boys' later careers omitted]

School continued much as usual although classes started slightly later and finished earlier, with no Saturday school, to accommodate long-distance travelling and the possibility of further air-raids.

We played games on the small fields and 'Lower Close' between the Fives Courts and Emmanuel Church and beyond; rugby and football plus cricket. Some matches versus local prep schools were arranged, including a fixture against Butcombe[1208] which we usually won; so much so that I recall in rugby that the HM (Mr E.G. Sharp[1209] – known by his nickname as EGGS) requested that we omit two/three of the bigger boys like Harding and myself!

Mr H.D. (Gilly) Gawne was in charge at Clifton. Gilly did an outstanding job in holding the fort as it were during the years 1941–44. Not only did he look after the buildings during successive air raids, ensuring that any incendiary bombs were extinguished promptly to prevent fire taking hold, but also was a tireless, patient, inspiring top class schoolmaster both in the classroom and on the games field. My era owe him a great debt.

[1204] Herbert Douglas Gawne [*M245*: 1919–50].

[1205] Henry Raymond Dodds [*M283*: 1926–60]

[1206] John Barclay Hope Simpson [*M300*: 1930–40]; later Head of History at Rugby, and author of *Rugby since Arnold* (1967), which intersects at many points with Clifton's story before and after Percival.

[1207] Sydney Parker Temple Wells [*M299*: 1930–66].

[1208] That is, of course, the Pre at Butcombe Court. The present Butcombe pre-prep opened in 1994, its name commemorating the evacuation.

[1209] Edmund Godfrey Sharp [*M288*]: see above **[69]**.

The pre-war Prep School staff were outstanding. Messrs Douglas (IIIa) [*M321*], Dodds (IIIb), Sharp (IIIc), Gawne [IIaG], Read (IIaR) [*M265*], Maclaren (IIb) [*M295*], Jenkins (IIc) [*M252*] in the Upper Pre, leaving Messrs Mackintosh (Ia), [*M276*], Collis (IbC) [*M315*], Jones (IbJ) [*M308*], Hamilton (Ic) [*M314*], Miss Imlach (Id) [*M258*] in the Lower Pre. The majority went off to war; some to Butcombe/Bude; some to us.

Two milestones stand out in the memory: the first morning after another fierce raid found a huge crater between Matthews' House and the main entrance to our beloved Prep School. Not only had this bomb caused considerable damage to nearby roofs and windows but, more importantly for us, had impaired our playground cricket pitch!

All was soon repaired ready for the second milestone when the front-line troops of the American V Corps disembarked at Avonmouth from the United States in late 1942, beginning the build-up to the D-Day invasion in 1944. Those few of us there were allowed to watch out of the windows with stark amazement at the sight of troops entering our sacred play area; and, what was more, calling out 'hud-two-three-four', 'turn about' – terms and smart uniforms the like of which we had never heard nor seen before.

I myself 'commuted' from Thornbury by 'bus every day from 1941 to mid-1942; I had been evacuated there, as were the likes of Sir Adrian Boult, the famous BBC conductor, who had been sent to Bristol as a 'safe' haven to London prior to Bristol coming into range of the Nazi bombers on the fall of France in 1940.[1210]

I well recall sheltering with Sir Adrian in the basement of the Colston Hall during a day raid when we were ordered to take shelter from the queue for the Thornbury 'bus which started its journey just outside.

Naturally the air raids and war-time conditions plus later the travelling were not particularly conducive to academic work. Sometimes we had been up all night, yet still managed to arrive at school promptly. It became a matter of pride to do so and crack on.

As far as I (remember, a twelve/thirteen year-old schoolboy) can recall the academic standards if anything rose; we specialised in both English and Latin grammar; English literature; for some, Greek; French; Maths; no Sciences, owing to the skills/experiences of those masters left to look after us; there was in any case no equipment left behind.

Messrs Dodds, Hope Simpson and Wells commuted between Butcombe and Clifton, with Mr Gawne on permanent duty at Clifton. This arrangement (to us boys) seemed to work well but it must have been a stressful period for those involved.

Mr Gawne had been in WWI; now an officer in the Home Guard. What was the original tea-room in the Zoo just aside the Prep School had been converted to a rifle range on the ground floor. Gilly arranged for some of the senior boys to practise their marksmanship there if, in his opinion, we had enjoyed an outstanding week both at work and games.

Another outing was to the Pre School Hall which the Americans had converted into a dining hall. I well remember being horrified as a guest being asked if I would like ice-cream added to my soup! Certainly in those days our new allies seemed to like ice-cream in everything. I was given some with a delicious pear and peach salad

---

[1210] The whole BBC Symphony Orchestra, of which Boult was conductor, was evacuated from London to Bristol at the start of the War, moving to Bedford when Bristol itself became a target.

as another starter; all this of course after we had not seen the like of such food for three years.

In retrospect we were possibly the 'forgotten few'; however those masters that were left and assigned to 'Clifton at Clifton' looked after us extremely well; our academic work only suffered in its breadth from lack of both appropriate teachers and facilities.

Although the working day was shorter with an abbreviated lunch time we became highly tuned to the effective use of time, especially with the five minutes end-of-lesson sessions on Latin and English grammar; symbols and underlining and coding the main clause and all the other conjunctive, adjectival, noun clauses; a *nominativus pendens* or a split-infinitive brought down upon one's head, with the black-mark book open at the ready.

They were anxious days; sometimes afraid that one would not see the morrow. When the church bells rang (which, despite reports to the contrary, they did), the sign for a Nazi invasion, would a storm-trooper be at the door or at the school next morning?

I certainly envied those at Bude and wish I had gone there. My father (with his brother, my uncle, both Old Cliftonians)[1211] was on a fixed pension and, despite lengthy discussions with Mr B.L. Hallward, the newly appointed Senior School Head Master, found himself unable to face the increased fees for Bude. New scholarships were suddenly withheld.

I myself stayed as nominal Head Pupil until December 1942 when I departed to Bristol Grammar School to take my Matriculation in the summer of 1943.

I later learned that the 'Clifton at Clifton' numbers reached between 75 and 90 before the College returned to take up normality again in the post-war Britain of 1945.

We certainly felt that we were proudly carrying the Clifton flag aloft whilst the main parts of the School were absent.

Butcombe, south of Bristol, we knew from our visits there, but Bude, in those days, was a long and tiring railway journey into Cornwall.

Halcyon, carefree, fraternal, pre-war days with quite magnificent staff, wrecked by an untimely wartime six years was not easy to cope with; but cope we had to do and did. I, for one, am mighty proud to have endured and achieved what we did during those dark days.

Doubtless some of my classmates have unhappily not survived to read this tribute to them. Those that have include Roger Whyte ('Whyte with a y' so called)[1212] with whom I had many a happy re-united railway journey in the 1950s travelling to London on a Saturday morning when Roger, a most talented, ubiquitous, sportsman was playing for Harlequins, I for London Scottish, using basic skills learned on those Prep School fields.

What then did we learn from our war-time experiences? Some erstwhile protected 11–12 year-olds had to grow up fast; we learned one salutary lesson – namely to take each day as it came – and above all, 'to count our blessings one-by-one'.

To 'commute' long before that word was in common parlance, sometimes after a serious air attack; to focus on one's work after being up all night; even to concentrate to do one's prep, which in the summer we began to do at school before journeying

---

[1211] Kenneth Grant MacEwen [*4469*: NT 1891–8] was the writer's father, St Clair Maling Grant MacEwen [*3672*: NT 1886–94] his uncle.

[1212] Roger Alan Malcolm Whyte [*11449*: NT 1938–47].

home; all helped to make us more resilient, able to accommodate life's ups and downs more easily. There is no doubt that we had been somewhat cosseted and spoilt, albeit hard-working, in our pre-war prep school life.

I myself, as Head Pupil, was made to learn basic leadership skills long before the normal age; such opportunities, experiences and exposures have to be grasped at the time and not lost; for example being forced to give a short speech at the US Army luncheon.

Butcombe and Bude would have been preferable, but for a few of us it was not to be.

MAPS

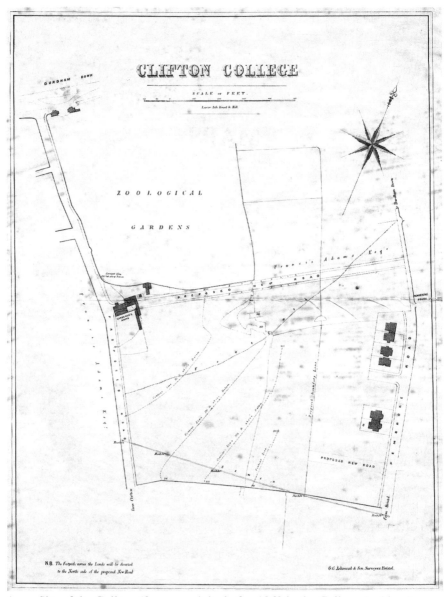

1   Site of the College (from an original of *c*. 1860 in the College Archives)

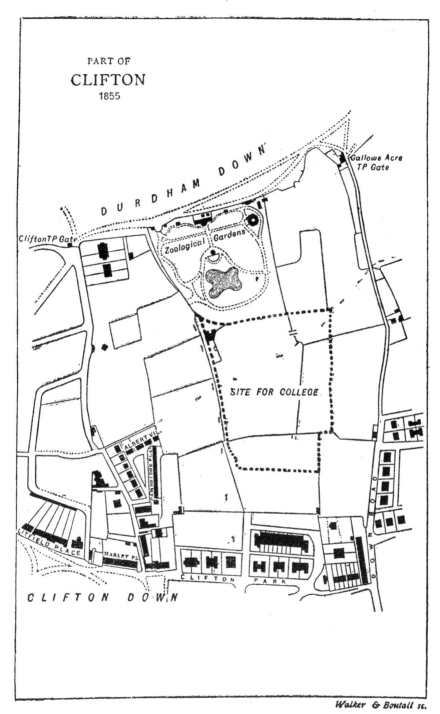

PART OF

CLIFTON

1855

Walker & Boutall sc.

2   The site outlined on a map of 1855, when only the Gardener's Arms, in the
     north-west corner of the purchased land, stood between the Zoo and Worcester
     Terrace

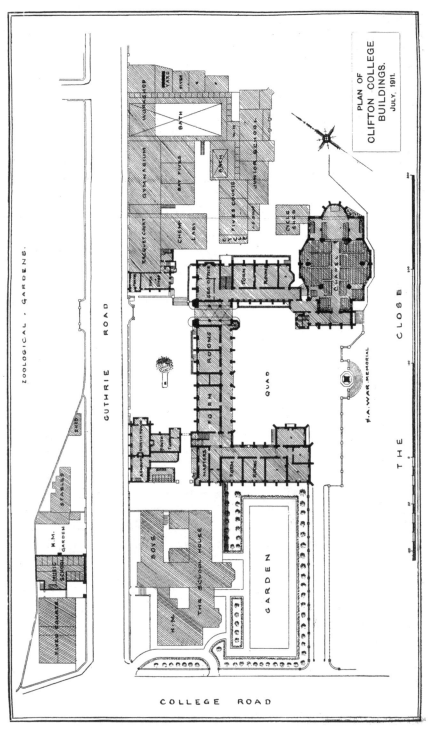

3   The College buildings in 1911 (from inset in the *Clifton College Register*)

INDEX

Peers are indexed under their family names. Places in the United Kingdom are identified by the counties existing before 1974 and by the parish boundaries at the Census of 1851.

As in the text, italic numbers in square brackets after names are keyed to entries in the *Clifton College Register*; with *HM* denoting Head Master and *M* teaching staff; President means President of Clifton College and Chairman means Chairman of the College Council; [*C*] indicates an ordinary member of the Council not also an OC or sometime master. HM is used for Headmaster of other schools.

An italic number without brackets refers to editorial text (in italic) above or below the document with that number (used for details not in the document itself). The introduction is indexed only for matter not occurring in the documents.

Most subjects relating to the School are arranged in various sections headed 'Clifton College'; other grouped entries are: aircraft; Bristol (1) to (6); health; military forces; munitions; newspapers and periodicals; Parliament (statutes); plays and films.

Trafalgar Square, 447n
Underground/Tube, 202, 428n
University, 156n
Imperial College, 187n
King's College, 3n
University College School, 64
Vauxhall Walk, Lambeth, 202n
Veriton Mantle Works, 202&n
Victoria and Albert Museum, 430n
Victoria Embankment, 447n
Victoria Memorial, 430n
Victoria St, 32, 34, 35, 251
Waterloo Station, 202
Westminster, Central Buildings, 426
Westminster Abbey [Collegiate Church of St
 Peter], xx, xxix, xlvii
Canon, 435&n
Dean, 22n
Organist, 334n
Westminster Bridge Road, 202n
Westminster Palace (Houses of Parliament),
 36, 202
Westminster School, xxi, xxvn, xxix,
 xxxiiin, 222n, *255*
Whitechapel, accent, 367
Whitehall, 100
Whitefriars, 90n
see also institutions beginning Royal
London (generally), much like Bristol, 202
London County Council School of Engineering
 and Navigation, 161n
London Necropolis Company, 202n
London Scottish Rugby Football Club, 464
Loos [en Gohelle, *dép* Pas de Calais, France],
 battle (1915), 177&n, 424&n, 442
Lorne, Marchioness of *see* Louise, Princess
Lorraine, Richard Cunningham [*10496*], 187
Robert Brodie [*10637*], 187
Los Angeles, CA, Olympic Games (1932),
 xlviiin
Loughborough, [Leics], College *later*
 University, 464n
Louise (Louise Caroline Alberta), Princess,
 Marchioness of Lorne, Duchess of
 Argyll (1900), 22n, 379
Lousada, Eric George Isidore [*9240*], 363, 365
Julian George [*4026*], 405, 407
Loveday, Thomas, Vice-Chancellor of Bristol
 University [*C*], 69&n, 71&n
Lucas, – , Miss, 410
E., 19&n

G.C., Malvern cricketer, 424n
Henry Arthur [*10672*], 187
Hugh Nathaniel [*3386*], scholarship, 130&n
Isabel Olga, 130
Owen David [*3607*], 19n
Ruth, 130
William Louis [*2715*], 130&n
Luce, William Henry Tucker [*8950*], 363,
 415
Luckman, Horace Pope [*M9*], 142, 211&n
Ludlam, Ernest Bowman [*M201*], 144&n,
 145–6
Ludlow, John [*2658*], 202&n
Lumley, Edward Adrian [*4359*], 405–6
Lüneburg, [*land* Niedersachsen, Germany],
 British Military Court, 297n
Lyon, Henry David John [*3786*], 119
Lyon King of Arms, Lord, 444&n
Lyons, Albert Leonard [*5014*], 407

McArthur, Charles [*41*], 1n
John, xxin, 1&n, 3, 8
MacColl (McColl), Alexander Malcolm [*6697*]
 or Hugh Herbert [*6696*], 424
Macdonald, Margaret *see* Steadman
McDowall, Charles, HM of Highgate School,
 22
MacEwen, Kenneth Grant [*4469*], 464&n
Robert Kenneth Gillespie [*11192*], 464&n
St Clair Maling Grant [*3672*], 464&n
McFall, Richard Graham [*10653*], 187
Macfarlane, John [*10585*], 187
Machiavelli, Niccolò di Bernardo dei, 129n
McKie, William (father of Sir W.N.), 334,
 339
Sir William Neil [*M284*], xlvii–xlviii,
 334&n, 335–40, 344–6, 348, 355
Mackintosh, David Forbes [*M276*], 464
MacLaren, Archibald, physical trainer, 277&n
Maclaren, Roderick [*M295*], 464
MacLellan, George Aikman [*6390*], 174&n
McLeod, Eric Ramsay ('Bunny') [*6449*],
 423&n
Norman Frederick [*732*], 142n
Reginald George McQueen [*812*], 142n
W.C., General, 142&n
McMillian, William, sculptor, 447&n, 448–50
Macpherson, Alexander Geldart [*4325*], 27n,
 292&n
Charles Gordon [*5678*], 27n
Kenneth Douglas Worsley [*4476*], 27n